Also by Gregory Woods from Yale:

*Articulate Flesh: Male Homo-eroticism and Modern Poetry*
*A History of Gay Literature: The Male Tradition*

# GREGORY WOODS

# HOMINTERN

## HOW GAY CULTURE LIBERATED THE MODERN WORLD

YALE UNIVERSITY PRESS
NEW HAVEN AND LONDON

For information about this and other Yale University Press publications, please contact:

U.S. Office:        sales.press@yale.edu        yalebooks.com

Europe Office:        sales@yaleup.co.uk        yalebooks.co.uk

Typeset in Minion Pro by IDSUK (DataConnection) Ltd

Printed in the United States of America

Library of Congress Control Number: 2016933354

ISBN 978-0-300-21803-9

A catalogue record for this book is available from the British Library.

10 9 8 7 6 5 4 3 2 1

*In memory of Guido Almansi (1931–2001)*

# CONTENTS

# LIST OF ILLUSTRATIONS

# PREFACE

The Homintern is the international presence of lesbians and gay men in modern life. Imagined as a single network, it is either one of the major creative forces in the cultural development of the past century, or a sinister conspiracy against the moral and material interests of nation states. You decide.

In the late nineteenth and early twentieth centuries, European scientists from a range of disciplines published research attempting to define and explain people who were attracted to their own sex. In the same period, a succession of public scandals also brought the existence of such people out into the open. It began to look as if there were a lot of them about.

So scandalous was their mere existence, so far beyond the pale their sexual behaviour – often illegal for men, for women virtually unthinkable – that they had to maintain varying levels of discretion or even total secrecy about their 'personal' lives. This in itself was then held against them, since it began to appear that they were secretly conspiring together – to do what? To undermine the collective moral framework; to question or ridicule acceptable standards of behaviour; even to subvert national security.

They allowed themselves, or were allowed, higher visibility in the leisured classes and in artistic occupations, where 'bohemian' styles and manners were acceptable, subject to various tacitly agreed restrictions. In some respects – the arts being of limited use to ideologues and bureaucrats – this made gay people seem harmless; but, before long, inevitably, they were said to be exerting too much cultural influence.

On the other hand, to those in the know, the presence of lesbians and gay men in the artistic avant-garde was energising, precisely because they looked at society from an unusual viewpoint and were apt to undermine previously long-accepted truths of human nature. By loving as they chose, they reminded the world that love is worth taking risks for. By living as they chose, they initiated a process of liberation by sleight of hand. Their very presence demanded a re-evaluation of fixed gender roles and more nuanced attitudes to all sexual behaviour. They could bring a completely fresh aesthetic to bear on over-familiar social conventions. The queerness of their artistic activities was often unnerving to those who sought, in both the method and content of the arts, a projection of the norm.

My book is about those people, and about changing attitudes to them. It is also about their own changing attitudes to sexuality and its role in their lives. Some of these individuals and their stories are exemplary, standing in for many similar experiences; others stand out for their strangeness, the unique radiance of which casts a peculiar light on the generality of the rest.

The independence of lesbian women had its own lessons to convey within the context of the broader struggle for women's equality. Despite being spoken of, and written off, as spinsters, whether single or in couples, such women were often more or less secretly admired for the spirit of their nonconformity: they had chosen to be free – or free of men, at least; which may be the same thing.

We are told that, in certain seasons, homosexuality was all the rage. Indeed, between the wars a certain kind of stylish, un-masculine, arty gay man was regarded as the very epitome of the modern. Acceptance of homosexuality came to be seen as one of the measures of modernity. I am interested in how ideas and images relating to homosexual people acquire status as lasting myths – the gay aesthete, the modern Sodom, the homosexual spy, the sirens' island, the tragic fall from grace, the Oriental pleasure dome, the sleazy dive, the pastoral idyll, the Homintern itself – which duly take their place in the common narratives not only of homosexuality's cultural status in the modern world, but of modernity itself.

The book is threaded with journeys, mainly by steamship or train. When my subjects travelled, either they or their art returned home with horizons broadened: Gide from Algeria, Forster from Italy, Isherwood from Germany, Stein from France, Lorca from the USA, Eisenstein from Mexico, Mishima from the USA . . . Many others were forced, or went voluntarily, into exile from home. For male travellers in particular, the sexual and the cultural were inti-mately connected. It is hard to disentangle journeys with sexual benefits from those with a cultural pay-off. (Many, of course, had both.) The main arena of our narrative consists of Europe and the shores of the Mediterranean, plus the two-way traffic across the Atlantic. Looked at from a global perspective, this cosmopolitanism is really quite local – as readers in the southern hemisphere will be quick to observe – but it is destinations that have accumulated mythic value, rather than any places in which gay people live or to which they have travelled, that interest me most.

I have no qualms about using literature as evidence, liberally quoting from novels with gay characters who travel abroad and scenes in gay clubs and bars in such cities as Berlin and Paris. I quote poetry to similar purpose. These texts are by authors who had observed the scenes they were describing. Many of them did not feel free to say so in print, except from behind the protective screen of literature: they could affect to be imagining what they had actually experienced first hand.

I crave the reader's indulgence for the fact that this is a poet's book. I often seek to cast an image, or sequence of images, on the reader's visual imagination, rather than persuade by linear argument. There are times when I make associative leaps which, judged as logical steps, might seem to be non sequiturs. I have always appreciated what Ezra Pound said of his *Cantos*: 'if the critic will read through them before stopping to wonder whether he or she is understanding them: I think he or she will find at the end that he or she has'. Optimistically, I would like to think of my own book's magical mystery tour in similar terms. It may be that I am an eccentric guide, but the reader will see the logic of our itinerary by the time the journey comes to its end.

# ACKNOWLEDGEMENTS

It passeth understanding that my publisher, Robert Baldock, has had confidence in my work for so long. I can hardly express how proud I am to have had three books published by him and Yale, one at the beginning, one in the middle, and now one towards the end of my academic career. Robert's enthusiasm, encouragement, polite scepticism and dry sense of humour have been crucial all the way. I'd like to thank the whole team at Yale for their dedication and unstirting professionalism; and I'm obliged to Melissa Bond and Beth Humphries, in particular, for their fiendishly thorough attention to my typescript.

The idea for this particular book began slowly to take shape around informal conversations I had with European colleagues at a series of British Council symposiums in Varenna, Italy (1994), Solothurn, Switzerland (1996), and Potsdam, Germany (1998); and at a Nordic Academy for Advanced Study conference on Russian literature at the University of Tromsø, Norway (1998), where discussions with Jostein Børtnes and Catriona Kelly, among others, added substance to some of my flimsy speculations. When I was starting the serious research for the book, in 2001, I was awarded a fellowship by the Arts and Humanities Research Board, matched by study leave from my own employer, Nottingham Trent University (NTU). A month-long residential fellowship in Gender, Sexuality and the Law at Keele University, in 2002, gave me access to texts I would not otherwise have seen, including most of those to which I refer in Chapter Six; as did two Hawthornden Fellowships, in 1999 and 2008, during which I was working mainly on new poetry collections but allowed myself to read about the Homintern between bouts of versifying.

For almost a decade I chaired the Gender Studies expert panel on the European Science Foundation's project to develop a European Reference Index for the Humanities (ERIH), the bibliographical research for which led to all sorts of useful discoveries. Other helpful, informal conversations took place around meetings of the panel in Tallinn, Strasbourg and Paris; and of the steering committee in Brussels, Budapest and Paris. My colleagues on the panel included Jens Nydström, Harriet Bjerrum Nielsen, Adelina Sánchez Espinosa and Ülle Must. Further illuminating conversations came out of a gathering of poets in Ljubljana, Slovenia, hosted by Brane Mozetič, to launch the gay poetry anthology, Brane Mozetič (ed.), *Moral bi spet priti: sodobna evropska gejevska poezija* (Ljubljana: Lambda, 2009).

Earlier versions of some parts of *Homintern* first appeared in the journals *Gay and Lesbian Review* (Boston, Massachusetts) and *Gragoatá* (Rio de Janeiro), as well as in Tony Sharpe (ed.), *W.H. Auden in Context* (Cambridge: Cambridge University Press, 2013).

Since most of the research was conducted in my own personal library (so to dignify the wandering drifts of books in my house), I must thank booksellers as well as librarians. In the first place, I have always relied on the information gathered on visits to Gay's the Word bookshop in Bloomsbury, especially when I get the chance to consult either Jim MacSweeney or Uli Lenart. In Nottingham I rely on advice from Ross Bradshaw and the rest of the staff of the Five Leaves Bookshop. Some late research for my project was done in the Bromley House subscription library in Nottingham, of which I am a member. I must also thank the inter-library loans department of the library at Nottingham Trent University.

I am grateful to my NTU colleagues on the course 'Reading Gender and Sexuality', especially Sharon Ouditt, Catherine Clay and Abigail Ward, as well as to students on that course and on 'Queering the Modern', all of whom had to put up with my thinking aloud. Beyond the classroom, I learned a huge amount from working alongside such colleagues as Catherine Byron, Phil Leonard, John Lucas, Gary Needham, Stan Smith, Nahem Yousaf and that selfless enabler of other people's research, Dick Ellis. Our department was home to a Centre for Travel Writing Studies, founded by Tim Youngs, which generated countless discussions of eventual benefit to my work. Sharon Ouditt and Joanne Hollows kept me sane during difficult times.

Finally, I have often enjoyed the hospitality of my friends Tim Franks and Peter Scott at their cottage in Herefordshire, visits that invariably both raised my morale and thickened my waistline. What more could one ask for?

# CHAPTER ONE

# THE HOMINTERN CONSPIRACY

## Beginning to Count Themselves

In a letter dated 22 June 1869, Friedrich Engels wrote to Karl Marx:

> The paederasts are beginning to count themselves and find that they make up a power in the state. Only the organization is lacking, but according to this it already exists in secret. And since in all the old and even the new parties, from [Johannes] Rösing to [Johann Baptist von] Schweitzer, such important men are counted, the victory cannot fail to arrive for them.

Engels was responding to Karl Heinrich Ulrichs' booklet *Incubus*, which seemed to portend a major shift in the sexual balance of power. Engels could not resist elaborating on a fantasy of his and Marx's about finding themselves on the losing side:

> It is only luck that we are personally too old to have to fear that on the victory of this party we must pay the victors bodily tribute. But the young generation!

It is clear from the rest of the letter, which evinces humour and distaste in roughly equal measure, that he was imagining being gang-raped by triumphant pederasts.[1]

There is some evidence that Marx had read and enjoyed the great American laureate of comradeship Walt Whitman – or, at least, the Whitman of 'Song of Myself' ('My right and left arms round the sides of two friends and I in the middle', 'Manhood balanced and florid and full!') and 'Pioneers! O Pioneers' ('All the hands of comrades clasping, all the Southern, / all the Northern, /

Pioneers! O Pioneers!').[2] Marx and Engels themselves knew a thing or two about the symbolic and actual force of comradeship. One of their main legacies would be the left-wing version of such symbolism ('Workers of the world, unite!'), but once desire was added to the mix, they were predictably discomfited.[3] Thus, at the very time that homosexuality was beginning to be examined and theorised as an individual state of being, verging on an aspect of identity, those who might be called homosexual were also beginning to be seen as a potential group with common interests; if overt, even a political movement capable of collective action, or, if covert, a subversive conspiracy. It is hardly surprising that they may have seemed like some kind of threat.

By the end of the nineteenth century, those theorisations of anomalous sexualities themselves amounted to a trans-European intellectual movement. The topic of what would eventually be called 'homosexuality' was studied from the viewpoints of a range of scientific disciplines by theorists who included Arnold Aletrino, Lucien von Römer and Jacob Israël de Haan in the Netherlands, Edward Westermarck in Finland, Cesare Lombroso and Paolo Mantegazza in Italy, Heinrich Hoessli in Switzerland, Károly Mária Kertbeny (an Austrian-born Hungarian), Karl-Heinrich Ulrichs, Carl Friedrich Westphal, Richard von Krafft-Ebing, Albert Moll, Iwan Bloch, Benedict Friedlaender and Magnus Hirschfeld in Germany, Vasily Vasilievich Rozanov and V.F. Chizh in Russia, Sigmund Freud in Austria, Arlindo Camillo Monteiro in Portugal, Edward Carpenter and Havelock Ellis in England, René Guyon in France and, later, Alfred Kinsey in the USA.[4] The outcome was a transnational sense of new subjectivities, but also of a potentially powerful collectivity.

It is hard not to see this wave of scientific enquiry as amounting to a bureaucratisation of identity and pleasure. Every twitch and quirk of desire had to be defined and categorised, a process that involved giving names to all sorts of things that had previously been considered unnameable because unspeakable. The immediate consequence was a neologising frenzy, in a babel of tongues, in which the bulk of the defining occurred around the so-called perversions. Only then did the standard form of acceptable desire get named, in contradistinction to what it was not. The man who first coined the term 'homosexual', in German in 1868, Károly Mária Kertbeny, originally set it in opposition to 'normalsexual'.[5] The preferred word 'heterosexual' followed in 1869. Neither caught on at once.

In 1869 Karl Westphal published a book on *Die conträre Sexualempfindung*, meaning 'contrary sexual feeling'. In *Psychopathia Sexualis* (1886), Richard von Krafft-Ebing concentrated his observations of same-sex sexualities on four main categories: psychosexual hermaphrodites (we would call them bisexuals); homosexuals (where he distinguished between 'inborn' and 'acquired' homosexuality);

effeminates and 'viraginites' (respectively, male and female persons with a psychic disposition corresponding to that of the opposite sex); and androgynes. In 1896, Marc André Raffalovich published a book entitled *Uranisme et unisexualité*. A book published in Rome in 1908 under the pseudonym 'Xavier Mayne' (actually by Edward Irenaeus Prime-Stevenson) was called *The Intersexes: A History of Similisexualism as a Problem in Social Life*. Mayne employed the terms 'uranian' and 'uraniad' to denote, respectively, homosexual men and lesbians. But his expression 'intersexual' was clearly ambiguous. For instance, René Guyon used it, not without good reason, to refer not to a status between the two sexes but to relations between men and women; in other words, to what we now call heterosexuality. 'Similisexualism' was probably dismissed as being too vague; had it caught on, I suppose male–female couples would have had to be called 'dissimilisexuals'. Edward Carpenter spoke of 'homogenic' love (that is, same-genus love).

The bureaucratising impulse is extreme in the theorisations of Karl-Heinrich Ulrichs. His main category was that of the 'drittes Geschlecht' or third sex. He divided the world into three sexes: men, women and urnings. The latter group he then subdivided into Mannlings (virile homosexual men), Intermediaries (virile passives, effeminate actives), Weiblings (effeminate homosexual men), Urningins (homosexual women), Uranodionings (bisexual men), Uranodioningins (bisexual women) and Hermaphrodites (the physically dually sexed). Uranodionings were further subdivided into the conjunctive (sexually bi-directional) and the disjunctive (with a sexual desire for women but a romantic desire for men). Of course, the whole of Ulrichs' scheme takes us back to the two first categories, which are left uninvestigated: (heterosexual) men and women. What are they? How are they to be categorised? Or what is it that leads to their being regarded as rising above the need for categorisation?

Surely the most flamboyantly inventive of these sexual bureaucrats was Lucien von Römer, a member of Magnus Hirschfeld's Scientific-Humanitarian Committee, who developed a model of intermediary sexes consisting of not two but 687,375 variations; but he did not give them all names. More usefully, surveying the sexual habits of his fellow students, he found that 2 per cent were exclusively orientated towards the same sex but that 20 per cent had had same-sex contacts of some kind.

Eventually, out of this hubbub of unisexuality, similisexuality, intersexuality, uranism, contrary sexuality, *per*version and *in*version, there slowly emerged a contingent consensus around the terms 'homosexuality' and 'heterosexuality', which has since proven hard to shake off.[6] This system soon became firmly entrenched in European languages.[7] In most, noun and adjective are the same, so that the same tautology is almost always available: the homosexual is homosexual. E.M. Forster's fictional representative of the newly named type, Maurice, finally tracks down a hypnotist from whom, for the first time, he hears the name of his 'trouble', 'Congenital homosexuality'. Maurice's impulsive response to this apparent gobbledygook is, 'Congenital how much?'[8] Meanwhile, legal statutes continued, in distinctly unscientific tones, to speak of such things as 'sodomy', the 'crime against nature', 'gross indecency' and so on.

When Maurice consults the family doctor over concerns about his sexuality, it turns out that Dr Barry knows only the Bible's attitudes to such things. 'He had read no scientific works on Maurice's subject. None had existed when he walked the hospitals [at the start of his career], and any published since were in German, and therefore suspect.'[9] Had his doctor been more up-to-date, better informed and less insular, Maurice might have found a quicker route to understanding the kind of man he had become. In Radclyffe Hall's novel *The Well of Loneliness* (1928), Sir Philip Gordon has a locked cabinet of books that he pores over when alone, making notes in the margins – notes which include the name of his daughter, Stephen. One book is by Karl Heinrich Ulrichs, another by Richard von Krafft-Ebing. After her father's death, Stephen finds them and reads them, beginning with the latter. She also finds his Bible, but hurls it away.[10] From a position of complete ignorance, Sir Philip has been trying to determine what category of person he has fathered. From a similar position of ignorance, but with the knowledge of first-hand experience, Stephen tries to solve the same conundrum. What the likes of Ulrichs and Krafft-Ebing provide is the knowledge that, although anomalous, Stephen is not unique and that hers is a natural state of being.

Such readings of the theorists were themselves far from theoretical: they were committed investigations into material reality, both physical and psychological, and into sexual practice. It may not be overstating the case to say that such texts actually conferred identity on those who dared consult them. At any rate, they maintained their value as primers for homosexual existence for many decades. The American poet and critic David Bergman, who was born in 1950, recalls: 'I first came to know about homosexuality from the yellowed pages of a copy of Krafft-Ebing that my parents kept in their bookcase'.[11]

To many, observing at a distance this cultural revolution among specialists, it seemed as if Love had somehow become a medical condition, the heart a sexual organ. As someone says in Aldous Huxley's novel *Those Barren Leaves* (1925), 'Too much light conversation about the Oedipus complex and anal eroticism is taking the edge off love'.[12] However, it is worth noting that hardly any of the freshly minted 'scientific' terms appear in the correspondence or quoted speech of the people I write about in this book. In part, this is because of the need for discretion; but, more importantly, it is because the new, formal terms simply did not feel right. This is not to downplay the significance of those academic/medical terms to the men and women who gathered strength from thinking of themselves as recognisable case studies, deserving of sympathetic treatment by the professionals and newly able to identify with others of their own kind. But the fact is that most people just got on with their lives, either ignorant of their status in the latest sexual theories or uninterested in it. Most homosexual men in Britain, for instance, were much less likely to use the academic terms in informal conversation with each other than such circumspect expressions as 'musical' or 'so' or 'that way' or 'TBH' (To Be Had) or even 'gay' – a wide-ranging term meaning sexually unconventional.[13] At once transparent (to those in the know) and opaque, they were the perfect currency for the open exchange of secret information.

Around the turn of the nineteenth and twentieth centuries, as never before, what had been unspeakable was now becoming a matter of prominent public record. Internationally, successive scandals – Oscar Wilde (1895), Georges Eekhoud (1900), Friedrich Krupp (1902), Sir Hector Macdonald (1903), Jacques d'Adelswärd-Fersen (1903), Nils Santesson (1907), General Kuno von Moltke and Philipp, Prince of Eulenberg-Hertefeld (1907, 1908), the Pemberton Billing case (1918), and the prosecution of *The Well of Loneliness* (1928) – brought the existence of homosexuality to the forefront of the collective consciousness in a manner that turned out to be both threatening and enabling to homosexual individuals.[14] (See Chapter Two.) Later, during the Cold War, many national security services on both sides of the Iron Curtain took seriously the existence of homosexual people as a potentially subversive conspiracy. Notoriously, the networks of homosexuality transcended many more formal and conventional social and political boundaries, reifying crossovers not only between national and racial cultures, but between class subcultures, between high society and the demimondes of bohemian artists, between the law-abiding and the criminal, between the respectable and the disreputable. Such refusals of fixed status seemed, to those of a bureaucratic and nationalistic cast of mind, inherently untrustworthy.

Thus, with the increasing visibility of a type came increased pressure on the individual to remain invisible. With that obligation to conceal oneself, however, came a corresponding distrust of homosexual surreptitiousness. Remember that, even in his light-hearted letter to Marx, Engels raised as a particular source of concern the fact that pederasts, having counted themselves, might then take the logical next step and organise themselves. This had not yet happened ('the organisation is lacking') and yet it had ('it already exists in secret'). In the twentieth century, a common pattern would take shape. Forced into the shadows, homosexual people would be distrusted for frequenting the darkness. What the blurbs of mid-century pulp fiction would often refer to as 'the twilight world of the homosexual' was both compulsory and blameworthy.

Coerced into a position where they became blackmailable, homosexual individuals could then be characterised as an intrinsic security risk. This logic was an inescapable snare.

## Natural Secret Agents and Natural Traitors

There was no such thing as the 'Homintern'. It was a joke, a nightmare, or a dream, depending on one's point of view; but, despite its lack of substance, it still occupied a solid and prominent site near the centre of modern life. The Comintern, or Communist International, was the international communist organisation set up by Lenin in 1919 and dissolved in 1943. (It was also known as the Third International.) The coining of the expression 'Homintern' is often attributed to Cyril Connolly, less often to Maurice Bowra, and sometimes to W.H. Auden; but Anthony Powell thought its source was Jocelyn Brooke, and Harold Norse claimed it for himself.[15] Most plausibly, it was the felicitous invention of many minds, unknown to each other, at more or less the same time. Anyone who pronounced the relatively new word 'homosexual' with a short first 'o' – and that is likely to have included anyone with a classical education – could have made the camp pun. 'Homintern' was the name Connolly, Auden and others jokingly gave the sprawling, informal network of friendships that Cold War conspiracy theorists would later come to think of as 'the international homosexual conspiracy'. In fact, the Homosexual International was sometimes only superficially international and sometimes only half-heartedly homosexual: it was also a matter of surfaces, fashions and styles. The term tended to be applied to networks only of men, in part because those who thought of such a potential conspiracy as a threat tended not to think of women, let alone lesbian women, as having sufficient influence to be worth worrying about. Yet, as I shall show in this book, the social networks in question often included both sexes; and the women who were active in them often wielded significant cultural influence in their own right.[16]

No less international than homosexual networks themselves is the fear of their undue influence. The likes of Connolly and Auden may have used the expression 'Homintern' in a light-hearted spirit, but there were official circles in many countries in which the idea was taken with the utmost seriousness. They had seen what Friedrich Engels saw, namely the prospect that the sexual minority might not only realise how big it was, but also organise itself to further its own interests. Foreign powers might harness this subterfuge. In England towards the end of the First World War, the *English Review* and the *Imperialist* published scare stories about Germany's plans to launch a moral attack on England by way of a list its secret agents had compiled of homosexual Englishmen and women. Germany stood ready both to debauch and to expose the debauchery of the English Establishment. (See Chapter Two.) In late 1933, Stalin and the Politburo were informed of a Nazi plot to undermine morale in the government and the party and to gather Soviet military intelligence. In the words of H. Montgomery Hyde, 'What was the more remarkable was that it was in substance a homosexual conspiracy.' As subsequently revealed in *The Letter of an Old Bolshevik* by Boris Nikolaevsky, said to have been written by, or under the influence of, Nikolai Bukharin,

> An assistant of the German military attaché, a friend and follower of the notorious Captain [Ernst] Roehm, managed to enter the homosexual circles in Moscow, and, under cover of a homosexual 'organisation' (homosexuality was still legal in Russia at that time), started a whole network of National Socialist propaganda. Its threads extended into the provinces, to Leningrad, Kharkov, Kiev, etc. A number of persons in literary and artistic circles were involved: the private secretary of a very prominent actor, known for his homosexual inclinations, an important scientific collaborator of the Lenin Institute, among others.[17]

The details matter less than the implications: foreigners, the notion of 'homosexual circles' rather than mere isolated individuals or couples, the possibility of the 'organisation' of something otherwise seen as being led by the passions, the 'network', the lengthening 'threads', a connection between the enigmatic and unpredictable arts and affairs of state, the mixing of classes, the sciences not so much objective as employing collaborators ... Each suggestion reinforces the one before with a further hint of secretive conspiracy.[18]

The salient feature of the widespread, paranoid association of homosexuality with espionage is the suspicion that homosexuals may form stronger allegiances to others of their own kind, across national boundaries, as well as across other social subdivisions such as classes, than to their own fellow nationals. In this respect, the cosmopolitanism of homosexual people was thought similar to, and congruent with, that of the Jews.[19]

Considering the similarities between the social situations of inverts and Jews, Marcel Proust concentrated less on prejudice against them than on their own accommodation of that prejudice. He compared their tendency to ingratiate themselves with, respectively, heterosexuals and Gentiles ('shunning one another, seeking out those who are most directly their opposite, who do not desire their company, pardoning their rebuffs, moved to ecstasy by their condescension'), their defensive togetherness ('brought into the company of their own kind by the ostracism that strikes them, the opprobrium under which they have fallen'), their tendency to despise those of their own kind who are least able to assimilate ('the mockery with which he who, more closely blended with, better assimilated to the opposing race, is relatively, in appearance, the least inverted, heaps upon him who has remained more so') and their search for historical predecessors in whom they can take pride ('taking pleasure in recalling that Socrates was one of themselves, as the Israelites claim that Jesus was one of them, without reflecting that there were no abnormals when homosexuality was the norm, no anti-Christians before Christ'). Proust also implicitly compared the martyrdoms of Alfred Dreyfus and Oscar Wilde.[20]

In addition to their similarities, there was also a conspicuous overlap between the two groups. For a start, of the theorists of (homo)sexuality, Hirschfeld, Raffalovich, Aletrino, Weininger, Bloch and, of course, Freud were all Jews. Sexology itself could be blamed on the vested interests of both groups: the Nazis' sacking of Magnus Hirschfeld's Institute for Sexual Research in 1933 was an act of anti-Semitism combined with violent intolerance of sexual dissent. (See Chapter Four.) Although laughed at or despised, by the 1930s the homosexual aesthete had come to epitomise the glamour of modernity, along with some of its imagined threat. (See Chapter Six.) The sophisticated, urban Jew was allotted a similar role. Thus, when D.H. Lawrence was writing the closing chapters of *Women in Love* (a novel he had begun in 1913) and needed a character to embody the cutting edge of Modernism in the arts, he came up with the sinister figure of Loerke, a German who is both homosexual and Jewish. Created at a time of intense and widespread anti-Semitism, some of it Lawrence's own, Loerke is referred to as being 'like a troll' and 'like a gnome'. Rupert Birkin says he is 'like a rat', adding a little later, 'I expect he is a Jew – or part Jewish'; and Gerald Crich agrees.[21]

It was during the Cold War period after the Second World War that the various national security services of the 'Free World' – the FBI under J. Edgar Hoover in particular – followed the Soviets and the Nazis by starting to take seriously the very existence of homosexuals as a potentially subversive conspiracy. Homosexual himself, Hoover was in the perfect position to generalise from his own experience of deviant duplicity: he knew better than virtually anyone how homosexual men could occupy positions of power. He was correspondingly aware of how they could be kept out of such positions. Others who worked alongside him – Roy Cohn, for instance – learned from Hoover the same lesson in both the acquisition of power and the inadmissible vulnerability that the powerful homosexual needed to keep under control.[22]

In 1950 the US Senate Subcommittee on Investigations produced a report entitled *Employment of Homosexuals and Other Sex Perverts in Government*, in which the tendency of perverts to congregate with other perverts was noted as a danger to the body politic:

Eminent psychiatrists have informed the subcommittee that the homosexual is likely to seek his own kind because the pressures of society are
such that he feels uncomfortable unless he is with his own kind. Due to this
situation the homosexual tends to surround himself with other homosexuals, not only in his social, but in his business life. Under these circumstances if a homosexual attains a position in government where he can
influence the hiring of personnel it is almost inevitable that he will attempt
to place other homosexuals in government jobs.[23]

The writers may never have noticed that every word could also be applied to
'the heterosexual' but, even if they had, they would not have thought much of
it, since the association of heterosexuals did not matter. Or rather, the association of heterosexuals was what was required for the smooth running of
American society – required to the extent of being taken for granted. In the
same year, 1950, John O'Donnell claimed in the *New York Daily News* that the
State Department was 'dominated by an all-powerful, super-secret inner circle
of highly educated, socially highly-placed sexual misfits, all easy to blackmail,
all susceptible to blandishments by homosexuals in foreign nations'.[24]

In an article called 'Homosexual International' in a 1960 issue of the
American magazine *Human Events*, R.G. Waldeck argues that 'the main reason
why' the US State Department was right to throw 119 homosexuals out of their
jobs in 1952 was that 'by the very nature of their vice they belong to a sinister,
mysterious and efficient International'. Rosie Goldschmidt Waldeck, the author
of the article, was born Rosa Goldschmidt to a prominent German-Jewish
banking family; she later converted to Catholicism and became an American.
She married at least three times. Warming to her theme, she goes on:

> This conspiracy has spread all over the globe; has penetrated all classes;
> operates in armies and in prisons; has infiltrated into the press, the movies
> and the cabinets and it all but dominates the arts, literature, theater, music
> and TV.

As a self-appointed, would-be expert on the topic, Waldeck kept a watch on the
situation from her relatively privileged vantage point. She writes that 'the
Homosexual International began to gnaw at the sinews of the state in the 1930s'
and that 'Until then it just nibbled'. At what was still this 'nibbling' stage, she
began to take notes on her observations of the phenomenon:

> With fascination I watched the little Sodoms functioning within the
> Embassies and foreign offices. Somehow homosexuals always seemed to

come by the dozen, not because they were cheaper that way but because a homosexual ambassador or chargé d'affaires or Undersecretary of State liked to staff his 'team' with his own people. Another reason was that the homosexuals really do look after their own[.]

Their biased exertion of influence may have been bad enough, but the real danger arose when these groups of homosexuals in positions of influence adopted a shared political view. 'The alliance between the Homosexual International and the Communist International started at the dawn of the Pink Decade [the 1930s]. It was then that the homosexual aristocracy – writers, poets, painters and such – discovered Marxism.' Waldeck does not explain why 'the homosexual aristocracy' does not simply consist of aristocrats, or why, having already mentioned embassies and foreign ministries, she suddenly places mere artists at the top of the pile.

With all these homosexual Marxists in place, one of their traits leads to the worst-case scenario: 'There is another even more sinister aspect of homosexuality in high places. It is that homosexuals make natural secret agents and natural traitors.' In support of this claim, Waldeck references the research of the Austrian-American psychoanalyst Theodor Reik's *Psychology of Sex Relations* (1945); and she names as the classic case of this syndrome Colonel Alfred Redl (the Austrian army officer who spied for the Russians before the First World War), who 'got an immense kick out of playing the role of both the traitor and of [*sic*] the one whose life work it is to apprehend and punish traitors'. Given such a risky state of affairs, merely clearing out the State Department can only be regarded as a start.

> At best the elimination of homosexuals from Government agencies is only one phase of combating the homosexual invasion of American public life. Another phase, more important in the long run, is the matter of public education. This should be clear to anyone who views with dismay the forebearance [*sic*] bordering on tenderness with which American society not only tolerates the infiltration of homosexuals everywhere but even allows them to display their perversion in public.[25]

So from 'natural secret agents' operating in the shadows, it is a short step to an 'invasion of American public life' and the open display of perversion. Whether the same individuals are involved in both fields of activity Waldeck does not vouchsafe. Nor is it at all clear which is worse: homosexual surreptitiousness or homosexual exhibitionism.

In Sweden, meanwhile, the attack came not from the Right but from so-called anti-fascists on the Left, led by the writer Vilhelm Moberg, who alleged that government had been corrupted by 'homosexual leagues'. In 1950 an investigation into allegations of sexual abuse in Swedish boys' homes had given rise to broader accusations of a high-level conspiracy and cover-up. The so-called 'Kejne affair' – after Karl-Erik Kejne, the cleric who had launched the first batch of accusations – led to the resignation of the Minister for Ecclesiastical Affairs, Nils Quensel, a bachelor with an interest in youth charities. Responding to the affair, the press fostered scare stories about a secret network of homosexual men in positions of power. No evidence of such a network was ever produced. There is no reason to regard this campaign as being substantially different from what was happening in the USA: essentially a shocked response to fresh knowledge of the sheer extent of homosexual desire at all levels of society.

Given the degree and volume of official rhetoric designed to stigmatise homosexual people as security risks, it is no wonder that, in the public imagination, perverts and spies became closely associated. Yet the item on 'Homosexuality' in Norman Polmar and Thomas B. Allen's generally reliable *Encyclopedia of Espionage* (1998) names just nine homosexual men and one bisexual: Alfred Redl, Guy Burgess, the bisexual Donald Maclean, Anthony Blunt, Alan Turning (*sic*), James A. Mintkenbaugh, William Martin, Bernon Mitchell, John Vassall and Maurice Oldfield.[26] The last-named had to resign his position as co-ordinator of UK security and intelligence in Northern Ireland after he was found to be homosexual; there was no suggestion that in his previous incarnation as Director General of MI6 he ever spied for anyone but his own Whitehall masters. Alan Turing helped break the Germans' most complex codes by developing the Enigma machine. The presence of these two figures reminds us that a genuinely representative list would include all those agents who spied *for* rather than *on* their nations, and all those lesbians and gay men who did secret work on behalf of the security of the collective. It may well be that because they were gay they were especially good at *keeping* secrets, rather than at betraying them.

From the *Encyclopedia*'s named group we arrive at a grand total of seven homosexual individuals and one bisexual who betrayed the interests of their own nations. To these we should add several unnamed cases – a US Embassy clerk in Moscow whom the Russians photographed with a male lover but then failed to blackmail into spying for them (he was sent home, along with two other homosexual employees of the Embassy); a French diplomat who was put in the same position by the Russians, but who simply thanked them for the rather flattering photographs; and 'dozens' of employees of the US National Security Agency who were dismissed when, not found to be, but suspected of being, homosexual – not a single one of them the betrayer of his own nation.

In brief, when one actually lays out the evidence it becomes clear that all the sound and fury about homosexual spies may have been ridiculously dispropor- tionate to the small number of actual cases: in the *Encyclopedia*'s account, one in the 1900s in Austria, three in the 1930s in Britain, one American in Germany in the 1950s, one in Britain in the 1960s, and the lovers William Martin and Bernon Mitchell, who defected to the USSR in 1960 because they disapproved of the intelligence-gathering methods of the US National Security Agency, by which they were employed. Each case may be serious enough in itself, if one believes in the sanctity of nations; but, put together, they do not amount to much. The fact that such cases have been used by so many agencies to deny security clearance to homosexual individuals says more about homophobia than about homosexuality itself.[27]

Ironically, there are times when the social habits of homosexual men arouse suspicion precisely because homosexual desire has *not* been considered a rele- vant factor. The English painter John Craxton attracted the interest of the authorities in Greece after the military coup in April 1967: 'Espionage was already suspected, since the liking of so cultivated a man for sailors' bars must surely signal an interest in naval intelligence. That raised a laugh from the suspect.'[28]

## The Girls' Friendly Society

Writers and artists with a grudge against those who, they feel, have excluded them from the inner circles of grace and denied them the glittering prizes can be quick with accusations of closed interests.[29] The Russian novelist Andrei Bely took something of a scattergun approach when complaining, in 1907, of those St Petersburgers he believed were ruining the integrity of Russian letters. He listed them:

> liberals, bourgeois, aesthetes, Kadets, whores and lechers, idlers, men and women alike, mediocrities, losers, ignoramuses, cynics and Mycaenases, vampires, the self-loving and self-indulgent, orgiasts and pederasts, sadists and the like[.][30]

In the face of such an army of conspirators how could any mere mortal writer survive? Bely's unrestrained rant could as well be one of his wilder fictional narrators' opinions, but this was no satire. At least he had the good sense to excise this passage when he republished the article in 1911. The American painter Thomas Hart Benton, a self-declared 'enemy of modernism', said in his 1937 autobiography:

If young gentlemen, or old ones either, wish to wear women's undergar-ments and cultivate extraordinary manners it is all right with me. But it is not all right when, by ingratiation or subtle connivance, precious fairies get into positions of power and judge, buy, and exhibit American pictures on the base of nervous whim and under the sway of those overdelicate refine-ments of tastes characteristic of their kind.[31]

The international avant-garde aroused much the same fury and distaste in Hitler and Stalin as in the critics of the 1913 Armory Show in New York. (Theodore Roosevelt: 'This isn't art!') Values previously taken for granted were deliberately being subverted; rules of perspective and harmony, even of logic, were deliberately being flouted; standards of decency and good taste were deliberately being violated . . . Later, the painter Francis Bacon had a peculiar rant about 'a Jewish, homosexual mafia' working against his interests in Manhattan when he failed to secure a collaboration with the photographer Peter Beard.[32]

In the liberal arts, where few great national interests are at stake, and matters of life and death tend to be only theoretically engaged, similar claims of influ-ential, enclosed cliques have often been made. For over a century, anxieties about gay exclusivity have consistently shaped the critical reception of work by artists known to be gay. Perhaps especially in the 1930s, and certainly in subse-quent accounts of the period, Modernism itself came under suspicion. The kinds of bohemian, cosmopolitan subcultures that were, to varying extents, accepting of homosexuals, communists and Jews, were themselves bound to be correspondingly subject to sceptical surveillance.

Commentators on British culture have continued, decades on, to purvey versions of inter-war literary culture in which it is taken for granted that groups of homosexual men were operating a professional bias in each other's favour. It is a standard cliché of our history of the 1930s. For instance, Valentine Cunningham flaws his major account of *British Writers in the Thirties* (1989) with a repeated suggestion that some cultural networks were less legitimate than others because they consisted of men who were homosexual. Speaking of the group around W.H. Auden, he seems both bewildered and disturbed to have to report that 'The shared male bed lay behind many of the coterie's [book] dedications', as if heterosexual people never dedicate their books to their lovers or spouses. The Auden group and others are described as 'guarded coteries bonded by shared private codes, covert languages and publicly inadmissible passions'. One group even becomes 'the magic homosexual circle'. Cunningham cannot leave the point alone. He speaks of 'the homosexual nature of much '30s cliquery', 'the period's crowd of homosexuals', 'the homosexual core of the

clique', and 'this homosexual coterie'. One group of friends and collaborators is
'a covey of homosexual chums'. (Gay men always have 'chums' in this book.)[33]

Although there is an implied triviality and foreignness in all of these expressions, Cunningham seems not to consider their triviality trivial. On the contrary,
such labels carry with them a strong suggestion of a potentially subversive
disengagement from the highly serious ideals of State (which are underpinned
by values of family and national religion). A coterie or a clique is assumed to be
held together by misplaced loyalties. Any group that sees itself as marginal is
likely to be only marginally committed to the national (or imperial) project.
When in the 1930s Wyndham Lewis spoke of 'the intense "outcast" *esprit de
corps* of the pathic', he sounded as though he was experiencing the caster-out's
anxieties concerning the consequences of his own hostility.[34] The phrase *esprit
de corps* evokes the militaristic togetherness of an enemy to describe what might,
from a different point of view, be described as the solidarity of the oppressed; or
else, merely, as a loose chain of contingent acquaintanceships. Cunningham,
writing in the 1980s, subscribes to the same view: 'affection for boys and among
the boys led naturally to jobs for the boys'. And the socialism of homosexuals is
fake because of its ulterior motivation: 'Much of the period's writing about the
proletariat is vitiated by the bourgeois bugger's specialist regard.'[35]

This critical tendency sometimes recurs with a quasi-subliminal brevity,
easily missed by the reader, perhaps a mere reflex on the part of the author.
There is such a moment in Hermione Lee's 1996 biography of Virginia Woolf.
In 1930, after dining with various homosexual men, including E.M. Forster
and Lytton Strachey, whose conversation strayed on to the topic of attractive
youths, Virginia Woolf said she had received 'a tinkling, private, giggling
impression. As if I had gone into a men's urinal.' Of Eddy Sackville-West she
said, quite simply, 'I can[']t take Buggerage seriously.' Hermione Lee comments,
dubiously, as follows: 'Like Simone de Beauvoir twenty years later . . . the feminist in her deplored the fact that gay men seemed to want to be women. And
she must also have felt that homosexuality was, for the next generation of
writers, an exclusive passport for literary success.' The latter sentence appears
out of nowhere, without evidence. Why 'must' she 'have felt' this? She was a
publisher, after all, and she published writers who were homosexual. Is Lee
suggesting Woolf was publishing them for that reason? Presumably not. But
the implication that the men were setting up each other's literary careers
according to sexual criteria is gratuitous and left unjustified.[36] That version of
1930s patronage has taken root in British literary history and is widely taken
for granted.

However, it was in the period after the Second World War that claims of
homosexual power brokerage in the arts flourished most often on both sides of

the Atlantic. In a 1953 essay in the *New Statesman and Nation*, J.B. Priestley wrote:

> There are some aesthetic enterprises that are hardly likely to succeed without some assistance from the Inverts' Block – called by a sardonic friend of mine 'the Girls' Friendly Society' – which enthusiastically gives its praise and patronage to whatever is decorative, 'amusing', 'good theatre', witty in the right way, and likely to make heterosexual relationships look ridiculous: all of which is probably the stiff price we are paying in London for our stupid laws against [male] inversion.[37]

Priestley is speaking of a broad cultural landscape, but his references to aesthetics, decoration, amusement, theatre and wit evoke the figure of Oscar Wilde (see Chapter Two) and the arena in which he scored the most spectacular successes of his career, the West End stage. He being out of the way, his place in the theatre has been taken by others, if lessers, of his sort – enough of them to distort the West End's representations of heterosexual life. So numerous and so clever are these pesky wits that they seem to be laughing at duller folk across every line of footlights. Dated though this lament may seem, it is purveying a myth that simply will not go away.

The actor Donald Wolfit is on record as having complained that 'the theatre is controlled by an international cartel of poufferie!'[38] In a 2001 biography of the actor John Gielgud, Sheridan Morley says that Wolfit, who was 'virulently anti-homosexual' as well as highly influential, 'already [in 1933] suspected John [Gielgud] to be at the heart of a precious West End clique which would, as Donald saw it, be specifically determined to keep his old-fashioned barnstorming virility in a state of semi-unemployment'. It is the influence of this 'precious . . . clique', rather than Wolfit's influential homophobia, that engages Morley's interest. The power of the producers H.M. Tennent and Hugh 'Binkie' Beaumont led to many accusations of undue influence, skewed in favour of particular young men for sexual reasons. Such accusations are absent from accounts of the influence of the West End's higher number of heterosexual producers. Expressions like 'mafia' are commonplace in this context. Of the young Richard Burton, for instance, Frank Hauser wrote: 'There is no doubt that the gay mafia around H.M. Tennent all fell for him, and although Richard was always resolutely heterosexual, I think he already knew how to play the gay game'. John Osborne said of his own experience, 'The first thing that struck me about the London stage was its domination at every level by poufs; I have been hag-ridden by these monsters ever since.' Kenneth Hurren, drama critic of the *Spectator* in the 1950s and 1960s, said of Hugh Beaumont's parties, 'there were more fag-ends walking around the rooms than in the ashtrays'. He added: 'the majority of actors and directors employed by Beaumont were homosexuals, and as he was the most powerful manager in London, that inevitably affected the climate of the West End'. One would like to see statistical proof of this claimed 'majority'. It looks suspiciously like a paranoid reaction against an unusual situation in which homosexual men were not actively being discriminated against. (I have seen no claim that these men acted in favour of lesbian women, too.)[39]

Interviewed by Keith Howes for *Gay News* in 1976, the influential drama critic Kenneth Tynan complained of this same period that the theatre in England had been very 'queer-dominated', trapped in what he called 'a homosexual hammer-lock'. Directors and producers who were 'queer' preferred to employ young male actors who were 'queer' too. One management 'made great use of homosexual actors and those glamorous female stars which the queer mafia goes for'. This bias even influenced the choice of plays to be staged: 'The more realistic, down-to-earth plays wouldn't have found favour.' When a particular producer had fourteen shows running at the same time, there was 'a disproportionate number of queer actors and directors' in evidence. Although he 'didn't thoroughly approve' of 'this imbalance', Tynan admitted, he never wrote about it.[40] The producer he referred to is likely to have been Hugh Beaumont. According to Arthur Miller, Beaumont was not beyond taking profitable advantage of anti-homosexual prejudice by staging club performances of banned texts and pocketing the additional membership fee paid by theatregoers. This happened, for instance, with Miller's own play *A View from the Bridge* with its brief reference to homosexuality.[41]

Once generated, it seems, such rumours do not go away. In *The Real Life of Laurence Olivier* (1996), despite the manifest success of Olivier, a man he mistakenly regards as entirely heterosexual, Roger Lewis gratuitously holds forth about a homosexual conspiracy not just in the theatre but in English public life generally:

> let's face it, in the acting profession, and in the arts in England (and in politics: there are over eighty homosexual Members of Parliament), it is practically impossible to become successful, or to garner honours, if you are too exclusively heterosexual ... It is a conspiracy – as bad as anti-Semitism. Literary editors, television producers, theatre critics, publishers, opera, ballet, museum curating: domains all controlled by [homosexual men].

Perhaps this author is an unsuccessful heterosexual – who knows? He also speaks of 'the extent of theatre's homosexual mafia' and compiles a little list of H.M. Tennent, Hugh Beaumont, the Ivy Restaurant, Terence Rattigan, the

Royal Court Theatre, Tony Richardson and John Dexter – important names, to be sure, but hardly the full extent of the post-war theatrical establishment in London.[42] Five men, a single theatre and a restaurant do not a culture make; nor do eighty parliamentarians fill a chamber of 650 members.[43] The idea that such clusters of homosexual men amount to 'a conspiracy – as bad as anti-Semitism' can only rebound on Lewis himself. It is as if he has never heard of Auschwitz. He has clearly never heard of homophobia.

Notwithstanding his perception that the London stage was dominated by 'poufs', John Osborne was well aware of a contrary force of anti-homosexual bias in the English theatre, in the mid-1950s at least. For instance, as he would write in his memoirs, 'The Denville Players of Scarborough [on the North Yorkshire coast] had made their conditions of employment brutally laconic: "No fancy salaries and no queer folk". This may sound like an endearingly bluff self-parody by stereotypical Yorkshire types; but this approach to the 'problem' of homosexuality's role in the theatre was not just a provincial trait. It was shared, in London, by George Devine: 'In the newly formed, middle-class liberal English Stage Company, principles would be applied as rigorously as by the Denville Players. No fancy salaries and the nod that queer folk were not to be considered, certainly not as officer material.' The English Stage Company had been founded in 1955, with Devine as its director, and the following year it began operating in the Royal Court Theatre in Sloane Square. Osborne reports that, in his first conversation with Devine, apropos of Terence Rattigan, 'he cut me short [by speaking] about the patent inadequacies of homosexual plays masquerading as plays about straight men and women'.

> He seemed to believe, in a simple-hearted way, that the blight of buggery, which then dominated the theatre in all its frivolity, could be kept down decently by a direct appeal to seriousness and good intentions from his own crack corps of heterosexual writers, directors and actors.

Even so, the Royal Court opened in April 1956 with a production of Angus Wilson's play *The Mulberry Bush*; Devine's associate director was Tony Richardson; and guest directors included Lindsay Anderson. So the embargo on queers can hardly be said to have been rigorously policed. And although Binkie Beaumont is supposed to have been so supportive of homosexual participants in theatre, he drew the line at writers, whom, as a class, he hated. According to Osborne again, 'Rattigan and [Noël] Coward had both suffered humiliation from his lizard tongue'.[44]

Even as recently as 2006, the English playwright Simon Gray spoke of 'heterophobes, which quite a few theatre critics are, or feel obliged to make themselves into'. Anticipating these critics' criticisms, he added: 'They can call me a homophobe, and it's thumbs down for me and my future, but if I call them heterophobes, it's also thumbs down for me and my future.'[45]

There were similar complaints about the American theatre during the 1950s, when the American stage was dominated by playwrights who were gay: Tennessee Williams, William Inge, Arthur Laurents, John Van Druten and Edward Albee. In a notorious 1966 article in the *New York Times*, Stanley Kauffmann claimed that 'The principal complaint against homosexual dramatists is well known. Because three of the most successful American playwrights of the past twenty years are (reputed) homosexuals and because their plays often treat of women and marriage, therefore, it is said, postwar American drama presents a badly distorted picture of American women, marriage, and society in general.'[46] (The writers he meant were Albee, Williams and Inge.) Another article in the *Times*, by drama critic Howard Taubman, similarly complained of the inauthenticity of male homosexual playwrights' representations of women.[47] Acknowledging the detachment of such writers from their material, Robert Patrick, a gay playwright himself, characterises the process as follows, for better or worse: 'The outsider inside, the homosexual, watched and saw and remembered, analyzed, distilled and idealized, criticized, satirized, commemorated, blessed, and cursed the beauty, passion, pain, poetry, harmonies, and contradictions of the all-encompassing heterosexual hegemony.'[48] Interestingly, Patrick reminds us that none of these playwrights were making gay characters. They were dutifully submitting to the taboo on the representation of homosexuality.

Interviewed by Keith Howes in London in 1978, Tennessee Williams said: 'Things are more advanced in America than they are here. There's been a lot of progress. But not enough. You see, there's still this hidden subterranean resentment. There are powerful critics in New York who still talk about "the gay conspiracy".'[49] Yet Williams himself, during an interview with George Whitmore in 1976, when asked the question, 'Do you think there is any such thing as a homosexual conspiracy in the theater?' had replied, 'In England, under H.H. Tenner [*sic*], the theater was dominated by great homosexual talents. H.M. Tenner was one of the leading producers of London's West End Theater. And I think [Hugh] Binky Beaumont did exercise a considerable tyranny . . . I think the theater was, in London [in the 1940s and 1950s], dominated by homosexuals, mainly because they offered the most talent. They don't anymore.' This interview was being conducted in New York City, so the fact that Williams only gave a reply about London is interesting in itself. Whitmore prompted him: 'Of course there are innumerable homosexual producers in New York', to which Williams unhelpfully replied, 'Probably. I don't know. I'm not interested in the sex lives of producers. They're not attractive enough to interest me.'[50]

Many similar complaints about undue influence cropped up with reference to music and musicians. In the immediate post-war period, we are told, 'So many important New York musicians were gay, one wit dubbed the American Composers League the Homintern.'[51] Addressing this period in his enormous overview of twentieth-century music, but without the ulterior agenda of the anti-gay conspiracy theorists, Alex Ross writes:

> Homosexual men, who make up approximately 3 to 5 percent of the general population, have played a disproportionately large role in composition of the last hundred years. Somewhere around half of the major American composers of the twentieth century seem to have been homosexual or bisexual: [Aaron] Copland, [Virgil] Thomson, [Leonard] Bernstein, [Samuel] Barber, [Marc] Blitzstein, [John] Cage, Harry Partch, Henry Cowell, Lou Harrison, Gian Carlo Menotti, David Diamond, and Ned Rorem, among many others.[52]

Mind you, it is all very well to identify all these important figures as being gay, but Ross does not mention that many of them were also Jewish. Their dual minority status should not be taken as an invitation to *choose*. That would be absurd. (Which was the more essential essence? Was Leonard Bernstein more gay than Jewish? More Jewish than gay? More himself than either?) A number of those who were both Jewish *and* gay had something else in common. In their youth, they had been to Paris to study composition under Nadia Boulanger: Aaron Copland in the early 1920s, Virgil Thomson in the mid-1920s (while there he met his lover, the painter Maurice Grosser), Mark Blitzstein in the late 1920s (his Russian-born lover, the conductor Alexander Smallens accompanied him to Europe in 1924), David Diamond in 1936 (his *Psalm*, an orchestral piece of that year, was inspired by a visit to Oscar Wilde's grave in Père Lachaise and dedicated to André Gide). You might complain that a certain type of Boulanger-styled music dominated the American scene for decades to come, as if an infection had occurred; or you might welcome Boulanger's powerful influence as having given American music the kiss of life.

Following a review of a book about Benjamin Britten, correspondence in the *Times Literary Supplement* (19 February 1949) hinted at Britten's homosexuality and spoke of 'the small but powerful sect that threatens to kill with kindness one of the most naturally gifted of contemporary British composers'. It is not clear whether this was a reference to the group of colleagues and friends with whom Britten surrounded himself professionally at Aldeburgh or, considering the hints these remarks follow, homosexual friends in particular. The ambiguity seems deliberate.

William Walton, too, responded to the feeling that Britten was eclipsing him, by conjuring up his own conspiracy theory. When Britten was offered the post of musical director at Covent Garden, Walton said 'There are enough buggers in the place already, it's time it was stopped'. According to Michael Tippett, Walton mixed with a group of composers (Constant Lambert, Elizabeth Lutyens and Alan Rawsthorne) and writers (Dylan Thomas, Louis MacNeice), as well as the critic Cecil Gray and the painter Michael Ayrton, who 'all had great chips on their shoulder and entertained absurd fantasies about a homosexual conspiracy in music, led by Britten and [his lover, Peter] Pears'. Tippett eventually said to Walton, at a Proms rehearsal in the Royal Albert Hall, 'You know, you can't be Ben, I can't be Ben, we none of us can be each other: so isn't it time you stopped all this nonsense about a conspiracy?' They became friends, but Walton did not give up his obsession. On one occasion he whinged, 'Everyone is queer and I'm just normal, so my music will never succeed.'

The heterosexual coterie of Walton, Lambert, Thomas Beecham and their chums coped with the conspicuous successes of Britten and Pears with sodomy jokes: 'Twilight of the Sods', 'The Bugger's Opera', 'The Stern of the Crew' and the like. On one occasion, Charles Mackerras, who was working as the musical director on Britten's *Noye's Fludde*, made a disparaging remark to John Cranko about the number of boys in the piece. Cranko, who was homosexual himself, passed on the remark to Britten. (Cranko explained: 'When suddenly you hear something like that, however long you may have worked together, suddenly you hate that person.') Disgruntled at having thus been betrayed to the maestro, Mackerras conjured up the usual spectre: John Cranko 'was a homosexual, and I'm not, and there is a sort of Freemasonry among them'.[53]

The presence of gay men in the vanguard of the visual arts gave rise to similar talk of a network of queer artists, dealers and curators conspiring to promote their favourites at the expense of more normal talent. Writing in the 1970s, the American art critic Calvin Tomkins said of the 1950s that there had been 'talk of a "homintern", a network of homosexual artists, dealers, and museum curators in league to promote the work of certain favourites at the expense of "straight" talents'.[54] The rumour was especially strong with reference to the Abstract Expressionists in New York. In 1959, in the magazine *Arts*, Hilton Kramer only thinly veiled his homophobia when attacking Robert Rauschenberg and Jasper Johns as purveyors of 'the window decorator's aesthetic'.[55] A major 5,000-word item by Robert Doty on the growing presence of homosexuality in New York was published by the *New York Times* on 17 December 1963. Doty said much the same about gay men in the theatre as the Senate Subcommittee had said, in 1950, about perverts in government:

There is a cliquishness about gay individuals that often leads one who achieves an influential position in the theatre – as many of them do – to choose for employment another homosexual candidate over a straight applicant, unless the latter had an indisputable edge of talent that would bear on the artistic success of the venture.[56]

The relatively new medium of television did not escape the homo-hunting zeal of the conspiracy theorists. A 1964 item in the American scandal rag *Inside Story* was entitled 'How the Homos Are Ruining TV'. An impression was sufficient substitute for evidence:

Nobody knows for sure how many pansies there are in TV. But things have gotten so out of hand in this new Sodom on the Coaxial Circuit that you can't tell the he-man from the she-men without a score card . . . Right now the twisted twerps not only are in a position to tell you what you can see as entertainment, they are recruiting others of the lavender set to give it to you! Their numbers are legion.

Taken together, the first and last sentences quoted here show a revealing example of the logic at play in such texts. In the same year, an item in *Whisper* magazine claimed that 'the gay guys and dolls have become the real rulers' of a 'make-believe empire' of television producers.[57]

A CBS television documentary, *The Homosexuals*, broadcast on 7 March 1967, included a reference to 'talk of a homosexual mafia in the arts'.[58] According to one report, during the 1967–68 season, 31 per cent of Broadway shows had gay producers, and at least 38 per cent had gay directors. *Time* magazine (21 January 1966) quoted the Broadway producer David Merrick as saying that 'In Hollywood, you have to scrape them off the ceiling.'[59] The unsigned article adopted an apparently measured approach: 'The notion that the arts are dominated by a kind of homosexual mafia – or "Homintern", as it has been called – is sometimes exaggerated, particularly by spiteful failures looking for scapegoats. But' – and there had to be a 'but' – 'in the theater, dance and music world, deviates are so widespread that they sometimes seem to be running a closed shop'.[60] Looking back on this period from the 1990s, Gore Vidal told Charles Kaiser that 'anti-homintern hysteria was absolutely out of control'. The reaction to gay dramatists began to follow a predictable pattern: 'Somebody would become successful, then the word would spread that he was a fairy . . . That meant that all the women were really men in disguise and the relationships were all degenerate ones. And this was a plot – by the fifties it was all a "homintern plot" – to overthrow heterosexuality'.[61]

As one cultural practice loses influence, another falls subject to the same type of scrutiny. In the mid-1990s, the fact that media moguls David Geffen, Barry Diller and Sandy Gallin, designer Calvin Klein, painter Ross Bleckner and writer Fran Lebowitz were all close friends gave rise to rumours of a 'Gay Mafia' (or 'Velvet Mafia') in charge of Hollywood, their showcase location of choice being the nightclub Studio 54 at 254, West 54th Street in New York City. Geffen regarded this as a 'silly' idea, adding, 'If they mean a group of people who are bonded to each other by virtue of friendship, *yes*, call it anything you want.'[62]

## Positions of Influence

In 1936 an unknown Swede called Kurt Haijby came close to causing a major scandal when, being sued for divorce on the grounds of adultery, he named as his lover the King of Sweden, Gustav V. Haijby was thirty-nine that year, the King seventy-eight. The state acted quickly to stifle the affair. Haijby would be paid 1,500 kronor to emigrate to the United States, where he would receive 3,000 kronor more. His wife, meanwhile, was given 15,000 kronor to withdraw her divorce application. Haijby duly sailed to New York, but he returned to Sweden when his second payment did not materialise. With the King's knowledge – indeed, with his signature – the court went on buying Haijby's silence in hefty instalments. In 1938, he was arrested for sexual offences involving two teenage boys but he was allowed, after a fortnight's appraisal in a mental institution, to slip away to Germany, where he continued to receive payment of 500 kronor a month. This was neither the place nor the time for indiscretion, and Haijby was soon arrested by the German authorities for homosexual activities and sentenced to nine months' imprisonment, at the end of which he spent a further four months incarcerated at Gestapo headquarters. (During this latter period the Gestapo were doing Sweden a favour by keeping him out of the way while Gustav was passing through Germany on his way to the south of France. The German authorities are said to have offered to consign him to a concentration camp, but their offer was declined.) On his release in 1939, Haijby returned to his homeland.

Despite the obvious danger he had faced, Haijby was unwilling to let the matter rest. He knew he had a secure income, at least for as long as the King was alive, and probably longer. In 1947, he fictionalised the relationship with Gustav in a novel called *Patrik Kajson Returns* (*Patrik Kajson går igen*). Rather than ban the book, the Stockholm police suppressed it by buying every copy. The King died in 1950, but still Haijby would not let go. He demanded an official investigation into the way he had been treated. As so often before, he got what he wanted: the investigation, if not its findings, for in the end he was charged with blackmail and given eight years' hard labour. He was paroled in 1956.[63]

Does it matter that the King of Sweden was gay? And if so, what does it matter? Are we seriously expected to believe that this would incline him to forge links of particular sympathy with (say) Ernst Röhm? Or Alfred Redl? Or Ivor Novello, for goodness' sake? The Swedish establishment might regard it as necessary to keep the King's sexual orientation secret, not least from his own citizens, but that secrecy cannot itself guarantee conspiratorial intentions subversive of national security. On the contrary. If we speak of Gustav V as an example of the presence of homosexuality in the highest reaches of a society, no matter how sententious or pious or prurient or scandalised our tone, there is little avoiding the impression that what we are saying is, ultimately, rather banal. It tells us nothing interesting about the generality of European royal families if we add that the last King of Italy, Umberto II, is said to have numbered among his lovers Luchino Visconti, Jean Marais and the boxer Primo Carnera. Is there more than the titillation of gossip to be gained from knowing that Cosmo Lang, enthroned as Archbishop of Canterbury in 1928, was homosexual? And what if we are to take seriously Roger Peyrefitte's repeated claims about Giovanni Battista Montini, who became Pope Paul VI? Truman Capote had received advice from Glenway Wescott on how to become 'kept'; one of his eventual keepers was Prince Paul of Greece, who became King Paul I in 1947. Rumour had it that Sir Anthony Eden was a lover of both Edward Sackville-West and Edward Gathorne-Hardy. Sackville-West was reminded of Eden when reading Mary Renault's pioneering gay novel *The Charioteer* in 1953.

According to his physician, Mao Tse-tung used to account for the hyperactivity of his sex life – if a man that powerful has any need for excuses – in terms of Daoist principles: in brief, his frequent sexual encounters were keeping him healthy. He did not restrict himself to the limits of heterosexuality. His male bodyguards, like their female comrades, were chosen for their looks. One of their special duties was to ensure that the old boy got a good night's sleep by giving him a genital massage at bedtime. Zhisui Li, his physician, first learned of this routine when one of the guards declined to do his duty, saying 'This is a job for a woman, not me.' In 1964, he saw Mao fondling another guard and trying to pull him into bed. Li gave the matter some thought: 'For a while I took such behavior as evidence of a homosexual strain, but later I concluded that it was simply an insatiable appetite for any form of sex.'[64] This is a reasonable deduction. But Li goes on to invoke a comparison with classical Chinese erotic fiction, adding, quite rightly, 'Catamites are part of Chinese tradition.' This would be a little easier to swallow if he were not referring to Mao's behaviour in his late sixties, shortly before the Cultural Revolution of 1966–69, which so violently and systematically swept aside what was left of Chinese reverence for tradition. The revolution dismissed homosexuality as bourgeois decadence and subjected homosexual individuals, at best, to the re-education afforded by hard labour. Officially, by the time about which Li is writing, homosexuality had been completely eradicated from the People's Republic, along with the class and culture to which it was supposed to belong. It may be through point-less adherence to this ideological position that Li chooses not to define Mao's homosexual activities as pertaining to homosexuality, nor even to bisexuality.

Zhisui Li's account tells us a lot about the character of Mao, and about how he exerted his power on an interpersonal level without fully recognising the humanity of the people around him. But otherwise it does not tell us much about the People's Republic. As with the King of Sweden, the sexual orientation of the head of state – once he has sired children (as both Gustav and Mao did) – is immaterial. Or rather, it is immaterial except insofar as it manifestly disproves the myth that homosexual orientation and/or activity is subversive.

If not powerful individuals, what about political movements? Did Ernst Röhm's prominence at the top of the Sturmabteilung (SA) confirm anti-fascist (and anti-homosexual) propaganda about the supposed sexual pathology of Nazism itself – or did the fact that he was purged on the Night of the Long Knives (30 June 1934) prove the contrary? Various prominent figures in the collaborative Vichy government of France are thought to have been bisexual or homosexual. Abel Bonnard, for instance, was minister of education; and Jacques Benoist-Méchin was secretary of state in charge of Franco-German relations. What does this tell us of Vichy? Is anything of import added to the mix if we take into account that the adventurer Alain Gerbault, who made the first solo transatlantic crossing in a small boat in 1923, was both homosexual and a Vichy apologist? On the other hand, what of Georges Mandel, who was deported after refusing to support the Vichy regime? (He had been Clemenceau's *chef de cabinet* in 1917 and was Minister for Colonies from 1938 to 1940. Sent back to France after his deporta-tion, he was assassinated in Fontainebleau forest in 1940.) What of the journalist and Resistance fighter Roger Stéphane, eventual founder of *France Observateur* (later *Le Nouvel Observateur*), who was imprisoned by the Gestapo? Must we conclude that both Vichy and the Resistance were gay conspiracies?

During the Nazi occupation of the Netherlands, the painter and writer Willem Arondeus, who had already carried out various minor tasks for the Resistance, developed a plan to destroy Amsterdam's citizen registration building, the hub of the national bureaucracy, where copies of all citizenship papers were kept. Destroying these documents would make it impossible for the authorities to check on the authenticity of any individual's identification papers. On 27 March 1943, Arondeus led a successful raid on the building, gaining entry by dressing his fifteen-strong group in German uniforms. The building burned down and the raiders escaped unharmed. However, the fifteen were all betrayed and were arrested five days after the raid. All but two of them were executed on 1 July. At least three of them – Arondeus himself, the writer Johan Brouwer and the tailor Sjoerd Bakker – were homosexual. Bakker's last request was to be provided with a pink shirt, and he instructed his lawyer to reveal his homosexuality after the war. The intention was to disprove the myth that pansies were cowards.

A Resistance activist who survived the war was the Marxist, homosexual Jew Niek Engelschman, who in 1940 had co-founded a short-lived magazine for homosexual men and women, *Levensrecht* (Right to Live). In 1946 the editors revived it, but it was suppressed by the police. Shortly thereafter they started another magazine, *Vriendschap* (Friendship). It was around this publication that a group of concerned men and women gathered to form the most significant group in the Dutch movement for homosexual rights, COC (Cultuur en Ontspannings Centrum: the Centre for Culture and Recreation). Others who were involved in the early stages of COC included Jef Last, the communist writer who had published two novels containing representations of homosexual relationships – *Zuiderzee* (1934) and *Huis zonder venster* (1935) – by the time he was invited to accompany André Gide on his celebrated visit to the Soviet Union in 1936. Jef Last fought for the Republicans during the Spanish Civil War, and then worked for the Resistance during the Second World War. Another early participant in COC, who joined up in 1947, was the Jewish interior designer Benno Premsela, one of only two members of his family to survive the Shoah. He served as a COC board member from 1953 to 1976, and for nine of those years as the board's chair.

One could go on listing names and influential positions indefinitely, but that would serve no practical purpose other than to reaffirm the fact that homosexual people have had a major role in most social and cultural developments in most societies. If you did not already know this it will come either as a shock or as a welcome surprise. It will either confirm your dreadful suspicion about the degenerate infiltration of society by perverts or reassure you that society thrives on diversity. Pierre de Frédy, Baron de Coubertin, established the modern Olympic Games. Philippe Erlanger, the historian and plenipotentiary minister of the Quai d'Orsay, founded the Cannes film festival. On a smaller scale, Bernard Dort and Roland Barthes set up the magazine *Théâtre Populaire* and Jean Hallier founded *Tel Quel*. We have seen that men like H.M. Tennent and Hugh Beaumont were considerably influential in the English theatre. France had comparable figures, including the arts entrepreneur Gabriel Dussurget, whose main protégé was the violinist Maurice Gendron; the director and theatrical administrator Antoine Vitez; and Michel Guy, the arts advisor to

President Georges Pompidou. But a cultural institution that was founded or run by a homosexual person is not itself a homosexual institution.

If there are few professions in which homosexual individuals are allowed to feel comfortable, homosexual individuals may gravitate to them. Then, where they proliferate, they may appear to be in league with each other against the rest. The theatre and fashion worlds are clear examples; and the material I have outlined above demonstrates some of the obvious, hostile responses from those who feel they are not getting adequate recognition because they themselves are not gay. It sometimes seems as if there has been a worldwide conspiracy amongst gay hairdressers to make the wives of rich men look ridiculous. If so, it is likely that they forged a secret alliance with the gods of haute couture: Giorgio Armani, Cristóbal Balenciaga, Pierre Balmain, Christian Dior, Erté, Charles James, Calvin Klein, Paul Poiret, Yves Saint Laurent Gianni Versace, . . . The idea is so absurd that it comes as a shock to find it was ever taken seriously. Yet Edmund Bergler, in his book *Fashion and the Unconscious* (1953), argued that the 'unconscious hatred of women' of homosexual men in the fashion industry resulted in 'the paradoxical fact that women are dressed by their bitterest enemies'. Although unlikely to have read Bergler's book, that most paranoid of US presidents, Richard M. Nixon, was arguing a similar case almost two decades later. During one of his homophobic rants in 1971, recorded on the Watergate tapes, he said: 'You know one of the reasons fashions have made women look so terrible is because the goddamned designers hate women. Designers [are] taking it out on the women.'[65]

That many homosexual individuals – as this book will show – did exert massive cultural influence in the twentieth century is obvious. They edited magazines and anthologies, founded publishing houses, directed theatrical production companies, administered prizes, wrote reviews, ran bookshops, held cocktail parties, hosted exhibitions, conducted private salons, controlled purse-strings. That is before we even begin to consider those who created the works of art. Yet the simple, banal fact is that, for every one of these individuals, it is possible to name ten or so (presumed) heterosexuals in equivalent positions of cultural power. The homosexuals look like a conspiracy precisely because they are *less* usual, and therefore more worthy of comment, than influential heterosexuals. It could be argued – if we are drawn to a paradox – that the true conspiracy is that of the homophobes in the less welcoming spheres of life, clubbing together to make life uncomfortable for queers.[66]

## All Queers Meet Each Other

The composer and lyricist Marc Blitzstein once said to Ned Rorem, 'sooner or later all queers meet each other'.[67] This is not true. It is an exaggerated reflection on the fact that, when lesbians and gay men were under pressure to hide from public view, still there seemed to be a lot of them about – and yet, few enough to seem as if one could soon meet them all.

But what if it were true?

Loyal alliances are creative and productive. A healthy culture will consist of many of them. You only have to think of a few such groups to be persuaded of this: Natalie Barney's salons, the Ballets Russes, the Ballets Suédois, the Beats, the Bloomsbury Group, the 'Nancy poets' (George Orwell's pejorative term for the Auden group), the George Kreis ... Where would modern culture be without them? Richard Davenport-Hines has pointed out that 'The cosmopolitanism of homosexuality was a distinct refrain in late-nineteenth and early-twentieth-century confessional memoirs.'[68] Men and women who travelled away from home were often pleasantly surprised to encounter others of their own kind, even without actively searching for them. The willingness of gay men and lesbians to associate across national boundaries throughout the last century led to extraordinary encounters, some fleeting, others more enduring; some social, some sexual, many creative.

To begin to understand the full cultural potential of such meetings, just imagine the conversations that took place between these pairs of individuals: Sergei Eisenstein and Noël Coward, Tamara de Lempicka and Adrienne Monnier, Yukio Mishima and James Merrill, Una Troubridge and Vaslav Nijinsky, Angus Wilson and Alberto Arbasino, Yves Saint Laurent and Andy Warhol, Edouard Roditi and Countee Cullen, Kenneth Anger and Roger Peyrefitte, Jean Cocteau and Arno Breker, Severo Sarduy and Roland Barthes, Roger Casement and Magnus Hirschfeld, Willa Cather and Stephen Tennant, John Minton and Gerard Reve, Anthony Blunt and Ludwig Wittgenstein, René Crevel and Gertrude Stein, Federico García Lorca and Hart Crane, May Sarton and Virginia Woolf, Witold Gombrowicz and Virgilio Piñera ... We could tell a large part of the story of modern culture by concentrating on its international love affairs or domestic partnerships: Virgil Thomson and Maurice Grosser, Natalie Barney and Renée Vivien, René Crevel and Eugene MacCown, Sylvia Beach and Adrienne Monnier, James Baldwin and Lucien Happersberger, T.S. Eliot and Jean Verdenal,[69] Christopher Isherwood and Don Bachardy, Patrick White and Manoly Lascaris, Salka Viertel and Greta Garbo, Angelo Rinaldi and Hector Bianciotti, Gian Carlo Menotti and Samuel Barber, Rudolf Nureyev and Erik Bruhn, Marguerite Yourcenar and Grace Frick, Luchino Visconti and Horst, Luis Cernuda and Stanley Richardson, Christian Bérard and Boris Kochno, Charles Henri Ford and Pavel Tchelitchew, Katherine Mansfield and Beatrice Hastings, Elizabeth Bishop and Lota de Macedo Soares, Glyn Philpot and Karl Heinz Müller, Robert Duncan and Werner Vordtriede ... Indeed, every one of these conjunctions deserves a novel or a play to itself. As W.H. Auden said in a completely different context, 'just reeling off their names is ever so comfy'.

When you think of modern culture, no less than of modern *gay* culture, you inevitably begin with the major cities of Modernism (London, Paris, New York, Berlin, Vienna, St Petersburg).[70] Focusing more sharply, you zero in on a range of narrower locations (Capri, Taormina, Tangier, Greenwich Village), cultural institutions (Cambridge University, Hollywood), cultural movements (San Francisco Renaissance, Beat generation, Abstract Expressionism), political contexts (Weimar Republic, the two world wars, the Cold War) and conspicuously productive combinations of period and location (1910s Harlem, 1920s Paris, 1930s Berlin, 1950s New York). Early in Marcel Proust's *Cities of the Plain* (*Sodome et Gomorrhe*, 1921), the volume of *À la Recherche du temps perdu* in which the narrator tells us he is going to study the 'descendants of the Sodomites' with 'greater thoroughness', something like Marx and Engels' apprehension arises in the narrator's recognition that inverts might be capable of taking collective action. Amateur on the topic though he is, he takes a strong stand against the possibility:

> I have thought it as well to utter here a provisional warning against the lamentable error of proposing (just as people have encouraged a Zionist movement) to create a Sodomist movement and to rebuild Sodom. For, no sooner had they arrived there than the Sodomites would leave the town so as not to have the appearance of belonging to it, would take wives, keep mistresses in other cities where they would find, incidentally, every diversion that appealed to them. They would repair to Sodom only on days of supreme necessity, when their own town was empty, at those seasons when hunger drives the wolf from the woods; in other words, everything would go on much as it does to-day in London, Berlin, Rome, Petrograd or Paris.[71]

For all the queasiness of his position, Proust establishes his knowledge that the cities he names have, as it were, already gone over to the Sodomite camp. Urbanity and modernity had combined to produce a favourable environment, so that in due course similar patterns of notoriety became attached to very different cities: Sodom-on-Spree, Sodom-on-Thames, Sodom-on-Seine, Sodom-on-Hudson, even Sodom-on-Tiber . . .[72]

Alan Sinfield has called 1895–1995 'the Wilde century', mindful of the reverberations of the 1895 scandal right the way through to the era of gay liberation. When David Halperin celebrates the completion of 'one hundred years of homosexuality' in 1992, he is marking the centenary of the word 'homosexual' in English; but his phrase refers to more than the minutiae of lexicographical history: it denotes that century in which homosexuality *came out* as a major cultural influence, and in which homosexuality was itself one of modernity's major cultural constructions. Wayne Koestenbaum has gone as far as to call the Modernist period itself 'The Age of Inversion, when heterosexuality was in the process of being undermined and traduced by its eerie opposite.' However, Dominique Fernandez is anxious to sound less sanguine about the actual effects of the new homosexual visibility. A chapter heading in his overview of homosexual culture refers to the period from the late nineteenth century to the birth of gay liberation, during which psychiatry and psychoanalysis held sway, as 'Cent ans de misère'.[73]

According to Susan Sontag, 'homosexual estheticism and irony' was one of the 'pioneering forces of modern sensibility'. According to George Steiner, 'Since about 1890 homosexuality has played a vital part in Western culture and, perhaps even more significantly, in the myths and emblematic gestures which that culture has used in order to arrive at self-consciousness.' According to Jeffrey Meyers, 'The homosexual writer in the modern period is analogous to the tubercular artist . . . in the eighteenth and nineteenth centuries, for inversion, like disease, puts its mark on a high percentage of artists and sets them apart from society.'[74]

The great Icelandic novelist Halldór Laxness said, in 1925, that Reykjavik had finally become a proper city, having recently acquired the necessary components of modernity: 'not only a university and a movie theatre, but also football and homosexuality'. To some elites in Western society, homosexuality itself was a distinctly modern (and, as we would later say, Modernist) style. Alan Pryce-Jones said of 1920s Oxford that 'it was *chic* to be queer, rather as it was *chic* to know something about the twelve-tone scale and about Duchamp's "Nude Descending a Staircase"'. When Frank Lloyd Wright tried to tar Modernism with the brush of homosexuality, asking his audience – at the Western Round Table on Modern Art, in 1949 – 'if this movement which we call modern art and painting has been greatly, or is greatly in debt to homosexualism', Marcel Duchamp responded: 'I believe that the homosexual public has shown more interest or curiosity for modern art than the heterosexual'.[75] In Raymond Chandler's novel *The Long Goodbye* (1953), Wade says to Marlowe, 'The queer is the artistic arbiter of our age, chum. The pervert is the top guy now.'[76]

One viable response to outspoken attacks on any sign of gay influence would be to embrace the notion of cultural conspiracy, ironically or in earnest.[77] Just as W.H. Auden and Harold Norse cheerfully took ownership of the Homintern joke, any number of us might indeed become mafiosi of queer cultural activism. Such imagery need not serve only homophobic purposes.

Indeed, from Marcel Proust ('a freemasonry far more extensive, more powerful and less suspected than that of the Lodges') to Gore Vidal in *The City and the Pillar* ('It was a form of freemasonry') and beyond, queer voices have agreed with the proposition that there is secretive work afoot. What Proust recognised, as a homosexual and a Jew himself, was that certain persecuted minorities are forced to adopt defensive formations, this 'freemasonry', but that society as a whole is just as likely to benefit as to suffer from the consequences.

The homosexual traitor may have been a travesty, an expedient lie promoted by governments during times of international tension; but, even so, if we concentrate our attention on bohemian individuals, producers and intensive consumers of the arts, it is true that we are not looking at people in the habit of wrapping themselves in national flags. For many, their personal commitment would be to, say, culture or civilisation, or simply to their fellow human beings, rather than to mother/fatherland. There is a wider humanity, and a wider morality. Many of the figures we shall encounter in this book were contributors to a cultural movement which, like Romanticism before it, overrode the borders of nations. Modernism demanded wider loyalties. Besides, if you were a member of a sexual minority that was denied legitimacy by a country's laws or social conventions, why should you choose to stay there if you could afford to move? Why bow to a Crown that would imprison you? Two well-known examples from Bloomsbury will suffice to convey the appropriate tone. At a military tribunal concerning his application for Conscientious Objector status, in 1916, Lytton Strachey was asked what he would do if he saw a German soldier raping his sister. He replied, 'I would try to get between them.'[78] And, in his essay 'What I Believe' (1939), E.M. Forster wrote, 'if I had to choose between betraying my country and betraying my friend, I hope I should have the guts to betray my country.'[79]

# CHAPTER TWO

# SCANDAL AND AFTER

## The Wilde Case (1895)

Wilde I can never forgive. You may maintain that he had a right to live his own life and, for the sake of sheer vanity, get himself into Reading Gaol. For there was no reason for his going to prison and the last thing that the British authorities wanted to do was to put him there.

So wrote Ford Madox Ford in a 1930 essay called 'The Death of English Poetry'. Ford castigates Oscar Wilde for not having taken the opportunity to flee the country when it became clear that he was about to be arrested. He adds the view of the Keeper of Printed Books at the British Museum, expressed to him at the time of Wilde's conviction: 'That means the death-blow to English poetry. It will not be resuscitated for fifty years.' It is a view which, thirty-five years later, Ford still holds. His implication is that the librarian's prophecy has been fulfilled.[1] For decades, Wilde was blamed for the knock-on effects of his decision to sue his lover's father for calling him a sodomite. To others the consequences were more human than literary. In his cultural history of male homosexuality, A.L. Rowse wrote: 'There is something we *can* blame him for: for having brought down upon himself the vindictiveness of philistines and allowing them to triumph. Thousands suffered unspeakably on account of his Irish irresponsibility and exhibitionism.'[2] On the other hand, he would eventually be celebrated as having highlighted the need for change. In 1908, Edmund Gosse wrote, in a letter to Robert Ross, who had just published a limited edition of the suppressed passages of Wilde's *De Profundis*: 'Perhaps poor Wilde (who alas! was in life so distasteful to me) may come to be honoured as a protomartyr to freedom, now he is in his grave.'[3] Indeed, so it would prove, once the life came to be retold in a succession of films and later biographies. So the Wilde case did not end in 1895 when the prisoner was sent down, his plaintive

'May I say nothing, my lord?' having been ignored; nor even in 1900, when Wilde died in exile, nudged into eternity by an unacceptable wallpaper.[4] Its ramifications were broadly cultural and social; but for homosexual men they could be personal, lasting and potentially dangerous. Timothy d'Arch Smith's claim that 'By 1908, the Wilde trial had been forgotten' is not credible.[5]

In truth, homosexual men's accounts of the consequences of Wilde's conviction are often both vague and hyperbolic. Even quite balanced versions are apt to stray into fantasy. For instance, according to Rupert Croft-Cooke, after Wilde's conviction 'There was no sudden or perceptible re-alignment but *fin-de-siècle* became a term of contempt, aestheticism a dirty word and art-for-art's-sake a discredited fallacy' – which seems fair enough. But Croft-Cooke goes on to claim that 'There was scarcely a titled man or woman in English fiction for more than twenty years', which is demonstrably untrue. So is his unsupported claim that 'There was a slump in sentimental friendships between men which hitherto wives had encouraged to keep their husbands from other women.' There is something to be said for the first part of Croft-Cooke's claim that Wilde's downfall partially explains why 'Rudyard Kipling became the most popular poet in England closely followed by A.E. Housman whose *A Shropshire Lad* was taken for open-air poetry of the healthiest kind'.[6] One can see that Kipling was a kind of solution to the decadent infection of English literature at the end of the nineteenth century, but quite how Housman got away with his wistfully homoerotic words – especially if what has already been said about sentimental friendships were true – is not a matter Croft-Cooke addresses. He is on safer ground when speaking of the lasting resonance of Wilde's cultural glamour: 'scarcely a book of name-dropping reminiscences, published in hundreds between, say, 1910 (when it became permissible, even chic, to remember Wilde in his dining-out period) down to, say, 1950 when it became a mark of senility, is without at least one entry under Wilde, Oscar, in its index'.[7] Although one had to avoid the taint of having been too close to Wilde, for decades it was considered a mark of good taste to have known him, heard his table talk and attended his first nights.

In the volatile year of Wilde's conviction, the young Winston Churchill was accused, in the weekly review *Truth*, of having taken part in 'acts of gross immorality of the Oscar Wilde type' while at the Sandhurst military academy. Churchill sued, and was awarded damages with an apology.[8] Reactions to the trials and Wilde's conviction were real and emphatic: they do not need the gratuitous aid of exaggeration to show a real atmosphere of hostility on one side and fear on the other. Dogs called Oscar were renamed. Modes of address were toned down. At the time of the trials Ferdinand Schiller wrote a letter to his beloved Goldsworthy Lowes Dickinson, beginning: 'My . . . (mustn't use the words since the Oscar Wilde trial).'[9] Wilde's crime was nameable – gross indecency – but generally had to be left unspoken, especially within earshot of the impressionable young. When Gerald Tyrwhitt-Wilson (Lord Berners) told his mother, in 1904, that Richard Strauss' *Salomé* was based on the play by Wilde, she responded, 'Oh, hush, dear.'[10] The name loomed like distant thunder over the English boarding school. Michael Davidson said of himself, as a youth in England just before the First World War: 'I still vaguely believed that I and Oscar Wilde – and, I suppose, that unlucky man [who had fruitlessly chatted him up] at the Southampton swimming pool – were the only people since the age of Alkibiades to be *born* with this yearning.'[11] At prep school at the time of the Great War, Cyril Connolly and two friends were once caught talking after lights-out in one of their dormitory cubicles by the school's matron. 'The locked door which our evidence of being a trio instead of the usual compromised pair could not palliate. It was Oscar Wilde over again.'[12] While still a schoolboy in the early 1920s, John Betjeman corresponded with Lord Alfred Douglas until banned from doing so by his father: 'He's a bugger. Do you know what buggers are? Buggers are two men who work themselves up into such a state of mutual admiration that one puts his piss-pipe up the other's arse. What do you think of that?'[13] When Wilde came up in conversation, Anton Dolin's father said, 'Never utter that vile man's name again.' Dolin comments: 'This of course only set my brain in motion, and from then until now I have read and listened to all I could glean about this tragic playwright.' As a young actor in his early teens, Dolin had an admirer called Charles, who used to write him letters and send him gifts until his father found the letters and forbade him to see the man again. Dolin writes: 'From then on I became suspicious of every look and any sign of the simplest affection, avoiding it in case it was wrong. And it was wrong to read Oscar Wilde, as I did again with deeper understanding. Was Charles another of those haunted creatures? Was I another Alfred Douglas?'[14] E.M. Forster's fictional character Maurice goes to his family doctor and declares, 'I'm an unspeakable of the Oscar Wilde sort.' The doctor replies 'Rubbish, rubbish!' and refuses to discuss the matter.[15]

Writing about one of Wilde's most avid followers, the English novelist Ronald Firbank, Brigid Brophy argued that publicity about the trials was caused by, and reinforced, a correlation of homophobia and philistinism in English public life:

Through the incidental fact that Wilde was the public personification of the aesthetic movement, two prejudices with not a rational leg to stand on between them were able to prop each other up. From 1895 on, an anti-homosexual challenged by the difficult question what exactly was *wrong* about homosexuality could reply that it tended towards the soppily arty, the morbidly affected and the frivolous (that is, the witty); and a philistine challenged to say what was wrong with art could reply that it was tinged with homosexuality.

This effect not only lasted for some decades (Brophy was writing in the late 1960s and early 1970s) but extended beyond Britain. As a consequence of the Wilde business, 'philistinism, nothing new in itself, went newly unopposed by any structure of argument. The lack, not wholly remedied yet, was bitterest in the post-Wilde generation of the Twenties and Thirties. The repercussive circle swept by the Wilde affair probably extended throughout western Europe. (An echo of the Wilde scandal was perhaps a small ingredient in the Nazi notion of the decadence of modern art.)'[16]

The opening sentences of André Gide's *Corydon* (1911) show how scandals tended to give rise to both anti-homosexual argument and pro-homosexual counter-argument:

> A sensational trial in 19— brought up once again the complicated and troublesome question of homosexuality. For a short while it was the sole topic of conversation. I grew tired of listening to the theories and observations of ignorant, bigoted fools, and I wanted to clarify my own ideas.[17]

So Gide's narrator goes to visit his old school friend Corydon, and a Platonic dialogue on the topic unfolds. Despite its pseudo-classical title and trappings, the book is rooted in current affairs; or recent affairs, at least. The opening section of the first dialogue refers to the sexological works of Albert Moll, Richard von Krafft-Ebing and Marc-André Raffalovich; the scandals of Oscar Wilde, Alfred Krupp, Sir Hector Macdonald and Philipp, Prince of Eulenburg; and to the related, hostile actions of the Marquess of Queensberry and Maximilian Harden. The implication is of quite urgent topicality.

Wilde's fame quickly spread far beyond Britain, the reputation of his person and his art, alike, acting as both a warning to those who might be tempted to overstep the mark and a model to be followed by those for whom overstepping the mark would be a matter of personal and artistic necessity. You could ally yourself with his name as a matter of sexual or aesthetic principle; and his name could be used against you as a slur on anything you were or did. In Alexandria in 1924, Socrates Lagoudakis launched a series of attacks not only on the poetry of Constantine Cavafy but also on his character, calling him 'another Oscar Wilde'. Cavafy's friends were so shocked that they took to heckling Lagoudakis' lectures.[18] The American gossip columnist Walter Winchell coined the term 'wildeman' for homosexual men in the 1920s.[19] Italians spoke of 'oscarwildismo' or 'wildismo'; the French used 'Dorian Gray' as a euphemism for homosexual. The duc de Gramont said to his daughter, apropos of the dismissing of a concierge, 'Don't get mixed up in this . . . It's a business of the Oscar Wilde type.'[20] Even in remote Friuli at the beginning of the 1940s, Pier Paolo Pasolini was made aware of the dead Irish playwright and his fate. As reported by his cousin Nico Naldini, 'It seems a schoolmate [Agostino Bignardi] had told him about Oscar Wilde, who had written a love letter to a boy and ended up in jail. In a letter dated 10 February 1950, Pasolini told Silvana Mauri, 'I bear the mark of Rimbaud, or [Dino] Campana and also of Wilde, whether I want it or not.'[21]

Wilde could, indeed, enter one's life at a tender age. In 1948, aged fifteen, the Swedish travel-writer-to-be Sven Lindqvist was seen reading André Gide's *The Fruits of the Earth* by a British composer, John, who invited the boy to visit him in London. Lindqvist went. Inevitably, then, John pointed out the implications of several passages in the Gide – which the boy had missed – and tried to kiss him. When Lindqvist threatened to report him, John defensively invoked the terrible fate of Oscar Wilde, persuading him not to do so.[22] In 1930s Japan, the young Yukio Mishima was only twelve or thirteen when he first read and became addicted to Oscar Wilde. The American poet James Merrill was, from an early age, self-educated in the manner of bookish queers: 'I'd read every word in print about Oscar Wilde and knew by avid, pounding heart the juiciest of Havelock Ellis's case histories.'[23] In England, one of those who, in a paradoxical way, derived the most strength from the Wilde scandal was Ronald Firbank. Indeed, Brigid Brophy went so far as to say of him, 'In several important respects, the crucial event in Firbank's life was the prosecution of Oscar Wilde' – which happened when Firbank was only nine.[24]

Of course, translation vastly extended Wilde's influence, as did critical reinterpretation. Each could highlight desirable aspects of the work and play down the less acceptable themes. There were 250 translations of Wilde into German between 1900 and 1934; the earlier of these were issued by Max Spohr, a publisher with a pioneering interest in texts on homosexual themes. Thomas Mann took Wilde's work very seriously, even to the extent of claiming that some of his aphorisms could have been formulated by Friedrich Nietzsche, and vice versa. The comedies went down well in the Third Reich. Wilde was the most frequently performed dramatist of the 1936–37 season, somewhat aided by Karl Lerb's translations, which emphasised the themes of self-discipline and moral conformity. Another factor in the plays' popularity was aesthetic escapism. The version of *The Importance of Being Earnest* that was performed at Gustav Gründgens' State Theatre was filleted of its social critique and served up as a kind of operetta or mere fairy tale. In Eastern Europe, on the other hand, censorship could be circumvented by downplaying Wilde's decadent individualism and portraying him as a great satirist of the class system.

In 1907, the Swedish newspaper *Dagens Nyheter* reported that Sweden had contracted 'Wilde fever', not only because his plays had become popular and *The Picture of Dorian Gray* and *De Profundis* had been published in Swedish translation, but also because dandyism had become fashionable in urban social circles. In Italy, Arnaldo De Lisle (pseudonym Giuseppe Garibaldi Rocco), the author of a gay-themed novel set in Naples, *L'uomo femmina* (*c*.1899), proposed to Wilde that he should translate *Salomé* into Italian. In the event, though, Eleonora Duse refused to act in it because of Wilde's reputation. Biagio Chiara was the first writer to introduce Wilde's work to Italian readers – among his translations were *The Picture of Dorian Gray*, *Lady Windermere's Fan* and the fairy tales in *A House of Pomegranates* – and his own work, especially the gay-themed stories in *L'umano convito* (1903), was itself influenced by Wilde. No great friend to homosexuals, Filippo Tomasso Marinetti, the godfather of Futurism, nevertheless denounced the British treatment of Wilde, especially given the well-known fact that all British gentlemen passed through a homosexual phase in their youth. Jean Cocteau made a dramatisation of *Le Portrait surnaturel de Dorian Gray* in 1908. Much later, the Swiss composer Hans Schaeuble, a married gay man who thought masculinity creative and therefore feared his own feminine element, made an opera of *The Picture of Dorian Gray* (1947–48). In the 1960s the gay Swiss composer Paul Burkhard turned *Bunbury* (as *The Importance of Being Earnest* had been called in German) into a musical comedy.

It was Herman Bang, as both admirer and plagiarist, who introduced Oscar Wilde into Danish culture. At more than a century's distance, it is difficult to disconnect the lampooning of Bang in the Danish press for his personal characteristics from deeper signs of critical discomfort in the face of his espousal of cultural modernity. Bang could easily be dismissed – or, on the contrary, built up – as a ridiculous figure, what with his habit of wearing make-up and scent in public, not to mention the latest French fashions in tight trousers and coloured socks: to the press, this self-conscious flamboyance signified nothing so much as decadence and effeminacy. (The Danish magazine *Punch* ran a campaign against Bang like that of the British *Punch* against Wilde – including attacking Bang's cosmopolitanism.) But the narrative stance of much of his writing was also open to attack. The novel *Lost Generations* (*Haablöse Slaegter*, 1880), published when he was in his early twenties, caused the first of a number of scandalised responses to his work, not only for its representations of drug-taking and heterosexual pleasure-seeking, but also for the more subtly disconcerting tone of its subjectivity: the narrative voice sounded, to those with such sensitivities, both unhealthy and unmanly. The influence of French writers is pervasive: the Romanticism of Musset, for instance, and the Naturalism of Zola. The investigation of heredity and degeneracy taps into a European cultural development for which the Danish literary establishment was unprepared and to which it responded with censorious instincts mirroring those of the cultural power brokers in Britain and across the Continent.

Bang had some success as a theatre director in Copenhagen and Paris, but his career as a writer was undermined by hostile responses to his personality, both as it manifested itself in that physical presence in the streets and salons and as the persona he adopted in his cultural journalism. He gained a reputation as a hysteric, accumulating around his perceived effeminacy the flaws attributed to the feminine itself: shrillness, illogicality and lack of objectivity. At the same time, his personal life was subjected to surveillance, even to interference, in several countries. Although his public appearance was blatantly different, like Wilde's before he was put on trial, it did not give rise to a quick supposition of homosexuality. Indeed, notwithstanding the use of make-up and so on, Bang actually made every effort to conceal his homosexuality, living as he did in acute fear of blackmail and exposure. He did not write about homosexuality in any works published while he was alive – the dour essay 'Thoughts on the Problem of Sexuality', written in 1909, was not published until after his death in 1912, when it came out not in Danish but in German – and what private references there are in his correspondence show that he thought of his sexuality as a diseased affliction, a heavy burden which he toted against his will. He did not even allow people to mention homosexuality in his presence. As one commentator puts it, 'rather than lend his homosexuality to literature Bang rejected it as unfit for Art'.[25] There were more important things to write about. In his own life, although he had experienced something close to the ideal in his love for the German actor Max Eisfeld – some of the effects of which are felt in his poetry collection *Digte* (1891) – the fact that he subsequently felt betrayed by Eisfeld could not fail to endorse his general scepticism about the viability of such relationships.[26] The closest Bang came to a positive representation of a male–male intimacy was in the novel *Mikaël* (1905), in which an artist develops a love for the beautiful young man whom he adopts as his son; but here, again, love is undermined by jealousy and ultimately collapses in betrayal.[27]

The cultural independence of the Latin American nations still being limited, their debates on, and models of, the new sexualities closely followed those of Western Europe. Fashions of aestheticism and decadence, although conceived in London and Paris, were later developed in Montevideo and Buenos Aires.

The Brazilian writer João do Rio, who translated *Salomé* into Portuguese, was a great admirer of Wilde. Another sophisticated man-about-town on the European *fin de siècle* model, he wandered the streets of his native Rio de Janeiro (hence the pseudonym; his real name was Paulo Barreto), every inch the dandified *flâneur*; but his prolific articles and stories about the urban life he observed around him were by no means confined to the class from which he had emerged, the bourgeoisie. His work was remarkable for its attention, not only to the decadence of the demi-mondes that had become the standard fare of European *fin-de-siècle* writers, but also to the detail of working-class life. Regardless of his fashionable adherence to a Wildean aesthetic of *art pour l'art*, João do Rio reported anthropologically on (for instance) the religious practices he had encountered in the city's slums. Even when reported objectively, without comment, such observations took on radical political significance: for merely to notice the working class was to accord it a degree of respect and value to which it was not accustomed. In this display of social concern, as in so much else, Wilde may have been his model. Of course, there were other good reasons for roaming – as he did – the nether regions of Rio de Janeiro by night, and his wanderings earned him a certain notoriety. Although he was circumspect in behaviour, if not in his 'effeminate' style and manner, João do Rio was often publicly attacked for being homosexual. Indeed, it seems that the novelist Machado de Assis twice tried to prevent his election to the Academy on moral grounds.

Wilde's influence in South and Central America was durable. Speaking to Clark Taylor in the 1970s, an anonymous interviewee ('a well known writer and political commentator who feels it is necessary to remain anonymous at the present time') said, 'In Mexico, for the last four or five decades, the most influential writer on homosexuality has been Oscar Wilde. All the educated Gay people have tried to act like Wilde ... to be that kind of witty person. The concept of the homosexual has been that of the witty, non-political, elegant, charming person trying to outdo everybody else in the Salon ... The dandies with their glamorous "chi-chi" gathering places, poetry readings and so forth.' He gives the poet and playwright Salvador Novo as an example.[28] Novo was widely known as the Mexican Oscar Wilde. Writing in 1967 about the reception in Cuba of José Lezama Lima's great novel *Paradiso* (1966), Julio Cortázar spoke of 'a conditioned, prefabricated culture ... with its rebellions and heterodoxies carefully controlled by the marquises of Queensberry of the profession,' which 'rejects all works that go truly against the grain'.[29]

As an adolescent in Colombia in the early 1960s, Jaime Manrique was shaken by a screening of Ken Hughes' 1960 film about the Wilde scandal. He later wrote: 'Guilt ran my life from my adolescence on. Guilt and secrecy. *The*

*Trials of Oscar Wilde*, starring Peter Finch, arrived in Barranquilla. It focused on the circumstances that led to Wilde's destruction as a man and as an artist ... I became terrified of my deepening homosexual feelings. Wilde's story seemed a story of what happened to men who transgressed the boundaries of heterosexual society: they ended up in jail and they were destroyed physically, socially, and spiritually.' He recalled that there was only one man known to be gay in Barranquilla, a certain 'Tarzan'. 'He was an outcast and an object of ridicule ... I put together the two images of homosexuality I knew – Oscar Wilde and Tarzan – and I thought this meant I was doomed to a life of ostracism.'[30]

In Czechoslovakia, the homosexual poet and novelist Jiří Karásek evidently tried to warn the public that what had happened to Wilde in England might happen to a man in their society too; yet he did nothing to avoid being influenced by Wilde: his own fiction, including *The Hidden Painting* (1923) and *Ganymedes* (1925) had various Wildean motifs. Progressive discussion of the Wilde case tended to be more common on the Continent than in Britain or Ireland. Homosexual writers could not ignore him. In the words of Stefano Evangelista, to such writers 'Wilde was an enabling precedent but he was also a figure to exorcize.'[31] In Germany, Hugo von Hoffmannsthal admired and imitated Wilde's aestheticism, but came to regard it as a dead end, perhaps especially after the events of 1895. His ambivalence extended to a 1905 essay, 'Sebastian Melmoth' (the name used by Wilde on heading into exile after his release from prison). One commentator writes that 'There are grounds for suspecting that the reasons for such ambivalence lie partly in Hoffmannsthal's shame about his own homosexual desires.'[32]

According to Evgenii Bershtein, 'Wilde's biographical legend shaped the formation of sexual identities and ideologies in *fin-de-siècle* Russia.'[33] Mikhail Kuzmin came to be regarded as 'the Russian Oscar Wilde' after the publication of his novel *Wings* in 1906; and, a touch more absurdly, 'the Russian Noël Coward'. He and his lover were very familiar with Wilde, man and myth, but ultimately Kuzmin repudiated the Wilde myth for something more positive, just as his work moved beyond decadent aestheticism towards Modernism. In a diary entry (6 June 1906), Kuzmin called Wilde 'that snob, that hypocrite, that bad writer and faint-hearted man, who besmirched that for which he was put on trial.'[34] Sergei Eisenstein, too, saw the espousal of Modernism as a way to prevent himself from eventually sharing Wilde's fate: he told the Soviet critic Sergei Tretiakov that, had it not been for the trinity of Marx, Lenin and Freud, he might have ended up as 'another Oscar Wilde.'[35] In the Russian press, which could not specify details on such matters, references to Wilde became 'common figures of speech which placed the transgressive sexual practice [of male homosexuality] in the West'.[36]

It is beyond doubt that the Wilde affair cowed other artists, having the effect of coercing them into conformity in both their personal behaviour and the art they produced. For instance, it can be argued that Somerset Maugham was open about his homosexuality until Wilde's conviction, which happened when Maugham was twenty-one. Bryan Connon describes the effects of the affair on Maugham:

Like his gay contemporaries, he was forced to create a façade of overt masculinity, and be on the alert for police activity. He even grew a moustache because it was well known that Wilde liked his young lovers to be clean-shaven. [Perhaps more significantly, Wilde was himself clean-shaven.] Sporting facial hair was therefore tantamount to a disguise and a statement to the public that the wearer was not queer. As he grew older he became a chameleon personality whose characteristics depended on the company he was in. But he was always haunted by the fate of Oscar Wilde and fear of public disgrace, although he continued to take risks when sexual need overcame caution.[37]

Frederic Raphael, too, considers the long-term effects of the Wilde case on how Maugham lived his life as a homosexual man:

The long shadow of Oscar Wilde lay across his life. Though he was to entertain many homosexuals at the Villa Mauresque [on Cap Ferrat, between Nice and Monte Carlo], which he bought in 1928, he never made any suggestion, however impersonal, that the brutal English laws against homosexual practices should be repealed or altered. Reformers solicited his help in vain. He had attended a dinner, during the days of Wilde's disgrace, in obstinate honour of the most scintillating wit of his time, but he never broke his silence over the love that dared not speak its name.[38]

Of course, to a considerable extent, Maugham was able to avoid the law by living abroad. There is no question, though, that the case had a pernicious effect on the cultural atmosphere not only in Britain but elsewhere too, affecting what writers and artists created, or what they chose not to create. As Brigid Brophy writes: 'Within earshot of the Wilde disaster, many artists who were tolerant or themselves homosexual (or both) were cowed into accepting discretion as a moral virtue, and one which could be substituted for aesthetic virtue. Open secrets were considered preferable to openness. In the practice of literature, discretion sometimes meant a joyless abstention from expressing emotions. The open secret concealed a void.'[39] One of the reasons for Brophy's massive celebration of Ronald Firbank, from which this quotation is taken, was that she believed Firbank wrote as he chose, ignoring all the contrary pressures.

The scandal continued to excite interest, even after the Second World War. On 28 August 1948, Dorothy Bussy wrote to André Gide: 'London is talking about two books. One is the report (verbatim) of Oscar Wilde's trials.'[40] Also in the late 1940s, in New York at the age of nine, Edmund White met his first Englishman, a soldier, while eating out with his parents. Already having read Oscar Wilde, he felt he ought to deliver an epigram. But when he did – 'I know a widow who just buried her husband and her hair has gone quite gold with grief' – the soldier 'looked genuinely repulsed. He winced with disgust and turned his attention to his chop.' White was probably right to infer that the man was 'sickened by my effeminacy and crazy interjection'.[41]

By 1955, when Peter Wildeblood's memoir of the later scandal of the Montagu case, *Against the Law*, was published, a normative image of the healthy, discreet, adult, homosexual man was starting to be taken seriously, at the expense of men whose homosexuality manifested itself differently. This move to claim respectability had to involve the repudiation of a figure like Wilde, whose reputation for bad behaviour, as the details of the trials faded into history, had become rather vague. As Wildeblood put it,

> I suppose that most people, if they were asked to define the crime of Oscar Wilde, would still imagine that he was an effeminate poseur who lusted after small boys, whereas in fact he was a married man with two children who was found guilty of homosexual acts committed in private with male prostitutes whom he certainly did not corrupt.[42]

As late as 1957, at Reading University, the poet and critic John Lucas and a friend went to a fancy-dress party as Oscar Wilde and Lord Alfred Douglas, and were hissed and booed as they passed through the dining hall beforehand.[43]

Saki's fictional aesthete Reginald, eponymous central character of the collection of stories *Reginald* (1904), says 'Scandal is merely the compassionate allowance the gay make to the humdrum.'[44] Two British movies, Gregory Ratoff's *Oscar Wilde* (1959), starring Robert Morley, and Ken Hughes' *The Trials of Oscar Wilde* (1960), starring Peter Finch, brought some of the details of the scandal back into focus for later generations. In his 1971 memoir *To Fall Like Lucifer*, Ian Harvey could still say with accuracy, 'the name most closely associated with homosexuality in the public mind in Britain is unquestionably that of Oscar Wilde'.[45]

## The Eulenburg Case (1906–09)

In Germany, the Krupp scandal of 1902 never reached its full potential. Whether by his own hand or from a heart attack brought on by stress aggravating an already weakened physical condition, the unexpected death of Germany's richest man, the industrialist Friedrich Alfred Krupp, snuffed out the story of his sexual activities with young men. In any case, since his rumoured transgressions had occurred abroad, on Capri, the scandal did not arouse the paranoid hostility that the Wilde debacle had generated in England. However, the German press had tasted blood, and the curiosity of its readers had been stimulated. While England had successfully sacrificed its scapegoat, Germany was in a state of readiness to create a victim of its own. There would not be long to wait, and when it blew up the scandal would involve the highest reaches of national life.[46]

It was in 1906 that a journalist and critic called Maximilian Harden started publishing allegations about homosexual relationships at the court of Wilhelm II. The Kaiser had left himself open to attack on the occasion of Krupp's funeral, when he accused the Social Democrats, who had published the initial allegations about Krupp's sex life, of having carried out an 'intellectual murder'. He affirmed that he had come to the funeral with the specific intention of protecting the reputation of Krupp and his family. Now Harden was writing openly that the Kaiser was surrounded by 'sick and degenerate' men. Among these was Philipp, Prince of Eulenburg, who had been an intimate friend of the crown prince, and then of the Emperor, since 1886. The two men had a shared interest in the arts, and Wilhelm became Eulenburg's ideal reader as he wrote more and more – eight volumes' worth – nationalistic poems based on Norse mythology; Wilhelm loved the things.

Harden's campaign of articles coincided with what might otherwise have passed as an isolated, minor scandal. The valet of Graf Johannes zu Lynar, brother-in-law of the Grand Duke of Hesse, asked to be assigned to another officer who would not, as Lynar had, expect to be allowed to masturbate him. Lynar resigned his commission and retired with a suitable pension. But the reverberant rumours about the case had the effect of confirming Harden's claims of corruption in high places. Similarly, when the anarchist paper *Der Eigene* outed the Reichskanzler Bernhard von Bülow, taking him to court for having committed unspecified offences, the very airing of the topic in connection with the name of a man so powerful as the Chancellor himself gave an impression that something profoundly unrespectable was happening among the governing classes. (On failing to prove his accusations, the editor of *Der Eigene*, Adolf Brand, who was homosexual himself, was jailed for libel.)

Harden had named both Eulenburg and Graf Kuno von Moltke as individuals at court who spoke and wrote to each other in excessively effusive terms
– terms which, between a woman and a man, would be the language of love.
While Eulenburg took the traditional course in such matters, lying low at a
quiet retreat on the banks of Lake Geneva, doubtless hoping for the fuss to blow
over, Moltke sued Harden for libel. There followed a sequence of trials: in
October 1907, Harden was found not guilty; in December 1907, despite having
withdrawn much of his original accusation, Harden was found guilty and
sentenced to four months' imprisonment; in April 1908, Harden successfully
sued a man who had accused him of accepting hush-money from Eulenburg; in
June 1908, as a result, Harden took Eulenburg himself to court for having
committed perjury in the December trial (but Eulenburg fell seriously ill during
these proceedings and went into retirement until his death in 1921); Harden's
appeal against his prison sentence was heard twice, in Leipzig and then at the
High Court in Berlin; and in April 1909, at a retrial forced by the prosecutor,
Harden was given a fine of DM600.

At every stage, the rumours of homosexuality at court were given a further
airing. One individual who suffered as a consequence was Magnus Hirschfeld,
who had given expert evidence at the first two trials. His testimony that homosexuality was an inborn condition, no more deserving of punishment than
heterosexuality was, incensed many editors, journalists and readers. Some of
their responses offered a bitter taste of things to come under Nazism, especially
when both Jewishness and homosexuality were used against him. Both *Das
Reich* (7 November 1907) and *Germania* (8 November 1907) said, 'We must
make an end of people like Dr. Hirschfeld.' Leaflets were distributed in the
street outside his house. Their message was unambiguous: 'Dr. Hirschfeld – a
Public Danger. The Jews are Our Undoing.'

Marcel Proust watched the case as closely as was possible from France. As
George D. Painter puts it, 'Proust took a keen interest in the Eulenburg affair.
Like many homosexuals and like [his fictional character] Charlus, he prided
himself on his knowledge of all the prominent, undiscovered inverts of Europe.'[47]
The English writer Frederick Rolfe reported that in 1908, after the Austrians
had been performing troop manoeuvres along the border with Italy, 'the
Venetians took a hatred of all Germans and went and smashed the windows' of
a male brothel, the 'Round Table' house on the Fondamenta Osmarin, 'calling
the boys and men there "Eulenbergs" [sic]'.[48] The more lasting effect of the
Eulenburg affair, in Germany and elsewhere, was the naturalisation of the relatively new term 'homosexual'. Newspaper accounts of the various trials used the
word and its variations repeatedly, to the extent of canonising them as the most
widely recognisable terms for male–male sexual and affectional relationships.

## The Pemberton Billing Case (1918)

The fact that the new sciences of sexology and psychoanalysis were of predominantly German and Austrian origins inspired in some British nationalists and jingoists the suspicion that sodomy itself was being promoted by a conspiracy of German-speaking perverts against the moral purity of the British Empire. Arnold White, editor of the *English Review*, had been reading the work of Otto Weininger and Iwan Bloch – 'all this German garbage', he called it – and had noticed German campaigns to repeal Paragraph 175 (banning male homosexual activity). From these he derived the paranoid theory that German 'urnings' (to use Ulrichs' term) were systematically infecting British urnings with anti-British feeling. In an article for the *Imperialist* entitled 'Efficiency and Vice', White proclaimed the crucial point about such people's perfidy, that 'Londoner urnings have more in common with Teuton urnings than with their own countrymen' and that they were erotically in thrall to their German counterparts: for 'When the blond beast is an urning, he commands the urnings in other lands'. He reported Iwan Bloch's estimate that there were 56,000 urnings in Berlin alone. By implication, that added up to 56,000 potential German agents ready to target the moral weakness of British urnings.[49]

The publisher of the *Imperialist* was Noel Pemberton Billing, a volatile inventor and adventurer, who had been elected to Parliament as an independent at the East Hertfordshire by-election of February 1916. In the issue of the *Imperialist* published on 26 January 1918, he printed an item entitled 'The Forty-Seven Thousand' in which he claimed that the German secret service had compiled a 'Black Book' containing the names of 47,000 English men and women who practised the vices of Sodom and Lesbia. These names had been meticulously amassed by German agents over the previous two decades – 'agents so vile and spreading such debauchery and such lasciviousness as only German minds can conceive and only German bodies execute'. (Billing was one of those polemicists who write in the heat of anger and do not spend much time checking their work for inconvenient contradictions. He clearly thought sodomy a practice beyond the capacity of the British physique, and yet one in which British degenerates had begun to indulge in their tens of thousands.) The most controversial aspect of his claim, if not the most surprising, was that the German list included the names of cabinet ministers, Privy Councillors and members of the royal household.[50]

When, on 10 February 1918, the *Sunday Times* advertised a forthcoming 'private' performance of Oscar Wilde's play *Salomé*, Billing detected yet another sign of the nation's moral decay. He seems to have taken particular exception to the fact that the play would star the dancer Maud Allan as Salomé, and would

be produced by Jack Grein, a cosmopolitan, Dutch, Jewish socialist and suffragist. On 9 February, the *Imperialist* had been renamed the *Vigilante*. In its first
issue under the new title, on 16 February 1918, the *Vigilante* carried a short
item headlined 'THE CULT OF THE CLITORIS', suggesting that if Scotland
Yard were to seize the list of people who applied to be in the audience when
*Salomé* was performed, 'I have no doubt they would secure the names of several
of the first 47,000'.[51] In other words, the audience was likely to include homosexual men and women – a deliberately scandalous claim. Jack Grein saw this
item on 5 March, and he and Maud Allan went to their solicitors. Against the
advice of Robbie Ross, who, as Oscar Wilde's most loyal supporter, had seen
more clearly than most what a libel trial can do to the reputation of the libelled
individual, they instituted proceedings against Noel Pemberton Billing and his
publication. When the case came to Bow Street Magistrates' Court on 6 April,
its details reached the mainstream newspapers for the first time. *Salomé* itself
was performed without incident on the 12th. When the libel case resumed,
Billing was committed for trial at the Old Bailey.

The trial began on 29 May 1918 and lasted for five days. Billing conducted
his own erratic and irascible defence. Given the nature of the case, a range of
topics was aired and debated with varying degrees of rationality. The clitoris
and its characteristics had to be defined (one witness said of its propensity to
play havoc with modesty, 'An exaggerated clitoris might even drive a woman to
an elephant'[52]); the word was accepted as being suitably Greek, scientific and
little-known, so not constituting obscenity in itself. The morality of Maud
Allan was called into question; rumours of the closeness of her relationship
with Margot Asquith, wife of the former prime minister, were allowed to hang
ominously in the atmosphere of the courtroom. Billing persuaded Eileen
Villiers-Stuart, who happened to be his mistress, to lie on oath that she had
actually seen and handled a copy of the German secret service's 'Black Book';
he even got her to say that the judge, Charles Darling, was named in it; gathering momentum, she also named Asquith and his wife, and Lord Haldane,
before Darling ordered her to stop. But Billing prompted his next witness,
Harold Spencer, who had actually written the item in the *Vigilante*, to repeat
the accusation against Asquith and Haldane.

Billing's star witness was Lord Alfred Douglas, a man after his own heart.
Douglas performed well, delivering the level of moral outrage that Billing had
hoped of him, until under cross-examination his own homosexual history was
turned against him. (One wonders what else he had expected.) In the end, he
had to be thrown out of court for heckling during Darling's summing-up. He
then provoked laughter in the gallery by trying to get a policeman to retrieve
his hat and cane, which he had left behind. The point which had provoked him

was that Darling had mistakenly referred to him as the author of *Salomé*, rather than its translator. It is a measure of how far he had travelled, emotionally, since he was Oscar Wilde's lover, that he took this slip as the worst possible insult rather than an inadvertent honour.

One minor point of interest about this trial is that it provided the moment at which the arcane scientific term 'orgasm' first entered public discourse in English. It was uttered in his evidence for the defence by Harold Spencer, who was explaining what effect, in the play, the kissing of the lips of the Baptist's severed head excited in Salomé. It 'produced an orgasm,' he said. 'What?' asked the prosecuting counsel. 'What is the word you used?' asked the judge. 'I am quoting from [Iwan] Bloch,' said Spencer. 'Repeat the word you used,' said the judge. Spencer repeated it. 'Some unnatural vice?' asked the prosecuting counsel. 'No,' said Spencer, 'it is a function of the body.' As the trial progressed, Billing had established, and not only to his own satisfaction, that this newfangled concept, the orgasm, would have featured strongly in any performance of *Salomé*, not least in the responses of members of its audience, especially if they were of the degenerate type listed in the 'Black Book'. Billing had successfully persuaded the jury of his viewpoint. They found him not guilty, but the judge denied him costs.

## Getting Away

It is hard to understand why some individuals went anywhere near the courts, putting their reputations at risk in order to protect them. English libel law has never been the suit of armour some people seem to have thought it. The obvious example is Oscar Wilde himself, who, to refute an accusation scrawled by a philistine on a mere visiting card, subjected his own personal life to the scrutiny not only of the Central Criminal Court but to that of the popular press as well. Within weeks he had lost his wife and children, his livelihood, many of his friends, and every last vestige of the reputation he had sought to shore up. For all that he did not know how to spell the word, Lord Queensberry knew Wilde was a sodomite and so, for that matter, did Wilde himself. From the moment any evidence was called in, the case was going to be indefensible. Or rather, Queensberry, whom Wilde was suing for libel, would be easily defended. Even until the last moment, when Queensberry had been acquitted and Wilde was waiting to be arrested in his turn, there was an alternative route to take. This was well known. Wilde could have left the country and lived somewhere under the liberal provisions of the Napoleonic Code.[53] Robbie Ross and Reggie Turner tried to persuade him to do so. When Ross told her what was happening, Constance Wilde said through her tears, 'I hope Oscar is going away abroad.'

By the time Wilde said, 'The train is gone. It is too late,' it was too late. Exile would have to come later, after hard labour.

The main rule regarding exile as a possible solution to the problem of scandal was, then, to get the timing right – not to miss the boat train, as it were. If you had portable assets, or access to money abroad, the whole process was relatively straightforward: you swapped one country for another and stayed put for life. Lord Arthur Somerset, who was caught up in the Cleveland Street scandal of 1889–90 as one of several high-born clients of Charles Hammond's establishment at number 19, a male brothel in all but name, fled the country as soon as it became clear that he was likely to be arrested, and spent the rest of his life in France, where he died in 1926. William Lygon, the seventh Earl Beauchamp, became governor of New South Wales in 1899, at the age of only twenty-seven. In 1931, long after he had returned to England to pursue a polit- ical career and had been appointed Liberal leader in the House of Lords, his wife petitioned for divorce. When it looked as if publicity about his homo- sexual activities might lead to a prosecution, he fled to the United States, where he died in 1938. It was of Beauchamp that King George V, on hearing of the sexual allegations, said, 'I thought men like that shot themselves', and it is to Beauchamp's credit that he asserted his right to an alternative.

Somerset Maugham spent most of his life in exile in the south of France, of course in part because he liked the place, but largely because his American lover Gerald Haxton had been declared an 'undesirable alien' in Britain. In 1915, on leave in London from active service in France, Haxton had been arrested and charged with 'gross indecency', but not convicted. When a hotel off the Strand was subjected to a routine military police raid in search of deserters, Haxton had been found in bed with a man called John Lindsell. Both men were represented, in the Old Bailey on 7 December 1915, by eminent lawyers, presumably found (with the help of his lawyer brother Freddie, destined to become Lord Chancellor) and paid by Somerset Maugham. According to subsequent rumour, Maugham himself had been arrested as well but used his influence to have his name removed from the details of the charge.[54] In later years, whenever Maugham travelled to London, he had to go on his own; Haxton, poor thing, was left to languish on the Riviera.[55]

If you were relatively unknown, and the scandal you were escaping was correspondingly little talked about, a temporary absence abroad might be sufficient; but even that might not be necessary. While at the University of Copenhagen, in 1877, Joachim Reinhard was accused by two students, who disliked his manner, of having attempted to seduce them. To escape the subse- quent flurry of rumours, Reinhard left for the United States on his nineteenth birthday, returning to Denmark only when he felt the rumour-mongering had died down, several months later. At the same time, another scandal was caused by Martin Kok, who groped a student who had attended a students' union party dressed as a woman. He, by contrast, opted to stay.[56] Both men later became writers, Kok publishing right-wing nationalistic poetry and Reinhard fiction; both became involved with the circle of literary homosexuals which, in the 1880s, centred on Herman Bang. By the end of the decade, Reinhard was again the object of public rumours of homosexuality, this time in the national press, and again, in 1889, he fled Denmark for the United States, where he remained for the rest of his life.

In some cases, exile comes as the last resort, after surviving a court case but not the subsequent disgrace. Leopold Ries was chief treasurer in the finance ministry of the Netherlands when, on 25 May 1936, he was arrested (along with eight other men) for having paid a seventeen-year-old, Henk Vermeulen, for sex. Only two of the accused were found guilty and given suspended sentences, but one of these committed suicide. As ever, publicity worked against the accused as perniciously as any official sanction. Ries was vulnerable both as a homosexual and as a Jew. He denied the accusation; in any case, Vermeulen was not a reliable witness. But Ries' reputation could not sustain a whispering campaign that brought up, among other things, a relationship with a soldier thirteen years previously, never even consummated; and Ries had to give up his job, with honour intact but without a pension. In 1941 he emigrated to New York, where he remained until his death in 1962.

To go back to the Wilde case: even if Wilde himself decided to stay, many others felt it expedient to leave Britain for the Continent. Many, but perhaps not as many as have settled into myth. It was Frank Harris who, in his 1916 biography of Wilde, gave the famously hyperbolic account of what happened in the immediate aftermath of Wilde's arrest:

> Every train to Dover was crowded, every steamer to Calais thronged with members of the aristocratic and leisured classes, who seemed to prefer Paris, or even Nice out of season, to a city like London, where the police might act with such unexpected vigour.

According to Harris, these men were astonished to have discovered that the authorities were aware of what men like them had been getting up to. Their privacies were being watched, their pleasures threatened. Harris revels in the consequence:

> Never was Paris so crowded with members of the English governing classes; here was to be seen a famous ex-Minister; there the fine face of a president

of a Royal society; at one table on the Café de la Paix, a millionaire recently ennobled, and celebrated for his exquisite taste in art; opposite to him a famous general. It was even said that a celebrated English actor took a return ticket to Paris for three or four days just to be in the fashion. The summer returned quickly; but the majority of the migrants stayed abroad for some time. The wind of change which had swept them across the Channel opposed their return, and they scattered over the Continent from Naples to Monte Carlo and from Palermo to Seville under all sorts of pretexts.[57]

For all that it coincides with instances of truth, this is the mythic version of the flight from Victorian Britain. Other writers have followed it, conjuring up images of first-class carriages on the boat trains to the south coast, full of effete aristos and their portable wealth. The truth was only different in being less spectacular. As Harris points out, exile was, for some, just a brief holiday until things in London settled down and they could return, not only to their homes and families, but even discreetly to their old habits. For others, as later for Wilde himself, it would be a wandering existence in search of pleasures or peace, peripatetic between the fashionable watering holes, both in and out of season. Anticipating that he would never settle, as we have seen, Wilde took the alias 'Sebastian Melmoth' – Sebastian the beautiful martyr, Melmoth the wanderer.[58]

## Radclyffe Hall and *The Well of Loneliness* (1928–29)

In 1920, Radclyffe Hall instituted proceedings against St John Lane Fox-Pitt, a member of the council of the Society for Psychical Research to which she aspired to be elected. He had referred to her as 'a grossly immoral woman'. When the case came to court on 18 November, Hall's counsel, Sir Ellis Hume-Williams, interpreted Fox-Pitt's accusations as openly implying that she was 'an unchaste and immoral woman who was addicted to unnatural vice'; this was, he said, 'as horrible an accusation as could be made against any woman in this country'. As Hall's biographer Diana Souhami rightly says, the trial of Fox-Pitt for slandering Hall as a lesbian 'ought to have proved historic'. Had Hall lost it, it might have been. It certainly aired significant issues about relationships between women, but never did so in a consistently coherent manner. There was a case to be made against Radclyffe Hall, and Fox-Pitt might have been the man to make it: he was the son-in-law of the very Marquess of Queensberry who had done for Oscar Wilde, and he shared many of Queensberry's worst habits of demonstrative moral outrage and self-righteousness. But he drew back. He claimed that he had never intended any slur on Hall's sexual morality; he had been referring only to her psychic research. On these lesser grounds, he was found to have slandered her, and she was awarded damages of £500 plus costs. Fox-Pitt appealed and a retrial was ordered, but eventually the case petered out.[59]

However, although Hall had won, hers was really only a victory in a technical sense. By bringing the case in the first place she had drawn attention to the accusations against her, and they were true. She was now widely understood to be lesbian – at least, by those who understood that the world had such creatures in it – and in that sense she had, indeed, been found guilty of sexual immorality. The seriousness with which the case had been taken in certain circles is demonstrated by the fact that Frederick Macquister, a Tory MP, soon proposed adding to the Criminal Law Amendment Act (1885) a clause outlawing 'acts of gross indecency by females' as well as those by males. Macquister's clause got through the Commons but was stopped in the Lords when Lord Birkenhead warned that to inscribe such sexual acts in law would be 'to tell the whole world there is such an offence, to bring it to the notice of women who have never heard of it, never dreamed of it'. It is possible that, had Radclyffe Hall been found as 'grossly immoral' as Fox-Pitt had originally stated, the conditions might have been created in which, the matter already having been scandalously aired in the press, Macquister's clause might have survived its passage through the Lords. British lesbians may owe Fox-Pitt's incompetence in presenting his case a debt of gratitude.

The year after the Fox-Pitt libel trial, Radclyffe Hall and Una Troubridge moved from the country, where they had been breeding dachshunds, into London. As they eased themselves into the cultural scene, they began meeting fellow lesbians, such as the writers May Sinclair and Vere Hutchinson. (Not that Surrey was empty of such women: they had met the composer Ethel Smyth on a golf course and gone to tea and dinner with her.) The painter Romaine Brooks courted Hall for a while, but to no avail. Undeterred, she invited the couple to visit her in the Villa Cercola on Capri. Hall's relationship with other lesbians was governed by her insistence on distancing herself from feminism in general and the suffragist campaign in particular. Another factor, given how many significant lesbian cultural figures were based in Paris, was the fact that she associated the French capital with Modernism and the superficiality of passing fashions. But Hall and Troubridge both liked Romaine Brooks, even if Brooks was upset by the portrayal of herself in Hall's first novel, *The Forge* (1924), and even if Troubridge hated the portrait Brooks painted of her. At about the same time, they met Tallulah Bankhead and her current lover Gwen Farrar; Bankhead invited them as special guests to her first night in *The Green Hat* at the Comedy Theatre. In the summer of 1926, notwithstanding their usual misgivings, Hall and Troubridge allowed Natalie Barney to show them around some of the main lesbian clubs in Paris: the Select, the Regina and the Dingo. They made a special trip to Passy to lay flowers on Renée Vivien's grave.

This had been Hall's most productive spell as a writer. *The Unlit Lamp* came out in 1924, the same year as *The Forge*; *Adam's Breed* followed in 1926, and won Hall the Femina Prize. (It was presented to her later in the year by John Galsworthy.) Then she wrote *The Well of Loneliness*, which would be published in 1928. As usual, it contained sketches of people she knew: Noël Coward as Jonathan Brockett, for instance, and Natalie Barney as Valérie Seymour. Hall had a strong sense that she was doing something momentous with this book. Here was a noble aim: she wanted it to be, as well as great literature, socially influential on the central question of the suppression of lesbian love. There was a difficult balance to be struck: for, ultimately, she was more interested in its quality as literature than that it should be successful propaganda. When it was completed, her own opinion was that she had managed the trick; *The Well of Loneliness* would change the world, and would bring her the admiration of those who knew anything about literature. She was wrong. Many prominent readers found the book boring or ridiculous. T.E. Lawrence said of it, in a letter to E.M. Forster, 'I read *The Well of Loneliness*: and was just a little bored. Much ado about nothing.'[60] Only on the grounds of freedom of speech and the book's social message would they want to defend it.

Hall knew, of course, that the book would provoke controversy. She and Troubridge were not going to be surprised by this. While *The Well of Loneliness* was in press, Troubridge was reading Wilde's *The Ballad of Reading Gaol* and *De Profundis* to her lover, as well as the Frank Harris biography of Wilde. As Diana Souhami puts it, 'Radclyffe Hall identified with Wilde's trials. If God willed she too would be spat at on Clapham Junction station, imprisoned, vilified, crucified.'[61] That, at least, was the rhetorical stance. Whether she and Troubridge felt there was a serious prospect of a catastrophic outcome is less clear. What is certain is that Hall was unwilling to compromise the various literary and social principles involved; nor would she make any attempt to lower her profile when the novel came out. She was putting her reputation on the line; which is more than many of those who mocked *The Well* would ever have been willing to do.

*The Well of Loneliness* has always suffered by unfair comparisons. By contrast with Faulkner, Joyce and Lawrence, it is untouched by Modernism; but then so are the novels of Arnold Bennett, Winifred Holtby, H.G. Wells . . . In terms of the craft of the novel, it is more accomplished than anything of the likes of 'Olivia' or Violet Trefusis. By contrast with Firbank, Waugh and Mitford, it is humourless; but then so are the novels of D.H. Lawrence, George Orwell, Virginia Woolf . . . Snobbish? So is Woolf. Right-wing? So are Céline, T.S. Eliot,

Wyndham Lewis, Ezra Pound . . . Dated in its conceptualisation of homosexuality? So is Proust. Cowardly and tentative? Think of Forster, who did not publish *Maurice* in his lifetime. Coy about sexual intercourse? Compare Hall's 'and that night they were not divided' with Forster's 'And now we shan't be parted no more, and that's finished'.[62]

When *The Well of Loneliness* was published in 1928, the first reviews were generally respectful, if not especially enthusiastic. But none of them – by, among others, Arnold Bennett, Vera Brittain, Cyril Connolly, L.P. Hartley and Leonard Woolf – took exception to the subject matter. Only when the popular press got hold of it did the book become controversial. On 19 August 1928, the *Sunday Express* published an editorial demanding that it be suppressed:

> Fiction of this type is an injury to good literature. It makes the profession of literature fall into disrepute. Literature has not yet recovered from the harm done to it by the Oscar Wilde scandal. It should keep its house in order.[63]

As so often, the invocation of the name of Oscar Wilde was itself a threat, and the book's publisher, Jonathan Cape, did indeed feel threatened. By acting defensively, he left the publication of the book in an even more vulnerable position. Cape took it into his head to send a copy of *The Well of Loneliness* to the Home Secretary, Sir William Joynson-Hicks, inviting him to pass it on to the Director of Public Prosecutions if he felt that there might be a case to answer. Then, in a letter to the *Daily Express*, he offered to withdraw the book if the DPP found it objectionable. Inevitably, Joynson-Hicks did pass the book on to the DPP's office – the Director being away at the time, the matter was dealt with by his deputy, Sir George Stephenson – and inevitably, the response came that there was indeed a case to be made against it. Joynson-Hicks told Cape so and advised him to withdraw the book. Although the 5,000 copies already in circulation were not interfered with, Cape cancelled a planned reprint. His sole act of defiance – which was not insignificant – was to have moulds made of the type so that he could smuggle the book out of the country and have it reprinted in Paris. Needless to say, demand for *The Well* had greatly increased since the *Sunday Express*'s first broadside against it; a Paris reprint was likely to prove popular.

Leonard Woolf and E.M. Forster rallied to defend the principle of freedom of speech, but Radclyffe Hall was not satisfied. Virginia Woolf takes up the story in a letter, dated 30 August 1928, to Vita Sackville-West:

> Morgan [Forster] goes to see Radclyffe in her tower in Kensington, with her love [Una Troubridge]: and Radclyffe scolds him like a fishwife, and says that she won[']t have any letter written about her book unless it mentions

the fact that it is a work of artistic merit – even genius. And no one has read her book; or can read it: and now we have to explain this to all the great signed names – Arnold Bennett and so on. So our ardour in the case of freedom of speech gradually cools, and instead of offering to reprint the masterpiece, we are already beginning to wish it unwritten.[64]

If there is a predictable element of Bloomsbury's aesthetic snobbery here, one can perhaps forgive the author of *Orlando* (to be published later that same year) her surprise at the egotistical ingratitude of the author of *The Well of Loneliness*. What is clear is that, whereas Hall sought to defend her book on the aesthetic grounds of her own genius, Bloomsbury was willing to defend it on the more sociological grounds of her right to speak about lesbianism. The latter was surely the more resonant issue. (Of course, *The Well* was sociologically a far more daring book than *Orlando*, even if the latter took far more aesthetic risks.) In the meantime, Sir Francis Floud, of Customs and Excise, expressed his view that *The Well* was not obscene; but the Home Secretary had made up his mind, and Jonathan Cape was issued with a summons to appear at Bow Street Magistrates' Court on 9 November 1928. While the wheels of the system ground into their slow motion, Una Troubridge read *Orlando* out loud to her lover.

In the event, the chief magistrate, Sir Chartres Biron, refused to consider cultural matters – he would not hear expert literary evidence for the defence from the likes of Forster and Virginia Woolf, who were both in court as the case began – and rather obviously leaned towards the prosecution in treating lesbianism as if it were against the law. As he said, 'These unnatural offences between women which are the subject of this book involve acts which between men would be a criminal offence.'[65] Not that any such 'offences' (there was no such offence in English law) ever occur in the book – it never goes further than a kiss on the lips – but Biron seems to have been adept at conjuring them up between the lines. After he had adjourned the trial for a week in order to reread *The Well*, it cannot have been much of a surprise to those present to hear him declare it obscene. He was especially horrified that Hall had depicted ambulance drivers at the front during the First World War as being 'addicted to this vice'; Radclyffe Hall was horrified that he thereby impugned the honour of those brave women. Having remained silent for days, she interrupted him at this point and he threatened her with eviction from the court.

Biron awarded costs against Hall and she had to sell the John Singer Sargent portrait of her late lover Mabel Batten. If she invested any hope in the prospect of an appeal, that hope was to be short-lived. If anything, the appeal, which opened on 14 December 1928, was even more absurd and biased than the original trial – all the more so since the Director of Public Prosecutions declined to release copies of the book for the appeal judges to read. The case in favour of *The Well* failed again. The following year, a similar prosecution was launched against it in New York; but this time Hall's book was well defended by Morris Ernst, and on 19 April 1929 the case was thrown out. Radclyffe Hall had been devastated by the fact that she was never called to give evidence in favour of her own work, and, of course, by the eventual judgment against *The Well*. As she said in a letter to Havelock Ellis, 'In the eyes of the law I am non existent.'[66]

Writing in 1958, Beverley Nichols said the word 'homosexual' was not widely known in Britain in the 1920s. 'Today the word is so common that one would hardly be surprised to see it over the entrance to one of the departments in a general store. But in the twenties it was taboo, and I think it is correct to say that the first time it began to come into general circulation was during the case of *The Well of Loneliness*, by Radclyffe Hall.'[67] The teenage Quentin Crisp, looking around him for cultural signs of what he felt he was about to become, found a few in newspaper accounts of court cases and in show-business gossip. According to these signs, homosexuality:

> was thought to be Greek in origin, smaller than socialism but more deadly – especially to children. At about this time *The Well of Loneliness* was banned. The widely reported court case, together with the extraordinary reputation that Tallulah Bankhead was painstakingly building up for herself as a delinquent, brought Lesbianism, if not into the light of day, at least into the twilight, but I do not remember ever hearing anyone discuss the subject except Mrs Longhurst and my mother.[68]

These tended to be matters for private gossip rather than dispassionate, public discussion; yet even so, the news was eagerly received by those who needed it most.

## Dolly Wilde: The Next Generation

Oscar's niece Dolly once said that reading *The Well of Loneliness* was 'like walking through a plowed field'. If she took her lesbianism seriously, knowing from family experience where the public fear of deviancy could lead, she nevertheless knew she must take it as lightly as the pleasures it afforded. She seems to have learned so much from studying the life of her uncle. The source of her fame and the seat of her tragedy were probably the same. In the words of her biographer, 'Everyone who met Dolly Wilde remarked on the disturbing ways in which she was like her famous uncle.' Her whole life was overshadowed by the Wilde scandal from the start. Oscar was imprisoned in May 1895, and

Dolly was born only weeks later, on 11 July. Her father was Oscar's elder brother, Willie. On one occasion Dolly had the wit to admit, 'I am more Oscar-like than he was like himself'. It is certain that some of the people who befriended her, including some of the women who had affairs with her, did so in part because of her association with him.[69]

At the beginning of the Great War she took one of the few active options open to women and went to join a women's ambulance unit in Paris. One of her Paris flatmates, and lovers, during the war was a seventeen-year-old girl who called herself Joe Carstairs. After the war Carstairs ran a chauffeuring company patronised by J.M. Barrie, among others. Carstairs had a brief affair with Tallulah Bankhead in the late 1920s and was acquainted with Radclyffe Hall and Una Troubridge. In 1934, fleeing the threat of imprisonment for not paying UK taxes, she bought Whale Cay in the British West Indies – now the Bahamas – for $40,000. In 1937 she met Marlene Dietrich in the south of France. They had an affair, which they had to keep secret from Dietrich's then lover, the novelist Erich Maria Remarque; he portrayed Carstairs as a man in *The Arch of Triumph*. At one point Carstairs gave Dietrich a beach.[70]

In 1925 or 1926, Dolly Wilde had a brief affair with the film star Alla Nazimova (later Nancy Reagan's godmother). Paris seemed to open up so many more possibilities than London had. She paid her first visit to one of Natalie Barney's Friday evening salons at 20 rue Jacob on 27 June 1927. Late in the same year she hawked Barney's novel *The One Who Was Legion* around London; but everyone she took it to, including Leonard and Virginia Woolf at the Hogarth Press, turned it down. A great intimacy developed between Dolly and Barney, to the extent that it was later said of her that Dolly was the only woman who could make Barney cry. Dolly appears as Doll Furious in Djuna Barnes' *Ladies Almanack* (1928), Natalie Barney as Evangeline Musset.

Natalie Barney once complained that her lovers were more interested in the *mot à mot* than in the *corps à corps*. This witticism suggests that there were times when she regretted that her lesbian salon was one of the most important centres of cultural ferment then active in Europe, containing as it did an extraordinary collection of clever and creative women. (See Chapter Four.) There seem to have been times when she wished it were less of a symposium, more of a boudoir. Not that she had great grounds for complaint: there was never any shortage of lovers at her beck. They included Lily de Gramont (duchesse de Clermont-Tonnerre), Romaine Brooks, Renée Vivien and, in what Barney referred to as a *demi-liaison*, the novelist Colette. It has been calculated that, from the time when she seduced her own governess at fifteen, she had forty significant affairs and hundreds of less momentous brief encounters. Remy de Gourmont called her *l'Amazone*.

In 1882, at the age of five, Barney had been rescued from some bullies by Oscar Wilde himself. Perhaps this is what gave her a lifetime of queer courage. In her twenties she was briefly engaged to Lord Alfred Douglas; then she had an affair with his fiancée Olive Custance. At twenty-two she had dressed as a pageboy to make love to Liane de Pougy. In 1902 she seduced Lucie Delarue-Mardrus, who was still married to Joseph-Charles Mardrus, the great Orientalist and translator of *The Arabian Nights*. In 1903 she and Renée Vivien went to Lesbos with the vague notion of setting up a lesbian colony there, but nothing came of it. If not exactly a colony, Barney's salon was certainly the centre of a subculture. Claude Mauriac called her 'the Pope of Lesbos'.

However, even if Natalie Barney was a great social organiser and cultural energiser, adept at forging networks to benefit fellow lesbians and women artists in general, she was not the only woman of her time who put such an effort into these things. Many women were looking after each other. Dolly Wilde's biographer suggests a network of female mutual aid, a women's Homintern, obviously dependent on various rich individuals, but also on a shared understanding that, when careers came to an end, those who were left destitute might be helped by others whose careers were in the ascendant. This is not a lesbian network, but it has many lesbian constituents:

> Shipping heiress Bryher, the writer born Winifred Ellerman, the only woman in the general milieu of European lesbians richer than Natalie Barney, gave money to Djuna Barnes, Sylvia Beach, Edith Sitwell and Dorothy Richardson, among others. Janet Flanner made certain that a near-destitute Alice Toklas did not want for necessities after Gertrude Stein's death; and she assisted Djuna Barnes as well. Solita Solano supported her lover, Margaret Anderson, founder of the *Little Review*, and Margaret's other lover, the soprano Georgette LeBlanc, out of her own meagre funds. Alice DeLamar, the retiring American heiress who came to Paris as an ambulance driver during the First War, bequeathed Eyre de Lanux and Eva Le Gallienne enough money to keep them through extreme old age. Even Peggy Guggenheim ... provided Djuna Barnes with a grudging monthly allowance (ungratefully received) that helped sustain her for the rest of her life.[71]

Where male patronage might be found wanting – when men distrusted women who chose not to take up the sacred roles of wife and mother – it must be replaced by something akin to female patronage.

F. Scott Fitzgerald was furious when, in May 1929, Dolly Wilde made a pass at Zelda Fitzgerald.[72] More often, with heterosexual men, she was something of a cock-tease. According to her cousin Vyvyan Holland, Oscar Wilde's son, 'she was always taking her horse to the water and then refusing to let him drink'.[73] The men who were more at ease with her sense of fun tended to be homosexual. She was a member of Stephen Tennant's circle and went to Brian Howard's famous Greek party dressed as Sappho.[74]

### Lord Alfred Douglas

The very name of Oscar Wilde set off its chains of associations, which were positive or negative according to the individual's attitudes to homosexuality. In his 1969 autobiography, Cyril Scott mentions an educational book about sex that he published anonymously during the First World War. 'Oscar Wilde's friend the late Lord Alfred Douglas of all people, brought an action against its publishers, who were ordered to burn the whole edition.' Wilde's name then triggers a personally defensive reflex: 'Mention of Oscar Wilde reminds me that anything in the nature of homosexuality has always been entirely foreign to my temperament.' This is, presumably, something he must establish, because he is later going to give an account of his chaste encounters with the German poet Stefan George and his circle. (See Chapter Five.) In case this disclaimer is insufficiently persuasive, he lays claim to a cleansing homophobia of which he has since duly been cured: 'Indeed, I owe it to Occultism for eventually ridding me of a strong intolerance towards homosexuals and lesbians by explaining its basic occult cause' – that is, by explaining that homosexual people have been reincarnated in the wrong sex, for which they are beyond blame.[75]

As a fifteen-year-old schoolboy, the writer Denton Welch saw a grumpy old man on a train who turned out to be Lord Alfred Douglas. Welch later wrote: 'I was thrilled. I had just read all about Oscar Wilde.' For Welch, who was born in 1915, Wilde continued to be a significant cultural and erotic forebear. In his late twenties in July 1943, after chatting with a brace of bathing boys he wrote in his diary: 'I began to think of Oscar Wilde ... and all the people who have longed to become young again. I don't know why 1890 should leap to my mind the whole time. Is it because they worshipped youth? Or is it because it always seems to me a rosy time for young men to be gay and wilful and wasteful?'[76]

For many younger homosexual men who wanted to establish some form of material connection with the myth that Oscar Wilde had become, meeting or corresponding with Bosie Douglas was a natural thing to try to do. The Canadian composer John Glassco did meet him in Paris in the 1920s and later said: 'Never was there a more sociable man, a man with better manners or more exquisite grace of movement, speech and behaviour.' Douglas was still convinced that he was the greatest living English poet.

It was however clear that the only important thing that ever happened to him was his friendship with Oscar Wilde, and he had been trading on it ever since. All that could have saved him from utter nonentity was some fund of genuine physical desire; but this (as I soon discovered) he did not have.[77]

As a teenager, Samuel Steward, used to write to famous writers, hoping thereby to store up contacts that he would cash in in due course. He wanted to be a gay literary groupie, and, if we are to believe his memoirs, that is what he became. The year 1937 seems to have brought particular successes. For a start, he visited Alfred Douglas in the hope of making a sexual connection with Oscar Wilde through the irascible remnants of Bosie. At first, Douglas maintained decorum and disclaimed any homosexual interest – until they had a drink. 'And that did it. Within an hour and a half we were in bed, the Church renounced, conscience vanquished, inhibitions overcome, revulsion conquered, pledges and vows and British laws all forgotten. Head down, my lips where Oscar's had been, I knew that I had won.' Thanking Steward afterwards, Douglas confided in him that all he and Oscar ever did was masturbate each other: 'We kissed a lot, but not much more.' Quite how this squares with Steward's suggestion that he fellated Bosie as Oscar had before him is not clear.[78]

Although he repudiated his homosexual past, and idiotically fought in the courts to save his reputation from being associated with it, Douglas continued to demand ownership of the topic. In the letters he exchanged with George Bernard Shaw, a correspondence which began in 1931, when Shaw was seventy-four and Douglas sixty, each time the topic of homosexuality cropped up both were already well informed. (Anthony Powell said of this correspondence, 'It was really a kind of flirtation between two elderly men, one not without its embarrassments.'[79]) Shaw was writing as a disinterested observer, and Douglas, since his self-reinvention as a respectably married Roman Catholic, was purporting to do so, even if the expression of his strongly held views always soon betrayed him as involved and obsessive on the topic. Shaw is the more authoritative commentator, perhaps the more so since he knows he is writing to a man with a greater practical knowledge of the matter than himself but who, as a consequence, has an anti-homosexual axe to grind. Writing on 16 August 1939, just before the outbreak of the Second World War, Shaw considers what has changed not only since Wilde's trials, but also since publication of the work of Wilde's first biographers:

[Frank] Harris and [R.H.] Sherard were hampered by the fact that in their time it was generally believed that homosexuality involved the most horrible depravity of character, and was unnatural and unmentionable. Since then the work done in England by Havelock Ellis and Edward Carpenter and abroad by Freud and the psychoanalysts has completely changed all that. Not only have sexual subjects become mentionable and discussable (compare Thackeray's novels with D.H. Lawrence's) but it is now known that a reversal of the sex instinct occurs naturally, and that the victim of it is greatly to be pitied and may be a person of the noblest character. Wilde's life must therefore be taken out of the old atmosphere in which Harris and Sherard wrote, and retold with a healthy objectivity which was impossible before the [First World] war.[80]

Robert Sherard's biography of Wilde had been published in 1906, Frank Harris's in 1918. The change that Shaw perceives, from 'unnatural and unmentionable' to natural and mentionable, has been slow, not necessarily because of wide-spread resistance to new ideas, especially new ideas like these – although that was undoubtedly a major inhibiting factor – but because the ideas in question have had to be disseminated through the culture beyond the relatively narrow social groups of those who were reading Freud and the others. (In the continental theorists' cases, of course, there was also a delay between initial publication and subsequent translation, if not always a long one.) The resulting slow changes might first, as Shaw implies, have affected intellectuals and artists, who then (like Lawrence) published work that was more widely read than that of the theorists, or was at least consumed in a different demographic pattern. Of course, the idea that the homosexual individual 'is greatly to be pitied and may be a person of the noblest character' is itself a rudimentary, intermediate position. It seems likely that Shaw knew pity was not the answer; he certainly knew that social policy cannot be based on the very few human beings who turn out to be 'of the noblest character'.

If the changes Shaw described had resulted in a 'healthy objectivity' about homosexuality, it had not rubbed off on Alfred Douglas. In his reply to Shaw, dated 18 August 1939, he said: 'I write as a devout Catholic (although I have the advantage of having known all about the homosexual question long before your Havelock Ellises and Freuds turned their attention to it).'[81] This intuitive response is pure Bosie, and to an extent one can sympathise with it. Despite the opening claim to an unassailable moral position – nobody who describes himself as devout is truly devout – Douglas is, at least, admitting to something of his past as Bosie. Claiming to have known 'all about the homosexual question' is not, of course, the same as admitting to having once been homosexual – although Shaw knew this of him well enough – but the implication of Douglas' remark is that he was present during the events of the 1890s, and that he had an interest, if not a part, in them. In 1939, Douglas was no longer interested in what sexology and psychoanalysis had to say about homosexuality. He was now investing his moral values in biblical tradition. His evident contempt for 'your Havelock Ellises and Freuds' – the 'your' is personal, associating them with other interests and opinions of Shaw's which Douglas regarded as modernistic fads – probably, also, has a tinge of class superiority and xenophobia. At any rate, he was not willing to take lessons on the topic from anyone, including George Bernard Shaw. It is worth noting, though, that Michael Tippett wrote to Shaw 'to obtain his views on homosexuality', some time in the 1930s, and received this reply from Shaw's secretary: 'Mr Shaw has asked me to say he has no knowledge of this matter, and that since it has nothing to do with the great march of evolution, it is irrelevant.'[82]

When Hesketh Pearson mentioned to Shaw, in January 1943, that he was hoping to write a life of Oscar Wilde, Shaw tried to dissuade him. Despite what he had said to Alfred Douglas about things having changed so much since the early biographies, he now argued that Frank Harris, Arthur Ransome and R.H. Sherard had already done what needed doing. Wilde's dazzling conversation could never be reproduced, his plays were still in print, and his poetry was negligible. Even the scandal, although memorable, would not always be remembered: 'some day, when the Queensberry business is forgotten, the Encyclopaedias will give an account of him in which it will be dismissed in half a line, like [Paul] Verlaine's similar misadventure [in 1873]; but that will not be in my time, and hardly in yours'.[83]

In 1939 a petition to the Prime Minister, Neville Chamberlain, asking for a Civil List pension for Douglas, was signed by James Agate, John Gielgud, Christopher Hassall, Harold Nicolson, Hugh Walpole, Evelyn Waugh, Virginia Woolf and others. It was apparently rejected, even after all those years, because of the Wilde scandal. The association of Wilde himself, or Wilde and Douglas paired, with homosexuality remained constant, insistent, and even incriminating, for many decades, as witness a ridiculous passage in Roger Shattuck's book about the French avant-garde *The Banquet Years* (1968), when Shattuck says the playwright Alfred Jarry appeared at the theatre several times with Wilde and Douglas – 'and there is further evidence of homosexual proclivities' in Jarry, as if merely having known the two notorious lovers were evidence in itself.[84]

# CHAPTER THREE

# THE NORTHERN EXOTIC

## Moonlight People

The history of homosexuality in Russia at the turn of the nineteenth and twentieth centuries is marked, among those classes who could afford to dream of such a drastic solution, by the growing desire to move out of the nation altogether. The cultural modernisation of Russia, which had begun at such a spectacular pace under Peter the Great, had now slowed to a crawl, restrained by the awesome reluctance of the tsarist bureaucracy. As elsewhere in Europe, the existence of homosexuality was silently understood among the upper classes, but barely spoken of until collective discretion was undermined by scandal or the threat of it.

Male homosexuality had been a recurrent theme of gossip surrounding the controversial figure of the faith healer Grigori Rasputin. In the early 1890s he had made a pilgrimage on foot to Mount Athos in Greece, but had been disgusted by the homosexual practices of the monks there; he left for the Holy Land and Jerusalem. All the same, Rasputin had a number of homosexual friends and allies, among them Prince Andronnikov, whose means of access to information was the plying of messenger boys with pleasures and then ransacking their sacks of whatever they were carrying. Late in 1915, Rasputin used his influence with the Tsar to get his ally Pitirim, who was homosexual, appointed Metropolitan of Petrograd. Prince Felix Yusupov, who had first met Rasputin in 1909 and been disgusted by him, became obsessed with him. Some say he was attracted to him, but others that he went to Rasputin to cure his own homosexuality. He plotted to have Rasputin assassinated. One of his co-conspirators, Grand Duke Dmitri Pavlovich, aide to the Tsar, may have been an ex-lover of Yusupov's. Yusupov did kill Rasputin on 30 December 1916; or rather, he left him for dead, but Rasputin drowned when disposed of in the river. Yusupov was subsequently banished.

As in German-speaking Europe and elsewhere, from the 1860s onwards, Russia saw a flurry of more or less scientific enquiry into sexual behaviour, accompanied by a feverish coining of terms, most of which did not survive the subsequent century.[1] One of the less convincingly scientific theorists was Vasily Vasilievich Rozanov, a philosopher and journalist who achieved popularity and notoriety through his writings on sexuality, which would lead to a blanket ban on his work in the Soviet era. At twenty-four, in 1880, the year of his graduation, he married a woman fourteen years his senior, Apollinaria Suslova, who had been the lover of Fyodor Dostoevsky. When they separated six years later she refused him a divorce, so he was never able to remarry. There was a short-lived correspondence between Rozanov and the poet Marina Tsvetaeva in 1914, prior to her affair with Sophia Parnok. Like his work on other subjects, what he wrote on sexuality contains many contradictions, but its consistent trend is against the grain of the faith-based validation of chastity and abstinence. A book he published in 1911 and then revised in 1913, *People of the Moonlight*, was not only his main statement on homosexuality but one of very few volumes on the topic published in Russia for many decades. For all its faults, therefore, it merits a respectable place in the cultural history of that nation. Central to his account is the belief that homosexual men (lesbians being absent from consideration) have an aversion to sex with women, for the most part because they have an aversion to sex itself. So homosexuals never masturbate – a rare view, this – and the receptive partner in anal intercourse never ejaculates – a far more common view. In any case, the vast majority of male–male couples – nine out of ten – do not indulge in this sort of thing. He was strongly opposed to the criminalisation of homosexual acts.[2]

The title of Rozanov's book does not refer to homosexual men as such, but to the more general category of those who have an aversion to procreative sexual intercourse. 'Moonlight people' (*liudi lunnago sveta*) are, however, linked throughout the book with 'sodomites' (*sodomliane, sodomity*), who often seem to be the same people. He also calls them 'congenital eunuchs' (*skoptsy iz chreva materi*) and the 'third sex' (*tretii pol*). Rozanov argues that undue medical and legal attention to the *actus sodomiticus*, anal intercourse, has led to a failure on the part of all the authorities of the law, religion and science to recognise the necessary contribution of 'moonlight people' to civilisation. Since only a tiny fraction of 'the vast organism of Sodom' actually practises *coitus per anum*, the filling of the prisons and madhouses with these 'male-females and 'female-males' is disproportionate to the scale and nature of their existence. Like the writer Mikhail Kuzmin, Rozanov regarded asceticism, the denial of the flesh as promoted by Christianity, as a greater perversion than homosexuality (if not greater than the practice of anal sex). Since each must act according to his nature, for a sodomite, procreative intercourse would be the perversion. As Lindsay Watton paraphrases this part of Rozanov's argument:

> For an actor to perform an act that contraindicates his or her own physical predisposition is, for that individual, sinful – and no external perspective can define it otherwise. Similarly, an actor fulfilling his or her own physical predisposition, in accordance with the biological imperative of pleasure, cannot be performing a sinful act, and no external perspective can legitimately claim it as such.[3]

To try to force a sodomite (say) to marry and procreate is equivalent to forcing a heterosexual into sodomy; and to act against one's own sexual nature, being a perversion, is a sin. There is a moral equivalence between the sodomite and the non-sodomite who act according to their nature, and between those who act against it. Where he draws the line, however, is at that point where 'moonlight people' cease to act as private individuals and start to gather as a public group. We are reminded of Friedrich Engels' anxieties on this score. Lindsay Watton summarises the point as follows:

> Sodomites, in Rozanov's scheme, are demonized only as an ideological community (Sodom), which dares to dispute the value of copulation and procreation of the 'normal' (that is, the heterosexual). Once the sodomite moves from the ethical and biological realms to the ideological plane, even in Rozanov's sympathetic argument Sodom is reconstructed as a threat. He is capable of vigorously attacking the ideal of Sodom, when he perceives it to be an outright attack on the importance of the family.[4]

Equality ends, then, once homosexuals start to behave like heterosexuals. The sexual system – with, above all, its primary term, the family – must not be called into question. This is a failure of nerve on Rozanov's part. It is as if, having understood how daring his rather odd book had become, he drew back from a wholehearted commitment to its implications; and yet it is not an uncommon failure. The same reluctance to countenance a collective, politicised existence among homosexual men and women characterises most of the twentieth century's approaches to homosexual law reform as, more or less reluctantly, espoused by heterosexual people. The spirit of the move appears to be something like: in return for our ceasing to harass and imprison them, they must vanish into the obscurity of discreet, lasting couples.

Leon Trotsky said of Vasily Rozanov: 'Even the most paradoxical exaggerations of Freud are much more significant and fertile than the broad surmises of

Rozanov who constantly falls into intentional [*sic*] half-wittedness, or simple babble, repeats himself, and lies for two.' Trotsky regarded Rozanov's influence on the intelligentsia as revealing nothing so clearly as the decadence of their bourgeois individualism. He had no time for the man or his crackpot theories, which could not be put to the service of the Revolution. 'Rozanov,' he said, in tones that invited no contradiction, 'was a notorious rascal, a coward, a sponger, and a lick-spittle.'[5] That may be so; or any part of it may be. But the fact is that Rozanov can now be seen to have engaged with what, for the whole of Western Europe, was one of modernity's insistent questions. It may be that the answers he came up with – out of the void on account of a lack of serious public discussion in Russia – were primitive, contradictory and just plain eccentric; but the fact that he had heard the question and tried to answer it was progressive in itself.

The Revolution's response was, as in so many things, to put the brakes on debate. For artists, one of the best options was to emigrate. Paris would seem the natural destination, especially since many educated Russians already spoke French. Those who remained submitted, or were forced to submit, to the conditions of debate; namely, silence. Simon Karlinsky has said that, 'among the numerous talented poets and prose writers who appeared on the literary scene *after* the October Revolution there was not a single lesbian or gay figure.'[6]

## Lovers of the Beautiful

On arrival in Petrograd from Moscow and, before that, his birthplace Konstantinovo in the Ryazan province, the twenty-year-old Sergei Esenin was surprised by the evidence he found of *muzhelozhstvo* (men lying with men) in the city. Esenin met Nikolai Klyuev, the leading figure in a group of 'peasant poets', in 1915. They had an affair that lasted until 1917, and Esenin addressed several love poems to the older man. One of his biographers says 'it is clear that Esenin met with the homosexual advances, not only of Klyuev, but of others', for he was moving in a distinctly gay cultural environment; and indeed, the writer coyly adds, 'He may have succumbed to the pressure of the milieu and discovered in himself a latent bisexuality.'[7] He later became associated with the Russian Imagist movement, which included the poets Ryurik Ivnev and Anatoly Mariengof, both homosexual; and appears to have had a three-year affair with the latter.[8] However, Esenin 'came to resent playing second fiddle to Klyuev' as a poet. On 25 December 1925, he visited Klyuev and got a lukewarm response to poems he read out. Some time early in the morning of 28 December, he hanged himself.[9]

When the Greek novelist and poet Nikos Kazantzakis visited what he referred to as the 'multicolored, multispermous chaos' of Moscow in 1927, to celebrate the tenth anniversary of the Revolution, he met Nikolai Klyuev, 'the most mystical and voluptuous of muzhik poets'. He thought the Russian looked nearer seventy than forty, but found his voice 'muted' and 'caressing'. Klyuev told him, 'I'm not one of those Russians who busy themselves with politics and cannons . . . I am part of the golden lode which makes fairy tales and icons. The true Russia depends on us.'[10] Klyuev's poetry is pervaded by images of fertilisation. This is ironic, less on account of the fact that he was homosexual than because he was an admirer of the Skopets sect who practised self-castration as a means to perfection. In the poem beginning 'Two youths came to me' his speaker deduces from the youths' visit, as well as from the scriptures, that 'I will conceive in my belly, / And bear twins into the world: / Love I will give over to the knife of the Skopets / And radiate immortality in song'. His severed testicles will seed an earth already liberally scattered with 'the grapes of fallen members'. The imagery of reproduction, focused as it is on spermatozoa rather than ova, seems entirely masculine, more masturbatory than heterosexual: 'For this embryo of the world do not spare your sperm, / Caress your testicles and couple as whales'. But his celebrations of ejaculation, as explicit as they are, hardly ever seem to celebrate physical pleasure. He is more interested in the idea of the copious scattering of sperm as a metaphor for non-sexual modes of creativity, including the composition of his own poetry. As he says in 'Mother Sabbath', as if draining the ejaculatory image of any erotic resonance: I 'spill my verse / As a catfish its milky sperm'.[11] Leon Trotsky, for one, was not impressed. He wrote, damningly: 'Kliuev's individuality is the artistic expression of an independent, well-fed, well-to-do peasant loving his freedom egotistically.' (This accusation of individualism – for which, read selfishness – was one that is often aimed at homosexual men and women, in part because they were assumed to define themselves in terms of pleasure alone, and in connected part because they were not traditionally regarded as forming families and reproducing satisfactorily.) In summary, Trotsky dismissed the man from his pantheon of writers likely to be of use: 'What will Kliuev's further road be – towards the Revolution or away from it? More likely away from the Revolution; he is much too saturated with the past.'[12] Klyuev was shot in 1937.

A memory of grey eyes between dark brows and pale cheeks, a private dynamic made public, generates the main erotic theme of Mikhael Kuzmin's major, six-part poem 'Alexandrian Songs' (1905–1908). Speaking from the imagined positions of different ages (eras and life-stages) and genders, Kuzmin adopts a variety of hieratic voices and tones of voice, which in one way or another keep reverting to that intensely remembered image of a love now lost. Alexandria itself provides, at a superficial level, the picturesque setting for a series of Orientalist fantasies whose homo-eroticism follows a number of available conventions: adopting female voices to express desire for male beauty;

comparing the beloved to the sun; invoking archetypes of male beauty from classical myth and history (Adonis, Antinous) ... Imitating not only the Muslim poets but also southern European poets who were themselves imitators of the Muslims (notably Pierre Louÿs), the sequence calls attention to material pleasures in the full knowledge of their ephemerality: 'Am I the less to love / these dear and fragile things / because they must decay?' In one poem a pretty boy, 'all but naked', entices the speaker into a brothel, offering a beautiful woman or, 'if such things do not tempt you ... other joys / not to be despised by a wise and courageous heart'. In another, one of Hadrian's soldiers witnesses the aftermath of the drowning of the Emperor's lover, Antinous. The sequence ends with the main speaker, having left Alexandria behind, wandering from Tyre to Ephesus, Smyrna, Athens, Corinth, Byzantium and, of course, the mighty Rome, experiencing many loves but never again encountering the grey eyes, dark brows and pale cheeks of his one true love. Kuzmin imagines the south and east of the Mediterranean and Asia Minor as an environment in which living cannot fail to involve loving, yet where love is at its most intense when refigured in retrospect as a yearning nostalgia.

In Kuzmin's novel *Wings* (1906), young Vanya Smurov is disappointed to see, when first arriving in St Petersburg by train, not the grand, cosmopolitan palaces he has been anticipating, but ugly suburban kitchen gardens and cemeteries, followed by a vast, polluted cityscape of tenements and shacks. He is also disappointed by the wan, bourgeois circles of school and extended family in which he finds he has to move. The only glimpse of the kind of cultural glamour he had been expecting is embodied in the person, behaviour and opinions of the sophisticated aesthete Larion Stroop, who befriends him. Stroop is aware of his disappointment and says to him, 'You're in bad surroundings; but that may be for the best, as you're divested of the prejudices of any kind of traditional life, and you could become a perfectly modern man if you wanted.' Stroop is himself such a man. Vanya overhears a long speech from him at one of his salons:

We are Hellenes: the intolerant monotheism of the Judaeans is alien to us, their turning away from the fine arts, their simultaneous attachment to the flesh, to posterity, to the seed [that is, to reproductive heterosexuality] ... Love has no other objective beyond itself; nature is also devoid of any shadow of the idea of finality. The laws of nature are of a completely different category to the laws of God, so-called, and men ... And men who link the concept of beauty with the beauty of a woman display only vulgar lust, and are further, furthest of all from the true idea of beauty. We are Hellenes, lovers of the beautiful, bacchanals of the future life.[13]

Virtually implicit in Vanya's first arrival in St Petersburg, and his meeting Stroop, is an eventual trip to Rome and Florence, and, as the novel closes, an imminent journey to Bari – so far south and east on the mainland of Italy that any next step might involve a crossing to Greece. Whether that is a necessary step for a Hellene, who carries Greek values within his person, is left open. Kuzmin himself had travelled with his lover 'Prince Georges', a cavalry officer, to Constantinople, Athens, Smyrna, Alexandria, Cairo and Memphis. In 1897 he took a trip to Rome and, having fallen in love with the lift boy, took him to Florence, intending eventually to take him all the way home to Russia 'in the capacity of my servant'. In the event, though, he sent the boy home to Rome instead. What he did take home was the Italian effect: 'he never severed the ties with Italy. It remained a source of personal and artistic inspiration for the rest of his life. He used his actual memories of his short stay in a number of works, and he made several journeys of the imagination to Italy, in cycles of poems or in individual lyrics.'[14]

Sergei Diaghilev thought very highly of Kuzmin's work. They saw so much of each other for a short time in 1907 that Kuzmin noted in his diary: 'Gossip is making the rounds about me and Diaghilev. *Quel farce*' (31 October 1907). Kuzmin was also greatly admired by such younger poets as Sergei Esenin and Marina Tsvetaeva, both of whom met him at the same St Petersburg literary soirée in January 1916. Diaghilev told him about a student in Moscow called Vladimir Ruslov, 'a proselytizer and *casse-tête*, who considers himself Dorian Gray, who always has about thirty comrades at the ready par amour'. Kuzmin corresponded with Ruslov, in the words of his biographers, 'fascinated as he was by the aura of legend that surrounded him and by the idea that a new kind of "gay society" of unprecedented sexual openness might be formed with Ruslov and his young friends as the Moscow nucleus'. Years later, on 1 March 1924, Ruslov wrote to tell Kuzmin about a 'small, very intimate circle made up in the main of young poets' that was meeting in Moscow under the name 'Antinous', its aim being 'the revelation of male beauty in print'. At their second meeting they had staged a dramatisation of the 'Antinous' section of 'Alexandrian Songs'. They were proposing to publish an anthology of gay poetry, but eventually had to abandon the idea. They asked Kuzmin to give them a reading, and after various difficulties, on 11 May he did so. 'Aunties and *jeunes hommes* assembled,' he reported; 'Very homespun but warm and courteous'. Even the agents of the secret police joined in the applause.[15]

Warm and courteous, perhaps, but not the sign of a wider thaw. Experimentation and innovation were now firmly discouraged, whether in form or theme. George Reavey writes that 'the effect of the Revolution in the

1920's was to bring an end to the interplay of [Modernist] "isms" [such as Acmeism and Futurism] and to make these poets individually face each in his own way the consequences of the Revolution, which had the effect of gradually stamping out the lyrical impulse'.[16] The great social experiment left those who did not fit in, at best, to fend for themselves; or it actively punished them for their failure to conform. Either way, it isolated them – in some respects the perfect, albeit unintended, strategy for producing vibrant, individual voices, which must then be silenced. Of course, this was by no means the fate only of gay and lesbian poets. To the bureaucrats of tyranny, anyone has the potential to be a deviant. If they speak, as poets do, anything they say is liable to incriminate them.

When she was twenty-two in October 1914, two-and-a-half years after she married Sergei Efron, the poet Marina Tsvetaeva met and fell in love with Sophia Parnok, a woman seven years older than herself, who published work as a critic and translator under the pseudonym 'Andrei Polianin'. (Simon Karlinsky says of Parnok, 'Throughout her life, she was openly and aggressively lesbian.'[17]) Their relationship lasted until February 1916, during which time Sergei Efron was at first a rather meek bystander, and then an absentee – he enlisted in the war effort, in March 1915, as a civilian nurse – but at the Front he received regular and detailed despatches on the affair from his wife. Notwithstanding the fact that Tsvetaeva once called her lesbian lover 'My fair stranger with Beethoven's face', by Karlinsky's account the affair with Parnok 'awakened her sensuality and gave her the kind of erotic fulfillment that she did not get . . . apparently, from her marriage'. Yet, because 'She always mistrusted the physical, carnal aspects of love', the resulting mood was conflicted, as can be seen in the varying tones of the sequence of poems 'Woman Friend' (also known in English as the 'Girlfriend' poems), which she originally thought of giving the title 'An Error'. The couple travelled together. In Petrograd, Tsvetaeva met the apprentice poet Leonid Kannegiser, who was almost certainly the lover of Sergei Esenin at the time. (He was certainly, later, the assassin of Moisei Uritsky of the secret police.) At the Kannegiser family's cultural salon, although she was disappointed not to encounter Anna Akhmatova, she did meet Osip Mandelstam and Mikhail Kuzmin. Of these, the first fell in love with her, but the second established a more welcome friendship with her. Parnok was in bed with a migraine, and Tsvetaeva had to hurry away to her bedside before she could hear Kuzmin, who was a composer as well as a poet, singing a selection of his own songs. She told him in a letter that she would never forgive Parnok for that; but this may just have been a polite gesture. In 1919–20, Tsvetaeva had an affair with the actress Sophia Holliday, which she wrote about in the prose piece 'Tale about Sonechka'.

In the early 1930s, Marina Tsvetaeva was invited to read 'Gars', the French translation of her poem 'The Swain' ('Mólodets') at Natalie Barney's salon at 20 rue Jacob in Paris. Simon Karlinsky's brief account of the occasion gives the sense of a lost opportunity, at which an ill-chosen text failed to establish a connection between two quite separate continents of lesbianism:

> The reading ended in a complete fiasco: the listeners had no idea of what it was Tsvetaeva was trying to do. In addition to the complexity of Tsvetaeva's style, the theme of the poem – a woman sacrificing herself, her mother and her child for the sake of a vampire she loves – could not have been very congenial to the predominantly lesbian audience.[18]

In any case, Tsvetaeva would have looked out of place even before she opened her mouth, since she must have been shabbily dressed by the standards of the Barney salon; and she had no great reputation, except among Russians, to excuse the oddity of her reading. In fact, she had no reputation at all – she was unknown. Tsvetaeva later claimed that Barney promised to help her find a publisher for the poem, and then not only failed to do so but even went and lost the manuscript. Tsvetaeva nurtured a grudge against her on that account. After the reading – and we have no record of the hostess' reaction – the only contact with Natalie Barney was literary: in December 1932, Tsvetaeva wrote a 'Lettre à l'Amazone' responding to Barney's *Pensées d'une Amazone* of 1920; and she revised it late in 1934, by which time Parnok, to whom Tsvetaeva was now indifferent, had died.[19]

The central argument of the 'Lettre' was that a woman cannot but make a choice between lesbianism and motherhood. (Tsvetaeva had a son she adored.) Even a lesbian couple whose love endures till death is marred by the void of their childlessness: 'Only for this and for no other reason are they a race of the damned.'[20] Diana Lewis Burgin reads the 'Lettre' as a statement about its author's discomfort with her own sexuality as much as it is about her discomfort with Barney's:

> Ample evidence in Tsvetaeva's life and work suggests that her struggle with Barney (as the embodiment of the lesbian Amazon) was a struggle with her own lesbian self, and, as an enemy beloved self, Barney was close to Tsvetaeva. Perhaps Barney even embodied the lesbian that Tsvetaeva wanted to be.[21]

Tsvetaeva does say in the 'Lettre' that 'two women who love each other are a perfect wholeness', but, as Burgin argues,

she could not believe that such 'a perfect wholeness', despite her own experience of it, could exist on earth, the realm of Mother Nature, where love
without biological issue seemed to her subject to absolute death. " 'Lovers
have no children,' " Tsvetaeva quotes one of Barney's pro-lesbian maxims
and adds bitterly, giving it a tragic dimension alien to Barney's thinking,
" 'True, but they die. All of them' ."

The literalism of this depressive outburst is depressing in its turn. The inter-
nalisation of homophobia is spectacular, all the more affecting for the fact that
it happened to a major poet with an incisive intelligence. Burgin displays an
understandable bafflement when she writes:

> Tsvetaeva so consistently championed the soul over the body in her life and
> her work, including parts of her 'Letter to the Amazon', that one can only
> marvel at her inability, or stubborn refusal, to recognize the potential for
> happiness in lesbian unions, a happiness she herself experienced with
> Parnok, and to break out of the confines of the most rigid biological deter-
> minism and choose to think symbolically.[22]

In her biography of Tsvetaeva, published two years after Karlinsky's, Viktoria
Schweitzer takes an almost entirely negative approach to the Tsvetaeva–Parnok
relationship. Pointing out that 'The air of the theatrical and literary salons in
those days was heavy with the scent of forbidden love' and that 'Such liaisons
were more or less openly acknowledged, and were not for the most part viewed
with disapproval', she nevertheless expresses her own disapproval in the unsubstantiated guess that, rather than the poet's being motivated by love, 'I should
not be surprised to learn that the thought of Sappho, and nothing more,
impelled Tsvetaeva to behave as she did.' In truth, Schweitzer does not want to
discuss the topic at all: 'I shall pass over the ups and downs of the relationship,
which dragged on for some eighteen months. I might have ignored it altogether, had it not played a dangerous part in Tsvetaeva's life, and left conspicuous traces in her writings.' At her most generously grudging, she does
acknowledge that 'There is no denying either Tsvetaeva's infatuation with
Parnok, or the affection she felt for her.' But she then quotes a poem – the thir-
teenth in the 'Girlfriend' sequence – in which Tsvetaeva speaks, not of 'infatuation' or of mere 'affection', but of 'love'. Perhaps the last word should go to
Marina Tsvetaeva's translator, Elaine Feinstein, who writes that 'The lyrics for
Parnok are both more sensual, and less tormented, than other love poetry
written by Tsvetaeva.'[23]

## The Russian Ballet

In her lengthy critical biography of the English novelist Ronald Firbank, Brigid Brophy writes:

> The strongest movement (and one adored by Firbank) to appear within vivid memory of the Wilde trials and make towards re-converting western Europe to aestheticism came from outside western Europe – that is, from outside the immediate repercussive circle of the trials – and was also comparatively frank and un-hangdog about the homosexuality of its leaders: the Russian Ballet.[24]

Even if it eventually involved an unparalleled collective effort of artists from most disciplines and many nations, this international movement was the responsibility of a single dynamic individual, Sergei Diaghilev.

As a teenager, Diaghilev went on a grand tour with his cousin and lover Dmitry Filosofov ('Dima'). As they made their way through Berlin, Paris, Venice, Rome, Florence and Vienna, their journey must have felt like nothing less than a honeymoon, given that they were in love with each other; and it is tempting to believe that Diaghilev's lifelong restlessness, manifested particularly in his constant touring of Europe for both work and leisure, derived from the bliss of this first experience of international travel. The precedent had been set for an amorous habit: the first thing he tended to do with any younger man he loved was take him to the south of France or down to Italy. Although he studied law in St Petersburg, and was awarded his law degree, he was constantly distracted by a greater interest in music. (He played the piano well, but Rimsky-Korsakov disabused him of the impression that he had a talent for composition.) Like Oscar Wilde, from whom they learned, he and his circle championed art for art's sake, and believed that morality had no part in the matter. In 1898 he toured Berlin, London and Paris, borrowing works of art to exhibit in St Petersburg. In Paris he sought out the exiled Wilde. Diaghilev was already a striking sight, tall and elegant, with an early white streak in his hair; the pair of them must have gone rather well together. Seeing them walking arm in arm, the women prostitutes are said to have stood on café chairs to hurl abuse at two such obvious threats to their business.

On 1 January 1899, Diaghilev started a cultural magazine, *The World of Art* (*Mir Iskusstva*), editing it fortnightly with Dima Filosofov. Simon Karlinsky calls the group of critics and artists behind the magazine 'predominantly gay'; and it did, indeed, publish gay-related articles, such as an essay on the homosexual colony at Taormina by Zinaida Gippius.[25] On 22 January his International

Exhibition opened at the Stieglitz Museum. When appointed Director of the Imperial Theatres in July 1899, Prince Sergei Mikhailovitch Volkonsky, who also happened to be gay, gave Diaghilev a job on the staff of the theatre directorate. It was when he was dismissed from this post, in 1901, that Diaghilev angrily went abroad, thereby unwittingly creating the conditions for the career in exile for which he is famous. Russia was a place to get out of when it became impossible to work there. That said, he returned to Petersburg at the end of the year. In 1903 he began to organise another great exhibition, this time of Russian portraiture. It opened in February 1905 at the Tauride Palace, with little short of 3,000 pictures on show. Meanwhile, in December 1904 Isadora Duncan had arrived in Petersburg. Her influence on the dancer Michel Fokine, converting him to a more naturalistic dance style than had yet been seen in Russia, would have a crucial influence on Diaghilev, returning him to an interest in ballet, the rigid conventions of which he had grown out of, or tired of, at least.[26]

In the spring of 1906, Diaghilev went to Italy and Greece with his new lover, Alexis Mavrine. Later in the same year, he took his skill as an exhibitor, plus a consignment of Russian art, to Paris, where he set up L'Exposition de l'Art Russe at the Salon d'Automne. He gained his first entrée to French society when he met the Comtesse Greffulhe, the model for Marcel Proust's Princesse de Guermantes. Not willing to confine his skills to a single art, he began to organise a series of concerts of Russian music, where possible to be conducted by the composers themselves. Five such concerts were staged in May 1907. Following on from the success of these, he quickly thought of staging an opera season for 1908. Thus, in due course, *Boris Godunov* opened in Paris on 19 May 1908, with Feodor Chaliapin as Boris. Diaghilev's next project was to bring the Imperial Ballet to Paris.

In May 1909, the various opera and ballet artists travelled down from Russia to France. At this time Diaghilev was gradually turning his emotional attention away from Alexis Mavrine, who was travelling as his secretary, to Vaslav Nijinsky, to whom he had been introduced by Nijinsky's then lover Prince Pavel Dmitrievitch Lvov the previous autumn. On 18 May, the ballet's season opened at the Châtelet. A day or two later, Mavrine eloped with the ballerina Olga Feodorova, leaving Diaghilev fuming with anger but free to concentrate on his new love interest. The ballerina Tamara Karsavina remarked that 'Diaghilev had become overnight a leader of the Paris homosexual set', by which she meant the circle that included Lucien Daudet, Reynaldo Hahn, Marcel Proust and Jean Cocteau.[27] This was not the only 'homosexual set' in Paris, nor was Diaghilev – or anyone else, for that matter – its 'leader'; but there was no reason why Karsavina should know that. What matters is the impression she had gained from his social connections: that Diaghilev was moving among homosexuals in particular. She may merely have thought he was a leader of the group because he was such a forceful personality and that it was inconceivable he could ever follow rather than lead. The season ended in mid-June, with the company deeply in debt and Diaghilev a declared bankrupt.

However, everything the Russian dancers had achieved in those few weeks had persuaded Diaghilev that he must make every effort to stage further seasons. He knew that the combination of Russian talent with the flexibility and adventurous spirit of French audiences and theatre managers could result in revolutionary innovations in the dance. His other main motivation was to provide a showcase for Nijinsky's talent. Also, he had just seen Nijinsky dancing with Anna Pavlova for the first time and been enchanted. When Nijinsky fell ill at the end of the season, Diaghilev rented a small flat and nursed him there himself. In August the two of them joined the designer Léon Bakst in Venice; then they travelled back to St Petersburg via Paris. Diaghilev commissioned *The Firebird* from Stravinsky, hoping that Pavlova would dance the title role.

The Ballets Russes opened their 1910 season on 20 May in Berlin, or rather at the Theater des Westens in the suburb of Charlottenburg; and they opened in Paris on 4 June. It was then that Marcel Proust said of their performance of Rimsky's *Schéhérazade*, 'I never saw anything so beautiful'.[28] As it happened, Pavlova turned out to be unavailable for *The Firebird*, so it was premiered on 25 June with Tamara Karsavina in the lead role. Because Diaghilev had not brought a Russian orchestra on this second season in Paris and was not having to pay Chaliapin and an opera company, the season proved financially secure.

On 5 February 1911, Nijinsky danced the male lead in *Giselle* without wearing trunks over his tights and was dismissed from the Imperial Ballet. Whether deliberate or not, this provided the opportunity Diaghilev needed to poach him for his own company. When he and Nijinsky left Russia in mid-March, the latter was leaving for good. On 9 April they opened their season in Monte Carlo. One of its highlights was a desexed Nijinsky in *Le Spectre de la rose*. His gender was made less specific by three means of costume (Léon Bakst devised a leotard with limp petals attached, in colours that merged, with the ultimate effect of rendering his physique softer and more vague), make-up (in Romola Nijinsky's words, his face looked 'like that of a celestial insect' with a mouth 'like rose petals') and, above all, Nijinsky's own choreography, which involved him in continuous, fluid movements, curling and swerving, swooping and turning, as though he were a rose leaf caught up in a flurry of wind.[29]

After Rome (from 14 May), the Paris season opened on 6 June. Nijinsky danced in *Carnaval*, *Narcisse* and *Le Spectre de la rose*, and as the puppet in *Petrushka*. (When rehearsals of *Petrushka* began, the orchestra thought Stravinsky's score was a joke.) The company opened its London season on

21 June 1911 at Covent Garden, where they were astonished to find themselves in the middle of a vegetable market. The city was packed for the Coronation of George V on 22 June. The King and Queen themselves attended the ballet on the 24th. The dancers were spooked by the applause at the end of their performance, which was muted by kid gloves. When Queen Mary got home she wrote, inscrutably, in her diary: 'The music and ballet were both extremely good.'[30] During an autumn season at Covent Garden, Pavlova danced at seven performances. While in London, Nijinsky went round to John Singer Sargent's studio in Tite Street, Chelsea, and Sargent sketched his head.

January 1912 saw the company in Berlin; May in Paris again. Nijinsky appeared with his skin painted blue in *Le Dieu bleu*, an Orientalist collaboration between Jean Cocteau and Reynaldo Hahn, designed by Léon Bakst. But the 1912 season is best known for a performance of Nijinsky's, which caused a particular scandal. The first performance of *L'Après-midi d'un faune* provoked both applause and booing, both extending for long enough to provoke an immediate second performance. Richard Buckle boils the narrative down to a single sentence: 'The idle Faun observes seven Nymphs, and his desire is aroused by one who undresses to bathe in the stream; but when he confronts her, she flees, and he has to console himself with the scarf she has left behind.'[31] The phrase 'console himself' is a euphemism for the scandalous suggestiveness of Nijinsky's actions at the climax of the ballet: he fucked the scarf. This celebration of sensuality was too strong for some. A front-page review in *Le Figaro*, written in bile by the editor himself, Gaston Calmette, pulled no punches:

> Anyone who mentions the words 'art' and 'imagination' in the same breath as this production must be laughing at us. This is neither a pretty pastoral nor a work of profound meaning. We are shown a lecherous faun, whose movements are filthy and bestial in their eroticism, and whose gestures are as crude as they are indecent. That is all. And the over-explicit miming of this misshapen beast, loathsome when seen full-on, but even more loathsome in profile, was greeted with the booing it deserved.[32]

What Nijinsky and Diaghilev regarded as beautiful could just as clearly be seen by others as the peak of bestial ugliness. However, recognising this, when the police attended the second night, Nijinsky judiciously toned down his sexual movements and the company was given the go-ahead for further performances.[33] The first performance of Ravel's *Daphnis et Chloë* was staged on 8 June, with Nijinsky as Daphnis. At a tense final rehearsal, the choreographer Michel Fokine, who was currently falling out of favour, called Diaghilev a bugger in front of the whole company.

Another Covent Garden season was staged between mid-July and the beginning of August. On this London trip Nijinsky and Bakst went to tea with Ottoline Morrell in Bedford Square and watched Duncan Grant playing tennis with a group of his friends. It is quite likely that this afternoon in Bloomsbury provided the initial inspiration for what was to become the ballet *Jeux*, premiered at the Théâtre des Champs-Elysées in Paris on 15 May 1913. Nijinsky's diary is revealing about this piece:

> the story of this ballet is about three young men making love to each other . . . Jeux is the life of which Diaghilev dreamed. He wanted to have two boys as lovers. He often told me so, but I refused. Diaghilev wanted to make love to two boys at the same time, and wanted these boys to make love to him. In the ballet, the two girls represent the two boys and the young man is Diaghilev. I changed the characters, as love between three men could not be represented on the stage.[34]

Even with the sexes normalised, a substantial part of the audience was inclined to laugh at a ballet based on a game of tennis. Diaghilev was still concentrating on finding vehicles suited to Nijinsky's extraordinary physicality. Richard Buckle gets a little carried away when he writes that 'No fairy with her three wishes, not Hadrian for Antinous, had ever had such rare gifts in store as Diaghilev had for Nijinsky that summer.'[35] Perhaps we should be indulgent towards the biographer, since the gifts in question included ballet scores by Richard Strauss, Claude Debussy and Igor Stravinsky. There was also a three-week vacation in Venice in September.

Notwithstanding the flashy surprises of *Jeux*, the real coup of the 1913 season was, of course, the première, on 29 May, of Stravinsky's *The Rite of Spring* (*Le Sacre du printemps*). The press, predictably and collectively, called it 'le massacre du printemps'. So much attention is given to *Le Sacre*'s effect on the audience that it tends to be forgotten that it was only the first part of the evening's programme. It was followed by Nijinsky in *Le Spectre de la rose*, and the evening ended with *Prince Igor*. It is hard to imagine a richer diet for balletomanes.

In mid-August, Diaghilev sent the company off on a South American tour, remaining in Europe himself. By the time they disembarked in Rio de Janeiro, Nijinsky was engaged to Romola de Pulszky. (He first met her in Vienna, earlier in the year, and she had been following him ever since.) They got married on 10 September in Buenos Aires. Romola became pregnant in Rio on the way home. When Diaghilev heard the news, he angrily took himself off to Naples for a holiday. By the end of the year, he had sacked Nijinsky. Seeking a replacement, his eye and instinct lit on an eighteen-year-old called Léonide Miassin, who later changed his name to Massine. Diaghilev soon developed an attachment to the boy; in August 1914 he took him on a long holiday in Italy – one of his most familiar modes of courtship – and although Léonide was heterosexual, they developed an understanding that encompassed both their personal friendship and the working relationship. In Florence, Diaghilev persuaded Léonide, who had never considered such a thing, to become a choreographer. Diaghilev rented a house at Ouchy on the north shore of Lake Geneva, within cycling distance of where Stravinsky was living (the latter's cycling distance, of course, not Diaghilev's own). Here, he restructured his company and had the sense to re-engage Nijinsky. Massine soon learned that his master expected the most of him. After the première of *Soleil de nuit* in December 1915 and a second performance for charity, the apprentice choreographer had good reason to believe his ballet had been a success. But Diaghilev merely said, 'I didn't hear them cheering.'[36]

On 1 January 1916 the company set sail for the United States. Diaghilev disliked travelling by sea and spent much of the voyage telling his rosary beads. (His many crossings of the English Channel were a source of acute anguish.) When they sailed into New York harbour on the 11th in thick fog, the foghorns that howled as they passed the Statue of Liberty convinced him the ship was sinking and he made for the lifeboat station. When the season opened at the Century Theater on 17 January, the New York censors made the company tone down the slaves' orgy in *Schéhérazade* and the onanistic climax of *L'Après-midi d'un faune*. In Boston the dancers were allowed to show no bare flesh but their toes. Miscegenation was objected to in Chicago, so Negro flesh had to be lightened. In Kansas City, Captain Ennis of the police department called Diaghilev 'Dogleaf' and insisted that he 'keep it toned down'. After a massive tour (also taking in St Louis, Cincinnati, Cleveland, Pittsburgh, Washington, Philadelphia and Minneapolis), they returned to New York City in time for Diaghilev to go down to the waterfront on 4 April to welcome Nijinsky and his family to the States. Tough negotiations about money ensued. On the 12th, Nijinsky danced *Petrushka* and *Le Spectre de la rose*. He was not well received by the Americans: both the *Herald* and the *Times* called him 'effeminate'; and indeed, when he appeared in *Narcisse* on the 22nd, some sections of the audience laughed at him and the *Herald* excelled itself by calling him 'offensively effeminate'.

Back in Paris, Diaghilev met Picasso for the first time. Soon afterwards, Picasso agreed to work with Eric Satie and Jean Cocteau on *Parade*. When the company sailed back to the States in the autumn, Diaghilev put Nijinsky in charge of the tour and went to Rome with Massine. Picasso and Cocteau joined him there in February 1917 to work on *Parade*. When Diaghilev took Massine down to Naples in the spring and he took a fancy to I Galli, a little cluster of rocky islands off the Sorrentine peninsula, Diaghilev set his heart on buying them some day. (This would prove complicated, since they belonged to different members of one extensive family.)[37] *Parade* was given its première in Paris on 18 May. It was not as poorly received as some famous accounts suggest; in fact, there was plenty of enthusiastic applause, plus a small amount of hostile whistling.

The following month the company was in Madrid, where the King and Queen attended every one of their performances. Diaghilev and Massine had made friends with Manuel de Falla; they suggested he turn his incidental music to *The Three-Cornered Hat* (*El Sombrero de tres picos*) into a ballet. (It would have its first performance at the Alhambra in Leicester Square, London, on 22 July 1919.) Relations between Diaghilev, Massine and Nijinsky were unusually peaceable until the moment when the latter, supported by his wife, announced that he would not be going on the forthcoming tour of South America. In the event, Nijinsky did go but Diaghilev stayed behind. So a performance at the Teatro Liceo in Barcelona on 30 June 1917 was the last time Diaghilev ever saw Nijinsky dance. At the end of the South American tour, Nijinsky stayed behind in Buenos Aires when the company left for Europe. A single performance he gave as a benefit for the Red Cross in Montevideo was the last occasion he ever danced in public.

The Treaty of Brest-Litovsk reduced Diaghilev and others in his company to stateless exiles. They continued to tour Europe, perhaps with a strong sense that to do so was now their official destiny. When the Armistice was announced on 11 November 1918, Diaghilev and Massine were dining with Osbert Sitwell in London. They made their way through the crowds in Trafalgar Square to a party at the Adelphi, off the Strand. Here, in Massine's words, they found that 'the Bloomsbury Junta was in full session'.[38] Lytton Strachey, Clive Bell, Roger Fry, the D.H. Lawrences, Mark Gertler, Ottoline Morrell, David Garnett, Duncan Grant and Maynard Keynes were all there; everyone except Diaghilev was dancing.

Diaghilev travelled with Massine many times in the ensuing months. They holidayed together in Naples and Venice in the summer of 1920. But the following January, Diaghilev sacked Massine for having a heterosexual affair within the company. At the end of February, Diaghilev took on Boris Kochno, a teenager, as his secretary. Although the boy was disappointed not to become his employer's lover as well, Diaghilev did look after him and their increasingly intimate relationship soon became indispensable to both of them. In 1923 another youngster arrived on the scene, materialising in Paris from Russia. He was the eighteen-year-old dancer Serge Lifar. According to Richard Buckle,

'He was (by his own admission) sexless, feeling no physical desire either for men or women, although he aroused the desire and love of both'.[39]

Next in line, as both dancer and lover, was Patrick Healey-Kay, otherwise known as Anton Dolin. As they travelled down to Monte Carlo, Diaghilev moved him into his sleeping compartment: 'Patrick, as Diaghilev always called him, understood the ways of the world. He had been seduced by a priest in the confessional when he was a boy.' Aptly, the new ballet *Le Train bleu* was created for Dolin. When they were in Venice, 'Patrick enjoyed himself on the beach [at the Lido], and Diaghilev occasionally interrupted his dipping into Proust and Radiguet to watch him through binoculars.' Mind you, Boris Kochno claimed Diaghilev never really read, but only 'counted the pages'.[40] Dolin was disappointed to receive a copy of *Death in Venice* from the older man for his twentieth birthday in July 1924; but in the evening a Cartier gold watch was added to the gift. Dolin left the company in June 1925, by which time Diaghilev was living with Serge Lifar.

In the summer of 1928, at the age of fifty-six, Diaghilev, who had been diagnosed with diabetes in June, fell in love with the sixteen-year-old composer Igor Markevich, who was to become his last protégé. Although Markevich was heterosexual – he would later marry Nijinsky's daughter, Kyra – he liked Diaghilev's company and was flattered by his affection. After a holiday with Markevich in Germany, Diaghilev went down to the Hôtel des Bains de Mer on the Lido at Venice and invited Lifar to join him there. The pace of life was catching up with him. Lifar nursed him alone until Kochno was called down from Toulon. The increasingly tired and weak Diaghilev was still euphoric about the successful holiday with Markevich, and whenever Lifar was out of the room he would share with Kochno the details of that last idyll. The two acolytes watched over him through his last days and were present when he died.

Virginia Nicholson has written that 'Until Diaghilev ballet had been an entertainment largely aimed at the heterosexual male, who came for a titillating evening looking up the dancers' skirts at the Alhambra . . . Ballet was never the same again, but neither were homosexuals'.[41] In his memoirs, the American dancer and choreographer Lincoln Kirstein remembers having cut out and saved a picture in *Vanity Fair*, an etching by Troy Kinney of Vaslav Nijinsky in his costume for *Les Sylphides*. Kirstein rather coyly says of it, 'this etching became an icon to which I constantly referred as the sum of masculine possibility'. It later turned out, when he met them, that both Osbert Sitwell and Richard Buckle remembered keeping the same clipping; Kirstein is naïvely surprised by this.[42]

In his pioneering book *A Queer History of the Ballet*, Peter Stoneley has summarised how the Ballets Russes transformed the presentation of masculinity in ballet:

Within a few short years, Diaghilev had transformed the ballet from a spectacle that focused on the female body to one that focused on the man.
Furthermore, the key figure, or the body in question, was not a limp form,
but a muscular man with an astonishing, explosive energy. Given the
different dramatic personalities in each of the roles, there was also an
implicit liberation from the idea of the homosexual as a singular sexological
type. Through Nijinsky, Diaghilev offered a range of personae and behavioural possibilities. Even though he drew on *fin de siècle* resources, this was
an escape from Wildean shame, and from physiological destiny, into a
joyous process of free association.[43]

After his death, Diaghilev's artistic work was carried on in France by Serge
Lifar, in England by Ninette de Valois, and in the United States by George
Balanchine. Through them, his influence went on to shape the ballet of the
Paris Opéra, the Royal Ballet and the New York City Ballet. Even elsewhere his
aesthetic continued to prevail. Alexander Schouvaloff has said that the most
damning criticism he ever heard of any ballet made after 1929 was, 'It's as if
Diaghilev had never existed.'[44]

## The Swedish Ballet

The Ballets Russes had many offshoots and influenced many dance styles in
many cultures, from the Kabuki theatre of Japan to Broadway and Hollywood.[45]
The Swedish Ballet (Ballets Suédois) was set up in direct imitation of the Ballets
Russes by Rolf de Maré as a showcase for his lover, the dancer Jean Börlin. Maré,
a rich Swedish aristocrat, was only semi-literate. He paid Börlin to leave the
ballet company at the Royal Opera in Stockholm and study choreography under
Michel Fokine. The latter had moved to Sweden in 1913 after leaving Diaghilev
and the Ballets Russes, and had set about modernising the Royal Opera's ballet;
but the management had disappointed his ambitions by refusing to allow him to
take the company on tour. When Maré then took Börlin to Paris and began to
put together a company there, the Swedish cultural authorities slipped easily into
a lasting habit of spreading smears about both him as an individual and the
Ballets Suédois as a group, making it practically impossible for Maré to return
home. The Ballet was often subjected to homophobic attack in Sweden, in particular because its name suggested it represented, or was representative of, the
nation. It was fostering a 'cult of Vaseline', for instance; and when the ballerina
Jenny Hasselquist left the company, the magazine *Fäderneslandet* claimed she
had written in her resignation letter: 'I no longer wish to sully myself by association with perverted quasi-aristocrats and their Vaseline-anointed catamites.'[46]

In 1920 the Ballets Suédois reopened the Théâtre des Champs-Élysées, which, although it had been built as recently as 1913, had been closed since the Great War. For the next five years it would form the centre of their experiment. They premiered on 25 October with *Iberia*, *Jeux* and *Nuit de Saint-Jean*. Here, as later in London, they were reviewed sceptically at first, suffering by constant comparison with the Ballets Russes, but they soon came to be seen as the equal of their older sibling. Diaghilev himself respectfully – even, perhaps, apprehensively – attended all their ballets, and often leased their theatre for his own company's use; but he always maintained a rather lofty distance from Rolf de Maré. A close friendship developed, though, between Maré and Jean Cocteau; and on 18 June 1921 the company performed *Les Mariés de la Tour Eiffel*, the ballet that had resulted from a collaboration between Cocteau and the radical group of Modernist composers, Les Six. On one evening, Jean Börlin danced, on points, the role of the Bathing Girl without anyone noticing that this masked dancer was actually a man.

The company paid its first visit to Berlin in the first half of February 1922, and was then well received all the way across central Europe; but they were consistently attacked in Stockholm, where they arrived on 16 May. Their tour continued through other Scandinavian cities, and then across to England. They did not return to Paris until May of the following year. On 25 October 1923 they performed *La Création du Monde* and *Within the Quota*, the latter with a libretto by Gerald Murphy and music by Cole Porter. Arriving in New York for the first time in November, they were again received coolly at first, but then gradually with more enthusiasm. An exhausting provincial tour of the USA followed. Like the Ballets Russes, they were welcomed as epitomising modernity even if they were somewhat distrusted as importing inexplicable European perversities into American cultural life.

Something of the company's position vis-à-vis modernity and Modernism is conveyed in remarks the Swiss poet and novelist Blaise Cendrars said he once addressed to Jean Börlin:

Listen, old man, you don't know how to dance. You have to understand. You're on a footing with sailors, half-castes, Negroes and savages, and that is what I admire most about you. You've planted yourself, on those Swedish peasant feet of yours, diametrically opposite the Ballets Russes, and you're jostling aside the French ballet tradition that has come down to us from St Petersburg via the ancien régime and Italianism. Listen to [Walt] Whitman's great heartbeat now and let yourself go in the arms of motorcar and aeroplane mechanics.[47]

The crux of Cendrars' version of the special quality of the Ballets Suédois is how they bridge the cultural gap between the 'primitive' and the industrial technology that underpins modernity. The association of the Russians – no less modern than the Swedes – with the long balletic tradition to which they had contributed and beyond which they had so radically moved, unkindly anchors them in the past; whereas the association of the Swedes with mere sailors, Negroes and mechanics asserts a fundamental connection with some of the icons of the Jazz Age and democratic modernity. Not only that: for, as the evocation of Whitman might have reminded him (although I am not sure that Börlin is likely to have read him), these are specifically homo-erotic icons. By encouraging the dancer to let himself go 'in the arms of motorcar and aeroplane mechanics', Cendrars wants him not only to think of himself as though he were a car or a plane, tuned to move with the speed and elegance of the new, but also, apparently, to give himself up to physical pleasure in the skilled hands of those who maintain and love such qualities. One doubts that Börlin needed either Cendrars' or Whitman's approval in the latter respect.

On 17 March 1925, Rolf de Maré announced that he was disbanding the company. Its financial state was dire, Jean Börlin was exhausted from having created twenty-four ballets and given about nine hundred performances, and Maré was in no mood merely to start repeating old successes. After Börlin's death from hepatitis five years later, at the age of only thirty-seven, Maré turned the Théâtre des Champs-Élysées over to music hall. Colette would perform there, as would Josephine Baker. Even long after the Ballets Suédois had closed down, Rolf de Maré tried to maintain a distance from his native Sweden. As his friend Åke Dubois later explained:

> It wasn't easy in those days. You often had to lead a double life. Rolf never made any secret of his leanings, but that didn't simplify matters. The scandals in high places [in Sweden] during the 1950s with their attendant witch-hunt of homosexuals didn't exactly contribute towards a more open society. All the more reason, then, to spend as much time as possible abroad. Living openly was of course easier in Paris or other places.[48]

## Sergei Eisenstein

Sergei Mikhailovich Eisenstein loved one man intensely for a long time. Grigori Alexandrov was a professional partner – as Eisenstein's assistant director – but probably not a sexual partner. Eisenstein's diaries of his 1926 trip to the flesh-pots of Berlin, where he is known to have visited both gay male and lesbian nightclubs as well as Magnus Hirschfeld's Institute for Sexual Science, seem to contain coded erotic references to Alexandrov. According to the Polish writer Waclaw Solski, on one occasion when Eisenstein said that, unlike the Hollywood film-makers, he was not interested in girls, 'Grigori Alexandrov suddenly burst into a short laugh, but quickly stopped and turned red' – which proves nothing, since one can think of many reasons for his embarrassment at having let slip the laughter.[49]

Eisenstein himself said to his biographer Marie Seton: 'A lot of people say I'm homosexual. I never have been, and I'd tell you if it were true.' But he did own up to having 'bisexual tendencies' in an 'intellectual way', like Balzac and Zola. In the United States in the early 1930s, as we have already seen, he said to Joseph Freeman that, 'had it not been for Leonardo, Freud, Marx, Lenin and the movies, I would, in all probability, have been another Oscar Wilde'. Yet if these cultural and political distractions led him away from Wildedom, or compensated him for the repression of it, he had other cultural interests that might just as easily have had the opposite effect. For a start, he had a particular interest in Oscar Wilde himself. To promote the Proletkult Theatre's production of an adaptation of Jack London's *The Mexican*, which he had designed, Eisenstein adapted the publicity that had heralded Wilde's arrival in New York. When he went to London in November 1929, he later said, 'I found the authentic atmosphere of Oscar Wilde'. It seems to have been what he was looking for.[50]

Eisenstein co-wrote a pantomime, *Columbine's Garter*, partly influenced by Jean Cocteau and Francis Poulenc's *Les Mariées de la Tour Eiffel*. He had a photograph of Cocteau, which he had cut out of the magazine *Je Sais Tout*, pinned to the wall in his flat. He must have been thrilled, then, to meet Cocteau when he went to Paris early in 1930; but embarrassed on the famous occasion a few nights later when he accompanied the Surrealist poet Paul Éluard to a performance of Cocteau's *La Voix humaine* at the Comédie Française, and Éluard shouted out at the traduced lover, on stage with her telephone, 'Who are you talking to? Monsieiur Desbordes?' Jean Desbordes being Cocteau's then lover, this was intended, and taken, as a ribald joke at the expense of the author. A row broke out, and Éluard had to be ejected from the auditorium before the play could continue. Cocteau did not associate the offence, if any, with Eisenstein and when, a short while later, the Russian was threatened with deportation – he had fallen victim to a flurry of anti-Soviet feeling in France – both Cocteau and Colette supported him, even getting him a meeting with Philippe Berthelot, Director of the Ministry of Foreign Affairs.[51] While still in Paris, Eisenstein frequented Sylvia Beach's bookshop Shakespeare and Company, where he was pleased to find Paul Verlaine's pornographic *Hombres* being sold, as he put it, 'under the counter quite openly'.[52] He attended the salon of Marie-Laure de Noailles and was invited to visit her husband the vicomte in his villa at Hyères, but never actually got there. James Joyce gave him a signed copy of *Ulysses*, which had just come out; and Gertrude Stein, whom he met at Tristan Tzara's home, gave him advice on his imminent trip to the United States.

He does seem to have been one of those men whose homosexual aspect could flourish only when they were away from home. One biographer sums up his active sexual life as follows: 'It seems likely that Eisenstein experimented with homosexual sex – mainly with young men for money in Western Europe and Mexico – as well as occasionally sleeping with women, something he was pleased to hint at in his memoirs.'[53] Travel took him to places where he found not only those young men but, perhaps more importantly, prominent cultural figures whom he respected and who were managing to live more or less openly with lovers of the same sex. Berlin, Paris and Wilde's London had all given him such glimpses of sexual and cultural possibility. As he set sail for New York on 8 May 1930, expecting Alexandrov to follow a short while later, he is likely to have anticipated more of the same.

The New World gave him a prickly welcome, however. He was greeted with an anti-Semitic and anti-Communist campaign against his presence. In California he met Greta Garbo and watched Marlene Dietrich being directed by Josef von Sternberg, but his own dreams of film-making in Hollywood came to nothing. Instead, he went down to Mexico to make *Que Viva México!* with Upton Sinclair. Although the film was never completed by Eisenstein himself – it existed in three inferior versions until the 1970s, when Grigori Alexandrov managed to obtain the rushes and reconstruct a more plausibly Eisensteinian version – it contains what have been seen as striking moments of directorial self-revelation when the camera lingers on the bodies of oppressed peasant workers. Any analysis of its political message should take into account that, like Gide's *L'Immoraliste* or Thomas Mann's *Der Töd in Venedig*, this is a northern homosexual's southern text and has important things to express in that regard.

On 19 April 1932, Eisenstein set sail from New York on the *Europa*. The world of, if not the desire for, the Mexican peasant was left far in their wake as, for the duration of the crossing, he shared a table with those two cosmopolitan queens, Noël Coward and the critic and actor Alexander Woollcott. Meanwhile, some trunks that Eisenstein had sent to Hollywood from Mexico were opened by US Customs and found to contain many of his homosexually explicit drawings and a sheaf of photographs of male nudes. On 27 October 1934, he married Pera Attasheva, an actress and journalist. This was clearly a marriage of convenience: the couple lived separately and, far from their relationship's ever being consummated, Eisenstein himself said that they never so much as kissed. He did not even mention his wife in his memoirs. To an extent, if intended to mask his true sexuality, the marriage worked: the mere fact of his having a wife, albeit one he did not live with, gave the impression of a man who was heterosexual but chaste.

Rumours of homosexuality continued to surface, it seemed, whenever Eisenstein formed a close relationship with another man. For instance, when Paul Robeson spent a fortnight in Moscow at the end of 1934, he saw Eisenstein virtually every day, giving rise to a shiver of suggestive gossip. Similarly, there would be unfounded rumours about the relationship between Eisenstein and Nikolai Cherkassov, the star of his films *Alexander Nevsky* (1938) and *Ivan the Terrible* (1942–44, 1946). Of the films Eisenstein never made, among the more intriguing was a proposal for a piece about Lawrence of Arabia, whose complex psychology the director felt he might capture, like that of Ivan, in pure images. However, the career of Grigori Alexandrov, after the two men's return from the United States, gives an impression of the film-maker Eisenstein could never have become, despite some of his enthusiasms. Alexandrov successfully turned his hand to making Hollywood-style musicals for the entertainment of the masses. The nearest Eisenstein came to such work – although Alexandrov's first musical was a project which Eisenstein had himself turned down – was the closing reel, in colour, of *Ivan the Terrible*, which, if arguably camp in some respects, is more genuinely sinister in its raucous glamour than any musical comedy could have survived being.

## Tamara de Lempicka

Born in 1895 to a Polish mother and Russian Jewish father, Tamara Gurwick-Gorska spent six months with her grandmother in Italy in 1907, and then moved to live in a hotel in Menton on the French Riviera. In St Petersburg in 1911, she met Tadeusz Lempicki, seven years her senior. They were married in 1916, by which time she was already pregnant. She had a daughter, Kizette, in September of that year. When her new husband, a counter-revolutionary activist, was arrested by the Cheka, she slept with the Swedish consul to buy his release and her own safe passage out of Finland. The couple were eventually reunited in Warsaw. In the meantime, she had an affair with a Siamese diplomat, with whom, unhindered by the Great War, she travelled to London and Paris.

In the summer of 1918, Tamara and Tadeusz moved to Paris, where there were already more than 200,000 Polish and Russian emigrants.[54] While she studied painting, he seemed to have lost the will to do anything. In the end, he took a job in a bank. They moved into a flat in Montparnasse, at 5 rue Guy de Maupassant. She was befriended by Adrienne Monnier, lesbian proprietor of the bookshop La Maison des Amis de Livres. Early in the 1920s she was taken to Italy by another woman, possibly her first lesbian lover. (It may be that this was Ira Perrot.) In terms of her development as an artist, too, the trip was momentous: for it was now that she discovered the work of two of her major influences, Antonello da Messina and Sandro Botticelli. At this time, contrary to the impression created by most art-historical narratives, there were more women painters working in Paris than men. Lempicka later remarked on this as a positive factor in her artistic education; but other women were less impressed. The writer Jean Rhys, for instance, said 'It's pretty awful to think of the hundreds of women round here painting away, and all that.'[55] In any case, there were strict, unwritten rules governing the lifestyles of such women. In particular, they were usually expected to be in a relationship with a male artist. By that means, a woman could be included in the prevailing male cliques and their conversations. Tadeusz Lempicki, of course, working in his bank, did not count.

Domestic life, if you can call it that, now followed a pattern. While Tadeusz and Kizette were at home, sleeping – he still in the thrall of the inertia which had afflicted him since leaving Russia – Tamara would frequent the respectable nightclubs for the first part of the night, dancing, flirting and snorting cocaine; and then, when her less perceptive friends imagined she was going home to her husband and child, she would head down to the less salubrious establishments along the banks of the Seine to consort with rough trade of both sexes. Apparently, she especially liked making love with a man and a woman at once. Then, still wide awake in the early morning, thanks to her heavy cocaine intake, she would go home to paint. A few hours' sleep would be snatched before a motherly breakfast with Kizette and the day's schedule of art lessons and café society.

Lempicka met Natalie Barney early in 1923, but found her salons pretentious. By contrast, she found Gertrude Stein's sufficiently lively and glamorous, yet lacking in that effortful clawing at high artistic achievement. Of her new friends Stein and Ernest Hemingway, she said, 'he wanted to be a woman and she wanted to be a man.'[56] She also made friends with André Gide and Jean Cocteau. Gide commissioned a portrait from her in 1924. However, early reviewers of her paintings noticed a tendency to depict 'Amazons' (always a code-word for lesbians), probably because her versions of the human body, female as well as male, invariably gave a sense of angularity and mass, and her female nudes tended not to be lying passively in wait for the imprimatur of the male gaze. Their sheer solidity, combined with the Ingres-like gloss of their surfaces, seemed more of a challenge to the viewer than a demure invitation to him to appreciate them.

Lempicka's own behaviour in mixed company was often a challenge in itself. She had a habit, at parties, of arranging food 'artistically' on naked female flesh (never male flesh) and inviting men and women to taste both the food and the platter. For all her apparent emphasis in her paintings on the power of the female physique, she was perfectly happy to serve up a passive girl to appease the jaded palates of her trendy friends. On one occasion in the summer of 1923 she shocked and thrilled the women around her in the lesbian night-club the Rose when she undressed a friend (both of them were wearing male evening dress), ostensibly to see if her body was worth painting. Feeling the other woman's breasts, she pronounced them 'Round enough'; then, thrusting one hand into the woman's naked groin, she added ' . . . but too wet for a painter to concentrate.'[57] Something of this exhibitionistic vulgarity sets the tone of her paintings.

In the winter of 1925 she held her first solo exhibition, showing fifty-one items in Milan, where she was lionised by the remnants of Italy's aristocracy. The following summer, she was invited with her Italian hosts to Gabriele d'Annunzio's eyrie on Lake Garda, Il Vittoriale.[58] He did them the honour of showing them his coffin, as well as the separate glass box in which his ears were to eavesdrop on eternity. Lempicka was impressed. Around the turn of 1926–27, she paid him two more visits, alone this time, on the pretext of painting his portrait but really for a taste of greatness. On the first occasion she fled his sexual advances in the middle of the night. On the second, she allowed him to kiss her armpits and feel her body through her clothes; still fully clothed himself, he ejaculated against her. When she fell ill after a flight in his aeroplane, he undressed her and ran his erection over her body. She continued to reject him, even when he sent her a poem in the middle of the night, delivered by a messenger on a white horse. The bottom line was that she found him both ugly and – yes! – vulgar. However, while still in Italy she allowed herself the time to fall in love with a bisexual marquis, Guido Sommi Picenardi.

When she was back in Paris, Tadeusz announced that he was in love with Irene Spiess, a Polish pharmaceuticals heiress. He spent much of that year (1927) with her in Poland, and in 1928 he decided to move there for good. Divorce proceedings began at once, but were probably not concluded until 1931; Tadeusz remarried in March 1932. After a trip to New York between October 1929 and January 1930, to paint a rich man's fiancée, Tamara Lempicka held a solo exhibition in Colette Weil's Paris gallery at 71 rue de la Boétie. Now in her mid-thirties and single again, she had become acutely aware of the passing years. She had started introducing her daughter as her sister, a sure sign. In 1933 she had a sexual relationship with Suzy Solidor (Suzanne Rocher), a singer in the club La Boîte de Nuit and a bad novelist. It was not a monoga-mous involvement. According to one observer, Tamara could be seen in the clubs, 'fondling quite openly a beautiful working-class boy one night, a girl the next. Her dates always looked mesmerized by her sophistication and beauty.'[59]

On 3 February 1934, seeking financial security, Tamara de Lempicka married Baron Raoul Kuffner in Zurich. It was to be an open marriage on both sides. They honeymooned in Egypt. At the beginning of 1939, they emigrated to the USA, pretending to their friends they were going for just a few months. Both were Jewish and, having only belatedly escaped the Russian Revolution, Lempicka was now keen, given the situation in Europe, to get out without delay. In 1940 they crossed the United States to California, where they leased King Vidor's villa in Coldwater Canyon, and Lempicka made friends with the likes of Charles Boyer, Greta Garbo and Tyrone Power. She hosted lavish showbiz parties from which her husband tended to stay away. She also did charitable work for Polish refugees. In 1942 they moved to New York and bought a $240,000 apartment on East 57th Street.

After the war, especially once she turned from the human figure to still life, her paintings came to be dismissed, increasingly, as facile decorations for the rich. It made no difference that she regarded herself as the originator of art deco, since deco had itself gone out of fashion. On fairly regular trips to Europe she could experience again the atmosphere of the good old days – as when lunching at the Ritz in Paris with Jean Cocteau and Prince Yusupov, and meeting the latter's 'son', Victor Manuel Contreras – but she was always, also, anxious to keep up with the times. In the 1960s she took one of her granddaughters to see the hippie musical *Hair* – twice: 'she liked seeing everyone take their clothes off'.[60] When public interest in art deco revived, in 1972, she held a successful solo exhibition, her first since the war, at the Galerie du Luxembourg in Paris. Not that she was always comfortably back in the swing of things. When Larry Rivers discovered her work in the 1970s and, in homage to her, painted a 'Resurrection of Tamara de Lempicka', she rejected his overtures. (He managed to speak to her only once on the phone.) She thereby probably missed yet another opportunity to connect with the contemporary art world. When she died in 1980, her ashes were scattered from a helicopter on to Popocatépetl, the Mexican volcano.

### Rudolf Nureyev

When Rudolf Nureyev joined the Kirov Ballet in Leningrad in 1958, he was the first male dancer to bypass the corps de ballet since Fokine and Nijinsky. In August of the following year he made his first Western trip, to the International Youth Festival in Vienna. But it was on 11 May 1961 that he began his famous trip to Paris with the Kirov. In the evenings he kept wandering off, without permission, with a group from the Paris Opéra Ballet. Among other treats, they took him to see *West Side Story*. A bisexual English fan, Michael Wishart, also took him several times to visit the Louvre. On 3 June Moscow ran out of patience with the young dancer and ordered his immediate recall. The Kirov adopted delaying tactics, since their Paris success was in large part dependent on Nureyev. When two more directives had arrived, to the same effect, the company decided to comply and send him home on the 16th, after their last night in Paris but before they went on to London. At the airport he was told that his mother was ill and that he was wanted for a perform-ance in front of Nikita Khrushchev. Seeing the obvious subterfuge, he threat-ened to kill himself. Everyone around him knew that if he went home he would never be allowed to perform abroad again. So, as the rest of the company boarded the plane to London, his French friends rallied round and persuaded the French police to stand near him. When he bolted from his Soviet minders there was a tug of war, but the French police managed to assert their authority and he was led away to a safe haven – but not before the Soviet cultural attaché had slapped his face. The first Soviet report on the matter denounced him for mixing with French homosexuals – by which it seems to have meant ballet dancers.

On 23 June, Nureyev danced the Sleeping Beauty at the home of the Ballets Russes and Suédois, the Théâtre des Champs-Elysées. He had twenty-eight curtain calls. Two of the people he most wanted to meet in the West were the choreographer George Balanchine and the best of the classical dancers, Erik Bruhn. When he happened to meet the American ballerina Maria Tallchief, once Balanchine's third wife and more recently Bruhn's lover, this became possible. Tallchief took him to Copenhagen to meet Bruhn, and before long Nureyev had fallen in love. (Nureyev was twenty-three, Bruhn thirty-two.) A friend later said, 'I doubt Rudolf ever knew he was homosexual until he met Erik.'[61] Nureyev's biographer Diane Solway has described the differences between these two great dancers:

> Bruhn was Nureyev's polar opposite, the Apollo to his Dionysus, poetic not powerful. Where the Soviet school favored big, soaring, powerful jumps with sustained poses, the Franco-Danish style of [August] Bournonville shunned fire for finesse, calling for crisp, nimble footwork, quick changes in direction, fluttering beats and incremental steps building to a crescendo. Bruhn moved audiences with the effortlessness of his dancing; Nureyev thrilled them with the effortfulness of his. Bruhn's performances were dignified, ethereal, elegant; Nureyev's were defiant, dangerous and unques-tionably sexual. The recognition that each possessed qualities the other desired kindled their mutual passion.[62]

Bruhn's friend the choreographer Glen Tetley said:

> Erik was totally smitten from the beginning and I don't recall his ever
> having that reaction to anybody else. It was the first time in his life that he
> was totally in love, that kind of hypnotic, physical, deeply erotic love. Erik
> was always rather veiled and immaculate and here was someone who was
> anything but. Rudolf could be the devil incarnate, one hundred percent
> animal, all impulse and just intuitively going after it. Eric was just flipped by
> the magnetism. And Rudolf saw this immaculate body and these perfect
> positions, this suave manner. Erik was the ideal, the god.[63]

Nureyev moved in with Bruhn and his mother. (The two men had separate
bedrooms.) Nureyev and Bruhn's mother soon learned to hate each other.

Nureyev made his London debut at the Theatre Royal, Drury Lane, on 2
November 1961. In a gala organised by Margot Fonteyn, Nijinsky's four-minute
*Feux d'artifice*, choreographed by Frederick Ashton, gave the audience more
than the thrill they had hoped for. Lady Diana Cooper whispered to Cecil
Beaton, 'He's better than Nijinsky!' To Beaton, he was 'a savage young creature,
half naked, rushing with wild eyes on an ecstatic, gaunt face, and a long mop of
flying, silk hair'. The hair would be important: for this boy had what the press
would call 'a Beatle haircut'. Alexander Bland spoke of 'the shock of seeing a
wild animal let loose in a drawing room'. It was on this night that Ninette de
Valois decided he must dance Giselle with Margot Fonteyn.[64]

Nureyev first arrived in New York on 15 January 1962. He asked if he could
join the New York City Ballet, but Balanchine was not interested. He told the
boy, 'You don't know how to dance the way we dance and it would take you too
long to learn.' When Nureyev protested to the contrary, Balanchine said, 'No,
no, go and dance your princes, and then when you're tired, you come back to
me.' His main objection, as he later put it, was that Nureyev was 'a one-man
show. I, me, a beautiful man, alone.'[65] Balanchine was also put off by the claque
of swooning boys who followed him from performance to performance. He
said, 'First time he danced in America at Brooklyn Academy of Music . . .
behind me were about twenty-five boys with red lips sitting and screaming
"God! oh God!" Frankly we don't need this.'[66]

The perceived eclipse of Bruhn by Nureyev was a problem. Bruhn was the
more technical dancer of the two, classical, less showy, more modest. He
became demoralised by the reception given his more mercurial lover, who was
indulged by the Royal Ballet's management and by Ninette de Valois. When, as
the major box-office draw, Nureyev was appointed permanent guest artist,
Bruhn was devastated. However, between them, they had managed to attract

an unprecedented public focus to male dance. Besides, the wildness of Nureyev could be overstated. No less an authority than Margot Fonteyn spoke of the precision of his method:

> I learned a great deal simply from watching him in class. Never had I seen each step practised with such exactitude and thoroughness. It was paradoxical that the young boy everyone thought so wild and spontaneous in his dancing cared desperately about technique, whereas I, the cool English ballerina, was so much more interested in the emotional aspect of the performance.[67]

Younger practitioners would learn valuable lessons from Nureyev's handling of his masculinity and sexuality. As the English dancer Christopher Gable put it:

> There was a tradition in my generation of dancers that you had to be really heterosexual onstage, because you had to prove that you weren't 'one of those' . . . So the English style was reticent, withdrawn male with a capital M, and self-effacing. Rudolf wasn't inhibited by any of that. He moved in a far more lyrical way than English dancers would have dared at that time . . . He was completely comfortable with his sexuality and his sexual orientation and he had no interest in anything other than expressing the music and the choreography in the way that seemed appropriate to him. People like me suddenly saw that there was no need to prove your maleness by using this sort of wooden and reserved style that said, 'I'm a man.' And so he gave us permission to take away all those barriers.[68]

In 1963 Gable became Nureyev's closest rival in the Royal Ballet. Along with Lynne Seymour they danced a threesome based on Shakespeare's sonnet 144, 'Two loves I have, of comfort and despair', with Gable, as Comfort, and Seymour, as Despair, struggling for possession of Nureyev.

In 1968 Frederick Ashton commissioned Derek Jarman to design a ballet, *Jazz Calendar*, to a score by Richard Rodney Bennett; Nureyev would dance one of its seven segments with Antoinette Sibley when it was premiered in January 1968. The young Jarman once turned down Nureyev's advances – more out of a naïve unawareness that they were happening than by design. By this time in the dancer's career, according to Jarman,

> Boys, and lots of them, were his sole interest; as far as I could see dance was just a means to this end. He was really only happy in the back room – I saw much more of him cruising the King's Road at four in the morning than

anywhere else. He was determined that you would fall for him, actually insisted that you did. It wasn't that he wanted to sleep with everyone – there wasn't enough time for that – but he wanted to be certain that if he clicked his fingers he could.[69]

On Christmas Day 1968 Nureyev opened in Rudi van Dantzig's *Monument for a Dead Boy* – about a boy becoming gay – with the Dutch National Ballet in The Hague. He then persuaded the Royal Ballet in London to commission van Dantzig to choreograph a new ballet, *The Ropes of Time*, which was premiered on 2 March 1970. In that year, there were plans for a film about Nijinsky – to be played by Nureyev – written by Edward Albee, to be directed by Tony Richardson. It would include a performance of *Jeux* as first intended, danced by three men. The project failed for lack of funding; and the funding had failed, according to van Dantzig, because the producers were 'worried about showing a ballet about three men'.[70]

Although both the Ballets Russes and Suédois had created important ballets using local folk tales and traditions – *The Rite of Spring* being the most prominent example – they also made extensive use of Oriental stories, thereby, when they toured, regularly bringing the East into the theatres and opera houses of the West. The Ballets Russes created a sequence of Orientalist ballets including *Prince Igor* (1909), *Ivan the Terrible* (1909), *Cléopâtre* (1909), *Schéhérazade* (1910), *Les Orientales* (1910), *Thamar* (1912), *Le Dieu bleu* (1912), *La Tragédie de Salomé* (1913) and *Aladdin ou la lampe merveilleuse* (1919). Léon Bakst's costume designs for *Schéhérazade* are among the most distinctive visual insignia of the company's style. (He also did the designs for *Le Dieu bleu* and *Aladin*.) Marcel Proust's Marcel is especially appreciative of the ways in which Bakst could conjure up an Oriental scene with the simplest of effects: he speaks of 'those properties used in the Russian ballet, consisting sometimes, when they are seen in the light of day, of a mere disc of paper, out of which the genius of a Bakst, according to the blood-red or moonlit effect in which he plunges his stage, makes a hard incrustation, like a turquoise on a palace wall, or a swooning softness, as of a Bengal rose in an eastern garden'.[71] Not surprisingly, the fashionable Orientalism of the Ballets Russes soon found its way into Parisian haute couture. For instance, as Cecil Beaton describes the experience, 'To enter [Paul] Poiret's salons in the Faubourg St Honoré was to step into the world of the Arabian Nights. Here, in rooms strewn with floor cushions, the master dressed his slaves in furs and brocades and created Eastern ladies who were the counterpart of the Cyprians and chief eunuchs that moved through the pageantries of Diaghilev'.[72] For their part, Jean Börlin and the Ballets Suédois staged exotic ballets that included *Derviches* (1920) and *Le Roseau* (1924).

Nor is it coincidental that two of ballet's most highly regarded leading dancers came equipped with the additional magic of appropriately Eastern looks. Both Vaslav Nijinsky and Rudolf Nureyev were renowned for the apparently Oriental exoticism of their physical appearance, which was at least as much imagined as real. Nijinsky was, after all, an ethnic Pole born in Kiev. As Richard Buckle describes him, he inherited from his father 'his high cheekbones and slanting eyes, which, in spite of the Nijinskys' Polish nationality, would seem to be indications of Tatar blood'. Such attributions of Eastern characteristics could be remarkably vague. For instance, the Brazilian composer Oswald d'Estrade-Guerra said of him, 'Sometimes one felt there was something mystical about him, but that did not strike me as anything unusual. I assumed it was typical of the Slav character.' More usually, the dancer was described as animal-like, as when Hilda Munnings said he was 'like a faun – a wild creature who had been trapped by society and was always ill at ease'.[73]

Nureyev was born near Irkutsk, on a train heading even further eastward. As a more reliable indicator, he was from a Volga Tatar family and was raised in a village near Ufa in Bashkortostan, east of the Volga but still west of the Urals. When she first saw him perform, Ninette de Valois was less impressed by his dancing than by the bow he took after it: 'I saw an arm raised with a noble dignity, a hand expressively extended with that restrained discipline which is the product of a great traditional schooling. Slowly the head turned from one side of the theatre to the other, and the Slav bone-structure of the face, so beautifully modelled, made me feel like an inspired sculptor rather than director of the Royal Ballet.' Of course, one of his most famous roles was as the slave boy in *Le Corsaire*. But he, too, tended to be most often described as an animal. As we have seen, Alexander Bland spoke of him as 'a wild animal let loose in a drawing room'. To Walter Terry, he was simply 'this animal'. Georgina Parkinson said, 'He was this passionate, fabulous-looking, gorgeous creature. [In behavioural terms, a] monster on the one hand, and a pussycat on the other.' Princess Margaret even went so far as to leave the planet to account for his striking looks: 'Here was this creature from the moon. He was more beautiful than I can describe with his flared nostrils, huge eyes and high cheekbones.'[74] It would be pleasing to imagine she had identified him as one of Rozanov's 'moonlight people'.

Estranged from their actual cultural origins, in one way or another, both Nijinsky and Nureyev remained strange to all who saw them. They shared with other Russian émigrés, if to a different degree, an air of mystery and distance that enhanced their northern exoticism. Both men were of ambiguous provenance, to the extent that one could never quite be sure whether there was snow or sand on their boots: having come from the North, they seemed to embody the South. As Modernism in Europe began to assimilate this exoticism into the mainstream of all the arts, the struggle, for artists, was to avoid becoming the norm. Perhaps, in this respect if not in many others, lesbians and gay men had an advantage.[75]

# CHAPTER FOUR

# FRANCE AND ITS VISITORS

## The Paris Scene

In *The Autobiography of an Ex-Colored Man* (1912), James Weldon Johnson contrasted the cultural atmospheres of Paris and London, whose very names seemed to him to express 'a certain racial difference'. The English were far more furtive in their pleasures, and the urban structures of London more stratified and enclosed, than was the case in Paris. (Contrast the London pub with the Paris café.) As a result, the pleasures of Paris were more visible to the visitor than those of London:

> Paris is the concrete expression of the gaiety, regard for symmetry, love of art, and, I might well add, of the morality of the French people. London stands for the conservatism, the solidarity, the utilitarianism, and, I might well add, the hypocrisy of the Anglo-Saxon . . . I saw many things in Paris which were immoral according to English standards, but the absence of hypocrisy, the absence of the spirit to do the thing if it might only be done in secret, robbed these very immoralities of the damning influence of the same evils in London.

Johnson made the same moral judgements about such differences as many Englishmen made when choosing to travel south:

> There is a sort of frankness about the evils of Paris which robs them of much of the seductiveness of things forbidden, and with that frankness goes a certain cleanliness of thought belonging to things not hidden. London will do whatever Paris does, providing exterior morals are not shocked. As a result, Paris has the appearance only of being the more immoral city. The

difference may be summed up in this: Paris practices its sins as lightly as it does its religion, while London practices both very seriously.[1]

Although the two cities are physically so close – little more than two hundred miles as the crow flies – one was predominantly Protestant, the other Catholic; one was on the North Sea, the other had, if only downwind of its magnificent sewers, a whiff of the Mediterranean. While London still had a reputation for stifling its artists in a shroud of post-Victorian convention, Paris, despite the best efforts of its stolid bourgeoisie, was thought of as a hotbed of bohemian creativity. Young artists from elsewhere in Europe or from America made their way there as soon as they could. Most went, if they could afford to, under their own steam. Others got help. A good example of how a young man of talent and good looks might receive the benefits of patronage and love, thereby gaining entry to a vibrant cultural scene, much of it gay, was the brief life story of the English painter Christopher Wood.

Wood had attended Marlborough College from 1914, and then Malvern College in 1918. In 1921, at the age of eighteen, he was invited to Paris by the homosexual Alphonse Kahn, who lived on the Avenue du Bois de Boulogne. Wood took up the invitation and attended a Parisian art school. Perhaps more educationally, he became the lover and protégé of a married Chilean diplomat, Antonio de Gandarillas. Under Gandarillas' sponsorship, Wood moved into a studio of his own (at first on the rue des Saints-Pères and then on the rue Balzac). They also travelled widely together. With Gandarillas in London, Wood met Ivor Novello and became the object of the painter Alvaro Guevara's romantic interest. (Guevara would later marry Wood's ex-fiancée Meraud Guinness.) In 1922 Gandarillas took him to Tunisia, Sicily (Taormina), Greece, Constantinople and Smyrna; then to Karlsbad, where both convalesced after bouts of malaria.

Back in Paris, Gandarillas introduced him to opium, and in 1924 he met Jean Cocteau, who told him he had more talent for painting than anyone he knew. (So much for Picasso.) Late in 1925, Wood discussed with Serge Diaghilev an idea for a ballet to be called *English Country Life*; the music was to be by Constant Lambert. Diaghilev encouraged Wood at first, but eventually the project fell through. Meanwhile, in 1926, Wood acquired a girlfriend – none other than Jeanne Bourgoint, the distaff half of Cocteau's *enfants terribles*. Picasso visited his studio and, genuinely impressed, recommended him to Diaghilev, who duly commissioned him to design *Romeo and Juliet*. However, Wood eventually resigned – he was not really up to the job – and the work was given to Joan Miró and Max Ernst. Later, though, Boris Kochno asked him for scenery for a piece called *Luna Park*, set to music by Lord Berners, for what was left of the Ballets Russes.

Through Gandarillas, Wood had made many close friends, most of them artists and many of them fellow homosexuals. In Marseille and Vence, the couple's company helped René Crevel in his long recuperation from tuberculosis. And a stay in St Malo in 1929 was enlivened by the presence of the designer Christian Bérard and the poet Max Jacob. Indeed, after Wood's sudden and unexpected death – he threw himself under a train on 21 August 1930 after lunch with his mother in Wiltshire – it is said that the individual who was most affected, after Wood's mother herself, was Max Jacob.

Crossing the Channel, although arduous in those days, was often, for the British, a significant, repeated event in narratives of love and its breakdown. In the summer of 1919, Violet Keppel's formidable mother manoeuvred her towards marriage to Denys Trefusis. Violet eventually agreed to the arrangement only because she saw it as a way of cloaking her actual love – for Vita Sackville-West, the wife of Harold Nicolson – in respectability. Poor Trefusis, a traumatised veteran of the Somme, saw none of the subclauses in their narrative of marital bliss. Violet and Vita went off to Paris, where they stayed in the flat of Edward Knoblock, the homosexual author of *Kismet*. Trefusis visited them there before they headed south without him. In a spirit of revenge, Harold Nicolson now embarked on an affair with the twenty-year-old Victor Cunard. Harold was furious when he heard that Vita and Violet had been seen dancing together publicly in Monte Carlo. When they finally returned to England Mrs Keppel announced her daughter's engagement to Trefusis and set a date for the wedding. Trefusis promised, in writing, never to demand sex from his wife. Not without reason, Violet felt he was beginning to hate her even before the wedding. She and Vita made a pact to elope before the dreadful event, but Vita backed out. On the day of the wedding (16 June 1919), Violet wrote to her, 'You have broken my heart, goodbye.' However, Vita intercepted Violet at the Ritz in Paris, abducting her from her honeymoon to a small hotel where they made love, and on the 19th they cruelly laid the facts before Trefusis. Later that evening, Vita dined alone at the Ritz, deliberately sitting where she could be watched by the married couple from the window of their suite. It comes as no surprise to learn that Trefusis did so in tears. He and his new bride began sleeping in separate rooms. Having thus made her point, Vita returned to Harold Nicolson to patch up their marriage.

When Vita and Violet finally did elope to France, in February 1920, Vita keeping Harold informed of their whereabouts, George Keppel, Mrs Keppel's husband and possibly Violet's father, tracked them down in Amiens but he could not persuade them to see sense. Lady Sackville, Vita's mother, sent the two husbands after them by private plane and, following a public row, the two heterosexual couples went their separate ways. Heading south, Trefusis, who was close to a nervous breakdown, promised to make his wife as unhappy as she had made him. He wanted a divorce, but Mrs Keppel, having much experience of marriages that had survived adversity, made every effort to prevent this. In the end, though, Trefusis did apply for a legal separation at the beginning of 1921. By now, Vita held no hope that she and Violet had any future together. In any case, Violet's lawyer had banned them from seeing each other. Under family pressure on both sides, the relationship ended that March.[2]

Trefusis and his wife had an awkward reunion and went to live together in a small flat in Paris, but they really lived separate lives. Mrs Keppel financed a move to a better flat. Violet began to write fiction. In 1923 Trefusis introduced her to Winnaretta Singer, the princesse de Polignac, and before long the two women were lovers. At the Polignac salon Violet met the likes of Colette, Proust, Cocteau and Jean Giraudoux. It was Proust who suggested she visit a place called St Loup, a hamlet near the town of Provins. She liked it so much that Winnaretta Singer bought and renovated a tower for her there. However, she seems to have had a habit of considering matrimony. For a while during the First World War, Violet and Osbert Sitwell had considered getting married, but they saw sense. Max Jacob once proposed to her, despite being the lover of Maurice Sachs at the time. And she and Lord Berners did actually become engaged when he visited her at St Loup in the autumn of 1933. But then – at least according to one of his better stories about himself – he put a notice in *The Times*, saying 'Lord Berners has left Lesbos for the Isle of Man', thereby indicating a return to his customary ways.

Like many other English visitors, the artist Robert Medley found the atmosphere of Paris distinctly relaxed: 'there were no parents to worry about, and under French law nobody had the right to interfere with our relationship'.[3] When he and his new lover, the dancer Rupert Doone, went there in May 1926, Medley found that Doone was already well known. He had been a lover of Jean Cocteau's, a status with which limelight came as a compulsory extra (the affair had ended in 1924). Doone introduced Medley to Djuna Barnes and to another of Paris's gay, expatriate denizens, Alan Ross MacDougall (Dougie), who had once been the secretary of Isadora Duncan. In the spring of 1928, Rupert Doone turned down the chance to tour as Anna Pavlova's partner; but this left him free, in July of the following year, to accept an invitation to join Diaghilev's Ballets Russes as a soloist. Diaghilev had never been particularly effusive with compliments, so Doone treasured the occasion when the great man said to him, even after watching a performance in which Doone had suffered a slight slip, 'Vous ne dansez pas mal.' It was, of course, through Doone that Medley met a succession of the great homosexual ballet dancers and choreographers. When introduced to Serge Lifar, he was especially impressed by 'his spectacular maquillage, the gold bangles and the varnished crimson fingernails'.[4]

Vincent Bouvet and Gérard Durozoi have written that, in Paris, 'Homosexuality and bisexuality were treated with relative tolerance in moneyed, cultural and artistic circles, and almost came to be regarded as a badge of modernity during the 1920s.' This was to change. 'During the 1930s, the attitude of tolerance and even permissiveness was gradually eroded, however, and records identifying "deviants" were established – giving rise to repressive laws under the Vichy regime.'[5] In the meantime, there was a gay scene in Paris, to which middle-class men and women had relatively easy access.

In Georges-Anquetil's novel *Satan conduit le bal* (1925), the owner of one Paris bar is quoted as lamenting patriotically, 'Isn't it shameful for Paris to be so far behind: in Berlin they have 150 establishments like this one, and here there are barely ten!'[6] In fact, Paris enjoyed a wide variety of gay and gay-friendly spaces, even if not in such a spectacular abundance as in Berlin. The most famous of the gay venues, although not generally spoken of as such in histories of Modernism, was Le Boeuf sur le Toit on the rue Boissy-d'Anglas. It opened in January 1922, taking its name from Darius Milhaud's ballet, based on a scenario by Jean Cocteau, which had been staged at the Théâtre des Champs-Élysées in February 1920. Among those who performed there were openly lesbian singers such as Dora Stroeva, Yvonne George and Jane Stick. Beverley Nichols reported having come across Cole Porter late one night, sitting alone in a corner of Le Boeuf sur le Toit – 'which in those days was a sweetly scandalous institution' – trying to think of a rhyme for 'duck-billed platypus' for inclusion in his lyric 'Let's Do It'.[7] Gay venues in Montmartre included La Petite Chaumière, a drag cabaret; Chez Bob et Jean, run by the dancer Bob Giguet and drag artiste Jean d'Albret; and the Brasserie Graff on the Place Blanche, a restaurant that became gay only late in the evening. On the night of the annual drag ball, the Magic City Ball, the Place Blanche would fill with onlookers who wanted to see the drag queens going into Graff's after the dance. Hustlers plied their trade on the rue Germain-Pilon, the Passage de l'Élysée-des-Beaux-Arts and the Boulevard de Clichy. The rue de Lappe near the Place de la Bastille was jokingly known as the rue de Loppe (Queer Street, in effect) because one of its dance halls (*bals musettes*) was gay-friendly.[8] Across the river, in the Bal de la Montagne-Sainte-Geneviève, both lesbians and gay men were welcome. A favourite lesbian haunt, Le Monocle, in Montparnasse, had an all-woman band. The English painter Edward Burra had a particular affection for the Place Pigalle, of which he wrote, in May 1931: 'The people are glorious. Such tarts all crumbling and all sexes and colours.'[9] Rupert Doone, Robert Medley, Burra and other gay friends used to congregate at the Select, a café in Montparnasse.

The Hungarian photographer Brassaï took many atmospheric photographs of the Parisian underworld in 1931 and 1932. Among his nocturnal shots of marginalised subcultures are those of 'Sodom and Gomorrah' – the brazen but somehow also secretive social environment of sexual inversion. Some of his written descriptions of what he observed are almost as resonant as his visual images. Of Le Monocle, on the Boulevard Edgar-Quinet, he wrote:

> From the owner, known as Lulu de Montparnasse, to the barmaid, from the waitresses to the hat-check girl, all the women were dressed as men, and so totally masculine in appearance that at first glance one thought they were men. A tornado of virility had gusted through the place and blown away all the finery, all the tricks of feminine coquetry, changing women into boys, gangsters, policemen . . . Even their perfumes – frowned on here – had been replaced by Lord knows what weird scents, more like amber or incense than roses and violets.

Brassaï also noted that 'These women, their passions slower to ignite, generally looked for more devotion and fidelity in their love affairs than do pederasts, most of whom cruise a lot and are often content with a quick trick.'[10] Of the broader nocturnal underworld he photographed, Brassaï said:

> I was eager to penetrate this other world, this fringe world, the secret, sinister world of mobsters, outcasts, toughs, pimps, whores, addicts, inverts. Rightly or wrongly, I felt at the time that this underground world represented *Paris at its least cosmopolitan*, at its most alive, its most authentic[.]'[11]

This is an important point, often overlooked. As we shall see in the case of Berlin, there is an important distinction to be made between venues catering to a local, working-class clientele and the more bohemian and/or touristic venues, more likely to be frequented by foreign visitors.

Even Germans who had sampled the delights of Berlin could be taken aback by what the French capital had to offer. When Klaus Mann went there in the mid-1920s he compiled a list of the reasons for his love of Paris, among them 'the many pissoirs – they are so convenient', but he did not specify the nature of the convenience. In almost the same breath he praised the atmosphere of the city because 'All things concerning sex are handled with that perfect casualness which is the proof of real civilization.' He meant, in part, the casualness of casual sex.[12] By contrast, Berlin was more self-conscious and more purposive. More frantic, even.

Besides, it was important for Mann to travel in Europe, and thereby to become an active internationalist. For his generation, he would later write,

To be a young European intellectual – it was an attitude, an ambition: it almost became a programme. The concept of European was meant, and accepted, as a protest against German nationalism, while the term intellectual defied the fashionable idolatry of 'blood and soil'.[13]

Back in Paris again in the spring of 1926, Klaus Mann met René Crevel, a committed internationalist for perverse reasons: 'He spent his days with Americans, Germans, Russians, and Chinese, because his mother suspected all foreigners to be crooks or perverts.' Sitting on Mann's bed, Crevel read out the early chapters of his novel *La Mort difficile*, with their 'venomous' portrait of his mother. On this trip, Mann also met Jean Cocteau ('The hours spent in his company assume in my recollection a savour both of burlesque show and magic ritual'), Eugene McCown, Pavel Tchelitchew, Julien Green, Jean Giraudoux and others. In the same year, 1926, Klaus' father Thomas Mann was surprised to find that the whores on the streets of Paris were predominantly male; and he observed striking new evidence of homosexual internationalism on the same streets. That this development should take place in Paris – the home of 'Proust and Gide, that friend of Oscar Wilde' – was, he felt, apt.[14]

Other young European intellectuals who returned home were less eager than Klaus Mann to sing the praises of Paris and thereby claim the benefits of its cosmopolitanism for themselves. Witold Gombrowicz, for one, was damned if he would admit to having been significantly bettered by his visit. Returning to Poland in 1928, he deliberately toned down his enthusiasm: 'It was important to me that people shouldn't say Paris had changed me – it seemed to me to be in the worst possible taste to be one of those young people who returned from the West civilized.'[15] Whereas Klaus Mann deliberately travelled against the grain of German nationalism, Gombrowicz was unwilling to replace pride in his own national culture with the self-serving adulation of a scene that most other Polish intellectuals had not had the opportunity to sample. He felt the adoption of a more sceptical tone was better suited to Polish cultural aspirations. Warsaw was just as civilised as the French capital.

Although Berlin later took the laurels, for much of the early part of the century Paris shared the honours as the joint Sodomite capital of Europe. Marc-André Raffalovich had published an article on 'Les Groupes uranistes à Paris et à Berlin' in 1904, mentioning Les Halles as a particular centre of activity. In an article entitled 'Invertis et pervertis' (*Le Journal*, 2 March 1910), Lucien Descaves expressed strong worries about the extent of male prostitution in Paris. Unlike women who became involved in the flesh trade, according to Descaves, the men developed habits of idleness, that most unmanly of conditions. Descaves was especially concerned about the proliferation of *vespasiennes*, the graffiti in which offered clear evidence that, far from being mere public urinals, these odoriferous constructions had become 'disgraceful trading posts'. André Gide cut out this article and added it to his own store of evidence, to be collated in the polemic of *Corydon*.[16] The homosexual magazine *Inversions* ran for a year – 'a few, earnest numbers that dealt with pressing issues and tried to elaborate a homosexual literature' – before it was suppressed at a 'complex and humiliating trial' in 1926.[17] The annual Magic City drag balls in Paris were said to be comparable with those in Harlem. In 1933, Brassaï attended the last of them:

> every type came, faggots, cruisers, chickens, old queens, famous antique dealers and young butcher boys, hairdressers and elevator boys, well-known dress designers and drag queens . . . Mature men accompanied by youths in drag were the rule. With hair by Antoine, clothes by Lanvin or Madeleine Vionnet, the great couturiers of the period, some of these ephebes on the arms of their rich protectors were extremely beautiful and elegant.[18]

In the Hungarian novelist Antal Szerb's *Journey by Moonlight* (*Utas és Holdvilág*, 1937), Paris is said to have had a reputation in Budapest of being 'full of perverts'. Erzi, who eventually lives there, apparently finds that its reputation is true, but is at ease with it: 'it all seemed perfectly natural'.[19]

Not all those who frequented them found the gay venues sympathetic to their tastes. When Radclyffe Hall first introduces the mixed lesbian and gay social scene of Paris early in the 1920s, in *The Well of Loneliness*, she is at her most ponderously depressive: 'That spring they made their first real acquaintance with the garish and tragic night life of Paris that lies open to such people as Stephen Gordon' – that is, to lesbian women.[20] We cannot help but be reminded of James Weldon Johnson's point about London's taking its sins 'very seriously', unlike Paris. Stephen and Mary accompany a small group of other women, first of all, to a bar presided over by Monsieur Pujol, 'the most aggressively normal of men', who, nevertheless, 'collected inverts' – or, at any rate, he collects and displays in a back room photographs of his past clients. Next, the group moves on to Le Narcisse, where Stephen actually dances with Mary. Finally, after a couple of interim stops at bars the narrative does not name, they go to Alec's.

> As long as she lived Stephen never forgot her first impressions of the bar known as Alec's – that meeting-place of the most miserable of all those who comprised the miserable army. That merciless, drug-dealing, death-dealing haunt to which flocked the battered remnants of men whom their

fellow-men had at last stamped under; who, despised of the world, must despise themselves beyond all hope, it seemed, of salvation. There they sat, closely herded together at the tables, creatures shabby yet tawdry, timid yet defiant – and their eyes, Stephen never forgot their eyes, those haunted, tormented eyes of the invert.

Is there something in these men's behaviour that is so disgusting? Or in the extremity of their campness? Apparently so:

Of all ages, all degrees of despondency, all grades of mental and physical ill-being, they must yet laugh shrilly from time to time, must yet tap their feet to the rhythm of the music, must yet dance together in response to the band – and that dance seemed the Dance of Death to Stephen. On more than one hand was a large, ornate ring, on more than one wrist a conspic-uous bracelet; they wore jewellery that might only be worn by these men when they thus gathered together. At Alec's they could dare to give way to such tastes – what was left of themselves they became at Alec's.

The level of debauchery seems fairly low: some jewellery worn by men who are sufficiently discreet to know that they cannot flaunt their rings and bracelets in more public spaces; some foot-tapping to the music, and then same-sex dancing (which even the ultra-restrained Stephen herself has recently indulged in at Le Narcisse); and that is all. Yet the language Hall uses for Stephen Gordon's reaction to this establishment is that of a Dantesque descent into Purgatory:

Bereft of all social dignity, of all social charts contrived for man's guidance, of the fellowship that by right divine should belong to each breathing, living creature; abhorred, spat upon, from their earliest days the prey to a ceaseless persecution, they were now even lower than their enemies knew, and more hopeless than the veriest dregs of creation. For since all that to many of them had seemed fine, a fine selfless and at times even noble emotion, had been covered with shame, called unholy and vile, so gradually they them-selves had sunk down to the level upon which the world placed their emotions.[21]

Throughout this chapter of the novel, while the emphasis is, ostensibly, on the homophobic treatment meted out to such men by society, the effect is to portray them as its ultimate cause. High levels of alcoholism and drug-taking are ascribed to the denizens of this scene, which evidence of having 'sunk down' seems to be taken as justification for the low 'level upon which the world placed their emotions'. This is written from Stephen's point of view, but it is doubtless also Hall's. Her social conservatism, to which we shall return, does not allow for much deviation from the norm. She expects her gender-dysphoric central character to behave with repressed, masculine dignity; but there is no evidence that Hall would permit even this level of indulgence to an effeminate man. The rings and bracelets, hidden or not, are as bad as the drug-taking.

The Anglo-Irish diplomat and writer Shane Leslie, dedicatee of F. Scott Fitzgerald's *The Beautiful and the Damned*, reported in his memoirs that, when he lived in Paris as a student before the Great War, he frequented 'two sub-worlds' in his efforts to learn French, 'the Catholic world and the world of Sodomy which has received many aliases since Lot's spectacular adventure in the city of that name.' Although he says little of it himself, Leslie does confirm the accuracy of Marcel Proust's version in *Sodome et Gomorrhe*: 'Realistic unto laughter is that study of genius which no moral textbooks and no Wolfenden Report can equal.' In a rather pedestrian response to these pre-Wolfenden hilarities, Leslie reduces Proust's art to that of the embalmer and his readers to professionals with ulterior motives:

> The Proustian world then existed and Proust's characters were deftly drawn from living folk but so cleverly disguised that no one could say they had known the despicable dandy called Monsieur de Charlus or the great actress Berman [*sic*] or the artist Elstir. But if one can trace the originals (whom I saw in the flesh!) one sees them embalmed forever. Proust comparing the hunted and secret lives of the queerly-sexed with the parallel world-wide difficulties encircling the Jews makes rare reading for doctor, cleric or snob.[22]

(Or, indeed, for fellow inverts.) Leslie's reduction of the novel's readership to those three classes suggests that it combines the contents of Richard von Krafft-Ebing's *Psychopathia Sexualis* – a compendium of sexual case histories – with those of the *Almanach de Gotha*. That would be an absorbing book, to be sure, but it is not the one Proust wrote.[23]

Notwithstanding his concentration on the upper classes, Proust does pay a little attention to a much less visible class of invert from the middle class. He speaks of young, professional men 'who are poor and have come up from the country, without friends, with nothing but their ambition to be some day a celebrated doctor or barrister'. Spending most of their time with teachers and fellow students, they still manage to find a parallel time and space into which to fit a parallel society 'composed exclusively of persons similar to themselves' – that is, of other inverts. 'In their quarter . . . they have speedily discovered other young men whom the same peculiar taste attracts to them'. They are able to meet in public places because they maintain strict levels of discretion:

> No one moreover in the café where they have their table knows what the gathering is . . . so correct is their attire, so cold and reserved their manner, so modestly do they refrain from anything more than the most covert glances at the young men of fashion, the young 'lions' who, a few feet away, are making a great clamour about their mistresses[.]

Proust adds that, in twenty years' time, they may discover that some of the latter group, even 'the most attractive among them', were, all along, 'akin to themselves, but differently, in another world, beneath other external symbols, with foreign labels, the strangeness of which led them [the first group] into error'. The point is that there is no single milieu of inversion, no single style of invert. Proust makes an interesting comparison with the political fragmentation of the Left:

> just as the 'Union of the Left' differs from the 'Socialist Federation' . . . on certain evenings, at another table, there are extremists who allow a bracelet to slip down from beneath a cuff, sometimes a necklace to gleam in the gap of a collar, who by their persistent stares, their cooings, their laughter, their mutual caresses, oblige a band of students to depart in hot haste, and are served with a civility beneath which indignation boils by a waiter who, as on the evenings when he has to serve Dreyfusards, would find pleasure in summoning the police did he not find profit in pocketing their gratuities.

The logic of this passage allows us to imagine, too, that the group of students whom these more open inverts have scared off may themselves be another, differently styled group of inverts, panicked less by the stares of the others, denoting desire, than by the likelihood that they may be identified with the starers, by association.[24] These groups of middle-class inverts do not play a substantial part in Proust's novel, which is located both above and below them on the social scale; but they do constitute a significant aspect of the broader context in which his more highly developed representations of upper-class inversion are presented. They are, after all, members of the narrator's own class. So, if he too is an invert – as his intense interest in the type often suggests he must be – these are the 'extremists' whose jewellery, carelessly exposed in a public place, rather than (as in *The Well of Loneliness*) in a nightclub catering specifically to inverts, might represent, to him, a real threat of potentially ruinous scandal.

Any homosexual individual had choices to make, in all the routines of everyday life, about degrees of discretion and disclosure. Many kinds of outré behaviour were, ultimately, forgivable if they occurred in the right place among people of the appropriate class and income level. If you found your way into the right kind of milieu, you could quite safely be open about being gay. Pierre Bergé once said of his experience: 'By the time I was twenty-one or twenty-two [in the early 1950s] I'd met people like Jean Cocteau. If you moved in those circles it was perfectly acceptable.'[25] It was less important to be secretive than it tended to be in London, given the state of English law and the post-Wildean atmosphere; but the ability to adjust one's behaviour to the occasion was always a useful skill. The generally accepted societal conventions applied, and could be stretched a little, in Francis Poulenc's career, as in so many others. He had a certain reserve, a discretion, about how he interacted in society. Although he was openly homosexual among his friends, he kept his relationships away from the glare of gossip. In the words of one of his biographers:

> If there was talking to be done about his personal life, as far as possible he would do it himself. Poulenc's society friends adored hearing him gossip about his boyfriends, but he almost never imposed them on hostesses. Unlike Cocteau, who brought his boyfriends everywhere he went, even to funerals, Poulenc preferred to attend society affairs alone. He had always a strong sense of what was socially acceptable, and revelled in gossiping about his private life, as if divulging naughty secrets.[26]

The phrase 'even to funerals' is redolent of an attitude more of the time of this biography's publication, 1996, than of the particular Parisian circles of the 1930s that are being referred to, in which, once the relationships in question were known and people were accustomed to seeing Cocteau in the company of his lovers, it would have been odd *not* to see him with them at funerals, of all occasions, when emotional support would be of most use. Of course, to those to whom the mere presence of homosexual lovers was a violation, the violation of a funeral might have been regarded as especially extreme. But there is no evidence to suggest that Cocteau went as one of a couple to such events in a spirit of exhibitionism. He expected things to be taken for granted. Poulenc, on the other hand, was simply a more inhibited personality. Perhaps he did not trust the discretion of certain lovers. Handling things the way he did, he must have felt he could maintain control over the release of information about himself. If it meant doing so 'as if divulging naughty secrets', that tone may have been imposed on him by the mere fact that he did not wish to show off his lovers; or it may have been a source of amusement to him; or he may, indeed, have felt that to speak of such things in such places was akin to 'divulging naughty secrets'. It may be a sign of residual shame. We know that he tended to think of himself defensively, and that, even when away from the familiar context of Paris, he denied himself certain pleasures in order to protect himself. When he toured Tunisia and Algeria as accompanist to the soprano Maria Modrakowska, he said he felt old. He encountered many handsome young soldiers, but rather primly contrasted himself with Reynaldo Hahn in saying that he was not going to put himself at risk by chasing them.[27]

### Pedestrians and Pederasts: Americans in Paris

In his novel *The Pilgrim Hawk* (1940), Glenway Wescott wrote:

> In the twenties it was not unusual to meet foreigners in some country as foreign to them as to you, your peregrination just crossing theirs; and you did your best to know them in an afternoon or so; and perhaps you called that little lightning knowledge, friendship. There was a kind of idealistic or optimistic curiosity in the air. And vagaries of character, and the various war and peace that goes on in the psyche, seemed of the greatest interest and even importance.[28]

This is the mythic version of the easy internationalism displayed by the so-called 'lost generation' of Americans who visited Europe between the wars. It is true that these travellers met many people whose paths they might not otherwise have crossed. For the most part, though, English-speakers mixed with English-speakers and, of course, among those whose language skills were up to it, bohemians mixed with bohemians. Nevertheless, Wescott does capture in this paragraph the idealistic atmosphere of the decade, when all kinds of cross-cultural exchanges seemed possible; and many, indeed, did take place.

In a study of American tourism, Harvey Levenstein writes that, although male homosexual acts were not criminal in France, as they were in the United States, 'there is no indication that pre-1914 Paris was any more attractive for visiting [American] gay males than any other city, including New York'. Cities allowed room for illicit activities and for those who sought to perform them, and were therefore attractive by mere virtue of their size. There is, however, evidence that, once such men did happen upon Paris – as so many did when the USA joined the First World War – they realised it was more attractive than the American cities in their experience. They tended not to know about Paris until they saw it for themselves, so the actual effect on levels of tourism from the USA was limited. Levenstein draws similar conclusions about lesbians.

Despite the presence of a thriving lesbian subculture, and many expatriate American lesbians, he says 'we know nothing of any American women who were encouraged by this to visit there as tourists'. He reiterates that, although 'The prewar underground of lesbian hangouts expanded into an extensive, varied, and quite public nighttime world . . . there is no evidence that this had any significant effect on American tourism.'[29] The men and women who ended up enjoying Paris as a relatively safe space in which to lead a homosexual exist-ence tended to have gone there for other reasons than tourism – as journalists, for instance, or as service personnel – or to join friends who were already there. Once they arrived, many stayed for as long as they could afford to do so. The stock market crash of 1929 would haul most of them home. Of those who could afford to remain, many would have left by the time of the German occupation of Paris in 1940; but even then, some stayed put. As Charles Glass writes, 'Until the Germans turned France into a version of their own prison-state, African-Americans, [male] homosexuals, lesbians and bohemians felt freer in Paris than in the socially more repressive United States. German occupation was not enough to send all of them home.'[30]

George Orwell did not approve of the kind of American visitor he saw in Paris. In his famous essay 'Inside the Whale' (1940), he wrote:

During the boom years, when [American] dollars were plentiful and the exchange-value of the [French] franc was low, Paris was invaded by such a swarm of artists, writers, students, dilettanti, sight-seers, debauchees and plain idlers as the world has probably never seen . . . The populace had grown so hardened to artists that gruff-voiced Lesbians in corduroy breeches and young men in Grecian or medieval costume could walk the streets without attracting a glance.[31]

One of the most famous of these American consumers of Parisian pleasures was Henry Miller. Prolifically engaged as he was, however, in what the city had to offer by way of heterosexual delicacies, his view of homosexual life in Paris was fragmentary and only grudgingly acknowledged. Of a dance hall he might observe: 'There were three or four whores at the bar and one or two drunks, English, of course. Pansies, most likely.'[32] In the streets and shops, too, he might remark on the appearance of 'those skinny little runts, who look like bell-hops and messenger boys, that one sees on pornographic post cards in little book-shop windows occasionally, the mysterious phantoms who inhabit the Rue de la Lune and other malodorous quarters of the city'. But the truth is that, although Miller spoke of the massed humanity of cities as 'pedestrians and pederasts' – an elementary piece of wordplay he liked so much that he used it twice in the same paragraph – he did not notice, or did not care to notice, much of gay Paris.[33] His lack of attention then fed into his slapdash attitudes to gay literary figures and their work.

For instance, it is not clear how much of Marcel Proust's fiction Miller had read by the beginning of 1932, but what is clear is that information about Proust's homosexuality both surprised and disconcerted him. When he heard it said that Proust's Albertine was the fictionalised transformation of a young man in Proust's life, he thought it unlikely. On 7 February 1932, he wrote in a letter to Anaïs Nin:

> Is it true that the prototype for Albertine was a man, a homo? . . . Personally, it is very difficult for me to believe this. I have tried rereading certain passages bearing in mind that Albertine was a fairy and not a lesbian. Some say – what difference does it make, it comes to the same thing? But I am sure you will agree it is not at all the same thing.

The tone is homophobic ('a homo', 'a fairy') but that in itself does not account for Miller's position. Part of the problem is the crudity of his sense of a purely homosexual transposition ('a fairy and not a lesbian') when the novel never reduces Albertine to such a narrow subjectivity as Miller's label 'a lesbian' might suggest. Marcel spends months, Proust tens of thousands of words, pondering this very question: *is* Albertine a lesbian? Even once it becomes clear that she does, indeed, have sexual relationships with other women, Proust does not allow that to pin down her identity in Marcel's mind, let alone the reader's. Not without reason does he compare her sleeping body with the protean ocean. Moreover, we might say much the same kind of thing about the 'homo'/'fairy' for whose maleness Proust has substituted the fictional Albertine's femaleness. Surely, if there has indeed been such a creative transposition between 'real' life and fiction, the indeterminacy of Albertine's sexuality is intended as a representation of the same, if obverse, mystery in Proust's beloved man friend: is he *straight*? Miller is quite right to dismiss the ease and banality of his interlocutors' 'what difference does it make'; but to replace it with an equally crude choice between mutually exclusive alternatives is hardly any less reductive.

Miller's position derives from the fact that he thought Proust had been married – '(into Bergson's family, wasn't it?)' – and was therefore demonstrably, definitively heterosexual. He does not allow for the possibility of a homosexual husband. (Again, because he wants the matter to be as clearly distinct as black and white, he never allows for any such intermediate, complicating shade as bisexuality.) As he says in the same letter, 'Proust I cannot think of in this way

[that is, as being homosexual] – and if he were an invert I can't imagine him
marrying'. Thus, two errors (Proust was married; homosexual men do not
marry) had hardened into an attitude, which made Miller resist reading
Albertine as anything other than a young woman – exactly as Proust must have
wished. It turns out that one of Miller's sources on the whole question was
himself homosexual, which in itself appears to have compounded the problem
in Miller's mind:

> There was a fairy, too, who insisted that Proust was a homo – 'a grand invert'
> – and regarded me rather contemptuously when I accepted it sceptically. He
> as much as said that my obtuseness was typically masculine.[34]

Note that while Miller distances himself from his interlocutor (the 'fairy') as
belonging to the opposite side of a binary distinction between sexualities, the
'fairy' (and I think I am justified in assuming he is a Frenchman) makes a more
flexible distinction between positions on a scale of gendered behaviour between
the masculine and, implicitly, the feminine. He seems not to have worried that
this would allow Miller to categorise him, the 'fairy', as being less masculine
and therefore feminine himself. The Frenchman's position is more aptly
Proustian in its pliancy than the American's rigid binaries.[35]

Enormous amounts of productive networking went on in Paris, whether or
not related to shared sexualities. Especially for young writers and artists, the
experience was educational, and its effects on subsequent American culture in
particular are immeasurable. In the summer of 1917, Cole Porter went to
France, where he seems to have served in an ambulance unit (although he
would always claim he joined the Foreign Legion). He was seen in Paris in a
wide array of different uniforms. Like so many others, he stayed on after the
Armistice. On 30 January 1918 he had encountered Linda Lee Thomas, a rich
divorcée, at a wedding at the Paris Ritz. At first he was offended by her, thinking
she regarded him as a paid entertainer, but by the end of the year they were
engaged. They got married in Paris on 12 December 1919. In 1920, Linda
bought them a house at 13 rue Monsieur, in the Invalides. Porter's closest
friend, Howard Sturgis, rented an apartment in the house. The Porters took up
with Gerald and Sara Murphy, who arrived in Paris in 1921. (Gerald had been
at Yale with Porter.) Porter met Darius Milhaud at the Princesse de Polignac's
house. Prompted by the Murphys, Milhaud invited Porter to create a ballet for
him and the Ballets Suédois. Porter invited the Murphys down to Venice so
that he could work on it with Gerald, who wrote the scenario and painted the
backdrop. *Within the Quota* ('the first jazz ballet') was premiered at the Théâtre
des Champs-Elysées on 25 October 1923. In 1925, while mixing with the

Diaghilev set in Venice, Porter appears to have fallen in love with Boris Kochno. He made the advances, Kochno the retreats. Porter occasionally contributed funds to Kochno and the Ballets Russes.

The photographer George Platt Lynes went to Paris at the age of eighteen in 1925. He met Gertrude Stein and, through her, Pavel Tchelitchew, Carl Van Vechten, André Gide and René Crevel. Crevel would be his occasional lover. Back in the States that year, he published booklets by Stein and Ernest Hemingway under his own imprint, As Stable Publications. On his second trip to France, in 1928, he stayed in Villefranche-sur-Mer on the Riviera with Glenway Wescott and Monroe Wheeler. There he met Jean Cocteau, Isadora Duncan and others. That year he posed as Apollo, naked, for a photograph by Man Ray.

In June 1921, Virgil Thomson went with the Harvard Glee Club to Europe for an eight-week singing tour of France, Germany and Italy, starting in Paris. They heard Poulenc play the organ in Notre-Dame and Albert Schweitzer in the Thomas Kirche in Strasbourg. Back in Paris in September, Thomson studied with Nadia Boulanger. (Aaron Copland was already one of her pupils.) For part of 1922 he shared expenses, meals, clothes and a bed with Eugene McCown, who was playing jazz piano in Le Boeuf sur le Toit. Through McCown he met Cocteau, Poulenc, Satie and others. In a letter to a friend (22 June 1922) he wrote: 'Whenever I go to call on a middle-aged or elderly person of either sex, but particularly men, I do my complexion with cold cream and hot water, I run all the way up the stairs, and then I slap myself as I ring the bell. Talk well, of course; put over your line, or whatever the cue is. But look your most adolescent.'[36] (He was twenty-five at the time.)

Thomson returned to Paris in September 1925. Although Paris was not Berlin – and, as he later said, 'Back then, if you wanted sex you went to Berlin' – most things were possible there. 'Everybody knew what everybody else was up to. But you did not talk about it' – which was just as he liked it. In a letter to Briggs Buchanan (2 November 1925) he was characteristically discreet: 'Paris is pretty dull. I think it's going to be an awful season. If anything happens in America, write me of it.' Through Sylvia Beach and Shakespeare and Company he met James Joyce, Ernest Hemingway, Ford Madox Ford, Ezra Pound and others. Dull indeed. Pound is said to have pointed out Ford to him, saying 'You see that little man there? That's the enemy,' meaning that he was the Modernist competition.[37] Among Thomson's other Parisian friends were Pavel Tchelitchew and Christian Bérard. In December 1925 he moved into a flat in St-Cloud with Maurice Grosser, a Harvard friend whom he had met three years previously. Although they shared the flat only for a short while, this became, for each of them, his lifetime's main relationship.

In 1926 Thomson slowly got to know Gertrude Stein and Alice B. Toklas, and on New Year's Day 1927 he cemented the friendship by giving Stein his setting of her poem 'Susie Asado'. Later in the year, he set her evocation of Provence, 'Capital Capitals' (1923). It was first performed at a costume ball given by Elizabeth de Gramont, duchesse de Clermont-Tonnerre. Stein now settled down to write an opera libretto for Thomson. In the late spring she delivered *Four Saints in Three Acts*. To Carl Van Vechten she wrote, 'I have written an opera and a rather amusing young American is making it put on the stage-able'. Thomson started composing the opera in a flat at 17 quai Voltaire, which he rented from that October. (He would later buy a bigger flat in the same building and eventually sell it in 1977.) Twenty years later, when Thomson was an important figure in the United States, Darius Milhaud said it was 'curious you all find Virgil so powerful here; in Paris he was just that little man in a dark suit'.[38] Thomson did know some French literary figures: André Gide and Marcel Jouhandeau, for instance, both called on him in his quai Voltaire apartment, and he tentatively recalled that 'a certain ease of intercourse developed' with Raymond Radiguet. By contrast, he found some of his own countrymen hard to deal with:

> Robert McAlmon I did find interesting [unlike Hemingway and his crowd]; I also esteemed him as a writer; but just like Hart Crane, who was around for a while and whom I also admired, he was too busy drinking and getting over it to make dates with. Both were better when casually encountered.[39]

Even Crane was by no means wasting time. In January 1929, he arrived at the Hotel Jacob (44 rue Jacob) with two letters of introduction: from Laura Riding to Gertrude Stein, and from Waldo Frank to André Gide. At Pavel Tchelitchew's, he discussed sex with Bill Widney; Widney thought sex was legitimate only 'where both enjoy it', whereas Crane said, 'It's legitimate if only one does'.[40] Crane introduced himself to Eugène Jolas, whose circle included Glenway Wescott, Klaus Mann and René Crevel. Jolas introduced him to Harry and Caresse Crosby. They very soon agreed to publish his great epic of the United States *The Bridge* with their Black Sun Press. When he went down to Provence in the spring he stayed with Roy Campbell – until asked to leave. He also, briefly, encountered the painter Marsden Hartley, whom he had previously met in New York, in Marseille. Hartley thought him a 'nice boy but a little flagrant in his methods'.[41] In June, having returned to Paris, Crane was thrown into the Santé for brawling, non-payment of a bar bill (quite a habit of his) and assaulting a gendarme. Character references were sought for him from Cocteau, Gide, Jane Heap and Jean Paulhan. On 17 July he set sail for the United States on the

*Homeric*, with a ticket bought for him by Harry Crosby. Although Crosby killed himself and Josephine Bigelow on 10 December, Crane completed *The Bridge* on 26 December and Black Sun published it in a limited edition in March 1930; Liveright published a larger edition the following month.

Writing about his own arrival in Paris in the early 1920s, Robert McAlmon said, 'I was hardly aware of Montparnasse, even as a legend, and Sylvia Beach informed me it was ghastly, a hangout for pederasts.'[42] To someone who was a part-time pederast himself, this was a considerable recommendation. But Montparnasse, however ghastly, also had to be visited for access to the bohemian crowd, and in particular to the writers with whom his name would become permanently associated. By 1925 McAlmon had published Ford Madox Ford, Mina Loy, Ezra Pound, Norman Douglas, Ernest Hemingway, Djuna Barnes, Havelock Ellis, William Carlos Williams, Edith Sitwell, Hilda Doolittle, James Joyce, Gertrude Stein, Marianne Moore, Wallace Stevens, Glenway Wescott, Marsden Hartley and Kay Boyle. McAlmon did claim to have put some effort into mixing with the French. He wrote: 'A few French writers – such as Jacques Baron, René Crevel, Cocteau, and [Philippe] Soupault – had gone in for cultivating Americans. I have had several passing friendships with French-Frenchmen, but there's always a drifting apart.' Although he did not attribute blame to either side for this 'drifting apart', later in his memoir he admitted the extent of the insularity of his own crowd: 'As a matter of fact, we were seeing far too much of Americans of every type at that time. It wasn't a French Paris at all.'[43] When newcomers arrived from the USA, he would take them to see the French, somewhat as if they were a species apart. For instance, he took John Glassco and his lover Graeme to a queer venue, the Bal des Chiffoniers. Glassco recalled it in his memoirs:

> These pale weedy youths in shabby tight-fitting suits, sporting so many rings and bracelets, these heavy men with the muscles of coal-heavers, rouged, powdered and lipsticked, these quiet white-haired elders with quivering hands and heads and the unwinking stare of the obsessed – all conveyed the message of an indomitable vitality, a quenchless psychic urge. Never had I felt the force of human desire projected with such vigour as by these single-minded devotees of the male; and I felt at the same time that this very desire, barely tolerated and so often persecuted by society, had already made its tragic marriage of convenience with the forces of a stupid criminality because both were equally proscribed and hunted down.[44]

(This closeness to crime was not unique to Paris, of course.) For most American expatriates, though, the French provided little more than evocative European background to the real drama: encounters with fellow anglophones. On another occasion, in a lesbian venue, the Gipsy Bar, Glassco encountered 'the famous Dr Maloney, the most-quoted homosexual in Paris, a man who combined the professions of pathic, abortionist, professional boxer and quasi-confessor to literary women'. The good doctor regaled Glassco with an account of an encounter he had just had with a sexton.[45] Maloney later appeared as that dynamic and dominating presence Dr Matthew O'Connor in Djuna Barnes' novel *Nightwood* (1936).

Leslie Hutchinson ('Hutch') was born in Grenada in 1900; he left for the United States when he was sixteen. In New York he studied medicine for a while, but he also started playing piano in Harlem clubs. Carl Van Vechten may have been his first male lover. In Paris, Hutch teamed up with the singer/dancer Ada Smith, who was popularly known as 'Bricktop' because she was a redhead; he worked as her accompanist as she taught whites how to dance. Her pupils included the Aga Khan and the Prince of Wales. The latter patronised Bricktop's new nightclub, the Music Box, and it took off as a result. Cole Porter, too, was performing there. The club was short-lived, but Bricktop then opened the legendary club Bricktop's, on the rue Fontaine, in October 1926. In November 1931, she opened Chez Bricktop, at 66 rue Pigalle. The lighting had been designed by the photographer Horst's lover George Hoyningen-Huene, also a photographer. Among Hutch's many lovers were both Tallulah Bankhead and Cole Porter. The three Porter songs most closely associated with Hutch would be among the best-known songs of the century: 'Let's Do It', 'Begin the Beguine' and 'Night and Day'.

For all that life in Paris could be liberating for expatriate American lesbians and gay men, they could not entirely escape American standards of behaviour. Especially if they continued to socialise with other Americans, even if only with other writers and artists like themselves, there was always the possibility that they would encounter on the streets of Paris the familiar strains of authentic American homophobia. They might, for a start, find themselves having to cope with the charismatic but combative Ernest Hemingway. Although, according to one writer, 'lesbians were a dark attraction' to Hemingway, he only put up with them for as long as they respectfully deferred to his testosterone.[46] When Gertrude Stein claimed, in *The Autobiography of Alice B. Toklas*, that his style was based on hers and Sherwood Anderson's, he retorted that she was 'queer and liked only queers' – whereas he had *cojones* and knew how to write.[47] Hemingway did admit that 'Miss Stein thought that I was too uneducated about sex and I must admit that I had certain prejudices against [male] homosexuality since I knew its more primitive aspects.'[48] (As a youth riding the boxcars in the Midwest, he had been threatened, or even raped, by an older man or men.) Hemingway's break with Robert McAlmon is described by one cultural historian in these terms:

> Yet the break came because, in his early twenties, Ernest found homosexuals disgusting. He wouldn't write about them, he said, because they were predictable. Given certain and usually unavoidable circumstances, they would act according to their perversion. One of their characteristics, Ernest believed, was the tendency to overreact or, better, to misreact, because their emotions were somehow short-circuited. Usually afraid to let their genuine feelings show, they would either amplify or suppress their response – keeping up a static of excitement, or affecting ennui – in order to hide themselves. In speech and writing, everything for them had to be more, or less, than it was.[49]

McAlmon was also guilty of having mischievously spread a rumour that Hemingway was having an affair with F. Scott Fitzgerald. This set Fitzgerald worrying about his reputation. (In the notebook section of *The Crack-Up*, Fitzgerald said of Hemingway: 'I really loved him, but of course it wore out like a love affair. The fairies have spoiled all that' – by which, presumably, he meant love between 'heterosexual' men.[50]) Yet this unforgivable sullying of masculine friendship was effected not merely by the salacious gossip of fairies, but by their very florescence in society. They smeared what should be the clear distinctions between masculinity and femininity. Implicit in it all, of course, is the characterisation of the non-homosexual, and himself in particular, as a precision instrument, never making anything 'more, or less, than it was'. This is why Jake Barnes, in Hemingway's 'lost generation' novel *The Sun Also Rises* (1926), mistrusts the fluent hands of homosexual men in a bar in Paris and clenches his own fists while watching them.[51] He feels far more comfortable in his admiration of the bodily fluency and ultra-precision of the beautiful (but flamboyantly heterosexual) matador Pedro Romero. Hemingway also took what Carlos Baker describes as 'a cordial dislike' to Glenway Wescott, especially to his bogus English accent. In *The Sun Also Rises* he briefly caricatured Wescott as the young novelist Robert Prentiss. When the author's mother publicly commented on the pessimism of the novel, 'No doubt, said Ernest sourly, Grace wished that her son Ernie were Glenway Wescott or some highly respectable Fairy Prince with an English accent and a taste for grandmothers.'[52]

The economics of expatriation had collapsed with the world economy in 1929 and remained precarious through the 1930s. As the political situation in Europe, too, began to deteriorate in the second half of the 1930s, many American visitors began to wend their way homeward. Reinserting themselves into American life after, in some cases, many years in France took a considerable effort. Observing this return of these expatriates to their native soil in 1936, Klaus Mann noticed a variety of responses to the difficult transition:

> Virgil Thomson managed to live in a New York hotel exactly as though it were situated somewhere in the Latin Quarter. Eugene McCown, too, carried a Parisian flavour along with his canvases and souvenirs when he moved his studio from the banks of the Seine to a building near Fifth Avenue. As for Glenway Wescott, he now appeared almost as conspicuously European in America as he used to be conspicuously American in Europe.[53]

## The Modern Sapphic Paris

In August 1910, Sabine Lepsius wrote a letter attacking one of the collective publications of the German poet Stefan George and his Kreis (his circle of younger, male acolytes) for those of its contents that concerned 'the woman question' and 'the love of boys' (*Jünglingsliebe*). In a pithy summary, she wrote: 'Culture is unthinkable without women. – Ancient Athens and the modern sapphic Paris are perversions.'[54] Athens stands for the cultural heritage of classically educated homosexual men, rather than for the modern city. The best Lepsius can cite by way of a lesbian equivalent, barring Lesbos itself, is modern Paris, which was more widely known for its specifically lesbian subcultures than was Berlin. Most of that renown came, not from clubs and cabarets, but from the artistic activities of a relatively small but very influential group of women, and from the salons in which they shared their ideas and developed their relationships.

Although women could wield considerable power in the cultural world of the Paris salons, as in the country houses of England, they tended to have to be the wives of already rich and powerful men. Correspondingly, the cultural activities of the salons themselves were geared towards endorsing the intellectual activities of men. As Shari Benstock writes:

> The salon world of the *belle époque* was, as it had traditionally been, entirely in the hands of a dozen or so women who provided French intellectuals [with] regular opportunities to prove their social worth. Gender roles were rigidly prescribed: it was women's duty to enhance the discourse of men. Despite the power held by the women who organized such gatherings, salon culture was dominantly male.

Within this milieu of private houses, apartments and gardens, it was possible for homosexual men to flourish; but they had to monitor the progress of their reputations with some care, for 'homosexuals were simultaneously protected by salon society and shunned by it – as were Jews. Both groups were feared by the larger society. The Dreyfus Affair [of 1894–1906] engendered fears that Jews had entered into a conspiracy for control of the government, and homo-sexuals were thought to be united in an effort to corrupt the morals of French society.'[55] It took economic independence, and mutual support, for equivalent pairs and groups of women to develop equivalent centres of cultural activity; and it took the determination of lesbian women to circumvent male social structures in this way. In *The Well of Loneliness*, Radclyffe Hall depicts a Paris of distinct zones, including that of the tourist sights (to which Jonathan intro-duces Stephen), the undifferentiated mass of the heterosexual city, the gay bars, and Valerie Seymour's salon. The last of these, as a private space, is the safest for Hall's moneyed, lesbian characters, even if it sees its own tensions and splits.

Natalie Barney once said, 'I am a lesbian . . . One need not hide it, nor boast of it, though being other than normal is a perilous advantage.' She moved into 20 rue Jacob in 1909. From that October, she held a salon every Friday from four o'clock to eight. Diana Souhami has said of it, 'It was at heart a lesbian arts club.'[56] Barney took pride in the variety in the origins of her guests. She said of her salons, 'I was an international person myself . . . and as I had a nice house I thought I should help other international people meet. The other literary Salons weren't international.'[57] Indeed, one guest is quoted as having said, somewhat hyperbolically: 'The universe came here . . . from San Francisco to Japan, from Lima to Moscow, from London to Rome.'[58]

The first of Barney's great loves was Renée Vivien, whom she had met in 1900. (At the age of twenty-one in 1898, the Englishwoman Pauline Tarn had been reincarnated as the Frenchwoman Renée Vivien when she ran away from her family to Paris. Vivien would die in November 1909, aged just thirty-one.) The second was the painter Romaine Brooks. Romaine had married John Ellingham Brooks, whom she met on Capri, in 1903. She left him and went to London, where she bought a house on Tite Street in Chelsea. When her husband tracked her down, she would not let him in. He went back to Capri, where, for a while, he shared a house with the novelist E.F. Benson. He would die on the island in 1929. Brooks bought herself a house on the avenue du Trocadéro in Paris in 1905. She had an affair with Renée Vivien in 1907, and then with Winnaretta Singer. After her first solo exhibition, in May 1910, she received commissions for portraits from Gabriele d'Annunzio and Ida Rubenstein. She rented a villa near Arcachon in the summer of 1910, living there with d'Annunzio while he wrote *The Martyrdom of Saint Sebastian*, in which Rubinstein was to star in the title role; but she found his life too troubled and left early. After the première of the play at the Théâtre du Châtelet on 22 May 1911, Brooks began an affair with Rubenstein. She painted her in varying degrees of nakedness. Brooks met Natalie Barney in 1915.

Natalie Barney needed Paris; Romaine Brooks hated it. Barney was promiscuous, Brooks not – nor even particularly sociable. Yet Brooks aroused Barney's jealousy when, on Capri, she attracted the attention of Luisa Casati and the pianist Renata Borgatti. Brooks painted Casati in the nude. In 1923 she painted Una Troubridge, who hated the result. Brooks and the British artist Gluck (Hannah Gluckstein) painted each other, but they were competitive and critical of each other's efforts. In 1930 Barney and Brooks had a villa built in a forest near St-Tropez, big enough for Brooks to isolate herself in her half while Barney surrounded herself with friends in hers. But this approximate approach to shared domesticity did not work. They drifted apart until the Second World War forced them together again – in Florence, where both were happily pro-fascist – but Barney returned alone to Paris in May 1946. When Barney showed Brooks' deserted studio, still full of portraits, to Truman Capote, he called it 'the all-time ultimate gallery of famous dykes' and 'an international daisy chain'.[59]

Barney presided over her salon for almost sixty years. As well as important male literary figures from France – André Gide, Anatole France, Max Jacob, Louis Aragon, Jean Cocteau – her visitors included major literary figures from abroad: Ford Madox Ford, Sinclair Lewis, Somerset Maugham, Ezra Pound, T.S. Eliot, F. Scott Fitzgerald, William Carlos Williams, Thornton Wilder, Rainer Maria Rilke, Rabindranath Tagore . . . But the main focus of the salon was its women guests: Colette, Mata Hari, Sylvia Beach, Gluck, Gertrude Stein and Alice B. Toklas, Edna St Vincent Millay, Isadora Duncan, Nancy Cunard, Adrienne Monnier, Peggy Guggenheim, Janet Flanner, Greta Garbo, Françoise Sagan . . . Its triumph was to have built a reputation as a mainstream cultural forum, in touch with the concerns of the era, rather than as some kind of curious sideshow, while yet functioning in the interests of its lesbian guests. Shari Benstock is right to maintain this point:

Not only did Barney's salon operate as a support group for lesbian women; Barney herself spent a lifetime trying to revise the public and private images held by the larger community and lesbian women themselves. She provided a role model in her own behavior, she wrote poetry in the tradition of Sappho (a tradition that had been systematically suppressed over the more than two thousand years separating Barney from Lesbos), she made a pioneer effort to rewrite lesbian history and experience, to deny that guilt, self-recrimination, drug abuse, suicide, unhappiness, and psychological torment were part and parcel of the lesbian's commitment to an alternative life.

Benstock adds that, in order to persuade the wider society that such views were valid, Barney believed lesbian women had a responsibility not to perpetuate old stereotypes:

> Barney herself objected to modes of lesbian behavior that seemed to confirm the scientific theories then prevalent. In particular, she objected to any form of dress or behavior that suggested homosexual women were really men trapped in women's bodies. Therefore, she objected to cross-dressing, to the anger, self-indulgence, and self-pity that marked the behavior of many of her friends, and to the need to mime the male in dress, speech, and demeanor.[60]

The point was to provide a robust alternative to male discourse by engaging with it face-to-face, and to refute male-authored theories of sexualities by living otherwise.

Barney's centrality to Parisian literary life is further demonstrated by the fact that she was depicted – and depicted *as a lesbian* – in fictional works by Liane de Pougy, Renée Vivien (as Vally in *Une Femme m'apparut*), Ronald Firbank, Remy de Gourmont, Colette, Lucie Delarue-Mardrus and Radclyffe Hall (as Valerie Seymour in *The Well of Loneliness*). Djuna Barnes wrote a lively bagatelle called *Ladies Almanack* in 1928. Natalie Barney featured here as Dame Evangeline Musset; Romaine Brooks as Cynic Sal; Lily de Gramont as the Duchesse Clitoressa of Natescourt; Una Troubridge as Lady Buck-and-Balk; Radclyffe Hall as Tilly Tweed-in-blood; Mina Loy as Patience Scalpel; Mimì Franchetti as Senorita Fly-About; and Janet Flanner and Solita Solano as Nip and Tuck. The book was privately published by Robert McAlmon.

Perhaps the most visible of the Frenchwomen who frequented Barney's salon was the novelist Colette; but she was only intermittently identified as a lover of women. Her first lesbian lover, Georgie Raoul-Duval, would later be the model for the mother in Jean Cocteau's novel *Les Parents terribles*. Natalie Barney enigmatically listed Colette as a 'half', rather than a 'full', conquest. But the most significant and lasting of Colette's lesbian relationships was with Sophie-Mathilde-Adèle-Denise de Morny, marquise de Belboeuf, otherwise known as 'Missy'. An inspiration to men as well as women, Missy was the model for the title character in Rachilde's *Marquise de Sade* and the protagonist of Jean Lorrain's *Âme de boue*. At one period in her life she kept a pair of carriage horses called Garlic and Vanilla; both garlic and vanilla come in *une gousse*, a clove or a bean – which just happened to be a slang term for a lesbian. Although Missy dressed mannishly herself, she had what Judith Thurman calls 'a straight man's contempt for pederasty' and was shocked if she saw a lesbian couple both in jackets and trousers. She was a skilful lover, by all accounts, but seems to have been unresponsive herself. Colette wrote that 'the salacious expectations of women shocked her very natural platonic tendencies'.[61] She was, of course, married.

Parisian literary society included many more or less openly homosexual women and men, and merely being 'literary' was enough to qualify one for moving among such people. Colette met homosexual men through her husband Willy (Henry Gauthier-Villars) before she ever met them through her new lesbian friends and lovers. Judith Thurman says of her relationships with these men, 'Colette was a fallen woman, but her somewhat campy, epicene charm had earned her a cult following among gay men, as both a writer and a performer.'[62] Even Robert de Montesquiou, who affected to maintain the highest standards in all things, admired her. They corresponded, respectfully exchanging publications. When *Chéri* was published, André Gide sent her a fan letter. Édouard de Max was a good friend; she wanted to write a play about Don Juan for him, but never got around to it. Robert d'Humières, a married homosexual, was a neighbour of hers and a friend.[63]

Colette's sapphic pleasures were as much cultural as sexual. Often, the two aspects were combined in erotic entertainments, as on an afternoon of amateur theatricals at Natalie Barney's, when Mata Hari did the Dance of the Seven Veils and Colette played a pastoral shepherd wooing a nymph. A year later, she played Daphnis in a piece by Pierre Loüys: she was already in danger of becoming typecast. An anonymous article about Colette, published at the end of 1906, speculated that 'she'll end her days either by taking the veil or running a Lesbian bistro in Monte Carlo'.[64] Either might have been an attractive alternative to her husband's bed.

Of the year 1905, in which Colette's father died, Thurman says, 'By the end of the year, Colette had formally entered Lesbos on Missy's arm.'[65] As if that were not potentially scandalous enough, in February 1906 Colette launched herself on a stage career in pantomime. By the end of the year she and Willy had ceased living together. Instead, she moved in with Missy, but she kept a small pied-à-terre of her own. Colette and Willy had stayed with Renée Vivien at her villa Cessole near Nice, in March 1906. A week later, Vivien sent Natalie Barney a poem she had written about Colette. Since the separation from Willy, Vivien had more assiduously cultivated her, but Colette found her poetry and her home stifling and unwholesome. Indeed, she once upset Vivien by taking her own lamp to brighten up a dinner there. She also deplored Vivien's heavy drinking, and Vivien's letters to her were nothing if not embarrassing. As Thurman puts it, 'There's a presumption of sexual complicity – one lesbian to another – which Colette, wary of intimacy, disdainful of identity politics, and indeed deeply ambivalent about lesbianism, could only find obnoxious.'[66] Many years later, when she came to realise that her own daughter, Bel-Gazou, was having relationships with other women, Colette was strongly disapproving.

One of the foreigners who contributed most to the international literary scene in Paris was Sylvia Beach, an American who arrived there in August 1916. (She had visited the city once before, with her family, in 1907.) In 1917 she met Adrienne Monnier, the proprietress of a bookshop which had not yet been named La Maison des Amis des Livres. Adrienne was five years younger than Sylvia. Beach had plans of her own to open a French bookshop in London, but Harold Monro advised her not to, perhaps fearing competition for his own Poetry Bookshop. Instead, on 17 November 1919, she opened the Anglophone bookshop and lending library Shakespeare and Company, at 8 rue Dupuytren in Paris. Visitors in the first few days included Louis Aragon, André Gide, Léon Fargue, Valéry Larbaud, Georges Duhamel and Jules Romains. On 16 March 1920, Gertrude Stein and Alice B. Toklas came into the shop for the first time. They would remain good friends until Beach published James Joyce's *Ulysses* in February 1922.[67] Beach and Monnier intermittently attended Natalie Barney's salon, when work allowed, and Barney regularly renewed her subscription to the lending library; but Beach was never convinced that Barney took literature seriously. Beach and Monnier began living together in 1920, an arrangement that would last until 1937.

In the summer of 1920 both Joyce and Ezra Pound materialised in Paris. Wyndham Lewis and T.S. Eliot, too, soon found their way to Shakespeare and Company. In March 1921, when Joyce was beginning to despair of ever finding a publisher for his new novel, Sylvia Beach offered to publish it. She once wrote, 'Probably I was stongly attracted to Joyce as well as to his work, but unconsciously. My only love was really Adrienne.' In July, Shakespeare and Company moved to 12 rue de l'Odéon, just across the road from Monnier's La Maison des Amis des Livres. That summer, Thornton Wilder arrived in the shop and made friends with Beach. As she later wrote, 'Adrienne and I were very fond of Wilder and liked to think of him as a member of the family'.[68] Other new arrivals that year included Sherwood Anderson, whom Beach would introduce to James Joyce and Gertrude Stein, and Ernest Hemingway, whom Beach would introduce to Ezra Pound in the shop. Beach met Robert McAlmon and Winifred Ellerman ('Bryher'), husband and wife in a *mariage blanc*, in May 1921, and made close friends of both.[69] On one festive occasion McAlmon took Beach and Monnier on a tour of the gay bars of Montmartre.

Shakespeare and Company regulars included Eric Satie (although he could not read English), Virgil Thomson, Aaron Copland, Sergei Eisenstein, W.H. Auden and Stephen Spender (in the late 1930s). (Beach had arranged for the publication of an abridged translation of Auden and Isherwood's *The Dog Beneath the Skin* in the spring of 1937.) Glenway Wescott and his lover Monroe Wheeler joined the lending library in February 1925. Elizabeth Bishop borrowed books while in Paris for three months in 1936, but she nervously backed out of attending a reception Beach invited her to, at which Joyce and Gide were to be present. Willa Cather visited the shop for the first time in the summer of 1933. Marianne Moore wrote to Bryher (7 November 1936): 'I could not say how fine I thought Sylvia Beach, or how much good it did me to meet her . . . I was much impressed with her cautious honesty of opinion and gracile youthfulness; and of course with her generosity.'[70]

In January 1939, when Americans were advised to leave Europe, Sylvia Beach decided to stay. She kept the shop open during the Occupation. When a Nazi officer threatened to confiscate all the books, she hid them upstairs in rooms on the fourth floor, where they remained until the Liberation. Shakespeare and Company, of course, went out of business as a result. Beach was finally arrested in late August 1942. The Germans had told her to dismiss a seventeen-year-old Jewish woman who worked for her, and she had refused. Beach was imprisoned with other American women in an ex-hotel at Vittel in eastern France, and was released the following year; but the young woman she had tried to protect was deported to a camp in Poland and never seen again. After the Liberation, Beach did not reopen the shop.

The other expatriate lesbian who played a major role in Parisian Modernism (if that is not too local a designation for her international influence) was Gertrude Stein. When they first went to Europe from the USA, Gertrude Stein and her brother Leo lived together in London. But Leo went to Paris in 1902, taking a studio and apartment at 27 rue de Fleurus. Gertrude joined him there and wrote her lesbian fiction *QED*. They started a collection of paintings by the likes of Henri Matisse and Pablo Picasso. As a natural consequence of doing so, they made friends with the artists and the artists' friends. (Yet Matisse later said Stein was in no position to comment on the avant-garde in France, since her command of French was so poor.[71]) Leo would go on to hate Modernist art, including his sister's writing, but Gertrude remained faithful for life. Speaking of which, Gertrude Stein and Alice B. Toklas met in Paris on 8 September 1907. Alice was staying across the Luxembourg gardens and started visiting every day; then she graduated to typing Stein's work; finally she started cooking for Stein the American meals she was missing. (They would spend the next thirty-nine years together, until Stein's death.) The following summer they went on a group trip to Italy. Alice and Gertrude explored Tuscany together. It was here that Gertrude proposed that Alice should come and live with her and Leo. Alice turned down this idea, however, and, once they had returned to Paris, rented an apartment of her own. But in 1910 she did move in with the Stein siblings. In the meantime, however, Gertrude and Leo were steadily growing apart, he becoming increasingly contemptuous of her writing. In 1913 he moved out, taking half their collection of paintings with him; Gertrude never spoke to him again.

Stein and Toklas made changes to the art collection and improved the apartment. When Stein held her artistic salons, Toklas took to sitting apart with the wives. In June, Carl Van Vechten visited them. He subsequently helped Stein find a publisher for *Tender Buttons* and became her main advocate in the United States. The two women spent part of the Great War in the Balearics, but returned to Paris in 1916 when the French victory at Verdun stopped the German advance on the capital. They acquired a Ford van, which they called Auntie, and joined the American Fund for French Wounded, distributing medical supplies. Toklas planned their itineraries according to the quality of the restaurants en route. They especially enjoyed the company of the young American servicemen they kept meeting. When Auntie conked out in 1920 they got a new Ford they called Godiva. Like Raymond Roussel, Toklas hated tunnels; so Stein would amuse herself by driving through as many as she could find.

Stein was more taken with the style of the men than the women in the Paris of the belle époque:

> In Paris around 1900–1914 the men were elegant and had almost more beauty than the women. When we came to Paris [in 1902] the men wearing their silk hats on the side of their head and leaning heavily on their cane toward the other side making a balance, the heavy head[,] the heavy hand on the cane[,] were the elegance of Paris. The women were plain, fashionable more than elegant in contrast with the men.[72]

Shari Benstock makes an important distinction between the cultural salons of Natalie Barney and Gertrude Stein: 'Barney's was a feminist effort that would eventually become an endeavour on behalf of lesbian literature and art', whereas Stein's was more self-centred: 'Stein began promoting herself as the resident genius of the Left Bank', which involved operating with men and by male standards.[73] In general, Stein preferred men to women. Diana Souhami somewhat understates the case: 'Gertrude was not a woman's woman when it came to affairs of the mind and she could be chauvinistic.'[74] Virgil Thomson wrote: 'Gertrude kept up friendships among the amazons, though she did not share their lives.'[75] The only time Adrienne Monnier visited Stein and Toklas at home she was insulted by a Stein monologue on how the French lacked any truly great literature. Understandably, Monnier thought this was a bit rich, coming from an American. Stein attracted the kind of reaction that W.H. Auden would attract in later years, and for similar reasons. Djuna Barnes said, 'I couldn't stand her. She had to be the centre of everything. A monstrous ego.'[76] Natalie Barney, though, was a friend. She and Romaine Brooks had first met Stein and Toklas at the Ballets Russes in 1926. In January 1927 Barney held a 'Homage to Gertrude' at which Mina Loy gave a reading from Stein and some of Virgil Thomson's settings of Stein songs were sung.

According to Thomson, Stein thought André Gide and Marcel Jouhandeau, in their habit of 'making fiction out of sex', were 'as banal as any titillator of chambermaids' – whatever that means.[77] She and Toklas did not appreciate Gide's high seriousness, or not when they had to endure it in person – 'André Gide turned up while we were at the Villa Curonia. It was rather a dull evening' – but many younger men who came and went through Paris amused them. The *Autobiography of Alice B. Toklas* does not go into detail or depth, but one gets the impression that their beloved young men, for all the depth of what creativity they might put on display for the two great ladies, were treated as harmless children or conveniently temporary pets. The book speaks of Marsden Hartley, 'whom we liked very much'. Glenway Westcott is said to have 'impressed us greatly by his [bogus] english accent' [*sic*], but ultimately he did not interest Stein: 'he has a certain syrup but it does not pour'. René Crevel 'talked with his characteristic brilliant violence'. They seem to have been fascinated by the way in which an allegiance to Surrealism had taken over his whole personality. Summarised in a characteristic sentence of Stein's, he gave the impression of having more dimensions than other men: 'He was young and violent and ill and revolutionary and sweet and tender.'[78] The Swedish painter Nils Dardel was introduced to Stein's salon by the German-Jewish art dealer Wilhelm Uhde. In the spring of 1929 Stein and Toklas rented a farmhouse at Bilignin in the Rhône valley. They would spend half of every year there for the next thirteen years. Paul Bowles stayed with them there in 1931, and Aaron Copland joined him. Cecil Beaton and Francis Rose stayed in the summer of 1939. Beaton later said of the house at Bilignin, 'Everything seemed to possess a patina that gave one's senses a delight. Everywhere was a feeling of perfection that can be acquired only by the most sophisticated people or by peasants.'[79] The American poet James Merrill and his lover Claude Fredericks visited in the 1950s. Merrill later said of the occasion: 'Alice and Gertrude had always kept a special fondness for male couples, if literary so much the better, and Alice's welcome, when she joined us, was the warmer for decades of practice.'[80]

When Stein and Toklas went to England in February 1936 so that Stein could lecture at both Oxford and Cambridge, they stayed with Lord Berners in

Berkshire. He wrote a ballet, *A Wedding Bouquet*, based on Stein's play, *They Must. Be Wedded. To Their Wife*. It was given its first performance at Sadler's Wells on 27 April; the musical director was Constant Lambert, the choreographer Frederick Ashton. Back in Paris, in November 1937, having to move out of 27 rue de Fleurus, they took a flat at 5 rue Christine. Janet Flanner inventoried their collection of 131 paintings. In the meantime, Stein wrote a libretto, *Dr Faustus Lights the Lights*, for Berners; but it was never produced because of the threat of war.

Although they were both Jewish, Stein and Toklas decided to stay in France. An arrangement was made with Marshal Pétain that they be protected. Although for a while a hundred German soldiers were billeted in their home, the two women survived the war unscathed. In December 1944, after the arrival of the Americans, they left the Rhône valley for good and returned to Paris, where they received constant visits from young GIs. In June 1945 they made a tour of US bases in Germany and even visited the Berghof, Hitler's home at Berchtesgaden. Stein died in 1946, soon after a cancer operation. Later in the year she was interred at Père Lachaise.

Alice B. Toklas wrote her renowned cookbook between February and May 1953. Among its highlights are many recipes contributed by old friends, including Sir Francis Rose (Chinese Eggs, Lemon Salad, Stuffed Italian Squash), Virgil Thomson (Shad-Roe Mousse, Gnocchi alla Piemontese, Pork 'alla Pizzaiola' of Calabria), Lord Berners (Roast Chicken in Cream, Steamed Spring Vegetable Pie), Natalie Barney (Stuffed Egg-Plant with Sugar), Cecil Beaton and Brion Gysen [*sic*] (Hashish Fudge: 'it might provide an entertaining refreshment for a Ladies' Bridge Club or a chapter meeting' of the Daughters of the American Revolution[81]).

## Indifferent Tolerance

During the Second World War, a new generation of foreigners experienced Paris for the first time. One young American serviceman who visited Le Boeuf sur le Toit while on leave in the city later reported:

> It was a *great* gay nightclub. Beef on the roof! You walked in, and suddenly you realized the *size* of homosexuality – the total global reach of it! There were hundreds of guys from all over the world in all kinds of uniforms: there were free Poles dancing with American soldiers; there were Scotsmen dancing with Algerians; there were Free French; there were Russians. It was like a U.N. of gays. It was just incredible. I mean there were men dancing with each other! I had never seen that before in my *life*! There was lots of

singing at the bar, and lots of arms around each other's shoulders. For me, it was like a sort of V-E Day for gays – before the real V-E Day.[82]

After the terrors, privations, embarrassments and worse of the Occupation, the post-war period saw a reimposition of conventions and norms. Liberation was subject to rationing. Even what some visitors experienced as excitingly louche was really, in the scheme of things, pretty subdued. Gay revellers were controlling their displays of pleasure. In Paris in 1947 with his lover, the art patron and collector Peter Watson, Waldemar Hansen wrote home to a friend in the USA that the gay nightclubs were 'like Berlin, 1941'. He seems to have meant the restrained gentility of the patrons' behaviour, which he certainly found worthy of note: 'the queens go round and round in those weird polkas or whatever they are. The Paris boys are a well-behaved lot, no rowdyism, very little painting up'. He added that 'Many of them are very masculine'.[83] Like the rest of Western Europe, France would follow the USA in using the threatened 'spread' of communism as a reason to crack down, not just on political dissent, but also on a whole range of unconventional behaviours. As elsewhere, homosexuality came under suspicion of subversion. When Charles Henri Ford and Pavel Tchelitchew arrived in Paris in June 1949, a Russian friend told the latter that 'Paris is very anti-paederast at the moment – orgies in the baths no longer take place; no "dancings" with boys only; no entertainers in drag'. But the *vespasiennes* were still, apparently 'working overtime'.[84]

In the late 1940s, Gore Vidal used to patronise the brothel Marcel Proust had set up in what was now called the Hôtel Saumon, in an arcade just off the Place de l'Humanité. The model for Jupien's brothel in *À la recherche du temps perdu* was now presided over by an elderly Algerian called Said, who had been there since Proust's time. Vidal questioned him about what Proust got up to ('Oh, he would just look. That's all. There were holes – you know, in the walls') before making proper use of the institution:

On the first floor there was a sitting room. One could look through a crack in the door at the room's contents, a half-dozen working-class boys, smoking, reading newspapers, drinking wine. Choice made, Said would send the one chosen to the room. To exoticize the Victorian solidity of Mme. Proust's furniture, Said had hung, wherever he could, beaded curtains while in dark dusty corners tarnished bronze pots and pipes gleamed.

Vidal connected the boys with the current talking point, Alfred Kinsey's *Sexual Behavior in the Human Male* (1949) and its famous 'scale' of sexual orientations:

The boys were polite and rather shy; and they urgently needed money. Whatever their primary sexual interest, they took easily to their own sex, and I often wondered how Kinsey would have rated them. The ghettoiza- tion of 'gay' and 'straight' had not begun. I suspect that all of them would marry and have children and then, in due course, with age, they would pay for women and perhaps boys, too, since that taste had been awakened, if nowhere else, amongst Said's Algerian beads.[85]

This harmless establishment was closed down in 1949, but France remained a potential refuge for those fleeing harsher social systems. In a diary entry for 20 October 1953, Jean Cocteau wrote, of a dinner-table conversation:

The English and Americans around the table didn't seem much more pleased with their governments than we are with ours. They asked me the secret of the charm which makes them want to live in France. I answered that French decadence was the extreme tip of a great civilization. Lord — might have found asylum in France. He could have slept with a thousand Boy Scouts without being condemned to hard labour.[86]

The reference is to Lord Montagu, who had been arrested earlier in the year and acquitted of the offences against the Boy Scouts; but who would be tried the following year for other offences and, on being found guilty, sentenced to twelve months' imprisonment – though not with hard labour. Cocteau seems haunted still, as well he might be, by the laborious fate of Oscar Wilde. At any rate, there was certainly still enough of a gay scene in Paris to maintain the city's reputation, for better or worse. When the painter Louis de Wet told his father – a white South African policeman – he was going to move to Paris and become an artist, his father said, 'If you go to that Sodium and Gomorrah you will be lost' [sic]. De Wet went to Paris in 1952, regardless, and his father stopped communicating with him.[87]

By the time of Raymond Queneau's novel Zazie in the Metro (Zazie dans le métro, 1959), the character Gabriel is a drag entertainer in a gay nightclub, 'the Mount of Venus, the most celebrated of all the pansy night-clubs of the capital, and there's certainly no serious shortage of them'.[88] But drag shows are not the same as a functioning gay scene, even if they might constitute part of one. Just as likely, at the more lavish end of the spectrum, they would be staged for the tourist market, for foreigners on the lookout for some vestige of the Naughty Nineties. For the young Englishman Angus Wilson, 'between 1930 and 1950 it was France . . . that stood for abroad for me . . . My sense of the nature of sexual licence (a particularly absurd thing when I reflect on the easy indifferent toler- ance the French, I believe, have towards homosexual life – but then I was a literary young man and inevitably Proust and Gide counted for so much for me), was sharpened and enriched there.'[89] But the fact that Wilson gives a cut-off date of 1950 should give us pause: he, too, had noticed a change for the worse. There is plenty of evidence of that 'easy indifferent tolerance', but some visitors were hard-put to find it.

James Baldwin is a case in point. Those haunted eyes of the Parisian inverts in Radclyffe Hall's *The Well of Loneliness* reappear almost thirty years later, in Baldwin's novel *Giovanni's Room* (1956) among the customers of the gay bar run by Guillaume:

> There were the usual paunchy, bespectacled gentlemen with avid, some-times despairing eyes, the usual, knife-blade lean, tight-trousered boys. One could never be sure, as concerns these latter, whether they were after money or blood or love. They moved about the bar incessantly, cadging cigarettes and drinks, with something behind their eyes at once terribly vulnerable and terribly hard. There were, of course, *les folles*, always dressed in the most improbable combinations, screaming like parrots the details of their latest love-affairs – their love-affairs always seemed to be hilarious. Occasionally one would swoop in, quite late in the evening, to convey the news that he – but they always called each other 'she' – had just spent time with a celebrated movie star, or boxer. Then all of the others closed in on this newcomer and they looked like a peacock garden and sounded like a barnyard.[90]

The book is narrated by David, an American who is every bit as homophobic about himself as he is about anyone else. His hatred of camp styles always raises the shrillness of his own voice. The more one rereads this novel, the more one is inclined to side with *les folles*, who are, at least, enjoying their lives. They may be indiscreet, but they have a lot to be indiscreet about. That David is never able to see them as human beings reflects as much discredit on his humanity as on theirs.

A backlash affecting the whole subculture follows the eventual murder of Guillaume by David's Italian lover, Giovanni:

> Editorials were written and speeches were made, and many bars of the genre of Guillaume's bar were closed. (But they did not stay closed long.) Plain-clothes policemen descended on the quarter, asking to see everyone's papers, and the bars were emptied of *tapettes* [queens].

The short-term closures of the gay bars are plainly intended as a terrorising technique rather than a serious attempt to clean up the city; as are the inspections of personal identity papers. The very visible *tapettes*, for whom the closet is no longer an option, can be treated by the police with less restraint than the more discreet clients of the bar. In that sense, they have a public identity that is public property. David now generalises about such scandals, perhaps from an implausibly knowledgeable position:

> Such a scandal always threatens, before its reverberations cease, to rock the very foundations of the state. It is necessary to find an explanation, a solution, and a victim with the utmost possible speed. Most of the men picked up in connection with this crime were not picked up on suspicion of murder. They were picked up on suspicion of having what the French, with a delicacy I take to be sardonic, call *les gouts particuliers*. These 'tastes', which do not constitute a crime in France, are nevertheless regarded with extreme disapprobation by the bulk of the populace, which also looks on its rulers and 'betters' with a stony lack of affection.

A bar that has been represented in David's narrative as the haven for a very narrow clique of gossiping queens, who scrutinised his relationship with Giovanni with searing amusement and scepticism, now turns out to have had a very broad reach across Paris, since the boys who lingered there also plied their trade on the streets.

> When Guillaume's corpse was discovered it was not only the boys of the street who were frightened; they, in fact, were a good deal less frightened than the men who roamed the streets to buy them, whose positions, careers, aspirations, could never have survived such notoriety. Fathers of families, sons of great houses, and itching adventurers from Belleville were all desperately anxious that the case be closed, so that things might, in effect, go back to normal and the dreadful whiplash of public morality not fall on their backs. Until the case was closed they could not be certain which way to jump, whether they should cry out that they were martyrs, or remain what, at heart, of course, they were, simple citizens, bitter against outrage and anxious to see justice done and the health of the state preserved.

Only for a moment does the ambiguity of these closing phrases prevail. It is not the justice meted out to their own kind – by way of social reform – that they are anxious to see done, but the calm-restoring justice of an arrest, trial, guilty verdict and execution. As the next sentence drily puts it: 'It was fortunate, therefore, that Giovanni was a foreigner.' That he is Italian absolves them all: it has no implications beyond the bar itself, no reach into the family homes and 'great houses' whose adult, male inhabitants had felt so threatened while the case remained unresolved. For a while it looked as if they might come out and declare themselves, albeit under extreme pressure, as 'martyrs' – an approach espousing victimhood as a political strategy. But that moment passes and the safer alternative prevails: they go back to being indistinguishable 'citizens', assured of the *égalité* their anonymity affords them. Their 'tastes' remain a personal secret, subject to state scrutiny only when another scandal should arise.[91]

In a 1954 essay on André Gide, without explicitly owning up to a personal involvement, Baldwin had given some hint of his disdain for the people frequenting the Paris scene:

> The really horrible thing about the present-day phenomenon of homosexuality, the horrible thing which lies curled like a worm at the heart of Gide's trouble . . . is that today's unlucky deviate can only save himself by the most tremendous exertion of all his forces from falling into an underworld in which he never meets either men or women, where it is impossible to have either a lover or a friend, where the possibility of genuine human involvement has altogether ceased. When this possibility has ceased, so has the possibility of growth.[92]

The 'underworld' of the gay scene in Paris caters only to an intersexual crowd, not 'either men or women', dedicated only to short-term sexual engagements and otherwise disinclined to involve themselves with, or support, each other. As depicted in the novel, they watch each other with a malicious intensity that then flourishes into destructive gossip; and they watch the door for any newcomer over whom they might compete for a sexual opportunity. Having escaped, to some extent, America's 'race problem' during his extensive sojourns in Paris, Baldwin would have to move to Istanbul before he felt he had escaped the equivalent 'problem' of homosexuality in both the USA and France.[93]

Baldwin was unconvinced by the credentials of the white Beat writers, whether as writers or as hipsters. He quite liked Allen Ginsberg, but did not identify with him merely because they were both gay. As his biographer puts it, 'How could they know what "hip" really meant? What did they know of what it cost to be "cool"? When their ersatz bohemianism failed them, they would simply go home and "take over the family business". Baldwin resented 'the way in which the hipsters appropriated and exploited the souls of black folk, without proper respect for the experience of the people in question.[94] Their time in Paris overlapped with his, but their lives did not.

In 1957, Allen Ginsberg and Peter Orlovsky had crossed the Atlantic and travelled to Tangier, Madrid, Barcelona, Venice (where they stayed for a month), Florence, Rome, Assisi ... After sightseeing in Naples, Ginsberg crossed to Ischia to visit W.H. Auden. He found him at Marie's Bar at 'a table-ful [sic] of dull chatty literary old fairies'. Auden told him that, although he admired it, he thought *Howl* was 'full of the author feeling sorry for himself'. Ginsberg got drunk and called them all 'a bunch of shits'. The next day, he wrote to his father: 'I doubt if Auden respects his own feelings anymore. I think his long sexual history had [sic] been relatively unfortunate and made him very orthodox and conservative and merciless in an offhand way ... Auden is a great poet but he seems old in vain if he's learned no wildness from life.'[95]

After Italy, Ginsberg and Orlovsky went on to Austria, Germany (pausing in Munich to visit Dachau) and France. They settled down in Paris, staying (on and off) for ten months in the so-called Beat Hotel (the name was Gregory Corso's), a run-down building at 9 rue Gît-le-Coeur in the Latin Quarter, which provided cheap accommodation for foreigners. Ginsberg, Orlovsky and Corso checked into room 32 on the top floor on 15 October 1957. The three of them shared a bed until Ginsberg and Orlovsky were able to move into room 25. Ginsberg was working on the fourth section of 'Kaddish'. When his mother Naomi had died in June 1956 the Kaddish was not said for her and Ginsberg did not attend the funeral; so he was now composing his own raw tribute to her. In November Orlovsky, too, began writing poems. William Burroughs arrived from Tangier on 16 January 1958; he would inhabit the Beat Hotel, on and off, until the end of 1962. In September, Brion Gysin joined him there. Maurice Girodias published Burroughs' *Naked Lunch* with his Olympia Press in July 1959. That summer Harold Norse started visiting Burroughs in the hotel. It was Norse who sent Burroughs off to meet Ian Sommerville in the bookshop where he worked. They became lovers (Burroughs was forty-five, Sommerville eighteen), and Burroughs sent the youth back to Cambridge to complete his degree. In September, Gysin showed Burroughs his new discovery, the 'cut-up' method of composition. Together they experimented with written texts, and then with tape recordings. When Harold Norse moved into the Beat Hotel in April 1960 he, too, began cutting-up. Burroughs used the technique to compile his novel *The Soft Machine* in 1960 and 1961. With his sensitive nose for a trend, Yves Saint Laurent launched his 'Beat' collection for Dior in the autumn of 1960. When Ginsberg arrived in Paris from New York in March 1961 he met Gysin for the first time and, although theirs was never an easy relationship, it was the two of them, rather than Burroughs, who prepared the book for publication. Girodias brought it out that June. It would be followed by *The Ticket That Exploded* in December 1962. Burroughs stayed on until December 1962, Norse until January 1963, and Gysin likewise. That was when the proprietor closed the hotel and sold it.

Barry Miles is uncompromising in his assessment of the extent to which these Beats mixed with French society: in short, they did not. In Miles' words, they 'preferred their own company, content to celebrate their own genius'. This was partly a matter of language: 'As non-French speakers, they had no involvement with French culture and the issues of the day, nor were they restricted by the rules with which the French lived, simply because they were ignorant of them.' The fact was that they were not really interested in what Paris – let alone France – had to offer beyond their own immediate needs: 'Many of the occupants of the Beat Hotel did not venture more than a few blocks from the rue Git-le-coeur from one month to the next; virtually everything they needed was on hand.'[96] There were plenty of Americans who did mix, of course, and who therefore gained massively, in the subsequent development of their careers, from cultural interaction with the French. For example, John Ashbery – of the same generation, but no Beat – lived in France for much of the decade between the mid-1950s and mid-1960s, earning his living mainly as an art critic for American journals (*New York Herald Tribune, Art International, Art News*), sharing his life with a Frenchman, Pierre Martory, and improving his own French all the time, until he became a fine translator of French poetry, including that of his lover.

Remarkably, the Beat writers had themselves become tourist attractions in Paris. In his memoirs, Harold Norse describes how 'Young people came to stare at the crumbling facade' of the Beat Hotel, 'hoping to catch a glimpse of a famous Beat writer'. On one occasion, he opened his window to communicate with a group of youths who had been 'gazing reverently upward' at the building.

> One of them waved shyly. I waved back. Gathering courage, he called in a German accent, 'Are you Jack Kerouac?' I might have known. 'No,' I called, 'but almost. Won't I do?' They didn't laugh. 'Is Kerouac there?' asked another. 'He's hiding in the closet.' 'Is Allen Ginsberg there?' 'In another closet.' They stared and lumbered off with hankering looks, still convinced that I was Kerouac. They would tell their friends they had seen and talked to 'The King of the Beats' at the Beat Hotel.

On another occasion, in the Mistral Bookshop on the rue de la Bûcherie, Norse annoyed a group of Oxford students, one of whom had asked him if he was Gregory Corso (who happened to be standing next to him). Having pretended that he was, Norse then failed to persuade them of the truth. Nor was Corso himself able to reclaim his identity. As for the students, 'They left in a huff as we doubled up with laughter.'[97]

# CHAPTER FIVE

# GERMANY AND ITS VISITORS

## The George Kreis

The German poet Stefan George had derived a significant legacy from the Wildean philosophy of 'L'art pour art', from the culture of 1890s 'Decadence' and from other aspects of Oscar Wilde's aesthetic.[1] But his contacts with young men were more selective than Wilde's. He gathered around himself a protective and admiring elite of disciples, the George Kreis, hand-picked as much for their good looks and 'aristocratic' mien as for their education and intelligence. Together, between 1890 and 1919, they published a cultural journal, *Blätter für die Kunst*. Not caring for an outside readership, they both wrote and read the journal for themselves. Intellectual and spiritual friendship was everything.[2] Young scholars who did not belong to the group hero-worshipped the Master from outside it. Walter Benjamin later wrote: 'It was not too much for me to wait for hours on a bench reading in the castle park in Heidelberg in expectation of the moment when he was supposed to walk by.'[3]

It is this position of George as a leader and teacher surrounded by a devoted, closed circle of disciples that all his life placed him at one remove from contact with ordinary humanity. It is as though he could be reached only through the medium of his disciples, to whom in the first place his words were addressed, for whom primarily his personality existed, and by whom his poems were more immediately comprehended.[4] Protected and insulated by the circle around him, he came to seem out of touch with – or, if you prefer, to have transcended – the everyday. And nothing was more everyday than women or, by extension, the love of women. E.K. Bennett is definite on this point: 'the love of women plays no important rôle in the poetry of George'.[5] Disciples who married were banished from the Kreis. Friedrich Gundolf, to whom this happened, later wrote: 'As a youth I trusted numbly, / Later gladly, to the Master, / Till one stronger came to free me.'[6] The sense of liberation from George was not uncommon, but it was a liberation gained at some expense and would often be described in wistful tones.

Although he kept a room in his family's house near Bingen on the Rhine for the whole of his life, George was a dedicated internationalist, living at various times in Austria, England, France, Italy and Switzerland, generally in simple rented lodgings or with friends. Even when in Germany, he tended to impermanence, living in Berlin, Heidelberg, Kiel and Munich. As a translator, he worked from English (Shakespeare), French (the Symbolists), Italian (Dante) and Spanish.[7] He first visited Italy at the beginning of 1889 when, after a stay on Lake Geneva, he briefly passed through Milan and Turin; but it was not until the spring of 1891, when he visited Verona and Venice, that the country really caught his imagination. After that, he made sure he went to Italy at least once a year until 1913; his last trip included a visit to the ruins at Paestum. What he found in the sunny South was not heat but light – a brightness that suffuses his most intensely idealistic poetry.[8] When he travelled to France after graduating in 1889, already thinking of himself as a poet, he met Stéphane Mallarmé, Paul Verlaine and Pierre Louÿs. In Vienna two years later, he had a close encounter with the aspiring poet Hugo von Hofmannsthal, who was only seventeen. Quite what happened between them is unclear, but Hofmannsthal's father felt he had to write to George, telling him to leave his son alone.[9] Hofmannsthal revered George as a poet, yet now and later he resisted the older man's attempts to enfold him in the embrace of the George Kreis, the elitism of which was personally distasteful to him and seemed also to be contrary to the principles of poetry, which, he felt, should spring naturally from the poet's position within – rather than above – the broader society. George, who had been trying 'to establish a salutary dictatorship in our literature', resentfully blamed Hofmannsthal for the fact that his sterile plans came to naught.[10]

George had a passionate interest, which he and his subsequent champions always claimed to be entirely spiritual, in teenage boys. (It is beyond doubt that they inspired his poetry.[11]) The most notable of them, because of his ultimate effect on the poetry, was the Bavarian youth Maximilian Kronberger, twenty years George's junior, whom he met in 1902. 'Maximin', as George called him, died of meningitis the day after his sixteenth birthday in 1904. In the poetry that followed, George deified him as an icon of immortal beauty. (Mortality has a habit of bringing on immortality.) Even readers who deny a homosexual relationship have to acknowledge, however reluctantly, the equivocal intensity of the poetry. For instance, Michael and Erica Metzger write that 'George's relationship to the boy, who greatly admired the poet, was that of a friend and teacher' – which is obviously an implicit denial that he was a lover – but they later say of the Maximin poems:

> The poems are passionate and poignant at once. Initially, we encounter the
> sense of the unseasonableness of the attachment of an older man to one
> much younger. This is resolved by their intellectual and emotional
> communion and by their mutual surrender to a friendship which is not
> lacking in strong sensual elements.[12]

This is slippery stuff. What the Metzgers cannot quite bring themselves to
acknowledge is, as any ancient Greek could have told them, that 'a friend and
teacher' may also, as in this case, be a lover. Unseasonable or not, the man–boy
relationship is presented by George as achieving the highest ideal, not least in
those 'strong sensual elements' which the Metzgers identify in the poems.

A year after Maximilian Kronberger's death, George established a close relationship with an Argentinian boy he had met once before, fourteen-year-old
Hugo Zemik ('Ugolino'). Poems would follow; as would other boys. A pattern
had been established. In the more forthcoming of his two autobiographies, the
English composer Cyril Scott gave an account of what it was like for a boy to be
on the receiving end of Stefan George's interest.[13] They met in 1896, when Scott
was seventeen and George twenty-eight. Scott went with a couple of friends to
visit the poet, who was living in his parents' home near Bingen. Scott was the
youngest of his party and the only one to arouse George's 'special interest'.
Further visits followed, Scott going to Bingen and George to Scott's lodgings at
Kronberg, where he 'stayed a few days each time'. It was on one of their walks in
the landscape around Bingen that 'Stefan George confessed that his attachment
to me was no ordinary one; though he had guessed from the beginning that I
was not of the type who would reciprocate his feelings'. Although one of the
friends with whom Scott first met George had warned him that 'the poet was
abnormal' and that he had once been intensely attracted to Hugo von
Hofmannsthal, Scott was surprised and embarrassed by the confession, and
'began to feel ill at ease in his presence as if a barrier had come between us'.

Scott takes issue with the often idolatrous approach to George by German
critics, and (given their homophobia) their consequent collective refusal to
deal with the fact of his homosexuality. Although he himself, as a teenager, was
distressed to discover that his cultural hero 'should have propensities which in
those days most normal people regarded with loathing and disgust', he did not
flee the man or reject his friendship; indeed, both then and in later life, what he
did reject was the notion that George's homosexuality must be recast as a purely
spiritual and intellectual interest in the relations between male souls, in order
to maintain his reputation as a great poet. As one who had been desired by
him, Scott felt he could legitimately bear witness to George's homosexuality,
but even he drew the line somewhere:

Yet let me not be misunderstood: I believe that Stefan George was too great an idealist to practise homosexuality in its grossest form. On the other hand, to pretend in these days of far greater tolerance [the late 1960s] that he was a man who merely admired youths, is to display that disregard for facts which simply turns biography into fiction . . . And, indeed, why should it be glossed over? George could no more help being a homosexual than, say, Chopin could help being a consumptive; and like many homosexuals and lesbians, he was not in the least ashamed of the fact, being almost obsessed, as he was, with Hellenistic ideas and ideals.[14]

The 'grossest form' of male homosexuality is usually anal intercourse. If Scott meant this, his reading of the situation seems entirely plausible. For many 'Hellenists', mutual masturbation and intercrural intercourse were just about as 'gross' as it got.

George published his last poetry in 1928. A self-imposed silence ensued. When he died on 4 December 1933 in voluntary exile at Locarno on Lake Maggiore, his friends protected his corpse from being taken back in triumph by the Nazis and interred on the sacred soil of the Third Reich. Among those who had stood vigil at George's deathbed was the twenty-six-year-old Claus Schenk Graf von Stauffenberg, who had joined the George Kreis at seventeen, along with his brothers. Many years later, on 20 July 1944, Stauffenberg, a lieutenant colonel wounded in action – he had lost one hand, two fingers of the other and the use of one eye – would place a briefcase bomb under the conference table in Hitler's East Prussian headquarters at Wolfsschanze and leave the room. The briefcase was moved, so that when it went off Hitler was only slightly injured. All of the conspiracy's leaders were executed. In the run-up to the assassination attempt Stauffenberg had taken to reciting George's poem 'The Antichrist'. As Joachim Fest puts it, 'Stauffenberg apparently found in the poem something that moved him, as it did many of his fellow conspirators: the projection of the enemy into the realm of myth, and hence the elevation of resistance into a sacred deed.' However, 'Although Stauffenberg was a great admirer of George, he always had an eye for simpler, rougher truths, and he led the debate within the resistance back to the political realm where it really belonged. Germans found themselves in a position, he argued, where they must inevitably commit some crime – either of commission or of omission.'[15]

Stefan George has had relatively few non-German admirers.[16] It is easy, on superficial acquaintance with his apparently sneering elitism, merely to ridicule or deplore him; and his poetry is not easily understood, let alone loved. After meeting him in Paris in 1908, André Gide declared himself 'Struck by the admirable head of St G. whom I had long hoped to know and whose work I admire every time I manage to understand it.'[17] In their libretto to Hans Werner Henze's *Elegy for Young Lovers*, W.H. Auden and Chester Kallman have the poet Gregor Mittenhofer refer dismissively to '*George* who so primly preaches / The love that dare not speak its name.'[18]

Nor was the lingering association with National Socialism of much help to George's international reputation. The great Polish poet Czesław Miłosz writes of some pro-Nazi, homosexual acquaintances of his, in Paris in 1935: 'They celebrated the age of chivalry, sacrifices and blood, and they had the sound of clanking swords.' One of them was Günter, who wrote poetry: 'Above all, that heavyset blond boy was imbued with Greece as it had been conceived by nineteenth-century German professors and with Hölderlin's nostalgia . . . His interest in Poles he justified by invoking the sacred tradition of friendship between Stefan George and Wacław Rolicz-Lieder', the Symbolist poet and translator of German poetry. Thus, George's choices of his own friends determined the choices of his younger admirers many years later. (Rolicz-Lieder had died in 1912.)

On the other hand, Miłosz also speaks of Stefan Napierski (Mark Eiger), a Jewish, homosexual aesthete and poet from a wealthy background, who translated Stefan George, Rainer Maria Rilke and Georg Trakl, and 'moved in elegant circles that took their cue from Weimar, Berlin or Paris'. He was eventually shot by the Nazis. Miłosz' language is no better than theirs when summing up this unfortunate man: 'Mark was the degenerate scion of a family of wealthy capitalists, owners of cement factories. He had all the earmarks of Middle Eastern Europeans of his type: money, a knowledge of foreign languages, a large collection of books, a neurosis, and homosexuality. In comparison with this pale, thin rodent in glasses . . . I was a specimen of vital, primitive strength.'[19]

One of the earliest enthusiasts in Britain for the idea of the George Kreis was the Oxford don Maurice Bowra, who may have been introduced to George's work by Edward Sackville-West. He was not impressed by the poetry – 'It all seems much of a muchness to me' – but he did like the idea of creating a sort of Bowra Kreis in Oxford. Indeed, he had done the ground work already. He told John Sparrow – also a don, also gay – 'I thought I would write to [George] and say that there is a circle of young man [*sic*] chosen for their looks who study his works in Oxford.' Unlike George, Bowra was able to take a light-hearted approach to lofty matters, but he was completely serious in admiring George's having revived and put into practice, in modern Germany, ancient Greek ideas. As Bowra's biographer puts it, 'Here were rules, Greek in origin, that offered some hope that the crucial values of the ancient world would not be lost and that poetry would always be a force in men's lives.'[20] Between 1928 and 1933, Bowra made frequent trips to Germany and even once caught sight of George in Heidelberg. Less fleetingly, he met several members of the Kreis and became especially close to one of them, Ernst Kantorowicz. They actually met in Oxford, when the German was a visiting professor at All Souls. It is possible that they were lovers; they certainly became lifelong friends. Bowra went to Germany to help Kantorowicz escape the Nazis, and later helped him land an academic post in the USA.

In Munich at the beginning of 1911 to improve his German, Rupert Brooke met Karl Wolfskehl, a member of Stefan George's circle, 'in appearance like a Bavarian Lytton Strachey'.[21] Wolfskehl attended George's salon and in turn would convene his own salons to pass on the master's wisdom. Brooke read some Swinburne at one of these latter events; George would doubtless have loved the look of him. In his autobiographical novel *In the Purely Pagan Sense* (1976), John Lehmann recalls his friend William speaking of a German boy for whom George's poetry appears to have been a necessary adjunct to his sexuality: 'He used to go about reciting the poems of Stefan George all day, believe it or not. He'd even go on reciting while he was doing it [that is, making love] – there's devotion to culture for you!'[22]

When the San Francisco poet Robert Duncan met fellow poet Jack Spicer in 1946, one of their first conversations was about Stefan George's Maximin cult. Duncan had been having an affair with Werner Vordtriede, who had had childhood connections with the George Kreis. As it happens, Spicer was studying medieval history with Ernst Kantorowicz. Spicer saw in Duncan an opportunity to set up an American version of the Kreis. Duncan moved into a communal household at 2029 Hearst Street, Berkeley, where nocturnal poetry readings and workshops were soon instituted.[23] On a visit to Berkeley, E.M. Forster called in on 2029, but he was unresponsive to the young poets until they served him tea and gin.[24]

## The Berlin Scene

In the 1931 census, Berlin recorded a population of 4,288,700. It was the third-largest city in the world, after London and New York. According to the French novelist Dominique Fernandez' reading of Europe's gay cultural history, 'The role played by Naples, Sicily, and North Africa at the beginning of the century passed, during the brief life of the Weimar Republic [1919–33], to a land in northern Europe' – namely Germany.[25] This is true, if not quite true enough. The fact is that, much as the name of Oscar Wilde acquired mythic status and came to stand for the type of the homosexual, so Weimar Berlin came to stand for urban homosexuality in both its identities, as both a place where dreams come true and a city of dreadful night. Its underworld was close to the surface and could easily be joined by interested parties or observed by fascinated outsiders, both friendly and hostile. It was a place that could change people's lives, for better or worse. Karl Heinrich Ulrichs' sister exclaimed, in response to his coming-out, 'Oh, if only you had never gone to Berlin!'[26]

A character in Stefan Zweig's novel *Confusion* (*Verwirrung der Gefühle*, 1927), while studying in Berlin, visits 'the underworld of the city' and has apparently homosexual encounters 'on dark street corners, in the shadows of railway stations and bridges' and in 'gloomy beer cellars whose dubious doors opened only to a certain kind of smile'.[27] The atmosphere of darkness, shadows and gloom in this brief sketch suggests furtive pleasures hidden away from the daytime streets, but gay life in Berlin was more varied and could be much more visible than this. To be sure, it had its share of clandestine spaces, indoor and out, its arcane penetralia, and its anonymous encounters and spurts of anti-gay violence; but there was also a gay political and social subculture in which the rights of homosexual individuals were argued for and law reform (repeal of the repressive Paragraph 175 of the penal code) was demanded. Homosexuality was being subjected to serious and intense scrutiny by sympathetic scientists, and openly discussed in many publications. There was also a vibrant tourist scene, in which visitors to the city could witness enactments of the 'decadence' for which the city was becoming famous. Looking back in 1976, Charlotte Wolff remembered the atmosphere of Berlin in the 1920s as having no boundaries: 'All the men came to these clubs and they *loved* lesbians. No nonsense. There were also masked balls at the Academy of Arts. I danced with women, I danced with men. We didn't think anything about it. You loved somebody or you loved nobody but you looked upon everything with delight.'[28]

In Alfred Döblin's great novel of Weimar life, *Berlin Alexanderplatz* (1929), Franz Biberkopf has his attention drawn to the city's homosexual population by the proprietor of a news-stand on the Hackesche Market in front of Oranienburger Strasse, from whom Franz is hoping for gainful employment. The old man thrusts a bundle of gay papers into Franz' arms and gets him to attend a public meeting the same evening, called in agitation against Paragraph 175 – 'Franz might hear something about the wrong done to a million people in Germany every day.' Although reluctant – 'A fellow might feel sorry for those boys, but they're none o' my business' – Franz allows himself to be taken to the meeting by the news vendor. In the hall they find 'almost nothing but men, mostly very young, and a few women, who sat apart in couples'. Embarrassed and self-conscious, Franz endures as much as he can bear of the meeting – 'it was too ridiculous for words, so many nancies in a bunch' – before making his escape. The last thing he hears as he leaves is a discussion of a new police ordinance in the city of Chemnitz: 'This forbids all inverts to go on the streets or use the public lavatories, and, if they are caught, it costs them 30 marks.' In the morning, notwithstanding his apparent lack of interest in the meeting, Franz settles down to read the gay newspapers still in his possession.

Döblin follows this sequence with the brief narrative of a married man who encounters a good-looking boy in the Tiergarten and is soon under his spell. Although 'he has noticed these things before', the man has apparently had no experience of them until now. More knowing than he looks, the boy gets the man to take him to a small hotel – 'You can give me five marks, or ten, I'm quite broke' – where they are shown to a room which is fitted with peepholes. Once the man has done enough to be blackmailed for, the hotel proprietor and his wife reveal themselves as blackmailers. He thinks of killing himself, but instead ignores the whole matter, hoping it will go away. However, he has been denounced to the authorities, and his wife and daughters get to hear of the case. In court, the man pleads his case with innocent eloquence – 'I went to a room, locked myself in. Is it my fault if they have those peepholes? . . . Did I steal anything? Did I commit a burglary? I only broke into a dear boy's heart. I said to him: my sunshine. And so he was' – and is, implausibly, acquitted.[29]

These two fragmentary glimpses of gay life are characteristically unspectacular in a novel that concerns itself with the daily routines of ordinary people. Döblin moves on. But one important point has been made: the lives of homosexual people take shape not in the scandalous cabarets and nightclubs, where stretching the boundaries of the permitted is a crucial component of a style directed at an excitable audience, but in the attempts by ordinary individuals to establish their own private lives. Hoping to bring love into their homes, they have to seek it where they can.

The novel *The Hustler* (*Der Puppenjunge*, 1926), by 'Sagitta', depicts fragments of the gay scene in 1920s Berlin while telling the story of a year in the life of a young male prostitute. 'Sagitta' was John Henry Mackay, who was brought up by his mother in her native Germany after his Scottish father died when he was two. He spent most of his adult life in Berlin. An anarchist much influenced by the philosopher Max Stirner, of whom he wrote a biography, early in the new century he embarked on a series of *Sagitta's Books of the Nameless Love* (*Die Bücher der namenlosen Liebe von Sagitta*), books including poetry, fiction and non-fiction, which, although subjected to a ban in Germany, were republished abroad in 1913. In one of the scenes in *The Hustler*, two men dressed as women celebrate one of their birthdays at a table in the Adonis Lounge, cheerfully dispensing champagne and schnapps to the boys who cluster around them. Two other men, inexperienced out-of-towners not wishing to be left out, run up a massive drinks bill to get themselves and two of the boys drunk. As the evening progresses the dancing begins and the Adonis Lounge delivers its tawdry magic. Men get boys and boys get money.

A far more varied economy is portrayed in the activities taking place, by day, in 'the Passage', a shopping arcade between Unter den Linden and the Friedrichstrasse. According to Sagitta's account, the Passage is alive with 'Crowds of the curious and indifferent, the casual and the occasional, as well as the seekers, amateur and professional in these matters – the native and the stranger'. Alongside the respectable routines of everyday life, 'Vice and inexperience, swindlers and racketeers of all kinds, carried on their business there . . . [T]here was no questionable livelihood that did not find its way there.' Penniless youngsters go there to barter their bodies for a meal and a bed for the night; 'apprentices and errand boys' go there to augment their meagre wages; boys who are not yet interested in girls go there to make friends or even lovers; schoolboys go there to make some pocket money or just to make fun of the 'queers' . . . This commerce of compatible interests goes on from early in the morning until late at night, when the Passage is locked, the schoolboys are in bed, as are many of the rent boys and their clients, and the remains of the day's cruising must happen elsewhere.[30] When W.H. Auden spoke to a rent boy in the Passage to arrange an assignation, he said he pictured himself as Proust's Baron de Charlus. In 'The Nowaks', one of the sections of *Goodbye to Berlin*, Christopher Isherwood writes about a boy called Pieps, a pickpocket who plies his trade on the Friedrichstrasse, 'not far from the Passage, which was full of detectives and getting too dangerous nowadays'. Isherwood makes it look as if he is referring to a crackdown on pickpockets, whereas it is more likely that the detectives are there to cut down on incidents of prostitution.[31]

Klaus Mann wrote about this same world in his novel *The Pious Dance* (*Der fromme Tanz*, 1925), the central character of which is a young teenager, Andreas Magnus, who leaves home and makes his way to Berlin. The usual encounters with low-life and bedbugs lead, eventually, to a minor role in a nightclub cabaret. From there, he goes on to frequent the haunts of his new friends, the rent boys in downmarket gay bars. These places serve as the boys' best refuge from the vastness of the city and, to some extent, as the last line of defence against the worst forms of exploitation. Above all, they provide the companionship of other disadvantaged boys. It is the infrastructure of the gay scene that keeps them from the streets – at the same time as it makes them more safely available to the men who patronise the bars. (More safely for both the boys and the men.) The men in whose arms the boys make their meagre living often offer to 'rescue' them from this communal life, but Andreas is never tempted by such offers. He always manages to preserve his own independence.

One of the more interesting aspects of this narrative is the way in which Klaus Mann represents Andreas' self-education as a homosexual man. Working in the bars and cabarets he soon becomes streetwise about how the scene and its denizens operate. Yet there is more to a mature identity than the necessary accumulation of that kind of defensive knowledge. There is also, for those boys with the appropriate intelligence and inclination, homosexual culture to be learned. After a long break, and for the first time since he left home, Andreas again gets into the habit of reading. His bibliography is both international and gay: he devours Knut Hamsun, Walt Whitman and Stefan George; then Hermann Bang, Paul Verlaine and Oscar Wilde. From each he draws profound conclusions about love and, given the nature of the age, about suffering. It is clear that the author, himself from a phenomenally bookish background, regards this period of placid introspection among heaps of books as equipping Andreas with the strength of character to survive the vicissitudes that merely being homosexual is likely to inflict on him. The scene and the culture, together, will enable him, above all, to tell false love from true.

## Magnus Hirschfeld

The scientific curiosity, bureaucratic method and sexual experimentalism of Germany in general and Berlin in particular became fused in the most practical way under a single roof: that of Magnus Hirschfeld's Institute for Sexual Science. It was a research centre, museum, library, guest house, social centre, campaigning organisation and therapeutic clinic – all, ultimately, to be destroyed by hostile ideologues.

Hirschfeld's first publication on homosexuality was an essay entitled 'Sappho and Socrates: How can one explain the love of men and women for people of their own sex?' It was published by Max Spohr of Leipzig in 1896.[32] Hirschfeld was in his late twenties at the time, with a questing intelligence and already reasonably well travelled. (He had been on a five-month trip to the United States, Morocco, Algeria and Italy in 1893 and 1894.) Before shooting himself on the eve of his marriage, a patient of Hirschfeld's had written to him, asking him to publicise his case – that of a human being cursed by homosexuality. The 1896 essay was the first of many pioneering contributions with which Hirschfeld may be said to have carried out the suicide's wishes, but it does not present homosexuality, male or female, as a curse. When speaking of the recent Wilde case, Hirschfeld does some familiar name-dropping:

> Oscar Wilde, this genius of a writer, who loves Lord Alfred Douglas with a passionate love, has been put into prison in Wandsworth. And this because of a passion which he shares with Socrates, Michelangelo and Shakespeare.

By now, Wilde was in Reading, not Wandsworth, and it is hard to imagine these three eminent boy-fanciers ever falling for Bosie Douglas. (Shakespeare, perhaps – but Socrates?) Regardless of the details, this is a restatement of a common position at the time (and, indeed, quite a common one ever since). The concentration on major artists and the concentration on love rather than sex (the pertinent matter in the case) follows Wilde's own attempted self-defence when on trial; and, although Hirschfeld would continue to repeat this argument throughout his career, he would soon turn his attention in a more undissembling fashion towards sexual desires and activities. In this same essay he refers to lesbians as 'those courageous "manly" women of high intelligence, rhetorical gifts and natural leadership', thereby engaging in a similar argument, which evidently leaves no room for lesser specimens, or even for the feminine lesbian. At this early stage, it was important not to cloud the issue with unrecognisable examples; a handful of stereotypes would be extremely useful for the time being.[33]

On 15 May 1897, Magnus Hirschfeld, Max Spohr and Edward Oberg drew up the Articles of Association of an organisation called the Scientific-Humanitarian Committee (*Wissenschaftlich-humanitäre Komitee*) whose main brief was to campaign for the repeal of Paragraph 175 of the 1871 Imperial Penal Code. (The paragraph stipulated a maximum sentence of five years' imprisonment for sex between men.) A petition they submitted to the Reichstag later the following year had 2,000 names on it, including those of Frank Wedekind, Rainer Maria Rilke and Heinrich and Thomas Mann (but the latter subsequently withdrew his). A tireless empirical researcher, Hirschfeld visited homosexual homes, bars and hotels in Berlin, and published his findings in *Berlin's Third Sex* (*Berlins drittes Geschlecht*, 1904). In December 1903 he sent sexual orientation questionnaires to 3,000 male students; in February 1904, to 5,000 metalworkers. Objecting to questions they did not want to answer, six of the students took him to court; found guilty of propagating obscene enquiries, he was fined and ordered to pay costs. (Of the students who did respond to the survey, 1.5 per cent were homosexual and 3.19 per cent bisexual.) By 1904, the Scientific-Humanitarian Committee had 365 members. One of these, who signed up in 1902, was the Baron Hermann von Teschenberg who had been a close friend of Oscar Wilde's when living in exile in England; he subsequently became Wilde's German translator. After the 1895 scandal, he had left London for Paris, and then returned to Berlin, where he spent the rest of his life fighting for homosexual rights. He died in Naples in 1911.

Even at this early stage in his career, Hirschfeld had to get used to being attacked, both as a corrupter of public morals and as a Jew. Because he was trying to maintain a reputation as an objective doctor and scientist, he was not generally known to be homosexual himself. If there were those who felt that his empathy for homosexual people amounted to the fellow feeling of identification, they seem to have been few. Anti-Semitism was probably always the greater threat to him and his work. After a sequence of attacks in 1908, he travelled south for a spell in the warmer atmosphere of Italy. Even in doing so, his identification travelled with him – he never ceased his investigations for anything so self-indulgent as a holiday – and he visited the grave of Johann Joachim Winckelmann in Trieste on his way home. Over the great art historian's bones he read out the passages in the *Italian Journey* (*Italienische Reise*) where Goethe heaps praise on Winckelmann. Such a cultural tribute obviously meant a great deal to Hirschfeld, and the more he learned about the history of men who loved other men, the more care he took to make connections between his own work and the lives of men he regarded as his cultural predecessors. So when he next went to Italy, in the spring of 1909, he chose to visit Aquila in the Abruzzi because that had been where 'Numa Numantius' (Karl Heinrich Ulrichs) had retired in 1882; he also made a pilgrimage to Ulrichs' grave.

Hirschfeld's international reputation was greatly enhanced by an address he delivered, accompanied by 150 slides, at an International Congress of Physicians convened in London by the British Medical Association in August 1913. He was especially impressed by suffragist demonstrators who livened up the proceedings in the Albert Hall with their shouts of 'Votes for women!' It was at this event that he met both Havelock Ellis and Edward Carpenter. The following year, he finally published his major work – 1,068 pages, based on 10,000 case histories – *Homosexuality in Men and Women* (*Die Homosexualität des Mannes und des Weibes*, 1914). Having thus established his credentials as at least one of the world's leading authorities on the topic, he did not allow himself to pause for breath. Nor did the outbreak of war permit him to do so. One task he set himself was to give homosexual men who had been turned down for active service a sense of collective purpose. (Too old at forty-six for the call-up himself, he was in any case a pacifist.) Whether he succeeded to any significant extent is doubtful, but his strategy of delivering as many lectures and writing as many articles for popular outlets as he could must have provided a degree of succour to the men he was talking about. The message was simple: that they sought, and deserved, equality with other men.

Early in 1919, he acquired the mansion at In den Zelten 10, Berlin, which became the world's first Institute for Sexual Science. Above the door he raised the inscription – in Latin, of course – 'Sacred to Love and Sorrow'. The fact that there was a need, and demand, for such a place seems proven by its first year's statistics: 4,000 people visited it, and within it no fewer than 1,250 lectures were given. Hirschfeld's younger lover, Karl Giese, whom he met soon after acquiring the building, had living accommodation on the same floor as the director's consulting room. Not surprisingly, even before the first year was over, it was clear that more space would be needed; so, in 1921, Hirschfeld bought the house next door, number 9A. On 2 February 1924, he handed over the Institute to the German State as the Dr Magnus Hirschfeld Foundation. It is a measure of the official respect accorded his work that the ceremonial occasion to mark the transfer was attended by the Minister of Justice, the Finance Minister, and the Minister for Art and Science.

In 1919, Hirschfeld had been approached by the film-maker Richard Oswald with a suggestion that they put together a film on the topic of homosexuality. The successful outcome was *Different from the Rest* (*Anders als die Andern*, 1919), starring Conrad Veidt. It included a performance by Hirschfeld himself as a doctor speaking out against blackmail and Paragraph 175. It was first screened on 24 May. Despite the superficially liberal atmosphere of the Weimar Republic, in this case manifested in positive responses to the film by a number of senior politicians, a campaign was successfully waged against it (by, among others, the sexologist Albert Moll) and by August 1920 it had been banned. From now on, those who opposed Hirschfeld and the work of the Institute seem to have sensed the vulnerability of the whole sexual health movement. They certainly learned that they would be able to wound it quite easily. When he gave lectures, Hirschfeld now had to get used to being heckled. Stink-bombs were often thrown into the halls in which he was speaking. After one lecture in Munich, a bunch of thugs spat in his face and then beat him unconscious. (No action was ever taken against them.) Although he came round in hospital, the wires carried news of his death across Europe. When he lectured in Vienna on 4 February 1923, Hirschfeld was interrupted by young Nazis, throwing stink-bombs and firing live rounds. Some audience members were beaten up, but this time Hirschfeld survived unhurt. A softer kind of attack had often come from other directions: his seriousness about sex was, after all, ripe to be satirised. René Crevel always mocked him and his Institute, and in his novel *Etes-vous fous?* (1929) lampooned him as the charlatan Dr Optimus Cerf-Mayer. Klaus Mann scolded Crevel for this lese-majesty.

In 1926 Hirschfeld accepted an invitation from the Soviet government to visit the USSR, taking the trip as an opportunity to observe the effects of Soviet sexual laws; he refrained from delivering any outright criticism while he was there. In the meantime, the internationalisation of the movement was gathering momentum. At a congress presided over by Hirschfeld, Havelock Ellis and August Forel in Copenhagen in 1928, the World League for Sexual Reform was founded. The next congress was held at the Wigmore Hall in London in

1929; Hirschfeld delivered the presidential address. The congress of 1930 was held in Vienna. Spreading his message further afield, Hirschfeld went to New York after the Vienna meeting, and then carried out an extensive lecture tour across the USA, receiving generous publicity all the way. By the time he left the USA on 1 March 1931, he had earned enough money to return to Germany the long way, by way of a world tour. He spent six weeks in Japan, then a further ten in China. There he met a twenty-three-year-old called Tao Li, who offered to travel with him as his interpreter. The boy's father, who had twenty-one other children, formally handed him into Hirschfeld's care. Tao Li went with him, far beyond the limits of his range as an interpreter, all the way home to Germany.

On 4 July, they set sail together for the Philippines; then, on the 10th, they went on to Bali. Like his earlier travels, for all its incidental pleasures, this was no holiday. Hirschfeld was both teaching and learning all the way. Even on the steamer to Bali, the *Tjinegara*, he gave a sexological lecture to the officers and first-class passengers. (Someone must have objected to the lower orders hearing about such matters.) He spent six weeks with Tao Li in Java, flew to Singapore – where they stayed, of course, in the Raffles Hotel – and took another steamer to Ceylon. On 8 September, while still on board ship, Hirschfeld gave the hundredth lecture of his tour. From Ceylon, they crossed to India. In Calcutta, where he delivered five lectures, they called in on the great poet Rabindranath Tagore. At Benares, although disturbed by what he regarded as Hindu fanaticism, Hirschfeld bathed in the Ganges. In Allahabad, they were met at the station by Jawaharlal Nehru, in whose house they stayed; Hirschfeld was allocated the bedroom Mahatma Gandhi had slept in. But in Agra, where the two lovers visited the Taj Mahal, Hirschfeld was bitten by Anopheles mosquitoes and subsequently developed malaria. Undeterred, he went on travelling and lecturing, usually in English. On 15 November they embarked for Egypt, via the Suez Canal, with Hirschfeld feverish most of the way. In Cairo, purely in the interests of science, he tried hashish. They went up the Nile to Luxor and Aswan, then down to Alexandria. Five weeks followed in Palestine, two of them in Jerusalem, where they stayed in the King David Hotel. As a Jew, Hirschfeld took a particular interest in this leg of the journey; he was especially concerned to find signs of developing tensions between Jews and Arabs. On 14 March 1932, the two men embarked on the *Byron* from Beirut, heading for Athens, where Karl Giese met them.

Giese's news was unwelcome. He had to warn Hirschfeld that he would not be safe if he returned to Berlin. For a brief moment, the three men enjoyed Athens together – as Charlotte Wolff puts it, 'With Karl Giese his beloved companion on one side, and his devoted pupil Tao Li on the other, life was still good for Hirschfeld' – before Giese returned to Berlin to run the Institute and Hirschfeld went to Zurich for a month.[34] In September, he went on to the fifth congress of the World League for Sexual Reform, which that year was held in Brünn (Brno), in Czechoslovakia. There was another trip to Italy early in the new year, before he returned to Zurich where he stayed for a while with both of the men he loved. This was no idyll, however, for Giese had just witnessed, in Berlin, between 6 and 10 May 1933, the sacking of the Institute by Nazi thugs and the public burning of all its unique records and the contents of its library. Some 20,000 books and 5,000 images were destroyed, and the Institute's list of names and addresses was seized, putting many lives and livelihoods in danger. The conflagration was also witnessed by Christopher Isherwood, who, many years later, briefly recorded the event, as usual referring to himself in the third person: 'A few days after the raid [on the Institute], the seized books and papers were publicly burned, along with a bust of Hirschfeld, on the square in front of the Opera House. Christopher, who was present in the crowd, said "shame"; but not loudly.'[35] There was a wave of copycat burnings around the country, mainly concentrated on the destruction of books by Jewish authors. Not until the development of Alfred Kinsey's institute for sexual research at Indiana University would any equivalent resource of sexual information be gathered in one place. The buildings were confiscated by the Nazis, and with them went that apparently safe space in which marginalised people had felt they could meet each other or read about themselves, and to which so many foreign visitors were attracted in order to affirm their sense of belonging to their own kind.

While Karl Giese took a three-week break in Locarno, Hirschfeld moved to Paris, where in April 1934 he founded the Institute des Sciences Sexologiques; Giese joined him there. The old man was shown a film of the destruction of the Institute in Berlin. However, by the autumn it was clear that the new Parisian institute was failing, and Hirschfeld moved to Nice, intending to stay for good. Giese went to London, meaning to qualify as a doctor, but moved on to Vienna instead; Tao Li went back to Zurich to complete his studies. On 14 May 1935, Hirschfeld had a stroke and collapsed on his doorstep, went into a coma and died. Karl Giese gave the funeral oration, calling his lover 'a gentle fanatic' (*ein weicher Fanatiker*).[36]

## Visitors to Berlin

Returning to Greece after three months in Russia in 1927, the Greek writer Nikos Kazantzakis found when he paused in Berlin and Vienna, either that 'The world had changed' or that he was now looking at it differently:

The brazen dances, barbaric modern music, mascaraed women, mascaraed men, the cuttingly ironic smile, the lust for gold and kisses – everything that had formerly seemed so strange and enticing to me, now called forth nausea and horror. I saw that they were portents of the end. An oppressive stink hung in the air, as though the world was rotting. Sodom and Gomorrah must have smelt the same.[37]

His chapter on an earlier sojourn in Berlin mentions none of this, whether 'strange and enticing' or not. Only when it seems ominous does he think it worth mentioning; but he only does so, now, very briefly. His literal journey is part of a metaphorical, spiritual one – the substance of his book – and the odour of materiality is not his point. Although his three masters are Christ, the Buddha and Lenin, it is the Old Testament he invokes, and the Cities of the Plain, to anathematise the modern pleasure-lovers of Berlin and Vienna. Also visiting Berlin in the late 1920s, but from Vienna, Elias Canetti wrote:

> Anything went. The taboos, of which there was no lack anywhere, especially in Germany, dried out here. You could come from an old capital like Vienna and feel like a provincial here, and you gaped until your eyes grew accustomed to remaining open. There was something pungent, corrosive in the atmosphere; it stimulated and animated. You charged into everything and were afraid of nothing ... Any attempt at shutting yourself off had something perverse about it, and it was the only thing that could still be regarded as perverse.[38]

Like Kazantzakis, Canetti was heterosexual, but even homosexual visitors could be shocked by the city, if only on first acquaintance. After initial doubts, the English writer Michael Davidson found Berlin 'the most exciting town one could conceive of: Babylon, Gomorrah, Rome in decay'. He first went there in 1928 and soon began to frequent Magnus Hirschfeld's Institute. He noticed that the cruising in the streets began as early as at nine in the morning. He found the authorities indulgent: seeing him in an argument with an aggressive youth, a policeman once said to him, 'You know, you should be very careful about what boys you pick up – there are some bad ones about.' With his Berlin lover, Werner, he explored the scene. He mentions such places as the Nüremberger Diele and the Kantdiele, where 'middle-aged stockbrokers danced with elegant pansies'; a bar called the Schnubart Diele, the moustache café, 'where men with magnificent moustaches went to meet other men with moustaches'; the Mikado, for cross-dressing women and men; an unnamed establishment 'devoted to plump, elderly men who came in little short knickers and sailor suits'; the Monte-Casino, full of teenage boys; and Davidson's own personal favourite – 'because, I suppose, it was so touching, and tore at my mother's heart' – the Adonis-Diele with its bored and hungry boys, all looking for a meal and a bed for the night.[39]

Robert McAlmon went to Berlin in the early 1920s and later described returning home from riotous nights, arriving 'at my huge room at eight in the morning accompanied by a retinue of various sexes'. He was both excited and disturbed by the street scenes that so many visitors commented on:

> At nights along the Unter den Linden it was never possible to know whether it was a woman or a man in woman's clothes who accosted one. That didn't matter, but it was sad to know that innumerable young and normal Germans were doing anything, from dope selling to every form of prostitution, to have money for themselves and their families, their widowed mothers and younger brothers and sisters.[40]

In 1924 Edward Sackville-West went to Freiburg to be psychoanalysed with regard to his homosexuality by one Dr Marten. Other homosexual friends were there, enjoying each other while trying to imagine enjoying women. Not surprisingly, Eddy liked Germany. He stayed in Dresden from the autumn of 1927 to the following spring. Christmas was spent with Harold Nicolson in Berlin: 'The night life of that city,' Eddy said, 'is really very strange indeed.'[41] He gave an account of that strangeness in a letter to E.M. Forster, and later he went back for more: he returned to Berlin for the winter of 1928–29. One evening in 1929, as if he had never been before, Nicolson got a detective to show him around Berlin's gay bars, but they depressed him. In a letter to his wife (12 April 1929) he commented, 'I do not like other people's vices.'[42] In November 1924, the novelist Hugh Walpole went to Berlin to hear his friend the Danish tenor Lauritz Melchior singing at the Opera, and found the city 'dirty and exceedingly wicked.'[43] The English painter Glyn Philpot visited the city in 1931, perhaps in large part because he was having a relationship with a young German, Karl Heinz Müller. According to one account, 'The inspection of the Berlin underworld celebrated in [his painting] *Lokal, Berlin* . . . was certainly a shock to his somewhat idealistic view of life and may well have induced a certain amount of self-examination.'[44]

W.H. Auden first travelled to the city in October 1928. Apart from brief visits home, he would spend ten months in Germany, seven of them in Berlin. Christopher Isherwood visited him there for a fortnight in March 1929. On a Saturday – the 16th or 23rd – they visited Hirschfeld's Institute, had a meal with John Layard, and ended up at the Cosy Corner, a bar at Zossenstrasse 7, in the working-class district, Hallesches Tor. There Isherwood found a boy called 'Bubi' and fell for him as if this were the real thing, the love of his life.

Auden watched them playing table tennis. He wrote in his diary, 'The sense of bare flesh, the blue sky through the glass and the general sexy atmosphere made me feel like a participant in a fertility rite.'[45] He also wrote a poem, 'This One', in which he casts a sceptical eye over Isherwood's self-delusive yearning for true love. Famously, it begins: 'Before this loved one / Was that one and that one.' John Sutherland says of Auden's attitude to rent boys: 'one paid them not for sex, but to go away after sex and leave one in peace to the more important business of writing.'[46] Although in *Christopher and His Kind* (1977) Isherwood claimed that 'To Christopher, Berlin meant Boys', Norman Page has counter-claimed that, in actuality, 'Isherwood went to Berlin primarily to work' – that is, to write *The Memorial* and to earn his crust by teaching English.[47] He was also, of course, learning German – for the sole purpose, he later claimed, of talking to his sexual partners. He wrote:

> For him, the entire German language – all the way from the keep off the grass signs in the park to Goethe's stanza on the wall [of Hirschfeld's Institute] – was irradiated with Sex. For him, the difference between a table and ein Tisch was that a table was the dining-table in his mother's house and ein Tisch was ein Tisch in the Cosy Corner.[48]

In his autobiographical novel *In the Purely Pagan Sense* (1976), John Lehmann wrote about having been taken by Isherwood to the same bar, the Cosy Corner. He spoke of this as 'a sensational experience' and 'a kind of emotional earth-quake'. His first sight of the place offered opportunities he had never dared imagine: 'The place was filled with attractive boys of any age between sixteen and twenty-one, some fair and curly-haired, some dark and often blue-eyed, and nearly all dressed in extremely short *lederhosen* which showed off their smooth and sun-burnt thighs to delectable advantage.' As soon as they arrived, Isherwood (here called William) sent him off to the toilets for a further lesson in availability: 'I was followed in by several boys, who, as if by chance, ranged themselves on either side of me and pulled out their cocks rather to show them off than to relieve nature as I was doing. I don't think a drop fell into the gutter from any of them; but many sly grins were cast in my direction'. When he went back to their table, he and William were joined by two other boys. William told him to put his hands in their pockets. 'I put one hand into the outer *lederhosen* pocket of the one on my left, and my other hand into the outer pocket of the one on my right. They were both now snuggling up to me. I had a shock of more than surprise when I found that the pockets had been cut off inside, and my hands went straight through to their sex.' He began to kiss both boys, but 'out of a shyness that I had not yet overcome' did not take either of them home.

He and William went on to several other *lokals*, but it was to the Cosy Corner that his thoughts kept returning. 'I was in a daze, my head swimming with pretty boys' inviting smiles and inviting thighs.'[49]

Other, more lavish establishments, were designed to cater for the needs of tourists from the provinces and abroad. Isherwood generalises about these lucrative joints in *Christopher and His Kind*:

> In the West End there were also dens of pseudo-vice catering to hetero-sexual tourists. Here, screaming boys in drag and monocled Eton-cropped girls in dinner-jackets play-acted the high jinks of Sodom and Gomorrah, horrifying the onlookers and reassuring them that Berlin was still the most decadent city in Europe.[50]

This was a 'decadence' staged to give an adequate frisson of transgression without the audience's having to mix with real transgressors; and, of course, they paid for this privilege. In *Goodbye to Berlin*, Isherwood concentrates these enactments of vice into the portrayal of a single nightclub, which we are to understand as being typical:

> The Salomé turned out to be very expensive and even more depressing than I had imagined. A few *stage lesbians* and some young men with plucked eyebrows lounged at the bar, uttering occasional raucous guffaws or treble hoots – supposed, apparently, to *represent* the laughter of the damned. The whole premises are painted gold and inferno-red – crimson plush inches thick, and vast gilded mirrors. It was pretty full. The audience consisted chiefly of respectable middle-aged tradesmen and their families, exclaiming in good-humoured amazement: 'Do they really?' and 'Well, I never!' We went out half-way through the cabaret *performance*, after a young man in a spangled crinoline and jewelled breast-caps had painfully but successfully executed three splits.[51]

Although a mere visitor to the city himself, Isherwood was more than theo-retically involved in the city's gay scene with particular gay Germans, and was actually living amid the social realities of Hirschfeld's Institute for a while. To the subjective objectivity of his camera-I, the Salomé's display of display is unbearable. Its portrayals of same-sex desire have nothing to do with the real lives of gay Berliners. The heterosexual audiences it caters for experience not desire but the satisfying superiority of their own judgemental tolerance. Not much will have to change before they decide that the tolerable is intolerable, after all.

On 7 November 1932, in Berlin, Count Harry Kessler had dinner with the French novelist Roger Martin du Gard, among others. Kessler recorded the Frenchman's impressions in his diary:

> It is his first visit and what fascinates him most is the life in the streets, 'la Rue de Berlin'. The people he sees there seem to him quite different from those in Paris; the future is reflected in their looks. The new man, the man of the future, is being created in Germany ... Martin du Gard is much impressed with the fine appearance of the German race. The handsome boys and beautiful young girls are, to him, a reincarnation of ancient Greece.[52]

Earlier in the year, in Paris (26 August 1932), Kessler had found the French mesmerised by developments in Germany – and not just the politics: 'Murky factors like bathing in the buff ("le nudisme"), dives where pretty boys substitute for girls, and the reassessment of moral factors among German youth have their part in the almost pathological interest taken in Germany.'[53]

Martin du Gard reported back to André Gide on the wonders and delights of Berlin, where he had found the young involved in 'natural, gratuitous pleasures, sport, bathing, free love, games, [and] a truly pagan, Dionysiac freedom'. He spent most of his time there wandering around 'the less salubrious districts of the city', noticing (relative to Paris) the many prostitutes of both sexes and the ready availability of pornography.[54] Encouraged by such reports, André Gide visited Berlin no fewer than five times in 1933. He, too, was delighted by, and seriously interested in, what he found there, although he did concede to Robert Levesque that Paris itself was slowly becoming more Berlin-like even if at the same time (to use that most erotically evocative of geographical terms) more 'southern'.[55] The two writers coincided in Berlin in October, Gide arriving for a fortnight, Martin du Gard for five weeks. They did their best to avoid each other on their forays into the sexual underworld, but always dutifully compared notes on what they had seen and experienced. They disagreed, for instance, on guesswork statistics concerning how many of the male prostitutes on the streets and in the clubs were actually homosexual.

Martin du Gard posed as a specialist in matters sexual in order to attend interviews with homosexual men at Hirschfeld's Institute. He also toured the gay clubs, nominating as his favourites the Hollandais and the lesbian Monocle. Christopher Isherwood was at Hirschfeld's Institute on the day that Gide was given a guided tour, Gide 'in full costume as The Great French Novelist, complete with cape'. Retrospectively calling him a 'Sneering culture-conceited frog!' from the safety of the mid-1970s – and in doing so sounding like a rather uptight, Francophobic D.H. Lawrence – Isherwood failed to consider that Gide's pose might have been a way of giving Hirschfeld's project the serious imprimatur of a symbolic cultural visit, to which the cape and the performed 'greatness' were essential embellishments.[56]

The English novelist William Plomer's wealthy friend Anthony Butts took him to Europe in May 1930. When they reached Berlin a friend of a friend showed them around the gay scene. In his memoir *At Home* (1958), Plomer would write of pre-Hitlerite Berlin: 'the then notorious night life was something well worth seeing. Blatant impudicity on such a scale was certainly exciting to youthful senses, but there was something desperately sad about it – and at times something grotesquely funny.' At times, he found, it was neither sad nor funny. In a club called The Sign of the Cross the floor-show included an enema display that he thought simply disgusting. On one occasion, Plomer and Butts encountered André Gide, 'apparently taking his pleasures with his usual seriousness.'[57] The travellers moved on to Venice and then Athens, but Plomer would later go back to Berlin in his fiction.[58]

One of the protagonists of Plomer's 1952 novel *Museum Pieces* is Toby d'Arfey, a standard (if heterosexual) aesthete in the Anthony Blanche mould (see Chapter Six), based on Tony Butts. One character says of him, 'He's an aesthete, but he's tough. He has a feminine streak, but the nicest men often have, don't you think?' When she first sees him, the narrator, Jane Valance, thinks his face suggests 'a man who loved pleasure although he saw through it'. What she thinks of as his 'Feminine ruthlessness', she comments drily, 'is not one of the qualities I like in a man'. He has a tendency to notice the lesbians around him – as when a distant female cousin's legacy goes to what he calls 'an ambiguous, or perhaps I had better say an *un*ambiguous female companion, a burning Sappho from Ilfracombe, by all accounts' – or to invent them – as when the housekeeper says to his mother, 'When I'm with you I feel just as I used to with my husband.' On his travels he has spent some weeks in Harlem. He reads Ronald Firbank and Vernon Lee. He thinks a school containing boys 'of all ages' from eight to eighteen is 'Very irregular. It must be a hotbed of vice.' He has a close relationship with Lydia Delap, a woman ten years older than he, who at the end of the Great War was in London, mixing with 'would-be aesthetes, and half-baked intellectuals, for the most part male, or ostensibly male, rather than female, though she had for a time an ambiguously close friendship with a young woman of striking appearance, who died of taking drugs'. She then moved to Paris, where 'She had a fatal attraction for the more effete of the younger American expatriates, to whom she became a sort of broody, fascinating, and corruptive elder sister.'[59]

It was in Paris, surrounded by these 'lost generation' nonentities that Toby
first met her; and it is with her that he travels to Berlin, at roughly the moment
of Isherwood's *Goodbye to Berlin*, when Communists and Nazis are vying for
possession of the streets. The idea of the trip came from Lydia, but the narrator
explains why it appeals to Toby:

> Berlin had the reputation at that time of being 'gay' with a freedom else
> where unknown and in some ways unprecedented. Of course he knew, as
> every thoughtful person knew, that it was gaiety and freedom of a kind that
> could not last, because it was morbid, desperate, and precarious; but the
> very precariousness and perversity of the 'life' it notoriously offered to the
> moneyed and enterprising visitor was an attraction to one who, like Toby,
> had at once a rage for life and a foreboding of finality.[60]

Jane's use of 'gay' is meant not in the specifically homosexual sense, restricted
at the time she is speaking of to a fairly narrow range of speakers, but in the
more general sense of an openness to pleasures which might, indeed, verge on
the scandalous. The 'unknown' and 'unprecedented' gayness of the place would
include nocturnal clubs and cabarets, including strip-shows catering to heterosexual men, jazz clubs frequented by both African and American Negroes, as
well as the queer haunts of homosexual women and men and cross-dressers of
all the genders. Whether the sense of foreboding emanates from the relative
primness of Jane Valance or from the hindsight of William Plomer, is not
immediately obvious. Jane does not yet know – or rather, she shows no sign of
knowing – that the streets are violently contested. (Toby will write to her later
about 'nasty attacks by gangs of political yahoos' from left and right.[61]) She has
no real reason to suggest that 'every thoughtful person' must be aware that the
gaiety of Berlin cannot last. But Toby, seeing the place at first hand, might get
an inkling of this possibility – if he really is as 'thoughtful' as Jane suggests.

We readers do not see Toby's Berlin at first hand; we receive it third-hand,
from Jane, via a long letter she receives from Toby. He reports that Lydia, who
'finds romantic what some people would find absurd or repulsive or merely
pointless', has discovered 'a Lesbian League' – 'She isn't one herself, of course',
he adds – which is 'organized like a sort of YWCA, with hostels, a magazine of
its own, and so on.' But she is 'more interested in the male counterpart of all
that, which is very much in evidence'. They want to visit 'a Lesbian *lokal*'
together, and then 'the other sort'. Outlandishly, they decide that in order to do
so without looking like heterosexual tourists, one of them must go to each
venue in drag – he as a woman to the lesbian bar, she as a man to the gay male
one. Toby describes the lesbians they encounter:

Such an extraordinary assembly of women you can't imagine – all shapes
and sizes and classes and nationalities, one might almost add 'and all sexes'
– some beautiful, others monstrous . . . On the whole their behaviour was
decorous, even prim. The atmosphere seemed to me sad and somehow
terribly respectable . . . They were like actresses determined to go through
with roles they hadn't chosen. Some of them were obviously enjoying themselves, while even the sad ones had a sort of dedicated look.[62]

For all its brevity, this sketch offers a version of homosexual subculture that
makes familiar claims: internationalism, the mixing of the classes, the coexist-
ence of a range of types, all adding up to an impression of the tolerance within
the subculture that it does not receive from without. Even 'all the sexes' are
represented here, so long as none of them is male – or, for that matter, heterosexual. As far as Toby can see – and he is, after all, only a one-off visitor with
decidedly partial vision – this is an exclusive subculture that bars its doors to
outsiders – men and unswervingly heterosexual women – but is open to all
types within its own catchment. Whether any bar really was as 'open' within
lesbianism as this seems to him is questionable; but, given so limited an
observer as Toby, Plomer is only conveying an impression of an impression.
The truth of the place is beyond both Toby and his correspondent.

Toby has found what he wanted in the 'extraordinary assembly' and some of
the outlandish individuals with it. (There is, for instance, a suitably grotesque
'hunchback Hungarian countess in jodhpurs *and spurs*' – Toby's emphasis –
whom I removed from the quoted description of the assembly.) But after the
initial shock of entering such a place, a major aspect of which is merely to be in
a club where no men are present (other than the observer himself, in drag),
ultimately Toby is disappointed. They usually are, such tourists. They go
looking for the outlandish and then, even when they have found a little of it, see
the mundanity behind it; the normality, even. Toby goes looking for a den of
sin and finds his admittedly 'extraordinary assembly' behaving well. They may
be lesbians, but they are just socialising with each other. This explains, I
suppose, the yoking of two assessments in his next sentence: 'The atmosphere
seemed to me sad and somehow terribly respectable.' The sadness is his, but he
wishes it on them for having disappointed him. The respectable homosexual is
always a let-down.

On the following night it is Lydia Delap who cross-dresses and Toby takes
her to a 'notorious' *lokal* called the Jugendquelle. He encloses a snapshot for
Jane: 'As you'll see from the photograph, she made a decidedly queer man, but
as we were going to a resort of queer men, that didn't matter much'. No detail is
offered of this place. (Was Plomer, in 1952, less willing to make an exotic and

humorous spectacle of his fellow homosexual men than of lesbians?) One detail, though, is of interest: 'There were several English present. I was introduced to a man who lives in Berlin and is writing a book. If it's as good as his conversation, it ought to be very good. He looked very quizzically at Lydia, who hardly spoke, and then at me. I feel deeply compromised.' (The watcher senses he is watched.) Doubtless, this is William Plomer's version of what it felt like to be captured by the fishy lens of Christopher Isherwood, as he made notes for *Goodbye to Berlin*.[63]

After all these accounts, written in letters and diaries at the time or retrospectively in memoirs and autobiographical fiction, it comes as a surprise to hear that the occasional visitor found the Berlin scene surprisingly tame. Duncan Grant, for instance, was disappointed when taken to some of Berlin's famous gay cafés in the summer of 1924. He wrote to Vanessa Bell: 'It was interesting to see but as you might imagine extremely proper and rather slow[,] not unlike a Cambridge party at a rather shabby undergraduate's rooms. The only thing that was a little bolder was that the pictures on the walls were sometimes photos of nude young men with horses – very teutonic.'[64] Even more surprisingly, perhaps, it was completely possible to overlook the notorieties of the sexual Berlin, if you had other things to do. In his memoirs, the art historian Kenneth Clark wrote: 'I made my way to Berlin, where I spent my time in museums and galleries, and so saw nothing of the ferocious depravities which made so great an impression on [his friend] Eddy [Sackville-West], and later on Stephen Spender.'[65]

Spender had travelled to Germany from England in 1930, attracted to its definitively modern environment and encouraged by Auden, Isherwood and others. He arrived in Hamburg in late July. Isherwood visited him there from Berlin in August, and Spender paid return visits to Berlin in September and December. In a famous passage in his memoir *World Within World* (1951), he wrote:

> Modernism in this Germany was (within certain limits of which I was not then aware) a popular mass-movement. Roofless houses, expressionist painting, atonal music, bars for homosexuals, nudism, sun-bathing, camping, all were accepted, and became like bright, gaudy, superficial colours in which the whole country was painted. Surrounded by this superficiality there were also serious artists, indignant Protestants, vengeful nationalists, Communists, many private tragedies, and much suffering. But such intense expressions of will and feeling were obscured by the predominant fashionableness of advanced attitudes. It was easy to be advanced. You had only to take off your clothes.[66]

Temporarily released from the post-Victorian inhibitions of England, he wanted to take part in the advance – in both of its aspects, superficial and serious. In a letter to Roger Senhouse (27 December 1930), Lytton Strachey reported that Spender 'Thinks of living in Germany with a German boy, but hasn't yet found a German boy to live with.'[67] Later, on the eve of war in September 1939, Spender wrote a diary entry looking back with rather hyperbolic fondness of his stay in Hamburg:

> I used to bathe, and I went to parties of young people. I had never enjoyed parties before and I never have since, but these were like living in the atmosphere of a Blue Period Picasso. Everyone was beautiful, and gentle, everyone was poor, no one was smart. On summer evenings they danced in the half light, and when they were tired of dancing they lay down in the forest, on the beach, on mattresses, on the bare floor. They laughed a great deal, smiling with their innocent eyes and showing well-shaped, but not very strong, teeth. Sometimes they let one down, sometimes the poorer ones stole, for example, but there was no Sin. I am not being ironic. There really was no sin, as there is in this kind of life in Paris or London.[68]

The need to distinguish Hamburg and Berlin from the likes of Paris and London is related to Spender's idealism and his sense of future possibilities, as distinct from the risqué, Wildean past of the Naughty Nineties. He was not seeking the freedom to be immoral, or even amoral, and his sense of sexual freedom was of a sunnier disposition, less moodily nocturnal, than the pleasures he associated with the *fin de siècle*. He was far less interested in the cabaret scene, with its self-conscious exhibitionism, than in cosy corners where relationships could be forged, even if initially on a commercial basis.

> I was twenty in those days, and I was caught up mostly with the idea of Friendship – *Freundschaft*, which was a very significant aspect of the life of the Weimar Republic. This, if it was frank, was also idealistic. It was not cynical, shame-faced, smart, snobbish or stodgy, as so often in England. It was more like Walt Whitman's idea of camaraderie.[69]

### Flirting with Fascism

It was all too easy to be seduced by fascism – as, indeed, by other tyrannies – if you did not live under its yoke and only judged it by its pageantry. With its polished leather, its gonfalons and its high-kicking chorus lines, Nazism provided the visitor to its formal parades with an uncommon spectacle, all the more exciting for its superficial contrast with the drabness of the Depression. It allowed you to imagine that a whole people could be enthusiastically *marched* into prosperity. Well, so it may have seemed. Some visitors were beguiled, and some of those eventually saw sense. A few examples should suffice.

The American architect Philip Johnson was an internationalist from the start, since his family's wealth enabled them to travel frequently. There was an extended trip to France in 1919, when Johnson was thirteen; then, in his late teens and early twenties, a second trip to Europe in the summer of 1925; a stay in England, where he studied a number of the cathedrals, in 1926; Heidelberg in 1927; and a family tour of Algeria, Egypt, Greece, Italy and France in 1928. It was on this last holiday that he first had a sexual encounter – with a guard in the Cairo Museum. Back in the United States he had his first affair, with an actor from Kansas City. He went to Heidelberg again in 1929, and during a fortnight in London enjoyed a brief flirtation with Noël Coward (never consummated). On the same trip he discovered Berlin, where he felt able to enjoy himself sexually, unencumbered by the guilt he always felt back home. He said of the city, 'It was a very open town because they'd lost the war . . . And that still rankled, of course. The defeated parties have to be sort of, "Well, I'm being fucked. I'm fucked. So I better make money doing it." And I enjoyed the payment part of it. They were Germans. They were boys. Very nice. Every summer I had a different friend.'[70] It was in Berlin, too, that he first started designing buildings (in the first place, merely, alterations to various Johnson family properties back home). He visited the Bauhaus in Dessau and met Walter Gropius. Not that his enthusiasm for Modernism in architecture precluded an interest in the Baroque, the best examples of which he studied in Dresden and Prague. One evening he sat next to the sixty-year-old Siegfried Wagner, son of the composer, in the Festspielhaus at Bayreuth, and was taken aback when the older man's hand began to explore the length of his thigh.

In 1924, Johnson's father had given him stocks in Alcoa, the Aluminum Corporation of America; by the time he graduated from Harvard in the spring of 1930, he was a millionaire in his own right. By now he was having a passionate affair with the would-be poet Cary Ross, whom he had met through friends associated with the new Museum of Modern Art in New York. Ross was said to have been a friend of Hemingway and the Fitzgeralds in Paris in the 1920s. They resumed the affair, with a little less frenzy, in Paris in the summer. They took to spending a lot of time with an architecture scholar, Henry-Russell Hitchcock, also gay. In Berlin, which he visited twice in the same year, Johnson met Mies van der Rohe, who was at that time the Director of the Bauhaus. Back in New York, he proposed that the Museum of Modern Art stage an exhibition of modern architecture. It did so in February 1932, and the exhibition subsequently toured thirteen US cities, introducing Americans to the concept of the International Style. In that same year, Johnson co-authored with Henry-Russell Hitchcock *The International Style: Architecture since 1922*. It was in the summer of 1932, in Berlin again, that German politics first impinged on his consciousness. A friend took him to one of Hitler's rallies, outside Potsdam; Johnson was thrilled to see 'all those blond boys in black leather'. This initial erotic enthusiasm would grow into a more perverse involvement in right-wing extremism as the decade wore on.

In New York, Johnson now ran with a smart young crowd of artists, many of them gay, working in a range of different art forms, but mainly in music. Virgil Thomson, whom he had found penniless in Paris and loaned the cost of his passage home, introduced him to John Cage in 1934; there was also Pavel Tchelitchew, Lincoln Kirstein, Thomson's lover Maurice Grosser, and Aaron Copland. Johnson and Cage had a fling together, which ended when Johnson failed to invite Cage to a society party at which Cage felt Johnson felt Cage did not belong. In the same year, Johnson had what he considered the first of his 'serious' relationships, with Jimmy Daniels, a black café singer he had met in Harlem. His association with the Museum of Modern Art saw its high point in the influential exhibition 'Machine Art'. He resigned from MoMA in December.

When Hitler came to power in 1933, Johnson was excited by German resurgence, and paradoxically fascinated by the National Socialist opposition to the Modernism to which he was himself committed. Over the next few years he did more than flirt with fascism; they seemed, for a while, to be made for each other. He and Alan Blackburn, an old school friend, founded something they called the National Party in 1934, holding informal meetings in Johnson's New York apartment. His friends in the arts were, for the most part, disturbed and embarrassed by this development. During the 1936 presidential election, which was won by Franklin D. Roosevelt, he worked with the Roman Catholic priest Charles E. Coughlin of the Union Party, in New London, Ohio. Then, in 1937, he and Blackburn founded the Young Nationalists, a band of youths who gathered mainly from backgrounds in the Ku Klux Klan, the German-American Band, and other right-wing groups. He kept on visiting Berlin, of course, still to sample its sexual opportunities, but now also to study fascism seriously. He attended the Nuremberg Rally celebrating the fifth anniversary of the Nazis' accession to power.

His 1939 trip to Germany was followed by a visit to Poland. According to his biographer, 'The Polish tour only reinforced Philip's preconceptions of backwardness among the Poles and the Jews, while reminding him of the superiority of German society and the German military force'. It really seems he had no sensitivity to the personal situation of those around him. For instance, when he was in Brno, in Czechoslovakia, he decided to call in on the architect Otto Eisler. It had not occurred to him to consider the consequences of the fact that Eisler was both a Jew and a homosexual; as it happened, he had been in the hands of the Gestapo just days beforehand. Eisler spoke to him only briefly. Johnson's American friends put up with staggering attitudes. Lincoln Kirstein, who was also both Jewish and homosexual, wrote of him in 1944, 'In his most rabidly fa[s]cist days, he told me that I was number one on his list for elimination in the coming revolution. I felt bitterly towards him, and towards what he represented.' When Britain and France declared war, following the invasion of Poland on 1 September 1939, the German Propaganda Ministry formally invited Johnson to follow the Wehrmacht to the front. He did so with enthusiasm, and blandly wrote home: 'We saw Warsaw burn and Modlin being bombed. It was a stirring spectacle.' He published five articles in *Social Justice* in 1939 (24 July, 11 September, 16 October and two on 6 November), all expressing his own anti-Semitism and approving of German politics. By June 1940, the US Office of Naval Intelligence had begun to investigate him as a possible German spy.[71]

In 1933, the American journalist Janet Flanner ('Genêt') travelled around Germany with a small group of other lesbian women, including her lover, Solita Solano, and another woman, Noel Haskins Murphy, with whom she had recently fallen in love. By now, there were plentiful signs of the repressive nature of the National Socialist regime. The women had to rein in their behaviour somewhat, and in public places lower their voices. On one occasion Solano was ordered to change out of the trousers she was wearing. Yet Flanner was slow to recognise what was happening under the Nazis. In 1935, having written a two-part profile of Queen Mary for the *New Yorker*, she then agreed to write a three-parter on Adolf Hitler – as far as possible, avoiding politics! When it was published in 1936, she was surprised to find that her piece was welcomed in Germany as being pro-Führer. (Malcolm Cowley of the *New Republic* called her a fascist to her face.) Sent to Berlin in the summer to cover the Olympic Games, she wrote of the Minister of Propaganda, Hermann Goering, that he was 'apparently the most liberal official patron of the arts in Germany today'. Her biographer adds: 'and she wasn't being ironic'.[72] As late as 1938, Flanner and Noel Haskins Murphy took their annual trip to the music festivals in Germany and Austria.

After the outbreak of war, Flanner and Solano went to New York on a previously planned visit. They had paid their rent in Paris up to April 1940, intending to return, but in the event they stayed in the USA. (Noel Haskins Murphy, on the other hand, decided to stay in France, even after the German invasion. She was interned by the Germans as an enemy alien in September 1942, once the

United States had finally entered the war. She was released in December.)
Flanner went on trying to be 'neutral' about fascism; indeed, she managed to
perform the peculiar contortion of supporting both Pétain and de Gaulle at the
same time. From the safety of Manhattan, she published *Pétain: The Old Man
of France* (1944). She went back to Europe to work as an official war correspondent for the *New Yorker*. In Paris, which by then had been liberated, she
met up with Noel again. For both print and broadcast media – she was now
recording despatches for the Blue Network, later to become ABC – she sent
reports to the USA from the front at Royan, then from various locations across
Germany, including Cologne and the newly liberated concentration camp at
Buchenwald. Yet even after the war had ended and the full extent of the Nazis'
atrocities was becoming apparent, Flanner's attitudes could be strangely ambiguous. For instance, in 1946, while covering the Nuremberg trials, she shocked
a group of women journalists and stenographers by asking them over breakfast
which of the Nazi defendants, if necessary, they would have slept with. She did,
however, write an admirable series of campaigning essays about the fate of
displaced people, after visiting the devastated cities of Vienna, Prague, Warsaw
and Berlin in March 1947. The French made her a knight of the Legion of
Honour in 1948.

The attraction to Nazism was often superficial, based on surface aesthetic
factors whose allure soon wore thin. Luchino Visconti seems to have associated
the political movement, romantically, with the German people – their language,
their culture, their looks – and then transferred that impression back home to
Italian fascism, before eventually seeing through, and fighting against, both.
Artistically literate from an early age, he developed a passion for the opera
when he was seven, and as a Milanese he was able to indulge it as often as he
wished in the family box at La Scala; but it was during his teens that family
connections began to bring him into contact with people who were or who
would become major figures in the Modernist revolution. At nineteen, for
instance, in 1925, he met Diaghilev, who had called on Donna Carla Visconti
with his new protégé Serge Lifar.

However, as he entered his twenties, two factors interrupted Visconti's life
as a leisured and well-heeled aesthete. In 1926 he joined the cavalry school at
Pinerolo in Piemonte; his military service lasted until 1928. Then, on 30
September 1929, he had an accident which would affect him permanently. He
crashed his new Lancia Spider on the way to Monza to race it, killing the family
chauffeur, who had been reluctant to go on the trip. Visconti did not drive
again for twenty years, and he continued to support the chauffeur's family for
the rest of his own life. As an immediate reaction to the disaster, he went into
retreat for two months in the Tassili mountains in the southern Sahara. When

he re-emerged, he consciously tried to quicken his emotional recovery. Intending actively to change his life, he travelled to Paris. There he met Serge Lifar again, as well as, among others, Jean Cocteau and Marie-Laure, the vicomtesse de Noailles. Coco Chanel took a fancy to him and they had an affair – for thus far in his life his sexual interests had been shared equally between women and men – but, although he had fluent French, he tended to remain silent in the face of Chanel's loquacity. One of only a few Italians under Fascism to have a passport, he compensated for the devastation of the car crash by launching himself into a life of rather frantic toing and froing; he was virtually commuting between Milan and Paris, but also made trips to London, Munich and Berlin. His great passion was for keeping racehorses. Not until the mid-1930s did his artistic involvements relegate the stud and the turf to the status of a mere interest.

Gaia Servadio's account of Visconti's travels in the early 1930s identifies another respect in which his interests were divided:

> Much as he was attracted by Paris, by the disorderly explosion of ideas, by sexual freedom and freedom of expression, his puritan side, his admiration for discipline and for the glorification of the body and youth ideally attracted him to the new Nazi regime.

His sister would recall his having attended a Nazi rally, probably in 1934, after which 'he described the discipline and strength of handsome youths who were carrying something, a huge pole, I think'. He later confided to a friend that he had watched with intense longing the ranks of uniformed, blond, sadistic boys. He was also an admirer of *Triumph of the Will*, Leni Riefenstahl's film of the Berlin Olympics. By contrast with National Socialism, he found Italian Fascism vulgar and parochial.[73]

Meanwhile, in Paris, Luchino Visconti made the reputation of an emporium selling smart luggage, when he bought all their suitcases stamped with the firm's initials, LV – Louis Vuitton. It was clear he had a lot more travelling to do, and no intention of travelling light. He went down to the Riviera for a while to stay in Coco Chanel's villa, La Pausa, between Roquebrune and Cap Martin. Here, at various times, other visitors included Cocteau, Lifar, Jean Marais and Francis Poulenc. But the affair with Chanel had ended, and in February 1935 he suddenly declared that he and a woman called Irma Windisch-Graetz had decided to get married. A conflict arose, since her father wanted them to wait until Visconti had found himself a profession, whereas Visconti was in a hurry to tie the knot at once. The fact was that he had fallen in love. The urgency came from the less convenient fact that it was not his prospective wife he had fallen in love with, but (for the first time) a man: the German photographer Horst P. Horst, whom he had met when lunching with Marie-Laure de Noailles.

It was from this time that Visconti could be regarded as predominantly homosexual; presumably, the relationship with Horst enabled him to recognise and accept this. Before long, he had given up his fiancée and, although he was still hiding his love for Horst from his friends, to his own satisfaction he had rejected bourgeois convention once and for all. There was an aesthetic and (eventually) professional pay-off, too: Horst taught him about photography. At the time they met, as Horst later recalled, Visconti wandered around with two books in his pocket: Mann's *Death in Venice* and one by Gide. He was still, by convention or habit, a fascist. Horst, though, had left Germany because of Nazism – he went to study architecture under Le Corbusier before turning to photography – and his personal influence soon began to change Visconti's view on the matter.[74] At the same time, a new political outlook was beginning to affect him via his unexpected involvement in film-making. In 1935 he had met Jean Renoir and taken the opportunity to observe him at work; both he and Henri Cartier-Bresson assisted Renoir in the making of *Une partie de campagne*; by 1936 he had been taken on as an unpaid member of Renoir's crew. This association accelerated his political awakening. His new friends introduced him to the films of Eisenstein; he also realised, at last, that to the Nazis and the Italian Fascists he and others like him were mere perverts.

Although his social whirl diminished slowly, Visconti threw himself into film work and, later, into the resistance to Fascism. Jean Renoir had suggested he film James M. Cain's 1934 novel *The Postman Always Rings Twice*; Visconti did so. When he showed its first rough-cut to Jean Marais, the film was called *Ossessione*. This magnificent debut was not welcomed by the Church in Rome, or by the Fascists, for reasons which Servadio makes clear in her account of a film

> which showed human weakness as a natural factor and recounted squalid episodes concerning unheroic characters. There was even a homosexual in the script, the Spaniard, who was depicted as a sympathetic character. The theme of male companionship as a better alternative to passion was offensive. The fact that a whore was a purer figure than Giovanna [the central character] was also at odds with contemporary ideas . . . The homosexual was the symbol of liberty.[75]

When the Allies landed at Salerno in September 1943, the King and Pietro Badoglio, who had taken over from Mussolini, fled Rome to evade the Germans.

Visconti likewise left the city, heading up into the Abruzzi, then turning south-ward with a group of Allied ex-prisoners of war. Circumstances forced them to turn again and, having escaped a brief spell of imprisonment by the Germans, they made their way towards Rome, where they arrived in February 1944. Having to remain in the city, Visconti started to work for the Resistance. On 15 April 1944, he was arrested and repeatedly beaten up, but not otherwise physi-cally tortured. He was, though, among a group who were subjected to a mock firing squad. He was released on 3 June 1944, by which time the Germans had commenced their retreat from the city. Not long afterwards, the Americans marched in.

As we shall see in Chapter Seven, a tenuous line of causation between homo-sexuality and the excesses of Nazism was often claimed, for propagandist purposes. Quite apart from the equation of Nazism and homosexuality, there is the contrary argument whereby the lax morals of the Weimar Republic could be used to justify, or could be blamed for, not only the Nazis' crackdown on homo-sexuality that followed – the closing of the clubs and pornographic bookshops – but also the labour camps and even the Second World War itself. In his novel *Funeral Rites* (*Pompes funèbres*, 1948), Jean Genet perversely yokes Nazism to homosexual history as the cold turkey from an opiate: before the Second World War, he writes, 'Germany, stunned and staggering, was just managing to recover from the deep, rich drowsiness, the dizziness, the suffocation fertile in the new prodigies into which it had been plunged by the perfumes and charms emitted slowly and heavily by that strange curly poppy, Dr. Magnus Hirschfeld.'[76] On the other hand, Genet also brings into occupied Paris an Adolf Hitler who is himself an addiction, political and sexual, an enemy ripe for the most intimate fraternisations.

In the anglophone world, it was Christopher Isherwood's very narrow version of Weimar Berlin and its eclipse that caught on and endured. A gay author's choice of a narrator of unspecified sexuality (based on himself) whose supposedly objective, camera-like curiosity surveys the scene without involve-ment, while his friend Sally Bowles stands in for him as a wholehearted partic-ipant in the pleasures the city afforded – albeit involving prostitution and an abortion – seems, objectively speaking, an unlikely narrative to have lastingly captured people's imagination. Having a sequence of German boyfriends, Isherwood was much more involved in German society than he was able to make his narrator, even though he lived in Berlin for just four years (1929–33). Perhaps this was to the benefit of his writing, which could only offer a pared down, narrowly subjective impression of the rise of Nazism – so pared down, indeed, that the narrative has a mythic simplicity amenable to apparently endless reworking and adaptation to other genres.

In truth, it is not so much *Goodbye to Berlin* itself as the later sequence of bastardisations of it that have fixed this view of Berlin. In 1952, John Van Druten dramatised Isherwood's story 'Sally Bowles' as *I Am a Camera*. The play was a success, but he and Isherwood argued over the balance of their respective shares in the royalties. Later in the decade, when Victor Chapin tried to turn the Berlin stories into a musical, Isherwood had the idea of getting W.H. Auden and Chester Kallman to write it. Auden was enthusiastic – he decided that the Isherwood character 'ought to be quite overtly queer'[77] – and Arthur Laurents told Isherwood that the Broadway producer Hal Prince was interested in the show. Isherwood wrote the treatment and Auden wrote some verses, but the project eventually failed and was shelved. Meanwhile, Isherwood was working on the book that would become *Down There on a Visit* (1961).

When *Cabaret*, the musical version of Van Druten's play, opened on Broadway in November 1966 it ran for 1,165 performances. (It was written by Joe Masteroff, with lyrics by Fred Ebb and music by John Kander.) Isherwood declined to see it, but his lover Don Bachardy went and said it was awful. On the other hand, they both liked Bob Fosse's 1972 movie version of the musical.[78] Liza Minnelli's Sally Bowles settled a particular phrase in the popular memory: 'divine decadence'. It is notable how few of the visitors to Berlin I have consulted referred to the experience as 'decadent'. That was still a word more closely associated with the *fin de siècle* of London and Paris.[79]

# CHAPTER SIX

# FROM FRIVOLITY TO SERIOUSNESS

## The Fashionable Vice

'Between the two German wars of the present century the fashionable vice was probably homosexuality.' So wrote T.H. White in 1950.[1] From the perspective of the twentieth century's mid-point it had become clear that this was no longer going to be the case – indeed, that it would become fashionable to denounce homosexuality as the worst of the vices. But the inter-war period was another matter: two public models of the visible homosexual (frivolous and serious) had appeared and lingered, almost to the extent of becoming tolerable – if only to the literati, and if only to some of them. In their 1941 social history of the same period in Britain, Robert Graves and Alan Hodge wrote:

> Homosexuality had been on the increase among the upper classes for a couple of generations, though almost unknown among working people. The upper-class boarding-school system of keeping boy and girl away from any contact with each other was responsible. In most cases the adolescent homosexual became sexually normal on leaving school; but a large minority of the more emotional young people could not shake off the fascination of perversity. In post-war university circles, where Oscar Wilde was considered both a great poet and a martyr to the spirit of intolerance, homosexuality no longer seemed a sign of continued adolescence ... [Male] homosexuals spent a great deal of their time preaching the aesthetic virtues of the habit, and made more and more converts.[2]

They added, with apparent approval, that lesbians 'were more quiet about their aberrations at first' – until they heard of the example of Weimar Berlin: 'in certain Berlin dancing-halls, it was pointed out, women danced only with women and men with men. Germany, land of the free! The Lesbians took heart and followed suit, first in Chelsea and St John's Wood and then in the less exotic suburbs of London.'

Looking back at the 1930s from the vantage point of the 1970s, Julian Symons wrote:

> The Thirties might also be called the homosexual decade, in the sense that in these years homosexuality became accepted as a personal idiosyncrasy: and became, too, a sort of password, so that several homosexual writers of little talent found their work accepted by magazines simply on a basis of personal friendship. It would probably be untrue to say that any writer of heterosexual instincts suffered seriously through this homosexual literary tendency among the young, but the assessment of writers on the basis of their sexual attractiveness can hardly be anything but damaging to literary standards.

Symons clearly had no conception of the difficulties a homosexual writer might have faced if he or she had chosen to write openly, rather than obliquely, about homosexual relationships – think of the undissembling openness of Radclyffe Hall's *The Well of Loneliness*, as against the complex codes of Isherwood's Berlin stories. He added:

> About all this, it may seem, there is nothing specifically new ... A, B and C, those well-known homosexual writers, were firmly established with their young men for years before the Thirties. That is true enough: the unique contribution made by the intelligentsia in the Thirties to the change in our sexual ethic rested in the attitude they adopted, by which the assertion of sexual freedom appeared to be a social duty.[3]

If to some limited extent 'fashionable', then, between the wars, male homosexuality adopted different styles in the two decades. The symbolic queer figure of the 1920s was an affluent and whimsical queen, dedicated to aestheticism and leisure, with a wandering eye for a burly sportsman. As this figure went out of fashion in the 1930s he was replaced by the more masculine and politicised artist, espouser of causes and befriender of workers. Middle- rather than upper-class himself, he nevertheless moved between exalted circles – having met the right people at Oxford or Cambridge – and the pubs and meeting rooms of the working class, romanticising the working man as the emblematic figure in an ideal future of social equality. It was to the latter group, broadly speaking, that W.H. Auden and his closest literary friends belonged.

Oscar Wilde was godfather to the 1920s aesthete-queen. Jessica Mitford said the aesthetes' heritage consisted of 'the Romantics, the England of Oscar

Wilde, [and] the France of Baudelaire and Verlaine'.[4] Men such as Ronald Firbank, Brian Howard, Harold Acton, Stephen Tennant and Cecil Beaton – although each unique in his way – and fictional characters like Reginald (in Saki's short stories), Anthony Blanche (in Evelyn Waugh's *Brideshead Revisited*), Ambrose Silk (in Waugh's *Put Out More Flags*), Cedric Hampton (in Nancy Mitford's *Love in a Cold Climate*) and Hew Dallas in Jocelyn Brooke's *A Mine of Serpents* – made a significant contribution to the visibility of homosexuality in English society.[5] Their variety boiled down to the unity of a popular, and not so popular, stereotype: the effeminate, arty, upper-class pansy.

For all the seriousness of this aesthete's involvement in the arts, it was playfully performed. For example, Cecil Beaton's country house Ashcombe barely existed in the real world at all. His bedroom was decorated with circus scenes, including a fat woman by Rex Whistler, a tumbler by Christopher Sykes, a naked Negro by Oliver Messel and, by Lord Berners, a Columbine with performing dogs. (All had been guests together on the same rainy weekend.) 'Meanwhile,' as Beaton later put it, 'unhampered by a social conscience, we gave parties.' Indeed, the eye grew so used to seeing people in fancy dress that, 'when Mr. H.G. Wells was brought over one Sunday wearing a Homburg hat and pinstripe suit, one felt he was the man from Mars'. There would be parodies of school sports days, with the prizes presented by John Sutro or Oliver Messel in drag. So full were the days with entertainment that Beaton was once shocked to find Tom Mitford reading a novel. Christian Bérard thought Ashcombe 'pure Lewis Carroll'.[6] A similar atmosphere prevailed at Lord Berners' Faringdon (where the doves were dyed in pastel colours during Easter) and Stephen Tennant's Wilsford.

Puerility may have been an important aspect of the mood, but behind it lay a sophisticated understanding of cultural forms. Even while they were still schoolboys, Brian Howard and Harold Acton were trailblazers in their espousal of the modern movement. Martin Green characterises their precocious values as follows:

What they stood for at Eton was modernism in general, understood as the movement against the consensus culture of Victorian and Edwardian England. They stood for French poetry – Mallarmé, Rimbaud, Verlaine, and Laforgue – and for French fiction – Proust, Huysmans, and Cocteau – and for France in general – Paris and [the couturier Paul] Poiret and Charvet (maker of the most exquisite ties) and just the sound of the French language. They stood for American poetry – Eliot, and Amy Lowell, and some Pound – and for cocktails and jazz. They stood for modern painting – Whistler and [Augustus] John, Picasso and Gauguin. Among English people and things they stood for the Sitwells, above all. And, of course, they stood for Diaghilev and everyone and everything associated with him, from Bakst and Stravinsky to Pierrot and Harlequin.[7]

A negative view of this list would be that it smacks of dilettante acquisitiveness, but if we are willing to be impressed by such highbrow schoolboy interests, we can see that Howard and Acton were already developing a comprehensive aesthetic that could style most aspects of a leisured, modern person's waking life. The pursuits implicit in the list are both serious and frivolous, profound and shallow. If they are taken as being of equivalent value – Mallarmé and a tie, Proust and a cocktail – we are well on our way to a developed and knowing espousal of the ethos of Camp. That said, despite everything one might assume about the Wilde scandal's having irreversibly linked effeminacy and homosexuality in the general consciousness, it was still possible to play the aesthete without being fingered as a sodomite. Speaking of an occasion when he appeared at a party in the 1920s in a tunic embroidered with chincherinchee and narcissus, Robert Medley later said, 'Nobody thought I was gay, dear, they just enjoyed the smell.'[8]

The most modern character in *Love in a Cold Climate* (1949), Nancy Mitford's novel set in the inter-war period and dedicated to Lord Berners, is a homosexual man, Cedric Hampton, whom Mitford seems to have based on both Stephen Tennant and Brian Howard. (David Warbeck was based on Eddy Sackville-West.) The moment of Cedric's first appearance in the narrative is striking:

> A glitter of blue and gold crossed the parquet, and a human dragon-fly was kneeling on the fur rug in front of the Montdores, one long white hand extended towards each. He was a tall, thin young man, supple as a girl, dressed in rather a bright blue suit; his hair was the gold of a brass bed-knob, and his insect appearance came from the fact that the upper part of the face was concealed by blue goggles set in gold rims quite an inch thick.

The next impression Fanny, the book's narrator, has of him is that he is foreign – yet foreign not by nation but by a quirk of individuality: 'He spoke with rather a curious accent, neither French nor Canadian, but peculiar to himself, in which every syllable received rather more emphasis than is given by the ordinary Englishman.'[9] Asked by Lady Montdore to remove his goggles, he demurs: 'In a mask one can face anything – I should like my life to be a perpetual bal masqué, Lady Montdore, don't you agree?' Although a serious approach to life, this is, of course, perceived to be frivolous. It smacks of Parisian superficiality and youthful inconstancy. It also suggests he has something less frivolous than his appearance to hide. He stands out from his surroundings not just because of his sexual ambiguity but because he is Canadian and much of his style is (European) continental, as is that of the circles in which he moves. A party he attends in drag – indeed, he changes his dress five times – is described as the best of its kind 'since the days of Robert de Montesquiou'. He is involved with a German, a frivolous and selfish boy called Klugg, who lives in Paris. Fanny learns that Klugg is 'hideous and drunken and brutal and German and unlettered' – all this, by Cedric's own account – but lovable all the same. Cedric creates an unmistakable impression wherever he goes, and is impervious to those who, on account of their prejudices, object to the impression they have received. However, such people often fail to sustain their embargoes on social interaction with him in the face of his charm. By being brazen, he can defeat the diffidence of English narrowness: 'It was extraordinary how fast he could worm his way through a thick crust of prejudice.' This is easier in London, though, than in the country: 'London society, having none of the prejudices against the abnormal which still exists among Boreleys and Uncle Matthews in country places, simply ate Cedric up.'[10] The family's neighbours, the Boreleys, are prejudiced against many groups: foreigners, well-dressed women, members of the Labour Party and so on.

> But the thing they could stick least in the world were 'aesthetes – you know – those awful effeminate creatures – pansies'. When, therefore, Lady Montdore . . . installed the awful effeminate pansy Cedric at Hampton, and it became borne in upon them that he was henceforth to be their neighbour for ever . . . hatred really did burgeon in their souls.

Fanny imagines they think of him as 'a terrible creature from Sodom, from Gomorrah, from Paris'.[11] The equivalence of Paris to the Cities of the Plain is only partial, for in some respects it is a lot worse, being full of the French. As another indication that knowing about homosexuality is regarded as a distinctly modern trait, it is to be noted that Mitford makes jokes about the ignorance of her parents' generation on this matter. Lady Montdore has heard that one of her guests, a prince, is 'a daisy, whatever that may be' (she means a pansy), and on another occasion she makes 'a fearful gaffe' when she confuses Sodomites with the Dolomites. As Polly says of her, with a hint of pity, 'she knows nothing, nothing whatever about all that'.[12]

In his 1975 biography of Mitford, Sir Harold Acton speaks of how Nancy and her brother Tom were allowed to bring friends home. Those friends included 'both athletes and aesthetes'. One among the latter, Oliver Messel, 'entertained the company with spicy monologues about tragic-comical White Russian refugee princesses, "refained" governesses afflicted with wind, and wriggling debutantes whose conversational gambit was limited to "Have you been to No, no Nanette?"'

The effect of such figures in the ancestral home was, according to Acton, akin to 'the invasion of Presbyterian Scotland, as it were, by Evelyn Waugh's Bright Young Things'. Writing so many years later, Acton found it hard to imagine how Brian Howard ('my former Eton crony') and Nancy's father, Lord Redesdale, 'coped with each other, if they were allowed to meet'.[13] However, Acton recognises as plausible the welcoming of the disruptive pansy into the ancestral home by bored hostesses:

> The conquest of tough Lady Montdore by Cedric Hampton . . . was what reviewers used to call audacious, but many dowagers whose names I could mention found youthful companions like Cedric who subjected them to a course of rejuvenation. Nancy herself was drawn to the ornamental type of homosexual, whose preoccupations were feminine apart from sex. She described Brian Howard as 'blissikins' and in Paris there were many others who brought grist to her comedic mill.

Acton knew what he was talking about: for there had been a time when he was 'blissikins', too. He quotes Mitford as saying of one social occasion, 'I had 12 people yesterday in before dinner and afterwards I thought I was the only normal one . . . It is rather strange one must admit. Nature's form of birth control in an overcrowded world I daresay'.[14]

Acton says of *Love in a Cold Climate* and Cedric Hampton: 'The novel was most original, perhaps, in depicting the dragonfly Cedric as a beneficent rather than as a pernicious influence: here for a change was a harmless fairy wand. Since then some of the social stigma attached to Cedric's type has faded and Nancy's witty tolerance might have helped the fading process. At the time, however [that is, in 1949], Cedric was generally considered an affront to normality by the English novel reading public, less sophisticated than the French.' Mitford found that in America, too, Hampton filled readers with unease. As she wrote to a friend: 'America is taking exception to Cedric the sweet pansy . . . It seems in America you can have pederasts in books as long as they are fearfully gloomy and end by committing suicide. A cheerful one who goes from strength to strength like Cedric horrifies them.'[15] By the time of the Cold War, frivolous people were being taken seriously. Whether they appeared in books or in public, they were expected to receive their comeuppance. Fear of such retribution took its toll on the public figure of the homosexual man.

## Modernity Outdated

Even in much earlier novels, the flamboyant modernity of the aesthete-queen had been characterised as paradoxically passé. There is already a moment in

Carl Van Vechten's novel *The Blind Bow-Boy* (1923) when the homosexual Duke of Middlebottom decides that Modernism has had its day, and the time has come to turn the cultural clock back. He says:

> Everything one called modern a year or two ago is old-fashioned: Freud, Mary Garden, Einstein, Wyndham Lewis, Dada, glands, the Six, vers libres, Sem Benelli, Clive Bell, radio, the Ziegfeld Follies, cubism, Sacha Guitry, Ezra Pound, *The Little Review*, Vorticism, Marcel Proust, The Dial, uranians, Gordon Craig, prohibition, the young intellectuals, Sherwood Anderson, normalcy, Guillaume Apollinaire, Charlie Chaplin, screens in stage d-d-d-d-decoration [the Duke has an occasional stutter], Aleister Crowley, the Russian Ballet, fireless cookers, The Chauve Souris, Margot Asquith, ectoplasm, Eugène Goossens, the tango, Jacques Copeau, Negro dancing. Let's not be modern. Let's turn back to the great period around 1910 – even a trifle earlier.[16]

The list is meant to sound improvised, but not merely whimsical. The duke is a highly educated arbiter of taste, knowledgeable across cultural forms and national boundaries. He has travelled widely, and knows several languages. His list implies a much longer list of items not mentioned. (He is not just naming everything he has heard of.) Although his vision ranges as broadly across popular culture as across 'high' culture, it is, nevertheless, arcane in some of its references. (He is not just naming the big names of the modern.) He is showing off, of course – as is the author – both in the compiling of the list and in the dismissal of it as old hat. His perverse recommendation that the arts be turned backwards to counter outdatedness comes from ingrained habits of going against the grain. He seems to have no real nostalgia for pre-Modernist culture. His recommendation is a deliberately paradoxical sign of ostentatious boredom. Already long committed to the new, he is looking around for a new newness – perhaps something as perversely new as the old.

Everything about Middlebottom bespeaks his involvement in a specifically homosexual version of modern culture – and a specifically modern version of homosexual culture. (No classicist, he.) His home contains a painting of orchids by Charles Demuth and 'a fountain inspired by Nijinsky's interpretation of Mallarmé's faun'. On a table there is a copy of Louis Couperus' novel about the dissolute Roman emperor Elagabalus, *Mountain of Light* (*De berg van licht*, 1906). Not only does he know his Firbank, but he even appears to know Firbank himself. One of his dogs is named Eskal Vigor, after the scandalous novel by the homosexual Belgian novelist Georges Eekhoud. He speaks of putting on a performance of Fernand Nozière's play *L'Après-midi Byzantine* (1908), with the participation of his friends. 'It's in one act and no costumes: cool for the actors, and hot for the spectators.' The main scenery is a low chair which looks like a bed. There is evidently a scene between a charioteer and a boy, but Middlebottom has little time for the straightforward erotics of pederasty: he wants the boy to be more queerly played by a girl. 'It is b-b-better so. It makes the piece more perverse.' When told to invite all his friends to attend the performance, he replies: 'I have no f-f-f-friends . . . only people that amuse me, and people I sleep with . . . The people that amuse me are all in the p-p-p-play . . . The theatre isn't b-b-b-b-b-big enough to hold the others.'[17]

Although he has recently come back to New York from Capri, where he spends two or three weeks in every year, he is no conventional tourist: clearly having more important things to get involved in, he has never bothered to visit the Blue Grotto. The only slightly backward-looking aspects to him are his association with a group that frequents the Café Royal in London, that haunt of Oscar Wilde's, and the Keatsian echo in his personal motto, 'A thing of beauty is a boy forever.'[18]

In Van Vechten's later novel *Parties* (1930), which bears the didactic and rather superfluous subtitle *A Novel of Contemporary New York Life*, the bisexuality of several of the central characters combines with other indicators such as the constant taking of cocktails and the free use of drugs as signs of their modernity. When David Westlake comes to after a drunken night of womanising, he groans 'I'm sick of sex . . . women anyway.'[19] Perhaps he is thinking of Roy Fern, the boy he loves. Hamish Wilding falls in love with both David and his wife, Rilda Westlake. Noma Ridge admits to having slept with both men and women, but says she prefers the former.

At the end of Compton Mackenzie's novel of life on Capri, *Vestal Fire* (1927), a new type has begun to arrive on the island (here called Sirene), bringing with them a new seriousness. Miss Virginia observes

> three owl-eyed young men of the moment with solemn and intelligent faces
> and dank devitalized hair – votaries of Athene who scoffed at romantic
> passion, looked askance at humour, and found a footnote of Dr. Ernest
> Jones as stimulating as cantharides.

(Ernest Jones was the first British psychoanalyst.) 'I guess I've lived too long,' the old lady laments, 'and maybe I've always been foolish and sentimental; but I think a man with queer ideas ought to look kinda bold and bad and picturesque.' Even Nigel Dawson, half her age, feels displaced, 'when sitting at one of the tables in Zampone's and surrounded by a group of these ruthless young moderns he was asked if he had been up at Oxford with Oscar Wilde. And they did not even pay either him or Wilde the compliment of pretending to be interested in the answer.'[20] By the mid-1920s, to be associated with the *fin de siècle* was to seem distinctly jaded. To be associated with the student Wilde was all the more so: for he left Oxford in 1878, long before the *siècle* was anywhere near its *fin*.

Of the characters in *The Rock Pool* (1936), Cyril Connolly's novel about a tightly interconnected, mainly expatriate community in the south of France, it is Jimmie who represents the now outdated type of the aesthete-queen. He has 'an intimate little voice of the "Vortex" period and a mop of peroxide hair'.

> There was a great deal to be said for his type, the oldfashioned Taormina young men [*sic*]. They had their roots in the past, and were naturally social and cultured. The tradition of Oscar was still preserved. They were the heirs of the dandies and inherited his metallic wit. They tended to be amusing and well-read rather than ignorant and sulky[.]

Early in their friendship, he and Naylor have a conversation about literature:

> Jimmy thought the two greatest modern writers were Firbank and Hemingway. Naylor proposed Norman Douglas, Eliot and Joyce. Jimmy praised [James Branch Cabell's novel] *Jurgen* and [F. Scott Fitzgerald's] *The Great Gatsby*, neither of which Naylor had heard of. Jimmy knew Gertrude Stein well, and Cocteau and Glenway Wescott, for he belonged to the charmingly dated Paris of the Select and the Bal Musette, and parties on the Ile Saint-Louis, having long been decoyed there from some ferocious small town by the *douceur de vivre*.

Naylor is attracted to the community in 'the rock pool' precisely because of its 'note of archaism' and 'the obsolete forms to be found within it'.

> Sicily, Capri, Majorca, Brioni [in Croatia], Corfu, all the island colonies of eccentric Anglo-Saxons, were, since the [post-1929] slump, one with Homburg and Spa: in Capri the untrimmed ilexes spread over Marsac's marble palace; the outraged Majorcans had jailed or exiled such picturesque characters as had descended on Palma and Pollensa; the Sicilian youth walked unmolested in Taormina and Cefalu.

(Count Marsac is the uranian central character of Mackenzie's *Vestal Fire*.) At the end of the novel, Naylor tries to imagine going back to London, but senses that he is even more out of joint than the times. He would be bound to feel more rejected there than ever: 'for if sex and snobbery, at which he was a failure, were going out, he was no better fitted for the Communism and hope that were coming in'.[21]

Decades later, as a freshman at the University of Sydney in the late 1950s, Clive James found himself among late inheritors of the tradition of the aesthete-queen, but did not yet understand their references: 'Spencer called something Firbankian. Who, what or where was Firbankian?' Spencer also delivers an impromptu speech that refers to Heinrich von Kleist, Lord Alfred Douglas and Jean Cocteau. Later, he co-directs the annual revue: 'Vocal music was by Palestrina. There were at least two sketches about Virginia Woolf. A third sketch might have been about her, but was more probably about Gertrude Stein. [A boy called] Grogan played Alice B. Toklas, or it could have been Vita Sackville-West.'[22]

## Becoming Serious: Evelyn Waugh

From Miles Malpractice in *Vile Bodies* (1930) onwards, Evelyn Waugh's novels are scattered with representations of the pansy-aesthete, all of them located somewhere beside, or even astride, a fault line between frivolity and seriousness. Towards the end of *Black Mischief* (1932), Sonia says to Basil Seal, 'people have gone serious lately'. Basil has been away in East Africa, attempting to modernise the island nation of Azania; on his return he has begun to notice the social consequences of the Wall Street Crash. Soon after a brief conversation with Seal, Sonia says to her husband, 'D'you know, deep down in my heart I've got a tiny fear that Basil is going to turn serious on us too!'[23] For all but the uppermost crust, turning 'serious' meant coping with economic reality – mainly by finding a way of earning a living. It meant, as in any period, growing up, settling down, perhaps getting married and starting a family. For some – like Waugh himself – it meant leaving their bisexuality behind. Yet when the Bright Young People looked back on their prime from the more sober times of the 1930s and 1940s, they often lit on their gaudiest homosexual friends as epitomes of all that was most vibrant and exciting about the 1920s. In Waugh's *Put Out More Flags* (1942), Ambrose Silk personifies modern culture, and his homosexuality is crucial to his modernity. Yet his heyday is past, as is that of the age he represents:

It had been a primrose path in the days of Diaghilev . . . at Oxford he had recited *In Memoriam* through a megaphone to an accompaniment hummed on combs and tissue paper; in Paris he had frequented Jean Cocteau and Gertrude Stein; he had written and published his first book there, a study of Montparnasse Negroes that had been banned in England by Sir William Joynson-Hicks [the Home Secretary from 1924 to 1929]. That way the primrose path led gently downhill to the world of fashionable photographers, stage sets for [C.B.] Cochrane, Cedric Lyne and his Neapolitan grottoes.

In 1929, the year of the Wall Street Crash, Silk turns from dalliance to austerity, moves to Germany and – ignoring the promiscuous pleasures for which so many Englishmen would have gone there – quietly falls in love with a Brownshirt called Hans. When the Nazis subsequently find out that Silk is a Jew, Hans is sent to a concentration camp: for them he represents 'something personal and private in a world where only the mob and the hunting pack had the right to live'.[24] So Modernism degenerates in two distinct ways: in England its aesthetic is watered down to the frivolous level of the Cochrane revues and fashion magazines (Waugh is mainly getting at men such as Noël Coward and Cecil Beaton), whereas in Germany its aesthetic side is discarded in favour of the drive for the industrial and military efficiency of fascism.

In *Brideshead Revisited* (1945), it is again the homosexual man who best represents international modernity: Anthony Blanche never succumbs to the nostalgia that afflicts the book's narrator (and, indeed, its author). Blanche, too, like Ambrose Silk, has experienced Modernism at first hand; and his Modernism, too, is of a distinctly homosexual sort:

> he dined with Proust and Gide and was on closer terms with Cocteau and Diaghilev; Firbank sent him novels with fervent inscriptions; he had aroused three irreconcilable feuds in Capri; by his own account he had practised black art in Cefalù [presumably with Aleister Crowley] and had been cured of drug-taking in California and of an Oedipus complex in Vienna.[25]

He has recited not *In Memoriam* but *The Waste Land* through a megaphone across an Oxford quad. Like Ambrose Silk, he has sought love not among the boys of Oxford, whose homoeroticism is represented as being a sign of arrested development (embodied in Sebastian Flyte's teddy bear, Aloysius), but among the men of Germany: he has a relationship with an unnamed policeman in Munich; and the man he later lives with in Morocco, Kurt, returns to Germany and becomes a storm trooper, has second thoughts but is not allowed to withdraw, and eventually hangs himself in a concentration camp.

When Waugh came to write *Men at Arms* (1952), the first volume of the *Sword of Honour* trilogy about the Second World War, he was aware of a very different type of homosexual man from the likes of Ambrose Silk and Anthony Blanche. Looking at himself in a mirror, the novel's protagonist Guy Crouchback appraises his new image and is reminded by it of other men: 'He had seen such moustaches before and such monocles on the faces of clandestine homosexuals, on touts with accents to hide, on Americans trying to look European, on business-men disguised as sportsmen.' In place of the flamboyant youth determined to stand out from the crowd, we now see the pre-Wolfenden homosexual-as-spy, the master of disguise whose mastery, while allowing him to fade somewhat into the crowd, falls short of rendering him entirely invisible as a type.[26]

The mental breakdown Waugh fictionalises from his own experience in *The Ordeal of Gilbert Pinfold* (1957) generates in the middle-aged Roman Catholic writer Pinfold a paranoid victimhood which is very much of its time. Central to it is the fear of being thought homosexual. Pinfold hears voices that keep returning to the same theme: 'Queer, aren't you, Gilbert? Come out of your wooden hut, you old queer'; 'Mr Pinfold was a sodomite. Mr Pinfold must be chastened and chastised'; 'he was Jewish and homosexual . . . he had stolen a moonstone and left his mother to die a pauper'; 'That cowardly, common little communist pansy'; 'He's attractive to women – homosexuals always are'; and, as well as having a '*peculiar* sense of humour', wearing his hair too long and wearing make-up, he is identifiable as a particular category of deviant: 'There are different types of homosexual, you know. What are called "poufs" and "nancies" – that is the dressy kind. Then there are the others they call "butch". I read a book about it. Pinfold is a "butch".' Cumulatively, these accusations, generated within his own failing intelligence, betray an extreme fear of seeming different. They emanate from a conformist mentality, not only of the individual mind they are preying on, but of the collective psyche. The sheer insistence of the sexual smear is indicative of the effect of increasing public awareness of homosexuality in the 1950s. By contrast, even communism seems a lesser threat. The fact that the bulk of the novel takes place on a slow ship to Ceylon – although Pinfold leaves the ship at Port Said and returns home – gives it an atmosphere of imperial decline. What Pinfold fears in himself is what so many imperialists feared in the Empire: communism, Judaism (the Shoah notwithstanding) and that sexual decadence which, since Gibbon's history of the decline of Rome, the British strongly associated with the death of empires. In the year of the Wolfenden Report, Evelyn Waugh sees English masculinity as having been seriously and irrevocably compromised.[27]

### The Nancy Poets and their Detractors

Jocelyn Brooke heard England's transition from the 1920s to the 1930s in the sounds of male voices. In *The Military Orchid* (1948), he wrote of the earlier decade:

> The Roaring Twenties . . .! But the label, perhaps, is a mistake. The true voice of the epoch was, surely, not so much a full-throated roar as a kind of exacerbated yelping; a false-virile voice tending, in moments of stress, to rise to an equivocal falsetto – half-revealing (like the voice of M. de Charlus

[in Proust's *Recherche*]) behind its ill-assumed masculinity a whole bevy of *jeunes filles en fleurs*.

When Brooke went on to speak of the decade's end, he was clearly thinking of one generation taking over from its predecessor. Having described the 1920s as a crowd of sissies verbally cross-dressing as men, he cast the 1930s, too, in terms of a homosexual style – but a very different one:

> The intellectual *chichi* which had marked the vanishing era was sternly rebuked; and the strident war-cries of homocommunism echoed from Russell Square [in Bloomsbury] all the way to Keats Grove [in Hampstead]. A number of ageing Peter Pansies wisely fled to the country, there to cultivate their Olde Worlde Gardens among the pylons and the petrol pumps; and an epoch which had begun with a bang came to an end, all too appropriately, with a whimper.[28]

In essence, Brooke was describing the ceding of cultural power by what was left, in the 1920s, of the pre-war belle époque to the brash young intellectuals of Modernism, the 'pylon poets' and the followers of Eliot (whose 'The Hollow Men' had ended 'Not with a bang but a whimper' in 1925). It had been Stephen Spender who famously published the poem 'The Pylons' in 1933, but it was to the wider Auden group, and the zeitgeist in general, that Brooke referred. Visiting the university in April 1936, Louis MacNeice found that 'Cambridge was still full of Peter Pans but all the Peter Pans were now talking Marx'. Stephen Spender later wrote of 'the Thirties when everything became politics'. The camp styles of the 1920s aesthete had given way to the more down-to-earth, in some respects duller, masculinity of the Auden group and those who followed in their wake. Writing in Shahi, Persia, on 22 April 1934, Robert Byron complained that:

> To asperse a sunset in these days is a political indiscretion; and equally so, to praise it, if there happens to be a cement factory in the foreground that ought to be praised instead. Somebody must trespass on the taboos of modern nationalism, in the interests of human reason. Business can't. Diplomacy won't. It has to be people like us.

People 'like us' are not necessarily homosexual, but they are aesthetes. By the end of the 1930s such men would seem irrelevant survivors of a less complicated era. On 27 October 1939, Spender had lunch with the ex-Bright Young Thing Brian Howard and then fixed him in his diary: 'rather silly, I thought, with his feminine way of tilting his head up as though under a cloche hat, and looking at you through half-closed eyelids'.[29]

In Britain, then, it was the Auden group that most visibly exemplified this cultural tendency. As the supposed leader of the group, and its most authoritatively vocal member, Auden was himself its embodiment. The schoolboy Auden was already at ease with talking dispassionately about homosexuality when he met his first adult of that kind, or the first adult he knew as such, Michael Davidson, who helped him get his first poem published. Already a fully paid up Freudian, Auden had a tendency to treat the matter as worthy more of analysis than of shame or embarrassment. In his final school year, when he fell in love with John Pudney, he lectured the younger boy about homosexuality, self-abuse, D.H. Lawrence, socialism and Sigmund Freud. When he went up to Christ Church, Oxford, he did not become an aesthete, in part because he was too poor to do so: he could not have afforded the necessary display of fine living. He did, though, become sexually active, and, within the bounds of sanity, was open about it. Uninhibited and apparently guiltless, he might have enjoyed himself more had he not been in the habit of falling in love with sturdily heterosexual athletes. Not until his trip to Germany, and to Berlin in particular, between October 1928 and July 1929, did he have the free access to such men's bodies that an economic depression offered relatively well off, foreign visitors.

Often flippant, most of his early writing's references to homosexuality are, by the standards of a later era, negative. He uses the epithets 'poof', 'pansy', 'pathic', 'bugger' and 'queer', and consistently refers to homosexuality as a weakness, or as a 'crooked' deviation from 'straight' logic. However, such references, each in itself apparently no more than glancing, do build up to a clear demonstration of interest – so much so, indeed, that as early as 1938 the American critic James G. Southworth wrote an essay characterising Auden as a campaigner on behalf of homosexuals (or urnings, in the terminology of Ulrichs), among whom he was himself to be numbered: 'Aware of the anomalous position of the urning in modern society he has sought by his frankness of utterance to rid himself of any guilt or inferiority.' On the evidence of *Poems* (1930), *The Orators* (1932) and *Look, Stranger!* (1936), Southworth concluded that Auden had made 'an impassioned plea for tolerance toward the Urning whose position in society is anomalous even though he is the product of that society'.[30]

His sexual boldness notwithstanding, Auden was aware of the need for strategic discretion. He had at least two scares, both involving written indiscretions. The first was in 1923, when his mother found and read a homoerotic poem he had written about his school friend Robert Medley. She passed the poem to her husband, who lectured the two boys about schoolboy intimacy, asked in coy terms if their friendship had ever been sexual, and destroyed the poem. The second incident, potentially far more serious, was in 1934, when he and Isherwood went to meet the latter's German lover, Heinz, at Harwich. An immigration officer, having read one of Isherwood's letters to Heinz, doggedly and suspiciously questioned him about the nature of his family's relationship with this working-class foreigner, before finally refusing to allow Heinz into the country. Auden's diagnosis of the situation was that the officer had seen through Isherwood at once because he was himself homosexual.[31]

The modern history of homosexuality is also, perforce, a history of homophobic responses to homosexuality. George Orwell springs to mind. When first dealing with the theme, journalistically, although he is speaking of a time when he felt vulnerable to assault, his language is relatively objective. In *Down and Out in Paris and London* (1933), Orwell speaks of having to fight off a man 'making homosexual attempts' on him in a hostel for homeless men at dead of night. Rather than attempt to go back to sleep, he stays awake, talking to his attacker. 'He said that his wife had promptly deserted him when he lost his job, and he had been so long away from women that he had almost forgotten what they were like. Homosexuality is general among tramps of long standing, he said.' Orwell describes a hostel in an alley off the Strand in London as being 'a dark, evil-smelling place, and a notorious haunt of the "nancy boys"'. Several men he sees in the kitchen, 'ambiguous-looking youths in smartish blue suits', he supposes to be of this sort: 'They looked the same type as the apache boys one sees in Paris, except that they wore no side-whiskers'. An alcoholic fellow Old Etonian who haunts the place seems not entirely poverty-stricken, therefore not needing to be in such a place: 'Perhaps he frequented common lodging-houses in search of the "nancy boys"'. Note that, at this early stage, he uses this expression in inverted commas. Before long, he would cease to do so.[32]

The central character of Orwell's novel *Keep the Aspidistra Flying* (1936), Gordon Comstock, a failing writer, is forced to make his living in the lesser trades of advertising and book-selling. While he is involved in the latter, a rich-looking young man of about twenty trips 'Nancyfully' into the bookshop. When he speaks he does so in what Comstock refers to as an 'R-less Nancy voice' ('I *adore* poetwy!'). He drifts away from the poetry shelves to leaf through the pictures in a book about the Ballets Russes, thereby betraying an allegiance to a particular strand of Modernism. It may be modern, but by implication it is closed to all but the unmanly.

Comstock has sent poems to the *Primrose Quarterly*, 'one of those poisonous literary papers in which the fashionable Nancy-boy and the professional Roman Catholic walk *bras dessus, bras dessous*' and 'by a long way the most influential literary paper in England'. He does not have any confidence that they will want to publish him. Indeed, when he finally receives the expected rejection slip from them he can hardly believe the stupidity of having bothered to send them anything in the first place. 'The idea of trying to horn in among that pansy crowd!' He wishes they would tell the truth: 'We don't want your bloody poems. We only take poems from chaps we were at Cambridge with.' Orwell appears to have in mind the crowd of ex-Apostles[33] who had moved to Bloomsbury and gained influence in various spheres associated with publishing. But they are not the only villains in Comstock's anti-Pantheon of forces arrayed against him. At an especially low moment, overwhelmed by his own paranoia, he surveys the whole Comstockophobic culture:

> He had a vision of London, of the western world; he saw a thousand million slaves toiling and grovelling about the throne of money. The earth is ploughed, ships sail, miners sweat in dripping tunnels underground, clerks hurry for the eight-fifteen with the fear of the boss eating at their vitals. And even in bed with their wives they tremble and obey. Obey whom? The money-priesthood, the pink-faced masters of the world. The Upper Crust. A welter of sleek young rabbits in thousand-guinea motor cars, of golfing stockbrokers and cosmopolitan financiers, of Chancery lawyers and fashionable Nancy boys, of bankers, newspaper peers, novelists of all four sexes, American pugilists, lady aviators, film stars, bishops, titled poets and Chicago gorillas.[34]

Not content to express this opinion in the borrowed voice of Comstock, which in any case generally sounds remarkably close in tone to his own, Orwell also did so under his own name in the following year's documentary book, *The Road to Wigan Pier* (1937). Here, he casually distances himself from current English poetry with a pair of references to 'the Nancy poets'. He apparently expects his reader, the typical subscriber to Victor Gollancz' Left Book Club, not only to know whom he means but also to agree with him about them. He does not mean the effeteness of poets in general but the homosexuality of a particular clique. In both passages, Orwell implicitly vaporises the claims of the writers in question to a socialist conscience:

> Practically everything we do, from eating an ice to crossing the Atlantic, and from baking a loaf to writing a novel, involves the use of coal, directly or indirectly. For all the arts of peace coal is needed; if war breaks out it is needed all the more. . . . In order that Hitler may march the goosestep, that the Pope may denounce Bolshevism, that the cricket crowds may assemble at Lord's, that the Nancy poets may scratch one another's backs, coal has got to be forthcoming.

In the second passage, he casts his net even wider:

> You and I and the editor of the *Times Lit. Supp.*, and the Nancy poets
> and the Archbishop of Canterbury and Comrade X, author of *Marxism
> for Infants* – all of us really owe the comparative decency of our lives to
> poor drudges underground, blackened to the eyes, with their throats full of
> coal dust, driving their shovels forward with arms and belly muscles of
> steel.[35]

Although Orwell was on the Left himself, he often seemed determined to tar the whole of the Left with the attitudes and tastes that he himself most despised. So London literary society was 'pansy-left circles' and 'the typical middle-class socialist' was a reader of Edward Carpenter 'or some other pious sodomite'.[36] One of the implied crimes of the poets is that the 'arms and belly muscles of steel' were apt to be noticed by them as the erotic outcomes of toil. In the early 1930s Julian Bell had accused Auden, Day Lewis and Spender of 'homosexual worker-worship'.[37] On receiving Nancy Cunard's famous 1937 petition to British writers about the Civil War in Spain – 'Are you for, or against, the legal Government and the People of Republican Spain?' – Orwell replied, 'Will you please stop sending me this bloody rubbish . . . I am not one of your fashionable pansies like Auden and Spender.' For good measure, he added a threat: 'By the way, tell your pansy friend Spender that I am preserving specimens of his war-heroics' in order to shame him later – 'when the time comes . . . I shall rub it in good and hard'. At no point did Orwell show any awareness that such language might put the victim in danger, threatening his employability if not his liberty.[38]

Orwell's biographers sometimes feel the need to explain, if not to excuse, his homophobia. Michael Shelden thinks his hostility to 'Nancy boys' – 'a term he used on several occasions' – was a result of the 'deep sense of guilt' he felt in later life about the homosexual phase he had passed through, as Eric Blair, at Eton College. Like his friend Cyril Connolly, Blair courted other boys who took his fancy; but Connolly is said not to have appreciated competition, and Blair was better-looking than he. On one occasion, when he had set his heart on winning the affections of a boy in Connolly's Election, Blair suspected, probably with good reason, that for that very reason Connolly would try to intercept the loved one and win him first. So Blair wrote to Connolly, asking him not to interfere. (The outcome of these rather genteel negotiations is not known.) When, many years later, Orwell reviewed Connolly's *The Rock Pool* in the *New English Weekly* (23 July 1936), he took a pompous line on the book's light-hearted portrayal of sexual reprobates:

Even to want to write about so-called artists who spend on sodomy what they have gained by sponging betrays a kind of spiritual inadequacy . . . The fact to which we have got to cling, as to a life-belt, is that it is possible to be a normal decent person and yet to be fully alive.[39]

Orwell's was not the only voice consistently harping on homophobic themes. On 30 December 1930 Stephen Spender wrote to Gabriel Carritt:

[Roy] Campbell, Wyndham Lewis and (now) [Robert] Graves are carrying on a great campaign against homosexuals. They all attack them in writing and by wild and inaccurate gossiping . . . It seems that every modern writer who happens to be normally sexed, is so overjoyed to find himself normal in one rather unimportant respect, when he is wildly abnormal in all other ways (as are C., W.L., and G.), that he must needs spend all his energy in attacking buggers.[40]

Roy Campbell's ostentatious determination to distance himself from homosexual men, their neuroses and their literature extended to his forthright poetry. In his 'Georgian Spring' he boils the supposed blandness of Georgian poetry down to one dismissive sentence: 'A thousand meek soprano voices carol / The loves of homosexuals or plants.' Although happy to celebrate the possibility of a healthy bisexuality, he insistently did so to the detriment of mere homosexual infirmity. In the first part of 'The Georgiad' he celebrates the figure of the heroic Androgyne: 'This was no neuter of a doubtful gender, / But both in him attained their fullest splendour, / Unlike our modern homos who are neither, / He could be homosexual with either / And heterosexual with either, too— / A damn sight more than you or I could do!' Not for him the pathetic pathic's reliance on the support of book-learning: 'With Edward Carpenter he had no patience / Nor from the Sonnets [of Shakespeare] would he make quotations.' This androgyne is a creature of instinct, with no need to excuse his identity or actions. 'He read no text-books: took himself for granted / And often did precisely what he wanted.' Besides, even if a man were to identify with or seek solidarity with his fellow homosexuals – more fool him – he would only be betrayed, for 'Cain had more Christian mercy on his brother / Than literary nancies on each other.'[41]

Writing about the new generation of poets, Campbell insisted on their interconnectedness to the extent of giving them the portmanteau surnames Spauden (Spender, Auden), Spaunday (Spender, Auden, Day Lewis) and MacSpaunday (MacNeice, Spender, Auden, Day Lewis). Even when naming them as individuals he did so only to meld them into a clique with a single brain: 'What Auden chants by Spender shall be wept'; 'the fat snuggery of Auden, Spender, / And others of the selfsame breed and gender.'[42] Again and again his homophobia and his anti-Semitism take a single track, as when, in 'A Letter from the San Mateo Front', he rails against 'Defrocked scoutmasters and wheedling Jews'; or, in 'Flowering Rifle', against 'the Invert and the Jew' whose 'racket' is to reduce the 'Human Spirit' to pulp. Indeed, a few lines further on in the latter poem, he commends Adolf Hitler for his oppression of 'the belittler, / The intellectual invert, and the Jew'. (The obscure first of these three groups seems to have been conjured up merely for the sake of the imperfect rhyme with 'Hitler'.[43])

Not unlike Orwell's Comstock, Campbell had come to regard the whole of English literary life as an effeminate and emasculate conspiracy against real men – and real poets – like himself. All around him he saw the effects of the 'All-Castrating Knife / Of London and its literary life'; and every male writer lesser than himself he regarded as a 'literary catamite / Who stands aghast at beauty and delight' ('Dedicatory Epilogue'). The leftist writers who supported the 'Reds' in Spain, apparently without exception, 'only by inversion can exist / As perverts' ('A Letter from the San Mateo Front'). Indeed, the leftists in general were laying waste to Spain so that 'crime might flourish, sodomy abound / And love be crushed'. In a footnote, he ridicules André Gide for having 'justified his vices by those of dogs' – presumably a reference to Gide's argument, in *Corydon*, that homosexuality cannot be unnatural since it is so prolific in the natural world. At the very lowest reach of his stooping, Campbell refers to the assassinated Federico García Lorca as 'The victim of the God that he defied', a point he underlines in a footnote excusing the 'natural reaction' of the fascists in Granada who 'rounded up and shot all corrupters of children, known perverts and sexual cranks' ('Flowering Rifle'). Campbell consistently wrote as if he thought the Homintern and the Comintern, along with international Jewry, were all involved in the same conspiracy.[44]

During the same period, the young Welsh poet Dylan Thomas was fulminating against homosexual men in his voluminous letters to Pamela Hansford Johnson. Like Orwell and Campbell, he tended to imagine them effeminising the culture, diverting critical praise from more deserving manly artists. In a letter of November 1933, he wrote:

Sodomhipped young men, with the inevitable sidewhiskers and cigarettes, the faulty livers and the stained teeth, reading [D.H.] Lawrence as an aphrodisiac and Marie Corelli in their infrequent baths, spew onto paper and canvas their ignorance and perversions, wetting the bed of their brains with discharges of fungoid verse. This is the art of to-day: posturing, shamming, cribbing, and all the artifice of a damned generation.[45]

He sounds like Thersites, railing against Achilles and Patroclus. It is certainly odd to see the man who would soon become the most celebrated boozer of his generation worrying about the state of other people's livers. He appears to be voicing a beginner's envy of the success of the previous generation, the Auden/ Spender group, who were now coming into their own. The following month, having seen a camp young man in a hotel, he fired off this diatribe to Johnson:

> Have you remarked upon the terrible young men of this generation, the willing-buttocked, celluloid-trousered, degenerates who are gradually taking the place of the bright young things of even five years ago? . . . They always existed, but in recent months – it seems months to me – they are coming, unashamedly, out into the open. I saw one with a drunken nigger last night.
>
> It is the only vice, I think, that revolts me and makes me misanthropic . . . But the sin of the boy with the nigger goes up like a rocketed scab to heaven.

Again, there is the disapproval of drunkenness in others; again, the sense of a general moral decline, aggravated by miscegenation. These homosexual men's real sin is not their degenerate behaviour – the sexual willingness of those hips and buttocks – but its visibility and its influence.

### Pansipoetical Poets

Similar changes, in both style and substance, were taking place across Europe. Superficial or not, the fashion for apparently apolitical aesthetics was giving way to a fashion for apparently artless political commitment. Curzio Malaparte outlined them in his novel *The Skin* (*La Pelle*, 1949):

> Those same noble apostles of Narcissus who had hitherto posed as decadent aesthetes, as the last representatives of a weary civilization, sated with pleasures and sensations, and who had looked to such as Novalis, the Comte de Lautréamont and Oscar Wilde, to Diaghilev, Rainer Maria Rilke, D'Annunzio, Gide, Cocteau, Marcel Proust, Jacques Maritain, Stravinsky and even [Maurice] Barrès to furnish the motifs of their played-out '*bourgeois*' aestheticism, now posed as Marxist aesthetes; and they preached Marxism just as hitherto they had preached the most effete narcissism, borrowing the motifs of their new aestheticism from Marx, Lenin, Stalin and Shostakovich, and referring contemptuously to bourgeois sexual conventionalism as a debased form of Trotskyism. They deluded themselves that they had found in Communism a point of contact with the

ephebes of the proletariat – a secret conspiracy, a new covenant, moral and social as well as sexual in character. From '*ennemis de la nature*,' as Mathurin Régnier called them, they had changed into '*ennemis du capitalisme*.' Who would ever have thought that among other things the [First World] war would have bred a race of Marxist pederasts?[46]

In this vivid sketch of the European cultural landscape, the internationalism of the Modernist movement in the arts is replaced by that of the labour movement. The distance from Decadence to High Modernism – a gulf, if that is what it was, spanned in Italian culture by Gabriele d'Annunzio – is presented as a continuum, even the later stages of which (Gide, Cocteau) are, it is suggested, beginning to seem as dated as the earlier (Novalis, Lautréamont). All are on their way out. By naming Narcissus, Malaparte invokes both their tendency to validate themselves with classical precedents, here further stressed by their desire for contact with proletarian 'ephebes', and a condition diagnosed by the definitively modern science of psychoanalysis. But their dedication to a cult (as 'apostles of Narcissus') and the washed-out weariness induced by their mental condition are now reconfigured and freshly imagined as a far more vigorous commitment – in politics rather than aesthetics. Although Malaparte does not name it as such, theirs is now a joint conspiracy of the Comintern with the Homintern.

More clearly than the quotations I have provided from English novels, Malaparte's identification of the move from d'Annunzio and Barrès to Marx and Lenin is a shift from the right wing to the left. The English version of this narrative tends to treat the earlier aesthetes as politically neutral, too innocently childlike to be committed to anything. The change is therefore presented as a politicisation of culture rather than an ideological about-turn. Contrasting his own generation with the previous one, that of the Bloomsbury Group, Stephen Spender wrote: 'A new generation had arisen which proclaimed that bourgeois civilization was at an end, and which assumed the certainty of revolution, which took sides and which was exposed even within its art to the flooding-in of outside public events, which cared but little for style and knew nothing of Paris.'[47]

In the United States, as in Europe, there were certain circles where *fin-de-siècle* styles of aestheticism were only reluctantly dropped. To some observers, the intellectual establishment still seemed ominously queer. When Malcolm Cowley went to Harvard, he found the atmosphere of the place backward-looking both culturally and sexually, in a manner which – not unlike other Ivy League generations – proved elitist and exclusive. Why, not even one's social standing could guarantee what might previously have been automatic rights:

'Even boys from very good Back Bay families would fail to make a club if they paid too much attention to chorus girls.' The fact is that Harvard had just caught up with the English *fin de siècle*, their reading of which, Cowley implied, was studiously decadent and to a large extent homosexual:

> The Harvard Aesthetes of 1916 were trying to create in Cambridge, Massachusetts, an after-image of Oxford in the 1890s. They read the *Yellow Book*, they read Casanova's memoirs and *Les Liaisons Dangereuses*, both in French, and Petronius in Latin; they gathered at tea-time in one another's rooms, or at punches in the office of the *Harvard Monthly*; they drank, instead of weak punch, seidels of straight gin topped with a maraschino cherry; they discussed the harmonies of [Walter] Pater, the rhythms of Aubrey Beardsley and, growing louder, the voluptuousness of the Church, the essential virtue of prostitution. They had crucifixes in their bedrooms, and ticket stubs from last Saturday's burlesque show at the Old Howard. They wrote, too; dozens of them were prematurely decayed poets, each with his invocation to Antinous, his mournful descriptions of Venetian lagoons, his sonnets to a chorus girl in which he addressed her as 'little painted poem of God.' In spite of these beginnings, a few of them became good writers.[48]

Whether this is a caricature is immaterial. What matters is the impression of a cultural backwater, albeit a sophisticated one, from which Cowley's own generation of American writers would make every attempt to escape. Although he is speaking of both apparent heterosexuals – reading Casanova and Laclos, and feasting with chorus girls – and possible homosexuals – reading Pater and Petronius, and writing poems on Antinous – it is clear that he thinks of the lot of them as being sexually perverse. The combination of their High Church and low-life interests marks them as weltering in their own sinfulness. Their self-conscious decadence, far from being daring – as it had been in the 1890s – comes across as a cliché, both unnatural and un-virile. Above all, un-American. All of their interests, at least as Cowley summarises them, are European, and none of them contemporary. Yet there is no evidence that any of these aesthetes have ever actually travelled to Europe; notwithstanding their knowledge of French, the implication is that they have not. Even their European artificiality is itself a mere pretence. The great irony is, of course, that Cowley's generation – which Gertrude Stein famously referred to as 'lost' – would soon effect their escape from what they regarded as the stagnation of American culture by heading for Europe. As we have seen, a generous exchange rate enabled many young American writers to live in Paris and London, at least until the Wall Street Crash, and, for the first time, to conceptualise an American avant-garde.[49]

There is another aspect, though, to Malcolm Cowley's resentment of the cliquishness of what was going on in the arts in the United States. Describing the atmosphere in Greenwich Village during the first summer after the Great War, he says that 'Revolution was in the air'. (The news from Russia in 1917 was still causing a thrill, of both hope and dread, in all the great Western cities.) Apart from the idea of a proletarian revolution, initiated by industrial strikes, Cowley imagines something else, 'another kind of revolt', oddly beginning with, as well as dancing in the streets, the drinking of cider and eating of ham. But this rather bucolic outburst of urban celebration – to which, presumably, New York's Jews would not be invited – would soon develop into something more actively interventionist:

> then you would set about hanging policemen from the lamp posts, or better still from the crossties of the Elevated, and beside each policeman would be hanged a Methodist preacher, and beside each preacher a pansy poet. Editors would be poisoned with a printer's ink: they would die horribly, vomiting ink on white paper. You hated editors, pansipoetical poets, policemen, preachers[.][50]

The coercive 'you' with which Cowley seeks to lure the reader into sharing his own personal prejudices is unconvincing: it really means 'I' or, at most, a paltry 'we' of like-minded young male writers whose rejection slips were getting them down. The hating of editors is easy enough to understand; that of policemen is an unremarkable convention on the left. The concept of the 'pansy poet' as a major foe, however, is worth following up, especially since it is expressed by a friend of Hart Crane's in a book whose revised edition (1951) contains an essay using Crane as a principal example of the generation of writers Cowley is ventriloquising as his pansy-bashing 'you'.

Pansy means 'homosexual' but not all homosexuals. The 'pansipoetical poets', similarly, are not all poets who were homosexual. While, on the one hand, Cowley recommends 'exile', or temporary expatriation, as a means whereby 'the artist can break the puritan shackles, drink, live freely and be wholly creative', on the other, being 'stopped by male prostitutes along the Kurfürstendamm' in Berlin strikes him as being on a par with 'machine guns in the streets of Berlin, Black Shirts in Italy' and an Arab revolutionary in France who said, by way of a toast, 'Let's imagine this vermouth is the blood of an English baby'. While happy to cast off his own shackles, he seems somewhat threatened by other men's excesses. Although his chapter on Crane is friendly – and pretty discreet about Crane's homosexual promiscuity – it is implicitly judgemental about the sheer amount of drinking into which, by escaping US

Prohibition, Crane chose to liberate himself. And all Cowley can find to say about the attitude of his generation of heterosexual male writers to feminism is: 'Female equality was a good idea, perhaps, but the feminists we knew wore spectacles and flat-heeled shoes.' He is ironic about his own crassness, here, but he does not rescind the thought.[51]

In the Germany of those 'male prostitutes along the Kurfürstendamm', of course, the move into seriousness had eventually accrued its own terrible significance. In Christopher Isherwood's *Goodbye to Berlin*, the boys with whom Herr Issyvoo has sunbathed and swum in a long season of freedom from commitment eventually find they have to take sides. Those, like Rudi, who choose the wrong side will soon pay the price. Christopher visits Rudi in his leftist clubhouse, barely more threatening to anyone than a scout hut, and is shown 'dozens of photographs of boys, all taken with the camera tilted upwards, from beneath, so that they look like epic giants, in profile against enormous clouds ... There were half-a-dozen other boys in the room with us: all of them in a state of heroic semi-nudity, wearing the shortest of shorts and the thinnest of shirts or singlets, although the weather is so cold.' The homoerotic iconography of the class struggle makes heroes of Rudi and his poor, working-class comrades. Yet this imagery might easily be mistaken for that of National Socialism: 'Above the table with the candlesticks was a sort of icon – the framed drawing of a young pathfinder of unearthly beauty, gazing sternly into the far distance, a banner in his hand.' One group of boys will prevail over the other and may take them at their own valuation, as warriors to be vanquished. On the closing page of the book the weather has changed for the better, but Hitler has taken control of the city and Christopher's mind goes back to Rudi:

> Rudi's make-believe, story-book game has become earnest; the Nazis will play it with him. The Nazis won't laugh at him; they'll take him on trust for what he pretended to be. Perhaps at this very moment Rudi is being tortured to death.[52]

Yet, no matter how dire the situation for many, there are always some who can exploit it to their own advantage. In *Mephisto* (1936), his great novel about the ways in which Germans managed to come to an accommodation with Nazism, Klaus Mann shows the homosexual Frenchman Pierre Larne complacently switching his sexual allegiance from young Communists to young Nazis with all the nimble footwork of true expediency: 'Now there were no more "young Communist comrades" at his side; they had been replaced by trim sturdy lads in their seductive and intimidating SS uniforms.'[53]

Some questions remained over the ability of the English officer class to cope with the demands of a war against fascism. Commenting on the introduction of conscription in the spring of 1939, Jessica Mitford reported: 'Philip Toynbee wrote us about a mutual acquaintance of ours who was a well-known London homosexual. As a young officer of "the new type," he had been required to write an official report on the visit of a captain to his regiment. "Captain — is an utter charmer," the report began.'[54] This is likely to be the kind of man Henry Miller had in mind when commenting on Lawrence Durrell's wanting to fight with the Greeks rather than the British:

> The Greek woman and the Orthodox priest – they sustained the fighting spirit. For stubbornness, courage, recklessness, daring, there are no greater examples anywhere. No wonder Durrell wanted to fight with the Greeks. Who wouldn't prefer to fight beside a [Laskarina] Bouboulina [the heroine of the Greek war of independence], for example, than with a gang of sickly, effeminate recruits from Oxford or Cambridge?[55]

Even if many had turned from frivolity to seriousness in keeping up with changing times, many others who observed them were still not convinced by the reliability of the conversion. It would take the war itself to test the matter.

# CHAPTER SEVEN

# BERLIN PROPAGANDISED

## Sodom on Spree

The reputation of Berlin as a city with a tolerant approach to the pleasures of homosexuality was of interest not only to those who might partake of such pleasures, even if only in their dreams of an emancipated life. Many were fascinated for contrary reasons by the lurid stories they heard. Berlin showed the depths to which other people could sink or from which they must be saved. Depravity was someone's fault, and it might as well be the fault of someone more important than a bunch of unfortunate perverts. The running narrative of the city's shameless excesses amounted to a myth, a usable scandal.

Visiting Berlin in 1919 in the aftermath of Germany's defeat in the Great War, Kurt von Stutterheim found that 'all kinds of dubious resorts had sprung up like mushrooms'. Censorship had been relaxed, with the result that 'Notorious magazines, which no chief of police of former times would have permitted, were sold openly on the *Potsdammer Platz*.' Having already deplored the open display of these unnamed publications on the streets, Stutterheim could not resist going into the 'dubious resorts' to see if they were any less shocking: 'An acquaintance took me into a dance-hall where painted men were dancing dressed in women's clothes. I was refused admission to another resort because it was only open to women, half of whom were dressed as men.' (He must have looked in the door and counted, or perhaps he asked a lesbian.) The whole of 'the public' appears to be behaving like him, searching out the frisson of the abnormal: 'The German theatre had become a home for the display of overheated and perverse sexuality, for which the public bought tickets with the expectation of witnessing something abnormal.'[1] Market forces gave them what they wanted.

As we saw earlier, Berlin had become *the* European city of erotic dreams and moral nightmares. If its reputation as a modern Sodom had a basis in the reality of the lives of Berliners – offering, among other delights, male gay bars and restaurants along the Friedrichstrasse, lesbian cafés on the Bülowstrasse, and male prostitutes along various avenues in the Tiergarten – in the rest of Germany and beyond, reports of that reality were simplified and repeated for ulterior purposes. Berlin became the symbol both of the wonderful things that could be achieved if one fought for them and of the terrible things that might happen if one did not fight against them.

In his 1962 novel *Down There on a Visit*, Christopher Isherwood recalls Mr Lancaster's having warned him, in 1928, about Berlin:

> Christopher – in the whole of *The Thousand and One Nights*, in the most shameless rituals of the Tantras, in the carvings on the Black Pagoda, in the Japanese brothel pictures, in the vilest perversions of the Oriental mind, you couldn't find anything more nauseating than what goes on there, quite openly, every day. That city is doomed, more surely than Sodom ever was.

The reference to Sodom narrows things down from a generalised, polymorphous Orientalism to something more precisely likely to appeal to Christopher's tastes (although Mr Lancaster apparently does not know this; nor, indeed, do the readers unless they are aware of the author's sexuality). The warning has an instantaneous effect, if not the one that was intended. Christopher writes: 'I decided that, no matter how, I would get to Berlin just as soon as ever I could and that I would stay there a long, long time.'[2] When Carl Van Vechten visited Berlin in 1929 with his second wife, Fania Marinoff, he said the city 'was like Rome under Caligula'.[3] This was definitely, from Van Vechten's viewpoint, a compliment; but others who could draw similar classical comparisons did so to warn of a dangerous decline in the city's moral standards. After all, had not the Roman Empire been destroyed from within, by its own moral laxity?

As often as not, observers of the economic and political crisis in the Weimar Republic during the 1930s allowed their scrutiny to shift in what they regarded as a logical association from financial disaster – the great inflation – to cultural decadence, especially as evinced in changes in sexual behaviour. Liberty had been sought, and liberties had been taken. For those to whom such things were scandalous, the sexual laxness of Berlin was used to represent the whole of the Weimar Republic. Both right-wing German commentators and anti-German voices abroad indulged in similar versions of the same argument. Under the provocative title *Is Germany Finished?* (1931) Pierre Viénot observed that in Germany 'sexual life, especially among the younger generation, is no longer regarded in itself from the standpoint of sin'. He identified three tendencies which were characteristic of this decline in the morality of young people: first, prospective husbands were no longer insisting that their wives be virgins; secondly,

'Homosexuality is no longer regarded as degrading, but is considered as a natural fact: witness the agitation for the rescinding of the clause in the German penal code [Paragraph 175] which makes homosexuality a criminal offence'; and thirdly, contraception had come to be widely regarded as legitimate.[4] The implication of Viénot's argument is that unless these degenerative trends can be reversed – as economic decline had to be reversed – Germany will be finished indeed. All three of his claims are overstated: they were really true of just a small proportion of the population, mainly concentrated in the big urban centres, and in Berlin especially. The mere existence of an argument against Paragraph 175 conjures up the familiar old fear: that unrestricted sodomy destroys empires.

The Nazis played on the same fears when they yoked their socially disciplinarian policies to an idealised vision of traditional sexual morality, embodied in the perfect wife. In *Germany Reborn* (1934), Hermann Goering connected the 'reds' who had presided over economic collapse with the issues of sexual and cultural decadence. He stated the case plainly, if with a flatulent rhetoric, in this passage on Weimar:

> The princes had been driven away and the red monsters climbed into the vacant thrones, but did not on that account become rulers. Above them all the Golden Calf was enthroned and the parties continue their grotesque dance. In every walk of life we see decadence and decay, the break-up of the Nation grows yearly more apparent, and the Reich is, from now on, a shadow, a framework held together with difficulty, already brittle in many places and without any sense of purpose. Corruption, immorality and indecency were the outward signs of the 'proud' Republic. And the decline of culture begins with the loosening of morals.[5]

It is easy to see in such a narrative of national decline, despite its brevity, a programme for rebuilding which involves the rooting out of those similar dangers to the state, leftists and perverts. (The third force, as it were, of the enemy within would be that which bore the brunt of the Nazis' vengeful reforms: the Jews.) If manifestations of sexual immorality were the 'outward signs' of a national sickness, then sending the boot-boys into the clubs and cabarets would, similarly, be a demonstration, a sign, of the resistance to decline. It would show that the Nazis meant business when they spoke of morality. The more spectacular sign would be the bonfire of books they lit after raiding Magnus Hirschfeld's Institute in May 1933.

Among many approving voices in Britain, voices of those who felt Britain itself would have been much improved by a moral clean-up on the scale the Nazis were attempting, was the Conservative member of parliament Sir Edward

Grigg. In *Britain Looks at Germany* (1938) Grigg expanded on a number of his pet obsessions, including the fecklessness of youth. He had observed and approved of Baden-Powell's achievements with the Boy Scout movement, his main reservation being that Britain had not used the scouts in the systematic way that the Nazis had. As he said, in a sentence with an especially telling parenthesis, 'One of the most salient points of the German system is that no section of German youth (except, indeed, an unhappy but exiguous minority of ostracized non-Aryans) is allowed to think of off-time spent in loafing.' He is thinking, mainly, of boys, and of what idle hands get up to. Later, he waxes lyrical about 'scouting', when what he is really talking about is the Hitler Youth:

> To put some romance and some sense of purpose into every young mind is surely one of the essential goals of education. Romance is quickening sunlight for boyish minds and hearts, and none should lack a share of its radiance. Scouting has been universal in its appeal, because it is compact of romantic interest. Few boys are not kindled to a keener sense of what can be made of life by the call of the open trail and the ancient knightly code of courage, truth and service to humanity.[6]

Because he had no ambitions as a writer, Baden-Powell never wrote as badly as this. Besides, his version of scouting was a much jollier affair, pig-sticking its way across the British Empire, romantic, if at all, at a less demonstrative level, and without much of the humbug of ancient codes, knightly or otherwise. Indeed, it is Grigg's heavy-handed attempt to mythologise the scouts that betrays his having moved beyond scouting as it existed in Britain to something, in his eyes, all the more rigorous, disciplined and purposeful: an enforced mass youth movement designed to eradicate the waywardness of the young and prepare them for a future – as what? Dutiful servants of the thousand-year Reich, it seems.

The Nazis' own mythology always represented their seizure of power as no less a moral than an economic crusade. A British sympathiser, Charles Domville-Fife, states the typical version of the matter on the first page of *This Is Germany* (1939): 'To have rebuilt a nation which had fallen from the high estate of a great empire to the chaotic human, economic and geographical debris left by defeat in war, disillusionment, penury, starvation, moral degeneracy and revolution, was a great task' – a great task, such commentators usually add, requiring the heroic puissance which only a great leader like the Führer could have provided.[7] The victory over degeneracy is as important an aspect of the myth as was the defeat of rampant inflation.

The first sentence of the Prologue of Sven Hedín's *Germany and World Peace* (1937), an unmediated screed of pro-Nazi propaganda, published in

London, pithily restates the moral myth: 'National Socialism has saved Germany from a state of political and moral disintegration.'[8] In his eighth chapter, Hedín enlarges on the standard claim by attempting to show the depths to which the Weimar Republic had sunk. Public life had degenerated, taking private life with it: 'Simultaneously with the disintegration of political life, one saw evidences in the streets and market-places, in drawing-rooms and in public bars, of immorality and the decay of family life.' Berlin was a kind of open sore, bringing to the surface the sickness within the national body. Cultural Bolshevism had infected the arts: 'The atmosphere of the theatre was pestilential – it was a fetid quagmire in which unhealthy sexual and porno-graphic plays sprang up like mushrooms in autumn.' Needless to say, it was not the true German who had created the conditions for this continuous festival of immorality, but the supposed outsider: 'Jewish writers and artists were largely responsible for this deplorable state of affairs, because they were the leaders of so-called Bolshevik culture.' Hedín does not dwell on homosexuality in the manner of so many other commentators at this time. For him, the mention of the Jew is sufficient on its own to conjure up the wraith of moral degeneracy and sexual perversion.

The *anti*-Nazi voice of Charles Wollf, who had been incarcerated in a concentration camp in France, presents the same case against Weimar, in the same terms, but not in order to praise Nazism for the successful subsequent clean-up; rather, to blame the indiscipline of the Weimar Republic for the exces-sive discipline of the Third Reich. In *Journey into Chaos* (undated, but published in London after 1942), Wollf says of Weimar: 'A dissolute liberty ruled here as never before. Desires and impulses, which before had been hidden according to the demands of morality, had at least been moderated by it, were flaunted in broad daylight, so to speak.' As ever, the prime evidence of this dissoluteness was provided by the new visibility and organisation of homosexuality: 'The homosexuals of both sexes no longer imposed any constraint on themselves. They had their clubs, their meeting-places and their own magazines.'[9] It takes something of a leap to deduce the first sentence from the manifestations of modest collective action in the second, but it is a leap which observers on all sides, most of them strongly opposed to homosexual emancipation, were able to take without much sign of effort.

## The Homosexuality of Hitler(ism)

Most anti-Nazi voices, instead of praising National Socialism for having sluiced out the stables of Weimar and reimposed a moral discipline on the German people, allowed the lax reputation of Weimar to linger over Germany as a whole for the sake of British and American readers, and then developed that sense by building up the myth of Nazism itself as sexually perverse. At the centre of this myth were claims, either that Hitler surrounded himself with homosexuals – although Ernst Röhm was usually the only one they could name – or that the Führer was himself homosexual. In *Hitler as Frankenstein* (undated, but probably written in 1939), Johannes Steel has a chapter called 'Men Around Hitler' in which he lists the known flaws and vices of senior Nazis. Thus: 'Roehm is a notorious homo-sexual, and he has frequently abused his military power as a supreme master over young men in a terrible manner'; and, a little further down the list: '[Edmund] Heines belonged to the circle around the homo-sexual Roehm' and was therefore, literally by association, homosexual himself. (He does not mention that Rudolph Hess was well known on the gay scene. When he visited the clubs he was known as 'Schwarze Maria'.[10]) Steel sums up the chapter in this closing flourish:

> The moral baseness of the Hitler Movement is clearly illuminated by the type of men Hitler has collected around him. This list could be prolonged into hundreds, for one lunatic in office gives another lunatic a post; one murderer, who is a Police Chief, makes another murderer a Captain of Police; one homosexual 'youth regenerator' makes another homosexual his A.D.C.[11]

There is hardly much point in arguing, on the contrary, that lunatic, murderer and homosexual alike – if one really must lump them together – are likely to *avoid* appointing lunatics, murderers and homosexuals, respectively, for fear of drawing attention to themselves. It is just as plausible that, as long as they had to hide the nature of their own personalities, they would actively discriminate *against* individuals of their own sort. But that is not the point. Nor is the fact that, if you wanted to present Nazism as a conspiracy, it would make a little more sense to present it as a clique of men who shared the same extreme political views. That would, at least, include most of them, whereas homosexuality does not. In addition, there are the Night of the Long Knives and the men with the pink triangles to be taken into account. Röhm's homosexuality could be overlooked so long as he remained useful; the moment he did not, it became a reason for getting rid of him – as is made perfectly clear in this entry in Goebbels' diary:

> What Röhm wanted was, of course, right in itself but in practice it could not be carried through by a homosexual and an anarchist. Had Röhm been an upright solid personality, in all probability some hundred generals rather than some hundred SA leaders would have been shot on 30 June [1934].[12]

In other words, it was ultimately his homosexuality that made him *and* his policies expendable. Nazism was, of course, fundamentally *anti*-homosexual, even if a proportion of Nazis were homosexual. But the myth of collective perversion had a purpose to serve in the anti-Nazi struggle – which was rarely noticeably pro-homosexual itself – and the facts of the matter could be allowed to lie fallow.

A measured, if brief, examination of the question of Hitler's possible homosexuality takes place in Karl Billinger's book *Hitler Is No Fool* (undated, but apparently written in 1939). Billinger was an anti-Nazi who had been incarcerated in a concentration camp and had then gone into exile in the United States. In his chapter 'Who Is Hitler?' a subsection headed 'The Bachelor' discusses the rumours of homosexuality, impotence and syphilis: 'Almost all of them are without foundation, because those who really know will not or can no longer tell.' The most Billinger will commit himself to is that Hitler 'undoubtedly is suffering from sexual repressions'. He mentions the open homosexuality of Röhm and Heines – 'The orgies which they held almost publicly more than once aroused storms of protest within the Nazi Movement itself' – and the fact that Count Helldorf's affair with 'the adventurer Hanussen, alias Steinschneider' did not cost the former his job as Berlin's chief of police. ('It cost only Hanussen's life.') He also reports that in 1927, when asked to dismiss various SA officers who were said to have been sexually abusing boys in the Hitler Youth, Hitler dismissed the matter, saying, 'I don't give a hoot whether they — from the front or the back!' Billinger disagrees with Goebbels' claim that Röhm and Heines were shot because they were homosexual. Yet, despite these signs of indulgence towards homosexuality within Nazism – 'He protected his followers as long as he believed he was sure of their faithfulness' – Billinger concludes by reiterating that 'there is no known basis for the assumption that Hitler himself is homosexual – or ever has indulged in homosexuality.'[13]

In *Germany Possessed* (1941), H.G. Baines implicitly purveyed the rumour of Hitler's perversion, via an attribution of unmanliness. Just as interesting is the contrast he establishes with Joseph Stalin:

> Stalin is a wolf: killing is natural to him. But Hitler is subtle, austere, effeminate, secluded. His make-up has probably a preponderance of feminine elements, albeit in a perverted form.

Baines adds a thumbnail sketch of Hitler in his jackboots, 'never unaware of the impression he is making, like a vain woman.'[14] There is something here about class: the difference between the 'natural' brutality of the peasant and the twisted wiles of the bourgeois ex-artist. By contrast with the later Yalta meeting's trinity of old men – Stalin, Roosevelt and Churchill – Hitler and Mussolini were often represented as blinded by personal vanity. Mussolini was more frankly ridiculed as a buffoon, but his masculinity was hardly ever impugned in the ways that Hitler's was. Homosexual, impotent, mono-testicular or infested with syphilis – Hitler's manifest cleverness had to be undermined by creating the impression of a volatile hysteric whose political perversity had origins in sexual perversion. August Kubizek, a close friend during Hitler's youth in Vienna, famously dismissed the possibility that Hitler was homosexual, in his post-war memoir:

> He could not bear the shallow superficiality of certain circles in Vienna, and I cannot remember a single occasion when he let himself go in his attitude to the other sex. At the same time, I must categorically assert that Adolf, in physical as well as sexual aspects, was absolutely normal. What was extraordinary in him was not to be found in the erotic or sexual spheres, but in quite other realms of his being.[15]

This is the period around which the rumours are most densely concentrated; there is an all-male hostel, where Hitler stayed, which tends to feature in them. Kubizek's book is generally persuasive, and he has usually been received as an honest witness. However, those who have credited the sexual rumours have argued that, if Kubizek, as an intimate friend, had himself been involved in that aspect of Hitler's life, he would later have covered it up. Apart from a few mavericks, subsequent biographers have taken the line that the matter needs raising, so persistently has it already been aired, even if mostly by writers with ulterior motives; but that no evidence has ever been found to support rumours which so clearly had their propagandistic uses. Even as relentlessly creative a psychological biographer as Robert Waite summarises the case in very few words:

> There is insufficient evidence to warrant the conclusion that Hitler was an overt homosexual. But it seems clear that he had latent homosexual tendencies, and it is certain that he worried a great deal about them.[16]

There is an obvious contradiction in the latter sentence – how can it be so 'certain' that he worried about something that it only 'seems clear that he had'? – but coming from a biographer who sounds as if he would have relished drawing a more positive conclusion on the matter, this position statement is admirably restrained. As ever, though, the rumours are served in being raised at all, even if they go on to be judiciously dismissed.[17]

For a while, the homosexuality of Ernst Röhm was a favourite topic among left-wing journalists, attracting a range of negative responses from ridicule to moral outrage, all designed to undermine the broader Nazi claim to social discipline and moral superiority. Finally, a man called Kurt Tucholsky wrote a short essay for *Die Weltbühne* (26 April 1932) straightforwardly entitled 'Röhm', in which he made a simple and rather touching plea for the homophobic propaganda to stop. 'I consider these attacks against the man improper,' he writes, for the well-mannered reason that 'one should not seek out one's enemy in bed'. It is not clear whom he means by 'we' in his climactic peroration – it is vaguely possible that he is a homosexual identifying with fellow homosexuals, but more probable that he means fellow leftists, in which case he is overstating the Left's commitment to homosexual law reform – but his rhetoric requires the collective first person to remind the Left of the requirement for solidarity:

> We oppose the disgraceful Paragraph 175 wherever we can; therefore we may not join voices with the chorus that would condemn a man because he is a homosexual. Did Röhm commit a public scandal? No. Has he abused young boys? No. Has he consciously transmitted venereal diseases? No. Such and only such can justify public criticism – everything else is his affair.

It has to be said that Tucholsky's is an isolated voice, certainly an untypical one. His argument that Röhm is, as it were, a 'good' homosexual and deserving of the courtesy of a private life cannot have carried much weight in anti-Nazi circles, where the slightest hint of sexual scandal among men who had laid such a substantial claim to the moral high ground would be developed to its fullest propagandistic potential. In a sense, Tucholsky's intervention cannot be accepted as valid in the struggle against Nazism; but it is a timely and persuasively generous contribution to the argument about homosexual equality. He does, though, allow one way in which the knowledge about Röhm's homosexuality can legitimately be used against the Nazis while not being used against homosexuals: 'If Goebbels screeches or Hitler thunders about the moral decay of modern times, then it should be pointed out that there are obviously homosexuals among the Nazi troops.' It is a reasonable argument, but one that would lose its validity on 30 June 1934, once Röhm and his friends had been killed.[18]

## Publications and Bookshops

In his chapter on Cultural Bolshevism (*Kultur-Bolschewismus*) in *Germany Puts the Clock Back* (1933), Edgar Ansel Mowrer lists the titles of books he found on display in a bookshop window in the very centre of Berlin in July 1932. He stood on the pavement in front of the shop and copied them down into a notebook; they included *The Witches' Love-Kettle*, *Flagellantism and Jesuit*

*Confessions, Sadism and Masochism, Sappho and Lesbos,* the magazine *The Third Sex* and a handy guide for all those sexual tourists, *Places of Prostitution in Berlin.* Mowrer sounds taken aback when he reports: 'While I stood and wrote down the titles, a crowd of adolescents gathered and made remarks about "lustful foreigners". They seemed as used to the sight of the sexual tourist they took him for as they must have been to the shop window itself. Meanwhile, according to Mowrer, the arts had relinquished their duty to uplift the spirit and unify the culture; instead, 'art had sickened, integral style given way to eclecticism, atonal music, cubism, futurism, experimental literature. After the defeat [of 1918] and revolution, nothing of the old order seemed to be left.' In its place, where once there were 'scruples' and 'discipline', the democrats of the Weimar Republic instated liberty – or, as Mowrer calls it, 'the liberty of catastrophe'. Of this disaster, one of the worst signs was a changing attitude to the 'sexual perversions' – by which he seems to mean only homosexuality (and male homosexuality, at that): 'After the war the laws punishing these practices were not changed, but they were ignored. An agitation was started to make perversions that did not entail the seduction or abuse of minors a purely private matter.' There had been, as he says, no change in the law; the very fact of a campaign against Paragraph 175 was sufficient proof of collective moral decay.[19]

Edgar Ansel Mowrer's list of the titles of dirty books, the collection of which cost him so much public embarrassment, reappears in its entirety in F. Yeats-Brown's *European Jungle* (1939), where it serves the same purpose as it did in Mowrer's book by illustrating, virtually unsupported by any other hard evidence, the depth to which the Republic had sunk before National Socialism came along. At least Mowrer had gone to Berlin and copied down his list on a real sidewalk, taunted by real victims of Germany's moral decline; and at least he presented it as an item of empirical evidence from which to draw wider conclusions. In Yeats-Brown's book, the evidence is the same and the prejudged conclusion is the same, but the leap between them is somehow even more breathtaking. From the one seedy bookshop in Berlin and the kids outside who taunted Mowrer, Yeats-Brown derives this grand overview of national change: 'Pornographic literature was displayed in the leading bookshops of the principal cities, and eagerly bought by boys and girls who thought themselves emancipated from the cramping complexes of their elders.' Of course, they have to be 'boys and girls' rather than young men and women, to emphasise the theme of the corruption of children; and that they are seeking to escape the 'complexes' of their parents suggests an impertinent Freudianism, the modernistic theories of the Viennese Jew which had seduced the younger generation away from the older generation's decent ignorance of the unconscious. Yeats-Brown cannot resist another racist slur in this account of Weimar's moral failure: 'There is a Slav element in the Germans, and the same dark forces as had captured Russia [Cultural Bolshevism, presumably] were working here in an underworld of failures, hysterics and sadists. All travellers to Germany at this time noted the corruption of manners and morals.'[20] For Slav read Jew, the infection from the East. For 'failures, hysterics and sadists' read sexual perverts, conjured into being by words ('hysterics', 'sadists') which had not existed before a pack of Jewish psychoanalysts and sexologists started inventing new perversions of the natural reproductive instinct.

In *Hitler's Wonderland* (1934), Michael Fry provides another list of 'pornographic' books available in Weimar Germany, all of them published by Magnus Hirschfeld's Institute of Sexual Science. They include *Stories of Morals in Paris*, *The Lustful Woman*, and *Picture Gallery of Erotic Practices*. Like Mowrer before him and Yeats-Brown after, Fry is not interested in the arguments of the publications he lists except to the meagre extent that their titles suggest their contents. Merely to raise certain topics at all, to name certain problems, is to promote them; and to promote them is akin to the publishing of pornography. (In a paragraph deploring a publication on abortion, Fry does not write the word itself. Instead he mentions 'illegal operations' carried out 'with the intention of facilitating "free love".') He mentions in passing 'Richard Linsert's masterpiece' *Unzucht unter Männern* (Male Sexual Offences), which offered 'a frank excuse of homosexuality' and 'pretended to show that particularly degrading vice in a favourable light'. Fry ridicules the defenders of such publications and the very idea that, in suppressing the Institute and its capacity to publish them, the Nazis were conducting a campaign against culture:

> Quite naturally, if the uncensored publications issued by the Institute and other publishers belong to the realm of 'culture', then Hitler should be severely condemned for retarding the progress of civilisation. On the other hand, if 'culture' and pornography are synonymous – as was undoubtedly the case in [pre-Nazi] Germany – then for the sake of Christian civilisation and the moral health of coming generations, it would be much safer to abolish 'culture'.

Note that he narrows the concept of civilisation down to 'Christian civilisation', a phrase which, in the context of National Socialism, has undisguised implications of exclusion. In claiming that Hirschfeld's Institute was the 'chief source of the lewd publications which flooded Germany's bookstalls', Fry has already made a point of adding that 'nearly all the members of this Institute were Jews'. For Fry, as for his ideological masters, resistance to the sexual reform movement was a racial project, since psychoanalysis and sexology were regarded as instruments in a Jewish plot to undermine the Aryan soul. The undissembling acceptance of the abolition of what others call culture, delivered with an irony that is every bit as complacent as it is clumsy, is an unexceptional attack on anything that might be stigmatised as un-Christian.

## Sexual Tourism

For obvious reasons, Berlin in the 1920s and 1930s attracted sexual tourists, both from the German regions and from abroad. As we have seen, various clubs and cabarets had been developed with an eye to such tourists, rather than as routine social facilities for the people of the city. These places were invariably expensive to frequent, and often seemed packed with observers rather than with the clientele they purported to serve. Gay clubs would end up catering to foreign heterosexuals who were looking for a hint of the 'decadence' which only Berlin – or so it was said – could provide. Christopher Isherwood described that party of young American men egging each other on to enter the Salomé.[21] Most of these observers, both German and foreign, must have gone for their own amusement. A significant number of others, however, went to be horrified, and then wrote up what they had seen, affecting the detachment of the anthropologist at the same time as they spluttered with moral self-righteousness; thereby affording their readers, at a distance, the same access to moral superiority. As well as this moral agenda, many of them also came armed with its adjunct political agenda.

Michael Fry's next gambit in *Hitler's Wonderland* is to attribute the evils of Berlin's gay scene to the same agency, by name the Institute of Sexual Science but by implication the Jews who were behind it:

> With the Institute, supported by many other sources, turning out pornographic magazines and books, it was only natural that the public should be supplied with places where all this 'culture' could be put into practice. The corrupt administration of the cities did not censure the Institute, so why should it forbid Pervert-Clubs, Homosexuality Leagues or 'Daisy' Bars?

('Daisy' bars were drag bars.) The implication is that, without the Institute, there would be no homosexuals in Berlin; or perhaps, slightly more logically, without the Institute to suggest the idea and to give them the necessary confidence, homosexuals would not have begun to gather in 'public' locations. Fry now takes us on a short tour of these locations, starting with the Eldorado. (In 1927, Otto Dix had painted a picture of this establishment.) At first, the place seems not unlike other nightclubs, although it does seem ominous that instead of *dancing* to the jazz that is being played, 'couples slither listlessly round the floor' to it. Using all his literary powers, including the galumphing irony to which he has already subjected his readers for some time, Fry sits down at a table in the corner and allows us to watch what he points out, starting with 'that rather pretty blonde girl over there'; we may ask her to dance if we wish to, but before we do he feels he should point out (in italics denoting an appropriate level of shock) that *she happens to be a man*. She is one of many such creatures in Berlin, although the prettiness that Fry has dared to notice sets her apart from many of her sort:

> Now that your eye is trained, you can pick out fifty of these 'Daisies' at a glance – most of them are rather unattractive. That is because we are in the 'Eldorado', the popular resort. For those who can afford them, there are smaller, more exclusive night-clubs, where you find no creatures with rough chins dressed in imitation Paris models. There you would see the cream of the 'Daisies' – the *beau-monde* of homosexuality – the better class of male prostitutes of which Berlin, Hamburg, Stuttgart, Munich, Cologne, etc. are full.

Although he has a 'trained' eye for these exotic creatures, and is willing to pass on his training to his readers, the extent of Fry's experience as a witness to such marvels is unclear. One must be generous in supposing that he had actually exercised his eye for a five o'clock shadow in the Eldorado, since he does describe the place, if only sketchily; he may even have visited one or two of the 'more exclusive' dives that someone has told him about, although that is less likely; but he shows no sign of actually having seen those whores on the streets and in the bars of the other major German cities. By now, his 'short tour' of visible vice has started to sound like hearsay. Hearsay, in the present context, means Nazi propaganda.

Our intrepid Virgil now leads us out into the street, pointing out the male 'street-walkers' as we pass on to the Kurfürstendamm and Potsdamer Strasse. He adds helpfully didactic comments: 'Notice how they accost the men – competing with women in the oldest profession in the world'. But in this cliché he reaches the limit of his familiarity with the homosexual degeneracy that has flooded not only Berlin but 'Christian civilisation' itself. For lack of any further revelations about man-loving men, he leads us instead into what he calls 'a Kaffir Dance Hall' and launches into a tirade of racist invective. So the sum total of his first-hand observation of homosexuality in Germany is one drag bar and some hustlers in the street; plus, of course, one pro-homosexual book by Richard Linsert (see above, p. 200). Yet the tone of this whole passage is set at a regulation pitch of hysteria, to give the impression that more is being revealed than actually is. It is then with summary satisfaction that Fry is able to report the beneficial effects of National Socialism: 'Hitler has cleaned up all the vice and filth which I have chronicled here – immoral Germany is a thing of the past.' As the men with the pink triangles and the women with the black triangles are given hard labour or worse, Fry is happy to be able to report that 'Things are different nowadays ... you can walk round the streets without being accosted by scores of male street-walkers ... the Institute of Sexual Science is no more ... The very air you breathe is purer.'[22]

In his pro-Hitlerite book *Hitler* (1931), Wyndham Lewis self-consciously conducts 'the Anglo-Saxon reader around a characteristic *Nachtlokal*' in the Berlin of 1930. The club in question is (again) the Eldorado. As we are led in, we find the usual atmosphere and jazz music – or, as Lewis calls them, 'the true appropriate glitter and nigger-hubbub'; and yet, indeed, this very expectedness is disappointing, since Lewis takes it for granted that the readers he is intro-ducing to the place are looking, not for a mere nightclub from the range of their own experience, but for 'the *frisson* of the exotic and the peculiar'. With that in mind, when we enter the Eldorado 'all at first is depressingly normal.' The idea is to sit down with one of the club's expensive-looking hostesses and buy her a drink; but, as Lewis points out in an almost impenetrably double-negatived sentence, the unsuspecting visitor's first impression will be that 'the exotic and the peculiar' are not on offer here: 'Still, he will have to be a sightseer of some penetration not to think that his sightseeing eyes may not this time be destined to gloat, upon what he had promised them he should find there.' All is not lost, though: for after a couple more expensive drinks the hostesses will confidingly whisper to their guests 'that they are *men*'. So we have got what we came for, and it serves us right. In case we doubt their word, since the appearance of these seeming women 'is too like, it is too true to nature by far', each of our hostesses 'will invite the sceptical tourist to pass his disbelieving paw beneath her chin'. (Is this the closest we shall come to a caress? It may depend on how many of those expensive drinks we can afford.) The proof of manhood will be found beneath their jawbones: 'a bed of harsh unshaven bristles as stiff as those of a toothbrush'. In an ironic reversal, Lewis leaves his Anglo-Saxon tourist so confused by the womanly normality of 'all these *trompe l'oeil*, spurious ladies' that, even after feeling the physical proof of the ill-shaven jaw, he is still asking himself 'What if after all he is being deceived?' What if these male transvestites are not men at all, but the very women they appear to be? Lewis wittily leads us to a point at which we must accept that these ladies, be they female or male, may be not only *trompe l'oeil* but also *trompe la taille*. He treats the matter pretty lightly, even to the extent of admitting from the start that he was himself deceived by the Eldorado's male prostitutes. But that is not the point of this guided tour of Berlin's underworld. He is describing a city – a whole culture, indeed – gone bad.

At the end of the decade, Wyndham Lewis published a second book about Nazism, *The Hitler Cult* (1939), this time expressing a disillusioned view. Knowing – and hating the fact – that he will be compared with André Gide, who famously reported his disillusionment with the Soviet system in *Retour de l'URSS* (1936) after he had actually observed it at first hand, Lewis claims never to have been truly taken in by fascism (as if he had seen the underside of its jaw from afar). He underlines this claim with a homophobic swipe at Gide and others: 'I could not "find out" Hitler or Mussolini because the nationalist uplift in which they traffic has never appealed to me. In a word, boy scouts are not my cup of tea.' As part of his justification for having believed that the arrival of Hitler on the scene had been beneficial for Germany, he restates the customary argument about the decadent state of Weimar Berlin:

> Pre-Hitler Berlin was a sink of iniquity – the fingers of any moderately fussy patriot must have itched to spring-clean it. Its male prostitutes alone, with their india-rubber breasts and padded hips – the fairy hostesses of *Eldorado* – were a standing invitation to the Puritan to organise a 'march on Berlin'.

This is the 'moral' argument at its crudest and most pared-down. No 'patriot' could have seen such a place as the Eldorado with Lewis' own light-heartedness when he described it in his earlier book. By implication, presumably, insofar as no 'patriot' could want to frequent such a dive – both because it is for tourists and because it contains particular kinds of Germans – no 'patriot' can be imagined as having a homosexual identity. The mere presence of ersatz women in the club is enough to foment and justify a right-wing putsch. At this point, Lewis reprints in full the description of the club from the earlier book. Somehow, that ironic account returns him to a good humour and, at a distance of a mere year, he makes the following comment on what Nazism has done to the Berlin he visited:

> In 1930 the German capital was the most diverting place in Europe for the sightseer, though, as you will have gathered from the above passage, the sightseer must not be morally squeamish. To-day it is strangely shrunken, and given over to political edification. For the Berliner, life has become like a never-ending film of *The Life of Adolf Hitler*.

Thus, although he felt the city needed spring-cleaning, he is sorry to find it no longer grubby. The posture is perverse, and he recognises it as such. The cleaner

Berlin is an altogether duller spot than it used to be. This is one of the rather flimsy bases of Lewis' sudden conversion to the anti-Nazi cause.[23]

One last tourist of Berlin dives, this one a conquering soldier. In his account of Germany in the inter-war period, *Assize of Arms* (1945), J.H. Morgan provides the customary report of moral disintegration in the arts and on the streets, throughout a nation brought low by military defeat and economic mismanagement. Morgan's grand narrative – it fills two volumes – of disarmament and rearmament includes in its undertones a related narrative of *moral* disarmament and rearmament, occurring at the same time, sharing the same participants, and driven by many of the same causal factors. Having described a stage review called *Harem Nights* (*Harem Nachte*) at Berlin's Apollo Theatre, in which naked women were ravaged by what the management described as 'genuine blacks from Africa' (*echte Schwarze aus Afrika*), 'almost as nude' as their victims, Morgan reflects that at least the ' "sex appeal" ' of the gyrating women was 'natural'. By contrast,

> What repelled British officers in Berlin and elsewhere with an almost physical nausea was the open and blatant evidence, which confronted us wherever we went, of the unnatural. That 'dark' offence . . . 'which is not so much as to be mentioned among Christians', flourished like a horrible fungus in the moral decay around us. It seemed to be accepted as a matter of course. 'Soliciting' by men was practised with the most shameless impudence in the streets, the Tiergarten, the foyers of fashionable hotels, as though they were licensed by the police. Even in polite society one German would say of another, and his tastes, 'Er ist homosexual' [*sic*], as one might speak of a man being fond of cricket or golf.

As in Fry's book, the invocation of the epithet *inter Christianos non nominandum*, for the love of which Christians dare not speak the name, is unfortunate in the context of inter-war Germany, if Morgan does not mean to suggest that Jews are more prone to indulging in that sort of thing. (It is certainly not a point he dwells on as Fry does; in fact, he states later on that homosexuality is no less shocking to the Jews than to the Roman Catholics.) It goes without saying that Morgan cannot have frequented such 'polite society' in England as might be found in Oxford colleges or houses in Bloomsbury, where it would have been far less shocking to call a man a bugger than to accuse him of liking golf.

Morgan reports that a Major Macmahon, a friend of his at the War Office, once wrote to him in Berlin, mentioning that he had heard there was 'a "Society" of homo-sexualists' in Germany who published their own magazine, and asking Morgan, for reasons best known to himself, if he could get him a copy of it. Morgan was taken aback – 'I thought at first that Macmahon was pulling my leg' – not by his friend's strange request, but by the very idea that such a 'Society' (*Verein*) should exist at all. It was not difficult to find out that the magazine was called *Freundschaft* or, indeed, to track down a copy: 'I bought a copy for my correspondent at a newspaper kiosk in the Unter den Linden, where I found it openly displayed. One glance at its contents was enough.' He was further surprised to discover that the magazine had been appearing regularly since before the war – and had not been suppressed. The issue he sent Macmahon contained one item which Morgan felt was especially pernicious: 'The character of this horrible periodical is sufficiently indicated by the fact that it flourished a leading article claiming Jesus Christ's affection for the beloved disciple [John the Evangelist] as a proof that the founder of Christianity approved and practised sexual perversion.'

On the whole, Morgan's strict homophobia is, in its way, more measured than that of many other of the shockable tourists who must have been as common on the streets of Berlin as they claimed the hustlers were. Morgan's account seems based on personally observed detail, and his footnotes show that he is joining a debate to which he has listened before opening his mouth. That said, Morgan takes a pretty standard anti-Nazi line by attributing the excesses of homosexuality to the Nazis themselves.[24] Adding 'lust', 'cruelty', 'bestiality' and 'homicidal fury' to the homosexuality he has been discussing, he says 'it is a simple fact that those whose practice of these vices was the most notorious were the very men who formed the spearhead of the Nazi conspiracy against the State. Almost without exception, the Nazi leaders were known and notorious as practitioners of these repulsive vices.' He cites with approval a German writer's claim that a 'homo-sexual taint . . . seemed characteristic of them all'.[25] He claims that Hitler only ever 'affected to discover' in Ernst Röhm, his 'boon companion and political bed-fellow', the 'vicious habits which had long been known to every one else' once he had decided to have him assassinated for reasons of political rivalry. Indeed, he cites with more approval the claim of a police commissioner that 'this nasty vice was and is in Germany at one and the same time the secret of political success, if practised discreetly, and the ruin of the practitioner if, in practising it, he is indiscreet'. Quoting the commissioner's preposterous claim that in Nazi Germany it is expedient 'to have homo-sexual tastes, or to affect to have them', Morgan concludes this stage of his argument with a flourish: 'So much for Hitler's claim to have cleansed Germany from vice'.[26]

What Morgan regards, with some distaste, as a failure on the part of the Nazi authorities can just as well be read, instead, as one of the social miracles of the war. Not all the destructive, homophobic zeal of National Socialism could wipe out the gay subcultures of Berlin. They survived. When Peter Adam explored the city's nightlife in 1949, he found plenty of interesting *lokals*. There was the Kleist Casino, which catered for men who wanted to dance with other men, and Die Ewige Lampe (The Eternal Lamp), which was exclusively lesbian. He especially liked Elly's Beer Bar, 'a rather friendly and sleazy working men's bar' run by a formidable transvestite. American and British soldiers used to frequent this place in mufti – for it was off limits – to watch the makeshift wrestling shows staged by Elly's half-naked gang of rent boys.[27] On 28 September 1959, Edward Albee went to West Berlin for the opening of *Die Zoo-Geschichte*, Pinkas Brown's translation of his play *The Zoo Story*, on a mind-blowing double bill with Samuel Beckett's *Krapp's Last Tape*. (Brown had been sent a copy of the play from Italy by his friend David Diamond.) While in Berlin, Albee observed a gay scene not much changed in its essentials since the 1930s. Boys from the eastern sector of the city would cross to the West to hustle. He wrote home to his lover, William Flanagan:

> Most of the boys seem pretty gay for me; they all dance at these saloons, with each other. Other places do this: One bar caters to middle-aged and old men, who go there, dance with each other etc. One bar is for drags, one bar is for drags over fifty and on, and on. One bar which, damn it, doesn't reopen until after I leave, has boxing and wrestling matches, with the winner going to the highest bidder. And then, there are some plain bars too. Just bars, with just people.[28]

Regardless of the viciously intrusive virtue of the puritans, the cheerful vices of Berlin's queer population, both native and transient, proved resilient. Weimar's legacy was not so much the vengeful righteousness of Nazism as the efficient fervour with which queer Berlin re-established itself and thrived after the war, even at the hostile epicentre of the Cold War.

Individual homosexuals, too, survived the Nazi assault on sexual minorities – though many did not. Having been imprisoned, tortured, raped, subjected to mock execution, deported and then forced to fight for the Germans in the Wehrmacht on the Russian front, the Frenchman Pierre Seel eventually made his way homeward towards Alsace on foot. There is a brief but heart-warming passage in his memoirs when he recounts having sheltered for the night in a deserted cottage in a forest. In the morning, he slicked his hair down with sewing-machine oil and made a few camp gestures, smiling at himself in the mirror, before walking on. In this moment, a young queen's rediscovery of himself in the other worldly remoteness of a fairy-tale setting, Seel enacts in miniature the survival of his kind.[29]

# CHAPTER EIGHT

# THE SOUTHERN EXOTIC

## That Southwards Drift

The Mediterranean Sea has been described as 'first and foremost an idealized dreamscape, a sentimental geography, whose real strength comes from the fact that we are not always in it, and thus imagine it all the more strongly'.[1] To those northern Europeans who could afford to travel there before the era of cheap flights and mass tourism, the South represented an idea of freedom. Even when, strictly speaking, liberty could not be found there, liberties could be taken. Very short distances could effect major transformations in living conditions, as well as in both climate and emotional climate. Little more than two hundred miles could take a man from London, where he was subject to the vicious restraints of the Labouchere Amendment, across the Channel to Paris, where he could relax into the ways of the Napoleonic Code. When Gustav von Aschenbach, in Thomas Mann's *Death in Venice*, has 'a youthful craving for far-off places', he need only cross the symbolic barrier of the Alps, travelling from Munich to Venice, a distance of less than two hundred miles; not so far off, after all. Even within Italy itself, quite short distances are intensely felt. For instance, the poet Sandro Penna lived in Perugia until he was twenty-two or twenty-three, but used to go on family holidays to the seaside in the summer. He visited Rome for the first time in 1923, when he was sixteen – a matter of barely a hundred, quite flat miles – and felt he was discovering the South much as an Englishman might. He later said, 'The sea, the summer and this trip to Rome influenced my poetry more than anything else.'[2]

Gilbert Adair has even called 'the homosexual diaspora' itself 'that southwards drift, as if by a gravitational force, of affluent gay northern Europeans, principally Germans, English and French'.[3] Robert Aldrich argues that 'the image of a homoerotic Mediterranean, both classical and modern, is *the* major motif in the writings and art of homosexual European men from the time of the Enlightenment until the 1950s'.[4] Substantiating this claim, and concentrating on the modern period, he writes: 'Throughout the nineteenth and early twentieth centuries homosexual men from many countries travelled to the Mediterranean, following in the footsteps of [Johann] Winckelmann and [August von] Platen, Byron and [John Addington] Symonds. They came for classical ruins and Renaissance art, for sun and sea and for the youths whom they could seduce with love or money. The writers or artists among them often brought homo-erotic themes of the Mediterranean to their work.' He says the Germans formed the largest contingent of such travellers, adding that 'this is not surprising considering the legal persecution of homosexuals in Germany, the importance of classical education there in the nineteenth century, increasing interest in the history of homosexuality with the homosexual emancipation movement by the late 1800s and general northern yearning for the warmth of the South'.[5] A detailed cultural knowledge of Greece and Rome, Florence and Venice, may have attracted such travellers, but pure knowledge was not the reason for the journey. Aldrich writes: 'The voyage south was a journey outside the library and into the "real world", but as well it formed a symbolic regression from "civilisation" to the natural state of mankind.'[6] The southward journey might be transformative, indeed.

Generally speaking, the European Homintern headed southward through Italy and thence to North Africa or Greece, rather than through the Iberian peninsula or the northern Balkans. The first symbolic step, though, was to leave Paris by way of the Gare de Lyon, built for the 1900 World Exposition, and make one's way down to the Riviera on the Train Bleu.[7] The two great port cities, Marseille and Toulon, were promising destinations in their own right, even if one did not use them to catch a steamer to North Africa. In his novel *Babylon* (*Babylone*, 1927), René Crevel calls Marseille 'the city of flesh'. It is full of working men, more profusely so than Paris: 'stevedores with skin the color of their hair, after the bath that cleanses them of the sweat of the docks at the close of day, bulge with far prouder chests than those of the whistling laborers of the capital'. Southern manners produce fresh erotic effects: 'The hoodlums of the city of flesh did not make eyes, but mouths. In three twists of their thick lips, they ran the gamut of all labial, and other, possibilities, and then whistled.' The roving eye is spoilt for choice: 'One lost, ten found, one needed only to choose among these sailors who produced from their seafaring pants splendid handkerchiefs freshly stained with love and perfumed with tobacco and cognac. Each one of these loafers of the old port, with an oblique glance, and for fifty francs, would promise a skilled and robust virility, a ruddy chest, a hard belly, and thighs that, having dispensed with the hypocrisy of underpants, had the good smell of coarse-grained cloth.'[8] Stephen Tennant found Marseille, and in particular the Vieux Port, inexhaustible. Revisiting it on the eve of the

Second World War, he noted that 'the town is far more complex & romantic & tempting than I had remembered. Such thrilling exciting things keep cropping up'.[9] Marsden Hartley once encountered Hart Crane in Marseille and thought him a 'nice boy but a little flagrant in his methods'.[10]

Jean Cocteau, in *Le Livre blanc* (anonymously published in 1928), gives a similarly enticing glimpse of Toulon: 'Men in love with masculine beauty come from all corners of the globe to admire the sailors who walk about idly, alone or in groups, respond to glances with a smile and never refuse an offer of love'.[11] Cocteau was adept at passing on his enthusiasms to his friends: 'There was the camp scene at Toulon, a real sailors' port, where an English crowd of Bohemian balletomanes congregated around Cocteau – Frederick Ashton, Sophie Fedorovitch, Edward Burra, Constant Lambert'.[12] Natalie Barney's salons were subject to seasonal transfer from Paris to Beauvallon, across the gulf from St-Tropez.

A different style of holiday was developed out of one rich couple's taste for bathing and sunbathing at the height of summer. Gerald and Sara Murphy, escaping Prohibition and their parents in the USA, rented the Hôtel du Cap at Antibes for the whole summer of 1923 – it usually closed once the English tourists had fled the sun in May – thereby creating a fashion for holidaying in the real heat of the region. They commandeered the Plage de la Garoupe, a relatively small beach on the west coast of the Cap, keeping it raked and clean for the more or less exclusive use of their friends. Something of their lifestyle is conveyed in the opening section of F. Scott Fitzgerald's *Tender is the Night* (1934), along with – sad to say – a good deal of its author's homophobia. The Murphys' many gay friends are reduced by Fitzgerald to the two stereotyped pansies, Dumphry and Campion.

At the Prince of Monaco's invitation, Sergei Diaghilev moved the Ballets Russes down to the Riviera in 1922, where they performed in the Théâtre du Monte Carlo, backing on to the casino. The company capitalised on the glamour of southward travel, and also on the newly fashionable beach culture, with the ballet *Le Train bleu* in June 1924. The libretto was by Jean Cocteau, the music by Darius Milhaud, curtain by Picasso, costumes by Coco Chanel. Jean Cocteau said of the ballet, '*Le Train bleu* is more than a frivolous work . . . It is a monument to frivolity!' The music critic Alex Ross has added: 'It was also a monument to the beauty of a boy, in the form of Anton Dolin. Diaghilev had long catered to a gay subculture, but he now became rather brazen, outfitting his favourite dancers in tight bathing suits or minuscule Grecian shorts'.[13] The train itself did not feature in the ballet named after it, which was instead located on the beach.

After the French Riviera, the Italian; and then onward into the warmth, further and further from the restraints of home and inhibition . . . Achille

Essebac's novel *Partenza . . . vers la beauté!* (1898) is rather picturesquely dedicated 'To the little shoe-shine boys of Marseille, the flower-sellers of the Piazza di Spagna in Rome, the brazen urchins of Naples, and Pio, the blind boy of Florence.' In 1952, taking a characteristically sceptical view of such men and their Italian adventures, Jean Genet described Italy as 'an immense whorehouse where fags from all over the world rented for one hour, for the night or for the duration of a trip a boy or a man'.[14] Samuel Barber laid the blame on the other party: he once told Ned Rorem, 'you'll find the Italians acquiescent. But even when they say I love you they still want to be paid.'[15]

Henry James' love affair with Italy began on his first visit there in August 1869. Having walked over the border from Switzerland, so taken was he with the landscape that he went back to Switzerland in order to walk into Italy again from another direction. Looking at a boy in Torcello, James commented: 'Verily nature is still at odds with propriety.'[16] After going down from Cambridge, E.M. Forster spent a year in Italy, which he famously called 'the beautiful country where they say "yes" ' – although he himself, poor man, was still inclined to say 'no'.[17] Lytton Strachey began a two-month European tour in March 1913. From Pompeii he wrote to Ottoline Morrell: 'Oh! I longed to stay there for ever – in one of those little inner gardens, among the pillars and busts, with the fountain dropping in the court, and all the exquisite repose! Why not? Some wonderful slave boy would come out from under the shady rooms, and pick you some irises, and then to drift off to the baths as the sun was setting – and the night! What nights those must have been!'[18] He seems to have been completely blind to the bourgeois oppressiveness of the city's narrow and crowded purlieux. After Ravello, he went up to Rome, which reminded him, absurdly, of Cambridge. The American painter Fairfield Porter appears not to have been aware of any erotic attraction to other men until a trip to Italy with his mother in the autumn of 1931. It was in Florence that he struck up an intense friendship with Arthur Giardelli, a youth four years his junior.

Late in 1920, Osbert and Sacheverell Sitwell had visited Gabriele d'Annunzio during the dying glory-days of his 'Regency' at Fiume.[19] Both of the brothers were oddly seduced by him, despite his obvious buffoonery. Osbert, who did not know Italian, thought him Byronic. He subsequently took a shine to Italian fascism, approving of Mussolini as embodying and enacting d'Annunzio's ideals. In 1931 he joined the New Party of Oswald Mosley. That August, they held a rally at his family home, Renishaw Hall in Derbyshire, but by the middle of the decade Osbert's interest in the party had dwindled. Italy was quite another matter. He had understood as early as 1904, when he was sent to convalesce from an illness in San Remo, that Italy would hold a special place in his heart: 'I realised that Italy was my second country, the complement and perfect contrast to my own'. He had the added attraction of a castle owned by his father at Montegufoni in Tuscany.[20]

Others, though, were more demonstratively attracted to what they saw of fascism in Italy. Like so many travellers to Nazi Germany, they developed a kind of touristic nationalism that allowed them to transfer their love of the location and its culture to the superficial aspects, often the mere spectacle, of its new political system. Shortly before his death in Palermo in 1933, Raymond Roussel sent a copy of his *Nouvelles Impressions d'Afrique* to Mussolini. The two had met in Rome in 1926, when Roussel had invited Il Duce to view his *roulotte*, a lavish precursor to the motor home in which he was travelling. The Frenchman found the Italian 'very simple and very kind'.[21]

After the debacle of *The Well of Loneliness*, Radclyffe Hall was inclined to look southward for an environment in which she could feel comfortable. On 4 February 1929, she and Una Troubridge left London for Paris, where old friends rallied round to support them. Natalie Barney held a party in their honour, and they had tea with Colette. (Colette had admired *The Well* as a work of literature, especially in its childhood passages, but from the relatively secure position of her Parisian bohemianism she was unable to understand why a true lesbian should suffer so.) When they went back to England they bought a house in Rye in Sussex, where they could live in relative seclusion but not in isolation. E.F. Benson lived down the road in Henry James' former home, Lamb House. Noël Coward and his boyfriend Jeffrey Amherst came to tea. London was easily accessible for further socialising, as when they had supper there with John Gielgud and his friend John Perry. Una Troubridge adapted Colette's *Chéri* for the stage, but it received bad reviews when it opened in London in October 1930. Hall's next novel after *The Well of Loneliness*, the awkward religious confection *The Master of the House* (1931), was also poorly received. Meanwhile, Troubridge's continuing physical ill health resulted in her having to have her uterus, cervix and appendix removed. Peace being hard to find, the couple became increasingly restless. Even in the placid atmosphere of Rye, two such irascible women were managing to make enemies. To top it all, Radclyffe Hall fell in love with Una Troubridge's nurse, a Russian refugee called Eugenia Souline.

On 21 June 1934, the three of them left for Paris, where they saw Colette, Natalie Barney and Romaine Brooks – and where Hall and the nurse became lovers. They headed south, then back to Paris, then down to Italy. At Sirmione on Lake Garda, near the supposed ruins of Catullus' villa, they stayed with Naomi Jacob.[22] They paid a courtesy visit to Gabriele d'Annunzio, who was briefly fascinated by their type. As they wandered restlessly to and fro, a difficult life as a threesome developed, Troubridge was forever understandably fearful of being abandoned; and, as if in murky reflection of personal discomfort, as the 1930s progressed Hall and Troubridge became increasingly, and demonstratively, right-wing. In Italy in 1935 they wore black shirts and Fascist lapel ribbons. Hall tried to meet d'Annunzio again, but he had lost interest. For a Christmas present in 1936, Hall gave Troubridge a pair of cufflinks in the shape of the fascist symbol, the *fascio*. The next month, a photograph of Mussolini, which Troubridge had sent to him, came back with the Duce's signature on it; Troubridge wept with pride. When they went back to Paris, they now found Natalie Barney's anti-fascist views insufferable; and a number of their other friendships came under similar pressure as a consequence of their wholehearted conversion to the fascist cause. For them, a highlight of this period came in 1938 when, while they were in the city, both Mussolini and Hitler visited Florence. Hall and Troubridge stood at their apartment window to watch the motorcade go by. As you would expect, they chanted 'Duce! Duce!' with the rest of the crowd, and gave the fascist salute. The absurdity of the picture they conjure up is hard to resist.

When Radclyffe Hall died of cancer on 6 October 1943, Una Troubridge took her meticulous revenge on the Russian nurse, Eugenia Souline, and also, to an extent, on Hall herself. Hall had written her will a few days before her death, but instead of giving Souline a substantial bequest she left her welfare in Troubridge's capable hands. Troubridge decided not to burn her own diaries, which she had promised Hall she would; instead she burnt the manuscript of Hall's novel *The Shoemaker of Merano*, as well as all of Souline's letters. She failed to inform Hall's ninety-one-year-old mother that her daughter had died; instead, the old woman read of it in a newspaper. Souline tried to challenge the new will, but in vain. Meanwhile, Troubridge settled down between 19 February and 18 March 1945 to write the definitive and incontrovertible version of *The Life and Death of Radclyffe Hall*. As one might guess from the fact that she set aside a mere month for this supposedly important task, the outcome was an unpublishably vague eulogy. When there were tears to shed, Troubridge shed them on hearing of the death of Benito Mussolini.

After the 1928 trial, Hall had found that because the judge had ordered the destruction of *The Well of Loneliness*, she no longer held the copyright; she was not legally able to exert any influence on some individuals who had decided to dramatise her novel. Now, in 1946, the Labour administration of Clement Attlee reconfirmed the ban on *The Well*. Una Troubridge moved to Florence, where she was somewhat lionised, to her delight, by young gay men. In grudging accordance with Hall's will, she had granted Eugenia Souline a pitifully small allowance. While Souline grew ill with cancer and died of it, Troubridge was single mindedly developing a fanatical admiration for an Italian man, an opera singer.

Some Americans who had experienced Europe before the Hot war, or during it, chose to escape there for the duration of the Cold. The economic conditions were by no means as propitious as after the First World War, but a Europe still recovering from the conflict was still a much cheaper place to live in than the United States; and social conditions in the nations in which the Napoleonic Code prevailed were far easier than those back home. Travelling through southern Italy with Peter Watson in 1947, Waldemar Hansen wrote to a friend that 'Rome is quite gay on the Via Veneto, where American soldier-queens sit in cars and camp with the local belles'. He added, 'I'm told that everyone in Italy is gay, for money. It's like pre-Hitler Berlin.'[23] The composer David Diamond had been spoilt for America by his trips to France in the 1930s. Having won a schol-arship in 1935 to travel to Paris and study composition under Nadia Boulanger, he stayed until the outbreak of war, making friends with such Modernist greats as Stravinsky, Picasso and Joyce. As well as these European expatriates – not to mention Frenchmen such as Maurice Ravel and André Gide – he also benefited from encounters with Paris's cornucopia of American escapees such as Carson McCullers, Georgia O'Keeffe and the by now Americanised Greta Garbo, all three of whom became his close friends. By contrast, after his enforced return there, he found the cultural world of New York narrower and, literally, harder work. Through a period of vibrant productivity in his own compositional work, Diamond had to earn his living by playing the violin in a popular radio orchestra. He returned to Europe in 1951 as a Fulbright scholar at the University of Rome, and after a year moved to Florence. He rode out the McCarthy era by absenting himself. It is easy to understand his decision, as an openly homosexual man, to remain in Italy during the worst of the anti-gay witch-hunts. He did not return to the United States for good until 1966.

Reporting back to New York from Rome in 1958, Frank O'Hara wrote: 'Everyone is so attractive it makes you wonder if you're not demented.'[24] Gore Vidal had found the Romans 'sad and confused' in 1948, but by the early 1960s they were 'coming to life': 'Every evening hundreds of boys converged on the Pincio in order to make arrangements with interested parties. Drugs were still the province of the few, mostly artists; there was thievery, but no violence; there was no AIDS, and sex was spontaneous and untroubled.'[25]

## Capri and its Visitors

In the romantic comedy *It Started in Naples* (1960), directed by Melville Shavelson and starring Clark Gable and Sophia Loren, Gable's voice-over says of the island of Capri, 'This place certainly had every nationality and every sex – including some I never heard of.' Peter Adam called Capri 'one of those dream destinations for the homosexual diaspora', but when he went there with his new German boyfriend, the latter was spirited away by an American.[26]

Capri's first tourist, the scholar and antiquarian Jean-Jacques Bouchard, when he went there in 1632 found the island's women and boys both good-looking and willing. Travellers have been making the same discovery ever since. The Marquis de Sade visited the island and set a scene in his pornographic novel *Juliette* there. Mendelssohn composed his *Walpurgisnacht* while staying in the Albergo Pagano in 1830. But it was not until the late nineteenth century that Capri gained its reputation as a watering hole for the Homintern and attracted an international community, not only of boy-loving men but of lesbian women, too. Many were active artists and writers; most were affluent, the crucial factor in the willingness of the Capresi to welcome them.

When the German artist Christian Wilhelm Allers arrived on the island in 1890 he started to draw local personalities. His first Caprese boyfriend was a lad called Alberino, from Marina Grande; but in 1902 the *quaestura* in Naples ordered his expulsion because of his relationships with local boys. He managed to escape before the police arrived, and spent much of his life on Samoa instead. That said, sexual relations between men had actually been decriminalised in 1891. The authorities were willing to reward discretion with a blind eye: it saved them any amount of trouble.

The Germans had begun the influx, but in the mid-1890s a number of English homosexuals began to patronise the island. In 1896, while Oscar Wilde was in prison, Alfred Douglas stayed on Capri; Robert Ross visited him there for two months. The following year, Bosie rented a villa at Posillipo, back on the mainland just north of Naples. He and the newly released Wilde crossed from there to Capri for three days; they lunched with Axel Munthe at the Villa San Michele, but were snubbed by English tourists at the Quisisana hotel and asked to leave. Other arrivals from England included, independently, John Ellingham Brooks, E.F. Benson and Somerset Maugham. (When Brooks was twenty-four and Maugham sixteen, they had had an affair in Heidelberg.) Brooks would say of Capri that he 'came for lunch and stayed for life'. In 1903 he married Romaine Goddard, an American artist who had inherited a fortune from her mother the previous year. The marriage lasted only a year; where-upon Goddard gave Brooks an allowance on the sensible condition that she never see him again. This enabled him to go on living comfortably on Capri. E.F. Benson often visited him there, and in 1913 they teamed up with Somerset Maugham to take a lease on the Villa Cercola, so that Brooks could live there and Benson and Maugham could visit whenever they wanted.

The German industrialist and arms manufacturer Friedrich Alfred Krupp came to Naples in 1898 to help develop the aquarium that had been founded there in 1872. He took up residence on Capri, taking a whole floor of the Quisisana, and crossed back and forth between the island and the city in a pair of private yachts, the *Puritan* and the *Maia*. He soon became highly popular with the Capresi, renowned for his generosity in both personal gifts and public works. Thanks to him, decent roads and a public park were built. On 28 April 1900 the general gratitude of the islanders was formalised when he was declared an honorary citizen of Capri. He returned each season for four years (1898–1901), carrying out scientific research on the marine life in local waters. His explorations of other local fauna were somewhat less academic. During orgies at the Grotta di Fra' Felice, it is said, every ejaculation was celebrated with fireworks. Photographs, inevitably compromising, were taken.

It was actually at the Hotel Bristol in Berlin that Krupp kept a harem of young Italian boys. Eventually, knowing what was going on and trying to protect his own reputation, the proprietor went to the police. In 1902, the Neapolitan press got wind of scandalous goings-on chez Krupp, and then the press in Rome took up the story. In the end, the German press tested the waters, but without using Krupp's name – not, at least, until 15 November 1902, when the socialist newspaper *Vorwärts* broke ranks. Krupp sued for libel, helped by the government, which ordered the police to seize every copy of the offending article. That was as far as official support went. Krupp himself solved the matter by dying, either of a heart attack or by his own hand, on 22 November. At his funeral Kaiser Wilhelm II defended Krupp's reputation. In 1904 the Kaiser travelled to Italy to visit Victor Emmanuel III and the Pope. Those formalities over and done with, he set sail for Sicily on his yacht, the *Hohenzollern*. At Taormina he visited Wilhelm von Gloeden to look at his photographs of young Sicilians. (Also signing von Gloeden's visitors' book that day were Kuno von Moltke and Philipp, Prince of Eulenburg.) The yacht then turned northward and put in at Capri.

Norman Douglas first went to Capri in 1888, in search of blue lizards; but it was at Posillipo that, in 1897, he bought a villa, aiming to spend time there to turn himself into a writer. The following year he married a cousin, who bore him a son. He visited Capri with his wife in 1901, then alone in 1902 and again alone, this time for three months, in 1903. Like Krupp's, his attention strayed from the local animal life to its human population: the island confirmed him in his pederasty. He went home to ask his wife for a divorce, and then returned to the island at the end of the year. By 1904 he had already written two books about Capri, researched both on the ground and in the libraries of Naples; four more followed in 1906.

In 1897, two American women, Kate and Saidee Wolcott-Perry arrived on Capri and stayed. They were distant cousins, brought up in the Wild West. When Kate was twenty-three, her father had adopted Saidee, who had been left orphaned and in poverty, aged nine. Kate Perry and Saidee Wolcott decided to present themselves to the world as sisters, hyphenating their surnames as well as their lives. It is said that after Kate's father's death they ran a brothel in New Orleans. They sold some land when they decided to go travelling; and when they decided to stay on Capri they sold the rest. They had the Villa Torricella built. Finished in 1907, it was an extraordinary Doric-Moorish-Romanesque-Gothic edifice, complete with minarets. Drifters who found sanctuary in this fantasy palace included Vernon Andrews, who was too effeminate to fit in anywhere else, and Godfrey Henry Thornton, who had exhausted most of his money on boys and blackmail.

The French poet Jacques d'Adelswärd-Fersen had visited Capri in 1896 or 1897, and then again in 1901. One historian of Capri refers to him as 'a decadent and retarded parnassian'.[27] When the scandal of his private life erupted into public court and a guilty verdict in 1903, he went into exile. Retiring to Capri in 1904, he had the Villa Lysis built. (While it was being erected he went off to taste the delights of Ceylon.) In Rome he met a sharp-witted and smooth-bodied fifteen-year-old, Nino Cesarini, whom he took on as his secretary/ factotum/lover. When they got home to Capri the two of them were befriended by the Wolcott-Perrys. Although rumours of the scandal which had sent Fersen into exile had filtered down from Paris, the Wolcott-Perrys, who were surely in the know, very publicly declared that they did not believe such libels. Anyone who thought otherwise was crossed off their guest list. (A further irritant was that the Capresi resented Nino Cesarini as an interloper: if the rich residents of their island were to adopt boys in this way, they should do so with the local talent, not with Romans. Nino would never fit into the community; not that Fersen needed him to.) Vernon Andrews rendered Fersen's poems into English, but could not smoke his opium, which made him sick. Norman Douglas found Fersen boring, egotistical and humourless, especially about himself. When the Villa Lysis was completed in July 1905, the finishing touch was put to its gardens in the form of a nude statue of Cesarini by Francesco Ierace. Fersen also commissioned portraits of Nino from the sculptor Vincenzo Gemito, a man whose attempts to suppress his homosexuality had sent him on a direct route to a lunatic asylum but who in 1909 was emerging from two long decades of intermittent confinement. Fersen's commission represented, for Gemito, his favourite subject: the unclad form of the young male. Not surprisingly, Fersen wrote a novel about Capri, *Et le feu s'éteignit sur la mer . . .* (1909), dedicated to the Wolcott-Perrys. It concerns a married man who becomes a misogynist when his boyish wife leaves him; but before succumbing to the charms of real boys he throws himself off a cliff. It contained recognisable portraits of the island and many of the people who lived there.

Nino Cesarini's inevitable military service was delayed for as long as Fersen could manage, but when it was finally imminent he was subjected to a formal ceremonial of initiation. James Money describes the scene:

> Fersen decided that before his departure Nino should be ceremonially flogged, with suitable Mithraic rituals, to consecrate him as a soldier. The ceremony, which took place at the Matermania cave, was attended by Kate and Saidee Wolcott-Perry, two other friends, and the Cinghalese boys from his household, who, with two of the Torricella maids, acted as 'slaves'. Elaborate Mithraic rites continued throughout the night until at sunrise the naked Nino was given twenty lashes with straps by the Cinghalese.[28]

These distinctly pagan rites were witnessed by a girl out cutting grass, and Fersen had to flee to Paris. (He was already in bad odour locally because his novel had presented a negative version of the island's climate.) Not until the decree of banishment was rescinded in 1913 could he return, with Cesarini, to the Villa Lysis. The faithful Wolcott-Perrys held a grand dinner to welcome them back. Perhaps by way of thanks, in October Fersen took them and Cesarini on a tour of South-East Asia; they returned via the United States late in the following year.

In March 1908 Norman Douglas' divorce came through. In May he moved to Massa Lubrense on the mainland and began writing *Siren Land*, his book about the Sorrentine peninsula. After the Messina earthquake on 28 December he collected money for the victims, and in June of the following year he went south with Vernon Andrews to distribute it. (One of their muleteers was shocked to see the latter applying make-up.) Douglas' philosophy is laid out in *Siren Land*, but with a light touch. The central point is that 'What you cannot find on earth is not worth seeking.' Given this fact, the Mezzogiorno is clearly one of the best places to live, since it provides so many earthly pleasures in such obvious abundance. One hardly need stir oneself to find them: at the height of summer 'The heat is too considerable for violent exertion, but time passes quickly doing even nothing, if one does it well.' His conception of the south is rooted in his classical education, since, for Douglas as for so many northern European visitors like him, around the Mediterranean 'every footstep is fraught with memories' – that is, with memories of the ancient world. In 1910, looking out across the Gulf of Naples from Sorrento, Henry James thought that 'the present appeared to become again really classic, to sigh with strange elusive sounds of Virgil and Theocritus'.[29] Similarly, watching an olive *vendemmia*, carried out by lamplight at night, Douglas sees 'half-naked, Praxitelean shapes of men and boys' turning the stone wheel of the olive press. It seems a general comment on his escape from England when he says, 'I, too, have dwelt with shepherds in Arcadia.'[30] It was reading *Siren Land*, published in 1912, that brought Compton Mackenzie to Capri in 1913.

In 1916 Douglas wrote his Capri novel *South Wind*, which appeared in 1917. Its opening glimpse of Capri, which he calls 'Nepenthe' after the Homeric potion that helps people to forget their woes, swathes the place in mystery of a rather standard, *fin-de-siècle* kind. Like one of Poe's cadaverous women, it seems both desirable and mephitic, a place to leave before one arrives:

> Viewed from the clammy deck on this bright morning, the island of Nepenthe resembled a cloud. It was a silvery speck upon that limitless expanse of blue sea and sky. A south wind breathed over the Mediterranean waters, drawing up their moisture which lay couched in thick mists about its flanks and uplands. The comely outlines were barely suggested through a veil of fog. An air of unreality hung about the place. Could this be an island? A veritable island of rocks and vineyards and houses – this pallid apparition?[31]

However, Douglas soon brings his portrayal of Capri down to earth and the earthy: for this island was nothing if not tangible. Mackenzie would start his own first Capri novel, *Vestal Fire*, in 1926; it would be dedicated to John Ellingham Brooks, but his second Capri novel, *Extraordinary Women*, which he wrote in 1927, was dedicated to Douglas. In both, the island is called 'Sirene'. The later of the two, unlike *The Well of Loneliness*, was published without any problem, probably because it dealt with sapphism lightly, as a matter for social comedy, rather than earnestly, as a matter for social reform. Although – and because – his wife was with him, Mackenzie bought himself a cottage in which to meet his boyfriends or to lend to friends for the same purpose. Such men knew what they were on the island for, and they arranged their lives accordingly, even if at great expense.

During the Great War, in Nino Cesarini's absence, Fersen became a drug addict (opium and cocaine) and allowed the garden at the Villa Lysis to become overgrown around him. Saidee Wolcott-Perry died in February 1917. Left on her own, Kate broke with Fersen once and for all. A cousin came from the United States to take her home. (She would die in 1924.) When the conflict came to an end, Vernon Andrews did his only known war work: he threw a party to celebrate. (Later, told of his own impending death in the flu epidemic of 1920, Andrews would maintain his standards of sangfroid by cracking open one last bottle of champagne.) Nino Cesarini returned to the Villa Lysis in triumph, bearing the Croix de Guerre.

After the war, as travel across Europe became easier again, there was an influx of affluent lesbians to this corner of the Mediterranean. Among them were the pianist Renata Borgatti, with whom Compton Mackenzie's wife Faith is said to have fallen in love, Mrs Francesca Lloyd and Mimì Franchetti. Most lesbian travellers would call on the Principessa Helène Soldatenkov, who had been living for many years at the Villa Siracusa, across the sound in Sorrento, waited on by an all-female staff. Her many lovers were 'governesses' to her daughter, who was also called Helène but known as 'Baby'. Mimì Franchetti succeeded in seducing the previously heterosexual Baby Soldatenkov, a matter which gave her mother, too, great satisfaction. (Compton Mackenzie wrote about them all in *Extraordinary Women*.)

In August 1919 Romaine Brooks arrived on the island. She threw her ex-husband out of the Villa Cercola and settled there. Faith Mackenzie, Compton's wife, gave a very vivid impression of Brooks and the effect her arrival had on the island's community of women:

> To be loved by Romaine for even five minutes gave any young woman who cared about it a cachet not obtainable since the days when young women could boast of being loved by the mighty Sappho herself. The arrival of this striking personality was a sensation. A heat-wave, hot even for Capri in August, sent temperatures up. Feverish bouquets of exhausted blooms lay about the big studio, letters and invitations strewed her desk, ignored for the most part, while she, wrapped in her cloak, would wander down to the town as the evening cooled and sit in the darkest corner of Morgano's terrace, maddeningly remote and provocative.[32]

Brooks painted a portrait of the Marchesa Casati lying naked on a bearskin rug. Casati left it behind when she vacated the Villa San Michele, which she had been renting from Axel Munthe; but when he came home he did not fancy keeping it.

In the summer of 1921 Fersen fell in love with Manfred, a schoolboy from a rich Sorrentine background. In October 1923 he took the boy to Sicily, where they visited the Baron von Gloeden in his Taormina studio. Soon after his return to Capri, Fersen committed suicide. By contrast, Norman Douglas returned home to Capri in March 1923 and flourished there again from the unexpected moment when he was met on the quay by the novelist Winifred Ellerman (Bryher) and hundreds of welcoming Capresi. When Hugh Walpole spent ten days on Capri in 1925, he complained of its expatriate community that 'No one here has a shred of reputation.'[33]

Although under fascism Capri was purged, and many homosexual foreigners were sent packing while others discreetly left of their own accord, after this gesture of moral action, the rest were left alone to get on with their lives. Nothing really stemmed the flow of such men to the siren isle. Newcomers included the artist Otto Sohn-Rethel, whose favourite subject was no surprise: a naked boy. In 1938 the bisexual Curzio Malaparte wangled permission, against local opposition, to build his Modernist house at Punta di Massullo. It was and is the most brazen building on the island, a glamorous violation of the rocky coastline, apparently designed to leave only its own occupants with the perfect view that had preceded it, but, if so, failing to the extent that it actually improves on nature; only its own occupants do not receive the benefit.

If prostitution had been a regional pastime for decades, during the Second World War in Naples it became a necessity for much of the starved population. Famously, flesh became cheaper than bread. The Allied troops provided the market but were also, themselves, marketable. Carlo Levi heard 'stories of drunken colored soldiers whose bodies the Neapolitan street boys passed from hand to hand, selling them like any other kind of merchandise'.[34] Curzio Malaparte tilts at the systematic prostitution of a whole city in his novel/memoir La Pelle (The Skin), but most notoriously speaks of how Naples became homosexualised by the circumstances of the Allied push from Salerno north-ward:

> The international community of inverts, tragically disrupted by the war, was reconstituting itself in that first strip of Europe to be liberated by the handsome Allied soldiers. A month had not yet passed since its liberation, and already Naples, that noble and illustrious capital of the ancient Kingdom of the Two Sicilies, had become the capital of European homosexuality, the most important world-centre of the forbidden vice, the great Sodom to which all the inverts of the world were flocking[.]

Malaparte is not the most reliable witness, in all his books being prone to spec-tacular, self-serving exaggeration; but even his highest flights of fantasy are at least based in observed reality. His sense of the depths to which the people of Naples had sunk through no fault of their own is ultimately persuasive: 'If the mothers didn't sell their children, do you know what would happen? To make money, the children would sell their mothers.'[35] When Malaparte's book was published (as Le Peau in 1949 and La Pelle in 1950), Neapolitans took its portrayal of themselves in bad part and Malaparte was treated accordingly. Somewhat less extremist versions of Naples in extremis, just after its liberation from the Nazis, can be found in John Horne Burns' novel The Gallery (1947) and in Norman Lewis' memoir Naples '44 (1978). Burns' novel includes a detailed representation of a gay bar in the Galleria Umberto. Momma, a rich, middle-aged Milanese, opens the bar after the city falls to the Allies in October 1943. The Military Police threaten to put it off limits if she does not stop Italians mixing with the US troops in an undesirable manner. The chapter about Momma describes one typical evening in the bar, leading up to the habitual late arrival of Captain Joe and a young Florentine, a fight at closing time, the arrival of the Military Police, and the crowning glory of Momma's strategic fainting fit.

In *Kaputt* (1944), his other terrifying novel/memoir of the war years, Curzio Malaparte records a conversation over dinner in the Italian Embassy on the Wannsee near Berlin. The assembled guests, who include both Germans and Italians, marvel at Malaparte's news, given him only days previously on Capri by Axel Munthe, that Eddi Bismarck is now a soldier. The object of their wonder and mirth is the Count Albrecht Edzard von Bismarck-Schönhausen, a homosexual man better suited to the Capri he left shortly before being called up than to the battlefields of the north. 'Thanks to Eddi, Germany will win the war,' jokes one very senior German. Malaparte himself is unsympathetic to poor Eddi's fate: 'The thought of the blond, delicate Eddi peeling potatoes in the Strasbourg barracks filled me with mischievous glee.'[36]

An English lady, one Mrs Hinde, felt sure it was the lack of a golf course that had weakened Capri's moral fibre. Mercifully, there is not enough room on the island for a course, so the fibre remained lax. Fascism and the war left the spirit of Capri undaunted. Even the dead hand of Cold War paranoia could not completely stifle its investment in perverse pleasures. Norman Douglas returned to Capri in October 1946 and was granted honorary citizenship. Bryher had married the homosexual writer Kenneth Macpherson. When the marriage was dissolved in 1947 she bought him a house on Capri, on condition that he provide accommodation for Douglas. The old boy made friends with the Baron von Schack, who shared many of his interests. In his old age, as a kind of sage, he was visited by younger homosexual men. Robin Maugham and Michael Davidson made the pilgrimage in 1951.

It may be that the best fictional celebration of the idea of the Homintern – not that the author ever names it as such – is Roger Peyrefitte's *The Exile of Capri* (*L'Exilé de Capri*, 1959). It is certainly, in the second and third of its three sections, the most detailed celebration of Capri as one of the Homintern's favourite watering holes. A fictionalised biography of Jacques d'Adelswärd-Fersen, maker of minor poems and major scandals, the narrative follows its protagonist from his first visit to Capri as a respectable seventeen-year-old, through the years of his homosexual notoriety in Paris, to the no less enjoyable years of his exile on Capri, further enlivened by forays to other parts of the world. On his first visit to the island, as a boy, Fersen actually witnesses the ejection of Oscar Wilde and Lord Alfred Douglas from the terrace restaurant of the Quisisana. When he returns to Capri as an adult, his career is in ruins and he has, like Wilde, served a prison sentence.

Just as Norman Douglas' *South Wind* begins with the ferry crossing and, in the renaming of the island as Nepenthe, a classical invocation of the means of forgetting the burdens of the world, so, too, does the second section of *The Exile of Capri* open with a view of the island from the deck of the ferry from Naples and a strategic reference to Greek myth:

> Crossing the bay of Naples on a limpid January morning he had the feeling of crossing the Lethe. Europe, an old hag bedizened with lies, had been left behind. The Sirens' isle floated on the horizon, much as it had been when, in Homer's day, its monstrous but seductive tenants seduced poor mariners.

But Fersen is no less aware of the more recent past. He remembers that 'the island had been Allers' downfall and the source of Krupp's misfortunes'. He disembarks at the Marina Grande with the firm intention of seeking love there, but of doing so with a connoisseur's discrimination rather than a mere collector's omnivorousness. The omens seem good when, mentioning Krupp to his cab driver, he receives in response a blank look – 'Capri was indeed the isle of forgetfulness'.[37]

Although magisterially well informed, in this book Roger Peyrefitte is as unreliable as ever, never allowing doubt to interfere with his enthusiasm for a peachy anecdote. The tale is full of gossipy speculation presented as fictional fact; yet it is all the more absorbingly readable for that. The second half of the book, located mainly on Capri, is threaded with the theme of the 'Uranism Service'. It is Norman Douglas who coins the term when Fersen, impressed by his encyclopaedic knowledge of all the sexual scandals behind the presence of so many northern Europeans in southern Italy, exclaims, 'Upon my word! . . . I believe you're in the *Intelligence Service!*' Douglas replies, 'No, only the Uranism Service – in other words I have a tolerably good knowledge of the planet Uranus, which controls our brotherhood's destiny.' We might think of it as the Intelligence branch of the Homintern. It is clear that Peyrefitte thinks of himself as being – and congratulates himself for being – no less distinguished a member of the service, a great purveyor of the many strands of gossip that, woven together, reveal the true extent of homosexual networks within the European elites.

Far from portraying the Uranism Service as an espionage network always working in support of those who have been driven into exile by scandal, Peyrefitte shows how it may also work in the interests of those who still have secrets to hide. Fersen is reminded of this when, a day after having met and exchanged gossip with Eulenburg and Moltke, he is snubbed by them. During their conversation on that first day, Eulenburg imagined transnational bonds being forged by fellow homosexuals, closing the cultural and political chasm between France and Germany:

> I am a friend to your country and would wish to be even more so. Moral and spiritual bonds are all very well, but bonds of quite another order strengthen them, and thus are born true pairs of soul-mates, and the real Platonic city. Certain of your generals – Gallieni who is in Madagascar and Lyautey who is in Africa – would get on better with General von Moltke, here, than with his cousin and namesake who has just succeeded Schlieffen as the Chief of our General Staff. Lieutenant von Lynar would come to terms with your Captain de Tinan, who was your war minister General André's collaborator. I dream of inviting them one day to what is called 'the Round Table of Liebenberg'. I should like to invite you, as a French poet, to meet our own Stefan George whose poems about France are the most beautiful ever written by a German. And your Saint-Saëns would compose one of his symphonic poems for us.

But the next day the two Germans escape down a side street to avoid having to talk to Fersen again. He understands at once what has happened: 'In the past twenty-four hours the Uranism Service had been operating to his detriment. The reign of love between the General Staffs had not yet started.' Between the dissembling spirituality of Stefan George and the all-too-physical indiscretions of Jacques d'Adelswärd-Fersen, it seems, there can be as little common ground as between Germany and France themselves. Even on Capri the lives of temporary visitors from the north are touched by the chill hand of propriety.[38]

On the eve of his return to England from Nepenthe, in Norman Douglas' *South Wind*, the Anglican bishop Mr Heard meditates on what he will find there in contrast to the oddities he has encountered on the island:

> And how would England compare with the tingling realism of Nepenthe? Rather parochial, rather dun; grey-in-grey; subdued light above – crepuscular emotions on earth. Everything fireproof, seaworthy. Kindly thoughts expressed in safe unvarying formulas. A guileless people! Ships tossing at sea; minds firmly anchored to the commonplace. Abundance for the body; diet for the spirit. The monotony of a nation intent upon respecting laws and customs. Horror of the tangent, the extreme, the unconventional. God save the King.[39]

1. Oscar Wilde, in caricature, infects the future of America with aestheticism, 1882.

2. Una Troubridge (left) and Radclyffe Hall taking themselves seriously in one of the greatest of lesbian swagger portraits, 1927.

3. Vaslav Nijinsky and Sergei Diaghilev enjoying themselves in the uniform of the ordinary, bowler-hatted to fit in, 1911.

4. Sergei Eisenstein in Mexico, seeking an alternative beyond Hollywood, 1931.

5. Tamara de Lempicka, self-portrait as an Art Deco icon of speed, style and independence, 1929.

6. Rudolf Nureyev and Erik Bruhn, a study in the harmony of contrasts, 1962.

7. Natalie Barney (left), whose salon was one of the engine rooms of Modernism, and her lover, the painter Romaine Brooks, c.1915.

8. From left to right, James Joyce with Sylvia Beach, the publisher of *Ulysses*, and her lover Adrienne Monnier, at Shakespeare and Company; by the great lesbian photographer Gisèle Freund, 1938.

9. Charles Henri Ford emerges, satisfied, from one of the *vespasiennes* of Paris: a mischievous portrait by Henri Cartier-Bresson, 1935.

10. Jean Cocteau, portrayed by Romaine Brooks as a totem of Parisian modernity, 1912.

11. Alice B. Toklas and Gertrude Stein, photographed at home by Man Ray, with part of their collection of Modernist art, Paris, 1922.

12. Marc Allégret and his lover André Gide, snapped by Ottoline Morrell, 1920.

13. The energy of desire yoked to more spiritual ideals: Stefan George with Claus and Berthold von Stauffenberg, Berlin, 1924.

14. Magnus Hirschfeld, second from right, holding hands with his beloved Karl Giese, while celebrating Christmas 1905 among queer friends.

15. The Eldorado, a showcase for people who needed to be both shocked and entertained by Berlin's nightlife.

16. Stephen Spender (right) and friend, embodying *Freundschaft*: photographed by Herbert List, Germany, 1929.

17. Luchino Visconti, photographed by his lover Horst P. Horst, who taught him how to see the world through the eye of a camera, 1936.

18. Cecil Beaton, self-portrait as aesthete, at home in Wiltshire: a study in calculated informality.

19. The Wolcott-Perry 'sisters', Kate and Saidee, taking tea on the terrace of their Villa Torricella, Capri, c.1910.

20. Constantine Cavafy, at a slight angle even to himself, let alone the universe, Alexandria, c.1925.

21. Pier Paolo Pasolini in Manhattan, unimpressed by the city's distinct gay subculture and the development of gay identity politics, 1966.

22. James Baldwin, enjoying a temporary, partial escape from racism and homophobia, Istanbul, 1965.

23. Jane Bowles and Amina Bakalia (Cherifa), putting a public face on their relationship, Tangier, 1967.

24. Paul Bowles with Mohammed Mrabet, whose voice he exploited or released, in his library in Tangier, Morocco, 1991.

25. Walt Whitman, the grand master of comradeship, adhering to Bill Duckett, 1886.

26. Yukio Mishima in Manhattan: the East goes West and finds the Broadway musical, 1964.

27. Underground Granada: Lorca and others (Adolfo Salazar, Manuel de Falla, Ángel Barrios, Federico García Lorca and, foreground, Francisco García Lorca) in the cellars of the Alhambra, *c.*1923.

28. Langston Hughes shows Carl Van Vechten his new book for children, *The First Book of Negroes*, 1952.

29. The Ubangi Club, at 131st Street and 7th Avenue, Harlem: the venue where Gladys Bentley headlined in the 1930s.

30. Louis Aragon at the congress of the Union des Femmes Françaises, 1971. He would later attend the first French Gay Pride march.

## Sicily and its Visitors

From October to November 1955, Alfred Kinsey and his wife Mac went to Europe, supposedly for a holiday. In London, when Kinsey lunched with Vyvyan Holland, the son of Oscar Wilde, Holland had to listen to a monologue on the homosexual habits of rabbits. Kinsey was shown around Rome by Kenneth Anger. Then he and Mac went down to Naples. Anger joined them again later for a whistle-stop tour of Sicily. In Taormina, Anger managed to winkle out a seventy-year-old who had once been one of Wilhelm von Gloeden's photographic models. He told them von Gloeden was a size queen – hardly a great contribution to gossip, let alone knowledge, but satisfying nonetheless.

What remained of the Grand Tour at the end of the nineteenth century included Sicily, mainly for its classical sites such as those at Syracuse and Agrigento; but Taormina, as well as having a Greek theatre, with spectacular views of Etna and the Straits of Messina, also had Wilhelm von Gloeden's celebrated studio. He had settled there in 1878, intending to paint, but had eventually set up a lucrative and fashionable photographic practice that for many years attracted visitors both distinguished and rich. His main subject matter was the local boys (and, less often, the girls), frequently posed against the town's classical ruins in pseudo-classical states of undress. Largely as a consequence of his photographs' popularity, the town became a tourist resort with good hotels. Many a postcard of his nudes would be slipped into travellers' copies of the Sicilian poets Theocritus and Moschus, as if the modern boy were a direct illustration of the classical poem of boy love. Carlo Levi once wrote of Taormina:

> This is one of the most renowned places on earth, and none of the trappings
> of its fame are sufficient to ruin it – not the luxury hotels, nor the tourists,
> nor the nightclubs, nor the literati, nor the questionable international demi-
> monde that assembles there, becoming all the more vulgar in the context of
> that austere and archaic nature, nor even the pathetic and famous follies of
> its eccentric guests. It appears that the volcanic atmosphere, this glistening
> sea, envelop everything, impassive, inducing a harmoniously contemplative
> state even in the most insensitive and demented visitors.[40]

Contemplative or not, Taormina in particular and Sicily in general were high on the list of places to be visited by homosexual northerners. When the composer Ethel Smyth, who rather liked gay men, visited Italy in 1920 with Edith Somerville, she was pleased to find 'colonies of Oscar Wilde-men' who made Sicily seem very cosmopolitan.[41]

In his novel *The Immoralist* (1902), André Gide projects his own experiences on to his central character, Michel. Travelling northward from the Maghreb, on his way home with his wife from a period of convalescence in Biskra, Algeria, Michel re-engages with his reading: 'I found myself back again on the classic ground whose language and history were known to me.' He does not mean Italian, which is no more a part of his cultural constitution than Arabic was. He is thinking of the Greek of Theocritus. But this reading paradoxically then connects him more intimately with the place he has left, and the boys he has left there: 'At Syracuse, I reread Theocritus and reflected that his goatherds with the beautiful names were the very same as those I had loved at Biskra.'[42]

Towards the end of the novel, Michel has been feeling smothered in France, 'smothered by culture and decency and morality', and has become certain that 'the searcher must abjure and repudiate culture and decency and morality'. He travels south again with his wife, heading into Italy on their way back to North Africa:

> That descent into Italy gave me all the dizzy sensations of a fall. The weather
> was fine. As we dropped into a warmer and denser air, the rigid trees of the
> highlands ... gave way to the softness, the grace and ease of a luxurious
> vegetation. I felt I was leaving abstraction for life, and though it was winter,
> I imagined perfumes in every breath.

He has brought a trunk full of books, but never opens it. Yet even in his attempt to escape culture, he is cultured all the same. In Taormina he flirts with his carriage driver ('a Sicilian boy from Catania, as beautiful as a line of Theocritus, full of colour, and odour and savour, like a fruit') and kisses him. The port scene in Syracuse releases him from some of his inhibitions: 'All the time I did not spend with Marceline [his wife] I spent in the old port. Oh little port of Syracuse! Smells of sour wine, muddy alleys, stinking booths, where dockers and vagabonds and wine-bibbing sailors loaf and jostle! The society of the lowest dregs of humanity was delectable company to me. And what need had I to understand their language, when I felt it in my whole body?' It is not until Tunis, though, that he feels he has arrived in 'A land free from works of art.' Art, he now feels, is a mere transcription of life, whereas 'The Arabs have this admirable quality, that they live their art.'[43]

The composer Karol Szymanowski, born into a privileged, landed family in the Ukraine, was able to travel from an early age; and his favourite southern destinations eventually exerted a strong influence on his music. As a young man he went with his close friend Stefan Spiess to Algeria, Tunisia and Italy, including Sicily. At Taormina the sight of boys bathing – 'I couldn't take my eyes off them' – typically made him think of Antinous. The atmosphere of North Africa and Moorish Sicily added a third dimension to his reading of such 'exotic' texts as the homoerotic poetry of Hafiz of Shiraz and the Persian mystic Jalal ad-Din Rumi. First he produced the two song cycles *Love Songs of Hafiz* (1911, 1914); then, beginning with sketches in September 1914, the Third Symphony, *Song of the Night*, based on Rumi.

When the family estate was destroyed during peasant riots in 1917, Szymanowski consoled himself in the drabness of Elizavetgrad, to which he had fled, by embarking on a novel, *The Ephebe* (*Efebos*). Brimming with nostalgia for the mythic South, the book exists now only in fragments – much of it was burnt in Warsaw in 1939 – but we know that its plot concerned the homosexual peregrinations of its central character, Prince Ali Lowicki. In his introduction, Szymanowski wrote of 'a magic vision of Italy rising in his mind's eye' and described Italy as 'the homeland of all dreamers about a heightened sense of living'. His cousin and collaborator, the writer Jarosław Iwaszkiewicz, who also was homosexual, said the book derived from his own *Legends* and from Walter Pater, but transcended both in its richness.[44]

The novel contained a description of Palermo around the time of the Norman king Roger II in the twelfth century. Szymanowski was fascinated by what he knew of Roger's enlightened rule and of a court which harmoniously drew together great scholars from both the Christian and Arab traditions. It was Iwaszkiewicz, visiting his cousin in Elizavetgrad during the summer of 1918, who suggested he base an opera on Roger's kingdom. In the event, Iwaszkiewicz wrote the libretto. They got together in Odessa in September, working together on the cliffs above the Black Sea. The composer was still adding chapters to his novel, while the poet was writing his Orientalist *Songs of an Infatuated Muezzin*. Szymanowski started setting these to music as soon as he returned to Elizavetgrad. The opera, *King Roger* (*Król Roger*, 1926), would progress less easily.

In October, Iwaszkiewicz settled in Warsaw, where he helped found the cabaret/café Under the Picadoro (*Pod Picadorem*) as a centre for writers dedicated to the cause of Polish national independence from Russia. The group, which included other homosexual writers such as Jan Lechón and Stanisław Baliński, also created the journal *Skamander* as an outlet for nationalist writing. Iwaszkiewicz did not give the *King Roger* project his full attention, with the consequence that he did not fill out the composer's scheme until 1920. Szymanowski was dissatisfied with what he received, and rewrote it himself. The score was, therefore, not completed until 1924, and the work was given its first performance in 1926. In some respects more an oratorio than an opera, lacking dramatic impetus, *King Roger* consists of a series of static tableaux representing the conflict between medieval Sicilian Christianity and pagan beliefs based on the virtues of beauty and pleasure. The latter are embodied by a beautiful young shepherd and prophet who arrives at the court, beguiling the Queen but being firmly resisted by the King. Each act contains a confrontation between the King and the Dionysian principle represented by the youth. In Iwaszkiewicz' original libretto, the King succumbed to the youth's arguments and became a disciple of Dionysus, but in Szymanowski's, having at least paid partial homage to Dionysus, Roger turns to salute the opposite principle, Apollo, and the sun comes up. The pure hedonism of the shepherd is thereby rejected.

The opera's evocations of southern and eastern landscapes and cultures are expressed, in the libretto, by an idiom unequivocally of the West and North. Announcing the approach of the mystic shepherd, the King's right-hand man Edrisi sings of his appearance – copper curls, goatskin garb, starlike eyes and enigmatic smile – as follows: 'To młodzik; włos ma miedziany, kędzierzawy, ubrany w skórę koźlęcia, jak każdy pasterz; oczy ma jak gwiazdy, i uśmiech pełen tajemnicy.' Like English, Polish has its own hyperborean harmonies which must be heard through the mediating instrument of a firm suspension of disbelief if it is to be accepted as plausibly expressing the atmospherics of Sicilian pastoral.

Szymanowski's time in the dreary surroundings of Elizavetgrad had been temporarily enlivened by the arrival of a beautiful, teenage refugee from Russia, Boris Kochno. They had a brief affair before the composer managed to get him safely out of the Ukraine to Warsaw. The affair, although fleeting, had a profound effect on the composer's life, irrevocably confirming his homosexuality and helping him to come out in a mood of positive self-belief, at least when abroad. (Elizavetgrad was another matter.) Not until he visited Paris, late in 1920, did Szymanowski discover what had happened to the boy. He had found his way to Paris and was now the secretary and lover of Sergei Diaghilev.

Jan Lechoń left Warsaw, which he loved, in 1930 and served as an unofficial cultural attaché at the Polish Embassy in Paris until 1939. Moving in prominent cultural circles, he knew Cocteau and Gide, as well as many other writers and artists. At the outbreak of war he fled, via Portugal and Brazil, to the United States, eventually settling in New York in 1944. He wrote patriotic verse and propagandist texts for the Polish government-in-exile, which was operating from London. After the war, staunchly opposed to the Communist regime, he did not return to his native land. He never came to terms with his exile, particularly since it left him no effective role as a Polish writer. The diary he wrote between 1949 and 1956, intending it for publication, made many references to gay writers from France and the United States, but never with any positive appreciation of their sexuality. Veiled references to his own lover, Aubrey Johnson, seem stifled by the language of sin and demonic possession. Lechoń jumped to his death from a hotel window on 8 June 1956.

Jarosłav Iwaszkiewicz published prolifically as a poet and novelist. His interest in the theme of *King Roger* had an obvious influence on his poetry collection *Dionysus* (*Dionizje*, 1922), and he wrote Orientalist fantasies such as the fable *Escape from Baghdad* (*Ucieczka do Bagdadu*, 1923); but more realistic fiction followed, based in the contemporary world. During the Nazi occupation he sheltered fugitives in his own home. After the war, he loyally supported the Communist regime, even to the extent of becoming a member of parliament. He was president of the Union of Polish Writers three times, and in 1970 was awarded the International Lenin Prize. Even so, notwithstanding the normative behaviour demanded of a man in such a sequence of prominent positions, Iwaszkiewicz allowed himself, in his published work, considerable leeway in dealing with the theme of homosexuality and to affirm – if somewhat more vaguely – his own homoerotic interests. He translated both Rimbaud and Gide into Polish.[45]

## The Intolerant South

If Englishmen ventured south in search of a touch of Greek love, many southerners looked northwards for their sense of an environment in which such things were openly tolerated. Speaking of French writers during and after the First World War, Theodore Zeldin writes:

> There were many minor novelists who wrote about England as though it was an island of poetry, aesthetes and athletes, beautiful young men and no women: in Paris, Oscar Wilde was its representative, and when English females did appear in French novels, they were usually simply French governesses, the 'miss'. This kind of England enabled Frenchmen steeped in the classics to reconstruct a sort of mirage of ancient Greece.

He adds that '*Moeurs oxfordiennes* became synonymous with homosexuality.' In Vita Sackville-West's novel *The Edwardians* (1930), set in 1906, the Italian ambassador teases Sebastian about Oxford's sexual segregation and young Englishmen's lack of interest in women. In Evelyn Waugh's *Brideshead Revisited* (1945), Cara, Lord Marchmain's Italian mistress, speaks to Charles Ryder about his relationship with Marchmain's son Sebastian. 'I know of these romantic friendships of the English and the Germans. They are not Latin. I think they are very good if they do not go on too long.' Her implication is that Charles and Sebastian's friendship has reached the limit of its value.[46]

The fact is that the southerners' South was not always what the northerners thought it was. A good deal was allowed, but the authorities in southern countries were far from being endlessly indulgent to the whims of northern travellers and expatriates; still less to those of their own nationals. A certain basic level of discretion was required of foreigners, but that was often the first thing that alcohol or drugs undermined. In Tennessee Williams' play *Suddenly Last Summer* (1958), partly based on the end of Hart Crane's life, Sebastian Venable travels from his native New Orleans to 'Cabeza de Lobo', where he is devoured by the boys whose sexual favours he has been soliciting. In even the most tolerant nations, the authorities would periodically purge the more disruptive elements, closing down especially lively venues. As his drug use, his drinking, his sexual behaviour and his tendency to cause public scenes became more obtrusive, early in the 1950s, Brian Howard was successively expelled from Monaco, France, Italy and Spain. And major cultural or political changes could demand the complete suppression of previously liberal conventions (as we shall see in the case of Tangier).

Individuals who managed to evade punishment found that being known as homosexual could initiate a lifelong relationship with homophobic authorities, who found a duty in harassment. Of all the modern artists, Pier Paolo Pasolini must have the dubious distinction, far in advance of the relatively untouched Oscar Wilde, of having had the most encounters with the law. By the end of his life they had given him reserves of experience and resentment that informed all of his public statements about the workings of the Italian state. Investigated for his active homosexuality and his active communism alike, and censored on account of the former if less often the latter, he found that both his body and his mind had somehow become the supposedly legitimate focus of public inquiry. Not that he exactly sought privacy – he was too much of the public intellectual for that – but he certainly found intrusions into his private life and his artistic processes, even as he got to used to them, increasingly frustrating.

As far as we know, the first, and surely the most damagingly serious, of his encounters with the law took place after a more willing encounter – with four boys, aged fourteen, fifteen, and two aged sixteen – in his native Friuli on 30 September 1949, when Pasolini was twenty-seven. Three weeks later the event came to the notice of the police, by way of an informer, and Pasolini was charged, under sections 521 and 530 of the Penal Code, with 'corruption of minors' and 'obscene acts in a public place'. One or several of the boys had masturbated him, and money had changed hands. One claimed that Pasolini had offered to pay his entry to a cinema but that he had declined, knowing what else was likely to be involved. This boy also claimed that the others had done with Pasolini what he himself had chosen not to. Pasolini's aunt Giannina attempted to buy off the boys' families. When questioned by the *carabinieri*, Pasolini admitted the acts in question, excusing himself on the grounds of having drunk too much wine and, according to the police report, 'having wanted to attempt an erotic experiment of literary origin and character, stimulated by reading a novel on a homosexual subject' by André Gide (or 'Gite', as the report put it). (Gide had won the Nobel Prize in 1947.) At one point, apparently, 'he even dared to say that by committing [the] said acts he was completing the education of [the] said boys'.[47] This desperate strategy could not counterbalance the damning fact that Pasolini was a schoolteacher and that his bookish instincts were expected to be channelled in other directions.

On 28 October, the affair hit the newspapers. On the 29th, the Italian Communist Party (PCI) voted to expel Pasolini. On 28 December, acquitted on the charge of corrupting minors but found guilty of public lewdness, Pasolini was given a suspended sentence of three months. More importantly, he had lost his teaching job and gained a reputation for what he had been acquitted of – the corruption of the young. An appeal was filed and the case rumbled on until April 1952, by which time, in a sense, the messy outcome did not much matter to Pasolini, who had left Friuli for Rome on 28 January 1950. He remained there for the rest of his life.

His next significant brush with the law came on New Year's Eve at the turn of 1950–51. He had spent the evening with his cousin Nico Naldini and the novelist Giovanni Commisso, also both homosexual. At some point they encountered a group of drunken youths, and Pasolini's wallet was stolen. When the police became involved it was he, and not the thief, who ended up in a cell. Although he was not there for long, the incident had a profound effect on him. He began, and for the rest of his life continued, to think of himself as the targeted victim of the malice of the state. The fact that he had been expelled by the PCI and deserted by some of his friends added to his distress. Nothing happened in the next twenty-five years to persuade him he was mistaken; indeed, plenty happened to confirm his view. As one of his biographers puts it, 'The decades brought more incidents – attacks, trumped-up charges, legal proceedings, evidence enough to seem not proof of paranoia but confirmation of a rightly reasoned theory.'[48] Once his career got into its stride, he was hardly ever *not* under investigation for one thing or another in one arena or another. No fewer than thirty-three actions would be brought against his books and films before he died.

The publication of his novel *Ragazzi di vita* in 1955 is a case in point. This pioneering account of the lives of a dispossessed underclass, narrated in Roman dialect, immediately made an impression on the bourgeois establishment, which expected far more anodyne and elegant contributions from its artists. On 21 July 1955 an action was filed against the author and Aldo Garzanti, the publisher, for the publication of obscene material, as forbidden by Article 21 of the 1948 constitution. It seems clear that the prosecutor who made this move was acting at the behest of either Fernando Tambroni, the Minister of the Interior, or Antonio Segni, the newly installed Prime Minister.[49] The Fascists' Code of Civil Procedure, which had not been repealed by the new Republic, was invoked to order the book's immediate removal from the shops. A court which convened in January 1956 had to be adjourned for ten months when it transpired that the judges had not yet read the book.

Meanwhile, Pasolini's novel was shortlisted for the 1955 Strega Prize (which was won by Giovanni Commisso's *Un gatto attraversa la strada*), was runner-up for the Viareggio Prize, and won the Colombi-Guidotti Prize (whose judges that year included Carlo Emilio Gadda). So the story of illiterate boys who sell their ejaculations for pocket money and find their food on rubbish dumps achieved its own unstoppable momentum as an object of impassioned disagreement between two powerful wings of the establishment. The book was subjected to outspoken attacks by the Left (the PCI) and the Right (the Movimento Sociale Italiano and the Roman Catholic Church). The publicity was invaluable, even if Pasolini himself was more in need of an immediate income from sales. When the matter came to trial at last, on 4 July 1956, the book was defended by many national literary figures, including Alberto Moravia and Giuseppe Ungaretti, and both author and publisher were acquitted. *Ragazzi di vita* was released from the warehouses and Pasolini had his first major success. For better or worse, he was now newsworthy and would remain so for the rest of his life; but, in the words of one of his biographers, 'to the general public Pasolini was presented as that admitted homosexual hauled up on obscenity charges and nothing more'.[50] By the end of the 1950s, his very name had entered the Italian language as a synonym for 'queer'; and in the vegetable markets, fennel (*finocchio*, which is also slang for 'queer') was often referred to as *pasolini*.

Pasolini's next major encounter with the law on account of his intimacy with boys came when he was thirty-eight. Late in the night on 29 June 1960, while driving along Rome's Corso Vittorio Emanuele, he stopped to give two boys a ride. When they came upon a fight in the Via di Panico, one of the boys recognised one of the participants and Pasolini gave him, a lift as well. The following morning, Pasolini was arrested at home for removing the instigator of a public disorder from the scene of a crime. The incident received massive publicity, in which the author was said to be leading the seedy life he described in his scandalous novels. The case first came to trial in November 1961, but dragged on until July 1963, when he was acquitted for lack of evidence. Less than a fortnight after that incident came a worse one. On 10 July 1960, a Sunday, Pasolini went for a drive along the seafront at Anzio. At about two in the afternoon he struck up a twenty-minute conversation with two twelve- or thirteen-year-olds before going into a restaurant for his lunch. With Pasolini out of the way, two reporters approached the boys, asking for details of the exchange. Quite how or why Alfredo Passarelli of *Il Tempo* and Costanzo Costantini of *Il Messaggero* happened to be in that place at that time, so conveniently on duty to pick up their scoop, is not known. Pasolini, of course, regarded it as a set-up. In any case, the details were compromising: he had asked the boys, who were watching some other boys in a boat, about those other boys' cocks, and then about their own. His interlocutors were embarrassed by this turn in the conversation and moved away. There was bad publicity, of course, thanks to the presence of the reporters; but the attempt to bring a case against Pasolini for the attempted corruption of minors was abandoned, though not until December, for lack of substantive evidence that any crime had been committed.

In the same year, Pasolini even came within the ambit of laws that had no validity in Italy. When the Soviet Union adopted Article 112 into its Penal Code, stipulating a penalty of five years' imprisonment for sexual acts between men, both Italy's right-wing press and the PCI used the Article as yet another argument with which to damn Pasolini: how could a homosexual be a communist, how could a communist be a homosexual? Trouble began to seem unavoidable, regardless of whether he instigated it himself. A mere two days after the start of the trial concerning the previous year's events in the via di Panico, he got into conversation with a nineteen-year-old, Bernardino De Santis, who worked at a petrol station next to a bar in Sabaudia. (These bleak places along the coast road would always mean trouble in Pasolini's life.) The next day, the boy told the police that Pasolini had tried to rob him of a mere 2,000 lire at gunpoint – a black pistol with a golden bullet, no less – but that he had run off when De Santis drew a knife. Given who Pasolini had become in the mythologies of the Italian press, the boy was taken seriously and, on 22 November, the police searched the writer's car and home. In the flurry of publicity that followed – attacks from the Right, defence, at last, from the Left – Pasolini's name was withdrawn from the shortlist for the Etna-Taormina Poetry Prize. When the case came to trial, Pasolini was absurdly assumed to have staged a fake hold-up as research for a film he intended making. The charge was reduced from armed robbery to threatening with a firearm, although no gun had ever been found, and he was given a suspended sentence of less than three weeks. The case eventually went as far as the Supreme Court

– six years later – and Pasolini was acquitted, but only on technical grounds, for lack of evidence. Alberto Moravia wrote of this case:

> The judges realized that what De Santis was saying was pure madness, but they wanted to deliver a verdict of condemnation anyway, for the simple reason that Pier Paolo is a homosexual. In Italy there is no article of the legal code that views homosexuality as a crime. Therefore, they have contrived a loophole.[51]

Indeed, Pasolini's whole life is the perfect example of how, even in a society where, strictly speaking, homosexual acts are not formally criminalised, the homosexual individual may be consistently treated as a criminal by reason of his sexuality.

Pasolini had no illusions about Rome in the 1950s as the sexual paradise that some northern travellers thought it was. He understood how bourgeois homosexuals were able to maintain some kind of respectability within the social system as it stood: 'Homosexuals stuck to careers in the Church, design, the bureaucracies, and hairdressing, and found one another at soirées, along the Tiber, and at the back balconies of movie houses. It was a world of hierarchy, clear roles, and fixed opinions.'[52] Above all, a world of cowed conformity. As late as 1962, in such a supposedly accepting, cosmopolitan city as Venice, Peggy Guggenheim, who in 1948 had bought and renovated the Palazzo Venier dei Leoni, once Luisa Casati's home, lost some of her expatriate gay friends when the Venice police decided to rid the city of such types. Those who went included the Beat writer Alan Ansen, the painter Robert Brady and the art dealer Arthur Jeffress.

In a 1956 diary entry, John Cheever listed various American types and reasons why they might feel liberated in Rome, beginning: 'First we have the two American homosexuals who have every reason to be pleased at finding themselves in Rome. Here they are not the talk of their landlady; rough boys do not whistle at them as they go down the street, nor do respectable householders look on them with loathing and scorn.'[53] That is as may be – and it rather depends on how the two Americans behaved in public places – but it is unlikely that the same indulgence would have been readily on offer to an Italian gay couple in Rome in 1956.

### In Every Land an Oriental Colony

Following the northern European's 'craving for far-off places', once courage has been plucked up and the loins have been girt, the traveller finds first the southern European nations; then the Mediterranean; the Maghreb and Egypt; then, heading naturally eastward, the Levant, Arabia, India, Indochina, Oceania, the Far East. Note that this itinerary coincides with Sir Richard Burton's 'Sotadic Zone' girdling the planet, in which 'pederasty is 'popular and endemic'.[54] Even as late as 1986, in his memoir *En los reinos de taifa* (*Realms of Strife*), the Spanish novelist Juan Goytisolo was thinking of the world in Burton's terms. He wrote: 'from 1963, my passion and longings would be aroused only by the rough, sunburned sons of the Sotadic Zone'. Exiled in Paris from Francoist Spain, he could find these rough, dark men in the Arab cafés of the French capital's Barbès district. Some he would recognise from his prior readings, 'in the iconography of Richard Burton'.[55]

Edward Said wrote of the West's strange obsession with the East:

> The Orient is *watched*, since its almost (but never quite) offensive behavior issues out of a reservoir of infinite peculiarity; the European, whose sensibility tours the Orient, is a watcher, never involved, always detached, always ready for new examples of what the *Description de l'Égypte* called 'bizarre jouissance.' The Orient becomes a living tableau of queerness.

Although Said is not referring specifically to a queerness of sexualities, his point remains relevant to our context, even to the extent of identifying voyeurism as being central to the lived experience of travel to the East. Near, Middle or Far, the East pre-exists the Western imagination's experience of actual locations: for, 'In the system of knowledge about the Orient, the Orient is less a place than a topos, a set of references, a congeries of characteristics, that seems to have its origin in a quotation, or a fragment of a text, or a citation from someone's work on the Orient, or some bit of previous imagining, or an amalgam of all these.' Part of the effect can be achieved in reverie after a visit to the library.[56]

Just as to Greece and Rome, travellers were initially attracted to the East by what they had read. The main literary source for Orientalist homosexuals was the great compendium of stories, the *One Thousand Nights and a Night* (*Alf Layla wa-Layla*). It had been translated, in bowdlerised form, into French (1704–17) by Antoine Galland, and this version had gone into English, German, Italian, Dutch, Danish, Polish, Russian, Flemish and Yiddish by the end of the eighteenth century. Gustav Weil's complete German translation (1837–41) was subjected to cuts by its publisher. The *Nights* was further translated into English in a more complete but still bowdlerised version by Edward Lane (1840, 1859); then unexpurgated in versions by John Payne (1882) and Richard Burton (1885); and more fully into French by J.C. Mardrus

(1898–1904). The young Marcel Proust read it in the Galland version. Mikhail Kuzmin read and reread the Mardrus. André Gide knew the Galland and the Weil, but eventually also the version of Felix Greve (1912–13) and that of Mardrus. Indeed, Mardrus dedicated his fourth volume to Gide. In 1918, while in Cambridge, Gide asked his friend André Ruyters to buy him in London a copy of the Burton version, complete with its 'Terminal Essay' on homosexual practices in the Orient.[57]

In the final volume of Proust's *Recherche*, when Marcel encounters M. de Charlus in the darkened streets of wartime Paris, surrounded by Senegalese soldiers, Charlus asks him, 'Don't you see all the Orient of [Alexandre] Decamps and [Eugène] Fromentin and Ingres and Delacroix in this scene?' But Marcel has a different point of reference:

> It was not the Orient of Decamps or even of Delacroix that began to haunt my imagination after the Baron had left me, but the old Orient of those *Thousand and One Nights* which I had been so fond of; losing myself gradually in the network of these dark streets, I thought of the Caliph Harun al-Rashid going in search of adventures in the hidden quarters of Bagdad [*sic*].[58]

Proust's reader may be reminded of an early passage in *Cities of the Plain* when Marcel declares that the numerous 'descendants of the Sodomites . . . form in every land an Oriental colony, cultured, musical, malicious, which has certain charming qualities and intolerable defects'.[59] It is as if the Sodomites of the present day were devotees of a cult rooted in a shared reading of the *Nights*. Certainly, there is much to be found in the stories that would be likely to appeal to their erotic interests, but there is also much of the contrary tendency. Robert Irwin has argued that, 'Because the *Nights* is an omnium gatherum, one can use its texts, through selective quotation from the stories, to support the argument that homosexuality was widely approved of, or to argue that it was indifferently accepted, or to demonstrate that it was absolutely abominated. It was certainly openly discussed.' He adds that 'the debate reverberates throughout the *Nights*. Some stories cheerfully celebrate homosexual seductions . . . On the other hand, some tales present the paedophile as a villain . . . A leitmotif in the *Nights* is the seclusion of a beautiful boy by his parents in order to protect him from lascivious men', even though 'the pursuit of beardless boys by likeable or villainous rogues features fairly frequently'. He adds, though, 'love or buggery between two mature men is not, I think, dealt with anywhere in the *Nights*'.[60] Other favourite literary sources from the East included the Persian poets Rumi, Hafiz and Saadi of Shiraz. In *Ioläus*, his 'Anthology of Friendship' (1902, 1906,

1915), Edward Carpenter wrote that 'The honour paid to friendship in Persia, Arabia, Syria and other Oriental lands has always been great, and the tradition of this attachment there should be especially interesting to us, as having arisen independently of classic or Christian ideals'.[61] But he bemoaned the lack of translations into English, or of accurate and complete ones; and his book (third edition) has only ten pages of this material.

For many male travellers who had not found or dared what they wanted at home, the Orient offered hands-on opportunities with impunity. The French Arabist and mystic Louis Massignon was first introduced to homosexual activity in Cairo, when his Spanish friend Luis de Cuadra led him to the right places. But he renounced this active sexual involvement before developing his career as an outstanding scholar of Islam. Similarly led by friendship, in his case with Oscar Wilde, André Gide lost his virginity among the boys of Algeria – and became an outstanding scholar of pederasty.[62] Holidaying in Tunis with Duncan Grant in 1911, John Maynard Keynes noted that 'The Arabs are wonderful – very beautiful and the first race of buggers I've seen.'[63]

Constantine Cavafy's modern Alexandria is very different from, and more modern than, that of Mikhail Kuzmin, which relies heavily on literary sources.[64] (See Chapter Three.) Much influenced by Baudelaire's Paris, it is a city full of erotic potential, a place of shopping, manual labour, bureaucracy, leisure and cruising. Strangers meet in cafés, shops and streets; they rent private rooms by the hour or for the night. Those without money but with sufficient capital of beauty sell their bodies while they can; those who buy them embrace them for as long as they can, and then remember them for the rest of their lives. Artists make art out of them, which lasts. For all its modernity, Cavafy's Alexandria sits on many layers of history, on the edge of a sea on which history and myth, far from being written on water, are lastingly inscribed as if on stone. Edmund Keeley says Cavafy 'apparently planned his work so that his readers would have before them a more-or-less continuous image of contemporary Alexandria alongside the historical and mythic territory his city served to evoke. In this way, they could not help keeping one eye directed at the poet's version of the actual city outside his window while they were being transported, through adjacent poems, into the world of history and myth beyond.'[65] Even within the quiet confinement of his flat, Cavafy's was a cosmopolitan life. Daniel Mendelsohn writes: 'Most evenings, as he grew older, found him at home, either alone with a book or surrounded by a crowd of people that was, in every way, Alexandrian: a mixture of Greeks, Jews, Syrians, visiting Belgians; established writers such as the novelist and children's book author Penelope Delta, Nikos Kazantzakis, a critic or two, younger friends and aspiring writers.'[66] He was equally fluent in Greek, French and English.[67]

Cavafy often wrote as a homosexual poet for a homosexual audience, albeit a small one: many of the poems were to be passed from hand to hand, otherwise unpublished. His knowledge of male love in the ancient world, applied to the modern, empowered him to celebrate the most stigmatised of loves and lovers. Taking ancient models of love commemorated in cultural artefacts, his poems often describe men who, by finding each other's beauty even in sordid circumstances, rise above those circumstances and the opprobrium associated with male love in the modern world. As an artist Cavafy sees himself as commemorating transience, thereby saving it for eternity. The briefest sexual encounter, should its beauty be harnessed to artistic ends, is amenable to such conservation.

Writing at a time when male homosexuality was routinely referred to in English culture as 'Greek love', while he does look back to a time and place where male–male love was celebrated, Cavafy does not follow the Socratic model of older lover nurturing and educating younger, a model much relied on by the English 'Uranians'. His ideal is not the *Greek Anthology*'s boy on the cusp of puberty, the faithless child who is about to find that the next generation of pretty boys will treat him just as cruelly as he has been treating his older suitors. Cavafy writes about young men in their twenties, often specifying their ages precisely, as between twenty-two and twenty-nine. (In this, he is more like Walt Whitman and E.M. Forster than he is like the Anglophone writers who were most inspired by Hellenism.) Robert Liddell reminds us that 'Cavafy's ephebes were not those of classical Greece, but those of the Hellenistic dispersion'.[68]

The other city (and its cultures) that interested Cavafy was Byzantium/ Constantinople: he was indifferent to Athens and the classical period. Born in 1863, Cavafy was the eighth child of a British merchant who died in 1870. He spent his early years in England, mostly in Liverpool, until his mother Haricleia decided to move to Alexandria in 1877. As a consequence of widespread anti-European rioting in the summer of 1882, the family left for Constantinople. There they remained until 1885. So it was in the great Byzantine capital that Cavafy came of age. Here he developed lifelong habits as a dedicated night owl, wandering the streets and observing the things other people only dared to do after nightfall. He frequented the houses of two separate branches of the family, so as to be able to stay out at night undetected.

It was E.M. Forster who famously recorded the sight of Cavafy in a street in Alexandria, 'standing absolutely motionless at a slight angle to the universe'.[69] Forster had been posted to Egypt in October 1915 as a Red Cross 'searcher', interviewing the wounded for information about the missing. He landed at Port Said on 20 November and took the train to Alexandria, where he booked into the Majestic Hotel. He had come to Egypt for three months but stayed for three years. Through Greek and Grecophile friends, on 7 March 1916, in the Mohammed Ali Club at 2 rue Rosette, he met Cavafy. It was Robin Furness – ex of King's College, now of the Press Censorship Department of the Egyptian Civil Service, translator of the *Greek Anthology* and of Callimachus – who first took Forster to Cavafy's flat on the rue Lepsius. When John Maynard Keynes went to Egypt in March 1913 to stay with Furness, he had been promised 'all the attractions which made Gomorrah such a popular resort in the good old days'.[70]

On 16 October 1916, Forster wrote in a letter to Florence Barger: 'Yesterday for the first time in my life I parted with respectability'.[71] He had had his first full sexual encounter, an anonymous meeting with a soldier on the beach; but the impersonality of this event plunged him into a depression for weeks. His spirits were then raised by his friendship with a tram conductor, Mohammed el Adl, aged about seventeen. Forster first spoke to him in January 1917. Matters developed slowly and it was not until May that they first met off the tram, in the Municipal Gardens, before going back to Mohammed's room. Their first kiss took place at the third of their off-the-tram meetings, this time in Forster's room. Obviously proud of himself, Forster wrote of their romance to friends back in England, including Edward Carpenter, Goldsworthy Lowes Dickinson and Lytton Strachey. However, in October 1917, Mohammed had to leave Alexandria, Robin Furness having found him a job with the military on the Suez Canal. Mohammed got married in October 1918. Forster left Alexandria on 2 January 1919 and was back in England by the end of the month.[72]

The Atelier des Beaux Arts in Alexandria was co-founded by the homosexual Gaston Zananiri, whose father was a Syrian Greek Catholic, his mother a Hungarian Jew. Among his lovers were Thomas Whittemore, of the Byzantine Institute of America, and a young American dancer called Kirk Prince. Zananiri was a friend of Cavafy's, and later became a friend of Lawrence Durrell's. Robert Liddell believed Durrell's *Balthazar*, the eponymous central character of his 1958 novel, was based on him.[73] Liddell taught at the universities of Cairo and Alexandria between 1941 and 1951. Cavafy's Alexandria becomes Liddell's 'Caesarea' in his novel *Unreal City* (1952). When Charles, its central character, goes out into the streets to look, but only look, at real life, with Christo Eugenides, 'Ah!' the latter cannot help exclaiming, 'There are beautiful boys in the bars of Caesarea!'[74]

The English artist Robert Medley served in North Africa in the Second World War. Initially, in January 1941, he sailed to Egypt to work in Camouflage, but later in the same year he joined the Eighth Army. As for so many others, the war became, for all its griefs and fears, a sexual carnival to which Medley later attributed significant developments in his art:

> it was from the commonplace promiscuity of wartime in a foreign place, in which affection, curiosity and lust, all played their part, that I date the capacity for the freer and more sensuous handling of paint which character-izes my post-war paintings, and which is in marked contrast to the puritanical and English dryness of my earlier work.[75]

Also in Alexandria during the war, the Australian writer Patrick White had a brief affair with the Baron Charles de Menasce. At one of Menasce's parties in July 1941, he met Manoly Lascaris, an Alexandrian with a Greek father and an American mother. (Working in the Bank of Athens in the early 1930s, Lascaris used to serve the aged and scruffy Constantine Cavafy, but was warned off meeting him outside work.) Menasce said of the relationship that developed between White and Lascaris, 'Of course you must realise it won't last. It never does with people like us.'[76] The two men took a flat together on the rue Safia Zaghloul, which they kept on for the next six years. Their relationship lasted until White's death in 1990.

Lucia Re has written of the Italian poet Giuseppe Ungaretti that his 'sense of eroticism, desire, and sexuality, including homosexuality, was profoundly influenced by his experience of Alexandria and the Arab world'. As we have seen, contrary to what travellers from northern Europe may have believed, the actuality of life in Italy for homosexual men and women often made them, too, crave the solace of more temperate climes. They too might choose to look southwards or eastwards for a more friendly environment. Re continues: 'Unlike Italian society, Alexandrian society was tolerant of a wide spectrum of sexual and erotic behaviors, including homo-erotic, homosexual, and interra-cial relationships.' Citing an interview for the 1964 documentary film *Love Meetings* (*Comizi d'amore*), during which Pier Paolo Pasolini asked him whether he had ever had a homosexual relationship and Ungaretti gave an evasive answer, Re nevertheless concludes that he was sympathetic to Pasolini's own plight: 'With a candor rather unusual among Italian poets, Ungaretti revealed that his first amorous passion as an adolescent in Alexandria was for another boy in his school.' It is not necessary to follow his official biographer Leone Piccioni, who anxiously assures us that this passion was 'pure': for the fact is that 'Ungaretti derived from his youth in Alexandria a sense of desire and pleasure less bound by a strictly heterosexual paradigm – and the pursuit of purity – than most Italian poets'.[77] But, although he developed it while living in Alexandria, Ungaretti's sense of Egypt is not urban: it has more to do with the romance and purity of desert heat and emptiness, with solitary yearning rather than sexual opportunity.

Not even the Arabists who eschewed the modern urban fleshpots, or the thought of them, for the rigour of life in the desert, were immune to a certain flamboyance of the imagination. At the very start of *Seven Pillars of Wisdom* (1922), his epic account of the Arab revolt against the Ottoman Empire, T.E. Lawrence ('of Arabia') raises the topic of male–male sex, characterising it unusually, for the time, as one of the signs of the *cleanliness* of desert life. In only the fifth paragraph of his enormous book, he writes:

> The Arab was by nature continent; and the use of universal marriage had nearly abolished irregular courses in his tribes. The public women in the rare settlements we encountered in our months of wandering would have been nothing to our numbers, even had their raddled meat been palatable to a man of healthy parts. In horror of such sordid commerce our youths began indifferently to slake one another's few needs in their own clean bodies – a cold convenience that, by comparison, seemed sexless and even pure.[78]

The Turks, too, he will characterise as being filthy by contrast with these Arab boys. The men in the Turkish ranks are 'kept chopping-blocks of their commanders' viler passions'. Lawrence goes on:

> So cheap did [the Turkish officers] rate [their men], that in connection with them they used none of the ordinary precautions. Medical examination of some batches of Turkish prisoners found nearly half of them with unnaturally acquired venereal disease. Pox and its like were not understood in the country; and the infection ran from one to another through the battalion, where the conscripts served for six or seven years, till at the end of their period the survivors, if they came from decent homes, were ashamed to return, and drifted either into the gendarmerie service, or, as broken men, into casual labour about the towns; and so the birth-rate fell. The Turkish peasantry in Anatolia were dying of their military service.[79]

As well as the mere fact that he was fighting on the Arab side, Lawrence's frank account of torture and (possible) rape at the hands of the Turks when he was taken captive in Deraa (now in Syria) helps to account for the extreme contrast between his versions of the two groups.[80] Yet Lawrence's appreciation of the beauty of the Arab men around him can seem intrusive, especially when he is describing moments in a battle. For example, when he is wounded during an

assault on the Turks, his companions rush to help him. Several are themselves
wounded. Lawrence writes:

> The others, in a rush, were about me – fit models, after their activity, for a
> sculptor. Their full white cotton drawers drawn in, bell-like, round their
> slender waists and ankles; their hairless brown bodies; and the love-locks
> plaited tightly over each temple in long horns, made them look like Russian
> dancers.[81]

To invoke the Ballets Russes at such a juncture seems frivolous, or perhaps just
misguided, in its privileging of aesthetics. Even in the heat of battle, Lawrence
is detaching himself to the extent of planning the work of art. His main source
of reference in narrative terms is the *Iliad*, but the reference to the Russians
conjures up something altogether more sumptuous, a corps de ballet of ener-
getic Nijinskys, more aptly dressed for a *battement* than a battle.

That said, maybe the reference to performance is not so jarring after all. The
recurrent element of role-playing, or of mere dressing-up, that is to be seen in
the approach to Arab cultures by various influential travellers (Burton, Thesiger,
Lawrence) arises again in the memoirs of the Hungarian poet György Faludi,
*My Happy Days in Hell* (1962), coming as a crucial step in the development of
his romance with a young Moroccan, Amar. So that Faludi can visit his home in
a zone forbidden to foreigners, Amar dresses him in embroidered linen trousers, a djellaba, leather slippers and a fez. 'The mirror showed two brothers',
different only in skin tone. (Faludi says to Amar, 'What is smoke on you is stain
on me.') As it happens, a Marabou –'a seer, a wise old man' – expresses his
approval of the relationship. He says to Amar:

> I am glad to note that for the sake of a foreigner you have deserted the
> young boys of Morocco. The fez looks good on the stranger, his eyes are
> beautiful, his waist narrow as if a snake were raising its body along the
> outline of his hips. But by the look of him I should say that he is at least as
> much of a rogue as yourself![82]

Clearly himself a connoisseur of the male body, the Marabou goes on to give
Amar advice on how to kill his wife. The subsequent conversation between
Amar and the irritated Faludi eventually boils down to the fine moral question
as to which is the greater crime – sodomy or murder? The unspoken implication is that both are justifiable in the pursuit of beauty.

Meanwhile, the Suez Canal – a mere obstacle on Lawrence's arduous
journey to Cairo to announce the fall of Aqaba – gave travellers more extensive

access, by steamer, to Asia and its narratives. E.M. Forster first went to India before his sojourn in Egypt. In 1906 he had tutored Syed Ross Masood, who was preparing to go up to Oxford. They became close, but Forster ruefully noted that 'He's not that sort – no one whom I like seems to be.'[83] They went to Paris together in 1909, but it was not until the last days of 1910 that Forster declared himself to Masood. The response was vague and distant. They travelled to Italy together in August 1911 and Forster declared himself again – but it was water off a duck's back. Meanwhile, he was autodidactically giving himself a homosexual education: a book list in the margin of his diary reads as follows: 'Sturge Moore, A.E. Housman, [John Addington] Symonds, [Walter] Pater, Shakespeare, [Thomas Lovell] Beddoes, Walt Whitman, E[dward] Carpenter, Samuel Butler, [Edward] Fitzgerald, [Christopher] Marlowe.'[84] On 7 October 1912, Forster set sail from Naples for India, where he made his way to Aligarh to visit Masood, and the two of them went on to Delhi together. In Chhatarpur he met the Maharaja Vishnwarath Singh Bahadur, lover of boys and seeker of Truth. (This was to be J.R. Ackerley's Maharaja of Chhokrapur.) Then, in December, he met the twenty-four-year-old Maharaja of Dewas. In their first conversation, the Maharaja made fun of Forster's sexual interests, which Forster thought ill-bred of him. In January 1913, he rejoined Masood in Bankipore.[85]

It was therefore not a particularly daunting prospect when, early in 1921, the Maharaja of Dewas invited Forster to spend six months as his secretary. Forster set sail on 4 March, and managed to spend a few hours with Mohammed el Adl in Port Said. Sea travel was never less than interesting. Heading eastward from Port Said on the same ship, Goldsworthy Lowes Dickinson later wrote: 'we discovered one interesting figure – a young officer called Searight, of a romantic Byronic temperament, homosexual and perpetually in love with some boy or other.'[86] Soon after his arrival in Dewas, Forster was visited by Masood. Despite a general disapproval of homosexuality, the Maharaja delivered one of the palace barbers into his hands. In November Forster went to stay with Masood in Hyderabad. On the way back to England in January 1922, he found Mohammed dying of consumption. He spent a month in Egypt, but seems not to have called on Cavafy. When he left, Mohammed's last words to him were, 'My love to you there is nothing else to say.'[87] In Marseille, Forster bought and began to read a copy of Proust's *Du côté de chez Swann*. Back home, he settled down, not without apprehension, to work on his Indian novel. At this time he seems to have cut a rather more pathetic figure than usual. It was while thinking of him on 12 March 1922 that Virginia Woolf wrote: 'The middle age of buggers is not to be contemplated without horror.'[88] On 17 May he heard that Mohammed el Adl had died.

It was Forster who suggested that the young J.R. Ackerley apply to be secretary to the Maharaja of Chhatarpur. (He was appointed in October 1923.) Letters from Ackerley in India helped Forster with the composition of his novel. So did a reading of T.E. Lawrence's *Seven Pillars of Wisdom*. (The last two chapters of *A Passage to India* were written under its influence.) He finished the novel on 21 January 1924. In May, the Woolfs published *Pharos and Pharillon*, his book of Alexandrian essays, under a dedication to Hermes Psychopompos, the 'conductor of souls' – in other words, to the tram conductor Mohammed el Adl. The book created a new interest in Cavafy's poetry among English readers. When Forster did go back to Alexandria in 1929, he visited Cavafy, who took the opportunity to say how much he admired *A Passage to India*. In June 1932, when throat cancer was diagnosed, Cavafy was taken to Athens for treatment. He died in Alexandria on his seventieth birthday, 29 April 1933. Among the speakers at his funeral was his friend Gaston Zananiri.

Unlike those for whom going to the Orient was an escape into a dream world of exoticism derived from memories of Aladdin and Ali Baba (perhaps in their uncensored versions), for others the escape from the West had a more immediate practical value. Between 1961 and 1971, James Baldwin lived for long periods in Turkey, mainly in Istanbul. Removing himself from the public arena of the USA, where he was an extremely famous and controversial figure in the movement for Civil Rights, allowed him to focus again on his work as a novelist. As Magdalena Zaborowska says, 'Like France before, Turkey helped Baldwin to escape some of the racist and homophobic climate of his home country and saved him as a writer during a tough period in his life.' He loved Istanbul, but he had no illusions about the ways in which his presence there was likely to be read in the USA, perhaps by admirers and detractors alike. Zaborowska writes: 'Baldwin was acutely aware that some of his readers, critics, and editors considered his Turkish visits a kind of "sex tourism" or "sex exile" – a perception that obviously revealed much more about their own voyeuristic approaches to race and sexuality than it "denuded" anything substantial about the writer.'[89] There must have been times – there were times – when Baldwin felt he could not win, so heavily was opinion stacked against him. Nevertheless, Istanbul was a solution for a while. It took him out of the transatlantic arena, far enough and for long enough, to give his place in his own nation the serious attention it merited.

The truth is that Baldwin was in Istanbul for what it was not, seeking a space that was free of the preordained scripts of American race relations. The travel of writers does not always produce travel writing, or even writing coloured by travel. Raymond Roussel said of his own experience:

I have travelled a great deal. Notably, in 1920–21, I travelled around the world by way of India, Australia, New Zealand, the Pacific archipelagos, China, Japan and America … I already knew the principal countries of Europe, Egypt and all of North Africa, and later I visited Constantinople, Asia Minor and Persia. Now, from all these travels I never took a single thing for my books. It seems to me that this is worth pointing out, since it illustrates so clearly how everything in my works derives from the imagination.

You might have thought that his far-ranging itinerary would have generated, at the very least, some local colour for the backgrounds of his fiction, but Roussel was determined to be, or seem, unmoved by the seeing of sights. When someone asked him about the sunsets he must have seen while cruising in the tropics, he replied that he had not had time to pay them any attention, for he had been working in his cabin. Michel Leiris said of him:

Roussel never really travelled … It seems likely that the outside world never broke through into the universe he carried within him, and that, in all the countries he visited, he saw only what he had put there in advance, elements which corresponded absolutely with that universe that was peculiar to him.[90]

Travel thus becomes an entirely imaginary pursuit, accomplished in material reality but most fully experienced in the mind. In 1925 in Cairo, a city which surely must have conjured up the sights and sounds of the Orient in his receptive consciousness, Ronald Firbank began a new novel – about New York. He wrote to a friend: 'I pitch a parasol, & a little French writing table (that opens & closes, the darling) every morning in the Libyan-desert, & sit & picture it all in the mirage – so beautiful & poetic it seems sometimes: I begin to love it – especially Harlem.'[91] Cairo serves as the stimulus for a Harlem that exists nowhere in reality. Even if of an inverted sort, surely this is the distilled essence of Orientalism.

Lord Berners remembered seeing Ronald Firbank, shortly before his death in Italy in 1926, 'ambling down the precipitous streets of Genzano [south-east of Rome] followed by a crowd of children'. Every now and then he would scatter a handful of change at their feet, a procedure which, far from satisfying them, excited them more and attracted an even larger crowd.[92] The Western traveller dispenses the cash that allows him to take the world for granted. Does he want anything in return? Of course he does: for even his dreams of the mysterious East are exploitative. On first arriving in Bombay in 1961, Pier Paolo Pasolini goes for a short evening walk with Alberto Moravia to the Gateway to India, and is enchanted by the sound of boys singing in the dusk. Too excited to go back to the hotel with Moravia, he continues wandering, especially interested in the beggar youths. When one propositions him he is taken aback and intimidated. He speaks to two others, a Muslim and a Hindu, both country lads who have come to the city to seek their fortune, like so many boys he has encountered in Rome. He gives them money.[93]

## Tangier and its Visitors

Although it is situated further to the west than all of the great European cities except Lisbon, but because it was therefore so easy to access from Europe or even the USA, during the post-war period Tangier was for many gay men *the* archetypal city of the Orient.[94] Speaking of the heyday of expatriate Tangier, a gay character in Robin Maugham's novel *The Wrong People* (1967) says the city 'had got very definite advantages – no income tax and almost unlimited license to indulge one's own peculiar tastes'.[95] Indeed, there seems not to have been much point in going there *unless* one had 'peculiar tastes'. In the novel *Let It Come Down* (1952), based in Tangier, Paul Bowles wrote: 'It was one of the charms of the International Zone that you could get anything you wanted if you paid for it. Do anything, too, for that matter – there were no incorruptibles. It was only a question of price.'[96] When Truman Capote wrote about Tangier in his unfinished late novel *Answered Prayers*, he said that 'virtually every Tangerine is ensconced there for at least one, if not all, of four reasons: the easy availability of drugs, lustful adolescent prostitutes, tax loopholes, or because he is so undesirable, no place north of Port Said would let him out of the airport or off a ship'.[97] (The Tangerinos were the city's European and American immigrants; the Tanjawis were the native Moroccan populace.) In a more measured estimate, the publisher John Calder said 'Tangiers [*sic*] was largely interchangeable with Paris as far as artists were concerned: less bohemian, but with more freedoms.'[98] The city had been given international status in 1912 – when Morocco itself was split into French and Spanish protectorates – to be governed by a commission representing Belgium, Britain, France, Holland, Italy, Portugal, Spain and the United States. Not until 1959 did the city become a part of the newly independent Morocco.

Paul Bowles first visited Tangier with Aaron Copland in 1931, on the recommendation of Gertrude Stein. He was much taken with the place, calling it a 'dream city', but Copland thought it 'a madhouse, a madhouse'.[99] They rented a house on the Mountain, the hill above the city, and installed a piano. Copland worked on his Short Symphony there, and Bowles on his Sonata for Oboe and Clarinet. Bowles returned to settle in Tangier a decade-and-a-half later, setting sail from New York on 1 July 1947. During the crossing he wrote the story 'Pages from Cold Point', in which a loving father suddenly becomes aware that his teenage son is cutting a sexual swathe through the boys and menfolk of the Caribbean island on which he has rented a remote house.[100] Iain Finlayson writes that

> Bowles had first settled in Tangier as a retreat from the actuality of the larger world. As a little condominium ruled by foreign powers but still possessing a lively native character, it had seemed ideal: a sort of stage set in which nothing that happened could be considered quite actual, where the various characters and choruses had their lines and their bits of business, where the plot was largely predictable and the dramatic conventions were immutable.[101]

Bowles bought an old house near the Place Amrah for $500 and began working on the novel that would become *The Sheltering Sky*. (John Lehmann would publish it in September 1949.) His wife Jane joined him at the beginning of 1948. John Latouche had introduced them in 1937; they had been married for ten years, but their sexual relationship had lasted only for the first year and a half.

For a time, Charles Henri Ford and Djuna Barnes stayed in the house, before it had been properly furnished, Ford typing up Barnes' novel *Nightwood*. Ford later complained that Bowles would wake them up at seven in the morning when he came to the house to practise the piano. Tennessee Williams and his new boyfriend Frank Merlo visited in December 1948, but they hated Morocco and left early. When Truman Capote and his lover, the writer Jack Dunphy, arrived from Gibraltar in 1949 he was dismayed to see Gore Vidal, with whom he was conducting a routine feud, on the quay with Bowles. (Seaboard arrivals had to be by ferry from Gibraltar since the harbour at Tangier was too small to accommodate ocean liners.) Largely because no one there had heard of him, the only thing Capote liked about Tangier was Cecil Beaton (who had). He and Jack soon left for greater renown. Whereas to Beaton and Capote 'Tangier was a *cul-de-sac*, an ante-room to limbo', to Barbara Hutton and David Herbert it was 'one of the few places on earth where they would not be heckled off the stage as hams'.[102]

At this time, Paul Bowles was involved with a Moroccan man, Ahmed Yacoubi, who lived at a safe distance in Fez, and Jane with a Moroccan woman, Cherifa, who did not. As these things happen, Jane did not like Yacoubi and Paul did not like Cherifa (Amina Bakalia). Nevertheless, a degree of harmonious tolerance was achieved.[103] (On 24 June 1957, Ahmed Yacoubi would be arrested for indecent assault on a teenage boy, a German. In subsequent

months, the police would call into question the nature of the Bowles' relationships with Moroccan nationals.) While their own home was being done up,
Jane and Paul Bowles went to stay with David Herbert in his Villa Mektoub. As
the second son of the fifteenth Earl of Pembroke, brought up in Wilton House
near Salisbury, Herbert had all the grandeur you might hope for, or dread, in
one who comes cloaked in an atmosphere of great privilege. Ian Fleming would
later refer to him as 'the Queen Mother of Tangier'. He had first visited Tangier
in 1936, and in 1939 he had rented a flat there with Cecil Beaton. Although the
Bowleses regarded Herbert as a good friend, the match was not perfect. In
particular, Paul was uncomfortable with the manner of Herbert's homosexuality. As Michelle Green puts it, 'while Paul had a writer's appreciation of gossip,
he abhorred frank discussions about homosexuality, and one could never enlist
him in the sort of bitchy gabfests that David [Herbert] loved'.[104] In fact, Herbert
would live to develop his own objections to the embarrassing behaviour of
other homosexual men. He wrote in his memoir *Second Son* (1971):

> Without wishing to sound pompous, there is one aspect of Tangier life that
> many of us who live here do find disagreeable, and occasionally embar-
> rassing. No doubt attracted by Tangier's old reputation as a city of sin, the
> summer months bring a swarm of European 'queens' who seem to imagine
> that every Moroccan they see is for sale. Great offence is caused by their lack
> of discrimination and if someone gets knocked on the head it is usually
> their own fault.[105]

By contrast with Paul, Jane Bowles was much more at ease talking about, and
more likely to joke about, her life as a Jew and a lesbian: having walked with a
limp since a riding accident, she used to refer to herself as 'Crippie the Kike
Dyke'. In her novel *Two Serious Ladies* (1943) she had portrayed a number of
seriously capricious women, women happy not only to act on their own whims
against the requirements of their menfolk but also, at times, happy to submit to
men's whims. The resulting narrative is unsettling in its willingness to make
light of weighty decisions. Early in the book, Miss Gamelon, who has made a
kind of living by typing manuscripts for authors, says to Miss Goering, whom
she met only the previous day:

> It's a funny thing. I always thought I should meet you. My cousin used to tell
> me how queer you were. I think, though, that you can make friends more
> quickly with queer people. Or else you don't make friends with them at all
> – one way or the other. Many of my authors were very queer. In that way I've
> had an advantage of association that most people don't have.[106]

Although by the early 1940s the homosexual meaning of 'queer' was well established, in this passage the word is ostensibly used to denote a more generalised strangeness. Yet by opening themselves to the life-enhancing possibilities of *strange* queerness, Bowles' women seem also to become at least curious about *lesbian* queerness. For instance, as soon as Mrs Copperfield slips away from her beloved husband into the carnival atmosphere of Panama City (the Copperfields being based on the newly married Jane and Paul), the psychological conditions have already been created in which she can decide, without warning, to run off with Pacifica, a rather ordinary Panamanian whore. There is a lot of Jane Bowles in the idea 'that you can make friends more quickly with queer people'. Perhaps more than her husband, she was open to eccentricity and difference in others, largely because she could recognise it in herself – not merely at some trivial level of behavioural mannerisms, but in the core of her own madness. There is certainly a lot of herself in the vulnerability of her strong women.

Although the authorities thought Paul Bowles' writing too obsessed with the 'exotic' aspects of Morocco – with folkloric aspects of native culture rather than with Morocco as a modern nation – Bowles was one of the few Tangerinos who were genuinely interested in Moroccan voices and what they had to say: as witness his field trips to tape-record native music and his transcription and translation of Moroccan story-tellers, such as Ahmed Yacoubi, Larbi Layachi and, most famously, Mohammed Mrabet. It was in the winter of 1964–65 that Bowles tape-recorded Mrabet narrating his novel *Love with a Few Hairs*. In the mere fact that it told its story in a Tanjawi voice, the book was remarkable. From this point of view, apparently unrecorded until then, the white man (Mr David, a hotel owner) recedes into the background, not necessarily unloved, but marginal to the emotional life of the boy (seventeen-year-old Mohammed), which is centred on the girl (Mina). In effect, the relationship with the man is represented as though it were the equivalent of a career to the boy: he chooses it, he needs it, it is not without its pleasures, but in the long term he finds it a drudge. He engages in it to better himself – that is, to raise his standard of living. Just as income from a career might make personal fulfilment easier to come by outside the office, so the relationship with the man makes possible the development of the relationship with the girl. To that extent, the boy may feel grateful to the man. The hard truth is, however, that the man's *love* has little intrinsic value to the boy; other than as a currency, it serves no purpose in his life. Some white men realised this; many did not. Some discovered it once they lost their hearts. Some used it as an excuse for abusing their boys. Some cynically regarded such boys as cynical and, feeling themselves exploited, happily exploited them.

Much as earlier generations of disgraced northerners went to Capri, in 1954 Rupert Croft-Cooke went to Tangier with his Indian friend Joseph Alexander after both had served prison sentences for homosexual offences and after Croft-Cooke had written his book on that experience, *The Verdict of You All*. Somerset Maugham had given him £500 to help him into exile. Croft-Cooke found the Tangerinos 'wary and crablike' because of the reputation he brought with him.[107] He stayed for fourteen years and wrote two books about his life in Morocco, *The Tangerine House* (1956) and *The Caves of Hercules* (1974). When the gangster Ronnie Kray went to Tangier for rest and recreation after spells in prison and an asylum, he befriended both Croft-Cooke and a boy called Hassan.

Francis Bacon spent the summer of 1954 in Tangier, along with Paul Danquah and Peter Pollock. They passed much of their time in Dean's Bar, since Bacon found himself on the same wavelength as Dean, its proprietor. Ahmed Yacoubi watched Bacon painting and introduced him to the Bowleses. Bacon liked Jane well enough, but said of Paul: 'I don't feel I was ever able to make much contact with him. He liked marijuana and I liked alcohol, and they create very different worlds.'[108] When he met William Burroughs on a later visit to the city, Bacon liked him but not the people he mixed with. He was especially concerned when one of Burroughs' friends delved into the garbage for a tin can, into which he then poured a drink to offer Bacon. Allen Ginsberg met Bacon and wrote of him to Jack Kerouac that he 'paints mad gorillas in grey hotel rooms drest in evening dress with deathly black umbrellas – said he would paint big pornographic picture of me & Peter [Orlovsky]'. The picture was never painted, alas.[109]

William Burroughs had materialised in the city in 1954, accompanied by Kiki, an eighteen-year-old Spaniard. Like Capote, he was not as well received as he might have hoped. 'A number of people seem to have taken a violent, irrational dislike to me,' he wrote. 'Especially people who run bars.' Contrary to the impression he had been given before he went there, he found the expatriate community narrow, disapproving and snobbish; and despite the fact that he had actually published a book, *Junky* (1953), albeit under the pseudonym William Lee, he was not treated as a writer. He commented: 'I have nobody to talk to except Kiki. Some artist and writer colony!' But there were compensations, the most obvious of them being Kiki's body and the local police's light touch when it came to sexual or narcotics offences.[110] Kiki was, famously, the boy who would blow smoke into his pubic hair and say 'Abracadabra' as his hardening cock emerged from the cloud. (Kiki would later be stabbed to death, back in Spain, by a male lover who was jealous of his relationship with a woman.) The boy's presence in Burroughs' novels is unvaryingly erotic, softened through a veil of nostalgia and kif smoke.

It was in 1955 that Burroughs' impressions of the city began to cohere in the idea of a place he called 'Interzone'. In the words of his biographer, 'Tangier was as much an imaginative construct as a geographical location, a metaphor for limbo, for a dead-end place, a place where everyone could act out his most extreme fantasies. On one level, Tangier was a reconstruction of the world in a small place.'[111] Above all, it was un-American, even if it was haunted by American misfits. With this setting in mind, as well as a title suggested by Jack Kerouac, *The Naked Lunch*, Burroughs began to write a novel. (Paul Bowles would appear in it as Andrew Keif.) Unlike, say, Isherwood's, the lens through which Burroughs wearily scrutinised the world was unwaveringly distortive:

> The Zone is a single, vast building. The rooms are made of a plastic cement that bulges to accommodate people, but when too many crowd into one room there is a soft plop and someone squeezes through the wall right into the next house, the next bed that is, since the rooms are mostly bed where the business of the Zone is transacted. A hum of sex and commerce shakes the Zone like a vast hive[.][112]

The vulgarity of the character A.J.'s extravagant parties is based on the self-indulgent celebrations of nothing in particular, held in her house near the Casbah by the Woolworth heiress Barbara Hutton, ex-wife of Cary Grant. Actually, the most extreme of these post-dated *The Naked Lunch*. For instance, her gala on 29 August 1960 had two hundred guests and thirty gatecrashers. The house had been freshly decorated – but so had the exteriors of all the neighbouring houses, which were to be floodlit. Hutton was to be found sitting on a throne on the roof terrace, courted by flatterers, visible to a silent audience of Moroccans at the windows and on the roofs of the houses all around hers.

Burroughs' is not so much a realistic view of Tangier as a hallucinated impression of the native community and the expatriate community's mutual exploitation and the latter's aimless promiscuities. There was much to be enjoyed, but what seems most to have caught Burroughs' attention was a growing sense of unease. Although it was often spoken of as such – most consistently by people who had never been there – Tangier was no paradise. The underlying inequities that made many of the expatriates' pleasures possible in the first place were the greatest threat to the stability on which the provision of such pleasures relied. Burroughs knew this, and, notwithstanding his own investment in the exploitative economies of Tangerino sexual and narcotic excess, he often seemed to be looking forward to the moment when the Europeans and Americans he had met there would get their comeuppance. When a nationalist riot occurred, he was prepared and eager. As he wrote to Allen Ginsberg, 'I went home and loaded my shotgun.' He wanted to go looking for action – 'I simply *must* see some of this bloodshed' – but he found he had come close enough when a man he knew, a strict young Muslim, ran amok with a meat cleaver, killing several Europeans. (A fortunate, slight change in his own routine may have saved Burroughs' life on this occasion.) At the same time, various homosexual Europeans received notes, signed 'The Red Hand', telling them to get out of town. Burroughs commented: 'As usual, puritanism and Nationalism come on together in a most disagreeable melange.'[113]

It was Paul Bowles who introduced Burroughs to the Swiss-Canadian painter Brion Gysin. Gysin had followed Bowles to Tangier in the summer of 1950. He installed a fifteen-year-old boy, Hamri, in his room and tried to turn him into a painter. Hamri stole his clothes. It was not until Paul Bowles organised an exhibition of paintings by Ahmed Yacoubi that Hamri finally saw the point in taking art seriously. Brion Gysin exploited tourists' Orientalist tendencies in 1954 by establishing a restaurant called the 1001 Nights, complete with live music, acrobats and dancing boys. For a while in the summer of 1966, he shared his flat with his new lover and collaborator, the poet John Giorno, until lately one of Andy Warhol's satellites. Gysin and Giorno worked on sound poems together, but the relationship faltered and Giorno went back home to New York in August.

Jack Kerouac arrived in February 1957, hoping to explore the 'City of Vice' about which he had heard so much, but his discoveries were somewhat determined by the fact that his guide was William Burroughs. Indeed, the first place Burroughs took him to was a 'dim queer bar', 'the lunching spot of most of the queer Europeans and Americans of Tangiers with limited means'. They then went rowing in the harbour and were accosted by a boatload of boys demanding to know if the handsome stranger was interested in what they had to offer. Burroughs – who was – said no. The seedy internationalism of the city disappointed Kerouac, who was seeking a more uplifting exoticism. In his own account, he saw: 'Dozens of weird expatriates, coughing and lost on the cobbles of Moghreb, some of them, sitting at the outdoor café tables with the glum look of foreigners reading zigzag newspapers over unwanted Vermouth. Ex-smugglers with skipper hats straggling by. No joyful Moroccan tambourine anywhere.' He spent much of his time typing up *The Naked Lunch* for Burroughs until it and the drugs he was on started giving him nightmares. He soon began to hate Tangier, complaining that 'mostly fags abound in this sinister international hive of queens'. He even had to endure the indignity of Burroughs' weeping on his shoulder, self-pityingly bemoaning his unrequited love for Allen Ginsberg. Although not averse to receiving the occasional blow job from a man, Kerouac had little sympathy. With characteristic incomprehension, he asked: 'What's all this *love* business between grownup men?' He was far more comfortable with Burroughs' dalliance with a string of boys. Adult male love was another country altogether: 'how on earth could they consummate this great romantic love with Vaseline and K.Y.?'[114] In any case, after a month in the city he was becoming seriously homesick for his mother and America.

Ginsberg and Orlovsky arrived in the city again on 21 March 1957. They were on a mercy mission, according to Ginsberg: 'Peter and I decided that since [Burroughs] was so lacklove, the two of us would take him on and do anything he wanted. Satisfy him. So we went to Tangier to fuck him – to exhaust his desires.' They were also attracted by Burroughs' account of the city: 'This place relaxes me so I am subject to dissolve. I can spend three hours looking at the bay with my mouth open like a Kentucky Mountain Boy.'[115] Despite his growing reputation in the USA for unexpectedly uninhibited behaviour – stripping off at parties and the like – Ginsberg took a while to become similarly relaxed in Tangier. Ned Rorem, an old friend of Paul and Jane Bowles', wrote in his diary that Ginsberg, 'the original obstreperous beatnik, tells me middle-classedly to "hush" when I ask Paul, in the Mahruba restaurant too loudly before the other diners, if the dancing boy is queer'.[116] Ginsberg met Jane Bowles in April. She was bewildered by him, especially by being asked over the phone, before they had even met, whether she believed in God.

Dr Timothy Leary arrived in the city in August 1961, joining Burroughs, Ginsberg, Alan Ansen, Gregory Corso and their friends with a bag of magic mushrooms. Burroughs soon left for New York to write *Nova Express*. When he came back in the summer of 1963, along with his two young acolytes Ian Sommerville and Michael Portman, he was disgusted to find the city full of American and European dropouts. The Moroccans, too, hated the recent influx of low-spending deadbeats and became increasingly hostile to foreigners as a result. The tide was even turning against the more affluent expatriates, especially insofar as they were perceived to be exploiting their hosts not just economically but morally. As Iain Finlayson says, 'Above all, the nationalists were not only ill-disposed to foreigners as a whole, they disapproved of homosexuality. There was some feeling that homosexuals, and particularly pederasts, had had their day in Tangier.'[117] So, by and large, it proved. A police purge had followed various scandals in 1958. A blacklist was compiled with the help of an informer – possibly the American David Woolman, a prolific paedophile whose own name, oddly, did not appear on the list. Many fled, a few were imprisoned, but most stayed. The most celebrated of the male brothels, Manolo's, closed down because its eponymous proprietor had been jailed. But then the mood passed and things returned to normal.

While visiting New York, Paul Bowles had invited the writer Alfred Chester, ex-drama critic of *Partisan Review*, to join him in Morocco. Chester, aged thirty-four, apparently 'inspired passionate devotion among friends like Susan

Sontag and the poet Edward Field.[118] He had spent nine years in Paris from 1951, one of those years on a Guggenheim Fellowship. Before leaving for the fringes of the Dark Continent in 1963, he held a farewell party, which he then described in a letter to Field:

> I learned today that I did the following things . . . bit Muriel's finger nearly to the bone, smacked Jay, bit Dennis' upper arm so hard that he's been in pain since, smashed Walter's precious teacups, tried to jerk off Jerry, threw a Bloody Mary at D. and then threw him on the floor and later tried three times to push him out the window . . . put my hand on the cunt of a girl named Sally [and] squeezed lime juice in everyone's eyes . . . After the party I went out and picked up a gorgeous Puerto Rican.[119]

Chester met up with Field and his lover, the novelist Neil Derrick, in Gibraltar and crossed to Tangier with them. Finely attuned to the needs of his guests, Paul Bowles immediately introduced him to a nineteen-year-old fisherman called Dris, whom he had lined up for the occasion. A few days later, Field and Derrick returned to Paris, whence they had come, but Chester stayed on. By mid-July, he was being fought over by Dris and a boy called Hamji. ('I feel like Carmen,' he said.) He had rented a small house near the Bowles' in Asilah, but before long he developed a rather demonstrative hatred of Paul. As Millicent Dillon describes it, 'Chester became obsessed with Paul, revering him one moment as a godlike figure and the next moment believing that Paul was poisoning him.'[120] Indeed, he reported to the US consulate that Paul was trying to kill him. He had been harbouring a grudge since Bowles refused to lend him some blankets, but a more general paranoia made the situation worse. One day, while lighting the gas stove, he set fire to his wig, which melted and had to be thrown away. From now on, perforce, he had to be open about his complete lack of hair. When Dris moved in with him, Chester was surprised to find that he was in love with the boy. For his own part, Dris proudly declared that he and Chester were 'the two craziest people in the whole of Morocco'.[121] Asked by a visitor, many years later, 'Of all the guys who came here, who was the craziest?' Paul Bowles unhesitatingly nominated Alfred Chester.[122]

Back in the city in the spring of 1964, Chester wrote an essay on Jean Genet for *Commentary* and began writing a new novel, *The Exquisite Corpse*, dedicated to Dris. His book of short stories, *Behold Goliath*, was due for publication by Random House in April. In the event, it was rather coolly received. One reviewer called him 'a very curious combination of innocence and depravity – a sort of cross between the Baron de Charlus and Huckleberry Finn'.[123] Several of the stories in *Behold Goliath* were on explicitly homosexual themes. In

'Behold Goliath' itself, Goliath used to love his schoolmate Bernard, but was treated with contempt by him. 'Sitting beside him at school was physic to Goliath, for then as now love gave him diarrhea as hatred constipated him. Eros' arrows were so many suppository tablets and Goliath's bowels serenaded the neighboring lad without pause.' Goliath is 'baptised' into his adult sexuality by a sailor on a beach, and gets a job as a stripper in a club. So important is sex to his identity that when he wakes with someone in his bed he comes up with the reassuring Cartesian thought, 'On m'encule, donc je suis.' Among his sexual partners is Raymond Tilt, who says of himself, 'I'm strictly bisexual: I like soldiers *and* sailors'.[124] In 'From the Phoenix to the Unnamable, Impossibly Beautiful Wild Bird', when his wife leaves him, Mario goes back to his ex-lover John, the narrator. But John is not willing to take up where they had left off on the eve of Mario's wedding. He leaves Mario and, on the way home, picks up a young mulatto man. In 'Ismaël', an ex-lover of the narrator's is converted from Judaism to Catholicism. The narrator subsequently picks up and makes love with a Puerto-Rican man called Ismael; tries in vain to find him the next night in a gay bar; then visits him at home and is shown his photograph albums. They make love before going out on a gay-bar crawl. They argue and part, but amicably.

The most celebrated of the stories in the collection is 'In Praise of Vespasian' (named after the legendary *vespasiennes*, or urinals, of Paris). In his quest for love ('From men he sought love – not theirs but his own') as a seventeen-year-old seminarian, Joaquin lusted after a gypsy; and at eighteen had sex for the first time, with a salesman, before leaving the seminary and Spain for France. 'He was no fraud. He was the real thing. And he was never offended if one mistook him for a heterosexual.' In Paris he follows an Algerian man from pissoir to pissoir, ending up in the man's room, making love. In England, he tries cottaging in a public lavatory, but his note-passing between stalls leads nowhere. In a restroom in New York he comes to the conclusion 'that perhaps the most pure and powerful expression of lust is utter indifference'. Finally, in a lavatory back in Paris, while he is dying of bowel cancer, Joaquin experiences a last, transcendent dream with a labourer before whom, as in a conversion or revelation, he kneels to take communion.[125]

Alfred Chester's novel *The Exquisite Corpse* (1967) is an adventurous and daring, if ultimately tiresome, assault on both social and literary convention. In a world apparently governed by reliable contingency, the characters shuttle between extremes of physical and psychological pleasure and pain. The stimulation of the nerve endings, whether inflicted by the self or by another, and whether experienced as agony or bliss, is the proof of life. All issues conventionally determined by moral preconceptions are released from the treadmill of social inhibition. Although impressive in the author's determination to slip the banal bonds of realism and bourgeois propriety, in the end the book does not achieve the sense of purposive control one gets from reading a novelist like William Burroughs (despite his cut-up technique's supposed adherence to chance). Sad to say, the enormous effort Chester obviously put into the book begins to look like self-indulgence. That said, *The Exquisite Corpse* is still capable of delivering some potent surprises in the daring of its representations of gay sex.

When Susan Sontag's 'Notes on "Camp"', later agreed to be a classic early intervention in gay cultural studies, were published in the autumn, Alfred Chester complained that she had stolen many of his ideas on the topic. Sontag herself had arrived in Tangier in August 1965 for a fortnight. In a state of more extreme paranoia than usual, Chester became convinced that she was taping his conversations – and yet, at the same time, he asked her to marry him. He was eventually thrown out of Morocco in May 1968. Having taken a cocktail of cognac and barbiturates, he died in August 1971 in the Arab quarter of Jerusalem.

Morocco's fame as the early home of the 'sex-change operation' added a further dimension to its sexual exoticism. There is a florid moment on this theme in *Cobra* (1972) by the Cuban novelist Severo Sarduy, who spent most of his working life in exile in Paris. The book's protagonists travel together

> to Moorish lands in search of a distinguished though hidden Galen, the conspicuous Doctor Ktazob, who in crafty Tangerian abortion houses uproots the superfluous with an incision and sculpts in its place lewd slits, crowning his cunning with punctures of a Muslim balm that changes even the voice of a Neapolitan brigand into a honeyed flute, that shortens the feet Ming fashion, Byzantinizes gestures, and makes two mother-of-pearl turgescences billow upon the chest, mimicries of those displayed by Saint Olalla upon a plate.[126]

With typical élan, Sarduy gathers into the backstreets of Tangier both Byzantium and pre-revolutionary China, transforming the sterilised precision of surgery into a festival of arts and artifice, camp performances elaborating femininity out of masculine superfluousness. This is not the sort of operation they carry out in the sterile hospitals of Paris and New York.

Many who came to Tangier in search of the freedoms they lacked in Europe or America found the city wanting and soon left. Either the pleasures it offered did not live up to stories of the city's heyday, or they proved monotonous in their availability, or they simply proved less pleasurable than had seemed likely. When Noël Coward visited in the spring of 1960 he was shown around by

David Herbert and given the juiciest gossip by Croft-Cooke, but he found the place cliquish and feud-ridden and was not sorry to leave. Joe Orton had first visited Tangier with Kenneth Halliwell in the summer of 1956; they came back the next two years. In May 1967, they stayed at 2 rue Pizarro, in the flat in which Tennessee Williams had written *Suddenly Last Summer*. Orton wrote in his diary:

> To be young, good-looking, healthy, famous, comparatively rich *and* happy
> is surely going against nature, and when to the above list one adds that daily
> I have the company of beautiful fifteen-year-olds who find (for a small fee)
> fucking with me a delightful sensation, no man can want for more.

But within weeks, on 25 June, he had recognised that one can have too much of a good thing and was writing that even sex with teenage boys had become monotonous.[127]

While Robin Maugham was writing his queer Tangier novel, his uncle Somerset Maugham wrote to him: 'Why do you think that Noël [Coward] and I have never stuck our personal predilections down our public's throats? Because we know it would outrage them.'[128] Terence Rattigan, though, was in favour of publication. *The Wrong People* was published in 1967 under the pseudonym 'David Griffin', but it came out as *Anders als die Andern* in Munich in 1969 under Maugham's own name. Sal Mineo, who had acquired the film rights, visited Maugham on Ibiza in 1971 to discuss the possibility of a film, but he was disappointed in the screenplay Maugham drafted for him, and in any case the project petered out when the authorities in Tangier, who were still trying to clean up the city's image, refused permission for filming there. Paul Bowles once said, 'Tangier doesn't make a man disintegrate, but it does attract people who are going to disintegrate anyway.'[129] He proved the first point by remaining in the city, whence so many others had fled, and not disintegrating. He was there still in 1990 when Bernardo Bertolucci filmed part of *The Sheltering Sky* there. Paul Bowles was the film's narrator.

### The Oriental Occidentalist: Yukio Mishima

The East, meanwhile, was often looking eastward to the West. Yukio Mishima was an internationalist from an early age. Born Kimitake Hiraoka in 1925 (Mishima was a pen name), he first read Oscar Wilde when he was only twelve or thirteen, around the same time as he was first taken to a kabuki theatre. Perhaps this can be taken as an emblematic conjunction, typical of the rest of his career: selectively adopting his Western influences – generally recent, and often in some regard homosexual – he would overlay them on a rigid sense of the continuity of Japan's traditions. His perception of himself as a lover of his own sex seems to have developed around the age of fifteen, when, according to his biographer, the poems in his notebooks became 'more overtly homosexual'.[130] Toshitami Bojo, whom he met in 1937, introduced him to the works of Joris-Karl Huysmans and Jean Cocteau. By 1940 his favourite reading included – as well as the Japanese classics and Jun'ichiro Tanizaki – Cocteau, Rilke, Proust and, above all, Raymond Radiguet's *Le Bal du comte d'Orgel*, which he read repeatedly. By all accounts, however, he was less interested in the book itself than in the legend of its precocious, twenty-year-old author. Mishima published his own first collection of stories in 1944, when he was still only nineteen. Of Oscar Wilde's work, what he liked most at this age was the decadence and necrophilia of *Salomé*. (One would like to imagine some connection between his later espousal of *Bunburyodo*, the dual way of literature [*Bun*] and the sword [*Bu*], and the queerness of 'bunburyism' in the *The Importance of Being Earnest*; but the only connection is coincidence, alas.) Yet, despite the aura of modernity that he felt he was acquiring through his cosmopolitan and, in the face of Japanese traditionalism, shocking reading habits, he soon found that events had left him behind. After the Japanese surrender in 1945, which came as such a heavy blow to the national self-image, Mishima began to feel the inadequacy of his cultural influences, both Western and Japanese. As he later put it, 'I could not avoid the bewildering discovery that at twenty I was already an anachronism. My beloved Radiguet, and Wilde, and Yeats, and the Japanese classics – everything – I had valued was now suddenly offensive to the tastes of the age.'[131] As the 1940s passed into the 1950s, he would respond to this discovery by turning away from European Modernist culture and towards contemporary American *popular* culture.

In 1949, Yukio Mishima published the autobiographical novel *Confessions of a Mask* (*Kamen no kokuhaku*), with its confessional accounts of masturbation, homosexual hero worship and fetishism. But it was not until late in the following year that he actually started to frequent the new post-war gay scene of bars and cafés in Tokyo, and when he did so he went armed with the excuse that he was making notes for what would later become the novel *Forbidden Colours* (*Kinjiki*, 1951 and 1953). According to his biographer, 'There is no evidence that Mishima had become actively homosexual until his first journey to the West in 1952.'[132] If so, we can see that his homosexuality must have acquired a sense of cultural duality virtually identical to that of his literary influences, firmly rooted in the traditional, formalised homoeroticism of *Shudo* and the Samurai, while yet dizzily spiralling off into the apparently limitless, liberatory possibilities of American teen culture.

It was on Christmas Eve 1951 that Mishima set sail from Yokohama, heading for San Francisco on the SS *President Wilson*, with the authorisation of a permit signed by General MacArthur. (There were no Japanese passports at the time.) Having crossed to the east coast, he spent ten days in New York City, where he attended performances of Richard Strauss' *Salomé* (revisiting his adolescent passion for Wilde, of course), *Call Me Madam* and, of all things, *South Pacific*. If he was, indeed, new to homosexual activity on this trip, by the time he moved on from New York to Rio de Janeiro for a month he was getting into his stride. In Rio, apparently, he would pick up teenage boys in the afternoons and take them back to his hotel room. His visit may have been all the sexier for the fact that he was there for Carnival, which began on 23 February 1952. On 3 March he flew to Paris, but he was robbed the next day, so his month there was spent in penury. While there, he met the film director Keisuke Kinoshita and the composer Toshiro Mayuzumi. He asked them to take him to a gay bar, but when they went to the Café Blanche he was irritated to find that the boys in the place were more interested in the composer than in him.[133] On 18 April he crossed to London, where he took the opportunity to see Benjamin Britten's new opera *Billy Budd*. For some unknown reason, he also took a day trip to Guildford.[134]

From London he went on to Athens, and soon after his return to Tokyo in May he enrolled on a course in Greek at Tokyo University. As the many references to ancient Greek culture in *Forbidden Colours* testify, he was not content simply to consume the entertainments of high capitalism. He wanted to explore their roots and, in doing so, to compare classical Greek traditions with the classical Japanese. It might be said that the catholicity of his cultural tastes would add to a sense of confusion which would ultimately destroy him. He once said to his architect, 'I want to sit on rococo furniture wearing Levi's and an aloha shirt; that's my idea of a life-style.'[135] This now sounds like a cliché of 1980s style magazines, but in its day, and in Tokyo, it must have sounded outlandish indeed. Utterly Western. (The architect was horrified.) Be that as it may, Mishima developed habits of cultural tourism which gave him more than just amusement; they profoundly changed his outlook on life as he was introduced both to new cultures and to new cultural practitioners. When Truman Capote was in Tokyo to observe the filming of *Sayonara* for the *New Yorker*, he met Mishima, who, on 6 January 1957, took him and Cecil Beaton to a kabuki play and then on a tour of the red-light district. In July 1957 Mishima went back to New York to promote Donald Keene's translation of his *Five Modern No Plays*, published by Knopf; and he spent a weekend at James Merrill's home in Connecticut. In August, not only did he meet Tennessee Williams, Christopher Isherwood and Angus Wilson, but he also saw no fewer than eight Broadway shows, including *My Fair Lady*, *West Side Story* and (again!) *South Pacific*.

After a massive trip that had taken him to Puerto Rico, Haiti, the Dominican Republic, Mexico, Yucatán, New York again, Madrid and Rome, he returned to Tokyo in mid-January – and started looking for a bride. (In June, when a magazine asked its women readers, supposing Yukio Mishima and the Crown Prince were the last men on earth, which of the two they would choose to marry, more than half of those who responded said they would rather commit suicide than marry either.) Stephen Spender dined with Mishima and others in Tokyo on 20 April 1958 and then noted in his diary: 'He is extremely frank about being homosexual, and started dinner by talking about a classic called *Great Homosexual Love Stories of the Samurai*.'[136] Nevertheless, Mishima married Yoko Sugiyama on May 1958; they had a daughter, Noriko, in June 1959 and a son, Iichiro, in May 1962. Meanwhile, he directed a production of the play he had first read and fallen in love with when he was fifteen, Wilde's *Salomé*.

In the last few years of his life, Mishima seemed torn between the cosmopolitan lifestyle, as initially glimpsed in the movies and then experienced on his world tour, and the closed orderliness of a traditional Japan. Although he took his wife on two world tours, in November 1960 and September 1965, and although he welcomed new Western friends such as Tennessee Williams into his home, he was increasingly disturbed by the fact that the opening up of Japanese society to foreign influences was causing what he regarded as a debilitating liberalisation, especially among the younger generation. The more he enjoyed the fruits of his own worldliness, it seems, the more he guiltily sought to deny them to others. Something of this ambivalence can be seen in his narcissistic body-building, in which the aesthetic values of American physique magazines were rather shakily applied to the ethics of the Samurai. Ian Buruma says of him, 'Mishima, like many nineteenth-century dandies, was raised with the kind of snobbery that comes with feeling one's class privileges slipping.'[137] Similarly, the cultural and material privileges he accorded himself as an internationalist seemed decadent and vulgar to him when they began to attract younger Japanese to Western popular culture. Such contradictions abound in the narrative of the end of his life, which we need not dwell on here. But to think of Yukio Mishima tripping down Broadway, humming 'There is nothing like a dame' or 'I'm gonna wash that man right out of my hair' with a spring in his step, is to evoke a sharp, representative image of the ironies of globalisation.

# CHAPTER NINE

# THE NEW WORLD

## Harlem and its Visitors

Introducing a 1985 reissue of Claude McKay's autobiography *A Long Way Home* (1937), St Clair Drake writes: 'There have been no black Marcel Prousts and André Gides. The traumatic effects of the black experience seem to have made confessional writing an intellectual luxury black writers cannot afford.'[1] Yet, from the slave narratives of the nineteenth century, through the memoirs of major figures such as Booker T. Washington (*Up From Slavery*, 1901) to Audre Lorde's 'biomythography' *Zami: A New Spelling of My Name* (1982), autobiography had been the distinctive mode of black American self-assertion. What was less characteristic of black American literature was the fictionalisation of personal experiences – although there are, of course, major exceptions, such as Richard Wright's *Black Boy* (1945) and James Baldwin's *Go Tell It on the Mountain* (1953). In general, the black autobiographers were more urgently concerned to contribute to the social record than to fashion an aesthetic object, as Proust and Gide had been. In fact, the black American first person singular has had an enormous range – from 'Nobody knows the trouble I've seen', through Frederick Douglass' 'My father was a white man', to Martin Luther King's 'I have a dream'. The range of women's voices runs from Phillis Wheatley's 'I, young in life, by seeming cruel fate, / Was snatch'd from *Afric*'s fancy'd happy seat', through Gwendolyn Brooks' 'What shall I give my children?', to bell hooks' 'Ain't I a woman?'

As for the other thing the two French Modernist novelists had in common – their homosexuality – there were obvious social circumstances, not least of them the Napoleonic Code, which allowed them to become pioneering homosexual theorists and 'gay novelists' with relative impunity. By contrast, hardly any black writers have enjoyed the financial independence and associated social protection that Proust and Gide could take for granted. Prousts and Gides do not emerge, fully formed, from nowhere. They are shaped over centuries by the Revolution and the first three Republics, the Renaissance and the Enlightenment, generations of cultural struggle between religious and secular authorities, and so on. In any case, if there have indeed been no black Prousts and Gides, it may be no bad thing. There were more important things to be. Claude McKay certainly thought so. Why not be the black Claude McKay?

Even though the black population was 90–95 per cent illiterate in 1860, as many as 1,200 black-owned newspapers were established in the USA between 1865 and 1900. In the half-century after 1860, illiteracy levels sank with astonishing rapidity from 61 per cent to 15 per cent. As immigration from Europe plummeted during the First World War, Negroes migrated northward from the South to take up employment opportunities in Chicago and New York. In the first decade of the twentieth century, 170,000 black migrants moved to the North; in the second, the number went up to 454,000; it only sank again in the fourth decade because of the Depression. New cultural ambitions were created by the transformation of agricultural workers into closely packed communities of industrial workers. When those black men who had gone to war in Europe returned to New York, a fresh sense of the Negro's dues was fomented in the black ghettos. Notwithstanding the many positive developments since the emancipation of the slaves, Harlem was still a community misshapen by disadvantage. Already one of the most populous black cities in the world, by the beginning of the 1920s Harlem still had few black-run businesses; as Claude McKay pointed out, 'The only Negro businesses, excepting barber shops, were the churches and the cabarets.' Nor did matters improve in the 1930s. Writing in 1937, McKay reported that 'Harlem is an all-white picnic ground with no apparent gain to the blacks. The competition of white-owned cabarets has driven the colored out of business, and blacks are barred from the best of them in Harlem now.'[2]

Zora Neale Hurston called the supportive whites 'Negrotarians'. But theirs was not the only support available to promising young black writers. There were black patrons, too, although they had less economic and social clout than their white counterparts; and there were also significant patrons who were both black and homosexual, such as the art collector Alexander Gumby and the literary editor Alain Locke. When Gumby had first arrived in Harlem, around the turn of the new century, he had been so excited by what he glimpsed of theatrical circles that he decided to establish a salon to attract their company. Although he was a mere postal clerk, he acquired a white patron, rented a studio on Fifth Avenue and successfully created what – because of all his books – became known as Gumby's Bookstore, a centre for cultural chatter, bathtub gin and louche goings-on. More famously, Alain Locke ran what he referred to (in an undated letter to Richard Jefferson) as a 'fraternity of friends' to which new members were introduced twice a year. The poet Countee Cullen was one such. Others more loosely associated with the group included Harold Jackman, Claude McKay and Bruce Nugent.

Cullen and the lover with whom he sustained a lifelong relationship, the schoolteacher Harold Jackman, were called 'the Jonathan and David of the Harlem Renaissance' by Arna Bontemps.[3] Cullen had other male lovers. His poem 'More Than a Fool's Song' is dedicated to one of them, Edward Perry. The coolly erotic poem 'To a Brown Boy' is dedicated to L.H., Langston Hughes. Yet despite such fine work David Levering Lewis still claims that, 'Like his lowly birth and orphanage, Cullen's homosexuality was to be a source of shame he never fully succeeded in turning into a creative strength.'[4]

Bruce Nugent did not always behave as the patrons wanted. A little too bohemian for their restricted version of bohemianism, he was likely to turn up to smart social occasions in an open-necked shirt and barefoot. (Bare feet were especially shocking in a cultured Negro: they tended to remind people of the cotton patch.) Although he would marry in 1952, he appeared to be at ease with his homosexuality; indeed, his fiction tends to portray homosexuals more positively than blacks. 'Sahdji', the short story he wrote for Alain Locke's anthology *The New Negro*, was dedicated to H.F., Hank Fisher, one of his white lovers.

It was generally known that involvement with Locke could be advantageous to one's career. (Or to one's grades: he was distinctly interested in his male students at Howard University. Women he would dismiss on the first day of classes with the promise of an automatic C grade.) Not only was literature on same-sex relationships discussed in his salons – he used to recommend that his young friends read Edward Carpenter's anthology on male love, *Ioläus* – but Locke liked to promote relationships between his protégés. When he was not trying to seduce them himself, he was match-making between them. The facts of the matter are unclear, but there were plenty of rumours. It is possible that he had a sexual relationship with Langston Hughes, perhaps also with Countee Cullen, and that he discriminated against Bruce Nugent's writing because Nugent had responded negatively to his sexual advances. However, evidence for such biased cultural promotion is inevitably hard to come by, and rumours to this effect may have been circulated by those whose writing Locke did not like, by those who did not like Locke, or by the usual homophobic voices that sound whenever patronage operates between homosexual men. In 1923, Locke introduced Countee Cullen to the idea of the German *Wandervogel* movement; indeed, he tried to arrange a trip to Germany for Cullen, but this never materialised.

The Harlem boarding house that Wallace Thurman shared with Bruce Nugent, Langston Hughes and others was known as 'Niggeratti Manor'. 'Niggeratti' was an expression of Thurman's coining, referring to the Harlem literati. The theatre critic Theophilus Lewis reported that the house's tenants 'spent wild nights in tuft hunting and the diversions of the cities of the plains and delirious days fleeing from pink elephants'.[5] In the summer of 1926, the Niggeratti produced the first issue of a deliberately controversial literary magazine, *Fire!*, with financial help from Carl Van Vechten. The magazine was not well received: while the white press ignored it, black critics were horrified. Langston Hughes said, 'The Negro press called it all sorts of bad names, largely because of a green and purple story by Bruce Nugent ['Smoke, Lillies, and Jade'], in the Oscar Wilde tradition, which we had included.' The reviewer for the *Baltimore Afro-American* began his review, 'I have just tossed the first issue of *Fire* into the fire'.[6] The magazine collapsed after this one issue. Wallace Thurman later satirised life in the 'Manor' in his novel *Infants of the Spring* (1932). He attacked black writers who wrote for aesthetically undiscriminating white patrons, but was also critical of American writers in general.

One individual who objected to Alain Locke was Claude McKay – who had read and discussed at an early age Walt Whitman, Oscar Wilde and Edward Carpenter with his white English mentor Walter Jekyll. He regarded Locke as an effete, white, Europeanised intellectual. McKay observed a lot of Uncle Tom-ism in the black writers he met. To his eyes, their 'renaissance' seemed mutually competitive and deferential to both the black bourgeoisie and whites. McKay tends to be called sexually indiscriminate because he is known to have had sexual partners both black and white, male and female, in the United States and abroad; but this looks to me more like a man of discriminating tastes, albeit broad ones. He was not going to be restricted in his pleasures by a fixed sense of identity; and even less so by a white, bourgeois sense of either the respectable or the exotically louche. Christa Schwarz says of him, 'He displayed disregard for respectability, barely concealing sexual relationships not only with black and white but also with female and male partners in foreign countries as well as within the United States.'[7] Frank and Francine Budgen remembered him as 'openly homosexual but not at all effeminate'.[8]

In the 1920s, tiring of what he would later refer to as 'the highly propagandized Negro renaissance period', McKay decided to go to Russia to observe the Revolution. As defined in his autobiography, his motive for the trip was: 'Escape from the pit of sex and poverty, from domestic death, from the cul-de-sac of self-pity, from the hot syncopated fascination of Harlem, from the suffocating ghetto of color consciousness.' He took ship across the Atlantic to Liverpool, working his passage as a stoker. On his way across Europe he paused in the notorious Sodom of Berlin: 'I visited many of the cabarets, which had sprung up like mushrooms under the Socialist-Republican régime, some of which seemed to express the ultimate in erotomania. The youngsters of both sexes, the hectic pleasure-chasers of the Berlin of that epoch . . . were methodically exploiting the nudist colony indoors, which was perhaps more exciting than the outdoor experiments.'[9] It was in Berlin in 1923 that he first met Alain Locke. He was fêted wherever he went in Russia, but found he was always having to speak of America's readiness for revolution. Nobody was interested in hearing his realistic scepticism about such an unlikely prospect. On his way home after a prolonged stay, he revisited Berlin, then went on to Paris, where he managed to avoid meeting Gertrude Stein. (When he did meet her, later, he found she shared something of Nancy Cunard's paradoxical Negrophile racism.) Heading south, he mixed with sailors on the Riviera, and observed prostitutes of both sexes in Marseille; his unpublished novel *Romance in Marseille* contains a sympathetic portrayal of gay life in that city. Being an exotic in Europe was not always to his taste:

> I remember that in Marseilles and other places in Europe I was sometimes approached and offered a considerable remuneration to act as a guide or procurer or do other sordid things. While I was working as a model in Paris a handsome Italian model brought me an offer to work as an occasional attendant in a special bains de vapeur. The Italian said that he made good extra money working there. Now, although I needed more money to live, it was impossible for me to make myself do such things.[10]

Having accompanied a Senegalese boxer to Barcelona, he went down to Morocco to complete *Banjo*, the book he was working on. In Paris he found, as well as Parisians, the 'cream of Harlem'. By now he had appeared in Locke's *Anthology of the New Negro* (1925) but, meeting Locke for the second time in Paris, McKay found him reactionary, not worth cultivating. In contrast, when he met Carl Van Vechten in the summer of 1929, McKay found him not at all patronising, but on this occasion they had little to say to each other. Van Vechten was drunk. When he saw a truckload of large carrots passing in the street, he made off in pursuit of it, exclaiming, 'How I would like to have all of them!' On another occasion Charles Henri Ford lingered long enough for them to become friends.

As a writer of the Left, McKay was open to even stricter leftist criticism than the other Harlem writers tended to receive. The characteristic attack would connect his associations with the wrong kinds of whites – the frivolous and spendthrift class enemy rather than the organised working class – to suggestions of deviant self-indulgence. In *The Liberator* (February 1921), Mike Gold complained that McKay's work was 'lacking in working-class content', which he blamed on the influence of Van Vechten: 'he has been the most evil influence – Gin, jazz, and sex – this is all that stirs him in our world, and he has imparted his tastes to the young Negro litterateurs. He is a white literary bum, who has created a brood of Negro literary bums.'[11] By thus casting all of Van Vechten's protégés as his stooges, misled into lassitude by the pleasures afforded by a rich, white man, Gold and others like him were able to dismiss the Harlem writers' 'race'-based critiques of American life as irrelevant to the supposedly more important class-based analysis. Thus did the Left also, for several decades, dismiss the politics of gender and sexuality.[12]

All of the best-known Harlem writers did travel far beyond Harlem itself. Although emergent from a narrow racial ghetto, both physical and symbolic, they were enthusiastically aware of the modern era's main political and artistic movements and their European origins. (The Garveyite back-to-Africa movement was international in its own way, of course.) McKay had been to England, where he met George Bernard Shaw and Sylvia Pankhurst, among others; as we have seen, in 1922 he went to Russia, via Berlin. Cullen was in France between 1928 and 1930. Hughes knew Mexico as a boy and shipped out to Africa, and then to Europe, at the age of twenty-one. In Paris he eventually found work as doorman in a club run by a lesbian from Martinique. Locke visited him in Paris to talk about his poems and took him on a trip to Venice.

Carl Van Vechten liked to quote – perhaps to the point of irritation – the old Arabic proverb 'It is unsafe to say, out of this fountain I will never drink.' It was a precept he attempted to live by. He began his career as a journalist on William Randolph Hearst's *Chicago American* in 1904. Two years later, he moved to New York City and landed a job as a staff reporter on the *New York Times*. In June 1907, he married Anna Snyder in London; they crossed to Paris and one of the first things they saw on their honeymoon was Colette performing in a music hall. In May 1908 Van Vechten was actually sent to Paris as the correspondent for the *New York Times*, but he was recalled a year later because he had shown far less interest in the news than in the arts. By the time he took up his new post in New York as the paper's deputy music critic, his and Anna's marriage was faltering; they eventually ended it in 1912, with a staged adultery on his part. Meanwhile, by virtue of being in the right place at the right time, Van Vechten became the first dance critic in the United States. It is a measure of his extraordinary good fortune in this respect that he saw and wrote about, in quick succession, Isadora Duncan at the start of her second New York season in November 1909, Louie Fuller in December, Maud Allan's *Salomé* in January 1910, and Anna Pavlova in March. In the summer of 1913, already fired up by the Armory Show, which in February had virtually introduced Modernist art to New York, Van Vechten went back to Paris. It was on this trip that he met and made friends with Gertrude Stein and Alice Toklas. He attended both the first and the second performances of *The Rite of Spring*, as well as many more of Diaghilev's company's productions. On his return to the USA, he took with him what was apparently the first wristwatch ever seen in New York.

In October 1914, Van Vechten married a Russian actress, Fania Marinoff; this time, the marriage lasted. By now, he had moved to the *New York Press* as drama critic. In 1924, he and Fania moved to an apartment at 150 West 55th Street, which was later referred to by one wag as the midtown branch of the NAACP (National Association for the Advancement of Colored People): for in that same year, within just a few weeks, he had met most of the luminaries of the new arts in Harlem. He had already, in any case, become something of an impresario, taking on the task of aiding the careers of artists he admired. He had championed Ronald Firbank's fiction in America – it was he who suggested Firbank change the title of *Sorrow in Sunlight* to *Prancing Nigger* – and by now he was, to all intents and purposes, Gertrude Stein's agent in her own country. It made sense that, when he discovered how many innovative and productive black artists were working in Harlem – yet without being known, let alone fêted, mere blocks away in white Manhattan – he should become a kind of publicist to the Harlem Renaissance. He and James Weldon Johnson quickly became friends, and through Johnson he soon met other key literary figures. For *Vanity Fair*, he wrote introductions to the poetry of Countee Cullen and Langston Hughes; and it was he who passed a collection of Hughes' poems to Knopf, who published them in 1926 as *The Weary Blues*. He even occasionally served as a judge at the racially integrated drag balls that were held in the Rockland Paris Casino.

Eric Garber has pointed out that, of so many bisexual and lesbian women at large in Harlem show-business circles – women such as Bessie Smith, Gladys Bentley, Jackie 'Moms' Mabley, Alberta Hunter, Gertrude 'Ma' Rainey, Josephine Baker and Ethel Waters – most favoured 'a "red hot mama" style, and kept their love affairs with women a secret', but a few, including Bentley and Rainey, were much more open.[13] Bessie Smith toured with Ma Rainey when still a teenager. One of her biographers writes: 'It is not known at what stage in her life Bessie began to embrace her own sex. Some have assumed that Ma Rainey, who was similarly inclined, initiated her', but there is no evidence to support this assumption.[14] She married a man called Jack Gee in 1923, but the marriage was disastrous: he beat her constantly and was unfaithful. When he eventually walked out on her, he kidnapped their adopted son. The marriage ended in 1929. Smith toured with her husband's niece Ruby Walker between 1923 and

1929, and an intimate friendship developed between them, but it is unlikely to have been sexual. That said, Smith did have relationships with both women and men while on the road; and she is known to have once beaten up Ruby for sleeping with a man *she* was sleeping with. She was far too intransigent and uncompromising for the Van Vechten scene. On one occasion when Fania (Marinoff) Van Vechten tried to kiss her, Smith knocked her down. Yet while she refused to be patronised by whites, she was professionally naïve, rarely taking advice, allowing herself to be commercially manipulated, and often taking one-off payments instead of negotiating better deals. Her heavy drinking was accompanied by frequent bouts of verbal and physical violence. After she died in a car crash in 1937, her ex-husband made a comfortable living on her royalties.

It was not only writers that benefited from patronage. Both Van Vechten and Locke were also interested in music and the visual arts. As much as with their active support, both were profligate with friendship. They cultivated the company of intelligent young men to the extent that a whole generation of Negro artists felt, for the first time, not only that they had a potential general audience, but that there were influential individuals who were, at least, interested in the progress of their careers. One such artist was Richmond Barthé. Born in 1901 in Bay St Louis, Mississippi, in an era when it was unthinkable for a Negro to take up an artistic career, Barthé had shown an early interest in virtually nothing but art. Luckily, he was protected and nurtured by white liberals in New Orleans. For Christmas in 1923 he was given his first set of oil paints, and in the following year he was sent to the Chicago Art Institute. In 1925 he worked from a black model for the first time. While still a student he modelled a pair of heads in plaster – one of a white man, the other of a black woman. His work was included in an exhibition of 'Negro art' and came to the attention of Alain Locke. When his studies ended in 1928, Barthé moved to New York, establishing his first studio in Harlem. In 1930 he met Carl Van Vechten and they became close friends. Another new friend was the lesbian novelist Winifred Ellerman. By the time of his first one-man show, in 1934, Barthé already had a reputation as one of America's leading sculptors. The Whitney Museum of Art bought his figure of an *African Dancing Girl*. During the 1930s he made a number of portrait busts of people from the theatrical world, including John Gielgud and Gypsy Rose Lee. Other major commissions followed. He received two Guggenheim Fellowships in the early 1940s, and in 1943 the Metropolitan Museum of Art bought his figure of *The Boxer*. The President of Haiti commissioned heroic figures of Toussaint–Louverture and General Dessalines. Towards the end of the decade Barthé bought a house in Jamaica. He called it 'Iolaus' (after one of Hercules' male lovers and Edward

Carpenter's anthology of male love) and lived there for twenty years, seeking the novel ease of living in a predominantly black society. However, as tourism began to take over the island in the 1960s he fled to Europe, at first to the shores of Lake Geneva and then to Florence, where he settled, only returning to the United States in 1976.

Carl Van Vechten had in the 1920s, and has had since, an ambiguous reputation with regard to his part in the Harlem Renaissance. While it is not in dispute that he showed more interest in African-American artists than any white man before him and most since, his interest could be voyeuristic and, at times, seem exploitative. Harlem was a playground for those who could afford to live outside it or who were not confined to it on racial grounds. Quite what kind of obscurity Van Vechten's young, black boyfriends disappeared into after the limelight of his company is, inevitably, unknown; the likelihood is that he helped them in their careers, but he can only have done so while his attention was on them. A field trip he took in the mid-1920s to a Harlem brothel in the company of Somerset Maugham and Gerald Haxton was not the only jaunt of its kind – and hardly calculated for the betterment of the Negro race. His 1926 novel *Nigger Heaven* was controversial not merely for its title – to which even Van Vechten's father objected – but for its representation of the 'authenticity' of Harlem life as being anti-rational and almost wholly given over to the pursuit of sex (albeit rather like his portrayals of white society). The venerable W.E.B. DuBois thought it racist, whereas Langston Hughes, whose own poetry was deplored in more conservative Negro circles as providing negative images, defended it. The Harlem Renaissance would have flourished without Van Vechten's help, although it would not so easily have come to the notice of white Manhattan and the broader American culture. One thing is certain: Van Vechten was an obsessive collector, throughout his life, of cultural artefacts, from first editions of books, through paintings and manuscripts, to the more ephemeral of texts such as theatre programmes. When he donated these to several major academic institutions late in his life, they formed the most substantial cultural record of the Harlem Renaissance, much of which would have evaporated without them. For all his failings, he also deserved the plaudits that came his way from significant African-American cultural figures. Zora Neale Hurston once said of him: 'If Carl was a people instead of a person, I could then say, these are my people.'[15]

A 1928 essay of observations of Harlem life by the English journalist Beverley Nichols begins:

At the table next to me sat six boys dressed as girls. Four were white and two were coloured. One was powdering his nose, another was rouging his lips, a third was sipping gin in a lady-like manner, a fourth was casting languorous glances in my direction. The two coloured boys, charmingly gowned in pale green, were so drunk that they had forgotten any of the conventions which apply to either sex.

As soon as you read these words you will, of course, hiss to yourself 'Berlin!' Only Huns go in for 'that' sort of thing! As all really nice people know, Germany is riddled, throttled, and overrun with every sort of perversion. Germany and nowhere else.

I greatly regret it, but the scene is not set in Berlin. It is laid in Harlem, half an hour by taxi from the Ritz Hotel, New York.

Knowing Berlin's notoriety for its perverse nightclubs, Nichols plays on the British reader's likely assumptions about location. Homosexual himself, but not saying so, Nichols adds, 'In this year of 1928 it should be evident even to the most clouded mentalities that there are as many grades of sex as there are grades of intellect, and that pity, rather than blame, is the only punitive attitude which a civilized community can decently adopt towards persons such as I saw that night.'[16]

White people often looked with envy at what they regarded as the relative freedoms available to black people in Harlem. Of course, their view of black people's lives was partial and distorted – hardly a view of reality at all. The high life they witnessed in the nightclubs bore little relation to the poverty and conformity that prevailed behind the scenes. The Negroes who were admired for being able to enjoy themselves so lustily in the palaces of jazz and bootleg liquor were, if employed, only insecurely so; while housed, usually cramped together in tenement conditions the white pleasure-seekers could not have endured; and if 'free' in their pleasures, liberated only to the extent that the moral lapses of an oppressed underclass are considered unimportant.

That said, however, the observation of, or peripheral and temporary participation in, Harlem's pleasures could be more than merely eye-opening. A visit to a nightclub might offer a revealing glimpse of life's possibilities. The 1931 novel *Strange Brother*, by Blair Niles, shows this happening to its central (white, gay) character. The book opens in a Harlem bar, but before long we learn that this establishment is just a showcase providing entertainment for a white clientele. As in Weimar Berlin, a clear distinction could be made between the 'genuine' gay bars frequented by the local gay population and the 'performed' ones – tourist traps designed to entertain the curious. Knowing this, June Westbrook decides that she wants to go on to a real Harlem bar. Mark Thornton suggests the Lobster Pot, which is then the setting for the second chapter. In the Lobster Pot, June is delighted by the Negroes' love of life, and Mark, who is secretly gay, is sickened by a group of powdered and effeminate queens. As he and Jane are leaving the bar, they witness the arrest of a queen called Nelly. Mark goes home in a depressed state and tries to calm himself by reading some Walt Whitman and Edward Carpenter. The next day, he goes to court to watch while Nelly is castigated for wearing make-up and sent to jail for six months.

Later, June attends one of the great Harlem drag balls – to which crowds of heterosexuals have flocked to watch the fairies – but Mark refuses to go with her. He remains uncomfortable with all things camp, preferring to think of his own homosexuality in terms of Whitmanesque masculinity: he is deeply involved in the quest for 'the comrade and the lover of whom Walt Whitman sang'. When June visits him at home, he reads out the Countee Cullen poem 'Heritage' from Alain Locke's anthology *The New Negro*. So moved is he by these lines, June can see he has 'always identified himself with the outcasts of the earth. The negro had suffered and that bound Mark to him.'[17] She is not quite right about this, of course: for he never manages to identify sympathetically with the queens whose example seems so threatening to his image of himself as a man. I suppose the important point here is that, even if he keeps his distance from the queens he sees in the Harlem subculture, he needs to see them. For this reason, the author seems to regard him as having a *right*, even as a white man, to his presence in the 'real' Harlem rather than the performed one. She allows him the distinction of being no mere tourist in search of the exotic, but a man who needs to learn from those 'in the life' how to inhabit his difference. It is not a lesson he is able to absorb.

The English writer James Stern had a more positive experience of Harlem and its inhabitants in the 1930s. Unlike Blair Niles' Mark, he was, or claimed he was, able to absorb the lessons he learned there. Consciously or not, Stern echoed what E.M. Forster had once said of Italy:

> it was in America, among Americans, in that gay, reckless, optimistic atmosphere, above all in the company of the Negro intelligentsia, that I began at last to break through the cement-like crust of my bourgeois British upbringing, to learn at last sometimes to utter an unhesitating Yes, where hitherto I would have withdrawn behind that cautious, instinctive, notorious No[.][18]

### A New Sodom

In a journalistic piece first published in November 1916, Djuna Barnes gave an account of a suburban woman's trawling of Greenwich Village for exotic signs of bohemianism, trailing her two daughters behind her. In a place called the

Dutch Oven, while the daughters giggled their way through some custard pie, she finally managed to catch 'what she thought might be risqué bits in the conversation between [the painters] Marsden Hartley and [Charles] Demuth'.[19] The sound is that of Modernism but also, if more covertly, that of homosexuality. Prohibition, which lasted from 1920 to 1933, from the Eighteenth Amendment to the Twenty-First, had a major effect, not only on drinking habits, but also on the sexual history of the USA. The Harlem scene could not have thrived without it. In the catalogue to a major exhibition of gay American art, David C. Ward has said:

> The twentieth century's sexual revolution took place, not in the 1960s, but in the 1920s, with the final shattering of Victorian conventions. Prohibition created a sense among many people that they were outlaws, which helped loosen morals and behavior in other ways. Moreover, it created a sense that other bounds could and even should be transgressed as well.[20]

George Chauncey makes the same point: 'By driving middle-class men and women to break the law if they wanted to socialize where they could have a drink and bringing them in contact with "low-life" figures, Prohibition encouraged them to transgress other social boundaries as well.' Correspondingly, the repeal of Prohibition in 1933 had negative effects on the presence of gay social life in the city: 'Repeal resulted in the segregation and isolation of the gay social world from the broader social life of the city, in which it had played such a significant role in the 1920s.' The sale of alcohol was brought back under control, though with many restrictive clauses. For instance, 'after Repeal, bar owners risked losing their entire business if they served a single homosexual'. As a consequence, 'Gay men hardly disappeared from the city, but for thirty years they became less visible to outsiders.' A certain amount of leeway was allowed for the tourist trade: 'A few pansy clubs managed to survive as tourist traps in the Village, but the gay subculture as a whole stopped being part of the spectacle of urban life.'[21] Nevertheless, a sizable gay scene still managed to flourish in the city, despite all discouragements. When Robert Byron went to New York, he wrote home to his Old Etonian friend Desmond Parsons (20 January 1935): 'the old Berlin isn't in it'. But he added, 'I have been celibate since arrival, why, heaven knows, but I suppose it is the result of curiosity, which drowns the grosser impulses at first.'[22]

Once the Nazis had clamped down on the freedoms enjoyed by homosexual men and women in Berlin, New York took over as the world's representative urban centre of homosexuality, and the symbolic heart of Sodom-on-Hudson eventually moved from Harlem to Greenwich Village. Speaking of the Village in particular, Chauncey argues that 'one of the central strategies deployed by gay men for claiming space in the city' lay in their seeking 'to emphasize the theatricality of everyday interactions and to use their style to turn the Life [Cafeteria on Christopher Street at Sheridan Square] and other such locales into the equivalent of a stage, where their flouting of gender conventions seemed less objectionable because it was less threatening'. Visibly (and audibly) camp gay men might embarrass or irritate their closeted counterparts, as is so often the case; but 'The very brilliance of the fairy left most men safely in the shadows, and made it easier for them to meet their friends in restaurants throughout the city without provoking the attention of outsiders.' This is a recurring theme in Chauncey's work on gay New York: the more visibly homo- sexual individuals, by appearing to embody the type, kept their less visible brothers and sisters safe in the ignorance of the wider community. He quotes Samuel M. Steward as having said of the 1920s, 1930s and 1940s, 'Those of us who could maintain our secret lived under an extraordinary protective umbrella: the ignorance and naiveté of the American public.' The visibility of the 'fairy' distracted their attention.[23]

Jim Willard, the central character of Gore Vidal's pioneering novel *The City and the Pillar* (1948), casts an inexperienced but apparently authoritative eye over the city's gay population soon after he himself has arrived there. He, too, notices the difference between the invisible and the visible:

It seemed that from all over the country the homosexuals had come to New York as to a centre, a new Sodom; for here, among the millions, they could be unnoticed by the enemy and yet known to one another. These were the practising ones. There were, as Jim knew, thousands of seemingly normal men with families who would never step into this society but who, in the small towns and villages, practised secretly with one another, or if they were too shy or ignorant, longed without words to consummate their dreams, to recapture certain happy days in their childhood when they had had rela- tions with schoolmates, now grown to be men, married like themselves, and seemingly free from troubling dreams. This group, the unorganized and submerged dreamers and practitioners, was much the largest. The thou- sands in New York were either the strong and brave or else the effeminate and marked, people who had nothing to lose by being free and reasonably open in their behaviour.[24]

These straight-acting, middle-class, married men from out of town are the constituency most keenly threatened by the stigmatising of discretion during the Cold War period. Secretive in their practices, like the adherents of a banned religion, they seek nothing more than to perform their obscure rites without interference; but they know that the slightest wrong signal – like those flashes of bracelets below the cuff that were so meaningful in both Radclyffe Hall's and Marcel Proust's novels – will expose them as, not 'normal men with families' at all, but dangerous subversives, their expedient discretion itself the proof of subterfuge.

Jim learns the current slang: 'fairy' and 'pansy' are out, while 'gay' is in. When Jim's own now grown ex-schoolmate Bob Ford visits the city, he remarks on a particular characteristic of post-war New York: 'There's a lot of queers here. They seem to be everywhere now.'[25] In a tone of voice that is not dissimilar, after spending a day in New York in 1953, John Cheever commented in his diary: 'A lot of homosexuals drifting around in mid-morning.'[26] Visiting the USA on a Ford Foundation Scholarship in 1959–60, Italo Calvino observed: 'The Third Sex is even more widespread than in Rome. Especially here in the Village. The unwitting tourist goes into any outlet to have breakfast and suddenly notices that everyone in the place, customers, waiters, chefs, are all clearly of that persuasion.'[27]

In Ann Bannon's novel *Journey to a Woman* (1960), when Beth arrives in New York City, her first thought is to explore Greenwich Village: 'The Village. The end of the rainbow. How she had wondered about this place!'[28] In Bannon's *Beebo Brinker* (1962), Beebo asks her gay friend Jack, 'aren't they just for men – the gay bars?' and he replies, 'Men, girls, and everything in between.'[29] The historian Joan Nestle has argued that, for a lesbian woman, 'Just going to the bar meant taking on fifties America. It meant being a woman who was different from the protected woman, the domesticated woman. It felt subversive just going out into the streets at two o'clock in the morning, knowing that I was going to a place that was illegal.'[30] According to Bannon, this impression of subversion did not even require a late night; for it extended even to the simplest aspects of women socialising without men in a public space. In the 2002 introduction to *Journey to a Woman*, she says: 'It was a conspiratorial act when a bunch of handsome, adventurous young women sat down to share a beer and cigarettes. But more than that, we were carrying a flag handed off from our mothers, both straight and gay, claiming autonomy and equality for women.' The use of beer and cigarettes for stress relief was a practice taken up by many during the war years: 'Freedom to smoke and drink without the intermediary of a protective male became associated at last, for better or for worse, with a defiance of past constraints on women's lives. It became, in short, an outward show of independence.'[31] Bannon does, though, see the negative side of this. In the 2001 introduction to her novel *I Am a Woman* (1959), she says: 'That some of the women from the '50s and '60s were sacrificed to the flow of liquor and smoke, lamentable though it is, is hardly to be wondered at. The options were so few and the need was so great that the bars were always crowded.'[32]

The title character of *Beebo Brinker* is thrilled to be taken by a gay male friend to a specifically lesbian bar in the Village for the first time:

> The other bars had been all male or mixed. In this one, [her friend] Jack Mann and the two bar tenders, and a small scattering of 'Johns', were the only men in a big room solidly packed with women. It excited Beebo intensely – all that femininity . . . For the first time in her life, she was proud of her size, proud of her strength, even proud of her oddly boyish face. She could see interest, even admiration, on the faces of many of the girls. She was not used to that sort of reaction in people, and it exhilarated her.

As a tomboy, Beebo has never gained complete acceptance in any social environment until now, in this crush of differentiated femininities. In the past, her boyishness has had the fortunate effect of deterring men from paying her any attention, but it also took its toll on her self-esteem. Suddenly, not only does she find a space full of feminine women who may welcome expressions of her desire, but she finds herself unexpectedly subjected to theirs. The description of the dance floor is hyperbolic and peppered with cliché, but it makes the crucial point about an entirely positive atmosphere and a related lack of disapproval:

> The music was rhythmic and popular. The floor was jammed with a mass of couples . . . a mass of girls, dancing, arms locked around each other, bodies pressed close and warm. Their cheeks were touching. Quick light kisses were exchanged. And they were all girls, every one of them: young and lovely and infatuated with each other. They touched one another with gentle caresses, they kissed, they smiled and laughed and whispered while they turned and moved together.
>
> There was no shame, no shock, no self-consciousness about it all. They were enjoying themselves. They were having fun in the most natural way imaginable. They were all in love, or so it seemed. They were – what did Jack call it? – gay.[33]

Thus do the two primary meanings of the word 'gay' affect each other in a successful subcultural venue. The description of what the women are doing is conveyed in a sequence of unexceptional verbs (touched, kissed, smiled, laughed, whispered, turned, moved) describing a scene which, to other eyes than Beebo's, might convey the shock of scandal. She knows this, and so, presumably, do all the women. The bar cannot erase this social context, but it can allow them to forget about it for long enough to shake off their self-consciousness about doing such an ordinary thing as dancing together.

As a black woman, however, the future poet and autobiographer Audre Lorde found the Village's lesbian bars less than welcoming. She says of the Bagatelle, which she first entered in 1956: 'There was an inner door, guarded by a male bouncer, ostensibly to keep out the straight male intruders come to gawk at the "lezzies," but in reality to keep out those women deemed "undesirable." All too frequently, undesirable meant Black.' As she came to frequent the place, she rarely saw another non-white face there. She later adds that 'Black lesbians in the Bagatelle faced a world only slightly less hostile than the outer world which we had to deal with every day on the outside – that world which defined us as doubly nothing because we were Black and because we were Woman.' Even so, Lorde does acknowledge that the bar did provide a much-needed sense of togetherness: 'It had a feeling of family'.[34]

James Baldwin, too, noted that the Village rationed its liberties. In his greatest novel, *Another Country* (1962), Rufus can only think of it ironically, as 'the place of liberation'. He is walking down the street with Leona (who is white) and notes the reactions of a white couple coming the other way. Assuming he and Leona are a couple too, the man gives them 'a swift, nearly sheepish glance', whereas his wife 'simply closed tight, like a gate'. (Rufus overlooks the fact of his own assumptions: that *they* are a couple and, indeed, that they are man and wife.) As people continue to take white Leona and black Rufus as a couple – or as Rufus feels they do – the discomfort of merely walking down the street becomes extreme: 'Villagers, both bound and free, looked them over as though where they stood were an auction block or a stud farm.' Leona, meanwhile, is oblivious to it all.

Much later in the novel, Baldwin points out another fault line across the supposedly unified community of the Village. Its Italian inhabitants, the narrator claims, have come to hate those 'who gave their streets a bad name' – among them 'the black-and-white couples, defiantly white, flamboyantly black'. They feel they are being held back by the less respectable elements crowding the streets: 'The Italians, after all, merely wished to be accepted as decent Americans and probably could not be blamed for feeling that they might have had an easier time of it if they had not been afflicted with so many Jews and junkies and drunkards and queers and spades.'[35]

Harlem and the Village were not the full extent of gay New York, of course, but they were the places that acquired particular mythic weight in this respect. The whole city was, and is, inhabited by gay people, and many other areas host gay venues. The midtown area is a case in point. W.H. Auden wrote his poem

'September 1, 1939', on the date of its title, in Dizzy's Club, a gay bar on West 52nd Street to which Harold Norse had introduced him the night before. The poem is generally taken as being a ceremonial farewell to 'a low dishonest decade' on the eve of the Second World War. Its location represents what must be preserved: 'Faces along the bar / Cling to their average day: / The lights must never go out, / The music must always play, / All the conventions conspire / To make this fort assume / The furniture of home[.]' It is an ordinary 'dive' but it holds the sum of its customers' hopes and desires.

The playwright Arthur Laurents wrote of his experience of midtown gay bars in the 1940s:

> On-the-prowl drinking led me first to the Bird Circuit: gay bars with bird names like the Blue Parrot (it looked like the Black Parrot). Brighter and better was the Astor Bar in Times Square, wall to wall with GI Joes and our allies, a sort of gay Stage Door Canteen. Socially higher but pissier was the Oak Bar at the Plaza; best was the old Savoy-Plaza Hotel on East Fifty-eighth Street: it was New York and you knew it the moment you walked in. The bar, at the end of a room that had music and a dance floor, was generous with drinks and attractive officers and enlisted men ready for action.[36]

Most sites of homosexual pleasure are also, in some measure, sites of homophobic attack. In Charles Henri Ford and Parker Tyler's novel *The Young and Evil* (1933), Gabriel gives an account of having been chased, at dawn, by four homophobic 'gangsters' who had emerged from a 'coffee pot' at the intersection of West 4th Street and Sixth Avenue, in Greenwich Village. Later, Karel and Frederick suffer a more serious, physical attack, also at night, on Riverside Drive on the Upper West Side.[37] Allen Ginsberg later expressed his gratitude that Frank O'Hara had shown him the existence of a gay scene beyond the Village: 'Frank taught me to really see New York for the first time, by making of the giant style of Midtown his intimate cocktail environment. It's like having Catullus change your view of the Forum in Rome.'[38]

It is not surprising that, to some visitors, the sexual manners of New York seemed very odd – even visitors from that supposedly relaxed, romantic and erotic paradise, Italy. The heterosexual Italo Calvino noted that the 'beatnik' poet Allen Ginsberg 'lives with another bearded man [Peter Orlovsky] as man and wife'. It was not so much two men living together that he found worthy of comment, as the fact that both of them had beards. The arrangement he was more used to seeing in Italy would more definitively have paired masculinity with effeminacy. Calvino was amused, though, to add that the two Americans had befriended the Spanish writer Fernando Arrabal, who was no less unshaven than they, 'and would like Arrabal to be present at their bearded couplings'. Far from scandalising America, as the ex-Surrealist Spaniard had hoped he might, Calvino wryly reported that Arrabal 'is totally terrified at his first encounter with the American avant-garde and suddenly is revealed as the poor little Spanish boy who up until a few years ago was still studying to become a priest'.[39]

Wherever one turns in the cultural history of New York – if it is honestly written – one stumbles across highly significant clusters of gay people living and working together. Were this not the case, there would never have been so many complaints about homosexual infiltration of the national culture. Such clusters might be concentrated around a single individual, in a single location, on a single project, and so forth. One Broadway musical is a good example. In the autumn of 1943, Jerome Robbins introduced himself to Leonard Bernstein, and on the same day they started collaborating on the ballet *Fancy Free*. It was premiered on 18 April 1944. Their next collaboration would be *On the Town*. Then, in January 1949, Robbins suggested they work together on a modern version of *Romeo and Juliet* – an urban love affair first conceived of as transgressing the boundaries between Jews and Italian Catholics. It had a catchy working title: *East Side Story*. Robbins suggested Arthur Laurents as a suitable author for the book. However, Laurents' heart was not in the project and it was shelved. A later conversation Bernstein had with Laurents about juvenile delinquency reignited the project, initially to be set in Los Angeles but eventually, because Laurents was more familiar with the Puerto Rican population of Harlem, in New York – but on the West Side rather than the East. Both Bernstein and Robbins were now all the more enthusiastic about the project because the music would involve plenty of Latin rhythms. So, in the end, the libretto of *West Side Story* was by Arthur Laurents, its lyrics by Stephen Sondheim, its music by Leonard Bernstein and its choreography by Jerome Robbins. If this was a gay collaboration, it was also a Jewish one. If *West Side Story* is a gay text, it is also a Jewish one. But if it was a conspiracy of either or both of the two networks, they were conspiring professionally to make an evening's entertainment out of the affirmation of heterosexual desire across two communities of Christians. It had its first night on Broadway on 26 September 1957.

In 1965, Arthur Laurents worked with Stephen Sondheim and Richard Rodgers on the musical *Do I Hear a Waltz?* based on his own play *The Time of the Cuckoo*. As well as on *West Side Story*, he also collaborated with Sondheim on *Gypsy* and *Anyone Can Whistle*. It was Jerome Robbins who had proposed a musical based on the memoirs of Gypsy Rose Lee. Laurents agreed to write the book of the musical, persuaded to do so, in part, because he had heard that both Gypsy and her mother Rose were lesbian. Sondheim agreed to do the lyrics for what would become *Gypsy*. Laurents later wrote: 'It was assumed that being gay didn't matter in the theatre. That may have been true when there were chorus boys in musicals, but they were pansy, not gay.'[40]

It is easy now, as it was at the time, to map connections between gay figures working in the arts and to draw conclusions, positive or negative according to one's inclination, about gay cultural influence. In *A Queer History of the Ballet*, Peter Stoneley highlights the case of the impresario and writer Lincoln Kirstein, an influential man if ever there was one:

> An incomplete list of the variously bisexual and homosexual men to be connected to Kirstein's work around mid-century – many of them suspiciously 'international' – would include the composers Aaron Copland, Paul Bowles, Virgil Thomson, Marc Blitzstein, and Samuel Barber; the artists and designers Pavel Tchelitchew, Paul Cadmus, Jared French, Eugene Berman, Cecil Beaton, and Christian Bérard; the choreographers Jerome Robbins, Eugene Loring, Anthony Tudor, and Frederick Ashton; and the literati who provided ideas, wrote essays and reviews, or were simply enthusiasts, such as Carl Van Vechten, Edwin Denby, W.H. Auden, Frank O'Hara, Charles Henri Ford, John Ashbery, Parker Tyler, Glenway Wescott, and Monroe Wheeler.[41]

The internationalism of this list is actually rather modest, mainly Anglophone; so the suspicion Stoneley mentions is baseless. Not all of these connections were made in New York, but it took a base in New York to make much of them – that 'much' being, principally, the New York City Ballet. Many other clusters benefited by, and helped to extend, the city's cultural primacy. According to the composer Ned Rorem, 'Manhattan during the war and up through the early 1950s was governed by Aaron Copland and Virgil Thomson, the father and mother of American music. Young composers joined one faction or the other, there was no third.'[42] Among other such groups were: in the 1950s, the painters Robert Rauschenberg and Jasper Johns (who were a couple), and Cy Twombly; the New York School of Poets, which included John Ashbery, Frank O'Hara and James Schuyler; Andy Warhol's 'Factory'; the Beat writers . . .

However, mere profusion was far from having created a fully accepting atmosphere, even on the cultural circuit. To take just one example from the 1950s: Patricia Highsmith, who in Paris had mixed with the likes of Jane Bowles, Jean Cocteau, Ned Rorem, Janet Flanner, Gore Vidal and Truman Capote, found the homophobic atmosphere in 1950s America hard to cope with. Having got drunk at a literary party in New York and given away the fact that her companion Marijane Meaker was her lover, Highsmith was furious, not with herself for having revealed it, but with her audience for having thought it salaciously worth knowing. Reminded of what had happened by Meaker some time later, she asked, 'Do you think anyone at a cocktail party in Paris or Rome would ever mention something like that? How vulgar!'[43]

In any case, the extent of New York's gayness and gay-friendliness should not be overstated. In the early 1950s, as restrictions on passports for radicals were threatened, Arthur Laurents and his lover, the actor Farley Granger, left for Paris and London. It is worth noting, given his extensive experience of both the theatre industry in New York and the film industry in Los Angeles, that Laurents thought London was very visibly gay:

> Being with [Farley Granger] in London induced a different feeling because he was an even more popular movie star there than he was at home. Especially with the gay world which was gayer than any I had ever seen at home. Not sexually: with two or three notable exceptions, I never found the English sexual. But gays were certainly ubiquitous. Married, not married, young, old, all shapes and sizes, all classes in a country still obsessed with a caste system, gay men were so many and so evident that I wondered were there any Englishmen who were totally straight.[44]

Edmund White observed a similar contrast in the mid-1960s: 'Whereas New York in the sixties had almost no gay bars, since Mayor [Robert F.] Wagner had closed them all in an effort to clean up the city for the [1964] World's Fair, London had dozens and dozens.'[45]

### Gay Hollywood

Hollywood runs a great international arts festival, one of the prime concerns of which has been to suppress its internationalism. Ditto its homosexuality. However, William J. Mann has argued that, contrary to the widespread impression of Hollywood as a place in which the closet was rigorously enforced by the studio system, the movie industry was often more accommodating to its homosexual workers at all levels. One of Mann's interviewees said to him, in answer to an obvious question, 'Who *didn't* have to lie? Who *didn't* have to pretend? The difference was, in Hollywood, our bosses lied *for* us. They protected us. We had a whole *community*, for God's sake. We had – dare I say it? – *power*. Where else in America did gays have such a thing?' The passionate tone offers its own evidence. Mann correctly points out what his interviewee seems not to have known, that there were other such protective communities and subcultures across the States at the time; but the point is well made, all the same. From the start, there were more than enough homosexual men and women in Hollywood for the operation of informal supportive systems. The disappointment is in the failure of that power to translate into a corresponding visibility in the cultural product: the movies.[46]

Mann found that his interviewees did not use such expressions as 'in' and 'out' (of the closet). Instead, they independently kept coming back to the words 'overt' and 'circumspect', and to degrees of both. Individuals, couples and groups tended to locate themselves where they felt most comfortable across a spectrum of degrees of openness. There was no general pressure to work towards a point at which it would become possible to come out; but, perhaps more surprisingly, there was no general imperative *not* to come out. The determining factors were many. There was a class difference, as elsewhere: 'The most overt gays tended to come from working-class backgrounds, while those from the middle classes invariably were more circumspect.' In certain professional areas, such as costume design and set design, it was possible to exploit the popular connection of male effeteness with aesthetic sophistication; yet that connection does not appear to have been applicable in relation to men who sought to direct movies. On the other hand, the few women who made it in major behind-camera creative roles had to shake off the stigma of whimsical femininity and demonstrate a willingness to get their hands dirty, metaphorically or not. One of Mann's interviewees summed up his own experience of being gay in Hollywood's early days as follows: 'My being gay and knowing all these people – the doors were always open. It was all this "understood" business. They knew I knew, I knew they knew. It was kind of a brotherhood.'[47]

Referring to Hollywood in the 1920s, Hart Crane said: 'O André Gide! No Paris ever yielded such as this!'[48] In the heyday of what Kenneth Anger would call 'Hollywood Babylon', one might argue that an artistic ethos combined with a pleasant climate to produce an atmosphere of sexual celebration, within limits that would soon be tightened up. The extent to which the ethos of the mode of production ever influenced the product – the movies themselves – has been a matter for much debate. In this context, William Mann asks a series of pertinent, rhetorical questions:

is it possible to see the gay influence in *The Wizard of Oz*, for example, because [the costume designer] Adrian created the Munchkins and Jack Moore the Yellow Brick Road? Can we reflect upon the gayness of the narrative of *Cat People*, written by DeWitt Bodeen? Might we consider the queerness of the very look of *Casablanca*, whose fantastic sets were designed by George James Hopkins? Or detect the gay soul of *Meet Me in St Louis*, because its direction was staged by Vincente Minnelli, its score orchestrated by Conrad Salinger, and its production arranged by Roger Edens? Might we consider the entire body of work of such directors as George Cukor or Dorothy Arzner or Edmund Goulding or James Whale, seeing their films as the creations of artists *who were gay*?[49]

The answer is probably affirmative in every case, if more convincingly so in some than in others; and acknowledging 'the creations of artists who were gay' is, of course, a long way from finding specifically 'gay art', especially since all of the named figures were working in collaboration with other artists who were not gay. However, Mann's list of questions gives a vivid sense of the creative possibilities of a specifically gay spectatorship.

Although the atmosphere in the film industry itself was quite relaxed, outside observers of that industry came to be less so. Ever since the late 1920s, varying degrees of pressure exerted from outside have had an effect on the atmosphere within the studios themselves and on the extent to which professionals in the industry – especially actors – have been able to reconcile their sexual orientations and their working lives. In 1926 the *Chicago Tribune* had published an article which denounced Rudolph Valentino as a 'pink powder puff' and posed the wider question, 'When will we be rid of these effeminate youths, pomaded, powdered, bejewelled and bedizened in the image of Rudy – that painted pansy?'[50] In a similar tone, an article in *Variety* in June 1930 approvingly reported that movie producers were winnowing out the pansies from the chorus lines. If any boy seemed 'too pretty, dainty or over-marcelled' he would be excluded from a picture: for 'It has been discovered the average American film fans resent effeminate men in operettas, musicals, etc.' The writer assumed that the flaw of insufficient masculinity was easy to identify. 'Even though a male chorus line might have only a couple of geraniums, the fans quickly spot 'em.' What might be allowable on the stage was less so on screen. The differentiating feature appears to be the medium itself: the 'Camera seems to intensify the effeminate mannerisms of the male crotcheters, making them much more conspicuous than in stage musicals.' By way of contrast, the writer specifies Broadway, where, presumably, audiences are either too far away from the chorus boys to spot their personal idiosyncrasies and their maquillage, or too undermined by the moral laxness of New York to worry about such things.[51]

There is a reciprocal relationship between Broadway and Hollywood, each feeding the other with talent, although the big money tends to be found in the latter. When James Dean appeared on Broadway in a stage adaptation of André Gide's *The Immoralist*, he was offered a screen test by Warner Bros., which, in due course, resulted in his being given a part in the film *East of Eden* (1955). Many performers from Europe began their American careers on stage on the

East Coast before graduating, as it were, to the movies on the West. This is true of Alla Nazimova, who had emigrated from Russia in 1905, and of Charles Laughton, who moved from London's West End to Broadway and then to Hollywood.[52]

For a short while in the early 1930s various live venues in Hollywood were renowned for their cross-dressing revues. The drag performer Rae Bourbon staged his *Boys Will Be Girls* shows at Jimmy's Back Yard. (For a while Harry Hay, later to become the celebrated gay activist, worked outside Jimmy's, enticing in the crowds.) Bobby Burns Berman, the proprietor of B.B.B.'s Cellar, used to stage a revue with ten boys in drag. But the 'pansy clubs' did not last. During a police crackdown in the autumn of 1932 both Jimmy's and B.B.B.'s were raided; five men were arrested at the former, nine at the latter. An item in *Variety* spoke of 'a drive on the Nance and Lesbian amusement places in town'.[53] Since cross-dressing was regarded as the most blatant of the pansy transgressions, various obscure local ordinances were invoked against it. By the end of the decade, when the drag star Julian Eltinge made a guest appearance at the Rendezvous Club, all he could legally do was appear on stage in a tuxedo and show off a rack of his best frocks. (The crackdown was not confined to Hollywood. In 1931, the very words 'pansy' and 'fairy' were banned from use in RKO vaudeville establishments, and in January 1933 pansy acts were banned from public entertainment venues in Atlantic City.) The Hays Code of self-censorship (1930) was unambiguous on the matter of homosexuality: 'Sex perversion or any inference to it [*sic*] is forbidden.' By 1933 there was a war against homosexuals in the movies. As one executive said, leaving no room for misunderstanding: 'I do not want any of them in Fox pictures.'

The public face of Hollywood was largely constructed, not by critics of the content of the movies themselves, but by gossip columnists with a sharp eye for the kinds of scandal that sell newspapers. Louella Parsons wrote for the *Los Angeles Examiner*; Hedda Hopper competed against her in the *Los Angeles Times*. Oddly enough, given the extent to which both were willing to use homophobic innuendo against a range of victims, both women had homosexual assistants. Indeed Parsons' gay sidekick King Kennedy would marry her lesbian daughter Harriet in 1939, even if they hardly ever lived together. Hopper employed a lesbian woman, Dema Harshbarger, as manager and general personal assistant. When Kennedy left Parsons, he joined Hopper. Later, Robert Shaw also worked for her. According to him, she often used gay men as informants.

By way of a more gay friendly contrast, in the late 1930s the magazine *Bachelor* – which had as its art director Jerome Zerbe, as its editor Lucius Beebe, and as its director of photography George Platt Lynes – profiled such eternal bachelors as Noël Coward and Cecil Beaton, published beefcake shots of the likes of Errol Flynn and Gary Cooper, and also included glamorous coverage of Marlene Dietrich, Greta Garbo and Mae West. Many of the women who have since come to be regarded as Hollywood's great 'gay icons' were shaped, or in a profound way designed, by gay men: Marlene Dietrich by Travis Banton, Greta Garbo by Adrian, Joan Crawford by William Haynes, Marilyn Monroe by Jack Cole, Judy Garland by Roger Edens, and so on. Correspondingly, Rudolph Valentino was tweaked into shape by lesbian women: Alla Nazimova and Natacha Rambova glossed and fluffed him up, in particular for his role in *Camille*. In the studios, few cameramen and technicians were gay, but there were exceptions, such as James Crabe. On the other hand, all of the most prominent decorators were gay – Arthur Krams, Henry Grace, George James Hopkins, Howard Bristol – as was virtually the whole of the MGM research department. Influential gay choreographers included Charles Walters, Robert Alton and Jack Cole (who created Jane Russell's number with the massed body-builders in *Gentlemen Prefer Blondes*).

The famous actors of popular 'sissy' roles – men such as Edward Everett Horton and Franklin Pangborn – were generally gay, too. As William Mann puts it, 'given that nearly all of the movie sissies were gay in real life, it is likely that there was a consciousness of what they were doing'. Indeed, Mann goes further: 'Just as the verisimilitude of talking pictures outdated blackface and demanded that real African Americans take on Negro parts, so, too, does it seem that actual homosexuals were frequently assigned the pansiest of pansy roles.'[54] Replacing those dangerous heart-throbs like Valentino, the sissies were safe because they were both funny and sexless. They never threatened, as Valentino had, to lure heterosexual women or, worse still, men away from the marriage market. Yet, by the early 1940s, the sissy started to take on a more sinister profile: in Mann's words, 'Conniving, manipulative, and dangerous, the sissy had suddenly turned lethal.' In general, at the same time, he now tended not to be played by gay actors so much as imitated – or travestied – by straight ones.

Various possibilities were available to same-sex couples, most of them involving the closet to a greater or lesser extent. The studio bosses expected absolute discretion, even while the social ambience of urban California encouraged something rather more relaxed. Many homosexual actors got married but kept their lovers in separate establishments. Another common solution, known as the 'twilight tandem', was the marriage of a homosexual man and a lesbian woman, with variable arrangements regarding their respective lovers. Such marriages included those between MGM's chief art director Cedric Gibbons and Dolores del Rio, or Edmund Lowe and Lilyan Tashman, or Rudolph Valentino and Jean Acker (the lover of Grace Darmond and, at another time, of Alla Nazimova), or Janet Gaynor (later the lover of Mary Martin) and costume designer Adrian, or Barbara Stanwyck and Robert Taylor. The actor William Haines, on the other hand, had no intention of either getting married or judiciously living apart from the man he loved: his boyfriend Jimmie Shields moved in with him, and Haines found him work at MGM as an extra.

With the advent of sound, many stars failed to make the transition from the silent movies, because they had either weak voices or strong accents. Men with 'effeminate' speech mannerisms stood no chance. William Haines, though, was the first MGM star to face the microphone in 1928. With a strong, deep voice, he and his queerness survived. All the actors had to go through extensive vocal training, of course, but when his voice coach said to him, 'The trouble with you, Mr Haines, is that you're lip-lazy', he had the presence of mind – and the confidence – to reply, 'I've never had any complaints before.'[55] Contrasting developments were taking place in the culture of Tinseltown. At the very time that the Hays Code was being drafted for the movie industry, late in 1929, and accepted by film producers, in 1930, the town of Hollywood saw the beginnings of an organised gay commercial scene. On New Year's Eve 1929, Hollywood's first gay club, Jimmy's Backyard on Ivar Street, was formally opened with a huge gala celebration. Haines was there; as was actor-director Lowell Sherman. Harry Hay would remember being there as a teenager, 'going from table to table and lap to lap'.[56] Other gay clubs opened during the next eighteen months, including Freddy's and Allen's. They tended to be speakeasies in private apartments, and were almost always short-lived. Yet, hardly had the atmosphere loosened up in this way than, in 1932, the police department began cracking down on such establishments, their first concern being to ban cross-dressing, that most obvious sign of wilful deviation from gender norms.

The gay actor Nils Asther had been on the verge of being fired in 1930 when he suddenly got married. His career was saved; but soon after it was announced, in September 1932, that he and his wife were to separate, Louis B. Mayer refused to renew his contract. His career ended. At about the same time, Mayer gave William Haines an ultimatum that resulted in his leaving MGM. Whether he resigned or was sacked is unclear; but it hardly makes a difference. The likelihood is that Mayer told him to get married, and that, in effect, Haines refused to give up his homosexuality – or, more importantly, his lover. Ramon Novarro's contract was allowed to lapse in 1934. There was a spate of expedient marriages: Gary Cooper in December 1933, Cary Grant in February 1934, Randolph Scott in 1936. (When Grant got married, Scott moved in next door. When Grant's wife left him, after an initial suicidal impulse, he moved in with Scott again. When Scott himself married, he and his wife never lived together.) The director Dorothy Arzner, who lived with her lover Marion Morgan, a dancer, was dropped by MGM in 1937. Vincent Price escaped a similar fate by eerily becoming heterosexual all of a sudden. William Haines' biographer puts the matter clearly: 'Those who played the game were rewarded with stardom, endurance, and protection: Cary Grant, Robert Taylor, Barbara Stanwyck, Rock Hudson. Those who refused – people like Dorothy Arzner and Billy Haines – were ushered out.'[57] George Cukor was reportedly sacked from directing *Gone with the Wind* in 1939 because the sexually reformed and newly wed Clark Gable said, 'I won't be directed by a fairy'. There was no question which of the two would be supported by the MGM management.

Thinking of the many homosexual and bisexual men and women who have worked in Hollywood leads us back, inevitably, to the question of cultural influence. Given such a significant presence in the studios throughout their existence, one might have expected their product, the movies themselves, to show at least some faint sympathy for people of that sort. If there is evident influence, it must be aesthetic rather than social. Surely only a workforce heavily blessed with queer people could have churned out so much High Camp; but the reluctance of the Hollywood system to temper its consistently hostile representations of homosexuality for most of the twentieth century shows that the considerable collective power so many individuals had was ceded to them under strict conditions.[58] No matter how many gay individuals we can identify among the film industry's writers, actors, designers, technicians and other creative participants, the fact is that Hollywood is too commercially in thrall to the presumed homophobia of its mass audience, even today, to be anything better than indifferent to lesbians and gay men. It might have taken an implausibly radicalised bunch of actively pro-gay studio bosses to make a significant difference for the better.

### New York to Havana and Back

*Fairies* de Nortamérica,
*Pájaros* de La Habana,
*Jotos* de Méjico,
*Sarasas* de Cádiz,
*Apios* de Sevilla,
*Floras* de Alicante,
*Adelaidas* de Portugal.

In the roll call of homosexual effeminates from the English-, Spanish- and Portuguese-speaking diasporas in these lines from his 'Ode to Walt Whitman', Federico García Lorca both repudiates and affirms a fellowship across national borders. On the face of it, the speaker is calling up the spirits of camp gay men, using derogatory epithets in Spanish, Portuguese and English, calling them up in order to denounce them. These lines have the sound of drunken, homophobic gangs yelling at their terrified quarry down city streets at night. The threat conveyed is palpable. And the implication of the list is that everywhere has its own version of the insult and the threat. Different nations and different languages merely provide variations on the single theme.

On the other hand, we should try to imagine a different tone of voice, perhaps more highly pitched, still echoing down the city streets at night. Might not these cries be affirming, whether singly or in groups, an identification that amounts to an identity? Might they not be recognisable as an affirmation of what would later come to be called gay pride? If so, this vocalisation conveys not threat so much as a frisson of erotic possibility. Again, different nations and different languages merely provide variations on the one theme.

Walt Whitman's mythic version of the United States offered an attractive optimism, a counter-discourse to that of 'degeneracy' and 'decadence' in *fin-de-siècle* Europe. For many literate Europeans, America *was* Whitman's America. For many homosexual Europeans, the Whitman of the imagination was a benign pander of comradeship, whose roving eye had taken the measure of American manhood and seen that it was good. His poetry conjured up Manhattan, a city of eye contact and spontaneous conversation; beyond it the great continent stretching all the way to the Pacific Ocean, a landscape of apparently infinite variety, on the face of which a man might shape his own destiny. Supposedly lacking in barriers of class and ethnicity, this was an environment in which one might, anywhere and at any time, befriend a stranger on equal terms.

Oscar Wilde's mother had read *Leaves of Grass* to him when he was thirteen. At Oxford he and his friends used to carry the book with them when they went for walks – or so Wilde told Whitman in January 1882, when they met. Wilde came away from his visit to Whitman uttering the proud words, 'The kiss of Walt Whitman is still on my lips.' He had charmed the old man, who thought him 'so frank and outspoken and manly'.[59] Whitman had little time for unmanly men. García Lorca, in his own mannerisms, was anxious not to be taken for such a man, a *marica*. Even if those multiple voices in his poem can be read positively, they are heard in the midst of a broader, homophobic attack. This 'Ode to Walt Whitman', like the collection *Poet in New York* (*Poeta a Nueva York*, posthumously published in 1940) as a whole, celebrates an urban environment profusely populated with young men, both white and black, most visibly of the working class. Lorca lays temporary claim to the New York City of Walt Whitman, but the fact is that Whitman's vision of 'adhesiveness' or fellowship between men was strictly 'manly'; and 'adhesiveness' is a comradeship of equals rather than of man over boy.[60]

Speaking of Polish poetry in particular but of European Modernism in general, Czesław Miłosz wrote that 'revolutions in versification were greatly indebted to Walt Whitman's poetry, which began to penetrate Europe around 1912'.[61] (It was also the year of Imagism and of Marcel Duchamp's *Nude Descending a Staircase*.) More indebted than most were poets who were homosexual and found in Whitman, as expressed by both form and theme, permission to speak of male love in a modern setting, especially an urban one, without recourse to the archaic sources of Greece and Rome. As well as that of Lorca, Whitman clearly influenced the work of writers such as Fernando Pessoa, Edward Carpenter, D.H. Lawrence, Hart Crane, Luis Cernuda, Yannis Ritsos, Vicente Aleixandre, Pier Paolo Pasolini, Mutsuo Takahashi ... To most of them, Whitman's verse was a welcome alternative to the 'decadent' tradition of Oscar Wilde and the *fin de siècle*. His labouring-class men could sling their arms around each other's necks in warmth of comradeship and give off the heady scent of sweat rather than those of incense and *les fleurs du mal*. They could (and did) routinely share their beds without causing a scandal. It also helped that Whitman was a much more interesting poet than Wilde.[62]

As well as referring to contemporary scandals, in the opening section of *Corydon* André Gide had invoked Whitman as his first representative figure of the homosexual man. Corydon has a photograph of him – 'an old man with a long white beard' – on his work table. The narrator asks why it is there, given that Léon Bazalgette's 1908 biography of the poet had established that he was a lover of women. Corydon points out some of Bazalgette's apparently deliberate mistranslations of the poetry, masking its homo-eroticism.[63] If Wilde was still the new century's most notorious representative of scandalous homosexuality, Whitman, although scandalous in his own way, stood for that more normative, masculine and natural (as opposed to effeminate and artful) version of same-sex love.[64]

Among the most striking of the homages to Whitman are those paid by the Portuguese poet Fernando Pessoa, under the heteronym 'Álvaro de Campos', in his 'Triumphal Ode' (London, June 1914) and the 'Salutation to Walt Whitman' (1915).[65] One critic goes so far as to say, 'Whitman was Pessoa's liberator'.[66] In the latter of the two poems, the speaker presents himself as a swaggering dandy, virtually daring Whitman to think him unworthy. Without any attempt to win it, he brazenly claims the older poet's love and carries it off to twentieth-century Lisbon:

> I, with my monocle and exaggeratedly tight-waisted coat,
> Am not unworthy of you, Walt, and you know it.
> I'm not unworthy of you, for the simple reason that I salute you ...

And although I never met you, being born around the year you died,
I know you loved me too, you knew me, and it gladdens my heart.
I know that you knew me, considered me and explained me,
And I know that that's what I am, whether on the Brooklyn ferry ten years
    before I was born
Or on the Rua do Ouro today, thinking about everything that's not the Rua
    do Ouro,
And as you felt everything, I feel everything, we walk hand in hand,
Hand in hand, Walt, hand in hand, dancing the universe in our soul.

Hart Crane, too, would hold hands with Whitman, at the end of part IV of *The Bridge* (published in 1930 by Harry and Caresse Crosby's Black Sun Press).[67] But Álvaro de Campos is far more explicit than either Crane or Lorca about Whitman's sexuality:

You, singer of vigorous professions, You the Poet of the Strong and the
    Extreme,
You, inspiration's muscle, ruled by male muses,
You, finally, an innocent in a state of hysteria,
Finally just a 'caresser of life,'
A shiftless idler, a pansy at least in spirit.[68]

(Whitman had called himself the 'caresser of life' in section 13 of 'Song of Myself'.) Despite any impression of effeminacy his own monocle and tailored jacket may convey, the speaker appeals to his forefather on the common ground of 'the Strong and the Extreme' as an appropriate bard for the purposes of urban modernity. For all his shiftlessness, his loafing about, Whitman is presented as being fully occupied with life, by virtue of hysterical engagement. His inspiration is muscular, inspired by muscularity. There is a fellowship, here, between poets who are man-loving men in an environment of masculine labour. Yet they themselves do not feel constrained to strut and strain in a performance of physical virility. Their pansy spirit is itself a sign of strength. Cyril Connolly once referred to Fernando Pessoa as 'Lisbon's Cavafy or Verlaine'.[69]

Lorca seems not to have been able to reconcile the two apparently opposed styles of manliness. To him, so anxious about his own masculinity, Whitman was the more reliable model for everyday life, as a rough-cut man's man, than Wilde and his like. So, to have found separatist subcultures of screaming queens in Whitman's Manhattan seems to have been more than Lorca could bear, even if it also rather excited him.[70] One line of the ode – 'los maricas, Walt Whitman, los maricas' – sandwiches the old bard between crowds of faggots in a manner that Lorca deplores; but one cannot help feeling that the old boy himself might have enjoyed the experience. Be that as it may, the ode makes for uncomfortable reading, especially when it descends to the crudest of homophobic epithets, 'Madres de lodo', literally 'mothers of mud' but very obviously euphemistic for 'mothers of shit'.

Daniel Eisenberg has claimed that 'in the early twentieth century Granada [where Federico García Lorca went to university] had the most important homosexual subculture in Spain'. One commentator testily responds that 'The existence of that subculture does not clarify Lorca's poems, whose terms of reference are international rather than local'.[71] Lorca became associated with the Rinconcillo (little corner) group, named after the space they occupied in the Café Alameda on the Plaza del Campillo and active between 1915 and 1922. Fellow homosexuals among them were the Republican journalist Constantino Ruiz Carnero and Lorca's childhood friend José María García Carrillo, a camp aesthete who made his living as a quantity surveyor. It was around 1917 that Lorca started to think of himself as a poet rather than a composer.

From 1919 to 1920 he went to Madrid, staying in the Residencia de Estudiantes, at various times in its history a significant crucible of the Spanish avant-garde, and was reunited with members of the Rinconcillo set who had moved there. Among others he met at this time was Luis Buñuel, with whom his friendship would always be rather uneasy. Perhaps because his younger brother Alfonso was homosexual, Buñuel was an enthusiastic queer-basher, lurking for his prey around the public urinals of Madrid. Although this was a passing phase and he soon gave up the practice, he never shook off the prejudice that motivated it. When someone suggested to him that the budding poet was homosexual, Buñuel, who liked to have such things clear in his mind, deeply offended (and perhaps frightened) Lorca by asking him, point-blank.

During the summer of 1922 Lorca worked with one of his gay friends, the composer and music critic Adolfo Salazar, on *The Tragedy of Don Cristóbal and Señorita Rosita*, hoping eventually to interest Diaghilev in staging it. They had a completed first draft by 5 August. He also worked with Manuel de Falla, whom he had met in Granada, on the folk songs known as *cante jondo*; and in the spring of 1923, after he had completed his law degree, he and Falla began to collaborate on a comic opera, *Lola, the Actress* (*Lola, la comedianta*). Lorca finished his libretto in the autumn, but Falla never delivered the music.[72] During the interval at the first performance of his play *Mariana Pineda* in Madrid on 12 October 1927, Lorca was introduced to a young poet from Andalucía, Vicente Aleixandre; and in Seville in mid-December he met the poet Luis Cernuda. Other gay poets of this and the next generation included Emilio Prados and Juan Gil-Albert.[73] Lorca's *Gypsy Ballads* (*Romancero gitano*), written between 1924 and 1927, appeared in the shops in July 1928. Luis Buñuel hated them, largely for homophobic reasons: 'It's a poetry that has the finesse and *apparent* modernity which any poetry needs nowadays in order to please the Andrenios, Baezas and homosexual, Cernuda-style poets from Seville.' He added that Lorca's poetry was 'the sort of thing that keeps Spanish beds full of menstrual blood'.[74] Thus, we see Lorca working, throughout the 1920s, in close collaboration with other gay artists and in heated dialogue with anti-gay ones.

In June 1929, Lorca embarked on the major overseas sojourn that would lead to *Poet in New York*. He went by train to Paris, where he paused only for a day, then on, via a choppy Channel, to London for two nights. Travelling through England, he formed the mistaken impression, conveyed by signs on the station platforms, that every town was called Bovril. He stayed with a friend for a few nights at Lucton School, near Ludlow. Then, after a day in Oxford, he took a train to Southampton to board the SS *Olympic* for New York. He arrived there on 25 June and stayed for six months of alternating enchantment and depression: enchantment with the modernistic city and its arts, depression at being so far from home and family and friends. Early in his stay, he met Nella Larsen, author of the novels *Quicksand* (1928) and *Passing* (1929). An important figure in the cultural life of Harlem, she introduced him to black American society and took him to his first Harlem nightclub. His poem 'The King of Harlem', in which he evokes the sight of 'your grand king a prisoner in the uniform of a doorman' and crowds of 'cooks, waiters, and those whose tongues lick clean the wounds of millionaires', is dated 5 August 1929. On 16 August he went to stay for ten days with his American friend Philip Cummings in a cabin in Vermont, before returning to New York City. Ángel Flores, editor of the magazine *Alhambra*, took him to Brooklyn to meet Hart Crane. Crane, who was currently putting the finishing touches to *The Bridge*, was in his element: they found him in a bar, surrounded by sailors as drunk as himself. He and Lorca managed some kind of conversation in tentative French – they are said to have talked about Whitman – but when Flores decided to leave, he looked back to see the two poets enjoying themselves separately, each in his own cluster of jolly jack tars.[75]

Lorca witnessed the Wall Street Crash in person. Indeed, to get a full sense of the atmosphere of the occasion, he joined the crowds outside the Stock Exchange for seven hours. He later claimed, also, to have seen on the sidewalk the body of one of the men who threw themselves from skyscrapers when they realised they had lost everything they owned. More cheerfully, he managed to get to see (and hear) his first 'talkie' at a New York cinema. At Christmas, as he watched the sailors on the wharves along the Hudson he felt threatened – a sailor had had his throat cut there – and yet ravaged by desire: 'Oh, the keen blade of my love, oh, the cutting blade!' ('Christmas on the Hudson', 27 December 1929).

On 4 March 1930, Lorca departed for Cuba, where he was already well known, arriving there three days later. During his three-month stay he gave five lectures in Havana. One of his biographers says, 'If New York had nudged Lorca toward an acceptance of his sexuality, Cuba allowed him to celebrate it.'[76] A friend who moved around the country with him recalled that he was never back in his hotel room before dawn, no matter where they went. He had an affair with one Lamadrid, a twenty-year-old youth of mixed race. He is said to have met the poet Porfirio Barba Jacob and stolen his lover, a Scandinavian sailor. He may also have spent a night in jail for some unspecified homosexual offence. While in Cuba, he was working on the play *The Public* (*El público*); and he also conceived of another about the Homintern, to be called *The Destruction of Sodom*, in which he would pay homage (in the words of his biographer) to 'the pleasures of the homosexual confraternity, who have made such a contribution to world culture.'[77] Adolfo Salazar arrived in Cuba on 16 May and joined Lorca for most of his last month there; and when Lorca left the island, Salazar sailed with him. He had completed the first draft of the 'Ode to Walt Whitman' just after he left Cuba on 12 June 1930.[78]

What seems clear in all the American poems, but especially so in the 'Ode to Walt Whitman', is that Lorca was both impressed and depressed by the sheer proliferation of same-sex activities that he witnessed being negotiated, if not actually carried out, during his visit to New York City. *Poet in New York* is full of both desire and envy. When the latter is dominant, Lorca erupts into a rage against his own kind. Perhaps because he himself most desired men who did not identify as homosexual, he sometimes affected to despise those who did. (This was not an uncommon pattern of behaviour.) In particular, what seems to have worried him about the New World's urban *maricones* was their tendency to associate with one another in what we might now call subcultures. The men Lorca most enthusiastically celebrates in his book – the industrial workers, 'singing, exposing their waists, / with the wheel, with oil, leather, and the hammer', and the glamorous Negroes of Harlem – would not have been seen dead in such compromised groups. But even the promiscuity of the manly men worried him. Down on the waterfront at Battery Place, a night-time crowded with servicemen and whores was saturated with urine and kept awake – or alive – by the foghorns of the transatlantic steamers.

> Everything is shattered in the night
> that spreads its legs on the terraces.
> Everything is shattered in the tepid faucets
> of a terrible silent fountain.

In this poem, 'Landscape of a Pissing Multitude', he seems to be sharing that thrilled but saddened sense Hart Crane expressed, in *The Bridge*, of love's having been reduced by urban promiscuity to 'A burnt match skating in a urinal'.[79] Yet, at the same time, what he witnessed in New York filled him with hope. One of his epigraphs, a quotation from Vicente Aleixandre, while acknowledging that the time for kissing is not yet ripe – 'el tiempo de los besos no ha llegado' – suggests that it might be imminent.

Lorca arrived back in Cádiz on 30 June and went straight home to Granada, arriving there the next day. Friends who encountered him after his year in the New World felt he had become less inclined to conceal his homosexuality. While in New York, he had read, in Spanish translation, both T.S. Eliot's *The Waste Land* (1922) and John Dos Passos's novel *Manhattan Transfer* (1925). In the latter, he will have read the scene in which, while they are walking along a residential street in the Flatbush area of Brooklyn, a drunken Tony Hunter unhappily comes out as gay to Jimmy Herf, who replies, 'But it all may be an idea. You may be able to get over it. Go to a psychoanalyst.' Tony says, 'I've tried to look it up in the encyclopaedia . . . It's not even in the dictionary.' Jimmy tries to cheer him up, patting him on the back and saying, 'There're lots of people in the same boat. The stage is full of them.' But Tony's self-hatred is not appeased, because, of course, this invocation of theatrical types is one of the things that troubles him about his situation. The theatre implies effeminacy and flamboyance. He does not want to be associated with such men; nor is he attracted to them. 'I hate them all,' Tony says. 'It's not people like that I fall in love with.' Tony takes Jimmy's advice, however, and does consult an analyst. He tells Nevada about the session while dancing with her: 'He said it was all imaginary. He suggested I get to know some girls better. He's all right. He doesn't know what he's talking about though. He can't do anything.' Nevada advises him against giving up on the doctor: 'He did wonders with Glen Gaston . . . He thought he was that way until he was thirtyfive years old and the latest thing I hear he's married an had a pair of twins' [*sic*].[80]

Following the great success of his play *Blood Wedding* in Buenos Aires, Lorca decided to visit Argentina, setting sail from Barcelona on 28 September 1933 and arriving on 13 October. He stayed for nearly six months, during which time the Argentine press covered virtually every aspect of his visit. As a result, by the time he left he was a major public figure and was seen off at the docks by a large crowd. He arrived back in Barcelona on 11 April 1934. In Argentina he had met and made friends with the Chilean poet Pablo Neruda. When the great matador Ignacio Sánchez Mejías returned to the ring in his early forties and was gored to death, Lorca began his 'Lament', most of which he wrote in Neruda's flat back in Madrid. It was finished by the beginning of

November. Although a lot of the evidence from this overseas trip suggests otherwise, Neruda said of Lorca in his memoirs, 'He was happy. He was always like that. Happiness was as much a part of him as his skin.'[81]

Lorca now thought of *Blood Wedding* and *Yerma* as the first two sections of a trilogy, which was to be brought to a close with *The Drama of Lot's Daughters*. This was the play that had begun life as *The Destruction of Sodom*. In his version of the narrative, Lot offers his daughter to the importunate angels, and then violates her himself – thereby avoiding sodomy by committing a worse sin. Lorca regarded this new play as being far in advance of anything anyone else he knew of had said about homosexuality: by contrast, he was convinced, Oscar Wilde would look timid and old-fashioned. At the start of 1935 he would be working on the new play again – it was apparently nearing completion – and he had restored its original title.

We have every reason to suppose that *The Destruction of Sodom* would have been thought extremely radical; to many, both obscene and blasphemous. Lorca was used, by now, to being treated as an extremist. When *Yerma* received its first public performance on 29 December 1934, right-wing elements in the audience directed shouts of 'Lesbian!' at the leading actress and 'Queer!' at Lorca himself. They were drowned out by a huge ovation at the end of the play, but reviews in the press divided along entrenched political lines. The right-wing press were increasingly inclined to make veiled remarks about Lorca's sexuality – a situation he began to take as a matter of course, hardly pausing to question whether he was in any real danger. (In Granada, he was quite widely known as *el maricón de la pajarita*, the queer with the bow tie.) He was certainly not going to be intimidated into discretion: the signs are that, had he lived, his work, both dramatic and poetic, would have become even more forthright about sexuality than it already was.

In 1935 Lorca re-encountered the poet Juan Gil-Albert, whom he had first met in Barcelona in 1933. Gil-Albert, who was about to publish an openly gay book of sonnets, gave him a caged dove. Lorca's subsequent 'Gongoresque Sonnet' ('Soneto gongorino') has the poet giving his lover a caged dove.[82] In 1937 Lorca read Vicente Aleixandre his own 'Sonnets of the Dark Love' ('Sonetos del amor oscuro'), but before he had given them that collective title. He planned a play, *The Black Ball* (*La bola negra*), beginning when a son tells his father he has been blackballed by the casino because he is homosexual. Renaming it *The Black Stone* (*La piedra oscura*), he subtitled it *Drama epéntico*, 'epéntico' being his own coinage, meaning one who can create but not procreate.

Meanwhile, to look southward from Lorca's Whitman's New York: the Hispano-Portuguese diaspora in Latin America had been taking its lead from Europe, in matters pertaining to sexual identity as in so many others. The regional equivalents of Lorca's *Fairies*, *Pájaros*, *Jotos*, *Sarasas*, *Apios*, *Floras* and *Adelaidas* developed their own variations on familiar models. In Mexico, the 'Contemporáneos' group had a somewhat marginal reputation, perhaps mainly because of their refusal to align themselves with any particular political faction and because their aesthetic principles were based on a shared internationalism at a time when to be cosmopolitan seemed suspiciously close to being anti-nationalistic. But they were also criticised because several of them – including Salvador Novo, Xavier Villaurrutia and Jorge Cuesta – were known to be homosexual. There was a related implication that the group's members, being too young to have experienced the revolution (1910–*c*.1920), were therefore untested as men. (By contrast, their rivals in the Estridentistas group celebrated an explicitly macho aesthetic.) Novo was instrumental in bringing work by Oscar Wilde, Jean Cocteau and Jean Genet to the Mexican stage. On 21 December 1924, Julio Jiménez Rueda stirred up a controversy in the newspaper *El universal* with an article complaining about the feminisation of Mexican literature and calling for a more virile national culture.[83] This signalled the start of a major reaction against suspiciously queer elements in modern Mexican writing.

In addition to the major precedents of Wilde and Whitman, a third literary figure exerted a strong, queer influence in South America: André Gide. For those who could not read French, Gide's *Corydon* was first published in Spanish translation in 1929. The very title of the book had become part of the lexical currency. Lorca's last lover Rafael Rodríguez Rapún told him that, 'according to [Eduardo] Ugarte I am a "Coridón" in the good sense of the word'.[84] Octavio Paz paired *Corydon* with Surrealism as Luis Cernuda's crucial influences: 'To the psychic commotion of surrealism must be added the revelation of André Gide. Thanks to the French moralist, Cernuda accepts himself; from that time on his homosexuality was not to be a sickness or a sin but a destiny freely accepted and lived. If Gide reconciles Cernuda with himself, surrealism will serve him to set his psychic and vital rebellion within a vaster, more total subversion.'[85] Although Cernuda had read *Corydon*, with deep personal interest, when he was in his teens, he did not fully acknowledge the fact that he was homosexual himself until his mid-twenties, by which time he had adopted a rather haughtily dandified façade which, while perhaps drawing attention to his sense of difference, defied anyone to confront him with it at a personal level. It is wrong, though, for a critic to claim that the acknowledgement of his own homosexuality then 'distanced him irreconcilably from mainstream society'.[86] It was merely one of a number of factors behind the unexceptional alienation of a poet who was subject to the common ailments of modernity. It makes far more sense to identify his bitterness as a republican exile (in Britain, the United States and, for the rest of his life, Mexico) after Franco's victory in

the civil war as the source of his estrangement from the Spanish cultural mainstream. As an earlier commentator, Derek Harris, points out, Cernuda was 'an
active homosexual, overtly defiant of the heterosexual society around him. The
image of a homosexual neurotic is reflected in the assessment of Cernuda as an
embittered, alienated poet, but the critics who see him in this way have failed
to separate the personality of the man from the *persona* he created in his poetry.'
For several decades Cernuda criticism, as Harris adds, either ignored his sexuality altogether or reduced it to a neurotic fault which, if applied to readings of
the poems, could only diminish them: 'It is tempting to believe that the way in
which so many critics studiously avoid this topic is a sign of unease and that
their emphasis on the neurotic elements of his personality is the result of a
suppressed moral judgement of his unnatural passion.'[87] Of course, having to
bear the stigma of the sodomite in a profoundly conservative, Catholic society
made him angry; it also helped to make him left-wing. Like Lorca, he found
that he could use the conventions of Surrealism to express himself in relatively
uncensorable ways. His way of establishing a personal identity as homosexual
was to adopt the controlled flamboyance of the dandy (as opposed to the outra-
geousness of the unguarded queen) in both clothing and manners, as well as in
the emotional precision of his writing. At the launch of Cernuda's *Reality and
Desire* (*La realidad y el deseo*) on 26 April 1936, Lorca gave a speech offering
implicit approval of Cernuda's courageous approach to his sexuality.[88]

     When Virgilio Piñera wrote about the homosexuality of his fellow Cuban,
the poet Emilio Ballagas, in an essay published the year after Ballagas' death,
'Ballagas en persona' (1955), it made sense to do so in terms of international
culture. Piñera asked, 'If the French write about Gide taking as a point of
departure this writer's homosexuality, if the English do the same with Wilde, I
don't see why we Cubans cannot speak of Ballagas as homosexual. Is it that the
French and English have the exclusive rights to that theme? Of course not.' José
Quiroga comments that, in Piñera's essay 'Ballagas becomes not solely a Cuban
poet, but part of a transnational network of male homosexual writers like Gide
and Wilde.'[89] After the revolution, however, the only acceptable form of internationalism was that of communism. To speak of homosexual internationalism was, as so often, to conjure up the threat of subversive conspiracy. In this
case, however, the Homintern was understood to be conspiring *against* the
Comintern, rather than in league with it.

     When the Spanish novelist Juan Goytisolo went to Havana in 1967, Piñera
told him all about revolutionary Cuba's persecution of gay men. Goytisolo could
not help thinking of all the gay writers he had met in the early 1960s, who had
now been either prosecuted or otherwise silenced: they included Reinaldo
Arenas, Antón Arrufat, José Lezama Lima, Heberto Padilla and Piñera himself.[90]

That said, the poems of Heberto Padilla show moments of irritation at the insensitivity of visitors to revolutionary Cuba and their assumption that the sexual-political platitudes of a Western counter-culture could uncomplicatedly be applied to Cuban society:

> Make love not war
> (slogans imported from Europe)
> are a kick in a prisoner's balls.

He was referring to the Allen Ginsberg generation, if not necessarily to Ginsberg himself. (The reference to Europe suggests not.) Ginsberg had been invited to attend a writers' conference in Havana in 1965. With little sensitivity to local cultural norms, and in tactless ignorance of the condition of the revolution, he behaved like a bull in a china shop until the authorities deported him to Prague. Padilla's poem 'Travellers' rails against those on the Left who visit the island for two or three weeks and then go home to write books about it:

> They are serious, civilized people, and all come provided
> with theories, which quite often cause them to go home frustrated
> by the lack of sexual freedom among Cubans,
> by the *inevitable* Puritanism of revolutions,
> and lastly by what they decide, with a certain sadness,
> they must call *the divorce between the theory and practice.*[91]

Sexual liberation is all very well – for those who are at liberty.

In a passage at the centre of his novel *Farewell to the Sea* (*Otra Vez el Mar*, 1982), Reinaldo Arenas performs a ceremonial repudiation of Walt Whitman's poetry in the light of his disillusionment with the Cuban revolution. Doubtless, García Lorca's 'Ode' is also at the back of his mind. As in that poem, Arenas' narrator addresses the old poet directly, but he does so without Lorca's ingratiating courtesies: 'Oh, Whitman, oh, Whitman / – you shameless old woman – / how you exasperate me, how impatient you make me!' Unlike most readers, he identifies aspects of Whitman's vision that are not broad and do not 'contain multitudes', but are, rather, narrow and exclusionary. He even finds Whitman inhibited. 'Were you never, at any moment, able to see that in even the most casual one-night (or -afternoon) stand, there is only defeat, that what excites you, provokes you most is not what promises to satisfy you, / but what gnaws at you, secretly, / and impels you at last, dregs upon dregs, to seek / one more momentary dreg?' He dismisses Whitman's work in the name of a broad range of gay men whose experience it overlooks: 'I refute your poetry with that look of that / sixty-year-old woman who devoted her life / to bringing up her son (and I quote) / "and just look what happened, he turned out to be gay, / and he's working in a forced-labour camp now" / I refute your poetry with the mute, angry, incontrovertible / pain of that son.' And: 'I refute your poetry with the painted face / of an old queen / in a provincial cabaret.' And again, but invoking that key urban location noted by Hart Crane: 'I refute your poetry with a tape recorder / in every public urinal (no water / in the private ones).'[92]

Concluding his account of four *Eminent Maricones* – Lorca, Reinaldo Arenas, Manuel Puig and himself – the Colombian-American poet Jaime Manrique points out that, for all its faults, the city of New York proved vitally important to all four of these Latina queens. 'Lorca came to accept himself as a gay man in New York. After his visit to the city he wrote his most original and daring works.' Here, too, 'Arenas wrote, at the end of his life, some of the most beautiful poems by a Latin American author in the twentieth century', as well as his autobiography. And here Puig wrote 'one of the few truly great works dealing explicitly with homosexuality and Marxism', his novel *Kiss of the Spider Woman*.[93] Arenas' *Farewell to the Sea* itself was first published in a third version. The first had disappeared in Havana in 1969; the second was confiscated in Havana in 1971; the third was smuggled out of Cuba in 1974 and eventually published in Barcelona in 1982. Arenas himself joined the Mariel Boatlift in 1980 and fled to the USA.

### Manuel Puig

Juan Manuel Puig was born on 28 December 1932 on the pampas in the province of Buenos Aires. From an early age he was an avid aficionado of Hollywood movies (and not only those of Hollywood), with an especial affection for the great female stars. As his biographer puts it, 'He always fell for the same movie, whether it was made in Germany in the twenties, Argentina in the thirties, Mexico in the forties, or Japan in the fifties. Suffering women, betrayals, abandonment: the stuff of melodrama was universal truth.' This was a passion he took seriously. He once ejected Nestor Almendros, who had just arrived from abroad, from his New York flat for making a disparaging remark about Lana Turner. He habitually made a comparison between macho attitudes to women and the cultural establishment's attitudes to 'minor', popular genres: 'Everybody enjoys them, but nobody respects them.'[94]

At school he was bullied for his sensitivity. Frequent sexual games always involved his being placed in, and accepting, a subordinate role. On one occasion he survived a rape attempt by a much bigger boy. At thirteen, in 1946, he was sent to a private boarding school, Colegio Ward, in a suburb to the west of

Buenos Aires, where an atmosphere of unrelieved Peronism prevailed. (Juan Perón was President of Argentina from 1946 to 1955.) During his teens Puig's favourite dramatist was the Tennessee Williams of *The Glass Menagerie*. Typically, in 1947, he discovered Sigmund Freud not in print but by way of Alfred Hitchcock's *Spellbound*. The mediating agency of Ingrid Bergman in a white coat and spectacles, at first with her hair tied back – in other words, impersonating a psychoanalyst – and then, once kissed by Gregory Peck, letting her hair down, was a most perverse way of taking in Freud's tenets, but it was, of course, a typically Puigian venture. As throughout his life, he transformed his learning into his own image.

Self-education was Puig's solution to the problem of trying to become an independent artist and homosexual man in the Argentina of the 1950s, even if that identity would involve not remaining in Argentina at all. In the words of his biographer, 'Manuel's facility and determination to learn languages was not only a gateway to the movies but a way out of Argentina. As a homosexual, an outsider, he was drawn to foreign languages, to otherness, and to other places where he could be himself.' He chose English, French and Italian because they were, as he put it, 'the languages of the cinema'.[95] Although in 1950 he enrolled in the School of Architecture at the University of Buenos Aires, he soon transferred to modern languages. He dropped out of university two years later, but continued to study at private institutes. At the Argentine Association for English Culture he was taught about detective fiction by no less an authority than Jorge Luis Borges.

Puig served his military service in 1953 as a clerk in the Air Force. By now he was living, as convention dictated, a double life, preserving his social and familial relationships by concealing his homosexuality, but within a closed circle of homosexual friends celebrating life's triumphs and disasters with the perverse paradoxes of camp. His biographer writes that 'camp became particularly subversive in a country obsessed with propriety and blind (like most nations) to its own kitsch'.[96] When he won a scholarship to spend a year in Italy, a long-term ambition had been achieved: at last he was going to escape Argentina, if temporarily.

He left for Rome in August 1956 and spent the year studying at the Centro Sperimentale di Cinematografia, next door to Cinecittà, in an unsympathetic atmosphere of dogmatic adherence to the tenets of *Neorealismo*. Although he met some of the major figures in Italian cinema – including Roberto Rossellini, Vittorio De Sica and Pier Paolo Pasolini (whose films he hated) – as well as other important cultural figures – the writers Dacia Maraini and Alberto Moravia, for instance – most of the people around him regarded his unrestrained love of Hollywood and its divas as frivolous and absurd. He did manage to find some allies, though. One of his classmates was fellow gay Nestor Almendros. Born in Catalonia in 1930, Almendros had fled with his family to Cuba when Franco won the civil war; he was a cinematographer who would go on to work with the likes of Eric Rohmer and François Truffaut and would win an Oscar for his work on *Days of Heaven* (1978). Almendros and Puig paired up to rebel against the Centro's prevailing ethos. As a non-Italian, Puig was granted no hands-on film-making practice; he just had to watch. But this turned out to be appropriate to his needs, for he gradually came to the realisation that he was better suited to appreciating films as a spectator than as a maker.

In 1957 Puig moved on from Rome, visiting France, Spain, England and Sweden. He arrived in London in February 1958 and made ends meet by giving private language lessons. His pupils included the screenwriter Paul Dehn, who would help him revise his own film scripts, and John Gielgud. The London spring was enlivened by sexual encounters with the film actors Stanley Baker and Yul Brynner. Early in 1959 he crossed to Paris, and then toured Europe. On the ship home, late in the same year, he had an affair with a woman. When she became pregnant, he paid for an abortion. Working on a preposterous movie, *Un americana en Buenos Aires*, he had an affair with the leading man, Jean-Pierre Aumont. His next crossing to Europe, in February 1961, was made in the company of Aumont and his wife. It was on this trip that Puig began working on his first novel.

Paris in the 1960s was as thick with South American expatriates as it had been, between the wars, with North Americans. Puig's biographer describes this subculture:

> The Argentine expatriates in Paris included writers Julio Cortázar and Hector Bianciotti (then a reader for Gallimard), Edgardo Cozarinsky (film-maker and critic), and Di Tella theater directors Jorge Lavelli and Rodolfo Arias. The Cuban group was equally diverse and accomplished: novelist Alejo Carpentier, then ambassador to France, film critic Carlos Clarens, playwright Irene Fornés, painters Wifredo Lam and Ramón Alejandro. National boundaries were erased in this Latin and largely gay network of artists and writers, but competing egos, aesthetic camps, and political views . . . would inevitably provoke rivalries and shift alliances.[97]

Puig made friends with Cozarinsky, who divided his time between Paris and Buenos Aires, where he lived with the film critic Alberto Tabbia. Among the other gay Argentines in Paris was the novelist Severo Sarduy, who was living with François Wahl, the wealthy proprietor of Editions du Seuil, and working as the Spanish-language acquisitions editor at Seuil. Sarduy was a member of the *Tel Quel* circle, a friend of Roland Barthes and Philippe Sollers, and a patient of Jacques Lacan. Nestor Almendros showed Puig's novel to Sarduy, but Sarduy failed to persuade Wahl to publish it; so Almendros passed it to the Spanish novelist Juan Goytisolo, who was also in Paris, working as a reader for Gallimard. Gallimard accepted it, and Goytisolo was instrumental in persuading Barral in Barcelona to consider it; but they then turned it down.

Puig returned to Argentina in May 1967 and stayed for six years until, as the political situation worsened, he left for Mexico in 1973. On a trip to Europe towards the end of 1973 he met the gay Italian novelist Alberto Arbasino, who would become an enthusiastic advocate of his work. In the meantime he published *Betrayed by Rita Hayworth* (*La traición de Rita Hayworth*, 1968), *Heartbreak Tango* (*Boquitas pintadas*, 1969) and *The Buenos Aires Affair* (*The Buenos Aires Affair: Novela policial*, 1973). In Puig's novels love is always a dangerous business; perhaps all the more so for women. His boisterous melodramas tend to end, at best, in tears. Leo, the heterosexual monster at the heart of *The Buenos Aires Affair*, embodies a masculine sexual pathology that fatally wreaks its needs on the bodies of women. The sexual pattern is fixed at adolescence: driving lust is marred by frequent bouts of impotence, which in turn is solved only by aggression. At a time of particular frustration, even a man will do: Leo lets a gay man fellate him, then kills him while anally raping him. (Later, while working as a diplomat in Europe, Leo sacks the gay man who is working as his secretary. Here, overt heterosexual pride is working, as it were, normally – that is, with civilised restraint.) Josemar, the central character in *Blood of Requited Love* (*Sangre de amor correspondido*, 1982), is a more moderate representation of prolifically lustful, heterosexual machismo. Even as a teenager he keeps two girls on the go at once, yet he routinely threatens to kill María Gloria if she ever goes with another man. He is so indulged by his mother – she tells him his good looks earn him so much love it is as if he were rich – that he seems to believe her womanhood endorses his mistreatment of any woman.

Early in 1974, Puig began the novel with which, by the time of his death, his name would be most closely associated all around the world; it was published as *El beso de la mujer araña* in 1976, and then in English translation as *Kiss of the Spider Woman* in 1979. Its dialogues between two prisoners, the apolitical queen and movie buff Molina and the radical Marxist Valentin, are often underscored by factual footnotes discussing various theories of homosexuality. Molina lavishly relates the plots of motion pictures – romance, espionage, horror and so forth – which form an ironic contrast with the footnotes. As a bourgeois queen, Molina paradoxically adopts and represents a position of extreme conventionality: unrelentingly passive, getting off on the fear of his sexual partners, identifying with movie heroines, speaking of himself as a woman, not interested in other queens, only interested in real (straight) men, claiming not to understand gay men who have relationships with men who identify as gay or who alternate sexual roles ... Yet this very insistence on opposing the reactionary radicalism of the drag queen to the revolutionary conservatism of the Marxist is what made *Kiss* so controversial. The book made waves across the stagnant establishment of leftist publishers in Paris. Juan Goytisolo was scathing in his account of their treatment of Puig:

> In an era in which the image of Latin America as an embattled continent turned pens into machine guns and writers into loudspeakers of revolution, a figure and work like his produced a reaction of distrust, scorn, and rejection. Julio Cortázar's ex-girlfriend ... vetoed the publication of *Kiss of the Spider Woman* [by Gallimard in Paris] because it no doubt hurt the clichéd image of the militant Marxist-Leninist upon presenting him as moved and carried away by the cinematic, Scheherazade-like arts of his apolitical and homosexual cell companion. These same moralizing and sectarian suppositions made other left-wing European publishers follow his example.

Goytisolo added that, to his mind, 'Manuel Puig is author of the best political novels of the sixties in Latin America because they're the work of a writer who knew no other commitment than the one he had contracted with writing and with himself.'[98] At Edmund White's suggestion, the April 1979 issue of the New York gay cultural magazine *Christopher Street* carried an interview with Puig and dedicated its front cover to him.

At one point Frank Ripploh, director of the earnest, gay-liberationist *Taxi Zum Klo*, expressed an interest in filming *Kiss of the Spider Woman*. Puig was understandably horrified: 'She makes gloomy films,' he said. Hector Babenco, who eventually made the film, was more obviously on the wavelength of the book. In the first instance, Burt Lancaster was somehow lined up to play Molina, despite the fact that he was so clearly too old for the role. He rewrote the screenplay himself, gratuitously increasing the amount of sex that occurs between Molina and Valentín. Most of the concerned parties were relieved when illness intervened and he had to withdraw from the project. Hans Werner Henze approached Puig in 1983 to write the libretto of an opera he wanted to base on *Kiss of the Spider Woman*, but this project never came to fruition. Instead, the gay American playwright Terrence McNally wrote the libretto of a musical based on the book. Puig referred to him, succinctly, as 'a horror'. Puig died on 22 July 1990; Nestor Almendros and Severo Sarduy followed, in 1992 and 1993, respectively. The McNally musical version of *Kiss* was a hit on Broadway in 1992.

# CHAPTER TEN

# THE NEW POLITICS

## A Lot of Privacy

It would be wrong to assume, during the decades when male and female homo-sexuality were subject to the heaviest of taboos, and male homosexual acts were illegal, a simple contrast between the need to conceal homosexual relationships and the opportunity to be completely open about heterosexual relationships. Marital coupling always had its public signs, of course: the engagement and wedding rings, the joint bank accounts, the joint mortgages, the joint member-ship of social organisations, the openly shared accommodation, the anniversary celebrations, the pregnancies, the children and so forth. As soon as we look at non-marital heterosexual relationships, on the other hand, the question of public signs of private lives is more clouded. In many social milieux for a substantial part of the twentieth century, non-marital heterosexual relation-ships had much in common with homosexual relationships. Indeed, in some contexts it might be said that the unmarried heterosexual couple had more in common with the homosexual couple than with the married couple.

John Bayley considers this question of the openness or otherwise of heterosexual affairs in mid-century England when trying to convey to readers at the end of the century the conditions under which Iris Murdoch, who would become his wife, conducted her love life in Oxford during her youth:

> Fifty years or so ago life in the university was more constricted and formal, but at the same time more comfortable and relaxed. For us, in those days, there was no paradox involved. We maintained public standards and conventions almost without being conscious of them, while leading our own private lives.[1]

The context is of interest. Bayley has just been speaking of a homosexual couple, but here he has turned to Murdoch and himself. It is in thinking of the other couple that he has raised the issues of 'public' and 'private' in relation to his own affair with Murdoch. No distinction is made between the two sexualities. His 'us' appears to refer not just to John-and-Iris, but also to both heterosexual and homosexual love. The 'standards and conventions' of 'public' life – where 'public' is understood to refer even to the enclosed hothouse of the Oxford colleges – were maintained without question, and therefore without any partic- ular sense of having been put under pressure to do so, by heterosexual and homosexual couples alike. Just as a small instance, there would be no question of either couple holding hands, say, or exchanging kisses in the public spaces of college or city. Inferences might, of course, be drawn even from lesser signals – such as the mere fact of being seen in each other's company on more than one occasion – but the need for discretion seems to have been generally accepted. A little later, Bayley goes on:

> There was a lot of privacy about in those days. An 'open' society is what we aim for now, or say we aim for, as an enhancement of our all being more classless and democratic. That was particularly true in Oxford, still a scho- lastic society in which one could be on good terms with a large number of people, meeting them most days in college, at dinner in halls or in lecture rooms and laboratories, without having any idea of how they were situated domestically, or socially, or sexually. Other people's lives might seem intriguing, which was part of the fun of privacy, but they remained what was on the whole an accepted and comfortable blank.[2]

We do not have to accept Oxford as typical of England, or Bayley as typical of Oxford, to take these remarks as contributing to a more general picture of social discretion and distance, in which, notwithstanding the understandably 'intriguing' nature of other people's lives – a human constant, one must suppose – they were allowed to remain 'on the whole an accepted and comfortable blank'. This lack of the enforced intrusiveness of the 'open' society that Bayley identifies as having developed in recent decades suggests an atmosphere in which it may well have been comfortable to develop a relationship with someone of the same sex as oneself. Being invisible, in common with other relationships around it, this one would be neither accepted nor un-accepted. It would merely take place.

This is a fine theory, up to a point – it may even be a fine ideal – but one is forced to introduce a range of caveats. In the first place, relationships do not simply evolve out of nothing. Human beings, whether heterosexual or homo- sexual, do not divide asocially like the amoeba. For lovers to meet in the first place, some kind of social interaction has to take place. The Capulets have to hold their ball. Two people have, at least, to be able to hold an intimate conversation without one aggressively turning on the other when its intimacy becomes too much for him. That is to say, the atmosphere Bayley describes may have been, if by default, quite friendly to same-sex relationships – but really only when the relationship had already developed. It may not have provided safe circumstances for homosexual individuals to seek each other's company; and it could not be relied on to remain safe if it became 'public' knowledge. The hothouse of privacy and discretion may seem safe, but it is an ideal atmosphere for the propagation of silent hostilities and resentments.

Besides all that, it becomes clear elsewhere in John Bayley's account of the same institutions in the same period that the impermeability of privacy was not complete. Gossip went on. In Murdoch's college, for instance, it was generally (if not universally) known that certain members of staff were lesbian. According to Bayley, who may or may not have been in the best position to tell, Murdoch never went further than flirtation with any of the women in question: 'She never went to bed with any of her colleagues, although the novelist Brigid Brophy tried very hard indeed to persuade her. That was both before and after we were married.'[3] This sounds suspiciously like gossip now, and the product of gossip then. Overall, it looks as if John Bayley approaches the whole issue with the complacent equanimity of the straight man. He cannot help that, poor fellow; but it does mean that, even if we accept it as a general principle of its times, we must apply a gentle scepticism, at least, to that whole area of interpersonal relations which he describes as 'an accepted and comfortable blank'. The lesbian adultery he accuses Brophy of attempting to put into practice might have been treated, had she succeeded, as 'accepted and comfortable' in the narrow confines of college hall – or it might not – but it surely would have been treated as a scandal if it had become truly public, for instance by reaching the ears of the press.

## The 'Good' Homosexual

In the light of his own experiences, Oscar Wilde developed a sense of what needed to be done with regard to homosexual law reform. In a brief letter to George Ives, postmarked 21 March 1898, he wrote: 'Yes: I have no doubt we shall win, but the road is long, and red with monstrous martyrdoms. Nothing but the repeal of the Criminal Law Amendment Act [1885] would do any good. That is the essential. It is not so much public opinion as public officials that need educating.'[4] The Act in question included the so-called Labouchere Amendment, proposed by a less than sober Henry Labouchere during a late-night parliamentary session on 6 August 1885, outlawing acts of 'gross indecency' between men, regardless of whether such acts were committed in public or in private. This is the offence of which Wilde would be convicted in 1895. It is clear from Wilde's subsequent letter that he was beginning to get a sense of the possibility of collective action on the part of those at risk of falling foul of this law. The 'we' he refers to are those who might easily, themselves, add to the law's list of 'monstrous martyrdoms'. He was anticipating the gay movement.

The terms of the outline argument for homosexual law reform in countries such as Germany and Great Britain remained more or less constant for decades. They are set out in the following passage from John Addington Symonds' essay on homosexuality *A Problem in Modern Ethics* (1891), in which he summarises Karl Heinrich Ulrichs' model for the way forward in Germany:

> Ulrichs proposes that urnings should be placed on the same footing as other men. That is to say, sexual relations between males and males should not be treated as criminal, unless they be attended with violence (as in the case of rape), or be carried on in such a way as to offend the public sense of decency (in places of general resort or on the open street), or thirdly be entertained between an adult and a boy under age (the protected age to be decided as in the case of girls). What he demands is that when an adult male, freely and of his own consent, complies with the proposals of an adult person of his own sex, and their intercourse takes place with due regard for public decency, neither party shall be liable to prosecution and punishment at law. In fact he would be satisfied with the same conditions as those prevalent in France, and since June 1889, in Italy.[5]

The guiding principles behind Ulrichs' formulation were those of the Napoleonic Code, according to which offences against religion or morality that did not do harm to either society or individuals should not be subject to prosecution by secular authorities. (Church law was beyond the remit of the Code.) With regard to male homosexuality, this ethic allowed for the abolition of medieval sodomy laws, with provisos governing public behaviour, violent behaviour and the corruption or violation of minors. Symonds might have added other Catholic countries in which the Code held sway, including Switzerland, Brazil and Mexico – and, indeed, a number of the German states, including Bavaria and Hanover.

Among homosexual men who were reading the latest European sexological work, it became a commonplace of the argument for legal tolerance to state the three limitations on sexual behaviour. For instance, in a letter dated 9 June 1895, Lord Alfred Douglas defended himself against accusations that he had abandoned Oscar Wilde, who had just been incarcerated in Reading Gaol. Douglas, who knew the work of Richard von Krafft-Ebing, argued that the law has no right to interfere with these people, provided they do not harm other people; that is to say when there is neither seduction of minors nor brutalisation, and when there is no public outrage on morals.[6]

As reasonable as such remarks may sound in the context of the Europe-wide sexological debate, in Britain they represented an extremist position, which would still look radical at the time of the Wolfenden Report of 1957. The Sexual Offences Act 1967 would shy away from Ulrichs' principles in several major respects. Indeed, UK law would not catch up with them until the equalisation of the ages of consent in 2000 – which, significantly, had to be prompted by Europe. Alfred Douglas' letter would be used against him during the Pemberton Billing case in 1918 – by which time he had become a married man, a Roman Catholic and a splenetic homophobe like his father.

One of the products of repeated references to the three taboos, on violence, on intergenerational sex and on offending the public, was the slow development of an image of the 'good' homosexual. In his way he was a concession – because an exception – to the lingering notion of homosexuality as an intrinsic evil. No pervert he, the 'good' homosexual was not morally responsible for his condition – he did not choose to be that way – for it was an inherent aspect of his being, a flaw with which he had quietly come to terms but without which he would have been, not only entirely normal, but even entirely conventional. In short, the 'good' homosexual was morally and politically conservative. He was sober and dressed soberly; if there were signs of effeminacy in his speech or bearing, he made every reasonable effort to suppress them; he never talked about his condition and he never allowed it to intrude on any of his interactions with normal people, whether at work or in his leisure hours. Men who were such creatures tended not to associate with 'bad' homosexuals lest they be tarred with the same brush, or more so than they already had been. Throughout the twentieth century, one often hears the voice of the 'good' homosexual distancing himself from the 'bad', seeking thereby to justify his own place in society: *he* does not like boys; *he* does not force his attentions on the unwilling; and, above all, *he* is discreet – unlike *them*, the ones who let the side down, the ones who give us a bad name, the ones who rock the boat, the ones who go on about it all the time, the obsessives, the perverts.

We do not yet have a cultural history of homosexual 'discretion', yet we need one: for 'discretion' is absolutely central to the formulation of homosexuality as a socially acceptable condition of life. It is a broader concept than the 'closet', but it occupies some of the same wardrobe space.[7] To be discreet is to refrain from shoving 'it' down other people's throats, in more senses than merely never to speak of it. Discretion involves your tone of speech as much as the things you actually say – or do not say. It involves how you dress in relation to conventional gender role play, but also how your body moves in and around whatever clothing you do allow yourself to wear. It obviously involves other aspects of style, such as coiffure and maquillage. It encompasses living arrangements and public behaviour – at work and leisure – but even opinions and emotions too, at least to the extent that either are expressed. Homosexual individuals, male or female, who manage to achieve discretion in spite of their inherent tendency to lapse into emotionalism and hysteria, although artistically inclined (virtually by genetic definition), should not really go into the arts since these indiscriminately encourage expressiveness. If they do, they must sublimate their flaw; and in doing so they are likely to improve their art. Explicit homosexual art is always aesthetically of less value than art which struggles to conceal the artist's sexuality. The same goes for real life: sublimation and repression will make you a better, if a tenser, person.

In the autobiographical account of his own involvement in the so-called 'Montagu trial' of 1954, *Against the Law* (1955), Peter Wildeblood is at pains to present himself as a perfect example of the 'good' homosexual. There is a certain amount of belatedly closing the stable door in this posture – since he has just emerged from a prison term as a consequence of his part in the scandal – but who can deny him his attempt at retrospective self-justification? Moreover, by the time of the writing of the book, he was increasingly turning his attention to the question of law reform, in which the 'good' and 'bad' homosexuals always play such prominent roles. In a celebrated passage, Wildeblood distances himself and his ilk from others; an argument worth quoting at some length, since it represents a very common position of the discreet:

Everyone has seen the pathetically flamboyant pansy with the flapping wrists, the common butt of music-hall jokes and public-house stories. Most of us are not like that. We do our best to look like everyone else, and we usually succeed. That is why nobody realizes how many of us there are. I know many hundreds of homosexuals and not more than half a dozen would be recognized by a stranger for what they are. If anything, they dress more soberly and behave more conventionally in public than the 'normal' men I know; they have to, if they are to avoid suspicion.

When I ask for tolerance, it is for men like these. Not the corrupters of the youth, not even the effeminate creatures who love to make an exhibition of themselves, although by doing so they probably do no harm; I am only concerned with the men who, in spite of the tragic disability which is theirs, try to lead their lives according to the principles which I have described. They cannot speak for themselves, but I shall try to speak for them.[8]

Wildeblood was not asking for tolerance for men such as Quentin Crisp; nor, for that matter, was the Wolfenden Committee. The whole campaign for law reform was centred on the *idée fixe* of privacy; as were the eventual reforms themselves. In this sphere 'privacy' was given an extremely rigorous, not to say draconian, definition. According to the train of thought typified by the above extract from Wildeblood's book, to have dyed hair or to flap one's wrists was equivalent, if not in degree, to public homosexual acts. Such exhibitionism was virtually its own argument against law reform: for the best argument in its favour, which Wildeblood spells out on behalf of the silent, was silence, coupled with invisibility.

(However, as we have seen, homosexual men and women were caught in a double bind over this issue. The very virtues that constituted the best aspect of the 'good' homosexual – silence and invisibility – were identical to the vices that made even the 'good' homosexual potentially 'bad'. The more silent and invisible you were, the more you could be trusted to fit in, and yet, ultimately, the less you could be trusted. If you were silent and invisible in the paranoid 1950s, you might be a Soviet spy.)

It was obviously necessary for would-be reformers to emphasise the large numbers of homosexual individuals so invisibly at large in society – the Kinsey reports of 1948 and 1953 had helped with creating this impression, even if they referred exclusively to the United States – but it was even more important to calm people's fear that to decriminalise male homosexuality would make queers both noisy and visible; would suddenly flood society, in other words, with replicas of the 'pathetic flamboyant pansy'. Yet, once such individuals no longer needed 'to avoid suspicion', there was clearly a danger that they might, indeed, start mincing and lisping their way into the public consciousness. The Wolfenden Committee was keenly aware of, and sensitive to, this possibility; and the framing of its decisions was governed, above all, by the urge to quell it. The age of consent would maintain the illegality of the corruption of youth, and assault laws could be used to punish violent coercion; but something had to be done to keep homosexuality where it belonged: in the shadows.

The spectre of offensively 'public' behaviour seemed to manifest itself in Parliament whenever homosexuality was discussed. (This is true of parliamentary debate on the topic for the rest of the century.) On occasion, such contributions were admirably prescient, as when a psychiatrist called Alfred Broughton, the Labour member for Batley, Yorkshire, conjured up the following image:

I can envisage men walking along the street arm in arm, possibly holding hands, and at dances perhaps wishing to dance together and even caressing in public places[.]

One does not catch the tone of this remark from the cold print of *Hansard*, but Doctor Broughton was no gay liberationist, and this was not a celebratory account of the joys of a future after decriminalisation. On the contrary, he was disgusted. He went on to say:

> if we see two men showing affection for one another in public it gives most people a deep sense of disapproval. It is unnatural, it is biologically wrong, and worst of all, because it is biologically wrong, it is a shocking example to young people.

If prostitution and homosexuality absolutely had to exist – and the good doctor sadly conceded that they did – 'I think it best we should keep them out of sight of the general public.' (As in the AIDS epidemic, many years later, the 'general public' did not have sex with prostitutes and was not homosexual.) In the same 1958 debate in the House of Commons, responding to the recommendations of the Wolfenden Report of the previous year, one speaker revealed how much was likely to be demanded of the 'good' homosexual, if Parliament ever did go ahead with decriminalisation. Having served on the Committee, Sir Hugh Linstead, Conservative member for Putney, was evidently speaking for more than himself when he said:

> If we no longer impose a legal code of sexual behaviour which we do not extract [*sic*] from anyone else, we can surely expect homosexuals to accept the same responsibility as the rest of us . . . [by] behaving themselves in public.[9]

He was not, of course, taking into account – if we look merely at those fears of Doctor Broughton's – that heterosexual couples are allowed to walk along the street arm in arm, or hand in hand; that they do, at dances, dance together; and even that they do end up 'caressing in public places'. (Look at London's South Bank during the 1951 Festival of Britain.) So, far from having 'to accept the same responsibility' as heterosexual people 'by behaving themselves in public', homosexual men – and, indeed, lesbians, whose spectral presence in society often seemed implicit in the hostile and threatening tone adopted by many speakers in these parliamentary debates and reporters on them in the press – would actually have far more limitations imposed on their 'public' behaviour, not only (for men) by the 'in private' clause of the eventual Sexual Offences Act 1967, but also by an array of public order statutes from which any police officers who were so inclined might pick and choose. When the Act was passed, the Earl of Arran (whose own decriminalisation bill had been lost in 1965) issued a sombre warning to the men who were supposedly to benefit from that night's events:

This is no occasion for jubilation; certainly not for celebration. Any form of ostentatious behaviour; now or in the future, any form of public flaunting, would be utterly distasteful and would, I believe, make the sponsors of the Bill regret that they have done what they have done.[10]

Arran was not the only man in the Lords who knew that the passing of the Act was no occasion for cracking open the bubbly. Even the Archbishop of Canterbury, Michael Ramsey, was well aware that little would be changed. As he had pointed out to the Lords back in 1965, the supposed decriminalisation

would still leave by far the greater number of homosexual crimes and convictions unaltered, and it would be a gross misrepresentation of this particular change to say, in sweeping words, that such a change would legalise homosexual behaviour[.][11]

This was said to reassure opponents of the measure. For all the fanfare and humbug that surrounded it, the 1967 Act was hedged about with caveats and conditions, among them the principle of 'privacy' and the restriction of legal behaviour to an encounter between two individuals only. As is well known, once the 1967 Act had been passed, the rate of convictions for homosexual offences went up.

The ideal inscribed in the 1967 Act is a lasting union between two 'good' homosexuals. Yet all it decriminalised was a limited range of sexual acts in a limited range of locations. As the speeches of even the more liberal legislators made perfectly clear, they had no intention of facilitating such acts in any way, let alone facilitating the coming together of such ideal couples. No leeway whatsoever was allowed for the social existence of homosexual people. They saw single homosexual people, male or female, only as a potential threat to public morality or to young people; and they saw groups of homosexual people as a potential conspiracy to carry out such threats, as a potential threat to public order, or as an implicit demonstration of collective identity; a form of 'ostentatious behaviour', in Lord Arran's telling phrase. It is difficult to establish quite how they imagined those two 'good' homosexuals were ever going to meet at all.

Thus, on the eve of Gay Liberation, a grudging and rather strange provision was made, but no official approval offered, for the carrying out of certain sexual acts between consenting male adults in private. Yet virtually anything those men might do to meet each other in the first place was, at best, unauthorised and, at worst, could be treated as illegal by police forces which needed to increase their arrest rates. To meet in a public place could be construed as soliciting; to meet in a group, as a conspiracy to commit indecent acts; to show affection outside the home, as behaviour likely to cause public offence or disorder. No space into which a third person might wander could be regarded as securely private; nor, in some jurisdictions, could a locked bedroom in a shared house or flat. Needless to say, a locked cubicle in a public toilet – which you would have hoped offered sufficient privacy for a whole range of private functions – was, in this one context, a public place. At its most extreme, the double bind created by the 1967 Act dictated that, no matter how secretly the two of you had sex, if a third party caught you at it you were in a public space and, therefore, breaking the law. Your defining third party could, if you were really unlucky, be a police officer.

### The 'Bad' Homosexual

All that would come later. The fact is that before decriminalisation, in many other countries as in Britain, if you were to live as a homosexual man, you could hardly *not* break the law. You might imagine you could; you would certainly hope to get away with it. But reality had a habit of intruding when you least expected it. Peter Wildeblood says of his own circumstances in 1946:

> I knew, of course, that homosexual conduct was illegal; but so were many other things which everyone did at that time, like trading in clothing coupons and buying eggs on the black market. Furthermore, it hardly seemed likely that the existing laws, antique and savage as they might be, would ever be used against men who were living, according to their lights, in a moral and discreet manner.[12]

The mistake Wildeblood made in judging the level of risk he was willing to take, as when shopping for eggs, was, of course, to assume that his own assessment of 'moral and discreet' behaviour was likely to be shared by those who policed the 'antique and savage' laws of the country. As he would find out in 1954, the legal system would regard cider as champagne, a picnic as an orgy, and the mere condition of homosexuality as de facto debauchery. Wildeblood was vaguely aware that certain daring voices were occasionally, tentatively suggesting that consenting relationships between adult men should be decriminalised.

> But most of us were not interested in law reform and hardly gave a thought to the possibility of prosecution. We always supposed – and the cases reported in the newspapers appeared to bear this out – that if we behaved ourselves in public, the police would leave us alone.[13]

Part of the problem was that – as he would discover in his own case – the newspapers, too, regarded cider as champagne, a picnic as an orgy, and homosexuality as debauchery. He and his friends had been misled into their sense of
security by the press's false reporting of lives and behaviour not so very unlike
their own. You could be discreet until you were caught, but from that moment
your story would be told in such a way, by reporters and prosecutors alike, that
you would appear indiscreet even to other homosexuals. Perhaps the most
plaintive sentence in Wildeblood's autobiography is this: 'I did not believe that
such things could happen in England, until they happened to me.'[14]

   A boy scout had falsely accused Edward Douglas-Scott-Montagu, Lord
Montagu of Beaulieu, of a sexual assault. Montagu's memoirs take up the story:
'While the Director of Public Prosecutions was dithering about whether or not
to bring a case his mind was made up for him by a threat of exposure by the
Beaverbrook press. I was always led to believe that this came from the very top
– from Lord Beaverbrook himself. He was certainly mischievous enough.' While
he was lying low in Paris, two men offered him the route of Burgess and Maclean
– escape to Moscow – but he declined. When the case came to court, the police
and the jury drank in the same pub during recess. Not unreasonably, Montagu
believed the police had been spinning against him. However, the case collapsed.
But then, on 9 January 1954 he was arrested again – as were Michael Pitt-Rivers,
his cousin, and Peter Wildeblood – on charges relating to two airmen. Montagu's
memoirs become temperately heated on this issue: 'This was supposed to be
England in the dawn of the new Elizabethan age, not Nazi Germany'; 'I could not
help feeling that someone was out to get me, dragging poor Michael and Peter in
my wake'; 'The unpleasant smell of McCarthyite persecution, which the British
people did not like, wafted across the Atlantic and there were many aspects of my
case which people found disturbing.' He started to receive many supportive
letters from the public. On 24 March 1954 all three men were found guilty.
(Montagu was sentenced to twelve months' imprisonment, Wildeblood and Pitt-
Rivers to eighteen months.) Montagu's mother wrote in her diary, of Mr Justice
Ormerod's notoriously one-sided summing-up, 'he was so wonderfully fair'.
When the two airmen, the accusers, left the court, the crowd outside attacked
their car with umbrellas and rolled-up newspapers. Montagu later said of his
time in prison, 'In some ways it was a relief to be away from all the drama and,
having lived in a state of acute mental agitation for so long, to have some private
time to oneself. Above all, it was a relief to be cut off from the intrusive media.'[15]

   What Montagu and Wildeblood's case tells us so clearly is that many
men who were homosexual, and chose to live as such, did so both in the full
knowledge of the fact that they could be prosecuted and yet in the hope – the
necessary hope – that they would not be. Thus, they made friends with each

other, they gave dinner parties, they shared accommodation, they shared beds, they wrote letters to each other, they gave each other presents, they went out together, they stayed in together – all in the condition of optimistic denial that was the nearest they had to what might be called a viable way of life. You could be discreet, you could be careful. You could even – as many, many examples demonstrate – be indiscreet and downright careless. In the end, whether or not you were prosecuted may have been, if not in the lap of the gods, an entirely contingent matter; crudely, a question of luck.

Peter Wildeblood once witnessed the entrapment of an old man by a good-looking police agent provocateur in a public lavatory just off the Brompton Road in London. While he sympathised with the victim of this officious ambush, he always distanced himself from men who sought each other out in such 'public' spaces, just as he refused to be associated with those who were attracted to young boys. Proudly belonging to neither of these groups, he persuaded himself he was safe. As he says:

> In spite of certain indications to the contrary, I still believed, with many others, that the police were only interested in invoking the existing sex laws against people who had corrupted children or committed a public nuisance. A man whom I knew had, in fact, been reassured on this point by a senior official at Scotland Yard, who told him that if he was ever blackmailed he would be quite safe in going to the police, who were more concerned with catching blackmailers than with persecuting their victims.[16]

Anyone who believed this had not reckoned with the homophobic zeal of the Home Secretary, Sir David Maxwell Fyfe, and Sir John Nott-Bower, who had taken over as commissioner at Scotland Yard in August 1953.

Another life story is worth telling at this point. Jeremy Wolfenden was born on 26 June 1934 at Uppingham School in Rutland, where his father was a master. He won a scholarship to Eton College in 1947 and narrowly escaped expulsion in 1951 for a homosexual indiscretion. In 1952, he won a further scholarship to Magdalen College, Oxford; but he was not quite finished with Eton. Towards the end of the year he wrote a letter to a boy at the school, advising him about his love life. When the letter got into the wrong hands, Wolfenden was banned from the school and his father was told. In the row that ensued, John Wolfenden learned that his son was homosexual. The boy was in no doubt of his sexual orientation and made no effort to deny it. Yet he already had an inkling of what he did not want to become. When he was eighteen he wrote: 'I am not going to end up as [Evelyn Waugh's] Anthony Blanche arty-tarting around the art galleries'. It was, indeed, a fate he managed to avoid.[17]

After his stretch of national service in the Royal Navy, learning Russian and cryptography, Wolfenden went up to Magdalen to read Philosophy, Politics and Economics. Among homosexual friends at the university were Anthony Page, later a distinguished theatre and film director, and Kit Lambert (son of the composer Constant Lambert), who later became manager of the rock group The Who. During his vacations Wolfenden started writing for *The Times*. In 1956, the National Union of Students sent a delegation, including Wolfenden, on a fact-finding tour of the Soviet Union. It is possible that their interpreter and guide, Yuri Krutikov, slept with him with the intention of entrapment into espionage at some future date. At any rate, for the time being he returned to Oxford uncompromised, and after being awarded a first-class degree he went to work for *The Times*. In 1960, the paper sent him to Paris as its number two correspondent there. Then, early in 1961, despite his increasingly heavy drinking and the related waywardness of his frequent sexual encounters, the *Daily Telegraph* offered him their post in Moscow. Having accepted it at once, he told a friend he expected to be caught and blackmailed within a fortnight. He set off from London on 11 April 1961.

Predictably, Wolfenden soon established a friendship with Guy Burgess, who was single mindedly drinking his way towards the grave. They had a lot in common. It is possible they were lovers. Inevitably, as he himself had forseen, he was indeed entrapped, photographed in his room with a young man, and black-mailed into snooping on other journalists for the KGB. (His biographer Sebastian Faulks has suggested that such an obviously unsuitable candidate may have landed the *Telegraph* job in Moscow because British Intelligence had wanted to get someone on the inside of the KGB working for them.) When Burgess died in 1963, he left Wolfenden first pick of his library, but the KGB got there first.

The last two years of Wolfenden's own life were hectic and complicated. In January 1964, the *Telegraph* withdrew him from Moscow for a year and sent him to New York instead. Two months later he got married. He went back to Moscow as a stopgap after a year, having asked not to be sent there permanently. He lived in fear of arrest until, having received a tip-off that the authorities were about to act, he left for London. At the end of the year he cheerfully took up an appointment in Washington, DC; but he was depressed to be contacted again by MI5, and then by the FBI. He was drinking more heavily than ever. He died on 27 September 1965, aged just thirty-one. We have no clear sense of what he had thought of his father's work chairing the Committee on Homosexual Offences and Prostitution from 1954; and we can only speculate on the ways in which having Jeremy as a son influenced the father's perception of homosexual men. The Wolfenden Report of 1957 certainly envisaged, in its apparent ideal, somebody less visible and better behaved.

In his memoirs, published in 1976, Sir John Wolfenden shows that he was well aware of the possible effects of his work on his children. On the original invitation from the Home Secretary to chair the Committee – whose members all called it CHOP to spare their female secretaries' blushes – Wolfenden wrote: 'There were the four children to consider, one [Jeremy] at university, the other three at school. What might they have to put up with in comment from their contemporaries if their father got involved in "this sort of thing"?' Throughout the period of the Committee's research he had to think carefully about his own behaviour, since there were obvious pitfalls, even for such a highly respectable family man: 'From time to time facetious gossip-column writers asked if we were undertaking first-hand experience in the relevant fields. For my part I thought it prudent to avoid public lavatories in the West End.' When the Report was published at last, receiving a huge amount of publicity, Sir John thought of the children again:

> I personally got landed with a label which has probably been more embar-
> rassing to my children than to me. At one time there was a rumour that our
> rather distinctive surname had passed into some Middle European
> languages as meaning a practising adult male homosexual. My legal friends,
> half-seriously, told me to watch out for anything similar in English and
> offered their services free in a libel action which would, they promised, set
> me up for life. But unfortunately English newspapers and magazines are too
> efficiently advised by their legal experts.

Whether the father was more embarrassing to the son than the son to the father is difficult to judge. Such things tend to balance each other out in the long run. Neither was without a sense of humour, but the father lacked the searing cynicism of the son's depressive streak. For all its limitations, the Wolfenden Report, which was not acted on for a decade – the Sexual Offences Act 1967 being its principal outcome – may have been seen by Jeremy as having its positive, progressive aspects, while by the time he was writing his memoirs in the mid-1970s, Sir John appears to have recognised that his son's generation could only have given it temporary approval, if any. In a final, wry reflection on the Report, Sir John wrote: 'What I find amusing is that we, who were thought by so many to be so outrageous in 1957, should now be regarded as Victorian fuddy-duddies. It is entertaining to have lived long enough to have made oneself obsolete.'[18]

Lord Montagu felt he had been well prepared for prison by public school and the army. He decided to remain celibate in prison, aware that to others he would have been a trophy fuck. The prison governor told him he had disgraced his class and would be despised and rejected for ever. But he knew he could not go into hiding or exile when released: one fellow prisoner had asked him, 'If you aren't brave enough to go to Beaulieu after this is over . . . how can I possibly go back to Leamington?' Montagu did, of course, go home. At Beaulieu he pioneered the opening up of stately homes to paying visitors and set up the famously successful motor museum. He married twice and fathered two sons and a daughter. He decided to keep quiet about the case, explaining in his memoirs (1976): 'It was, after all, the invasion of my privacy which had been one of the most repugnant aspects of my prosecution.'[19]

The terms of decriminalisation proposed by the Wolfenden Report and then signed into law in England and Wales a decade later were so narrow as to make most homosexual men 'bad' homosexuals after all. The same paradox arose wherever the law and social conventions were liberalised during the 1960s and 1970s. A certain leeway was offered, but more was demanded and taken. By trying to take the option of liberty, gay men and lesbians looked as if they were taking liberties. For a start, the gay movement very quickly became insistent on the principle of coming out; and yet the provision that had been made for the meagre liberty that was on offer was located in the very place the movement deplored: the closet. Just as the Sexual Offences Act 1967 spoke of sexual acts between two individuals *in private*, the wider expectation was that, tolerated within the limits of common decency, lesbians and gay men would continue to live even those gay aspects of their lives that took place outside the bedroom *in private*. But coming out demanded a completely different use of space.

At the end of his autobiography, *To Fall Like Lucifer* (1971), Ian Harvey issued a warning about the likely consequences of what he regarded as the extremism of the 'permissive society' and its adherents: 'the new tolerance towards homosexuality would suffer if the homosexuals by their behaviour became involved [in such extremism]. The younger element in the homosexual society should walk warily.' As an ex-minister in Harold Macmillan's Conservative government, Harvey was precisely attuned to the tones required of homosexual men by the reformers of the Wolfenden Committee in 1957 and, to no less an extent, by the reformist members of parliament who passed the Act in 1967. He was an ex-minister because, in November 1958, he had been caught with a guardsman in St James's Park and charged with 'gross indecency'; so he also had an insight into the consequences of intolerance: despite the dropping of the charges, both men had been fined for a breach of the park regulations and Harvey had lost his parliamentary seat as well as his ministerial position. It is noticeable, however, that his own behaviour before decriminalisation does not seem to have tempered his attitude to the pleasures of younger men after it.

The idea that scruffy, young gay liberationists were likely to spoil things for everyone else – especially since the change in the law was so recent, the Queen's signature still wet on the Act – was widespread among older homosexual men in the 1970s. They had not struggled quietly for so many years (those of them who had) for a bunch of hairy hippies to take up the freedoms the new legal situation had handed them and thereby, by association, brand all homosexual men as hedonistic weirdos. Especially irritating was the gay liberationist claim that homosexuality was intrinsically radical and subversive of the heterosexual, patriarchal status quo. For many older men, the quietism imposed by the illegality of homosexual acts had led to an extremely cautious social conservatism that was never likely to welcome the raucousness of the new liberationist politics. Ian Harvey sums up the 'Sexual Revolution' of the 1960s as follows: 'Things have reached such a pitch in some directions that it has become difficult to avoid coming to the conclusion that heterosexual behaviour is "old hat". In order to restore the balance the protagonists of heterosexuality have had to resort to talking off all their clothes in public.'[20]

Writing in the late 1950s, Beverley Nichols remarked on how much had been lost in the way of (hetero)sexual glamour since the 1920s: 'A dinner-jacket was folded over the back of a chair and a brightly beaded dress was hung on a hook. It wasn't a question of an old pair of jeans tossed into a corner and a drab jumper pushed into the linen basket.' Similarly, the alluring formality of social occasions was being lost: 'When a modern hostess writes the words "black tie" on her invitation cards she means that it is a comparatively formal party; when a hostess of the twenties wrote these words, she meant that it wasn't.'[21] It should not come as a surprise that aesthetes of an earlier period would be aghast at some of the laid-back styles being adopted by later generations. The objection of older homosexual men to the gay liberation generation was often sartorial; or, to put it more broadly, a matter of style. While young men's bodies were no less sexy than they had ever been, the habit of negligently clothing them in torn and faded jeans and a mere T-shirt was a major shock to the system of those who had come to regard the homosexual type as having an inbred sense of style. (For lesbians the problem was less obvious. Clearly, the fact that women, whether heterosexual or lesbian, could now wear trousers, at least in informal situations, without causing adverse comment was a welcome development for many lesbian women to whom trousers were a natural home.) Long, unkempt hair and unshaven faces, too, violated the standards of older generations of queens.

Some older men, though, were happy to adjust their sartorial standards to the carnival of the new era. In March 1963, Cecil Beaton had a night out in San Francisco: 'We went to louche bars. At one called the Toolbox the decorations were of men in black mackintoshes with tin hats, and on the walls still lives of parts of motorbicycles. The atmosphere was quite frighteningly tough until one realized that the jeans and leather jackets were in many cases a fancy dress.' And, indeed, he picked up a tall Scandinavian-American art historian half his age and they had a relationship that lasted a couple of years.[22]

## From the Covert to the Overt

If we think back to Federico García Lorca's 'Ode to Walt Whitman', we may hear an echo of his objections to the 'fairies' of North America in the objections of some older, homosexual men and lesbians to what they considered the excesses of the gay liberation period: the perceived separatism of gay subcultures (or the 'gay ghetto'); the brazenness of the visibly, and even proudly, unmanly and unwomanly; the glorying in their difference. For some, the increasing toler- ance, even acceptance, of homosexuality had the effect of tarnishing the brand. It began to lose its aspect of the daring, the dangerous, the truly forbidden. Why, once it became respectable, it might even cease to be sexy! There is an element of this in Luchino Visconti's response, when dining with gay friends in New York City towards the end of his life, to an invitation to go on afterwards to a gay bar. He dismissed with contempt the very idea of such a place: 'When I was young, homosexuality was a forbidden fruit, something special, a fruit to be gathered with care, not what it is today – hundreds of homosexuals showing off, dancing together in a gay bar. What do you want to go there for?'[23] That he regarded as a form of exhibitionism ('showing off') what others might regard as an entertainment concerned with, as well as sexual connection, subcultural connectedness ('dancing together in a gay bar') suggests that he always felt gays were being watched, and judged, by straight people; and that he still cared how he looked to them. Many others felt the same.

In the late 1960s Janet Flanner grew increasingly uncomfortable with the sexual openness she witnessed. She tended to regard it as a breach of class-based etiquette: 'She was shocked by the overt homosexuality in New York, which to her showed a definite lack of propriety and class.'[24] Ambivalent about increasing gay visibility in the USA, Noël Coward was extremely uncomfortable when taken to the profusely gay resort Fire Island but, typically, enjoyed the adulation he received there. In his diary he wrote that he found the atmosphere of the place 'sick-sick-sick'. He went on:

Never in my life have I seen such concentrated, abandoned homosexuality. It is fantastic and difficult to believe. I wished really that I hadn't gone. Thousands of queer young men of all shapes and sizes camping about blatantly and carrying on – in my opinion – appallingly. Then there were all the lesbians glowering at each other … I have always been of the opinion that a large group of queer men was unattractive. On Fire Island, it is more than unattractive, it is macabre, sinister, irritating and somehow tragic.

He had an off-Broadway, drag performance of his play *Private Lives*, in which the action had been transferred from the French Riviera to Fire Island, closed down. ('It wasn't even amusingly camp, it was just terrible.') He himself went on combining openness in his social life with professional discretion. When Sheridan Morley drafted *A Talent to Amuse*, his biography of Coward, the latter demanded that it be purged of references to his sexuality – to protect the sensitivities of his ageing fans. He told Morley, 'I can't afford to offend their prejudice, nor do I really wish to disturb them this late in their lives; if I had a very young audience, I might think differently.' When Morley pointed out T.C. Worsley's openness about being gay in his 1967 memoir *Flannelled Fool*, Coward replied: 'There is one essential difference between me and Cuthbert Worsley. The British public at large would not care if Cuthbert Worsley had slept with mice.'[25] Again – and one can see how this might be especially acute for a celebrated performer – the sense of being watched prevailed.

In 1954, the American composer Harry Partch refused the film-maker Kenneth Anger permission to use his *Plectra and Percussion Dances* on the soundtrack of *Inauguration of the Pleasure Dome*. (This despite holding the view that 'The rebelliously creative act is also a tradition.'[26]) According to his biographer, 'Such an overt treatment of homosexual subject matter as some of Anger's films contain made Partch uncomfortable; he remained discreet about his sexuality, not discussing the matter even with close friends.'[27] The idea that sexual orientation was an entirely private matter was a hard one for many people to discard. For obvious reasons, it also determined people's attitudes to some of the main tenets of gay-liberationist politics. In Partch's case:

On the one hand, as many friends have testified, Partch approved of the act of personal liberation implicit in the practice of homosexuality … Harder for him to accept was the gay movement's principal tactic, that of 'coming out' … [I]t was not simply that as a member of an older generation he felt shy about declaring allegiance with a cause espoused by the young: he felt also that coming out assumed that one had a fixed sexual identity that could confidently be declared in public … The act of coming out seemed to him less of an avowal of personal liberty than a personal gesture of political alignment, and thus was of secondary interest to him.[28]

Fellow composer Virgil Thomson organised his friends into two groups, the openly 'queer' and the 'proper'. Among the latter he had a long sequence of women friends who accompanied him to concerts and dinners. Almost all of these reported that his homosexuality had been understood from the start but never mentioned, let alone talked about at any length. Gay men who belonged to the 'proper' set were only those who could be trusted to keep private matters private. He later disapproved of the gay liberation movement's insistence on openness. He never used the word 'gay', and was not pleased when, in the late 1980s, his own favoured term 'queer' was radically politicised by the AIDS movement and its coalition of adherents to non-normative identities and practices.

Thomson continued to forge new friendships with younger gay men, among them the novelist Christopher Cox, the pianist and voice coach Craig Rutenberg, the painter Mark Beard and the photographer Ron Henggeler; he lived above the composer Gerald Busby and his lover Sam Byers in the Chelsea Hotel. But he made few concessions to their ways of living. As his biographer puts it, 'Their openness about being "queer" seemed to him an enormous mistake. He chided them about queer politics and refused to use the word "gay". Sometimes someone would try to argue with him that things were changing. Mostly the topic was avoided.' When Maurice Grosser developed symptoms of AIDS in 1986, Thomson persuaded him not to be open about this. 'He persuaded Maurice that were his condition to be made public, he would be stigmatised as the oldest known person with HIV. This would completely overshadow his reputation as an artist.' Grosser died on 26 December 1986; the given cause of death was 'congestive heart failure'.[29]

For much of the century, as we have seen throughout this book, the lives of many gay men and lesbian women – especially those who were affluent or those who worked in the arts – were led according to the unspoken principle of the 'open secret', whereby the presence of homosexuality was accepted without explicit acknowledgement. Christopher Reed has argued that 'Homosexuality, inscribed by sexology as the secret status of the artist as a "type," became the paradigmatic secret of avant-garde art. Its status as an "open secret" – constantly suspected and hinted at, but never frankly acknowledged, is among the defining characteristics of the Modernist avant-garde.'[30] One can see why many who had lived their lives, and conducted their careers, by these informal conventions might later object to being asked to 'come out' by younger gay liberationists. Refuting the accusation that they had been living in 'the closet', they often replied: but I've never been 'in'! Discussing how open secrecy works, Alan Sinfield has written:

The secret keeps a topic like homosexuality in the private sphere, but under surveillance, allowing it to hover on the edge of public visibility. If it gets fully into the open, it attains public recognition; yet it must not disappear altogether, for then it would be beyond control and would no longer effect a general surveillance of aberrant desire. The open secret constitutes homosexuality as the 'unthinkable' alternative – so awful that it can be envisaged only as private, yet always obscurely available as a public penalty for deviance.[31]

In their attempts to make the unthinkable thinkable, and in their concomitant argument that sexual identity was not merely something you do in bed, the politicised members of the younger generation were now, if only implicitly, pointing out the existence of the secret. While not actively outing their elders, their politics sometimes felt as if it were threatening to do so. The attribution of greater virtue to being out-of-the-closet was a particular irritant.

Using the familiar phrase, the novelist and screen writer Gavin Lambert said, of the film director Tony Richardson, that his 'bisexuality was an open secret to his friends, a locked closet to the world'. Living in the aftermath of Burgess–Maclean and Montagu–Wildeblood, 'he placed his female lovers centre stage and relegated his male lovers to the wings'. In a sentence that seems to reek of score-settling after the deaths of all concerned, Lambert says that, 'as a realist, Tony had no hesitation in following the examples of Noel Coward, Somerset Maugham, Cecil Beaton, Stephen Spender, Terence Rattigan, Angus Wilson, and all the others who took care never to cross that line'. This is an unjust yoking together of men with a variety of approaches to the issue; there may be a certain amount of envy of the success these men enjoyed in their careers, perhaps as a consequence of their varying strategies of concealment, discretion and coded affirmation. Lambert is, of course, speaking of the 1950s in particular. In another mood he might have acknowledged that Spender (say) had been more open in earlier times – indeed, by the 1950s he was living as a predominantly heterosexual family man with children, which might explain his discretion more than that of the others named here – and Wilson would be more open later. But Lambert's implicit contrasting of his life with theirs expresses an increasingly common position adopted by gay men in the second half of the century. You might call it competitive outness. It tends to operate, at its crudest, as a reproach to earlier, and a challenge to later, generations. One is tempted to respond to Lambert by asking him why such a man in such a period would *not* have followed such eminent examples, positive role models in their own ways? The answer has to do with a gay liberationist ethic imposed retrospectively (Lambert was writing in the late 1990s) on individuals who had, to a greater or lesser extent, begun both their careers and their adult lives as homosexual men in the long shadow of the Wilde scandal. Alternatives were, as Lambert suggests, open to them; but who is to say, in the manner of a self-appointed commissar, that such alternatives should override the choice of personal comfort, say, or of artistic ambition? Lambert writes from the position of a man who took the option of openness and, as he may have predicted, survived it – as other men may not have thought possible. Richardson's spotlighting of his female lovers must have seemed an apt solution to the problem of living as a bisexual at that particular moment in history. Lambert believed it was the wrong solution. That is, pretty much, all we can say. It is worth noting that when Lambert visited Richardson in the summer of 1970 at his estate in the south of France, far from the restrictive rules of the movie industry, he found the atmosphere 'Completely homosexual in a charming, unforced, well-mannered way.'[32]

Of course, there are degrees of outness, and occasions for the closet. There are conventions and an unwritten etiquette. No one could seriously call the Christopher Isherwood of the 1970s closeted, yet his diaries show that he was reluctant, at times, to be associated with gay-liberationist events because, as something of a public figure, his presence at, or involvement in, such events would be noted by the media, and he did not want to embarrass his swami by association.[33] Similarly, you could not call Rudolf Nureyev closeted. The singer-songwriter and AIDS activist Michael Callen claimed to have watched Nureyev in a New York bathhouse having sex with with four men (black men, he specified) in sequence. According to a friend and biographer of Leigh Bowery, who provided the costume designs when Nureyev commissioned a ballet from Michael Clark for the Paris Opéra, 'Rudolf continually chased Michael and was always trying to lift up his kilt and feel his packet. Michael ignored his advances and got on with his work.' Yet Nureyev is said to have been furious when, at dinner in his apartment, Clark broke the rules by openly kissing his boyfriend.[34]

Much of the resistance to the new identity politics was superficially focused on the use of the word 'gay'. The only reference to homosexuality in any of Sir Osbert Sitwell's letters was '(!)' after 'gay' in a 1967 letter to Lincoln Kirstein.[35] Mary Renault disliked 'gay' and objected to gay liberation itself as 'sexual tribalism'.[36] Bruce Chatwin hated it: 'I'd much rather be called a bugger,' he said.[37] Elizabeth Chanler, to whom he was married from 1965 to 1981, later said of him: 'I knew Bruce was ambidextrous. He was never obvious about it and it embarrassed him that he had this tendency, but he wasn't going to give in to it completely. Looking back, I think he was very uncomfortable at having got himself into this situation, but given his background he didn't see any alternative, and he thought men living together completely unnatural. Once I said:

"What about famous couples like Benjamin Britten and Peter Pears?" Bruce said, "No, it's still not right".[38] According to Peter Pears, in later life Benjamin Britten was gratified by the increasing social acceptance of homosexuality, but 'The word "gay" was not in his vocabulary'. When Pears himself first publicly acknowledged his homosexuality, three years after Britten's death, in an interview in *The Advocate* (12 July 1979), he said: 'I've always rather resisted gay demonstrations because I feel that we have to fit into a society and we don't particularly want to make ourselves an extra nuisance. I'm all for plugging away and making it clear to those who have eyes to see what the situation is.'[39]

Among those who had not yet come out, there were many who thought they had missed the boat: it was a young person's thing. Some regretted this, others not. In a diary note of 1972, John Cheever wrote: 'I am tired of worrying about constipation, homosexuality, alcoholism, and brooding on what a gay bar must be like. Are they filled with scented hobgoblins, girlish youths, stern beauties? I will never know.' In 1978, thinking back on one of his affairs with another man, Cheever wrote: 'I was determined not to have this love crushed by the stupid prejudices of a procreative society. Lunching with friends who talked about their tedious careers in lechery, I thought: I am gay, I am gay, I am at last free of all this.' But he added: 'This did not last for long.'[40]

In Britain, the actor Alec Guinness, who had led a life of Roman Catholic guilt, furtive cruising and keenly disapproving observation of fellow queers, had such an extreme reaction to sexual explicitness that he set fire to his copy of Alan Hollinghurst's novel *The Swimming-Pool Library* (1988), calling it 'too unsuitable'. He deplored the recent 'flaunting [of] homosexual causes' by the younger, gay actor Ian McKellen, tersely commenting: 'Very tiresome and it is bound to create a horrid backlash' – this in 1988, when the horrid backlash already caused by the AIDS epidemic was one of the motivating factors behind McKellen's pro-gay advocacy.[41]

In France, despite being increasingly relaxed about including homosexuality as a theme in his books, even if always in tandem with the concept of sin, the novelist Marcel Jouhandeau objected to public expressions of, or organisations around, the topic. According to André Baudry, founder of the homophile organisation Arcadie and the journal of the same name, 'Marcel Jouhandeau dealt with his homosexuality in private.' Speaking from his own clearly opposed position, Baudry added, 'He did a brisk business with his books and did not want homosexuality placed on the public square. He was one of those people who saw only their own little self-interest.' Jacques de Ricaumont, another Arcadien but further to the right on the political scale, made the same point in a gentler tone: 'For Jouhandeau, homosexuality had to be a purely individual matter. He did not accept the esprit de corps of Arcadie or the very idea of a homophile movement.'[42] When Baudry founded the group in 1954 he had written to various prominent homosexual men and women, including Marguerite Yourcenar, to enlist their support. Yourcenar remained silent on her own behalf, but she did privately chide Marcel Jouhandeau for his aggressively angry response to Baudry.

Of course, the *événements* of 1968 had the effect of accelerating change, so that Arcadie itself began to look distinctly out of date. Not only that, but its elitist politics were now out of joint with the times. Frédéric Martel says, 'Before 1968, homosexuality located itself on the political right; now it was part of the left.'[43] (As we have seen, something similar had happened, in terms of cultural dominance, in Britain at the end of the 1920s as the Bright Young People gave way to the Auden generation.) Along with the political realignment there was a cultural shift. Where once the scholars of homophile self-esteem had gathered precedents for their desires from classical sources, anchoring themselves in the respectability of the past and the stability of the written text, the younger generation of activists were now engaging with what they could garner from cinema. As Martel puts it, 'Just as homosexuals in Arcadie drew up lists of writers in the 1950s, militants in the 1970s compiled lengthy filmographies and organized screenings.'[44]

Not until late in his life was Roland Barthes beginning to come out. Or rather, the man who had lived with his mother until her death in October 1977 and had not wanted to upset her with the knowledge of his homosexuality (the assumption being that Madame Barthes was psychologically blind), but who had evolved a life for himself as a gay man with close gay male friendships and a more active sexual involvement only when abroad – in Morocco he had encounters with local youths, and also went to brothels – was, before his death, seeking a way to make a more public, cultural affirmation of his sexuality. An important, if odd, instance was his writing of a preface for Renaud Camus' explicitly gay (and gay liberationist) novel *Tricks* (1981), apparently without having read it. (Barthes puts in one of his cameo appearances as a librarian in Romania in Renaud Camus' 1983 novel *Roman Roi*.) His reaction to the new gay movement was ambivalent, as his biographer explains:

> He was struck by the way homosexuals behaved differently from in the past, particularly by the fact that they no longer felt ashamed. But he did not personally care for what, in his eyes, amounted to a form of collective indoctrination, the moment when liberated individuals formed new groups and regimented their behaviour. He thought that by virtue of their 'liberated' behaviour homosexuals were conforming to another stereotype.[45]

Perhaps he might have endorsed the view of one of those homosexual men from the past, Raymond Roussel, who once said, 'We mustn't strip away the charm of the taboo, or lose the cult of the secret garden.'[46]

## Culture and Gay Culture

The South African novelist Mary Renault was generally happier in male company than among women. Or rather, she had little patience with the kind of women she tended to meet, who accepted being treated as second-class citizens. Her biographer says that it was 'men, preferably good looking and gay, who most easily claimed her attention.'[47] This was, in part, because the kind of gay men she met were actively involved in the arts: 'her actor and dancer friends were a last bulwark against the encroaching tide of barbarism, a travelling cosmopolitan brotherhood, free from the fettered, tribal obsessions of the despised Afrikaners. She was fascinated by their craft and traditions, and admired the way they wore their homosexuality like a masonic badge.'[48]

In 1962 Renault and her lover Julie Mullard travelled around Europe for several months. In Athens her translator Kimon Friar managed to arrange entry, for her and the American poet James Merrill, to restricted parts of the Acropolis Museum; but Renault was glad only to have to shake hands with Merrill before being left on her own. It was also while in Athens that she was introduced to the novelist Colin Spencer, a man whom she liked at once, and to Robert Liddell, whose books she already knew. He amused her over dinner with gossip about Ivy Compton-Burnett and Margaret Jourdain. At her insistence, they all went on to a gay nightclub, and when a young man danced on the table with rolled-up socks under his shirt as breasts, Renault held forth on her own theory of sexuality: 'all men, she declared, should love someone of their own sex until just over twenty, when they should marry and raise a family. They should, however, return to their own sex in middle age.' Characteristically, 'she had no corresponding theory for women.'[49] The fact is that she appears to have put more thought into male homosexuality than into lesbianism. Perhaps it was enough for her merely to live the latter without complicating it.

Her radicalism was reserved for the struggle against apartheid. In 1956 she was one of the first to join the Black Sash (Women's Defence of the Constitution League) to protest against the Nationalist government's racialist policies. In 1960 she would help re-establish PEN in Cape Town, but she was less interested in the movement for gender equality once it broadened out from the practicalities of gender segregation and employment rights. 'I've never been a feminist,' she said, 'simply because all those years my inner persona occupied two sexes too indiscriminately to take part in a sex war.' This very personal identification with men had obvious benefits in the conceptualisation of male lives in her novels. She went on: 'I do have sympathy for the *early* feminists, because they were then subject to rigid apartheid and job-reservation, unable to show what, as individuals, they could do. But immediately it became a Cause people felt justified in saying quite idiotic and untrue things, like how women had never produced a Shakespeare or a Beethoven or a Michelangelo because they had been kept at the kitchen sink . . . and doing totally unjustifiable things like chucking themselves under horses in the Derby.'[50] Renault did not think of herself as a woman writer. She believed feminist arguments about the 'great men' of the artistic canons were a distraction from the fact that women had the capacity to compete with men in the arts, regardless of gender.

In Renault's novel *The Charioteer* (1953), Ralph Lanyon warns Laurie Odell ('Spud') of the dangers of over-reliance on an untrustworthy network of homosexual and bisexual people, apparently of both sexes: 'we all have to use the network some time,' he says, but:

Don't let it use you, that's all. Ours isn't a horizontal society, it's a vertical one. Plato, Michelangelo, Sappho, Marlowe; Shakespeare, Leonardo and Socrates if you count the bisexuals – we can all quote the upper crust. But at the bottom – Spud, believe me, there isn't any bottom. Never forget it. You've no conception, you haven't a clue, how far down it goes.[51]

Ralph's use of a deeply conventional list of famous homosexuals and bisexuals from the past in order to suggest the virtues of the best of the present-day network establishes both his own pride and his shame at being associated with others – pride in the highbrow cultural tradition, but shame in having to connect with those who do not live up to it. He seems to despise most of the men he meets in gay circles: their promiscuity, their effeminacy, their unreliability . . .

However, Laurie seems not to need warning: for he, too, has an innate sense of his own superiority. When he and Ralph are deep in conversation with each other at a wedding, Laurie fleetingly catches the eye of 'one of the decrepit waiters':

Laurie's gaze travelled out from Ralph's face to meet a cold, flat, withdrawing eye, glaucous and sunken, the eye of yesterday's fish rejected by this morning's buyers, wrinkling on the slab. The face could still be read, as it were, between the lines; faint traces were left in it of a mincing, petulant kind of good looks. The glance, so quickly caught away, lingered on like a smell; it had been a glance of classification.[52]

It is hard to imagine a more repellent description of the mutual recognition of two gay strangers. The gay men Renault approves of do not like to be associated with the likes of this anonymous waiter, still less to be recognised by such a person as having anything in common with him. So, what is wrong with this man, as far as we can gather from such a brief glimpse and Laurie's instinctive reaction against it? Just a whiff of effeminacy (the strange evidence of 'mincing' in his face) and the petulance that stereotypically goes with it, good looks gone to seed, and, of course, the fact of his being a mere waiter. It is clear that Renault herself subscribed to the notion of a 'vertical society' or moral hierarchy of homosexual behaviour. Much of her fiction endorses an elite.

Many mid-century writers objected to the prospect of being categorised according to the criteria of identity politics. After May Swenson had alerted her to a forthcoming anthology, edited by Ann Stanford, Elizabeth Bishop replied on 7 November 1971:

> I thought at some point in the past I must have told you that I have always refused to be in any collections, or reviews, or special numbers of just women? *Always* – this has nothing to do with the present Women's Lib Movement (although I'm in favour of a lot of that, too, of course). I see no reason for them and I think it is one of the things to be avoided – and *with* 'Women's Lib' perhaps even more so. WHY 'Women in Literature'? No – it's *The Women Poets in English*, I see. But still, WHY? Why not *Men Poets in English*? Don't you see how silly it is?[53]

(Stanford's major anthology *The Women Poets in English* was published in 1972.) As for her lesbianism, although she lived openly with her partner, the Brazilian architect Lota de Macedo Soares, Bishop is quoted by Frank Bidart as having recommended the benefits of 'closets, closets, and more closets'. In fact, Bidart added, 'I can't quote her words exactly, but she felt that certain kinds of directness and ambition . . . had been impossible. Out of her distrust of the straight world she didn't want people to know she was gay. She certainly didn't want people to talk about it.'[54] Other lesbian writers had similar qualms, but often felt the contrary pressure to stand up and be counted. The argument in favour of anthologies was similar to that in favour of coming-out itself. To refuse to be included might seem closeted, yet to allow yourself to be included might restrict your reputation to that of a mere 'lesbian writer' or 'gay writer' rather than – what? – a writer. Some took evasive action on their own behalf. James Baldwin did not want to be just a black writer, forever dealing with 'the Negro problem' in the USA; so he wrote *Giovanni's Room*, a novel about a relationship between two white men, an American and an Italian, living in Paris.

Once identified as lesbian or gay, writers were then assumed to have something in common with others of that sort. May Sarton came round only slowly
to accepting an association with a broader subculture of lesbians and gay men.
But come round she did, and after a book-signing at a gay bookstore in
Greenwich Village on 29 April 1977, she wrote to her gay friend, the painter
William Theo Brown: 'I do have some reservations about being affiched as gay
or lesbian, but they are our people, and I am coming to rather like being with
them.' That said, she did have difficulties accepting the criteria by which writers
and their work were discussed at certain feminist or specifically lesbian events.
Giving a reading with Audre Lorde in Chicago, she felt conservatively dressed
and old-fashioned. Sarton was 'introduced as a writer who who was a total
failure until the women's liberation movement came along' (an assessment that
she found 'a little hard'). Furthermore, 'She did not like Lorde's poetry, or the
way she attacked the audience for not being on the streets of Soweto.' Nor did
she approve of a discussion the next day, during which the prevailing view
appeared to be that one wrote with the body. (One woman said, 'I write with my
womb.') 'Finally she blew up. Art was written with the mind and soul, not the
body. Art should be judged as art, not as propaganda.' For the most part,
however, she was conciliatory; and in the end, as far as sexual orientation was
concerned, she preferred to keep a foot in both camps: she felt she functioned
best as 'a bridge between the hetero and homosexual worlds'.[55]

Sarton's pensive novel *Mrs Stevens Hears the Mermaids Singing* (1965) might
be said to be bogged down in matters that Virginia Woolf had raised more
angrily, many years earlier, in *A Room of One's Own* and *Three Guineas*. It is no
weaker, as a novel, however, for what could be regarded as its dislocation from
the then-current centres of feminist debate. Indeed, a not inconsiderable part
of its enduring interest lies in the signs it shows of changing consciousness. If it
seems out of date for the year of its publication, that is largely because its central
character is an old woman. What is open to question is the extent to which
Sarton deliberately and knowingly voiced, through her, an already redundant
approach to gender relations. Looking back on her life in October 1977, Sarton
said: 'I didn't come out as a lesbian until *Mrs Stevens*, when I was in my forties.
I didn't want to be labeled too soon, set off like Radclyffe Hall. More important,
I waited until my parents were dead.'[56] (Her mother had died in 1950, her father
in 1956.) The extent to which the writing of a novel whose central female
character is bisexual, and whose main male character is gay, can be regarded
as a coming-out on the part of its author varies, of course, depending on the
viewpoint.

When it comes to Sarton's ill-judged (and poorly edited) final novel, *The
Education of Harriet Hatfield* (1989), with its sixty-year-old central character,

you might well feel you were reading a book from the early 1970s, or even in parts the 1950s, until you came up against a reference to the AIDS epidemic. Implausibly, Harriet sets up a feminist bookshop in a blue-collar suburb of Boston, the distinguished example of Sylvia Beach playing in her conscious- ness (albeit somewhat tepidly: 'my heroine among women booksellers'), with no experience of book-selling or even much of feminism. At this late stage in her career, Sarton, through Harriet, is still hot and bothered about whether a woman-loving woman should call herself a 'lesbian' ('That awful word' which to Harriet's ear 'seems primarily sexual'). Cumulatively, the book deploys more arguments against such 'labels' than in favour of them. Just at the point in history when, largely in reaction to homophobia aroused by the AIDS epidemic, the word 'queer' was being readopted as an indicator of radical impatience with the claimed quietism of 'gay' identity politics, Sarton's central character was still saying, 'As far as the words go, "gay" seems to me even worse than "lesbian".'[57]

The Australian novelist Patrick White did not go out of his way to mix with, or in, the gay subculture, which he regarded with distaste. Indeed, he probably went out of his way not to do so. He is on record as having said,

> Homosexual society as such has never had much appeal for me. Those who discuss the homosexual condition with endless hysterical delight as though it had not existed, except in theory, before they discovered their own, have always struck me as colossal bores. So I avoid them, and no doubt I am branded as a closet queen.[58]

He had little but contempt for the gay liberation movement's public demonstra- tions. His biographer says, 'White never marched. His advice to those who suggested that he take part was to get off the streets and get on with their lives.' His recorded opinions on the matter were of a piece: 'I've marched in the streets, but only to get myself a man'; 'Screaming about the streets and waving your handbag in people's faces. That gets me down.' In fiction, he believed, homo- sexuality was 'a theme which easily becomes sentimental and/or hysterical. It is, anyway, rather worn.' He said of James Baldwin, 'If he had been a white queen shrieking instead of a black, the world would have shouted back, "Enough!" long ago.' On the other hand, he admired David Malouf's novel *Johnno* (1975) for dealing with male–male intimacy without making an issue of homosexu- ality. Indeed, he went so far as to recommend Malouf, who had become a friend, for the Nobel Prize in Literature. He was willing to accept the potential social benefits of such respectable kinds of publicity. When Angus Wilson was knighted in Britain in 1980, White said, notwithstanding his staunch republi- canism, 'The knighthood may help advance the homosexual cause.'[59]

By the time he had become a major public figure in Australia, White did feel he had to come out in some way that was more than merely casual. He chose to do so by writing his memoirs, which would be entirely open about his relationship with Manoly Lascaris. According to his biographer, 'White's urgent purpose in writing *Flaws in the Glass* was to make a public and dignified declaration of his homosexuality' – even if only, in White's words, 'To stop some other bastard getting in first.' His affectionate, private title for the memoir was *The Poof's Progress*. For a while he did toy with other, lesser schemes – 'I am compiling a list of Superpoofs in history who have contributed to the arts, and shall spring it on this philistine colony at the end of the year' – but in the end he did not bother; instead, he concentrated on the memoir. Lascaris was horrified by the typescript of *Flaws in the Glass*, but he demanded no changes.[60]

When, on the book's publication in 1981, Sidney Nolan saw what White had written about him, he made a series of retributive drawings, depicting White among the sodomites in Dante's Hell. Nolan fell back on homophobia as his mode of defence. Among other angry responses to White, he said: 'He doesn't understand much about life does he? He's just lived with a man for forty years.' A similar jibe from Geoffrey Dutton, in response to one of White's attacks, brought another friendship to an end. Dutton wrote to White: 'Your homosexuality, since you mention it, has indeed given you great insight, but it has also denied you the give and take, the interaction of love with human frailty, that comes not only from one's own life with wife and children but from those of the children's friends.' White quite reasonably responded, 'You seem to imply there's no give and take in a homosexual marriage. My God if you knew!'[61]

On a visit to London in the early 1980s, the American literary critic Robert K. Martin mentioned to the Greek publisher and poet Nikos Stangos that he was about to visit Gay's the Word bookshop in Bloomsbury. Martin recorded their conversation in his diary: 'Nikos can see no need for such a thing. England, he declares, has no need of liberation; it has always been liberated. That sort of thing – gay bookshops and the like – is typical of America.' Martin further ventriloquises Stangos (who had an American lover, the novelist David Plante), as follows: 'Literature is literature . . . there is no such thing as gay literature. You can buy any book you want in any bookstore. He is convinced that Americans are the enemies of culture, exporting a political strategy that can have no relevance to enlightened societies like England.'[62] In diaries published many years later, David Plante wrote that he and Stangos 'do not participate in the gay movement, would not, for example, go to a reading of gay poets because they are gay to support them for being gay'. He adds, in obvious bad faith, 'Our failing.'[63]

Degrees of liberation from enforced discretion had major implications within the arts. The French novelist Dominique Fernandez believed that an ethos of letting-it-all-hang-out would undermine the Apollonian principles of artistic creativity: 'Although it has just been liberated, homosexuality – a hotbed of intellectual questioning and a cultural stimulant while it was repressed – can find nothing better to do than cater for its every last fantasy, forgetting the need for inner restraint without which genuine creativity is impossible.' Referring to the explicitness of some recent gay photography, he wrote: 'Without sublimation, without the need to search for a language, the monotony of the real is difficult to escape from. By showing everything, one ends up saying nothing.' The changing status of homosexuals was making homosexuality itself less worthy of note: 'the banal nature of homosexuality has today deprived those who practice it of a substantial slice of what used to make them interesting. Perhaps this condemns homosexual art to live on solely in the form of nostalgia and pastiche – or else in advertising exhibitionism and lucrative scandal-mongering.'[64]

Marguerite Yourcenar had taken a comparable approach several decades earlier, in 1953, when François Augiéras sent her a copy of his novel *Le Vieillard et l'enfant* (published under the pseudonym Abdallah Chaamba). She wrote back on 16 May, criticising the book's 'tone of excitement and unhealthy pride', and in a later letter (undated) she warned him not to become 'a bird that always emits the same cry'. This is a bit rich, considering how often she wrote about gay men herself. Augiéras was open with her about his own life as well as his work, telling her about his work as a prostitute. After a gap, several letters were exchanged between 1960 and 1964. At one point, 21 June 1960, he complained, 'you have always had a way of minimizing my efforts that distresses me'. He expressed the desire to meet her, but she apparently allowed the correspondence to die out.[65]

Following a related line in the mid-1970s while considering the sexually explicit novels of William S. Burroughs, Jean Genet, John Rechy and Hubert Selby Jr, and contrasting them with the earlier writers Joseph Conrad, André Gide, Thomas Mann and Marcel Proust, the literary critic and biographer Jeffrey Meyers declared that 'The emancipation of the homosexual has led, paradoxically, to the decline of his art.'[66] Ignoring the fact that none of the four more recent novelists was simply a chronicler of liberation or liberated attitudes, Meyers argued that the need for concealment required the development of a literature that was oblique and nuanced, using metaphor rather than graphic description – a better literature, therefore. This was quite a common view; still is. The suggestion was (although Meyers did not explicitly say this) that the oppression of homosexuals happily accounted for the profusion of major homosexual authors in the Modernist period. The universality of their themes was not compromised by the literalism and virtual obscenity of attention to the details of gay sexual activity. Their books were subtle, complex, coded, oblique, even at times obscure.

On the other hand, Kingsley Amis, who had a negative view of literary obscurity, saw no such qualitative pay-off in the obliqueness of gay writers, which he seems to have regarded as perversely secretive. Amis subscribed to a simplistic view of pre-liberation homosexual men's defensive development of complex literary styles – and even did so with reference to later generations – as can be seen in references in his letters to W.H. Auden and James Fenton. Of the latter he wrote to Robert Conquest on 9 November 1982: 'James Fenton . . . you can't make head or tail of half the time. That's because he's queer, you see. You must never give yourself away about anything. I bet you could explain a lot of Auden's obscurity in the same way.' Similarly, he wrote to Philip Larkin on 9 March 1983: 'I think Fenton's obscure because he just has the habit of covering everything up because he's queer, even when what he's covering up has nothing direct to do with being queer. Like Auden.' This is, then, the flip side of the Jeffrey Meyers critical line, praising the obliquity of pre-liberation gay writers for precisely this quality.[67]

Edward Albee spoke at Out Write, a conference for gay writers held in San Francisco in 1991. He later reported:

> I pointed out a whole bunch of writers in the twentieth century who happened to be gay: Henry James, Gertrude Stein, Thornton Wilder, Tennessee Williams. They didn't write about gay themes. It was just a small part of their identity. Why concentrate on it? This has nothing to do with trying to be popular or to avoid censure. But it could be a limitation. In my own writing, I have a couple of gay characters, but I never felt the need to write about a gay theme.[68]

Was there, could there be, should there be, any such thing as 'gay literature'? In his 1987 book *Homosexualität und Literatur*, the German novelist Hubert Fichte waxed sceptical about the division of novelists into sexual categories: 'To speak of homosexual authors, and a homosexual style, presupposes that there is such a thing as a heterosexual literary style and heterosexual standards of judgement.'[69] Jean Genet firmly ruled out the idea that his own work was shaped by any subcultural intent. Edmund White writes that, in 1970, while developing his relationship with the Black Panthers, Genet 'was careful not to be drawn into discussions of the women's movement and gay rights. At this point he still conceived of both movements as a *personal* struggle in overcoming *psychological* oppression caused by societal taboos', in contrast to the collective and physical oppression suffered by the Panthers and their constituency. But he did successfully press Huey Newton to temper the homophobic language habitually used by the Panthers. 'In France Genet would lend his name to an early gay liberation publication, but the fight for gay rights was never high on his list.' In an unpublished 1983 interview he said, 'I did not write my books for the liberation of the homosexual.'[70]

## Madness Begets Madness

In Italy in the 1960s, Pier Paolo Pasolini had found himself increasingly out of step with the social aspirations of gay men. His own brand of radicalism was likewise out of step with the feminism that sought to end the sequestering of young women that made young men sexually available to men like him. Not for him, either, the emergent gayness that considered itself a distinct identity, collectively a distinct subculture. As one of his biographers puts it, 'faced with politicized, public homosexuals gathering in ghettoed bars, he stuck (some thought defiantly) to rough trade he found on the streets and in the fields, where he began.'[71] A trip to New York in September 1966, when he met Allen Ginsberg, among other young gay cultural figures, did nothing to change his mind. This was partly a matter of sexual taste: Pasolini was turned on by the kind of young, working-class boys who would not have been allowed into a gay bar in Rome, had such a place existed; and his boys would not have wanted such access in any case (unless to look for paying trade), since they did not identify as gay. But there is more to his response than this. Pasolini's politics were inextricably bound up with his sexuality, and his politics were not concerned with the recommendation of assimilationist, bourgeois lifestyles.

The German film-maker Rainer Werner Fassbinder was similarly convinced of the futility of the urge to assimilate. His biographer writes: 'As a homosexual he was outside normality. At the same time it was evident to him that homosexual relationships are based on structures which amplify the normality from which homosexuality distanced him – they were not an alternative.'[72] Indeed, this is one of the preoccupations of his film *Fox and His Friends* (*Faustrecht der Freiheit*, 1974). The German title means something like 'freedom's law of the jungle'. Fassbinder said of it, 'It is certainly the first film in which the characters are homosexuals, without homosexuality being made into a problem.' This is not to say that his characters are much enjoying themselves in their newly achieved openness: for, as he adds, 'here homosexuality is shown as completely normal, and the problem is something quite different, it's a love story, where one person exploits the love of the other person, and that's really the story I always tell.'[73] His biographer writes that 'for Fassbinder a different sexuality did not in itself provide a guarantee of more human and less exploitative behaviour. The exploitation of emotions is always frighteningly present in his work, because exploitation has to do with the social, and not the sexual, orientation of the characters.'[74] Unlike so many gay artists of the era, Fassbinder was still interested in class, for instance.

Fassbinder was convinced that 'Someone who wants to liberate himself for a new society must go down to the deepest depths of this society.'[75] One implication of such remarks, of which there were many, was that American gay liberationists, whose main aim seemed to be unquestioningly to assimilate themselves into the cultural mainstream, even if it was homophobic and sexist and racist, were moving in precisely the wrong direction. The self-indulgent idea of many gay liberationists that gayness was automatically a revolutionary subject position – despite more than ample evidence to the contrary – gave Fassbinder, who thought it absurd, one of his most consistent dialectical positions on the politics of sexuality. He did not regard gayness as either revolutionary or even alternative. As his biographer puts it, 'For him the gay scene was a magic mirror, in which it is possible to discern the mechanisms of established society more clearly.'[76] At the time of his death in June 1982, he had plans to film James Baldwin's novel *Giovanni's Room*. Such a film of a 1957 novel beginning in murder and ending in execution would also have been a bold statement of intent: Fassbinder was going against the grain of 1980s 'positive images'.

Baldwin had written a screenplay of *Giovanni's Room*, but all attempts to get it filmed had failed. In an anachronistic fragment of dialogue he added to the text, he had Giovanni say: 'Chez Guillaume they are always talking about *gaie* Liberation. But they are afraid – to be free. That is why they always sound like a barnyard. *Gaie!* They are always asking me, I say them, it is nobody's business, sometimes I am *gaie* and sometimes I am sad, and I do not have no club to love – whoever I love. And I do not have to answer to nobody, except just the good God who made me.'[77] There seems to be little distance between this utterance of Giovanni's and its author's own attitude. Certainly, Baldwin had a habit of dismissing the gay movement as 'a club', thereby suggesting it could be joined at will – or one could be expelled from it – without any real connection to the matter in question: personal sexuality.

If assimilation into heterosexual society raised certain fears, so, too, did the prospect of being assimilated into the narrowly gay 'club' that Baldwin speaks of, or the 'gay ghetto'. The word 'ghetto' arises in the mid-century, borrowed from aspects of the American Civil Rights movement – but also, of course, has terrifying echoes of the Jews under Nazism. The ghetto is a place into which

members of a despised minority group are either literally herded after confisca-
tion of their homes and belongings, or more subtly coerced by poverty and
rising rental costs elsewhere. In relation to gay men and lesbians, the 'gay ghetto'
was something much more positive: the urban area in which gay clubs and bars
had accumulated and, therefore, in which the gay presence on the streets was
overt and relatively safe. Gay tenants might move into rental properties here in
order to take part in this positive atmosphere. Gay men having relatively high
disposable income, they would look after their homes and the areas around
them, with the consequence that property prices would rise and the area
become gentrified. Daytime venues, such as cafés and bookshops, would join
the clubs and bars. Gay business associations and gay residents' committees
would consolidate the safety and gentility of the area.

W.H. Auden, who had known Berlin in the 1930s, felt comfortable with
many of the social developments around homosexuality in 1960s America, but
he disliked the idea of a ghettoised gay social life. Charles Osborne puts the
case as follows: 'Although he was never to make any public pronouncement
about his homosexuality, in the later nineteen-sixties he was always willing to
talk to homosexual student societies at universities where he was lecturing or
giving poetry readings. He saw no reason to pretend, but he also saw no reason
to proclaim.' He did, however, refuse to let any of his poems appear in specifically gay anthologies, 'for the reason that he had written his published love
poems to be read without reference to the sex of the person addressed'. He also,
in general terms, opposed gay separatism, saying: 'I'm no advocate of the purely
Uranian society myself. I mean, *I* certainly don't want to live only with *queers*.'[78]

The poet Frank O'Hara, two decades younger than Auden, was accepting of
and open about his gayness, but he likewise objected to the exclusiveness of
gay-only locations and events. Joe Le Sueur writes:

> if he was going to be adamantly opposed to the gay ghetto principle as
> exemplified by Cherry Grove on Fire Island, Lenny's Hideaway downtown,
> the Bird Circuit uptown, any gay gathering where straights were excluded
> or not wanted – in other words, a way of life that promoted compulsive
> cruising, misogyny, and homosexual separatism – he must have felt it
> necessary, as a point of pride and as a moral obligation, to hammer home to
> straight people the clear, unmistakable message that he was an uncontrite,
> arrogant queer who was not about to sing *miserere* or fall on his knees to
> anyone.[79]

In an essay in *Playboy* (January 1979), Gore Vidal argued that what he saw as
the current stance of the gay movement – in its development and affirmation of

gayness as an identity – was slavishly tied to the Judaeo-Christian stigmatisa-
tion of the sodomite, modernised in his incarnation as the 'homosexual person':

> Actually, there is no such thing as a homosexual person, any more than
> there is such a thing as a heterosexual person. The words are adjectives
> describing sexual acts, not people. Those sexual acts are entirely natural; if
> they were not, no one would perform them. [The 'irrational rage' of
> 'Judaism'] has triggered an opposing rage. Gay militants now assert that
> there is something called gay sensibility, the outward and visible sign of a
> new kind of human being. Thus madness begets madness.[80]

When Angus Wilson used to go and stay with Douglas Cooper and John
Richardson at their château in France, they distinguished between two distinct
spheres of interest of his. As Richardson puts it in his memoirs: 'A shrill street-
corner orator when discussing politics or gay lib, Angus was a scream when he
regaled us with stories in his countertenor's voice about the British Museum
Reading Room.'[81] The distinction between welcome screaming and unwelcome
shrillness is instructive. The tone of voice is not the point; the topic of conversation is. For his part, Wilson was scathing about other writers who refused to
come out. During an interview with Denis Lemon, the editor of *Gay News*, he
said of E.M. Forster, Somerset Maugham and Noël Coward, apropos of their
failure to campaign openly for homosexual law reform, 'They were three
terrible men.' Yet, like so many others, Wilson was uncomfortable with the new
use of the word 'gay' – because he found it too 'zissy'.[82]

When looking to their own past sexual history, some individuals, understandably, had great difficulty making any clear sense of the future. In his 1976
novel *In the Purely Pagan Sense*, after a long, fictionalised account of his sexual
conquests in London, Paris, Vienna, Berlin and elsewhere, John Lehmann
reflects on his failure to establish a lasting relationship with any of his sexual
partners. Apparently now settled in both Britain and middle age, he sees around
him many men of his own class who are living with younger, working-class men
(guardsmen, sailors, even policemen), such relationships across classes and age
groups being the only kind of homosexual 'marriage' he and the circles he moves
in seem able to envisage; and he imagines a time in the near future when class-
based incompatibilities will have evaporated. He describes this future entirely in
terms of the consumption of culture:

> Your doughty guardsman m[a]y be as ardent an *aficionado* of the ballet as
> his gentleman friend, and will compare notes with him on the latest middle-
> brow bestseller. The guardsman will, perhaps, provide his friend with the

rare sporting print or Rowlandson he needs to fill the gap in that enchanting series on the staircase; and offer, when the friend is down on his luck, to take him for a package tour among the Greek islands.[83]

If there is to be any compromise between such men – horror of horrors! – it will be in the older, higher-class man's descent to 'middlebrow' reading matter and the 'package tour'. There appears to be no question, for instance, of their going to the cinema together, let alone a football match ... To my mind, what is remarkable about this coda to his fictionalised memoirs is that, even though the book was published in 1976 as a 'Gay Modern Classic', Lehmann seems totally unaware of any recent developments in sexual politics: he does not even mention the Sexual Offences Act 1967, let alone the women's movement or gay liberation. He is vaguely aware that the British class system has begun to break down, but not the sex/gender system. There is no sexual-political conscious-ness on show in his book. Lehmann had let himself get out of touch. This might not have mattered if his book were not being marketed for a new (post-decriminalisation) generation of readers.

The idea of a politics of sexuality was often the stumbling block. Roger Cook said of the painter Patrick Procktor, 'He was really pre any sense of queer politics or gay politics. He had a negative view of the whole gay politics thing.'[84] Although Francis Bacon objected to Section 28 of the Local Government Act 1988 (in effect, banning the use of public money in the UK to 'promote' homosexuality), he refused to sign petitions about it. His biographer Daniel Farson's explanation of this position is no clearer than the position itself: 'He did not feel at ease in "groups". He detested such militancy, and though he laughed as he did so, he told me several times: "I really hate gays".'[85] Having felt like outsiders to mainstream society, many older men and women now felt like outsiders to the gay subcul-ture, which they found too politicised, too organised, apparently coercive in its uniformity. In a 1974 diary entry in New York, John Cheever observed: 'Two young men with their arms around each other frisk off to the East. Gay Liberation is electing its officers at the other end of town. Do they have a president, a secre-tary, and a treasurer?'[86] He was joking, and yet he may have unwittingly hit on a banal truth: the movement for gay rights did have to submit itself to a degree of organisation. Why should its groups not keep records and balance its books? On the other hand, for all Cheever knew, the two men might have been heading off to a meeting of the residents' association or even the PTA.

Thinking back to that moment in the late 1860s when Friedrich Engels noticed that pederasts were waking up to the possibility of some kind of collec-tive empowerment, we can see that he was right, even if he was joking at the time. By sheer, unexpected weight of numbers (often calculated by guesswork and partisan exaggeration), gay men and lesbians were indeed capable of becoming what Engels referred to as 'a power in the state'. This both exposed them to terrible vulnerability, as under Nazism, and yet gave them the potential for considerable strength. What was needed was not mere 'coming out' in enormous numbers – for, as we have seen throughout this book, many men and women *had* been out for decades, and could not have gone back in again – but an openness that was more than individual. Real social change demanded mutual identification on a grand scale. Being known to be gay on the cocktail circuit, or in the salons and the country houses, was not enough. The benefits of subcultural solidarity would be amply displayed in many countries during the first years of the AIDS epidemic, early in the 1980s, when the hostility of politicians, journalists and even large sections of the medical establishment left gay communities (in the first instance) to make their own arrangements: to share information, for instance, to provide new institutions of mutual care, to hypothesise the possibility of safer sex, and, of course, to engage in the scandalously long struggle for proper research into, and access to, effective and affordable drug treatments. Countries that did not have strong gay movements were slower in their responses to AIDS.

When Leonard Bernstein urged Aaron Copland, who was in his eighties, to come out, Copland drily replied, 'I think I'll leave that to you, boy'.[87] (Copland was born in 1900, Bernstein in 1918.) On the other hand, the poet Louis Aragon, who was born in the nineteenth century three years before Copland, felt able to join the French gay movement – after the death of his wife. One writer speaks of him 'appearing at Gay Pride parades in a pink convertible, surrounded by ephebes'.[88] Aragon was a veteran of Natalie Barney's salons and of literary gatherings at Sylvia Beach's bookshop, Shakespeare and Company. Having previously taken part in the *événements* of 1968, joining the students in the streets, Aragon had recent experience of collective action. It may be that, when deciding to go on a gay pride march, he was also remembering the liberatory principles of the Surrealism to which he had once been a prominent subscriber. (In Paris in the mid-1920s, he had been a member of the Bureau of Surrealist Research, along with André Breton and Antonin Artaud.) Rather than end my narrative in a committee room or a closet, therefore, I would like to offer this final image of an elderly gay man, facing the public world with pride and not a little amusement. We can imagine him laughing and singing and chanting slogans, eyeing up the boys and girls along the way, blowing kisses to the bikers and drag queens . . . His presence is an affirmation of both subcultural belonging and still-flourishing desire. Life is not a gay pride march, of course. People go back to their routines. When the march has dispersed and the marchers have gone home, they may be reminded that desire is both astonishing and unremarkable.

# NOTES

## Chapter 1: The Homintern Conspiracy

1. Hubert Kennedy, *Ulrichs: The Life and Works of Karl Heinrich Ulrichs, Pioneer of the Modern Gay Movement* (Boston: Alyson, 1988), p. 134. *Incubus*, subtitled *Urning-Love and Blood Lust*, concerned the case of a man accused of the violent rape and attempted murder of a five-year-old boy. For Ulrichs, the case raised three crucial questions: was the accused responsible for his sexual orientation; did his treatment of the child amount to 'Urning-love'; and was the crime committed in a state of diminished responsibility? (Kennedy, pp. 136–140). The friendship between Marx and Engels was built on frankness in all areas of their lives: 'They had no secrets from each other, no taboos: if Marx found a huge boil on his penis he didn't hesitate to supply a full description': Francis Wheen, *Karl Marx* (London: Fourth Estate, 1999), p. 84.
2. Maurice Mendelson, 'Life and Work of Walt Whitman: A Soviet View', in Gay Wilson Allen and Ed Folsom (eds), *Walt Whitman and the World* (Iowa City: University of Iowa Press, 1995), pp. 336–338; p. 338. I am grateful to Steve Jones for this reference. See also Walter Grünzweig, *Constructing the German Walt Whitman* (Iowa City: University of Iowa Press, 1995), pp. 159, 253 n. 37.
3. In his book on male collaborations, Wayne Koestenbaum writes: 'I lack the temerity to venture a gay critique of *The Communist Manifesto*, but it is tempting to compare Marx and Engels forging communism, and Freud and Breuer labouring over psychoanalysis': Wayne Koestenbaum, *Double Talk: The Erotics of Male Literary Collaboration* (New York & London: Routledge, 1989), pp. 12–13.
4. On the further international dissemination of sexological texts, see Heike Bauer (ed.), *Sexology and Translation: Scientific and Cultural Encounters Across the Modern World* (Philadelphia, Pennsylvania: Temple University Press, 2015).
5. On 6 May 1868, in a letter to Karl Heinrich Ulrichs, Kertbeny used the word *Homosexualisten* (homosexuals), cannibalised from the Greek *homos* (the same) and the Latin *sexualis*. He used it again a year later in two anonymous pamphlets about the laws criminalising homosexual activities.
6. 'Bisexuality' remained, and to an extent always has remained, ambiguous: to biologists, zoologists and botanists it has generally meant having the characteristics of both sexes; whereas to lay speakers it came most often to mean having an attraction to either sex or to both sexes.
7. Variations on the original German (homosexuell) include: Norwegian (homoseksuell), Swedish (homosexuell), Finnish (homoseksuaali), Danish (homoseksuel), Estonian (homoseksuaalne), Latvian (homoseksuāls), Lithuanian (homoseksualus), Polish (homoseksualny), Czech (homosexuál), Slovakian (homosexuál), Slovenian (homoseksualni), Hungarian (homoszexuális), Croatian (homoseksualac), Albanian (homoseksual), Turkish (homoseksüel), Maltese (omosesswali), Italian (omosessuale), Portuguese (homossexual), Spanish (homosexual), French (homosexuel) and Dutch (homoseksueel). The other term to have survived well is, of course, 'lesbian' and its variations: Icelandic (lesbía), Norwegian (lesbisk), Swedish (lesbiak), Finnish (lesbo), Danish (lesbisk), Latvian (lesbiete), Lithuanian (lesbietê),

Polish (lesbijka), Czech (lesbička), Slovakian (lesbička), Slovenian (lezbyka), Hungarian (leszbikus), Croatian (lezbijka), Albanian (lezbike), Turkish (lezbiyen), Maltese (lesbjani), Italian (lesbica), Portuguese (lésbica), Spanish (lesbiana), French (lesbienne), Irish (leis-piacha), Dutch (lesbisch) and German (lesbisch). Note that neither term was taken up in modern Greek.

8. E.M. Forster, *Maurice* (Harmondsworth: Penguin, 1972), p. 158. The pioneering gay activist Harry Hay first saw the word 'homosexual' when reading Edward Carpenter's *The Intermediate Sex* at the age of eleven in 1923.

9. Forster, *Maurice* p. 140.

10. Radclyffe Hall, *The Well of Loneliness* (London: Virago, 1982), pp. 22–23, 207. The novel's first edition had a foreword (or an 'Appreciation') by Havelock Ellis.

11. David Bergman, *Gaiety Transfigured: Gay Self-Representation in American Literature* (Madison, Wisconsin: University of Wisconsin Press, 1991), p. 5.

12. Aldous Huxley, *Those Barren Leaves* (Harmondsworth: Penguin, 1951), p. 39. This develops into something of a running joke later in the novel. Two characters visit Assisi, where, 'in the upper and lower churches of St Francis, Giotto and Cimabue showed that art had once worshipped something other than itself. Art there is the handmaid of religion – or, as the psychoanalysts would say, more scientifically, anal eroticism is a frequent concomitant of incestuous homosexuality' (pp. 244–245). In Spoleto, they look at the frescoes of Lippo Lippi: 'Anal-eroticism was still the handmaid of incestuous homosexuality, but not exclusively. There was more than a hint in these bright forms of anal-eroticism for anal-eroticism's sake. But the designer of that more than Roman *cinquecento* narthex at the west end of the church, he surely was a pure and unmixed coprophilite.' After naming Freud the narrator adds, 'Can we doubt any longer that human intelligence progresses and grows greater?' (p. 246). The current intellectual trend also enables characters to interpret each other. Discussing a man they know, one woman says: 'Fundamentally, unconsciously, I believe he's a homosexualist.' Her interlocutor replies, 'Perhaps.' The narrator adds, 'She knew her Havelock Ellis' (p. 222). Ellis' *Sexual Inversion* had been published in German in 1896 and then in English in 1897. Ellis crops up again in Evelyn Waugh's 1928 novel *Decline and Fall*: 'Downstairs Peter Beste-Chetwynde mixed himself another brandy and soda and turned a page in Havelock Ellis, which, next to *The Wind in the Willows*, was his favourite book'– Evelyn Waugh, *Decline and Fall* (Harmondsworth: Penguin, 1937), pp. 127–128. At the climax of Samuel Barber's opera *A Hand of Bridge* (1959), David sings of his desire for 'twenty naked girls, twenty naked boys, tending to my pleasures' in a hectic schedule of ecstasies, 'every day another version of every known perversion, like in that book of Havelock Ellis hidden in the library behind the "Who's Who"': Michael S. Sherry, *Gay Artists in Modern American Culture: An Imagined Conspiracy* (Chapel Hill, North Carolina: University of North Carolina Press, 2007), pp. 168–169. The opera was premièred at the Spoleto Festival of Barber's lover, Gian Carlo Menotti.

13. Of course, in the mouths of others, even the neutral terms can be applied with venom, and their use may escalate to the more venomous. In Giorgio Bassani's Italy, between the wars, Dr Fadigati is generally said to be 'così' (like that) or 'di "quelli"' (one of those): Giorgio Bassani, *Gli occhiali d'oro* (Milano: Mondadori, 1980), p. 36. Deliliers refers to him as 'un vecchio finocchio' (p. 51). Later, Signora Lavezzoli begins by genteelly saying he has 'certi gusti' (special tastes) and is 'così', but very quickly escalates the negativity of her language and calls him a 'sporcaccione' (filthy person) and a 'vero degenerato' (real degenerate) (p. 85). Eventually, Nino Bottecchiari suspects Deliliers himself of having taken up with some other 'facoltoso finocchio' (rich pansy) like Fadigati (p. 132). But at no point in this narrative does anyone use the newly minted psychological/medical terms.

14. Jean Cocteau wrote of his boyhood having been punctuated by public scandals of various kinds: 'The luck of having been too young to understand the Dreyfus Affair ... The Adelswärd-Fersen Affair ... Schoolboys recruited after school to take part in black masses, crowned with roses. The trial of the princes in Germany and the newspapers hidden away and the conversations cut short when one enters the room': Jean Cocteau, *Souvenir Portraits: Paris in the Belle Époque* (London: Robson, 1991), p. 80. The Baron Jacques d'Adelswärd-Fersen and his friend Hans de Warren were found guilty of inciting minors to commit debauchery (those rose-crowned black masses), sentenced to six months' imprisonment, fined and deprived of their civil rights for five years. Fersen subsequently moved to Capri, where he built the Villa Lysis. (See Chapter Eight.) Fersen is the central character of Roger Peyrefitte's novel *The Exile of Capri* (*L'exilé de Capri*, 1959).

15. Patrick Higgins (ed.), *A Queer Reader* (London: Fourth Estate, 1993), p. 287. Harold Norse quotes a letter he wrote to Auden and Chester Kallman in 1939: 'As for me, I believe in the Homintern; leave the Comintern to the Party'. Since Auden subsequently used the word in an essay in *Partisan Review* in 1941, it was then attributed to him, much to Norse's irritation: Harold Norse, *Memoirs of a Bastard Angel* (London: Bloomsbury, 1990), p. 77. Noel Annan repeats the attribution to Maurice Bowra, whom he refers to as 'an immensely masculine bisexual', in *The Dons: Mentors, Eccentrics and Geniuses* (London: HarperCollins, 1999), p. 165.

16. The '-intern' half of the expression is sometimes neglected. For instance, of thirty-three individuals represented in a section called 'Homintern' in Patrick Higgins' anthology *A Queer Reader*, twenty-five are Anglophone (eighteen UK, seventeen US) and only eight continental European (three French, one German, one Greek, one Spanish and two Italian). None is so 'international' as to hail from anywhere other than North America and Europe.

17. H. Montgomery Hyde, *Stalin: The History of a Dictator* (London: Rupert Hart-Davis, 1971), pp. 291–292. Elsewhere, we are told of a US senator who believed Hitler had a 'world list' of homosexuals which subsequently fell into Stalin's hands: Nicholas von Hoffman, *Citizen Cohn* (London: Abacus, 1989), p. 130.

18. Evidence would be superfluous. When homosexuality itself is the incriminating factor, little more is needed than a narrative of innuendo, even at the end of the twentieth century. For instance, in a 1998 book that makes much of the supposition that Adolf Hitler and Ludwig Wittgenstein were in the same school class – they certainly went to the same school – Kimberley Cornish uses Wittgenstein's homosexuality as a key factor in the argument that he was a spy for the Soviet Union: Kimberley Cornish, *The Jew of Linz: Wittgenstein, Hitler and Their Secret Battle for the Mind* (London: Century, 1998). I have not read Cornish's book, but as Alan Bennett reports it, 'we have lists of Trinity [College, Cambridge] men who were Apostles, which of them were homosexual and so on, Cornish dodgily assuming, as did Andrew Boyle and John Costello before him, that homosexuality is itself a bond and that if two men can be shown to be homosexual the likelihood is that they're sleeping together. So we trail down that road looking for cliques and coteries with even G.M. Trevelyan's sexual credentials called into question because he happens to have recommended the homosexual Guy Burgess for a job at the BBC': Alan Bennett, *Untold Stories* (London: Faber and Profile, 2005), p. 255.

19. The playwright Jamie Wooten once declared that 'Jews and gays are very close in sensibility . . . It's just a chromosome away, really': David Ehrenstein, *Open Secret: Gay Hollywood, 1928–2000* (New York: Perennial, 2000), p. 311. Eve Kosofsky Sedgwick discusses the parallel between Jewish and gay identities in *Epistemology of the Closet* (Hemel Hempstead, Hertfordshire: Harvester Wheatsheaf, 1991), pp. 75–82.

20. Marcel Proust, *Cities of the Plain, Part One* (London: Chatto & Windus, 1968), pp. 22–23, 22. Giorgio Bassani compares anti-Semitism with homophobia in his novel *The Gold-Rimmed Spectacles* (*Gli occhiali d'oro*, 1958).

21. D.H. Lawrence, *Women in Love* (London: Grafton, 1988), pp. 373, 379, 395. This is the definitive Cambridge edition of a novel written between 1913 and 1920, when it was first published.

22. On Hoover's homosexuality, see William J. Maxwell, *F.B.Eyes: How J. Edgar Hoover's Ghostreaders Framed African American Literature* (Princeton, NJ: Princeton University Press, 2015), pp. 290–91.

23. Charles Kaiser, *The Gay Metropolis, 1940–1996* (London: Weidenfeld & Nicolson, 1998), p. 79. US Senate document 241, 15 December 1950.

24. William J. Mann, *Behind the Screen: How Gays and Lesbians Shaped Hollywood, 1910–1969* (New York: Penguin, 2002), p. 295. See also John D'Emilio and Estelle B. Freedman, *Intimate Matters: A History of Sexuality in America* (New York: Perennial Library, 1988), pp. 292–293; and Nicholas von Hoffman, *Citizen Cohn: The Scandalous Life and Times of Roy Cohn, Lawyer, Fixer, Destroyer* (London: Abacus, 1989), pp. 127–128.

25. R.G. Waldeck, 'Homosexual International', *Human Events*, 29 September 1960. Reprinted in extract in Martin Bauml Duberman, *About Time: Exploring the Gay Past* (New York: Sea Horse, 1986), pp. 199–202. Paul Hallam comments on this article in *The Book of Sodom* (London: Verso, 1993), pp. 28–29.

26. Norman Polmar and Thomas B. Allen, *The Encyclopedia of Espionage* (New York: Gramercy Books, 1998), pp. 264–266. The spy books often pre-empt questions about the (un)trustworthiness of homosexual men by describing homosexuality in entirely negative terms. For

instance, Andrew Boyle speaks of 'the sad pleasures of sodomy' with specific reference to the exuberantly cheerful Guy Burgess; and characterises the 'two most obvious weaknesses' of Donald Maclean as follows: 'the first, an urge to drink himself into a stupor when depressed; the second and more repelling, a desire, in that condition, to consort with homosexuals': Andrew Boyle, *The Climate of Treason: Five Who Spied for Russia* (London: Hutchinson, 1979), pp. 107, 184. One study of spies, oddly, does not mention Burgess' homosexuality when discussing him, although on the same page it does introduce Anthony Blunt as 'a discreet homosexual': Jeffrey T. Richelson, *A Century of Spies: Intelligence in the Twentieth Century* (New York & Oxford: Oxford University Press, 1995), p. 93. Even more oddly, on the same page, Richelson so intimately associates Guy Burgess and Donald Maclean that he conflates them when introducing the former, whom he calls 'Donald Burgess'.

27.  As late as 1982, the parliamentarian Leo Abse gave the queers-as-spies myth especially repellent expression: 'treachery is uncomfortably linked with disturbed homosexuals unable to come to terms with their sexual destiny . . . It was always so: did not Judas embrace and kiss Christ as he betrayed him?': Leo Abse, 'The Judas Syndrome', *Spectator*, 20 March 1982, quoted in Francis Wheen, *The Soul of Indiscretion: Tom Driberg, Poet, Philanderer, Legislator and Outlaw* (London: Fourth Estate, 2001), p. 167. Tony Judt is drily dismissive of network claims in narratives of homosexual spies, and of spies falsely accused of being homosexual – in both cases, to suit the propagandising needs of the accuser. Writing of the case of Alger Hiss and his ex-Communist accuser Whittaker Chambers, and reflecting on the fact that the former's lawyers considered using the latter's bisexuality against him, Judt writes: 'Nobody, to my knowledge, has suggested that Margarete Buber-Neumann, David Rousset, Viktor Kravchenko, or the many other European ex-Communists who spoke out about Stalinism in the 1930s and 1940s – men and women such as Victor Serge in Russia, Ruth Fischer in Germany, and Ignazio Silone in Italy, not to mention Arthur Koestler – were driven by some peculiar combination of ressentiment and repressed sexuality to betray former colleagues, embarrass friends, or avenge themselves on an inhospitable world': Tony Judt, 'An American Tragedy? The Case of Whittaker Chambers', in Tony Judt *Reappraisals: Reflections on the Forgotten Twentieth Century* (London: Vintage, 2009), pp. 299–313; p. 310. It is not as if there was any lack of other available motives for the actions people took, whether they were gay or straight. For further discussion of the association of homosexuality and espionage in a British context, see Simon Shepherd, 'Gay Sex Spy Orgy: The State's Need for Queers', in Simon Shepherd and Mick Wallis (eds), *Coming On Strong: Gay Politics and Culture* (London: Unwin Hyman, 1989), pp. 213–230. See also Alan Sinfield, *Literature, Politics and Culture in Postwar Britain* (Berkeley & Los Angeles: University of California Press, 1989), chapter 5: 'Queers, Treachery and the Literary Establishment'.

28.  Ian Collins, *John Craxton* (Farnham, Surrey: Lund Humphries, 2011), p. 132. Craxton once said, 'I love sailors and hate navies, love soldiers and hate armies' (p. 148).

29.  Norman Mailer satirised this sort of axe-grinding when he complained that 'the London literary scene had been rigged against him by a homosexual coterie dominated by' the overtly *hetero*sexual Christopher Hitchens, Martin Amis and Ian Hamilton: Christopher Hitchens, *Hitch-22: A Memoir* (London: Atlantic, 2011), p. 279 n.

30.  Quoted in John E. Malmstad and Nikolay Bogomolov, *Mikhail Kuzmin: A Life in Art* (Cambridge, Massachusetts & London: Harvard University Press, 1999), p. 142. None of those pederasts found their way into Andrei Bely's great novel *Petersburg* (1916).

31.  Quoted in Peter Stoneley, *A Queer History of the Ballet* (London & New York: Routledge, 2007), p. 93. Benton added that the typical American museum was 'run by a pretty boy with delicate wrists and a swing in his gait'.

32.  Daniel Farson, *The Gilded Gutter Life of Francis Bacon* (London: Vintage, 1994), p. 225.

33.  Valentine Cunningham, *British Writers of the Thirties* (Oxford: Oxford University Press, 1988), pp. 148, 149, 150, 151, 153, 374, 378. When Cunningham speaks of 'the' homosexual writers of the 1930s, he apparently means about six men: W.H. Auden, Christopher Isherwood, Stephen Spender, E.M. Forster, William Plomer and J.R. Ackerley.

34.  Cunningham, p. 149.

35.  Cunningham, p. 150. After the latter sentence, there is a seamless transition, without a paragraph break, from these 'buggers' to the statement: 'Misogyny was rife in the writing of this period' – followed by a list of *hetero*sexual misogynists (p. 151). Douglas Dunn's poem 'Audenesques for 1960', addressed to Auden, invokes another expression of this approach to the poet and his generation: 'I was angered once by Glaswegians dismissing you as / "The

Grand Panjandrum of the Homintern". / Poetry has too many enemies to contend with. / "A nancy poet, not a real one; and a fake socialist". / One genius tends to use another as a doormat': Douglas Dunn, *Dante's Drum-Kit* (London: Faber, 1993), p. 91. Even as late as 2007, according to Erin G. Carlston's readings of the British press, 'Auden remains reflexively tied to the Cambridge spies by a series of associations, sometimes quite romanticized, between aesthetes and intellectuals, homosexuality, a commitment to left-wing causes, and illicit conspiracy': Erin G. Carlston, *Double Agents: Espionage, Literature, and Liminal Citizens* (New York: Columbia University Press, 2013), p. 189.

36. Hermione Lee, *Virginia Woolf* (London: Chatto & Windus, 1996), pp. 613–14.

37. J.B. Priestley, 'Thoughts in the Wilderness: Block Thinking', *New Statesman and Nation* 46, 1182 (31 October 1953), pp. 515–516; p. 516. Quoted in Dan Rebellato, *1956 and All That: The Making of Modern British Drama* (London & New York: Routledge, 1999), p. 185.

38. Jonathan Croall, *John Gielgud: Matinee Idol to Movie Star* (London: Methuen, 2011), p. 223.

39. Sheridan Morley, *John G: The Authorised Biography of John Gielgud* (London: Hodder & Stoughton, 2001), pp. 97, 204, 240. Morley adds: 'The London theatre was still, in these long pre-AIDS days, a very homosexual place to live and work' (p. 241). Presumably – unless the reference to AIDS is just a gratuitous stab – he means that the epidemic fundamentally changed the sexual demographic of the industry, but nowhere does he examine this claim in detail; nor does he even refer to it again.

40. Keith Howes, *Outspoken: Keith Howes' Gay News Interviews, 1976–83* (London: Cassell, 1995), p. 33.

41. Arthur Miller, *Timebends* (London: Methuen, 1999), pp. 429–430.

42. Roger Lewis, *The Real Life of Laurence Olivier* (London: Century, 1996), pp. 106n, 107. There is one obvious omission from Lewis' list, John Gielgud; but then he was still alive at the time it was compiled, and might have bitten back. Lewis dismisses Donald Spoto's 1991 biography's 'unsubstantiated theory that Olivier was a committed homosexual – as if that had anything to do with the price of tea' (p. xii, n). Well, if the homosexuality of Tennent, Beaumont, Rattigan, Richardson and Dexter is so important, it seems reasonable to deduce that Olivier's bisexuality might also add up to more than the price of tea. That Lewis is taking a line on homosexuality more than on Olivier is revealed by his conclusion: 'Homosexuality is a mockery of nature; Olivier's duty was through acting to try and control nature' (p. 107).

43. An account that is both more scholarly and more temperate – even if it provides far more material for those who are inclined to subscribe to Roger Lewis' conspiracy theory – is offered by Dan Rebellato: 'Gay men *were* powerful in the British theatre of the forties and fifties. After all, a list that includes Terence Rattigan, Noël Coward, Ivor Novello, Rodney Ackland, John Gielgud, Max Adrian, Wynyard Browne, Michael Benthall, Cecil Beaton, Laurence Olivier, Robin Maugham, Melville Gillham, Frith Banbury, Emlyn Williams, Alan Webb, Loudon Sainthill, Eric Porter, Eric Portman, Michael MacLiammóir, Hilton Edwards, Frankie Howerd, Paul Dehn, John Van Druten, Alec MacCowan, Laurence Harvey, Richard Wattis, Kenneth Williams, Vivian Ellis, Peter Bull, R.C. Sherriff, Richard Buckle, Esmé Percy, John Cranko, Somerset Maugham, Binkie Beaumont, Benjamin Britten, Philip King, Peter Shaffer, James Agate, T.C. Worsley, Charles Laughton, Alfred Lunt, Denholm Elliott, Rupert Doone, Michael Redgrave, Robert Helpmann, Sandy Wilson, Oliver Messel and Alan Melville is not just a list of homosexual or bisexual men; it is a roll-call of one generation in British Theatre': Rebellato, p. 163. But even this longer list does not justify the hyperbole of the end of Rebellato's sentence. Apart from anything else, not all of these men are from the same 'one generation'. More importantly, looking at the wide range of roles of these very different writers, administrators, enablers and performers, one could very easily produce a much longer list of men in the same areas of British theatre who were probably *not* gay or bisexual.

44. John Osborne, *Almost a Gentleman: An Autobiography, Volume II, 1955–1966* (London: Faber, 1992), pp. 8, 9, 10, 58. The idea of Terence Rattigan's ever discriminating *in favour of* fellow homosexuals, rather than against them, seems implausible. His reaction to John Gielgud's arrest for cottaging in the autumn of 1953 was characteristically self-centred. 'There'll be no Sir Terry now,' he said: Michael Darlow and Gillian Hodson, *Terence Rattigan: The Man and His Work* (London: Quartet, 1979), p. 228. When one of the defendants in the Lord Montagu case (1953, 1954) sought refuge with him, Rattigan turned him away. Elsewhere, Osborne complained of 'Binkie Beaumont's lily empire with its praetorian guard of Godfreys, Terrys, scuttling agents, managers, poison bum-boys and their hacks': John

Osborne, *A Better Class of Person: An Autobiography, 1929–1956* (Harmondsworth: Penguin, 1982), p.142.

45. Simon Gray, *The Smoking Diaries: The Year of the Jouncer* (London: Granta, 2006), p. 263.
46. Stanley Kauffmann, 'Homosexual Drama and Its Disguises', *New York Times* (23 January 1966), section 2, p. 1. See also Doug Arrell, 'Homophobic Criticism and Its Disguises: The Case of Stanley Kauffmann', *Journal of Dramatic Theory and Criticism* 16, 2 (Spring 2002), pp. 95–110.
47. Howard Taubman, 'Not What It Seems', *New York Times* (5 November 1961), section 2, p. 1. See also Sherry, pp. 128–129.
48. Robert Patrick, 'The Inside-Outsider', in Jackson R. Bryer and Mary C. Hartig (eds), *William Inge: Essays and Reminiscences on the Plays and the Man* (Jefferson, North Carolina: McFarland, 2014), pp. 25–29; p. 2 7.
49. Howes, p. 69.
50. Winston Leyland (ed.), *Gay Sunshine Interviews, Volume One* (San Francisco: Gay Sunshine, 1978), pp. 309–325; p. 323. The misnaming of H.M. Tennent is, presumably, a mistaken transcription of Williams' often slurred speech on Whitmore's part.
51. Charles Kaiser, *The Gay Metropolis* (London: Weilenfeld & Nicolson, 1998), p. 17. See also Humphrey Burton, *Leonard Bernstein* (London: Faber, 1995), p. 43.
52. Alex Ross, *The Rest is Noise: Listening to the Twentieth Century* (London: Harper Perennial, 2009), p. 450. On this topic, he does not venture much further afield. He does add, apparently with less conviction, that 'In Britain, too, the art of composition skewed gay', but he names only Benjamin Britten and Michael Tippett.
53. Humphrey Carpenter, *Benjamin Britten: A Biography* (London: Faber, 1992), pp. 303, 313, 384–385. Michael Tippett, *Those Twentieth Century Blues: An Autobiography* (London: Pimlico, 1994), pp. 214–215. See also Michael Wilcox, *Benjamin Britten's Operas* (Bath: Absolute Press, 1997), p. 57. By the time his biography was being written, Mackerras felt he should put on record that he 'was distressed and ashamed that he had so thoughtlessly offended one who had been so good to him and whom he revered as a musician': Nancy Phelan, *Charles Mackerras: A Musicians' Musician* (London: Gollancz, 1987), p. 120.
54. Calvin Tomkins, *Off the Wall: Robert Rauschenberg and the Arts World of Our Times* (New York: Doubleday, 1980), p. 260.
55. Jill Johnston, *Jasper Johns: Privileged Information* (New York & London: Thames & Hudson, 1996), p. 144.
56. Kaiser, p. 158.
57. William J. Mann, Behind the Screen, p. 337.
58. Kaiser, p. 165.
59. Kaiser, pp. 190, 168.
60. Anonymous, 'The Homosexual in America', *Time*, 21 January 1966, pp. 40–41. Quoted in Alan Sinfield, *Out on Stage: Lesbian and Gay Theatre in the Twentieth Century* (New Haven & London: Yale University Press, 1999), p. 8.
61. Kaiser, pp. 169, 167. Vidal often returned to this point. In 1970, he wrote: 'The Homintern theory . . . is a constant obsession of certain journalists and crops up from time to time not only in the popular press but in the pages of otherwise respectable literary journals': Gore Vidal, 'Doc Reuben', in *Sexually Speaking: Collected Sex Writings* (San Francisco: Cleis Press, 1999), p. 52.
62. Anthony Haden-Guest, *The Last Party: Studio 54, Disco, and the Culture of the Night* (New York: William Morrow, 1997), pp. 56–57. See also David Ehrenstein, *Open Secret: Gay Hollywood, 1928–2000* (New York: Perennial, 2000), pp. 110–112. Although rejected for service in the Vietnam War because he ticked the 'Yes' box next to the homosexuality question, David Geffen did not officially come out until 18 November 1992: Tom King, *David Geffen: A Biography of New Hollywood* (London: Hutchinson, 2000), pp. 63, 489. Elsewhere, we are told that Roy Cohn had access to the Reagan administration via a 'lavender Mafia': Nicholas von Hoffman, *Citizen Cohn: The Scandalous Life and Times of Roy Cohn, Lawyer, Fixer, Destroyer* (London: Abacus, 1989), p. 423. In a major discussion of the infiltration of the American power elite by members of minority groups, lesbians and gay men are described as only being able to gain entry 'by asserting as many similarities as possible and by managing differences that might rekindle discomfort. Most of all, they must behave in traditionally masculine or feminine ways': Richard L. Zweigenhaft and G. William Domhoff, *Diversity in the Power Elite: Have Women and Minorities Reached the Top?* (New Haven & London: Yale University Press, 1998), p. 174.

63. Jens Rydström, 'Haijby, Kurt', in Robert Aldrich and Garry Wotherspoon, *Who's Who in Gay and Lesbian History from Antiquity to World War II* (London & New York: Routledge, 2001), pp. 196–197.

64. Zhisui Li, *The Private Life of Chairman Mao: The Memoirs of Mao's Personal Physician* (London: Arrow, 1996), pp. 358–359.

65. Sherry, p. 54.

66. In some notorious cases, though, these homophobes were themselves queer. Perhaps it would not be entirely perverse, or if perverse rationally so, to claim that the McCarthyite assault on Communists and homosexuals in the USA in the 1950s, spearheaded by Joseph McCarthy and Roy Cohn, with the fervent support of J. Edgar Hoover, was indeed a homosexual conspiracy.

67. Quoted in Stoneley, p. 93.

68. Richard Davenport-Hines, *A Night at the Majestic: Proust and the Great Modernist Dinner Party of 1922* (London: Faber, 2007), p. 193.

69. Carole Seymour-Jones gives an account of the Eliot–Verdenal relationship in her biography of Eliot's first wife, *Painted Shadow: A Life of Vivienne Eliot* (London: Constable, 2001), pp. 49–54. Other intense relationships with young men followed, including one with a German known as Jack, whose bad behaviour disrupted the poet's marital home life (pp. 359–362). With contrasting brevity, Robert Crawford writes: 'there is no evidence that Tom [Eliot] and Jean Verdenal slept together or even that their mutual attraction was essentially homoerotic'. He adds, rather oddly: 'Certainly they liked each other enough to be daft with one another': Robert Crawford, *Young Eliot: From St Louis to* The Waste Land (London: Cape, 2015), pp. 155–156.

70. On the proliferation of homosexual subcultures in late-nineteenth-century cities of many nations, see Graham Robb, *Strangers: Homosexual Love in the Nineteenth Century* (London: Picador, 2003), pp. 156–167. Julie Abraham opens her account of homosexual metropolitanism with a bold claim: 'My fundamental assertion is that homosexuals became, over the course of the past two centuries, simultaneously model citizens of the modern city and avatars of the urban; that is, models of the city itself': Julie Abraham, *Metropolitan Lovers: The Homosexuality of Cities* (Minneapolis & London: University of Minnesota Press, 2008), pp. xviii–xix.

71. Marcel Proust, *Cities of the Plain, Part One* (London: Chatto & Windus, 1968), pp. 44–45.

72. Berlin acquired the Spree nickname in France after the Eulenburg scandal. London: see Morris B. Kaplan, *Sodom on the Thames: Sex, Love, and Scandal in Wilde Times* (Ithaca, New York: Cornell University Press, 2005). Paris: Arthur Koestler refers to the city he first visited in 1929, when he was 24, in his memoir *Arrow in the Blue* (first page of chapter XXIII). New York: Frank O'Hara used the Hudson nickname in his poem 'Commercial Variations'. Rome: in a historical novel, Simon Peter (Saint Peter) asks, 'Has Rome become Babylon? . . . Has the capital of the world degenerated into a new Sodom on Tiber?': Paul L. Meier, *The Flames of Rome* (Grand Rapids, Michigan: Kregel, 1981), p. 279. More recently, this latter name is more often used by Protestants to denote the Vatican City.

73. Alan Sinfield, *The Wilde Century: Effeminacy, Oscar Wilde and the Queer Moment* (London: Cassell, 1994). David Halperin, *One Hundred Years of Homosexuality, and Other Essays on Greek Love* (New York & London: Routledge, 1990). Koestenbaum, *Double Talk: The Erotics of Male Literary Collaboration*, p. 128. Dominique Fernandez, *Le rapt de Ganymède* (Paris: Bernard Grasset, 1989), p. 83.

74. Susan Sontag, 'Notes on "Camp"', *Partisan Review* 31, 4 (Fall, 1964), pp. 515–530; p. 529. George Steiner, 'Eros and Idiom', in *On Difficulty, and Other Essays* (Oxford: Oxford University Press, 1978), pp. 95–136; p. 115. Jeffrey Meyers, *Homosexuality and Literature, 1890–1930* (London: Athlone, 1977), p. 10.

75. Laxness: Gunði Thorlacius Jóhannesson, *The History of Iceland* (Santa Barbara, California: Greenwood, 2013), p. 100. Oxford in the 1920s: Alan Pryce-Jones, *The Bonus of Laughter* (London: Hamish Hamilton, 1987), p. 49; see also Humphrey Carpenter, *The Brideshead Generation: Evelyn Waugh and His Generation* (London: Faber, 1989), p. 81. Wright and Duchamp: Jonathan Weinberg, *Speaking for Vice: Homosexuality in the Art of Charles Demuth, Marsden Hartley, and the First American Avant-Garde* (New Haven & London: Yale University Press, 1993), p. 205.

76. Raymond Chandler, *Later Novels and Other Writings* (New York: Library of America, 1995), p. 626.

77. Truman Capote liked to play International Daisy Chain, a gossip game establishing unlikely links by tracing chains of people who had had affairs, or sexual encounters at least, with each other. For instance, one chain led from Henry James to Ida Lupino, by way of Hugh Walpole, Harold Nicolson, the Hon. David Herbert, John C. Wilson, Noël Coward and Louis Hayward. Capote's favourite chain led from Cab Calloway to Adolf Hitler: see Gerald Clarke, *Capote: A Biography* (London: Cardinal, 1989), p. 213. Such matters are beyond the limited scope of the present book.
78. Michael Holroyd, *Lytton Strachey* (London: Vintage, 1994), p. 349.
79. E.M. Forster, *Two Cheers for Democracy* (Harmondsworth: Penguin, 1965), p. 76.

## Chapter 2: Scandal and After

1. Ford Madox Ford, *Memories and Impressions* (Harmondsworth: Penguin, 1979), pp. 73, 78. Wilde was convicted of 'gross indecency' under the terms of the 'Labouchere amendment', Section 11 of the Criminal Law Amendment Act 1885, and sentenced to two years' hard labour.
2. A.L. Rowse, *Homosexuals in History: A Study of Ambivalence in Society, Literature and the Arts* (London: Weidenfeld & Nicolson, 1977), p. 188. Rowse's gratuitous sneer at Wilde's Irish origins is characteristic of hostile responses to his behaviour from British homosexual men: his Irishness can be substituted for his homosexuality as the blameworthy aspect of his character. Over the years, Wilde has been blamed for many things. In later life, the English *flâneur* Quentin Crisp would wryly hold it against him that 'he dragged the fair name of Mr Plato into this sordid case': Tim Fountain, *Quentin Crisp* (London: Absolute Press, 2002), p. 30. Graham Robb has argued the importance of not attributing the Wilde debacle solely to homophobia, still less to homophobic unanimity. Many people sympathised with Wilde and continued to admire him; and those who took against him did so, or had already done so before the trials, for many reasons other than his sexual behaviour: his tendency to ridicule social norms, for instance, and his Irishness – see Graham Robb, *Strangers: Homosexual Love in the Nineteenth Century* (London: Picador, 2003), pp. 36–39.
3. Ann Thwaite, *Edmund Gosse: A Literary Landscape* (London: Tempus, 2007), p. 367.
4. The lesbian couple Katherine Bradley and Edith Cooper – aunt and niece, who called themselves, jointly, 'Michael Field' – were able to reconcile their divided cultural loyalties when it came to mourning. Emma Donoghue writes: 'As fussy Tory spinsters and free-thinking suffragist Aesthetes, they wept for the deaths of both Queen Victoria and Oscar Wilde': Emma Donoghue, *We Are Michael Field* (Bath: Absolute Press, 1998), p. 9.
5. Timothy d'Arch Smith, *Love in Earnest: Some Notes on the Lives and Writings of English 'Uranian' Poets from 1889 to 1930* (London: Routledge & Kegan Paul, 1970), p. 21. Hugh Kenner identifies Wilde's death as a crucial moment, one of the births of Modernism: 'Joyce seems to have begun what was finally the *Portrait* [*of the Artist as a Young Man*] just after Oscar Wilde died; was it to have offered a lower-class Catholic analogue to Wilde's upper-middle-class Protestant career[?]': Hugh Kenner, *The Pound Era* (London: Faber, 1975), pp. 272–273.
6. Rupert Croft-Cooke, *Feasting with Panthers: A New Consideration of Some Late Victorian Writers* (London: W.H. Allen, 1967), pp. 285, 288, 290.
7. Croft-Cooke, p. 170. Later in the book, Croft-Cooke writes: 'If we have had enough of Wilde we have had more than enough of every kind of literature dealing with homosexuality, which is not a subject in itself of remarkable interest and nearly always a bore in fiction' (p. 259).
8. Michael Paterson, *Winston Churchill: Personal Accounts of the Great Leader at War* (Newton Abbot, Devon: David & Charles, 2005), pp. 86–88.
9. G. Lowes Dickinson, *The Autobiography of G. Lowes Dickinson, and Other Unpublished Writings* (London: Duckworth, 1973), p. 104.
10. Mark Amory, *Lord Berners: The Last Eccentric* (London: Chatto & Windus, 1998), p. 31.
11. Michael Davidson, *The World, the Flesh and Myself* (London: GMP, 1985), p. 71.
12. Cyril Connolly, *Enemies of Promise* (Harmondsworth: Penguin, 1961), p. 191.
13. Bevis Hillier, *Young Betjeman* (London: John Murray, 2003), p. 117.
14. Anton Dolin, *Last Words: A Final Autobiography* (London: Century, 1985), pp. 2, 16. Dolin did, indeed, become another Bosie: for when he joined the Ballets Russes de Monte Carlo in November 1923, he also, reluctantly, became Serge Diaghilev's lover (pp. 38–39). For his next birthday, on 27 July 1924, Diaghilev gave him a copy of Thomas Mann's *Death in Venice*.

15. E.M. Forster, *Maurice* (Harmondsworth: Penguin, 1972), p. 139.
16. Brigid Brophy, *Prancing Novelist: A Defence of Fiction in the Form of a Critical Biography in Praise of Ronald Firbank* (London: Macmillan, 1973), pp. 244, 245. It is also important to remember that, as Alan Sinfield has convincingly argued, 'Until the Wilde trials, effeminacy and homosexuality did not correlate in the way they have done subsequently' in Britain and elsewhere – see Alan Sinfield, *The Wilde Century: Effeminacy, Oscar Wilde and the Queer Moment* (New York: Columbia University Press, 1994), p. 4.
17. André Gide, *Corydon: Four Socratic Dialogues* (New York: Farrar, Straus & Co., 1950), p. 3.
18. Robert Liddell, *Cavafy: A Critical Biography* (London: Duckworth, 1974), p. 188.
19. Mitt Machlin, *The Gossip Wars: An Exposé of the Scandal Era* (no place specified: no publisher specified, 1981), p. 64.
20. Richard Davenport-Hynes, *A Night at the Majestic: Proust and the Great Modernist Dinner Party of 1922* (London: Faber, 2007), p. 191.
21. Barth David Schwartz, *Pasolini Requiem* (New York: Pantheon, 1992), p. 197. See also Enzo Siciliano, *Pasolini* (London: Bloomsbury, 1987), p. 53. Pasolini to Mauri: Pier Paolo Pasolini, *The Letters of Pier Paolo Pasolini, Volume I: 1940–1954* (London: Quartet, 1992), p. 325.
22. Sven Lindqvist, *Desert Divers* (London: Granta, 2000), pp. 100–101. Lindqvist rewrites the ending of Gide's *The Immoralist* from the viewpoint of the narrator's wife Marceline, and then from that of the child prostitute Meriem.
23. James Merrill, *A Different Person: A Memoir* (San Francisco: HarperCollins, 1994), pp. 38, 9.
24. Brophy, p. 243.
25. Pål Bjørby, 'The Prison House of Sexuality: Homosexuality in Herman Bang Scholarship', *Scandanavian Studies* 58 (1986), pp. 223–255; p. 228.
26. Eisfeld would play Jokanaan in Max Reinhart's production of Wilde's *Salomé* in Berlin on 29 September 1903.
27. Henning Bech says of *Mikaël*: 'It is the most pronounced portrayal of homosexuality precisely because it does not speak of homosexuality. It is the exposition of homosexuality's most common mode of being in modern societies: the dialectics between presence and absence, knowing and ignoring, desire and denial': Henning Bech, *When Men Meet: Homosexuality and Modernity* (London: Polity, 1997), p. 38. One response to this novel, which had the collateral effect of implicating Bang, however remotely, in the Wilde case, was to accuse him of having plagiarised *The Picture of Dorian Gray*. When Bang was under attack for his writings about homosexuality, Björnstjerne Björnson came to his defence. One of the most distinguished writers of his time – he wrote the lyrics of the Norwegian national anthem and won the Nobel Prize for Literature in 1903 – Björnson was fascinated by the topic of male love and had a number of close friendships with homosexual men.
28. Clark L. Taylor Jr, 'Mexican Gaylife in Historical Perspective', *Gay Sunshine* 26/27 (Winter 1975–1976), pp. 1–3; p. 3. Taylor's interlocutor adds that Wilde's influence dated from the 1920s. In the 1890s, 'the influence was French, not English. The Mexican Gay people were trying to be French and decadent in the symbolistic image. They tried to be decadent like Montesquiou' (p. 3).
29. Julio Cortázar, 'To Reach Lezama Lima', in José Lezama Lima, *Selections* (Berkeley, California: University of California Press, 2005), pp. 138–166; p. 149.
30. Jaime Manrique, *Eminent Maricones: Arenas, Lorca, Puig and Me* (Madison, Wisconsin: University of Wisconsin Press, 1999), pp. 27–28. The earlier Colombian writer Bernardo Arias Trujillo, whose first novel, *Sodom's Way: Confessions of a Homosexual* (*Por los caminos de Sodoma: Confesiones de un homosexual*), was published in 1932 under the pseudonym Sir Edgard Dixon (*sic*), also published a translation of Wilde's *The Picture of Dorian Gray*.
31. Stefano Evangelista, 'Introduction: Oscar Wilde, European by Sympathy' in Stefano Evangelista (ed.), *The Reception of Oscar Wilde in Europe* (London: Continuum, 2010), p. 18.
32. Robert Vilain, 'Tragedy and the Apostle of Beauty: The Early Literary Reception of Oscar Wilde in Germany and Austria', in Evangelista, pp. 173–188; p. 179.
33. Evgenii Bershtein, '"Next to Christ": Oscar Wilde in Russian Modernism', in Evangelista, pp. 285–300; p. 285.
34. John E. Malmstad and Nikolay Bogomolov, *Mikhail Kuzmin: A Life in Art* (Cambridge, Massachusetts, & London: Harvard University Press, 1999), p.105.
35. Simon Karlinsky, 'Russia's Gay Literature and Culture: The Impact of the October Revolution', in Martin Bauml Duberman, Martha Vicinus and George Chauncey, Jr (eds), *Hidden From*

*History: Reclaiming the Gay and Lesbian Past* (London & New York: Penguin, 1991), pp. 347–364; p. 361.

36. Evangelista, p. 289.
37. Bryan Connon, *Somerset Maugham and the Maugham Dynasty* (London: Sinclair-Stevenson, 1997), p. 31.
38. Frederic Raphael, *Somerset Maugham and His World* (London: Book Club Associates, 1978), p. 63.
39. Brophy, p. 247. I return to the 'open secret' in Chapter Ten.
40. Richard Tedeschi (ed.), *Selected Letters of André Gide and Dorothy Bussy* (Oxford: Oxford University Press, 1983), p. 286. Bussy was referring to H. Montgomery Hyde (ed.), *The Trials of Oscar Wilde* (London: Hodge, 1948). The other talked-about book was Graham Greene's novel *The Heart of the Matter*.
41. Edmund White, *My Lives* (London: Bloomsbury, 2005), p. 182.
42. Peter Wildeblood, *Against the Law* (Harmondsworth: Penguin, 1957), p. 11. It should come as no surprise that Wilde even found his way into people's sexual lives, for better or worse. According to his autobiographical novel *In the Purely Pagan Sense*, John Lehmann once had a boyfriend who insisted on their acting out fantasy roles in their love-making: master and slave-boy in ancient Greece, squire and page in a medieval castle, and so on. 'One afternoon he suddenly decided that we were exiles in a café in Boulogne at the turn of the century and cried out, "Look, Oscar, there's Robbie Ross coming down the street! Oh, I do hope he's got some more money for us." But this didn't somehow work quite as well [as the other fantasies], perhaps *because it was too real*, and it was not added to the repertoire': John Lehmann, *In the Purely Pagan Sense* (London: GMP, 1985), pp. 222–223. My italics.
43. John Lucas, *Next Year Will Be Better: A Memoir of England in the 1950s* (Nottingham: Five Leaves, 2010), p. 254.
44. H.H. Munro, *The Penguin Complete Saki* (London: Penguin, 1982), p. 24. For all that the lumpen majority are excluded from the fun and its potentially disastrous consequences, as its audience they accrue the benefit of the vicarious entertainment it provides. John Carey has said of Saki's work in general, 'This kind of cruel wit, which can be matched in Oscar Wilde, and later in Evelyn Waugh, who greatly admired Saki, was a new departure in English literature, and it represented a response to a new pressure – the encroaching mass, with its demands for common human sympathy': John Carey, *The Intellectuals and the Masses: Pride and Prejudice among the Literary Intelligentsia, 1880–1939* (London: Faber, 1992), p. 54.
45. Ian Harvey, *To Fall Like Lucifer* (London: Sidgwick & Jackson, 1971), p. 128. Michael Bronski, a member of the later, gay-liberationist generation, wrote: 'Oscar Wilde is perhaps the most important figure in the history of gay sensibility': *Culture Clash: The Making of Gay Sensibility* (Boston: South End Press, 1984), p. 58.
46. News travels far, if not necessarily fast. In Yukio Mishima's novel *Forbidden Colours* (*Kinjiki*, 1951, 1953), Nobutaka Kaburagi (himself a rich homosexual) asks Shunsuké, 'Do you know, sir, why the third president of the Krupp Steel Works committed suicide before the First World War? A love that turned all values upside down took over his sense of dignity and destroyed all the balance by which he had supported himself in society': Yukio Mishima, *Forbidden Colours* (Harmondsworth: Penguin, 1971), p. 34.
47. George D. Painter, *Marcel Proust: A Biography, Volume II* (London: Chatto & Windus, 1965), p. 106.
48. Baron Corvo, Frederick Rolfe, *The Venice Letters* (London: Cecil Woolf, 1987), p. 33. Rolfe was not present on this occasion, but was reporting what he had been told by one of the ex-boys of the establishment, a 16-year-old stevedore, Amadeo Amadei.
49. Philip Hoare, *Wilde's Last Stand: Decadence, Conspiracy and the First World War* (London: Duckworth, 1997), p. 56.
50. Hoare, *Wilde's Last Stand*, pp. 57–58.
51. Hoare, *Wilde's Last Stand*, p. 91.
52. Hoare, *Wilde's Last Stand*, p. 141.
53. When E.M. Forster's Maurice consults a hypnotist in the hope of being cured of his homosexuality, Mr Lasker Jones offers no cure but only a rational suggestion: 'I'm afraid I can only advise you to live in some country that has adopted the Code Napoleon . . . France or Italy, for instance. There homosexuality is no longer criminal' – Forster, *Maurice*, p. 184.
54. Connon, *Somerset Maugham*, p. 67.

55. As Gerald Haxton's case reminds us, exile from certain countries in certain others had its own compensations and rewards. A life of luxury in the south of France could well distract one from the grief of missing London, especially if one's lover was rich enough, as Maugham was, to keep a villa filled with friends old and new. As well as sunshine, exile from the North in the South also gave access to the freer sexual morality of the Mediterranean rim, where Catholicism and Islam created such a different atmosphere from the hyperborean chill of Protestantism. Moreover, in the minor exile of tourism, being caught by the police of a foreign country often had only minor consequences. On the night of 28 January 1932, in Taxco, Mexico, the American poet Hart Crane was caught in flagrante delicto with the houseboy of a friend and had to spend the night in jail. (Not for the first time. On previous occasions he had been banged up overnight for disorderly drunkenness.) The matter was expedited in the morning when Crane was told to get out of town.

56. In 1893, Martin Kok was arrested for sexual offences against a 16-year-old butcher's boy, but released after three weeks, since the relationship had not, in actuality, contravened any law.

57. Quoted in H. Montgomery Hyde, *The Other Love: An Historical and Contemporary Survey of Homosexuality in Britain* (London: Mayflower, 1972), pp. 172–173.

58. In a letter to Dr Trigant Burrow dated 13 July 1927, D.H. Lawrence wrote: 'I'll try and find your paper on the "Genesis and Meaning of Homosexuality" – you should have said "Genesis and Exodus". It is possible that this latter remark is a reference to the aftermath of the Wilde trials: D.H. Lawrence, *Selected Letters* (Harmondsworth: Penguin, 1950), pp. 164–165.

59. Diana Souhami, *The Trials of Radclyffe Hall* (London: Weidenfeld & Nicolson, 1998), pp. 105–112. One writer concluded, even as late as 1975: 'She had made the same mistake that Oscar Wilde had made. Egotism is a symptom of the disturbed psyche, and the invert, as Havelock Ellis had shown, finds an irresistible attraction in taking risks': Lovat Dickson, *Radclyffe Hall at the Well of Loneliness: A Sapphic Chronicle* (London & Toronto: Collins, 1975), p. 95.

60. David Garnett (ed.), *Selected Letters of T.E. Lawrence* (London: Reprint Society, 1941), p. 296.

61. Souhami, *Trials*, p. 171. Others have made similar uses of Wilde's works. In prison again after a spell of freedom during which he had met many prominent artistic figures in Paris, Jean Genet had much to complain of. His contacts with the outside world had spoilt him for prison. He wrote from jail, 'Pas de lettre de Jean Cocteau. Ni de Jean Marais. Ni de Picasso.' But then, a few days later, 'Reçu une lettre de Cocteau. Une autre de Marais. Très gentil.' He railed against Picasso again when forced to erase the pornographic murals he had executed on the walls of his cell. Everyone, including even art itself, was letting him down. At the beginning of July 1943 he wrote that he had been reading Oscar Wilde's *De Profundis*. He seems to have been creating an elevated, tragic sense of his own fate: Jean Genet, *Lettres au petit Franz (1943–1944)* (Paris: Le Promeneur, 2000), pp. 47, 49, 84, 75.

62. Radclyffe Hall, *The Well of Loneliness* (London: Virago, 1982); Forster, *Maurice*, p. 210.

63. Souhami, *Trials*, p. 178.

64. Souhami, *Trials*, p. 185.

65. Souhami, *Trials*, p. 203.

66. Souhami, *Trials*, p. 207.

67. Beverley Nichols, *The Sweet and Twenties* (London: Weidenfeld & Nicolson, 1958), p. 104.

68. Quentin Crisp, *The Naked Civil Servant* (London: Fontana, 1977), p. 25.

69. Joan Schenkar, *Truly Wilde: The Unsettling Story of Dolly Wilde, Oscar's Unusual Niece* (London: Virago, 2000), pp. 89, 8, 217.

70. See Kate Summerscale, *The Queen of Whale Cay* (London: Fourth Estate, 1997).

71. Schenkar, pp. 190–191.

72. Matthew J. Bruccoli, *Some Sort of Epic Grandeur: The Life of F. Scott Fitzgerald* (London: Cardinal, 1991), p. 325.

73. Schenkar, p. 124.

74. However, not completely blind to male charms herself, she was enchanted for a while by Jean Bourgoint, Jean Cocteau's male *enfant terrible*. Jean and his sister Jeanne were the models for Paul and Elisabeth in Cocteau's novel *Les Enfants Terribles* (1930).

75. Cyril Scott, *Bone of Contention: Life Story and Confessions* (London: Aquarian Press, 1969), pp. 34–35.

76. Michael De-la-Noy, *Denton Welch: The Making of a Writer* (Harmondsworth: Viking, 1984), p. 47. Jocelyn Brooke (ed.), *The Denton Welch Journals* (London: Hamish Hamilton, 1973), p. 82.

77. John Glassco, *Memoirs of Montparnasse* (Toronto & New York: Oxford University Press, 1970), p. 203. The matter in parentheses remains unexplained.

78. Samuel M. Steward, *Chapters from an Autobiography* (San Francisco: Grey Fox, 1981), p. 51.
79. Anthony Powell, *Under Review: Further Writings on Writers 1946–1989* (London: Heinemann, 1991), p. 37.
80. Mary Hyde (ed.), *Bernard Shaw and Alfred Douglas: A Correspondence* (London: John Murray, 1982), p. 120.
81. Mary Hyde, p. 122.
82. Michael Tippett, *Those Twentieth Century Blues: An Autobiography* (London: Pimlico, 1994), p. 53.
83. Hesketh Pearson, *The Life of Oscar Wilde* (London: Methuen, 1946), p. 1. Arthur Ransome's *Oscar Wilde: A Critical Study* was published in 1912.
84. Roger Shattuck, *The Banquet Years: The Origins of the Avant-Garde in France, 1885 to World War I* (New York: Vintage, revised edn 1968), p. 197.

## Chapter 3: The Northern Exotic

1. Vladimir Nabokov rather proudly recorded the fact that his father had coined the 'convenient' Russian term for 'homosexual', *ravnopolïy*, in a 1902 essay, 'Carnal Crimes': Vladimir Nabokov, *Speak, Memory* (Harmondsworth, Middlesex: Penguin, 1969), p. 139.
2. Vitaly Chernetsky, 'Rozanov, Vasily Vasil'evich', in Robert Aldrich and Garry Wotherspoon (eds), *Who's Who in Gay and Lesbian History: From Antiquity to World War II* (London & New York: Routledge, 2001), pp. 384–386. I am grateful to Catriona Kelly for first drawing Rozanov to my attention.
3. Lindsay F. Watton, 'Constructs of Sin and Sodom in Russian Modernism, 1906–1909', *Journal of the History of Sexuality* 4, 3 (1994), pp. 369–394; p. 384.
4. Watton, p. 386.
5. Leon Trotsky, *Literature and Revolution* (Ann Arbor: University of Michigan Press, 1960), pp. 42–43, 42. For the ultimate dismissal, Trotsky invoked the New Testament narrative: 'Rozanov sold himself publicly for pieces of silver' (p. 44). Even Rozanov's staunchest academic defenders eventually prove squeamish, as when George F. Putnam writes that 'Rozanov is tender to the point of embarrassment when he speaks of love': 'Vasilii V. Rozanov: Sex, Marriage and Christianity', *Canadian Slavic Studies* 5, 3 (Fall 1971), pp. 301–326; p. 320.
6. Simon Karlinsky, 'Russia's Gay Literature and Culture: The Impact of the October Revolution', in Martin Bauml Duberman, Martha Vicinus and George Chauncey, Jr (eds), *Hidden From History: Reclaiming the Gay and Lesbian Past* (London and New York: Penguin, 1991), pp. 347–364; p. 360. My italics. Making the same point elsewhere, Karlinsky goes on to mention the emigration of Marina Tsvetaeva, the critic Georgy Adamovich, poet Anatoly Steiger and poet Valery Pereleshin – see Simon Karlinsky, 'Introduction' to Kevin Moss (ed.), *Out of the Blue: Russia's Hidden Gay Heritage, An Anthology* (San Francisco: Gay Sunshine, 1997), pp. 15–26; p. 25.
7. Gordon McVay, *Esenin: A Life* (London: Hodder & Stoughton, 1976), p. 68.
8. Moss, p. 153.
9. John Glad, 'Preface' to Nikolai Klyuev, *Poems* (Ann Arbor, Michigan: Ardis, 1977), p. xiv. Esenin's much-anthologised suicide note, which he transcribed in his own blood before killing himself, is an ardent valediction addressed to a friend. As translated by Robert Chandler and Anthony Rudolf, it begins: 'Farewell, dear friend, farewell – / you're present in my heart. / We'll meet again, the stars foretell, / though now we have to part': Robert Chandler, Boris Dralyuk and Irina Mashinski (eds), *The Penguin Book of Russian Poetry* (London: Penguin, 2015), p. 349.
10. Nikos Kazantzakis, *Report to Greco* (London: Faber, 1973), pp. 396, 398.
11. Klyuev, pp. 14–15, 18, 32.
12. Trotsky, pp. 60–61, 66. When Klyuev died in exile in Siberia in 1937, his ex-lover Nikolai Arkhipov preserved his correspondence and unpublished poems, but they all vanished when Arkhipov was himself later arrested.
13. Mikhail Kuzmin, *Wings* (London: Hesperus, 2007), pp. 14, 28–29. Vladimir Nabokov took the name of Vanya Smurov for Vanya and Smurov, two characters in his novel *The Eye*, the first version of which was written in Berlin in 1930. The book's narrator watches Smurov closely, and is finally revealed to *be* him. A letter he reads denounces Smurov as one of the class of 'sexual lefties': a homosexual man with a platonic passion for a woman, Vanya – see Vladimir Nabokov, *The Eye* (London: Penguin, 1992), pp. 85–86.

14. John E. Malmstad and Nikolay Bogomolov, *Mikhail Kuzmin: A Life in Art* (Cambridge, Massachusetts & London: Harvard University Press, 1999), pp. 30–31, 35, 42.
15. Malmstad and Bogomolov, pp. 81, 138–139, 321–323.
16. George Reavey, 'Russian Poetry: Introduction', in Willis Barnstone et al. (eds), *Modern European Poetry* (Toronto, New York & London: Bantam, 1966), pp. 371–373; p. 372.
17. Simon Karlinsky, *Marina Tsvetaeva: The Woman, Her World and Her Poetry* (Cambridge: Cambridge Unviersity Press, 1986), p. 51.
18. Karlinsky, *Marina Tsvetaeva*, p. 208.
19. Sophia Parnok died in August 1933, amply supported by the woman who had been her lover for eight years, Olga Tsuberbiller, her ex-lover Liudmila Erarskaya, and her last lover Nina Vedeneeva.
20. Karlinsky, *Marina Tsvetaeva*, p. 211.
21. Diana Lewis Burgin, 'Mother Nature Versus the Amazons: Marina Tsvetaeva and Female Same-Sex Love', *Journal of the History of Sexuality* 6, 1 (1995), pp. 62–88; p. 72.
22. Burgin, p. 88.
23. Viktoria Schweitzer, *Tsvetaeva* (London: Harvill, 1992), p. 98. Elaine Feinstein, 'Introduction' to Marina Tsvetaeva, *Bride of Ice: New Selected Poems* (Manchester: Carcanet, 2009), pp. ix–xix; p. x.
24. Brigid Brophy, *Prancing Novelist: A Defence of Fiction in the Form of a Critical Biography in Praise of Ronald Firbank* (London: Macmillan, 1973), p. 247.
25. Simon Karlinsky, 'Introduction: Russia's Gay Literature and History', in Moss (ed.), p. 22.
26. In 1922, Duncan married Sergei Esenin, eighteen years her junior. The marriage lasted a year.
27. Richard Buckle, *Diaghilev* (London: Hamish Hamilton, 1984), p. 146.
28. Buckle, *Diaghilev*, p. 172.
29. Buckle, *Diaghilev*, p. 192.
30. Buckle, *Diaghilev*, p. 208.
31. Buckle, *Diaghilev*, p. 224.
32. Buckle, *Diaghilev*, p. 226.
33. According to some commentators, the incipiently heterosexual Nijinsky was expressing himself in ways which were not apparent to Diaghilev: 'The *Faun* expresses an awakening longing in one of nature's creatures for members of the opposite sex. Diaghilev seems to have missed the importance of this point – had he not done so, it would certainly have given him cause for concern, if not alarm': Richard Philp and Mary Whitney, *Danseur: The Male in Ballet* (New York: McGraw-Hill, 1977), p. 66.
34. Diane Solway, *Nureyev: His Life* (London: Weidenfeld & Nicolson, 1998), pp. 362–363.
35. Buckle, *Diaghilev*, p. 236.
36. Léonide Massine, *My Life in Ballet* (London: Macmillan, 1968), p. 77.
37. Massine bought the largest of the islands, Gallo Lungo, in 1922, and, with design advice from Le Corbusier, built a house there. The island was bought by Rudolf Nureyev in 1988, after Massine's death.
38. Buckle, *Diaghilev*, p. 350.
39. Buckle, *Diaghilev*, p. 409.
40. Buckle, *Diaghilev*, pp. 417, 436.
41. Virginia Nicholson, *Among the Bohemians: Experiments in Living, 1900–1939* (London: Penguin, 2003), p. 46.
42. Lincoln Kirstein, *Mosaic: Memoirs* (New York: Farrar, Straus & Giroux, 1994), pp. 212–213.
43. Peter Stoneley, *A Queer History of the Ballet* (London & New York: Routledge, 2007), p. 77. A much cruder account of the influence of the male dancers in the Ballets Russes runs as follows: 'Diaghilev's own homosexuality . . . left its stamp on ballet and created a lasting question about male dancers, whose public image has for years been unfairly regarded as homosexual': Joy Melville, *Diaghilev and Friends* (London: Haus, 2009), p. 33. On the theme of homosexuality, Jennifer Homans moves outward from the Ballets Russes to the broader culture: 'homosexuality at the time was not only a personal preference, it was also a cultural stance: against bourgeois morality, with its stiffly constraining style and etiquette. It was also an assertion of freedom – freedom for a man to appear "feminine" or (in Nijinsky's case) androgynous, perhaps, but above all to be experimental and follow inner instincts and desires rather than social rules and conventions. It is no accident that so many twentieth-century modern artists and those involved with dance in particular were homosexual, or that sexuality was a genuine source of artistic inspiration': Jennifer Homans, *Apollo's Angels: A History of Ballet* (London: Granta, 2010), p. 306.

44. Alexander Schouvaloff, *The Art of Ballets Russes* (New Haven & London: Yale University Press, 1997), p. 10.
45. See Steven G. Marks, *How Russia Shaped the Modern World: From Art to Anti-Semitism, Ballet to Bolshevism* (Princeton, New Jersey: Princeton University Press, 2003), pp. 199–202.
46. Erik Näslund, *Rolf de Maré: Art Collector, Ballet Director, Museum Creator* (Alton, Hampshire: Dance Books, 2009), p. 224.
47. Bengt Häger, *Ballets Suédois* (London: Thames & Hudson, 1990), p. 280.
48. Näslund, *Rolf de Maré* pp. 508–509. In 1931 he bought the Cotswold Estate, a coffee plantation in Kenya, eventually having to sell it during the Mau-Mau rebellion, in 1957.
49. Ronald Bergan, *Sergei Eisenstein: A Life in Conflict* (London: Warner, 1999), pp. 161, 122.
50. Bergan, pp. 119, 167. The reference is to Marie Seton, *Sergei M. Eisenstein: A Biography* (London: Bodley Head, 1952).
51. On 4 March 1930 he was given two weeks to leave the country, but his permission to stay was subsequently extended.
52. Bergan, p. 185.
53. Bergan, p. 119.
54. Another Russian who had to move to Paris in order to flourish, both professionally and personally, was Romain de Tirtoff, who came from an affluent naval background in St Petersburg. When he first started publishing early versions of what would become his trademark Orientalist fashion designs, to protect his family's crusty reputation he did so under a pseudonym derived from the French pronunciation of his initials, Erté. He went to Paris in 1912, at the end of his teens, and moved in with his lover, Prince Nicholas Ouroussoff, for the next two decades, until the latter's death in 1933. Like Lempicka a major figure in the art deco movement, Erté gained a popular international reputation when *Harper's Bazaar* adopted his style as theirs, using almost 250 of his designs for their front covers. For a short time in the 1920s, he also designed costumes for Hollywood movies. A prolific survivor, he was still working in Paris when art deco came back into style in the mid-1960s.
55. Laura Claridge, *Tamara de Lempicka: A Life of Deco and Decadence* (London: Bloomsbury, 2001), p. 83.
56. Claridge, p. 98.
57. Claridge, p. 103.
58. D'Annunzio was bisexual. Natalie Barney once said of him, 'He was not just a man who loved women, he was a man who loved.' Or, as his biographer Philippe Jullian puts it, 'the hero, like Jupiter, after so many Ledas, Danaës and Europas, had his Ganymedes': Philippe Jullian, *D'Annunzio* (London: Pall Mall, 1972), p. 345. He is known to have consorted with young men at Fiume, where he was dictator from 1919 to 1921, and later in his stronghold at Gardone. Reminiscing about him on Italian radio in 1956, Jean Cocteau said: 'Every day I go to talk about him with the boys in the Piazza di Spagna' – ostensibly an innocent remark about how widely the great man was still being read by ordinary Italians, but, since the boys he refers to would have been hustlers plying their trade, Cocteau was mischievously referring to the more direct contact an earlier generation of such boys had with d'Annunzio (Jullian, p. 356). As much as he admired both sexes, this dynamic little egotist was also admired by both. Indeed, when he went to Paris in 1910, even the haughtily stand-offish Robert de Montesquiou 'was smitten at first sight': Frances Winwar, *Wings of Fire: A Biography of Gabriele D'Annunzio and Eleonora Duse* (London: Alvin Redman, 1957), p. 242.
59. Claridge, p. 188.
60. Claridge, p. 301.
61. Solway, p. 194.
62. Solway, p. 192.
63. Solway, p. 195.
64. Solway, p. 212.
65. Solway, p. 222.
66. Solway, p. 233.
67. Solway, p. 225.
68. Solway, pp. 284–285.
69. Derek Jarman, *Smiling in Slow Motion* (London: Vintage, 2001), p. 288.
70. Solway, p. 363.
71. Marcel Proust, *Within a Budding Grove, Part Two* (London: Chatto & Windus, 1967), p. 344.

72. Cecil Beaton, *The Glass of Fashion: A Personal History of Fifty Years of Changing Tastes and the People Who Have Inspired Them* (New York: Rizzoli Ex Libris, 2014), p. 148.

73. Richard Buckle, *Nijinsky* (Harmondsworth: Penguin, 1980), pp. 5, 472, 337.

74. Solway, pp. 215, 212, 244, 246, 227. Jerome Robbins took things one step further than most when he said, 'Rudi – is Rudi – an artist – an animal – & a cunt': Deborah Jowitt, *Jerome Robbins: His Life, His Theater, His Dance* (New York: Simon & Schuster, 2004), p. 392. We return to the Orient in Chapter Eight. Nureyev said of himself, 'I had animal power, yes, but there was a finesse. I am not a brutal force. There's a subtlety': quoted in Julie Kavanagh, *Rudolf Nureyev: The Life* (London: Fig Tree, 2007), p. 262. Jennifer Homans links his Eastern manner and looks with his animal sensuality as key factors that contributed to his popularity in the 1960s: 'even in the most classical of steps, he flirted with the image of a virile Asian potentate, and his unrestrained sensuality and tiger-like movements recalled a clichéd Russian orientalism (first exploited by Diaghilev's Ballets Russes), which also linked to the escapist fantasies of 1960s middle-class youth: Eastern mysticism, revolution, sex, and drugs': Jennifer Homans, *Apollo's Angels: A History of Ballet* (London: Granta, 2010), p. 434.

75. Post-USSR Russia has continued to provide, both deliberately and by neglect, a hostile environment for lesbians and gay men, as well as for their cultural activities. The writer and artist Slava Mogutin, under threat of imprisonment for 'open and deliberate contempt for the generally accepted moral norms', fled Moscow in 1995 and applied for political asylum in the USA. In addition to his own writing, he had translated selections from Allen Ginsberg, William Burroughs and Dennis Cooper into Russian, and had edited translations of Baldwin's *Giovanni's Room* and Burroughs' *Naked Lunch*, as well as the collected works of Yevgeny Kharitonov. He developed a successful career in New York, where he became best known for his work in the visual arts.

## Chapter 4:  France and its Visitors

1. James Weldon Johnson, *The Autobiography of an Ex-Colored Man* (New York: Penguin, 1990), pp. 100–101.

2. Violet is 'Eve' and Vita is 'Julian' in the novel they wrote together but published under Vita's name, *Challenge* (1923). Vita is 'Mrs Gellybore Frinton' in Ronald Firbank's *The Flower Beneath the Foot* (1923). Firbank is 'Lambert Orme' in Harold Nicolson's *Some People* (1926).

3. Robert Medley, *Drawn from the Life: A Memoir* (London: Faber, 1983), p. 71.

4. Medley, pp.103–104, 122.

5. Vincent Bouvet and Gérard Durozoi, *Paris Between the Wars, 1919–1939: Art, Life and Culture* (New York: Vendome, 2010), pp. 398–399, 400. After the Second World War, Saint-Germain-des-Prés became markedly gay, to the extent that one newspaper report said, 'Let's have [the] courage [to] say it: Saint-Germain-des-Prés has been invaded by the Third Sex.' We are told that its most famous gay venue, on the rue du Cherche-Midi, was Le Fiacre, which 'enjoy[ed] an international reputation. Its upstairs restaurant served a cosmopolitan elite that included international stars of stage and screen, while its ground-floor gay bar welcomed more plebeian customers': Michael D. Sibalis, 'Paris', in David Higgs (ed.), *Queer Sites: Gay Urban Histories since 1600* (London: Routledge, 1999), pp. 10–37; pp. 30, 29.

6. Georges-Anquetil, *Satan conduit le bal* (Paris: Éditions Georges-Anquetil, 1925), p. 237. Quoted in Michael D. Sibalis, 'Paris', in Higgs, *Queer Sites*, p. 28. But Noel Annan writes that 'it was Paris, the cultural capital of Europe, that was the international capital of the [homosexual] fraternity', and not Berlin: Noel Annan, *Our Age: Portrait of a Generation* (London: Weidenfeld & Nicolson, 1990), p. 116.

7. Beverley Nichols, *All I Could Never Be: Some Recollections* (London: Cape, 1949), p. 150.

8. On the Paris dance halls, see Florence Tamagne, *A History of Homosexuality in Europe: Berlin, London, Paris, 1919–1939* (New York: Algora, 2004), pp. 68–72. On male prostitution, see pp. 73–78.

9. Jane Stevenson, *Edward Burra: Twentieth-Century Eye* (London: Pimlico, 2008), p. 119.

10. Brassaï, *The Secret Paris of the 30's*, trans. Richard Miller (London: Thames & Hudson, 1976), pp. 153, 158.

11. Brassaï, p. 3. My emphasis.

12. Klaus Mann, *The Turning Point: Thirty-Five Years in This Century* (London: Gollancz, 1944), p. 94. Brassaï said of the Parisian pissoirs, 'Neither the smell nor the dirt of these places repulsed the devotees of Greek love. On the contrary. The more malodorous the chapels, the more popular they became': Brassaï, p. 50.

13. Klaus Mann, *The Turning Point*, pp. 101, 102, 143, 103.
14. Anthony Heilbut, *Thomas Mann: Eros and Literature* (London: Macmillan, 1996), p. 537.
15. Witold Gombrowicz, *Polish Memories* (New Haven & London: Yale University Press, 2004), p. 74.
16. Patrick Pollard, *André Gide: Homosexual Moralist* (New Haven & London: Yale University Press, 1991), pp. 244–245.
17. Adrian Rifkin, *Street Noises: Parisian Pleasure, 1900–40* (Manchester: Manchester University Press, 1995), p. 140.
18. Brassaï, pp. 162–163.
19. Antal Szerb, *Journey by Moonlight* (London: Pushkin, 2007), p. 127.
20. Radclyffe Hall, *The Well of Loneliness* (London: Virago, 1982), p. 384.
21. Hall, p. 393.
22. Shane Leslie, *Long Shadows* (London: John Murray, 1966), p. 94.
23. As early as 1928, Walter Benjamin complained about the German literary critics who treated the *Recherche* as if it were merely 'a literary supplement to the *Almanac de Gotha*': Walter Benjamin, *Illuminations* (London: Fontana, 1973), p. 208.
24. Marcel Proust, *Cities of the Plain, Part One* (London: Chatto & Windus, 1968), pp. 25–27.
25. Alice Rawsthorn, *Yves Saint Laurent: A Biography* (London: HarperCollins, 1996), p. 39.
26. Benjamin Ivry, *Francis Poulenc* (London: Phaidon, 1996), p. 151.
27. The daftest, even if perhaps the most funniest, accounts of homosexuality in inter-war Paris comes in Rebecca West's *Cousin Rosamund*, a novel West left unfinished on her death in 1983. According to Rose, its English narrator: 'After the First World War it had become fashionable in Paris to be silly, and an appalling measure of French intelligence and spirit, and even some of its classical spirit, was devoted to establishing silliness as a way of life. Men loved men and women loved women, not because there was a real confusion in their flesh, such as Mary and I often noted in those with whom we worked [as musicians], but because a homosexual relationship must be nonsense in one way, since there can be no children, and it can be made more nonsensical still. Where there can be no question of marriage there is no reason against choosing the most perversely unsuitable partner; and often we met gifted Frenchmen who took about with them puzzled little waiters or postmen or sailors, flattered and spoiled but never acclimatised': Rebecca West, *Cousin Rosamund* (London: Virago, 1988), p. 4.
28. Glenway Wescott, *The Pilgrim Hawk: A Love Story* (New York: New York Review Books, 2001), pp. 3–4. Kegan Doyle attempts to revive the reputation of Glenway Wescott, specifically as a gay writer, in 'The Moral of Glenway Wescott: The Closet and the Second Act', *Canadian Review of American Studies* 28, 1 (1998), pp. 43–61.
29. Harvey Levenstein, *Seductive Journey: American Tourists in France from Jefferson to the Jazz Age* (Chicago & London: University of Chicago Press, 1998), pp. 203, 204, 245.
30. Charles Glass, *Americans in Paris: Life and Death under Nazi Occupation* (New York: Penguin, 2009), p. 3.
31. George Orwell, *Essays* (London: Everyman, 2002), p. 2.
32. Henry Miller, *Quiet Days in Clichy* (New York: Grove, 1965), p. 80.
33. Henry Miller, *Tropic of Cancer* (London: Harper Perennial, 2005), pp. 193, 288.
34. Henry Miller, *Letters to Anaïs Nin* (London: Peter Owen, 1965), pp. 48–49.
35. Not until the Kinsey Reports of 1948 and 1953 would the model of a spectrum of sexualities become an accepted commonplace in public discussions of sexuality in the USA.
36. Anthony Tommasini, *Virgil Thomson: Composer on the Aisle* (New York & London: Norton, 1997), p. 105.
37. Tommasini, pp. 123, 126, 133.
38. Tommasini, pp. 171, 175.
39. Virgil Thomson, *Virgil Thomson* (New York: Knopf, 1967), pp. 55, 110.
40. John Unterecker, *Voyager: A Life of Hart Crane* (London: Blond, 1970), p. 588.
41. Townsend Ludington, *Marsden Hartley: The Biography of an American Artist* (Boston: Little, Brown, 1992), p. 195.
42. Robert McAlmon and Kay Boyle, *Being Geniuses Together, 1920–1930* (London: Hogarth, 1984), p. 30.
43. McAlmon and Boyle, pp. 113, 224.
44. John Glassco, *Memoirs of Montparnasse* (Toronto & New York: Oxford University Press, 1970), p. 54. In this memoir, Graeme is never presented as what he really was, Glassco's lover,

or Robert McAlmon as his occasional bedmate (although there is one moment suggesting that Graeme and Glassco shared a bed, and that McAlmon once drunkenly crept in between them); all the sexual detail is about Glassco and women. Andrew Lesk says that 'much of the published recollections are factually misleading and were not written in 1929–1932 but in the late 1960s': Andrew Lesk, 'Having a Gay Old Time in Paris: John Glassco's Not-So-Queer Adventures', in Terry Goldie (ed.), *In a Queer Country: Gay and Lesbian Studies in the Canadian Context* (Vancouver: Arsenal Pulp Press, 2001), pp. 175–187; p. 176. Perhaps so, but surely a memoir is just that – a compilation of retrospective memoirs – rather than a journal written at the time of the experiences it describes.

45. Glassco, p. 24.
46. Michael Reynolds, *Hemingway: The American Homecoming* (Oxford: Blackwell, 1992), p. 98.
47. Anthony Burgess, *Ernest Hemingway and His World* (London: Thames & Hudson, 1978), p. 64. One commentator's analysis of Hemingway's homophobia comes down to apparently bland but quite plausible deductions: 'Perhaps his dislike of homosexuals stemmed also from a personal experience, and perhaps it was involved, like his sports, with some inner fear or doubts about his own masculinity': Robert W. Lewis, Jr, *Hemingway on Love* (New York: Haskell, 1973), p. 222.
48. Ernest Hemingway, *A Moveable Feast* (London: Cape, 1964), p. 23.
49. Peter Griffin, *Less Than a Treason: Hemingway in Paris* (New York & Oxford: Oxford University Press, 1990), p. 50.
50. Matthew J. Bruccoli, *Scott and Ernest: The Authority of Failure and the Authority of Success* (London: Bodley Head, 1978), p. 163. See also Matthew J. Bruccoli, *Some Sort of Epic Grandeur: The Life of F. Scott Fitzgerald* (London: Cardinal, 1991), p. 325: at the same time, Zelda 'became concerned that she was a latent lesbian'.
51. Jeffrey Meyers reads this scene as follows: 'the inverts do not present the usual threat to masculinity since Jake's virility has already been destroyed. But their psychological wounds match his physical wound, and these men who are not men remind him of his own incapacity. Jake wants to reassert his male force against his repressed fears': Jeffrey Meyers, *Hemingway: A Biography* (London: Macmillan, 1985), p. 200. See also Gregory Woods, 'The Injured Sex: Hemingway's Voice of Masculine Anxiety', in Judith Still and Michael Worton (eds), *Textuality and Sexuality: Reading Theories and Practices* (Manchester: Manchester University Press, 1993), pp. 160–172.
52. Carlos Baker, *Ernest Hemingway: A Life Story* (New York: Charles Scribner's Sons, 1969), pp. 164, 188–189.
53. Klaus Mann, *The Turning Point*, p. 232.
54. Robert E. Norton, *Secret Germany: Stefan George and His Circle* (Ithaca & London: Cornell University Press, 2002), p. 448.
55. Shari Benstock, *Women of the Left Bank: Paris, 1900–1940* (London: Virago, 1987), pp. 44, 46–47.
56. Diana Souhami, *Wild Girls: Paris, Sappho and Art: The Lives and Loves of Natalie Barney and Romaine Brooks* (London: Weidenfeld & Nicolson, 2004), p. 60.
57. Suzanne Rodriguez, *Wild Heart, A Life: Natalie Clifford Barney and the Decadence of Literary Paris* (New York: Ecco, 2003), p. 180.
58. Rodriguez, p. 183.
59. Souhami, *Wild Girls*, p. 183.
60. Benstock, p. 11.
61. Judith Thurman, *Secrets of the Flesh: A Life of Colette* (London: Bloomsbury 1999), p. 153.
62. Thurman, p. 208. Colette's husband was Henri Gauthier-Villars, a writer fourteen years her senior, who published under the pseudonym 'Willy'.
63. The translator of Conrad and Kipling, Robert d'Humières had helped Proust, whose English was not very good, to translate Ruskin; in return, Proust used him as one of the models for his much-loved character the Marquis de Saint-Loup. Robert d'Humières died bravely in the Great War, half deliberately exposing himself to unnecessary danger in order to escape a looming scandal.
64. Thurman, p. 170. Colette would return to the story of Daphnis and Chloe in her novel *The Ripening Seed* (*Le Blé en herbe*, 1923).
65. Thurman, p. 160.
66. Thurman, p. 214.

67. Much subsequent effort went into smuggling copies of it into the United States. Beach's role as the book's publisher lasted for a decade. Beach declined D.H. Lawrence's request that she publish *Lady Chatterley's Lover*. Privately, she referred to it as a 'sermon-on-the-mount – of Venus': Noel Riley Fitch, *Sylvia Beach and the Lost Generation: A History of Literary Paris in the Twenties and Thirties* (London: Penguin, 1985), p. 280.

68. Fitch, pp. 79, 82.

69. Robert McAlmon married Winifred Ellerman in New York in 1921. She was the lover of Hilda Doolittle (the poet H.D.). He said, in a 1921 letter to William Carlos Williams, 'The marriage is legal only, unromantic, and strictly an agreement': McAlmon and Boyle, p. 45.

70. Marianne Moore, *The Selected Letters of Marianne Moore* (London: Faber, 1998), p. 369.

71. Quentin Bell, *Bloomsbury Recalled* (New York: Columbia University Press, 1996), p. 158.

72. Gertrude Stein, *Paris France* (London: Brilliance, 1983), p. 111.

73. Benstock, p. 15.

74. Diana Souhami, *Gertrude and Alice* (London: Phoenix, 2000), p. 159.

75. Thomson, p. 179.

76. Souhami, *Gertrude and Alice*, p. 159.

77. Thomson, p. 175.

78. Gertrude Stein, *The Autobiography of Alice B. Toklas* (Harmondsworth: Penguin, 1966), pp. 143, 110, 216, 236, 244, 256.

79. Cecil Beaton, *The Glass of Fashion: A Personal History of Fifty Years of Changing Tastes and the People Who Have Inspired Them* (New York: Rizzoli Ex Libris, 2014), p. 148.

80. James Merrill, *A Different Person: A Memoir* (San Francisco: HarperCollins, 1994), pp. 74–75.

81. Alice B. Toklas, *The Alice B. Toklas Cookbook* (London: Folio Society, 1993), p. 256.

82. Charles Kaiser, *The Gay Metropolis* (London: Weidenfeld & Nicolson, 1998), pp. 36–37.

83. Adrian Clark and Jeremy Dronfield, *Queer Saint: The Cultured Life of Peter Watson, Who Shook Twentieth-Century Art and Shocked High Society* (London: John Blake, 2015), p. 237.

84. Charles Henri Ford, *Water from a Bucket: A Diary, 1948–1957* (New York: Turtle Point, 2001), p. 52.

85. Gore Vidal, *Palimpsest: A Memoir* (London: Abacus, 1996), p. 178.

86. Jean Cocteau, *Past Tense: Volume II Diaries* (London: Methuen, 1990), p. 263.

87. Christopher Logue, *Prince Charming: A Memoir* (London: Faber, 1999), p. 158.

88. Raymond Queneau, *Zazie in the Metro* (London: Penguin, 2001), p. 122.

89. Angus Wilson, *Reflections in a Writer's Eye: Writings on Travel* (London: Secker & Warburg, 1986), p. 4.

90. James Baldwin, *Giovanni's Room* (London: Penguin, 2000), p. 30.

91. Baldwin, *Giovanni's Room* pp. 141–142.

92. James Baldwin, 'The Male Prison', in James Baldwin, *The Price of the Ticket: Collected Nonfiction, 1948–1985* (London: Michael Joseph, 1985), pp. 101–105; p. 104.

93. See James Campbell, *Talking at the Gates: A Life of James Baldwin* (London: Faber, 1991), p. 211.

94. James Campbell, p. 138.

95. Barry Miles, *The Beat Hotel: Ginsberg, Burroughs and Corso in Paris, 1957–1963* (London: Atlantic, 2001), p. 230. Much later, on 30 September 1973, when he heard of Auden's death, Ginsberg spent the afternoon weeping.

96. Miles, *The Beat Hotel*, pp. 66, 19, 24.

97. Harold Norse, *Memoirs of a Bastard Angel* (London: Bloomsbury, 1990), pp. 348–349.

## Chapter 5: Germany and its Visitors

1. See Guido Glur, *Kunstlehre und Kunstanschauung des Georgekreises und die Aesthetik Oscar Wildes*, special issue of *Sprache und Dichtung* (Neue Folge Band 3), 1957. In his 1929 Preface to St.-John Perse's *Anabasis*, Hugo von Hofmannsthal traces another line of influence: 'New reflexes appear, visions of a violence barely tolerable to the eye; it is a road which leads from Rimbaud's *Bateau Ivre* to the earliest versions of Stefan George. Both share what the Romans describe with the word *incantatio* – the dark and violent self-enchantment induced by the magic of sound and rhythm': St.-John Perse, trans. T.S. Eliot, *Anabasis* (London: Faber, 1959), p. 85.

2. Impressive evidence of this active, systematic involvement in comradeship can be seen in a published portfolio of 175 black-and-white photographs of George's colleagues and disciples,

including the Stauffenberg brothers (but not including Maximin). See Robert Boehringer, *Mein Bild von Stefan George* (München & Düsseldorf: Helmut Küpper vormals Georg Bondi, 1951).

3. Robert E. Norton, *Secret Germany: Stefan George and His Circle* (Ithaca & London: Cornell University Press, 2002), p. 475.

4. E.K. Bennett, *Stefan George* (Cambridge: Bowes & Bowes, 1954), pp. 12–13.

5. E.K. Bennett, p. 34. Mario Pensa makes a similar point: 'Evidentemente la donna non poteva rappresentare per George il tipo di perfezione umana. Al suo posto invece subentra l'uomo': Mario Pensa, *Stefan George: saggio critico* (Bologna: Nicola Zanichelli Editore, 1961), p. 182.

6. Golo Mann, *Reminiscences and Reflections: Growing Up in Germany* (London: Faber, 1990), p. 165.

7. George translated the sonnets of Shakespeare – as A.L. Rowse later put it, remounting one of his hobby-horses – 'under the mistaken impression, usual with homosexuals, that they are homosexual': A.L. Rowse, *Homosexuals in History: A Study of Ambivalence in Society, Literature and the Arts* (London: Weidenfeld & Nicolson, 1977), p. 211.

8. See Emmy Rosenfeld, *L'Italia nella poesia di Stefan George* (Milano: Malfasi Editore, 1948).

9. See Norton, pp. 98–107.

10. H.A. Hammelmann, *Hugo von Hofmannsthal* (London: Bowes & Bowes, 1957), p. 20.

11. For an early response to George's homoerotic themes, see Peter Hamecher, 'Der männliche Eros im Werke Stefan Georges', *Jahrbuch für Sexuelle Zwischenstufen* 14, 1 (1914), pp. 10–23.

12. Michael M. Metzger and Erika A. Metzger, *Stefan George* (New York: Twayne, 1972), pp. 35, 132.

13. The earlier memoir, *My Years of Indiscretion*, lacks mention of Stefan George's homosexuality. It does, though, give an atmospheric sense of Scott's inability to fit in with the high seriousness of the hero-worshippers clustered around the poet. After he committed such indiscretions as saying 'I don't care for Beethoven' at the dinner table, 'altogether the Stefan George circle came to regard me as an unusually outspoken young man who lacked the much admired quality of *reverence*': Cyril Scott, *My Years of Indiscretion* (London: Mills & Boon, 1924), p. 44.

14. Cyril Scott, *Bone of Contention: Life Story and Confessions* (London: Aquarian Press, 1969), pp. 103–104.

15. Joachim Fest, *Plotting Hitler's Death: The German Resistance to Hitler, 1933–1945* (London: Phoenix, 1997), pp. 216, 240.

16. Even so, Noel Annan has identified George's seriousness as being part of a broader European trend: 'The austere homosexual was to be found more on the Continent than in England: in Montherlant, Wittgenstein, and especially in the Stefan George Kreis in Germany. The spirit was fierce, even puritanical. Those possessed by it wanted to purify society, rid it of worldliness, shabbiness and equivocation and, while idealizing young men, to protect them from the corrupting influence of women': Noel Annan, *Our Age: Portrait of a Generation* (London: Weidenfeld & Nicolson, 1990), p. 110.

17. Ernst Morwitz, 'Stefan George', in Stefan George, *Poems* (New York: Schocken Books, 1967), pp. 9–36; p. 15, n.

18. W.H. Auden and Chester Kallman, *Libretti and Other Dramatic Writings by W.H. Auden, 1939–1973* (London: Faber, 1993), p. 202. Auden, Kallman and Henze dedicated the opera to Hugo von Hofmannsthal. George Steiner takes a similar tone in his characterisation of the *Kreis* as 'George and his coven', in which homoeroticism 'turned histrionic': George Steiner, *Lessons of the Masters* (Cambridge, Mass. & London: Harvard University Press, 2003), pp. 121, 120. On Marsden Hartley's interest in George, see Jonathan Weinberg, *Speaking for Vice: Homosexuality in the Art of Charles Demuth, Marsden Hartley, and the First American Avant-Garde* (New Haven & London: Yale University Press, 1993), pp. 149–151.

19. Czesław Miłosz, *Native Realm: A Search for Self-Definition* (Berkeley & Los Angeles: University of California Press, 1981), pp. 177, 178, 199–201.

20. Leslie Mitchell, *Maurice Bowra: A Life* (Oxford: Oxford University Press, 2009), pp. 105, 106.

21. Christopher Hassall, *Rupert Brooke: A Biography* (London: Faber, 1972), p. 253.

22. John Lehmann, *In the Purely Pagan Sense* (London: GMP, 1985), p. 95.

23. Ekbert Faas, *Young Robert Duncan: Portrait of the Poet as Homosexual in Society* (Santa Barbara, California: Black Sparrow, 1983), pp. 172–175, 225. Kantorowicz had written one of the George Kreis's more important texts, a life of the medieval emperor Frederick II. Such biographies by George's disciples had a particular purpose. As Peter Watson puts it, 'their

intention was to highlight "great men", especially those from more "heroic" ages, men who had by their will changed the course of events': Peter Watson, *The German Genius: Europe's Third Renaissance, the Second Scientific Revolution and the Twentieth Century* (London: Simon & Schuster, 2010), p. 574. As a Jew, Kantorowicz had been forced out of Germany and had made his way to Berkeley by way of Oxford.

24. Forster was scathing about George: 'he had an intense personal experience which exalted his poetry but did not improve his judgement, and as a result of that experience the circle of friends hardened into a cult, and George almost assumed the airs of a priest. Domineering and humourless, he trained his young disciples and began to send them out into the world': E.M. Forster, *Two Cheers for Democracy* (Harmondsworth: Middlesex: Penguin, 1965), p. 233.
25. Dominique Fernandez, *A Hidden Love: Art and Homosexuality* (Munich: Prestel, 2002), p. 256.
26. Graham Robb, *Strangers: Homosexual Love in the Nineteenth Century* (London: Picador, 2003), p. 132. He went there as a postgraduate student, aged 21, in 1846.
27. Stefan Zweig, *Confusion: The Private Papers of Privy Councillor R Von D* (London: Pushkin, 2002), pp. 130–131.
28. Keith Howes, *Outspoken: Keith Howes' Gay News Interviews, 1976–83* (London: Cassell, 1995), p. 25.
29. Alfred Döblin, *Berlin Alexanderplatz* (Harmondsworth: Penguin, 1978), pp. 70–71, 72–73.
30. John Henry Mackay, *The Hustler* (Boston: Alyson, 1985), pp. 99, 130–131. *Puppenjunge*, the term Mackay used for the title of his novel, means 'doll-boy'. The actual term for a rent-boy was *pupenjunge*, 'fart-boy'. The latter term is used within the novel, but not on its cover.
31. Norman Page, *Auden and Isherwood: The Berlin Years* (London: Macmillan, 1998), p. 19. Christopher Isherwood, *Goodbye to Berlin* (Harmondsworth: Penguin, 1945), p. 119.
32. Max Spohr was a publisher whose fiction list included Siegfried Moldau's *Wahreit* (1906), Hans Waldau's *Aus der Freundschaft sonnigsten Tagen* (1906), Konradin's *Ein Jünger Platos* (1913) and Theo von Tempesta's *Aus dem Liebesleben zweier Freunde* (1914). All of the firm's publications adhered to the Hirschfeld theory of the Third Sex.
33. Charlotte Wolff, *Magnus Hirschfeld: A Portrait of a Pioneer in Sexology* (London: Quartet, 1986), p. 33.
34. Wolff, p. 366.
35. Christopher Isherwood, *Christopher and His Kind, 1929–1939* (London: Eyre Methuen, 1977), p. 101.
36. Wolff, p. 414.
37. Nikos Kazantzakis, *Report to Greco* (London: Faber, 1973), p. 419.
38. Elias Canetti, *The Torch in My Ear* (London: Granta, 1999), p. 299.
39. Michael Davidson, *The World, The Flesh and Myself* (London: GMP, 1985), pp. 150, 151, 154. On the male gay scene in Berlin, see Florence Tamagne, *A History of Homosexuality in Europe: Berlin, London, Paris, 1919–1939* (New York: Algora, 2004), pp. 51–53. On the lesbian scene, see pp. 53–57. On mak prostitntima see pp. 58–61.
40. Robert McAlmon and Kay Boyle, *Being Geniuses Together: 1920–1930* (London: Hogarth, 1984), pp. 97, 98.
41. Michael De-la-Noy, *Eddy: The Life of Edward Sackville-West* (London: Arcadia, 1999), p. 117.
42. James Lees-Milne, *Harold Nicolson: A Biography, Vol. 1, 1886–1929* (London: Chatto & Windus, 1980), p. 368.
43. Rupert Hart-Davis, *Hugh Walpole: A Biography* (London: Rupert Hart-Davis, 1952), p. 256.
44. Robin Gibson, *Glyn Philpot, 1884–1937: Edwardian Aesthete to Thirties Modernist* (London: National Portrait Gallery 1984), p. 27. Gibson's rather overheated catalogue note to the painting itself reiterates the point and takes it further: 'Nothing is known of what Philpot may have seen in the way of modern German art, but this grotesque scene of pre-war Berlin night life, which might have been culled from the pages of Isherwood, offers evidence of an acquaintance with [George] Grosz and [Otto] Dix ... Philpot was clearly shocked and disturbed by what he saw there ... [I]t is a vivid indictment of the decadence of the times. The dregs of society are observed as if in an icy blue goldfish-bowl, beneath a searing red inferno' (p. 74). Why, one of them is even reading a book!
45. Humphrey Carpenter, *W.H. Auden: A Biography* (London: George Allen & Unwin, 1981), pp. 96–97.
46. John Sutherland, *Stephen Spender: The Authorized Biography* (London: Viking, 2004), p. 83.

47. Isherwood, *Christopher and His Kind*, p. 10; Page, p. 41. On another occasion, reviewing Gerald Hamilton's *Mr Norris and I*, Isherwood wrote: 'One of my chief motives for wanting to visit Berlin was that an elderly relative had warned me against it, saying that it was the vilest place since Sodom': Christopher Isherwood, *Exhumations: Stories, Articles, Verses* (London: Methuen, 1966), p. 86. In the same review he wrote: 'The "wickedness" of Berlin's night-life was of a most pitiful kind; the kisses and embraces, as always, had price-tags attached to them, but here the prices were drastically reduced in the cut-throat competition of an overcrowded market. (I remember hearing of a boy who told a psychiatrist quite seriously that he was "homosexual – for economic reasons"!)' (pp. 86–87).

48. Isherwood, *Christopher and His Kind*, p. 23.

49. Lehmann, *Purely Pagan Sense*, pp. 44–46.

50. Isherwood, *Christopher and His Kind*, p. 29. He adds: 'Wasn't Berlin's famous "decadence" largely a commercial "line" which the Berliners had instinctively developed in their competition with Paris? Paris had long-since cornered the straight-girl market, so what was left for Berlin to offer its visitors but a masquerade of perversions?'

51. Isherwood, *Goodbye to Berlin*, p. 190. My italics. There is another of these tourist dives in Anthony Powell's novel *Agents and Patients* (1936). Maltravers leads a group of visitors through the side streets of the city until they come to a doorway 'by which stood a notice saying that this was the real Berlin'. Indeed, it says so in several languages. This is the first of several night-spots they visit. In the next, 'two business men in black-striped suits' are among the couples on the dance floor. Chipchase claims to be 'making observations for my new book on psychology'. He watches closely as Commander Venables is 'joined on one side by a tall blonde in evening dress, carrying an ostrich-feather fan, and on the other by a young person in a dinner-jacket with wavy dark curls and a precise little mouth'. These are Willi[e] and Fritzi. But Maltravers has to point out to Mrs Mendoza that she has 'fallen into the common error of thinking that Fritzi is the boy and Willie the girl'. More importantly, 'The Commodore seems to share your misapprehension': Anthony Powell, *Agents and Patients* (Harmondsworth: Penguin, 1961), pp. 130, 131, 133.

52. Count Harry Kessler, *The Diaries of a Cosmopolitan: 1918–1937* (London: Weidenfeld & Nicolson, 1999), pp. 434–435.

53. Kessler, p. 428.

54. Catharine Savage, *Roger Martin du Gard* (New York: Twayne, 1986), pp. 448–449.

55. Savage, p. 452.

56. Isherwood, *Christopher and His Kind*, p. 20.

57. William Plomer, *At Home* (Harmondsworth: Penguin, 1961), p. 67.

58. In Athens, Plomer had an affair with a Greek sailor called Nicky. For a while he was more deliriously in love than at any other time in his life, and he thought Nicky was, too. But the sailor moved on to another (by his standards) rich foreigner, taking Plomer's savings with him. The shock of this betrayal remained with Plomer for the rest of his life, and he seems never to have fully regained his faith in love.

59. William Plomer, *Museum Pieces* (Harmondsworth: Penguin, 1961), pp. 8, 13, 72, 17, 20, 112, 48.

60. Plomer, *Museum Pieces*, p. 93.

61. Plomer, *Museum Pieces*, p. 102.

62. Plomer, *Museum Pieces*, pp. 102–103.

63. Plomer, *Museum Pieces*, p. 103.

64. Frances Spalding, *Duncan Grant: A Biography* (London: Chatto & Windus, 1997), p. 259.

65. Kenneth Clark, *Another Part of the Wood: A Self-Portrait* (London: Book Club Associates, 1974), p. 114.

66. Stephen Spender, *World Within World* (London: Readers' Union, 1953), p. 93.

67. Lytton Strachey, *The Letters of Lytton Strachey* (London: Viking, 2005), p. 637.

68. Stephen Spender, *The Thirties and After: Poetry, Politics, People (1933–75)* (London: Fontana, 1978), p. 105.

69. Spender, *Thirties and After*, p. 106. He adds, a few sentences later, 'The Germans had a reputation at that time of being homosexual, but I think it would be truer to say that they were bisexual, though there were of course a few of those zealots and martyrs who really hate women, whom one finds everywhere.' I shall return to Whitman in Chapter Nine.

70. Quoted in Charles Kaiser, *The Gay Metropolis, 1940–1996* (London: Phoenix, 1999), p. 210.

71. Franz Schulze, *Philip Johnson: Life and Work* (New York: Knopf, 1994), pp. 136, 164, 139.

72. Brenda Wineapple, *Genêt: A Biography of Janet Flanner* (London: Pandora, 1994), p. 149.

73. Gaia Servadio, *Luchino Visconti: A Biography* (London: Weidenfeld & Nicolson, 1981), pp. 45, 47.

74. Once, when they were staying in Horst's house in Hammamet, Tunisia, they had a row about Horst's refusal to stand up during the broadcast of a news item about an Italian victory in Somalia.

75. Servadio, pp. 81–82.

76. Jean Genet, *Funeral Rites* (New York: Grove, 1969), p. 38. It was not uncommon for homophobic observers on both the Left and the Right to blame the liberties of Weimar Berlin for the restrictions and subjection that followed. Genet was being typically, knowingly contrary, by purveying such an argument from the subject-position of an openly man-loving man. Less forthcoming about his own sexuality, in one of his memoirs the English journalist Beverley Nichols breezily claimed that 'Such German as I can manage was picked up in the streets of Berlin and, of course, in bed, where at least one gets down to fundamentals.' He went to Berlin in 1936 but did not enjoy the experience. The Nazis' clean-up had not yet taken effect: 'My main reason for hating it was because everybody in the city, by which I mean every pair of arms and legs, was for sale.' From this understandable reaction against the social and sexual consequences of economic collapse, and looking back from the late 1970s, Nichols developed a theory that the widespread prostitution he had witnessed in the city was one of the major causes of the subsequent war: 'I imagine that in the entire history of civilisation there has never been such a sexual extravaganza as was presented by Berlin at the beginning of the last decade before the [Second World] war, and I have a feeling that this chaffering in young bodies was in no small degree responsible for the war itself.' Not only that, but even the excesses of the war had their origins in what he had so disliked in Berlin: 'Some of the brutality [of the German troops], I believe had its origin in memories of the male brothels which sprang up in all the great German cities, with the tacit approval of Goebbels, who realised that they were not only a tourist attraction but also a convenient setting for espionage. The youth of Germany was getting its revenge': Beverley Nichols, *The Unforgiving Minute: Some Confessions from Childhood to the Outbreak of the Second World War* (London: W.H. Allen, 1978), pp. 1, 227, 228.

77. Peter Parker, *Isherwood: A Life* (London: Picador, 2004), p. 665.

78. Isherwood discusses the different versions of Sally Bowles in Isherwood, *Christopher and His Kind*, pp. 51–54.

79. Berlin remained the mythic point of reference. Thus, reflecting on a post-war visit to Tokyo, Angus Wilson wrote: 'Defeat in war seems to have a rather peculiar effect on the "pleasure life" of a nation, and, as in Berlin of the nineteen-twenties, there are many rather strange "private shows" at which the unsuspecting inquisitive visitor may find himself': Angus Wilson, *Reflections in a Writer's Eye: Writings on Travel* (London: Secker & Warburg, 1986), p. 29. But Wilson gathered that by 1957, the time of writing, such places had been closed down.

## Chapter 6: Frivolity to Seriousness

1. T.H. White, *The Age of Scandal* (London: Folio, 1993), p. 102.

2. Robert Graves and Alan Hodge, *The Long Week-End: A Social History of Great Britain, 1918–1939* (Harmondsworth: Penguin, 1971), pp. 97–98.

3. Julian Symons, *The Thirties: A Dream Revolved* (London: Faber, 1975), pp. 40–41.

4. Jessica Mitford, *Hons and Rebels* (Harmondsworth: Penguin, 1962), p. 35.

5. There is an extended analysis of this generation in Martin Green, *Children of the Sun: A Narrative of 'Decadence' in England After 1918* (London: Pimlico, 1992). To the list of fictional characters we should add Lord Risley in E.M. Forster's *Maurice* (written in 1913–14, revised in the 1930s and late 1950s, but not published until 1971); and Donald Butterboy, a portrait of Brian Howard, in Wyndham Lewis' *The Roaring Queen* (finished in 1936 but suppressed as libellous and not published until 1973). One relatively feeble, late flaring of the pansy-aesthete is Denis Porson in Frederic Raphael's novel *The Glittering Prizes*. Soon after graduating, he is arrested at a party with some guardsmen and given two years. He later opens a pub restaurant. Raphael underlines the fictional origins of his novel by giving his central character Adam Morris *Brideshead Revisted* to read during his first year at Cambridge – see Frederic Raphael, *The Glittering Prizes* (Harmondsworth: Penguin, 1976), p. 36.

6. Cecil Beaton, *Ashcombe: The Story of a Fifteen-Year Lease* (Stanbridge, Wimborne, Dorset: The Dovecote Press, 1999), pp. 57, 32–33, 81.

7. Martin Green, *Children of the Sun*, pp. 158–159. Nothing could be further from the spirit of this internationalist modernity than that silly remark of John Betjeman's, 'Isn't abroad *awful*?':

Humphrey Carpenter, *The Brideshead Generation: Evelyn Waugh and His Friends* (London: Faber, 1989), p. 181.

8. Keith Howes, *Outspoken: Keith Howes'* Gay News *Interviews* (London: Cassell, 1995), p. 39.

9. Nancy Mitford, *The Pursuit of Love, and Love in a Cold Climate* (Harmondsworth: Penguin, 1980), p. 392.

10. Nancy Mitford, *Pursuit of Love*, pp. 455, 394–395, 405, 428, 436. The novel's title is borrowed from George Orwell's *Keep the Aspidistra Flying*: 'It is not easy to make love in a cold climate when you have no money.'

11. Nancy Mitford, *Pursuit of Love*, pp. 410, 411.

12. Nancy Mitford, *Pursuit of Love*, pp. 288, 444.

13. Harold Acton, *Nancy Mitford* (London: Gibson Square Books, 2004), pp. 32–34.

14. Acton, p. 78.

15. Acton, pp. 78–80.

16. Carl Van Vechten, *The Blind Bow-Boy* (New York: Knopf, 1925), p. 128. Mary Garden was a Scottish soprano, Sem Benelli an Italian playwright, Sacha Guitry a French playwright, Gordon Craig an English actor-director-designer (son of the actress Ellen Terry), Eugène Goossens an English composer, and Jacques Copeau a French actor-director-playwright. La Chauve-Souris was a revue company founded in Moscow by Nikita Balieff. After the Revolution, Balieff went into exile, re-establishing the company in Paris in 1920. C.B. Cochrane invited it to London, and it made frequent visits to the USA throughout the 1920s.

17. Van Vechten, *Blind Bow-Boy* pp. 130, 131, 139.

18. Van Vechten, *Blind Bow-Boy* pp.124, 126, 129, 130, 117.

19. Carl Van Vechten, *Parties: A Novel of Contemporary New York Life* (London & New York: Knopf, 1930), p. 32.

20. Compton Mackenzie, *Vestal Fire* (London: Cassell, 1927), p. 410.

21. Cyril Connolly, *The Rock Pool* (Oxford: Oxford University Press, 1981), pp. 27, 37, 38, 58, 131.

22. Clive James, *Unreliable Memoirs* (London: Picador, 1981), pp. 131, 132, 137.

23. Evelyn Waugh, *Black Mischief* (London: Penguin, 2000), pp. 231–232, 233.

24. Evelyn Waugh, *Put Out More Flags* (London: Penguin, 1943), pp. 43, 42.

25. Evelyn Waugh, *Brideshead Revisited: The Sacred and Profane Memories of Captain Charles Ryder* (Harmondsworth: Penguin, 1962), p. 47.

26. Evelyn Waugh, *The Sword of Honour Trilogy* (London: Penguin, 1984), p. 97.

27. Evelyn Waugh, *The Ordeal of Gilbert Pinfold* (London: Penguin, 1998), pp. 36, 60, 61, 70, 84–85. Hoping for a peaceful time on a transatlantic crossing, Beverley Nichols was dismayed to be latched on to by Waugh, who threatened to put him into one of his books. Sitting down to dinner one night, Waugh murmured 'Pederasty.' Nichols: 'What about pederasty?' Waugh: 'You must instruct me in it.' Nichols goes on, barely managing to suppress his awareness of Waugh's potential for malice: 'Regarding him across the table I suggested that it might be rather late in the day for that sort of thing. Besides, I happened to dislike small boys. The subject was therefore dropped, with some regret, I suspect, for a little spot of pederasty would have added a nice touch of colour to his imaginary portrait': Beverley Nichols, *The Sun in My Eyes: Or How Not to Go Round the World* (London: Heinemann, 1969), p. 272.

28. Jocelyn Brooke, *The Orchid Trilogy* (Harmondsworth: Penguin, 1981), pp. 57, 58.

29. Louis MacNeice, *The Strings Are False* (London: Faber, 1965), p. 156. Stephen Spender, 'Introduction' to *The Temple* (London: Faber, 1988), p. xi. Robert Byron, *The Road to Oxiana* (London: Picador, 1994), p. 257. Stephen Spender, *Journals 1939–1983* (London: Faber, 1992), p. 53. In 'Where Engels Fears to Tread', which purports to be the review of a memoir tellingly called *From Oscar to Stalin: A Progress*, Cyril Connolly satirises Brian Howard and other aesthetes as the memoir's author, 'Christian de Clavering'. In his progress from Eton to Oxford to London ('The 'twenties. Parties. Parties. Parties') to Paris, Berlin, Munich and Greece, Christian meets all the usual suspects and voices all the expected attitudes. Then, back in London, he wanders into a bookshop: 'It was full of slim volumes by unfamiliar names – who were Stephen, Wystan, Cecil, and Christopher?' Thus begins his political awakening. He eventually changes his name to 'Chris Clay' and, in the last sentence of the review, denounces Cyril Connolly as a fascist: Cyril Connolly, 'Where Engels Fears to Tread', in Marie Jacqueline Lancaster (ed.), *Brian Howard: Portrait of a Failure* (London: Blond, 1968), pp. 602–613.

30. James G. Southworth, *Sowing the Spring: Studies in British Poets from Hopkins to MacNeice* (Oxford: Blackwell, 1940), pp. 136, 142.

31. Richard Davenport-Hines, *Auden* (London: Heinemann, 1995), pp. 48–49. Christopher Isherwood, *Christopher and His Kind, 1929–1939* (London: Eyre Methuen, 1977), pp. 123–125.

32. George Orwell, *Down and Out in Paris and London* (Harmondsworth: Penguin, 1974), pp. 131, 141, 142.

33. The exclusive Cambridge Conversazione Society, or Apostles, counted among its members, at various times, Anthony Blunt, Rupert Brooke, Guy Burgess, Goldsworthy Lowes Dickinson, E.M. Forster, Roger Fry, John Maynard Keynes, George Rylands, Lytton Strachey, Ludwig Wittgenstein and Leonard Woolf.

34. George Orwell, *Keep the Aspidistra Flying* (London: Penguin, 1989), pp. 12–13, 35, 84, 166–167.

35. George Orwell, *The Road to Wigan Pier* (Harmondsworth: Penguin, 1962), pp. 29–30, 31.

36. George Orwell, *Essays* (London: Everyman, 2002), p. 397. George Orwell, *A Life in Letters* (London: Penguin, 2011), p. 60.

37. P.N. Furbank, *E.M. Forster: A Life, Volume Two* (Oxford: Oxford University Press, 1979), p. 223.

38. Orwell, *Essays*, p. 74. Wyndham Lewis constructed a hostile, fictional portrayal of Stephen Spender as Dan Boleyn, a 'tall melting glowing young debutante . . . standing suffused with a hot maidenly bloom': *The Apes of God* (London: Nash & Grayson, [1930]), p. 63.

39. Michael Shelden, *Orwell: The Authorised Biography* (London: Minerva, 1992), pp. 76, 503–504, n. 24. Orwell, *Essays*, p. 41.

40. John Sutherland, *Stephen Spender: The Authorized Biography* (London: Viking, 2004), p. 120.

41. Roy Campbell, *The Collected Poems of Roy Campbell, Volume One* (London: Bodley Head, 1949), pp. 181, 203–204, 232.

42. Roy Campbell, *The Collected Poems of Roy Campbell, Volume Two* (London: Bodley Head, 1957), Spauden: p. 49; Spaunday: pp. 85, 92; MacSpaunday: pp. 86, 87, 89, 90; 'What Auden chants . . .': p. 45; 'the fat snuggery . . .': p. 143. Reviewing a 1976 National Portrait Gallery exhibition of 'Young Writers of the Thirties', Orwell's biographer Bernard Crick scathingly described it as 'the MacSpaunday Family Album' because it excluded so many writers outside the Auden circle, Orwell among them. He wrongly assumed this was a somewhat belated response to the 'Nancy' label: Sutherland, pp. 489–490.

43. Roy Campbell, *Collected Poems, Volume Two*, pp. 43, 213.

44. Roy Campbell, *Collected Poems, Volume Two*, pp. 133, 134, 46, 170; Gide: 175; Lorca: 199.

45. Paul Ferris, *Dylan Thomas* (London: Hodder & Stoughton, 1977), p. 130.

46. Curzio Malaparte, *The Skin* (London: Panther, 1964), p. 91. Mathurin Régnier was the French satirist of the 16th–17th centuries, whose sonnet 'Contre les sodomites' begins with the line 'Sodomites enragés ennemis de nature'.

47. Stephen Spender, *World Within World* (London: Readers' Union, 1953), pp. 121–122.

48. Malcolm Cowley, *Exile's Return: A Literary Odyssey of the 1920s* (New York: Penguin, 1994), pp. 34, 35. First published in 1934, *Exile's Return* was revised and expanded in 1951.

49. Even the most notable exceptions, the insurance executive Wallace Stevens and the paediatrician William Carlos Williams, although they stayed in the States, kept themselves steeped in the works of European experimentalism, principally in poetry and painting.

50. Cowley, pp. 51, 52.

51. Cowley, pp. 61, 82, 73.

52. Christopher Isherwood, *Goodbye to Berlin* (Harmondsworth: Penguin, 1945), pp. 195, 196, 204.

53. Klaus Mann, *Mephisto* (New York: Penguin, 1995), p. 187.

54. Jessica Mitford, *Hons and Rebels*, p. 193.

55. Henry Miller, *The Colossus of Maroussi* (Harmondsworth: Penguin, 1972), pp. 39–40. It is worth noting that the war did not stop students choosing their own sexual manners. The playwright John Mortimer, who was briefly up at Brasenose College before being sent down in 1942 for writing love letters to a schoolboy, claimed that 'At Oxford after Dunkirk [1940] the fashion was to be homosexual': Valerie Grove, *A Voyage Round John Mortimer* (London: Penguin, 2008), p. 48. Mortimer was later credited with having scripted the famous Granada Television adaptation of *Brideshead Revisited* (1981), but in fact his scripts were not used.

### Chapter 7:  Berlin Propagandised

1. Kurt von Stutterheim, *The Two Germanys* (London: Sidgwick & Jackson, 1939), pp. 163, 172.

2. Christopher Isherwood, *Down There on a Visit* (New York: Four Square, 1964), pp. 26–27. In fact, this warning came from Isherwood's cousin, Basil Fry.

3. Bruce Kellner, *Carl Van Vechten and the Irreverent Decades* (Norman, Oklahoma: University of Oklahoma Press, 1968), p. 242

4. Pierre Viénot, *Is Germany Finished?* (London: Faber, 1931), p. 39.

5. General Hermann Goering, *Germany Reborn* (London: Elkin Mathews & Marrot, 1934), pp. 38–39.

6. Sir Edward Grigg, MP, *Britain Looks at Germany* (London: Nicholson & Watson, 1938), pp. 194, 200.

7. Charles W. Domville-Fife, *This Is Germany* (London: Seeley Service, [1939]), p. 13.

8. Sven Hedín, *Germany and World Peace* (London: Hutchinson, 1937), p. vii.

9. Charles Wolff, *Journey into Chaos* (London: Heinemann, n.d.), pp. 70–71.

10. Charlotte Wolff, *Magnus Hirschfeld: A Portrait of a Pioneer in Sexology* (London: Quartet, 1986), p. 429.

11. Johannes Steel, *Hitler as Frankenstein* ([London]: Wishart & Co., n.d.), pp. 143–144, 146, 147.

12. Hugh Trevor-Roper, (ed.), *The Goebbels Diaries: The Last Days* (London: Secker & Warburg, 1978), p. 248.

13. Karl Billinger, *Hitler Is No Fool* (London: Hurst & Blackett, n.d.), pp. 29–30.

14. H.G. Baynes, *Germany Possessed* (London: Cape, 1941), pp. 222, 223.

15. August Kubizek, *Young Hitler: The Story of Our Friendship* (London: Allan Wingate, 1954), p. 169.

16. Robert G.L. Waite, *The Psychopathic God: Adolf Hitler* (New York: Basic Books, 1977), p. 234. The issue of Hitler's supposed homosexuality was raised for a new century in Lothar Machtan's 2001 book *Hitlers Geheimnis: Das Doppelleben eines Diktators*, translated as *The Hidden Hitler* (New York: Basic Books, 2001). Charles Stone discusses the book, and the issue in general, in 'What if Hitler *Was* Gay?', *Gay and Lesbian Review* 9, 3 (May–June, 2002), pp. 29–34.

17. Hitler's *Mein Kampf* (1925) waxed erotic about the ideal condition of the German people, hoping to base a northern future on the southern past: 'What has made the Greek ideal of beauty immortal is the wonderful union of a splendid physical beauty with nobility of mind and spirit.' He had a clearer idea of, and more interest in, how to achieve the former, the 'splendid physical beauty', than the latter, the 'nobility of mind and spirit'. Perhaps he assumed, as so many others have assumed, that once you had achieved the former the latter would somehow evolve of its own accord: *mens sana* springing spontaneously from the fertile principle of the *corpus sanus*. Not unlike many other political commentators of his day, he felt that the state 'ought to allow much more time for physical training in the school', so that the young generation could be prevented from becoming soft: 'Not a single day should be allowed to pass in which the young pupil does not have one hour of physical training in the morning and one in the evening.' Such remarks tempt one to fantasise a meeting between Adolf Hitler and Dr Thomas Arnold of Rugby; they would have discovered plenty of common ground. Both had a nationalist purpose in their theories of education; Hitler declared, and Arnold might not have disagreed, that 'it is not the purpose of the People's State to educate a colony of aesthetic pacifists and physical degenerates'. But here Hitler's language takes on its own sinister momentum, leading in its suggestion of expendable types to the labour camp and the ovens. Moreover, both types – the aesthete and the degenerate – have a particular resonance in the context of homosexuality. Indeed, in his very next sentence he makes a sexual distinction between the reproductive and unproductive: 'This State does not consider that the human ideal is to be found in the honourable philistine or the maidenly spinster, but in a dareful personification of manly force and in women capable of bringing men into the world.' Notice that Hitler had more interest in women than Arnold had, but only insofar as they could bear children – and male children, at that. Quite who the 'honourable philistine' might be is not clear, but the suggestion seems to be that, by contrast, reproductively productive men and women are culturally involved – which is to say, nationally involved. The whole purpose of physical and mental fitness is to strengthen the national body politic: 'The individual has to regain his own physical strength and prowess in order to believe in the invincibility of the nation to which he belongs.' Under the Third Reich, fitness regimes, the education system, the armed services and the arts would be united in the pursuit of national goals. Among these, 'beauty' was, if not quite synonymous with, as important as 'strength'. Hitler was sufficiently well educated himself to know that this was a characteristic of the ancient Greek civilisations. When he spoke of 'beauty' he meant 'strength', and, confident of the Greek precedent, he knew there was nothing particularly philistine about that. Following the spirit of these passages of *Mein Kampf*, the Nazis would make it a matter of nationalistic

policy to use a particular kind of (Aryan) beauty as the centrepiece of its propaganda: for, as Hitler had written: 'it is in the interests of a nation that those who have a beautiful physique should be brought into the foreground, so that they might encourage the development of a beautiful bodily form among the people in general': Adolf Hitler, *Mein Kampf* (London: Hurst & Blackett, 1939), pp. 342–345. Not that the senior Nazis were very good models, but a well-tailored uniform might, from certain camera angles, do the trick.

18. For a useful discussion of relevant aspects of Röhm, see Eleanor Hancock, ' "Only the Real, the True, the Masculine Held Its Value": Ernst Röhm, Masculinity, and Male Homosexuality', *Journal of the History of Sexuality* 8, 4 (1998), pp. 616–641.

19. Edgar Ansel Mowrer, *Germany Puts the Clock Back* (London: John Lane the Bodley Head, 1933), pp. 192–194.

20. F. Yeats-Brown, *European Jungle* (London: Eyre & Spottiswoode, 1939), pp. 142–143.

21. Christopher Isherwood, *Goodbye to Berlin* (Harmondsworth: Penguin, 1945), pp. 190–191.

22. Michael Fry, *Hitler's Wonderland* (London: John Murray, 1934), pp. 20–21, 21, 22, 19, 20, 24–25, 27, 30.

23. Wyndham Lewis, *The Hitler Cult* (London: Dent, 1939), pp. 24–25, 22, 23, 25. When Robert Byron revisited the Eldorado, one of his old Berlin haunts, with his sister and brother-in-law in 1938, it had reopened as the Golden Horseshoe, with three circus horses on which customers could ride a dirt track around the dance floor. Byron and his sister both did so.

24. Among the texts he has been reading is a paper by R.T. Smallbones, whom he had known while in Germany. Dated 14 December 1938, it used homosexuality to account for Nazism. See Gregory Woods, *A History of Gay Literature: The Male Tradition* (New Haven & London: Yale University Press, 1998), pp. 250–251.

25. The reference is to Hans von Treschkow, *Von Fürsten und anderen Sterblichen* (Berlin, 1922).

26. J.H. Morgan, *Assize of Arms: Being the Story of the Disarmament of Germany and Her Rearmament (1919-1939) in Two Volumes*, vol. 1 (London: Methuen, 1945), pp. 195, 238, 195–196, 236–238.

27. Peter Adam, *Not Drowning but Waving: An Autobiography* (London: André Deutsch, 1995), p. 128.

28. Mel Gussow, *Edward Albee: A Singular Journey* (New York & London: Applause, 2001), p. 114.

29. Pierre Seel, *I, Pierre Seel, Deported Homosexual: A Memoir of Nazi Terror* (New York: Basic Books, 2011), p. 73.

## Chapter 8: The Southern Exotic

1. Xavier Girard, *Mediterranean from Homer to Picasso* (New York: Assouline, 2001), p. 8. David Attenborough views the ecological history of the Mediterranean – 'the place where we became so powerful that we were able to transform landscapes wholesale, where we started to keep exotic animals and plants brought from all over the world, [and] where we turned half a continent into a market garden' – as representing the Earth itself: 'It is the planet': David Attenborough, *The First Eden: The Mediterranean World and Man* (London: Guild, 1987), p. 230.

2. 'Ho vissuto a Perugia tutta la mia giovinezza fino a ventidue-ventitré anni, ma soprattutto d'estate andavo a mare e a sedici anni ho conosciuto Roma, che è stata per me la scoperta del Sud, un po' come per un inglese. Il mare, l'estate e questo viaggio a Roma hanno influenzato più di tutto la mia poesia': quoted in Elio Pecora, *Sandro Penna: una cheta follia* (Milano: Frassinelli, 1984), p. 38.

3. Gilbert Adair, *The Real Tadzio: Thomas Mann's* Death in Venice *and the Boy Who Inspired It* (London: Short Books, 2001), p. 98.

4. Robert Aldrich, *The Seduction of the Mediterranean: Writing, Art and Homosexual Fantasy* (London: Routledge, 1993), p. x, my italics.

5. Aldrich, p. 101. Winckelmann was the great theorist of Neoclassicism, 'whose leaden flights of pederastic dogma make even the longueurs of modern "queer theory" look almost sprightly': Robert Hughes, *Goya* (London: Harvill, 2003), p. 72.

6. Aldrich, p. 167.

7. The Train Bleu was the sleeper that connected the English Channel at Calais with Paris and then the Côte d'Azur. It provided First Class accommodation only. In *The Mystery of the Blue Train* (1928), Agatha Christie points out that it was also known as 'The Millionaires' Train'.

8. René Crevel, *Babylon* (London: Quartet, 1988), pp. 112, 141.

9. Philip Hoare, *Serious Pleasures: The Life of Stephen Tennant* (London: Penguin, 1991), p. 241.

10. Townsend Ludington, *Marsden Hartley: The Biography of an American Artist* (Boston: Little, Brown, 1992), p. 195.

11. Jean Cocteau, *The White Paper* (London: Brilliance Books, 1983), p. 53.

12. Virginia Nicholson, *Among the Bohemians: Experiments in Living, 1900-1930* (London: Penguin, 2003), p. 232.

13. Alex Ross, *The Rest is Noise: Listening to the Twentieth Century* (London: Harper Perennial, 2009), p. 115.

14. Essebac: Aldrich, *Seduction*, p. 123. Genet: Edmund White, *Genet* (London: Chatto & Windus, 1993), p. 429.

15. Ned Rorem, *The Paris Diary of Ned Rorem* (New York: George Braziller, 1966), p. 55.

16. Fred Kaplan, *Henry James: The Imagination of Genius* (Baltimore & London: Johns Hopkins University Press, 1999), p. 4.

17. P.N. Furbank, *E.M.Forster: A Life, Volume One* (Oxford: Oxford University Press, 1979), p. 96.

18. Michael Holroyd, *Lytton Strachey* (London: Vintage, 1994), p. 284.

19. After a glance at some of the evidence, a recent biographer concludes of d'Annunzio: 'Probably not an active homosexual, then, but certainly a sadomasochist': Lucy Hughes-Hallett, *The Pike: Gabriele d'Annunzio, Poet, Seducer and Preacher of War* (London: Fourth Estate, 2014), p. 160.

20. Philip Ziegler, *Osbert Sitwell: A Biography* (London: Pimlico, 1999), p. 31. See my dramatic monologue 'Sir Osbert's Complaint' in Gregory Woods, *Quidnunc* (Manchester: Carcanet, 2007), pp. 59–70.

21. Mark Ford, *Raymond Roussel and the Republic of Dreams* (London: Faber, 2000), p. 170.

22. Naomi Jacob disapproved of their increasingly fascistic sympathies. She turned down the Eichelberger Prize in 1935 because it was also being awarded to Adolf Hitler: Paul Bailey, *Three Queer Lives: An Alternative Biography of Fred Barnes, Naomi Jacob and Arthur Marshall* (London: Hamish Hamilton, 2001), pp. 151–152.

23. Adrian Clark and Jeremy Dronfield, *Queer Saint: The Cultured Life of Peter Watson, Who Shook Twentieth-Century Art and Shocked High Society* (London: John Blake, 2015), p. 240. The Via Veneto would be a crucial location in Federico Fellini's *La Dolce Vita* (1960).

24. Brad Gooch, *City Poet: The Life and Times of Frank O'Hara* (New York: Knopf, 1993), pp. 311–312.

25. Gore Vidal, *Palimpsest: A Memoir* (London: Abacus, 1996), pp. 388–389.

26. Peter Adam, *Not Drowning but Waving: An Autobiography* (London: André Deutsch, 1995), p. 178.

27. Edwin Cerio, *The Masque of Capri* (London: Thomas Nelson, 1957), p. 73. Paul Morand recalled seeing Fersen among the many pederasts in the piazza San Marco in Venice in 1908. Morand *père* refused to shake hands with any such creature, 'never suspecting that he was doing so all day long': Paul Morand, *Venices* (London: Pushkin, 2002), p. 44.

28. James Money, *Capri: Island of Pleasure* (London: Hamish Hamilton, 1986), pp. 110–111.

29. Fred Kaplan (ed.), *Travelling in Italy with Henry James* (London: Hodder & Stoughton, 1994), p. 285. Of course, the topography of the whole of the Gulf of Naples is resonant with its classical legacy, from the Phlegraean Fields (Campi flegrei) in the north, where the lake of Avernus still marks the entrance to Hades, by way of the baths at Baia (Baiae), the Roman amphitheatre at Pozzuoli, the supposed tomb of Virgil above the fishing port of Mergellina, past Herculaneum and Pompeii at the foot of Vesuvius, to the terrifying cliff on Capri where Tiberius' villa stands sentry over the tip of the Sorrentine peninsula; and even further southward to where, in the far distance, the ruins of Paestum would be liberated from malarial mosquitoes by the marsh-draining zeal of Benito Mussolini.

30. Norman Douglas, *Siren Land* (Harmondsworth: Penguin, 1983), pp. 198, 38, 196, 19, 178. Men like Douglas must have been an acquired taste. Having read Nancy Cunard's book on him, Samuel Beckett once drily remarked that he thought he and Douglas 'would not have got on': Deirdre Bair, *Samuel Beckett: A Biography* (London: Picador, 1980), p. 400.

31. Norman Douglas, *South Wind* (Harmondsworth: Penguin, 1953), p. 6. Arriving on the island, the bishop Mr Heard has heard of 'its beauty and historical associations: they attracted strange tourists from every part of the world. Queer types! Types to be avoided, perhaps' (p. 8). Cyril Connolly's parody-aesthete Christian de Clavering declares that 'Before one can understand Oxford one must have lived in Capri.' So, between Eton and the House (Christ

Church, Oxford), he spends a few months on the island, supposedly cramming. Before long, he has figured in five Capri-based novels in three languages. He has also sampled 'poppy after poppy' in Adelswärd-Fersen's villa: Cyril Connolly, 'Where Engels Fears to Tread', in Marie Jacqueline Lancaster (ed.), *Brian Howard: Portrait of a Failure* (London: Blond, 1968), pp. 602–613; p. 606.

32. *Money*, p. 156.
33. Rupert Hart-Davis, *Hugh Walpole: A Biography* (London: Rupert Hart-Davis, 1952), p. 258.
34. Carlo Levi, *The Watch* (South Royalton, Vermont: Steerforth Italia, 1999), p. 315.
35. Curzio Malaparte, *The Skin* (London: Panther, 1964), pp. 87, 128.
36. Curzio Malaparte, *Kaputt* (New York: Dutton, 1946), pp. 272–273.
37. Roger Peyrefitte, *The Exile of Capri* (London: Panther, 1969), p. 101. It was often also experienced, with great relief, as an escape from Naples, that magically anarchic city in which it has always been possible for travellers to get into all sorts of trouble, both delightful and dreadful. After going down from Cambridge in 1903, Ronald Storrs made his way to southern Italy, where Naples gave him mixed feelings: 'Of Naples I seem to remember nothing but the beauty of the bronzes and the ugliness of nature's most intimate rites performed before a listless public in the open streets': Ronald Storrs, *Orientations* (London: Ivor Nicholson & Watson, 1937), p. 17. Of Naples in the 1920s, Klaus Mann wrote: 'I thought it depressingly dull, although I was persecuted by a gang of veritable apaches and almost assassinated in a sinister sort of maison de rendezvous': Klaus Mann, *The Turning Point: Thirty-Five Years in This Century* (London: Gollancz, 1944), p. 95.
38. Peyrefitte, pp. 137, 142, 143. On this novel, see also Gregory Woods, 'Roger Peyrefitte, *The Exile of Capri*', in Tom Cardamone (ed.), *The Lost Library: Gay Fiction Rediscovered* (New York: Haiduk, 2010), pp. 151–158.
39. Douglas, *South Wind*, p. 304.
40. Carlo Levi, *Words Are Stones: Impressions of Sicily* (London: Hesperus, 2005), p. 62.
41. Louise Collis, *Impetuous Heart: The Story of Ethel Smyth* (London: William Kimber, 1984), p. 156.
42. André Gide, *The Immoralist* (Harmondsworth: Penguin, 1960), pp. 49, 50.
43. Gide, *The Immoralist*, pp. 137, 139, 144, 145, 148.
44. Teresa Chylińska, *Szymanowski* (New York: Twayne & The Kościuszko Foundation, 1973), p. 89.
45. Czesław Miłosz said of Iwaszkiewicz: 'He travelled much all over Europe, served for a while as a diplomat in Copenhagen and Brussels, and puzzled literary critics by the amoral, Dionysiac and, at the same time, pessimistic character of his work. The younger generation reproached him for a complete indifference to social and political causes, yet they were attracted to his demoniac art ... The most controversial of the *Skamander* group, he has always had many detractors and admirers': Czesław Miłosz (ed.), *Post-War Polish Poetry* (Harmondsworth: Penguin, 1970), p. 23.
46. Theodore Zeldin, *France 1848–1945: Intellect and Pride* (Oxford: Oxford University Press, 1980), pp. 110, 111. Vita Sackville-West, *The Edwardians* (London: Virago, 1983), pp. 45–46. Evelyn Waugh, *Brideshead Revisited* (Harmondsworth: Penguin, 1962), p. 98.
47. Barth David Schwartz, *Pasolini Requiem* (New York: Pantheon, 1992), p. 225.
48. Schwartz, p. 243.
49. Schwartz, p. 276, claims the former; Enzo Siciliano the latter, in *Pasolini* (London: Bloomsbury, 1987), p. 179.
50. Schwartz, p. 285.
51. Schwartz, p. 388.
52. Schwartz, p. 233.
53. John Cheever, *The Journals* (London: Cape, 1991), pp. 75–76.
54. It is in section D ('Pederasty') of the 'Terminal Essay' to his 1885 translation of *The Arabian Nights* that Burton writes: 'Within the Sotadic Zone the Vice is popular and endemic, held at the worst to be a mere peccadillo, whilst the races to the North and South ... practise it only sporadically amid the opprobium [*sic*] of their fellows who, as a rule, are physically incapable of performing the operation and look upon it with the liveliest disgust': Richard Burton, 'Terminal Essay', in Brian Reade (ed.), *Sexual Heretics: Male Homosexuality in English Literature from 1850 to 1900, an Anthology* (London: Routledge & Kegan Paul, 1970), pp. 158–193; p. 159.
55. Juan Goytisolo, *Forbidden Territory and Realms of Strife* (London: Verso, 2003), pp. 344, 352.

56. Edward Said, *Orientalism* (London: Penguin, 1991), pp. 103, 177.

57. Patrick Pollard, *André Gide: Homosexual Moralist* (New Haven & London: Yale University Press, 1991), pp. 176–178.

58. Marcel Proust, *Time Regained* (London: Chatto & Windus, 1970), p. 148. For the type of image Charlus is thinking of, see Eric Karpeles, *Paintings in Proust: A Visual Companion to In Search of Lost Time* (London: Thames & Hudson, 2008), pp. 308–309.

59. Marcel Proust, *Cities of the Plain, Part One* (London: Chatto & Windus, 1968), pp. 44–45. Proust's Marcel knows the *Nights* from boyhood, as do other boys in gay fiction. For instance, the title character of Umberto Saba's *Ernesto*: 'Ernesto had spent the most enchanting summer of his life when he was thirteen . . . reading *The Arabian Nights* as he lay on his tummy on the brass bed in the only room in the house with a sloping roof. He was so engrossed that he even forgot to go swimming in the sea, which he normally looked forward to so much': Umberto Saba, *Ernesto* (Manchester: Carcanet, 1987), p. 75. Marcus Matthews, in Angus Wilson's *No Laughing Matter*: when he wakes up from a nightmare, he sculpts the shapes around him into a more comforting décor, 'making wilder and wilder arabesques, ever more involuted spirals, draping the room in sables and furs and crimson velvets, adorning it with domes and minarets until at last it was Scheherazade's room and not his own at all, except that there in the centre of the gorgeous East he sat, cross-legged, round-eyed (a page, a mommet, Scheherazade herself, slave master-mistress), crowned absurdly, fantastically, wonderfully with a vast jewelled tiara almost his own height again': Angus Wilson, *No Laughing Matter* (London: Granada, 1979), p. 46.

60. Robert Irwin, *The Arabian Nights: A Companion* (London: Allen Lane, Penguin, 1994), pp. 69, 170–171.

61. Edward Carpenter, *Anthology of Friendship: Ioläus* (London: George Allen & Unwin, 1929), p. 109.

62. See Jonathan Fryer, *André and Oscar: Gide, Wilde and the Gay Art of Living* (London: Allison & Busby, 1999).

63. Robert Skidelsky, *John Maynard Keynes, 1883–1946: Economist, Philosopher, Statesman* (London: Pan, 2004), p. 153.

64. One biographical note says 'Kuzmin had visited Alexandria ten years earlier; it is unlikely that he and Constantine Cavafy knew of each other, but Alexandrian Songs is similar to Cavafy's poetry in both tone and subject matter': Robert Chandler, Boris Dralyuk and Irina Mashinski (eds), *The Penguin Book of Russian Poetry* (London: Penguin, 2015), p. 168. I am not convinced of the claimed similarity.

65. Edmund Keeley, *Cavafy's Alexandria: Study of a Myth in Progress* (London: Hogarth, 1977), p. 46. Of Cavafy's two Alexandrias, Keeley writes: 'It seems that the major thematic purpose of the parallel between the Sensual Cities of Cavafy's ancient and modern worlds was to under-line areas of continuity, even of identity, between past and present in the erotic experience of the lovers portrayed, while at the same time underlining the vast differences between past and present in the station and social roles of these lovers. Put in its simplest terms, the lovers of Cavafy's ancient Alexandria are not only accepted by their society, but are often depicted as representing the best which that society has to offer – the best of the young, anyway – whereas Cavafy's contemporary lovers are generally depicted as impoverished outcasts' (p. 72).

66. Daniel Mendelsohn, 'Introduction' in C.P. Cavafy, *Collected Poems* (New York: Alfred A. Knopf, 2009), pp. xv–lix; p. xxiv. It is worth pointing out that Arabs are conspicuous in their absence from this list of visitors. There were limits to Cavafy's internationalism: he spoke no Arabic, visited no Egyptian homes, and went to Arab boys for sex only as a last resort.

67. Having read Forster's essay on Cavafy, Malcolm Muggeridge visited him in Alexandria in 1932. He reported that Cavafy was 'a passionate lover of the English language, which he spoke fluently, having learnt it almost entirely from reading works like Milton's *Areopagitica*, Johnson's *Rasselas* and Macaulay's Essays. The result was indescribably funny and touching; such splen-didly rounded phrases and sonorous words coming from so seemingly alien and frail a figure, applied indiscriminately to any subject, weighty or frivolous, which might arise': Malcolm Muggeridge, *Chronicles of Wasted Time, I: The Green Stick* (London: Collins, 1972), p. 164.

68. Robert Liddell, *Cavafy: A Critical Biography* (London: Duckworth, 1974), p. 164.

69. Quoted in P.N. Furbank, *E.M. Forster: A Life, Volume Two* (Oxford: Oxford University Press, 1979), pp. 32–33.

70. Skidelsky, p. 164.

71. Michael Haag, *Alexandria: City of Memory* (New Haven & London: Yale University Press, 2004), p. 32.

72. Philip Mansel makes the point that, by restricting himself socially and erotically to Europeans, Cavafy missed out on that undercurrent of urban, Egyptian life that tolerated male homosexuality as a way of protecting the virtue and value of Muslim women; and missed the possibility of a relationship like that between E.M. Forster and the tram conductor Muhammad el-Adl. Mansel's conclusion is heavy with irony: 'The foreigner [Forster] crossed racial frontiers; the Alexandrian [Cavafy] did not': Philip Mansel, *Levant: Splendour and Catastrophe on the Mediterranean* (London: John Murray, 2010), p. 143.

73. Asked how he regarded the role of Cavafy in *The Alexandria Quartet*, Lawrence Durrell replied, 'As the expresser of the essence of the city.' He went on: 'I used him as precisely the poet of the city I was trying to build, you see, because he expressed the absolute amorality of the city, the irony of it, the cruelty of it, all in a sort of shorthand. And if you really wanted to say to somebody very quickly: "Let me give you a sketch of the Alexandrian temperament," you could easily put Cavafy's poetry into his hands': Robert McDonald, 'Jumping About Like Quanta', in Earl G. Ingersoll (ed.), *Lawrence Durrell: Conversations* (Cranbury, New Jersey: Associated University Presses, 1998), pp. 149–162; pp. 150, 151. This interview was conducted in London on 22 November 1975.

74. Robert Liddell, *Unreal City* (London: Peter Owen, 1993), p. 80. On the same page, Eugenides refers to Charles as the type of 'the English male virgin'.

75. Robert Medley, *Drawn from the Life: A Memoir* (London: Faber, 1983), p. 183.

76. Patrick White, *Flaws in the Glass: A Self-Portrait* (Harmondsworth: Penguin, 1983), p. 100.

77. Lucia Re, 'Alexandria Revisited: Colonialism and the Egyptian Works of Enrico Pea and Giuseppe Ungaretti', in Patrizia Palumbo (ed.), *A Place in the Sun: Africa in Italian Colonial Culture from Post-Unification to the Present* (Berkeley, California: University of California Press, 2003), pp. 163–196; p. 184. Maurizio Sanzio Viano says of this same interview with Pasolini: 'Faced with more personal questions, Ungaretti extricates himself with a coy answer: "I am a poet. I transgress all laws just by writing poetry." Pasolini does not succeed in legitimizing "the pressing reality" of homosexuality through an open confession by Ungaretti. Only those among the viewers who know of Ungaretti's homo-erotic tendencies are able to understand what Pasolini is trying to do': Maurizio Viano, *A Certain Reality: Making Use of Pasolini's Film Theory and Practice* (Berkeley & Los Angeles, California: University of California Press, 1993), p. 126.

78. T.E. Lawrence, *Seven Pillars of Wisdom: A Triumph, Volume 1* (London: Reprint Society, 1939), p. 28. Sounding not unlike T.E. Lawrence or Wilfred Thesiger, the Hungarian explorer and aviator László Almásy wrote: 'In the infinity of the desert body and mind are cleansed.' Almási did not, it seems, show much interest in Arab youths when in the desert – his wartime lover in the Libyan desert was Hans Entholt, a German actor – but R and R in Cairo before the Second World War does seem to have involved local contacts: 'unsubstantiated rumours exist of his purportedly predatory sex life in the darker corners of Cairo'. The seediness of the city could not compare with the purity of the desert: John Bierman, *The Secret Life of Laszlo Almasy: The Real English Patient* (London: Penguin, 2005), pp. 247, 132. Almásy was the original of the central character in *The English Patient*, the novel by Michael Ondaatje (1992) and the film adaptation directed by Anthony Minghella (1996). Wilfred Thesiger did not identify as homosexual, probably because he associated male homosexuality, definitively, with anal intercourse. Referring to his days at Eton College, he once said, 'I never heard of anyone being sodomized . . . which is what homosexuality is. I can conceive of nothing more unpleasant than sodomy. To me it would be absolutely appalling.' However, according to his biographer, 'He would later admit that he was physically attracted to the adolescent youths with whom he was to form close relationships throughout his life, while maintaining that these liaisons were essentially platonic.' It is likely that his Platonism stretched to modes of physical contact short of sodomy, although he had a low sex drive and said that when he was in the desert he did not miss sex any more than good meals or other physical indulgences. Certainly, what drive he had was directed towards males. As he once said, 'I do prefer men to women physically . . . In statues and everything, the shape of a man is much more appealing': Michael Asher, *Thesiger: A Biography* (London & New York: Viking, 1994), pp. 67, 63. In a striking but simplistic phrase, Ian Buruma has said, 'Thesiger is in love with racial macho': Ian Buruma, *The Missionary and the Libertine: Love and War in East and West* (London: Faber, 1996), p. 48.

79. T.E. Lawrence, p. 55.

80. T.E. Lawrence, pp. 452–455.

81. T.E. Lawrence, p. 440.
82. György Faludy, *My Happy Days in Hell* (London: Penguin, 2010), p. 144.
83. P.N. Furbank, *E.M. Forster: A Life* (Oxford: Oxford University Press, 1979), vol. 1, p. 168.
84. Furbank, I, p. 159, n.1. Francis King writes: 'As a young man, Forster, like many homosexuals of his day, had felt a community of spirit with [A.E.] Housman, as with Whitman': *E.M. Forster and His World* (London: Thames & Hudson, 1978), p. 88.
85. Interviewed by Farrukh Dhondy in 2001, a characteristically sour V.S. Naipaul said of Forster and *A Passage to India*: 'Forster of course has his own purposes in India. He is a homosexual and he has his time in India, exploiting poor people, which his friend Keynes also did. Keynes didn't exploit poor people, he exploited people in the university; he sodomised them, and they were too frightened to do anything about it. Forster belonged to that kind of nastiness really. I know it might be liberally wonderful now to say it's OK, but I think it's awful.' Naipaul added that Forster 'was somebody who didn't know Indian people. He just knew the court and a few middle-class Indians and the garden boys whom he wished to seduce': Farrukh Dhondy, 'Farrukh Dhondy Talks to V.S. Naipaul', *Literary Review* 278 (August 2001), pp. 28–36. (I am grateful to Mahendra Solanki for calling my attention to this interview.) A more balanced, more detailed and more sympathetic account of Forster's relationships in Egypt and India is given in Damon Galgut's fine novel *Arctic Summer* (London: Atlantic, 2014).
86. G. Lowes Dickinson, *The Autobiography of G. Lowes Dickinson, and Other Unpublished Writings* (London: Duckworth, 1973), p. 178.
87. Haag, *Alexandria*, p. 106.
88. Furbank II, p. 105.
89. Magdalena J. Zaborowska, *James Baldwin's Turkish Decade: Erotics of Exile* (Durham, North Carolina: Duke University Press, 2009), pp. 24, 20.
90. Mark Ford, *Raymond Roussel*, pp. 19, 30, 20. Why, then, travel at all? Roussel's close friend and ostensible girlfriend Charlotte Dufrène once hinted that many of his foreign trips were motivated by the need to escape the demands of blackmailers.
91. Miriam J. Benkovitz, *Ronald Firbank: A Biography* (London: Weidenfeld & Nicolson, 1970), pp. 289–290.
92. Benkovitz, pp. 292–293.
93. Pier Paolo Pasolini, *The Scent of India* (London: Olive Press, 1984), pp. 9–19.
94. Conversely, the pansy uncle – 'though maybe I should have called him "auntie"' – of the narrator of Raymond Queneau's novel *Odile* (1937), classifying countries by their latitude, regards the Orient as belonging solely to the East, and therefore thinks Morocco much the same as Brittany – see Raymond Queneau, *Odile* (Normal, Illinois: Dalkey Archive, 1988), p. 11.
95. This novel was originally published under a pseudonym: David Griffin, *The Wrong People* (New York: Peacock, 1967), p. 92.
96. Paul Bowles, *Let It Come Down* (London: Penguin, 2000), p. 21.
97. Truman Capote, *Answered Prayers* (London: Penguin, 2001), p. 77.
98. John Calder, *The Garden of Eros: The Story of the Paris Expatriates and the Post-War Literary Scene* (London: Alma, 2014), p. 180. (Calder adds the British 's' to the name of the city.)
99. Iain Finlayson, *Tangier: City of the Dream* (London: Flamingo, 1993), p. 93.
100. Although father and son are extremely close, it is not strictly true to say, as Millicent Dillon does, that the story 'tells of an incestuous affair between the [narrator] and his son': Millicent Dillon, *You Are Not I: A Portrait of Paul Bowles* (Berkeley & LA: University of California Press, 1998), p. 177. Atlantic crossings were productive times for Bowles. He wrote 'The Delicate Prey' on board ship in 1948. His fellow passenger Tennessee Williams said that the story – in which an Arab man castrates and then rapes a boy from an enemy tribe – was unpublishable; Dillon, pp. 219–220.
101. Finlayson, p. 146.
102. Finlayson, p. 245.
103. In 1956 Paul signed over the house to Jane, so that she in turn would be able to pass it on to Cherifa.
104. Michelle Green, *The Dream at the End of the World: Paul Bowles and the Literary Renegades in Tangier* (New York: HarperCollins, 1991), p. 72.
105. Finlayson, p. 298.
106. Jane Bowles, *Two Serious Ladies* (London: Virago, 1979), p. 11.

107. Finlayson, p. 298.
108. Michelle Green, p. 153.
109. Michelle Green, p. 192.
110. Finlayson, pp. 194, 195.
111. Ted Morgan, *Literary Outlaw: The Life and Times of William S. Burroughs* (New York: Avon, 1990), p. 253.
112. William Burroughs, *The Naked Lunch* (London: Corgi, 1968), p. 202.
113. Michelle Green, pp. 157, 158, 162.
114. Jack Kerouac, *Desolation Angels* (London: Flamingo, 2001), pp. 337, 339, 340–341, 344. Michelle Green, pp. 174, 176.
115. Barry Miles, *Ginsberg: A Biography* (London: Viking, 1990), p. 214.
116. Finlayson, p. 225. The Moroccan writer Tahar Ben Jelloun had a certain grudging respect for Ginsberg's frankness about his reasons for having gone to Tangier in the 1950s: 'boys and hashish – and neither is expensive'. By contrast, Ben Jelloun said of Paul Bowles: 'I didn't like Bowles, the man or the writer. He loved young Moroccan boys and preferred them illiterate. He'd write books in their words; it was an ambiguous relationship': Maya Jaggi, 'Voice of the Maghreb', *The Guardian: Review* (6 May 2006), p. 11. Having emigrated to Paris in 1961, Ben Jelloun was literally better placed to speak back to imperialism (albeit in French rather than Arabic) and to the white gay men who had treated Tangier as their sexual playground. See, for instance, his novel *Leaving Tangier* (2009).
117. Finlayson, pp. 232–233.
118. Michelle Green, p. 264.
119. Michelle Green, p. 269.
120. Dillon, p. 307.
121. Michelle Green, pp. 271, 274.
122. Dillon, p. 145. One reason why George Plimpton would not publish a story of Chester's in an early issue of the *Paris Review* was the biographical note Chester had provided: '*Alfred Chester is an impenitent atheistic Jew, a heavy drinker, continually smoking nicotine – with or without marijuana – a pill-popping hairless albino homosexual who cannot keep a lover and an American citizen of exemplary right-wing views*': Christopher Logue, *Prince Charming: A Memoir* (London: Faber, 1999), p. 163.
123. Michelle Green, p. 300.
124. Alfred Chester, *Behold Goliath* (London: André Deutsch, 1965), pp. 54, 67, 79.
125. Chester, *Behold Goliath* pp. 158, 163, 174.
126. Severo Sarduy, *Cobra and Maitreya* (Normal, Illinois: Dalkey Archive, 1995), p. 46. As director in charge of Spanish and Latin American writing at Éditions du Seuil, Sarduy published José Lezama Lima's novel *Paradiso* in a French translation; and in a similar role at Gallimard he published Juan Goytisolo. Philippe Sollers wrote the French translation of *Cobra*.
127. Finlayson, pp. 318, 319.
128. Bryan Connon, *Somerset Maugham and the Maugham Dynasty* (London: Sinclair-Stevenson, 1997), p. 255.
129. Michelle Green, p. 258.
130. John Nathan, *Mishima: A Biography* (Cambridge, Massachusetts: Da Capo, 2000), p. 32.
131. Nathan, pp. 63–64.
132. Nathan, p. 106.
133. Mishima once told Frank O'Hara he liked sleeping with Caucasian men because they had bigger cocks. 'Come to Japan, see for yourself,' he added: Joe LeSueur, *Digressions on Some Poems by Frank O'Hara: A Memoir* (New York: Farrar, Straus & Giroux, 2003), p. 189.
134. On his various travels, Mishima was routinely introduced to many writers, but was keen also to meet ordinary men – and not only for sexual reasons. At the end of a British Council trip to Britain, when asked who was the most interesting person he had met, he replied, 'Bill Brown' (rather than, say, Stephen Spender or Angus Wilson). Brown was the man who had driven him to visit Francis King in Brighton – see Francis King, *Yesterday Came Suddenly* (London: Constable, 1993), pp. 253–254.
135. Nathan, p. 150. Philip Core said of Mishima's hybrid styles: 'Frequently photographed in "bikey" gear, or as a naked musclebound porn star, Mishima wanted to be both a traditional Samurai hero at home, and a New York underground star abroad. To a certain extent he was – befriended by Tennessee Williams, Cocteau, and even the Rothschilds – but all the camp

of kimonos and cockrings jumbled together reveals the alienated son of an American GI in war-torn Japan that was his real creative self': Philip Core, *Camp: The Lie that Tells the Truth* (London: Plexus, 1984), p. 130.

136. Stephen Spender, *Journals 1939–1983* (London: Faber, 1992), pp. 189–190. The text in question, *Comrade Loves of the Samurai*, was a selection of tales by Ihara Saikaku (1642–1693). An English translation by F. Powys Mathers was privately published in 1928.

137. Buruma, p. 11.

## Chapter 9: The New World

1. Claude McKay, *A Long Way from Home* (London: Pluto, 1985), p. x.
2. McKay, pp. 49, 133.
3. Eric Garber, 'A Spectacle in Color: The Lesbian and Gay Subculture of Jazz Age Harlem', in Martin Bauml Duberman, Martha Vicinus and George Chauncey, Jr (eds), *Hidden From History: Reclaiming the Gay and Lesbian Past* (London & New York: Penguin, 1991), pp. 318–331; p. 327.
4. David Levering Lewis, *When Harlem Was in Vogue* (New York: Oxford University Press, 1989), p. 77.
5. Garber, p. 329.
6. Langston Hughes, *The Big Sea: An Autobiography* (London: Pluto, 1986), p. 237.
7. A.B. Christa Schwarz, *Gay Voices of the Harlem Renaissance* (Bloomington & Indianapolis: Indiana University Press, 2003), p. 89.
8. Wayne F. Cooper, *Claude McKay: Rebel Sojourner in the Harlem Renaissance, A Biography* (Baton Rouge & London: Louisiana State University Press, 1987), p. 131. It is interesting how often one encounters variations on the 'not at all effeminate' qualification after the 'homosexual' definition. For much of the twentieth century, heterosexual people were taken aback by male homosexual masculinity.
9. McKay, pp. 154, 150, 156.
10. McKay, pp. 315–316.
11. Christopher Lasch, *The Agony of the American Left* (New York: Vintage, 1969), p. 51. Gold also attacked Marcel Proust (as a 'masturbator') and other 'politically imbecile' writers, denouncing them as 'pansies' (p. 52).
12. On the homoerotic literature of the Harlem Renaissance, see Gregory Woods, *A History of Gay Literature: The Male Tradition* (New Haven & London: Yale University Press, 1998), pp. 209–216.
13. Garber, p. 326.
14. Chris Albertson, *Bessie* (London: Barrie & Jenkins, 1972), p. 117.
15. After the publication of *Parties* in 1930, Van Vechten more or less gave up writing – certainly as his main artistic interest – and turned to photography, mainly portrait photography. Even as a relative beginner – though a beginner with the best of connections and influence – by 1933 he had produced enough work of high quality to show in an exhibition alongside Cecil Beaton, Edward Steichen, Man Ray and George Platt Lynes. The subjects of his individual portrait photographs would include Aaron Copland and Norman Douglas (1935); Langston Hughes, Alec Waugh and Glenway Wescott (1936); Cecil Beaton (1937); Bryher (1938); Marsden Hartley (1939); Janet Flanner and Charles Laughton (1940); Countee Cullen (1941); Paul Bowles and John Latouche (1944); Marc Blitzstein and Virgil Thomson (1947); Gore Vidal, Evelyn Waugh and Tennessee Williams (1948); Marcel Jouhandeau and Marie Laurencin (1949); Jane Bowles (1951); William Inge (1954); James Baldwin and Donald Windham (1955); Ned Rorem (1956); James Purdy (1957); Edward Albee (1961); Lincoln Kirstein (1964); plus W.H. Auden, Julien Green, Christopher Isherwood, Gian Carlo Menotti, Leonard Bernstein, Samuel Barber, Truman Capote, Marlon Brando, Bessie Smith, Carson McCullers and Raymond Massey.
16. Beverley Nichols, *Oxford – London – Hollywood: An Omnibus* (London: Cape, 1931), pp. 617, 673. One historian sums up the gay clubs and cabarets of Harlem as follows: 'Many of Harlem's least reputable clubs featured transvestite acts known as "pansy parades." While the Ubangi Club attracted crowds of gays and lesbians, "Queerosities" ruled the Clam House, a West 133rd Street dive owned by a lesbian named Gladys Bentley dressed up as a man and performed double entendre numbers while she flirted with women in the audience. One male performer even dressed up as Gloria Swanson and wowed audiences with the risqué song "Hot Nuts". In a codicil fifty pages later, he adds: 'Whites from downtown looking for interracial homosexual

action could still [after the Cotton Club closed down in 1935] find it at a cheap, seedy night-club called Chez Clinton': Jonathan Gill, *Harlem: The Four Hundred Year History from Dutch Village to Capital of Black America* (New York: Grove, 2011), pp. 271–272, 322. In Ralph Ellison's 1952 novel *Invisible Man*, when he first gets to New York, the narrator is invited by Mr Emerson's son to accompany him to a Harlem nightclub called, with a nod to Walt Whitman, the Calamus Club. It has, he says, 'a truly continental flavour'. The narrator turns down his invitation: Ralph Ellison, *Invisible Man* (Harmondsworth: Penguin, 1965), pp. 147–158.

17. Blair Niles, *Strange Brother* (London: T. Werner Laurie, 1931), pp. 188, 234.
18. Jane Stevenson, *Edward Burra: Twentieth-Century Eye* (London: Pimlico, 2008), pp. 216–217. If Stern had stayed in London he might have found an establishment called the Shim Sham Club (at 37, Wardour Street). With black jazz performers and customers, it was also welcoming to a crowd that included Jews, Communists and lesbians and gay men. An item on it in the magazine *Melody Maker* was aptly headlined 'Harlem in London': Judith R. Walkowitz, *Nights Out: Life in Cosmopolitan London* (New Haven & London: Yale University Press, 2012), p. 236.
19. Djuna Barnes, *New York* (London: Virago, 1990), p. 238. For details of the Greenwich Village gay scene during the First World War and the Prohibition period, see Neil Miller, *Out of the Past: Gay and Lesbian History from 1869 to the Present* (London: Vintage, 1995), pp. 141–145. For greater detail, see George Chauncey, *Gay New York: Gender, Urban Culture, and the Making of the Gay Male World, 1890–1940* (New York: Basic Books, 1994), pp. 228–244.
20. Jonathan D. Katz and David C. Ward, *Hide/Seek: Difference and Desire in American Portraiture* (Washington, DC: Smithsonian Books, 2010), p. 91.
21. Chauncey, pp. 327, 348, 351, 358.
22. James Knox, *Robert Byron* (London: John Murray, 2004), p. 347.
23. Chauncey, pp. 168, 177, 103.
24. Gore Vidal, *The City and the Pillar* (London: John Lehmann, 1949), p. 211. Speaking of Sodom: in Saul Bellow's 1970 novel *Mr Sammler's Planet*, Sammler says, 'New York makes me think about the collapse of civilization, about Sodom and Gomorrah, the end of the world': Saul Bellow, *Mr Sammler's Planet* (Harmondsworth: Penguin, 1972), p. 244.
25. Vidal, *City and the Pillar*, p. 261.
26. John Cheever, *The Journals* (London: Cape, 1991), pp. 33–34.
27. Italo Calvino, *Hermit in Paris: Autobiographical Writings* (London: Penguin, 2003), p. 30.
28. Ann Bannon, *Journey to a Woman* (San Francisco: Cleis Press, 2003), p. 116. Julie Abraham writes that 'the heroines of the lesbian novels of the 1950s and 1960s were routinely pictured in public in the city – in bars or at work – their lives routinely contrasted with those of married women immured in the suburbs. When they were not out in public, the lesbians of the 1950s and 1960s were to be found in their own city apartments': Julie Abraham, *Metropolitan Lovers: The Homosexuality of Cities* (Minneapolis & London: University of Minnesota Press, 2008), p. 261.
29. Ann Bannon, *Beebo Brinker* (San Francisco: Cleis Press, 2001), p. 38.
30. Quoted in Charles Kaiser, *The Gay Metropolis, 1940–1996* (London: Phoenix, 1999), p. 86.
31. Bannon, *Journey*, pp. ix, xi.
32. Ann Bannon, *I Am a Woman* (San Francisco: Cleis Press, 2002), p. xiii.
33. Bannon, *Beebo Brinker*, pp. 40–41.
34. Audre Lorde, *Zami: A New Spelling of My Name* (London: Pandora, 1996), pp. 191, 196, 194.
35. James Baldwin, *Another Country* (London: Penguin, 1990), pp. 37, 38, 292.
36. Arthur Laurents, *Original Story By: A Memoir of Broadway and Hollywood* (New York & London: Applause, 2000), pp. 32–33.
37. Charles Ford and Parker Tyler, *The Young and Evil* (London: GMP, 1988), pp. 46, 182.
38. Barry Miles, *Ginsberg: A Biography* (London: Viking, 1990), p. 391.
39. Calvino, p. 27. Arrabal told Calvino that 'at home the beatniks are very clean, they have a beautiful house complete with fridge and television, and they live as a quiet bourgeois ménage and dress up in dirty clothes only to go out' (pp. 27–28). Further evidence of the perversity of New York arose when Calvino and another Italian man picked up two women – who then paired off with each other instead (p. 29).
40. Laurents, p. 404.
41. Peter Stoneley, *A Queer History of the Ballet* (London & New York: Routledge, 2007), p. 103.
42. Ned Rorem, *Knowing When to Stop: A Memoir* (New York: Simon & Schuster, 1994), p. 207.
43. Marijane Meaker, *Highsmith: A Romance of the 1950s* (San Francisco: Cleis Press, 2003), p. 79. Highsmith began her career using the pseudonym 'Claire Morgan'; Meaker published

mystery/crime novels under the pseudonym 'Vin Packer', but is now perhaps best known as the author of *Spring Fire* (1952), generally credited as launching a wave of lesbian pulp fiction.

44. Laurents, p. 179.
45. Edmund White, *My Lives* (London: Bloomsbury, 2005), p. 178.
46. William J. Mann, *Behind the Screen: How Gays and Lesbians Shaped Hollywood, 1910–1969* (New York: Penguin, 2002), p. x.
47. William J. Mann, *Behind the Screen*, pp. xv–xvi, xxii.
48. Quoted in Thomas Yingling, *Hart Crane and the Homosexual Text: New Thresholds, New Anatomies* (Chicago: University of Chicago Press, 1990), p. 77.
49. William J. Mann, *Behind the Screen*, pp. xxii–xxiii.
50. William J. Mann, *Behind the Screen*, pp. 123–124.
51. William J. Mann, *Behind the Screen*, p. 128.
52. Nazimova reversed the process in the mid-1920s, returning to the New York stage and then to Europe, where she did work that was far more serious and experimental than she was ever likely to have found in Tinseltown.
53. William J. Mann, *Behind the Screen*, p. 146.
54. William J. Mann, *Behind the Screen*, p. 132.
55. William J. Mann, *Wisecracker: The Life and Times of William Haines, Hollywood's First Openly Gay Star* (New York: Penguin, 1999), p. 143.
56. William J. Mann, *Wisecracker*, pp. 152–153.
57. William J. Mann, *Wisecracker*, p. 236.
58. Vito Russo audited the extent and quality of those representations in his ground-breaking 1981 book, later revised, *The Celluloid Closet: Homosexuality in the Movies* (New York: Harper & Row, 1987).
59. Richard Ellmann, *Oscar Wilde* (London: Penguin, 1988), pp. 163–164, 163.
60. Allen Ginsberg would bring Whitman and Lorca together again, but in 'A Supermarket in California' rather than New York, in 1955. But the two dead poets, although lurking in the same retail outlet, have nothing to do with each other: Lorca is up to something unidentified 'down by the watermelons', perhaps looking for young black men of the kind he knew from Harlem, while Whitman follows a different drummer, 'poking among the meats in the refrigerator and eying the grocery boys': Allen Ginsberg, *Collected Poems 1947–1980* (London: Viking, 1985), p. 136.
61. Czesław Miłosz, *The Witness of Poetry* (Cambridge, Massachusetts: Harvard University Press, 1983), p. 70. Walter Grünzweig has followed Whitman's trail into German and Austrian culture as far as the Wandervogel and nudism movements of the first two decades of the twentieth century – see Walter Grünzweig, *Constructing the German Walt Whitman* (Iowa City: University of Iowa Press, 1995).
62. Emile Delavenay has argued that Whitman was, for the English social reformer, sexologist and poet Edward Carpenter, 'the guide and the master, the beacon showing the way to the accomplishment of his own destiny. There is not one of [Carpenter's] books in which he does not name [Whitman], quote him, describe his personal magnetism, and invest him with the attributes of divinity': Emile Delavenay, *D.H. Lawrence and Edward Carpenter: A Study in Edwardian Transition* (London: Heinemann, 1971), p. 222. (In the broader argument of Delavenay's book, it follows that Whitman had a comparable influence on D.H. Lawrence.) For Carpenter, it was Whitman and not Oscar Wilde who was both herald and model of the new breed of man-loving men. In his account of a visit to Whitman in Camden, New Jersey, on 17 June 1884, Carpenter's notes are revealingly brief on what the great man had to say about having met Wilde: 'have just [*sic*] had a visit from Oscar Wilde – who told me about England; I made him do the talking – rather liked him'. It is hard to believe this is all Whitman said of the occasion, but it is certainly all that Carpenter subsequently felt like repeating – see Edward Carpenter, *Days with Walt Whitman, with Some Notes on His Life and Work* (London: George Allen, 1906), p. 36. There is nothing of Wilde in *Ioläus*, Carpenter's wide-ranging 'anthology of friendship', whereas its first edition (1902) actually ended with poems from Whitman ('Recorders ages hence', 'When I heard at the close of the day' and 'I hear it was charged against me'.)
63. André Gide, *Corydon: Four Socratic Dialogues* (New York: Farrar, Straus & Co., 1950), pp. 4–8.
64. Patrick Pollard discusses what is known of Gide's readings of Whitman, and summarises Gide's disagreements with Bazalgette, in *André Gide: Homosexual Moralist* (New Haven & London: Yale University Press, 1991), pp. 270–278.

65. Unlike Lorca, Pessoa was well able to read Whitman in the original. The sophistication of his English is best displayed in his translations of the poetry of his gay protégé António Botto, first published in 1948. See *The Songs of António Botto*, edited and introduced by Josiah Blackmore (Minneapolis, Minnesota: University of Minnesota Press, 2010). The *Canções* were published in January 1922. In July, Pessoa published a long essay announcing Botto as 'the only true aesthete in Portugal'. In the controversy that followed, what was referred to as the 'Literatura de Sodoma' was alternately denounced and defended. See R.W. Howes, 'Fernando Pessoa, Poet, Publisher, and Translator', *British Library Journal* 9, 2 (1982), pp. 161–170; pp. 164–165. See also Josiah Blackmore, 'Introduction: António Botto's Bruises of Light', *The Songs of António Botto*, pp. ix–xxxvi; pp. xiv–xvi.

66. Susan Margaret Brown, 'Pessoa and Whitman: Brothers in the Universe', in Robert K. Martin (ed.) *The Continuing Presence of Walt Whitman: The Life After the Life* (Iowa City: University of Iowa Press, 1992), pp. 167–181; p. 177.

67. The closing lines of 'Cape Hatteras': 'yes, Walt, / Afoot again, and onward without halt, – / Not soon, nor suddenly, – no, never to let go / My hand / in yours, / Walt Whitman – / so—': Hart Crane, *The Complete Poems and Selected Letters and Prose of Hart Crane* (London: Oxford University Press, 1968), p. 95.

68. Álvaro de Campos, 'Salutation to Walt Whitman', in Fernando Pessoa, *A Little Larger than the Entire Universe: Selected Poems* (London: Penguin, 2006), pp. 197–214; pp. 198, 212–213. Pessoa once wrote of 'the insatiable, unquantifiable longing to be both the same and other': Fernando Pessoa, *The Book of Disquiet* (London: Serpent's Tail, 1991), p. 25. If his various heteronyms were any help in achieving this ambivalent balance, clearly, Álvaro de Campos was of the 'other' camp.

69. Eugénio Lisboa and L.C. Taylor (eds), *Fernando Pessoa: A Century Pessoa* (Manchester: Fyfield/Carcanet, 2003), p. 298.

70. Paul Binding sees an ambivalence even in Lorca's response to Whitman alone: 'Lorca in his own crisis of love must have found Whitman's proclamatory pride in his sexual condition both assuring and disconcerting. His ode to Whitman reveals this double attitude [which] helps to give the poem its haunting ambiguity': Paul Binding, *Lorca: The Gay Imagination* (London: GMP, 1985), p. 134.

71. C. Brian Morris, *Son of Andalusia: The Lyrical Landscapes of Federico García Lorca* (Liverpool: Liverpool University Press, 1997), pp. 405–406. If you wanted to engage in discussion with this peevish point, you could reply that the local subculture in question – like so many we are seeing in the present book – actually had rather a lot of international links. Morris is referring to Eisenberg's item 'Granada' in Wayne R. Dynes (ed.), *Encyclopedia of Homosexuality* (Chicago & London: St James Press, 1990), pp. 489–490. In their history of male homosexuality in Spain, Richard Cleminson and Francisco Vásquez García are not a lot more generous about the Granada group. Their few paragraphs on it give a paltry impression of the group's significance, even if they concede that 'what cannot be denied is the existence of a lively intellectual and artistic culture in Granada based a round [*sic*] the group of friends that included Federico García Lorca, Manuel de Falla and Manuel Angeles Ortiz, amongst others, and in bars and cafés, such as "El Polinario" in the grounds of the Alhambra'. Some members of this group of friends 'articulated a voice which spoke of homosexuality' quite clearly, 'working between silence and expression': Richard Cleminson and Francisco Vásquez García, '*Los invisibles*': *A History of Male Homosexuality in Spain* (Cardiff: University of Wales Press, 2007), p. 230.

72. Falla's sexuality is rarely discussed with any clarity by his commentators, even if they sometimes raise relevant questions. For instance: 'How was it that this celibate, ascetic, monkish man could feel the pulse and emotional heartbeats of women in music with so absolute a certainty of touch? It is by no means a common gift': Burnett James, *Manuel de Falla and the Spanish Musical Renaissance* (London: Gollancz, 1979), p. 102.

73. Bruce Swansea and José Ramón Enríquez, 'Homosexuality in the Spanish Generation of 1927: A Conversation with Jaime Gil de Biedma', *Gay Sunshine* 42/43 (Spring 1980), pp. 18–20; p. 14.

74. Ian Gibson, *Federico García Lorca: A Life* (London: Faber, 1989), p. 220. The reference is to the journalist and literary critic Andrenio (pseudonym of Eduardo Gómez de Baquero) and the poet José Frutos Baeza.

75. 'Ángel Flores, the New York editor and translator who introduced the two men, remarks that, unfortunately, neither was aware of the other's poetic accomplishment. It was almost as if two transatlantic liners had passed each other without signals in the black of night': Edwin Honig, *García Lorca* (London: Cape, 1968), p. 14.

76. Leslie Stainton, *Lorca: A Dream of Life* (New York: Farrar, Straus & Giroux, 1999), p. 248.
77. Ian Gibson, *Lorca,* p. 293.
78. With characteristic hostility, Roy Campbell wrote that 'Lorca went and stayed in the U.S.A. for some time, but was unable to establish a real contact with the Americans or their way of life. The result on his poetry [*sic*] was entirely negative.' Campbell does not even mention the 'Ode to Walt Whitman': Roy Campbell, *Lorca: An Appreciation of His Poetry* (Cambridge: Bowes & Bowes, 1952), p. 71.
79. The line is in section VII of *The Bridge,* 'The Tunnel' – see Crane, p. 110.
80. John Dos Passos, *Manhattan Transfer* (Harmondsworth: Penguin, 1986), pp. 213, 280–281.
81. Pablo Neruda, *Memoirs* (Harmondsworth: Penguin, 1978), p. 115. Ignacio Sánchez Mejías was predominantly heterosexual, but, according to Gibson, 'It came as a shock to many people, including Lorca, that the bullfighter also had a liking for pretty young men': Ian Gibson, *Lorca,* p. 198.
82. Ian Gibson, *Lorca,* p. 419.
83. The article was called 'El efeminamiento de la literature mexicana'. See Viviane Mahieux, 'The Chronicler as Streetwalker: Salvador Novo and the Performance of Genre', *Hispanic Review* (Spring 2008), pp. 155–177; p. 161.
84. Ian Gibson, *Lorca,* p. 360.
85. Octavio Paz, 'Luis Cernuda: The Edifying Word', in Luis Cernuda, *Selected Poems* (Riverdale-on-Hudson, NY: The Sheep Meadow Press, 1999), pp. xiii–xli; p. xx.
86. Neil C. McKinlay, *The Poetry of Luis Cernuda: Order in a World of Chaos* (London: Tamesis Books, 1999), p. 6. Gide would always be a mentor of his: 'In him he found some answers to the more personal concerns posed by his homosexuality and an echo of the deeply ethical considerations that pervade most of his poetic output': Salvador Jimenez-Fajardo, *Luis Cernuda* (Boston: Twayne, 1978), p. 25.
87. Derek Harris, *Luis Cernuda: A Study of the Poetry* (London: Tamesis Books, 1973), pp. 2, 13.
88. Ian Gibson, *Lorca,* p. 432. Neruda, Aleixandre and many others were present. It may be that Lorca had a sexual relationship with Cernuda at some point. Gibson refers to Emilio Garrigues y Díaz-Cañabate, 'Al teatro con Federico García Lorca', *Cuadernos hispanamericanos* 340 (1978), pp. 99–117; pp. 106–107.
89. Quoted in José Quiroga, *Tropics of Desire: Interventions from Queer Latino America* (New York: New York University Press, 2000), p. 115, 118.
90. Juan Goytisolo, *Forbidden Territory and Realms of Strife* (London: Verso, 2003), pp. 307, 327.
91. Heberto Padilla, *Sent Off the Field* (London: André Deutsch, 1972), pp. 88, 110–111.
92. Reinaldo Arenas, *Farewell to the Sea: A Novel of Cuba* (New York: Penguin, 1987), pp. 269–273. G. Cabrera Infante has written, of Arenas: 'His pansexuality is, always, homosexual. Which makes him a country Cuban version of a Walt Whitman of prose and, at times, of a poetic prose that is on occasions a brown man's burden': *Mea Cuba* (London: Faber, 1994), p. 413.
93. Jaime Manrique, *Eminent Maricones: Arenas, Lorca, Puig, and Me* (Madison, Wisconsin: University of Wisconsin Press, 1999), p. 113.
94. Suzanne Jill Levine, *Manuel Puig and the Spider Woman: His Life and Fictions* (London: Faber, 2000), pp. 269, 271.
95. Levine, pp. 60, 62.
96. Levine, p. 76.
97. Levine, p. 169.
98. Levine, pp. 302–303.

## Chapter 10: The New Politics

1. John Bayley, *Iris: A Memoir of Iris Murdoch* (London: Duckworth, 1998), p. 12.
2. Bayley, p. 14.
3. Bayley, p. 20.
4. Wilde, Oscar, *The Complete Letters of Oscar Wilde* (London: Fourth Estate, 2000), p. 1044.
5. Brian Reade (ed.), *Sexual Heretics: Male Homosexuality in English Literature from 1850 to 1900* (London: Routledge & Kegan Paul, 1970), pp. 248–285; p. 269.
6. Philip Hoare, *Wilde's Last Stand: Decadence, Conspiracy and the First World War* (London: Duckworth, 1997), p. 157.
7. In his novel *Count d'Orgel* (*Le Bal du Comte d'Orgel,* 1924), Raymond Radiguet makes an interesting distinction between discretion and secrecy. Of the character Paul Robin, he

writes: 'Paul believed he was discreet, [but] he was only secretive. Thus he divided his life into compartments: he thought he alone could pass from one to another. He did not yet know how limited the world is and that one may meet anyone anywhere': Raymond Radiguet, *Count d'Orgel* (London: Calder & Boyars, 1968), p. 23.

8. Peter Wildeblood, *Against the Law* (Harmondsworth: Penguin, 1957), p. 13.
9. Patrick Higgins, *Heterosexual Dictatorship: Male Homosexuality in Postwar Britain* (London: Fourth Estate, 1996), pp. 123–124.
10. Higgins, p. 141.
11. Higgins, p. 145.
12. Wildeblood, p. 30.
13. Wildeblood, p. 31.
14. Wildeblood, p. 54.
15. Lord Montagu of Beaulieu, *Wheels Within Wheels: An Unconventional Life* (London: Weidenfeld & Nicolson, 2000), pp. 100, 106, 108, 118. One of the boy scout party – not one of the accusing scouts – later explained to Montagu how the false accusations in the earlier case came about (pp. 134–135).
16. Wildeblood, pp. 47, 50.
17. Sebastian Faulks, *The Fatal Englishman: Three Short Lives* (London: Hutchinson, 1996), p. 222.
18. John Wolfenden, *Turning Points: The Memoirs of Lord Wolfenden* (London: Bodley Head, 1976), pp. 132–133, 137, 145, 146.
19. Montagu, p. 132.
20. Ian Harvey, *To Fall Like Lucifer* (London: Sidgwick & Jackson, 1971), pp. 169, 128. From the year following the publication of his memoirs, Harvey became a vice-president of the Campaign for Homosexual Equality.
21. Beverley Nichols, *The Sweet and Twenties* (London: Weidenfeld & Nicolson, 1958), pp. 109, 110.
22. Hugo Vickers, *Cecil Beaton: The Authorized Biography* (London: Weidenfeld & Nicolson, 1985), p. 477.
23. Gaia Servadio, *Luchino Visconti: A Biography* (London: Weidenfeld & Nicolson, 1981), p. 154.
24. Brenda Wineapple, *Genêt: A Biography of Janet Flanner* (London: Pandora, 1994), p. 279.
25. Philip Hoare, *Noël Coward: A Biography* (London: Arrow, 1997), pp. 477–478, 516, 509.
26. David Ewen, *American Composers: A Biographical Dictionary* (London: Robert Hale, 1983), p. 497.
27. Bob Gilmore, *Harry Partch: A Biography* (New Haven & London: Yale University Press, 1998), p. 227.
28. Gilmore, p. 378.
29. Anthony Tommasini, *Virgil Thomson: Composer on the Aisle* (New York & London: Norton, 1997), pp. 518, 537, 544.
30. Christopher Reed, *Art and Homosexuality: A History of Ideas* (Oxford: Oxford University Press, 2011), p. 137.
31. Alan Sinfield, *Cultural Politics – Queer Reading*, 2nd edn (Abingdon, Oxon: Routledge, 2005), p. 47. Here, Sinfield is referring back to David A. Miller's original theorisation of the concept of the 'open secret' in *The Novel and the Police* (Berkeley: University of California Press, 1988), pp. 205–206. Understandably, David Ehrenstein used this expression as the title of his book *Open Secret: Gay Hollywood, 1928–2000* (New York: Perennial, 2000). Near the end of her life, Susan Sontag said of her own decision not to come out: 'I grew up in a time when the modus operandi was the "open secret." I'm used to that, and quite okay with it. Intellectually, I know why I haven't spoken more about my sexuality, but I do wonder if I haven't repressed something there to my detriment': quoted in Edmund White, *City Boy: My Life in New York During the 1960s and 1970s* (London: Bloomsbury, 2009), p. 273. White admitted resenting the relative ease with which closeted individuals developed their public careers: 'I thought a bit resentfully that all these "blue-chip" artists – Jasper Johns, Cy Twombly, John Ashbery, Elizabeth Bishop, Susan Sontag, Robert Wilson – never came out. We openly gay artists had to deal with the dismissive or condescending judgements all around us – "Of course since I'm not gay myself your work seems so exotic to me" – while the Blue Chips sailed serenely on, universal and eternal. It paid to stay in the closet, obviously . . . They definitely knew how to shape their careers': *City Boy*, p. 215.
32. Gavin Lambert, *Mainly About Lindsay Anderson* (London: Faber, 2000), pp. 8–82, 155.

33. See, for instance, Christopher Isherwood, *Liberation: Diaries, Volume Three, 1970–1983* (New York: HarperCollins, 2012), pp. 97, 161–162.
34. Sue Tilley, *Leigh Bowery: The Life and Times of an Icon* (London: Sceptre, 1997), p. 181. Otis Stuart, *Perpetual Motion: The Public and Private Lives of Rudolf Nureyev* (London: Simon & Schuster, 1995), pp. 156, 157.
35. Philip Ziegler, *Osbert Sitwell: A Biography* (London: Pimlico, 1999), p. 389.
36. David Sweetman, *Mary Renault: A Biography* (London: Chatto & Windus, 1993), p. 273.
37. Nicholas Shakespeare, *Bruce Chatwin* (London: Vintage, 2000), p. 335.
38. Shakespeare, p. 168. Peter Adam said of him, 'Chatwin was, like so many of us, drawn to the darker sexual possibilities of foreign places, and for a man of his uptight mature, travelling was almost the only way to catch a bit of living': Peter Adam, *Not Drowning But Waving: An Autobiography* (London: André Deutsch, 1995), p. 416.
39. Humphrey Carpenter, *Benjamin Britten: A Biography* (London: Faber, 1992), pp. 578, 586.
40. John Cheever, *The Journals* (London: Cape, 1991), pp. 289, 292, 347.
41. Piers Paul Read, *Alec Guinness: The Authorised Biography* (London: Simon & Schuster, 2003), pp. 463, 468.
42. Frédéric Martel, *The Pink and the Black: Homosexuals in France since 1968* (Stanford, California: Stanford University Press, 1999), p. 59.
43. However, most on the Left, including many who were gay themselves, regarded the push for gay rights as being subordinate to the wider struggle: liberation of the mass would bring that of the minority in due course. Thus, we are told of the Greek writer Costas Taktsis, 'As a homosexual, he was acutely aware of the oppressively authoritarian nature of Greek society, but he believed that liberation should be for everyone, and that homosexuals would cease to be oppressed only when the whole of society is liberated': Peter Mackridge, 'The Protean Self of Costas Taktsis', *European Gay Review* 6/7 (n.d.), pp. 172–184; p. 173.
44. Martel, pp. 62, 95.
45. Louis-Jean Calvet, *Roland Barthes: A Biography* (Bloomington & Indianapolis: Indiana University Press, 1995), pp. 183–184.
46. Mark Ford, *Raymond Roussel and the Republic of Dreams* (London: Faber, 2000), p. 75.
47. Sweetman, p. 253.
48. Sweetman, p. 213.
49. Sweetman, p. 227.
50. Sweetman, pp. 252–253.
51. Mary Renault, *The Charioteer* (London: Virago, 2013), p. 212.
52. Renault, p. 347.
53. Elizabeth Bishop, *One Art: Letters* (London: Pimlico, 1996), pp. 548–549.
54. David R. Jarraway, *Going the Distance: Dissident Subjectivity in Modernist American Literature* (Baton Rouge: Louisiana State University Press, 2003), p. 140.
55. Margot Peters, *May Sarton: A Biography* (New York: Knopf, 1998), pp. 321, 326, 367.
56. Margot Peters, p. 4.
57. May Sarton, *The Education of Harriet Hatfield* (London: Women's Press, 1990), pp. 24, 114, 121.
58. Patrick White, *Flaws in the Glass: A Self-Portrait* (Harmondsworth: Penguin, 1983), p. 80.
59. David Marr, *Patrick White: A Life* (London: Cape, 1991), pp. 526, 583, 599, 583, 599.
60. Marr, *Patrick White*, pp. 595, 599. There were 'terrible storms' in their house 'when his partner, Manoly Lascaris, read the scathing portrait of his family' in the memoir – see David Marr, 'A Note on *The Hanging Garden*', in Patrick White, *The Hanging Garden* (London: Vintage, 2013), pp. 217–224; p. 217.
61. Marr, *Patrick White*, pp. 607, 613–614.
62. Robert K. Martin, 'London Diary', in Michael Denneny, Charles Ortleb and Thomas Steele (eds), *The Christopher Street Reader* (New York: Wideview/Perigee, 1983), p. 231. (I am grateful to Jim MacSweeney, of Gay's the Word, for this reference.) Robert K. Martin's pioneering book *The Homosexual Tradition in American Poetry* had been published in 1979.
63. David Plante, *Becoming a Londoner: A Diary* (London: Bloomsbury, 2013), p. 408. In the 1980s, however, Plante and Stangos became sufficiently activist to organise the publication of a letter opposing 'Margaret Thatcher's Clause 28' (p. 422).
64. Dominique Fernandez, *A Hidden Love: Art and Homosexuality* (Munich: Prestel, 2002), pp. 300–302, 307, 315.
65. Josyane Savigneau, *Marguerite Yourcenar: Inventing a Life* (Chicago & London: University of Chicago Press, 1993), pp. 267, 268–269.

66. Jeffrey Meyers, *Homosexuality and Literature, 1890–1930* (London: Athlone, 1977), p. 3. Meyers' book has chapters on Oscar Wilde, André Gide, Thomas Mann and Robert Musil, Marcel Proust, Joseph Conrad, E.M. Forster, D.H. Lawrence and T.E. Lawrence.

67. Kingsley Amis, *The Letters of Kingsley Amis* (London: HarperCollins, 2000), pp. 953, 960–961. Amis regarded this secretive quality in gay writers as having done for Christopher Isherwood. He wrote to Philip Larkin (8 September 1952): 'I have re-read the memorial and thought about mr norris and berlin and have come to the conclusion that what shagged our Chris was not coming clean about being a homo' [*sic*] (p. 292). Yet Richard Crossman was disappointed by his friend Auden's later poetry, feeling that the earlier work had a certain clarity: 'What I want from Auden,' he said, 'is good homosexual love poetry, like "Lay your sleeping Head". Show me any good homosexual love poem from the later poetry. That's what I want!': Charles Osborne, *W.H. Auden: The Life of a Poet* (New York & London: Harcourt Brace Jovanovich, 1979), p. 297.

68. Mel Gussow, *Edward Albee: A Singular Journey* (New York & London: Applause, 2001), pp. 350–351.

69. Hubert Fichte, *The Gay Critic* (Ann Arbor, Michigan: University of Michigan Press, 1996), p. 403.

70. Edmund White, *Genet* (London: Chatto & Windus, 1993), pp. 606–607, 610.

71. Barth David Schwartz, *Pasolini Requiem* (New York: Pantheon, 1992), p. 473.

72. Christian Braad Thomsen, *Fassbinder: The Life and Work of a Provocative Genius* (London: Faber, 1997), p. 27.

73. Thomsen, p. 180.

74. Thomsen, p. 183.

75. Thomsen, p. 304.

76. Thomsen, p. 182.

77. James Campbell, *Talking at the Gates: A Life of James Baldwin* (London: Faber, 1991), p. 254.

78. Charles Osborne, pp. 256, 330.

79. Joe LeSueur, *Digressions on Some Poems by Frank O'Hara: A Memoir* (New York: Farrar, Straus & Giroux, 2003), p. 227.

80. Gore Vidal, 'Sex Is Politics', in Gore Vidal *Sexually Speaking: Collected Sex Writings* (San Francisco: Cleis Press, 1999), p. 110.

81. John Richardson, *The Sorcerer's Apprentice: Picasso, Provence and Douglas Cooper* (London: Cape, 1999), p. 147.

82. Margaret Drabble, *Angus Wilson: A Biography* (London: Secker & Warburg, 1995), p. 481.

83. John Lehmann, *In the Purely Pagan Sense* (London: GMP, 1985), pp. 251–252.

84. Ian Massey, *Patrick Procktor: Art and Life* (Norwich: Unicorn, 2010), p. 178. Despite having been openly gay for many years, Procktor got married in 1973 at the age of 37.

85. Daniel Farson, *The Gilded Gutter Life of Francis Bacon* (London: Vintage, 1994), p. 218.

86. Cheever, *The Journals*, p. 292.

87. Humphrey Burton, *Leonard Bernstein*, (London: Faber, 1995), p. 473.

88. Benjamin Ivry, *Francis Poulenc* (London: Phaidon, 1996), p. 134. This claim of plural such appearances has itself proliferated online. It seems more likely that this happened only once, at Paris's first gay pride march, on 25 June 1977.

# BIBLIOGRAPHY

Abraham, Julie, *Metropolitan Lovers: The Homosexuality of Cities* (Minneapolis & London: University of Minnesota Press, 2008)

Acton, Harold, *Nancy Mitford* (London: Gibson Square Books, 2004)

Adair, Gilbert, *The Real Tadzio: Thomas Mann's Death in Venice and the Boy Who Inspired It* (London: Short Books, 2001)

Adam, Peter, *David Hockney and His Friends* (Bath: Absolute Press, 1997)

Adam, Peter, *Not Drowning But Waving: An Autobiography* (London: Andre Deutsch, 1995)

Adams, Stephen, *The Homosexual as Hero in Contemporary Fiction* (London: Vision, 1980)

Albertson, Chris, *Bessie* (London: Barrie & Jenkins, 1972)

Alderson, David, *Mansex Fine: Religion, Manliness and Imperialism in Nineteenth-Century British Culture* (Manchester: Manchester University Press, 1998)

Aldrich, Robert, *The Seduction of the Mediterranean: Writing, Art and Homosexual Fantasy* (London: Routledge, 1993)

Aldrich, Robert, and Garry Wotherspoon (eds), *Who's Who in Gay and Lesbian History: From Antiquity to World War II* (London & New York: Routledge, 2001)

Aldrich, Robert, and Garry Wotherspoon (eds), *Who's Who in Contemporary Gay and Lesbian History: From World War II to the Present Day* (London & New York: Routledge, 2001)

Allen, Gay Wilson, and Ed Folsom (eds), *Walt Whitman and the World* (Iowa City: University of Iowa Press, 1995)

Alpert, Hollis, *Fellini: A Life* (London: W.H. Allen, 1987)

Amis, Kingsley, *The Letters of Kingsley Amis* (London: HarperCollins, 2000)

Amis, Kingsley, *Memoirs* (London: Penguin, 1991)

Amory, Mark, *Lord Berners: The Last Eccentric* (London: Chatto & Windus, 1998)

Anderson, Reed, *Federico García Lorca* (London: Macmillan, 1984)

Annan, Noel, *The Dons: Mentors, Eccentrics and Geniuses* (London: HarperCollins, 1999)

Annan, Noel, *Our Age: Portrait of a Generation* (London: Weidenfeld & Nicolson, 1990)

Anonymous, 'The Homosexual in America', *Time*, 21 January 1966, pp. 40–41

Arenas, Reinaldo, *Before Night Falls* (New York: Penguin, 1994)

Arenas, Reinaldo, *Farewell to the Sea: A Novel of Cuba* (New York: Penguin, 1987)

Arrell, Doug, 'Homophobic Criticism and Its Disguises: The Case of Stanley Kauffmann', *Journal of Dramatic Theory and Criticism* 16, 2 (Spring 2002), pp. 95–110

Asher, Michael, *Lawrence: The Uncrowned King of Arabia* (London: Penguin, 1999)

Asher, Michael, *Thesiger: A Biography* (London & New York: Viking, 1994)

Atlas, James, *Bellow: A Biography* (London: Faber, 2000)

Attenborough, David, *The First Eden: The Mediterranean World and Man* (London: Guild, 1987)

Auden, W.H., *Collected Poems* (London: Faber, 1976)

Auden, W.H., and Chester Kallman, *Libretti and Other Dramatic Writings by W.H. Auden, 1939–1973* (London: Faber, 1993)

Baden-Powell of Gilwell, Lord, *Rovering to Success: A Book of Life-Sport for Young Men* (London: Herbert Jenkins, 1930)

Bailey, Paul, *Three Queer Lives: An Alternative Biography of Fred Barnes, Naomi Jacob and Arthur Marshall* (London: Hamish Hamilton, 2001)

Bair, Deirdre, *Samuel Beckett: A Biography* (London: Picador, 1980)

Baker, Carlos, *Ernest Hemingway: A Life Story* (New York: Charles Scribner's Sons, 1969)

Baldoni, Luca (ed.), *Le parole tra gli uomini: Antologia di poesia gay italiana dal Novecento al presente* (Milano: Robin Edizioni, 2012)

Baldwin, James, *Another Country* (London: Penguin, 1990)

Baldwin, James, *Giovanni's Room* (London: Penguin, 2000)

Baldwin, James, *The Price of the Ticket: Collected Non-fiction 1948–1985* (London: Michael Joseph, 1985)

Bannon, Ann, *Beebo Brinker* (San Francisco: Cleis Press, 2001)

Bannon, Ann, *I Am a Woman* (San Francisco: Cleis Press, 2002)

Bannon, Ann, *Journey to a Woman* (San Francisco: Cleis Press, 2003)

Barber, Michael, *The Captain: The Life and Times of Simon Raven* (London: Duckbacks, 2001)

Barber, Stephen, *Edmund White: The Burning World* (London: Picador, 1999)

Barea, Arturo, *Lorca: The Poet and His People* (London: Faber, 1944)

Barker, Richard H., *Marcel Proust: A Biography* (London: Faber, 1959)

Barnes, Djuna, *New York* (London: Virago, 1990)

Barnes, Djuna, *Nightwood* (London: Faber, 1979)

Barrett, William, 'New Innocents Abroad', *Partisan Review* 17, 3 (March 1950), pp. 272–291

Barthes, Roland, *Roland Barthes* (London: Macmillan, 1977)

Bassani, Giorgio, (*The Gold Rimmed Spectacles Gli occhiali d'oro*) (Milano: Mondadori, 1980)

Bauer, Heike (ed.), *Sexology and Translation: Cultural and Scientific Encounters Across the Modern World* (Philadelphia, Pennsylvania: Temple University Press, 2015)

Bayley, John, *Iris: A Memoir of Iris Murdoch* (London: Duckworth, 1998)

Baynes, H.G., *Germany Possessed* (London: Cape, 1941)

Beaton, Cecil, *Ashcombe: The Story of a Fifteen-Year Lease* (Stanbridge, Wimborne, Dorset: The Dovecote Press, 1999)

Beaton, Cecil, *Beaton in the Sixties: The Cecil Beaton Diaries As They Were Written* (London: Weidenfeld & Nicolson, 2003)

Beaton, Cecil, *The Glass of Fashion: A Personal History of Fifty Years of Changing Tastes and the People Who Have Inspired Them* (New York: Rizzoli Ex Libris, 2014)

Bech, Henning, *When Men Meet: Homosexuality and Modernity* (Cambridge: Polity, 1997)

Bejel, Emilio, *Gay Cuban Nation* (Chicago & London: University of Chicago Press, 2001)

Bell, Quentin, *Bloomsbury Recalled* (New York: Columbia University Press, 1996)

Bellow, Saul, *Mr Sammler's Planet* (Harmondsworth: Penguin, 1972)

Bely, Andrei, *Petersburg: A Novel in Eight Chapters* (London: Penguin, 1995)

Benjamin, Walter, *Illuminations* (London: Fontana, 1973)

Ben Jelloun, Tahar, *Leaving Tangier* (London: Arcadia, 2009)

Benkovitz, Miriam J., *Ronald Firbank: A Biography* (London: Weidenfeld & Nicolson, 1970)

Bennett, Alan, *Untold Stories* (London: Faber and Profile, 2005)

Bennett, E.K., *Stefan George* (Cambridge: Bowes & Bowes, 1954)

Benstock, Shari, *Women of the Left Bank: Paris, 1900–1940* (London: Virago, 1987)

Berg, James J., & Chris Freeman (eds), *The Isherwood Century: Essays on the Life and Work of Christopher Isherwood* (Madison: University of Wisconsin Press, 2000)

Bergan, Ronald, *Sergei Eisenstein: A Life in Conflict* (London: Warner, 1999)

Bergman, David, *Gaiety Transfigured: Gay Self-Representation in American Literature* (Madison, Wisconsin: University of Wisconsin Press, 1991)

Beurdelay, Cécile, *L'Amour bleu* (Cologne: Evergreen, 1994)

Bierman, John, *The Secret Life of Laszlo Almasy: The Real English Patient* (London: Penguin, 2005)

Billinger, Karl, *Hitler Is No Fool* (London: Hurst & Blackett, n.d.)

Binding, Paul, *Lorca: The Gay Imagination* (London: GMP, 1985)

Bishop, Elizabeth, *One Art: Letters* (London: Pimlico, 1996)

Bjørby, Pål, 'The Prison House of Sexuality: Homosexuality in Herman Bang Scholarship', *Scandinavian Studies* 58 (1986), pp. 223–255.

Blackmore, Josiah (ed.), *The Songs of António Botto* (Minneapolis, Minnesota: University of Minnesota Press, 2010)

Boak, Denis, *Roger Martin du Gard* (Oxford: Clarendon Press, 1963)

Boehringer, Robert, *Mein Bild von Stefan George* (München & Düsseldorf: Helmut Küpper vormals Georg Bondi, 1951)

Bookbinder, Paul, *Weimar Germany: The Republic of the Reasonable* (Manchester: Manchester University Press, 1996)

Booth, Mark, *Camp* (London: Quartet, 1983)

Borland, Maureen, *Wilde's Devoted Friend: A Life of Robert Ross, 1869–1918* (Oxford: Lennard, 1990)

Botto, António, *The Songs of António Botto* (Minneapolis, Minnesota: University of Minnesota Press, 2010)

Bouvet, Vincent, and Gérard Durozoi, *Paris between the Wars, 1919–1939: Art, Life and Culture* (New York: Vendome, 2010)

Bowles, Jane, *Two Serious Ladies* (London: Virago, 1979)

Bowles, Paul, *Let It Come Down* (London: Penguin, 2000)

Boyle, Andrew, *The Climate of Treason: Five who Spied for Russia* (London: Hutchinson, 1979)

Brassaï, *The Secret Paris of the 30's*, trans. Richrd Miller (London: Thames & Hudson, 1976)

Brée, Germaine, *Gide* (New Brunswick, N.J.: Rutgers University Press, 1963)

Brée, Germaine, *The World of Marcel Proust* (London: Chatto & Windus, 1967)

Breese, Charlotte, *Hutch* (London: Bloomsbury, 2001)

Bristow, Joseph, *Effeminate England: Homoerotic Writing After 1885* (Buckingham: Open University Press, 1995)

Brodsky, Joseph, *Watermark* (London: Penguin, 1997)

Bronski, Michael, *Culture Clash: The Making of Gay Sensibility* (Boston: South End Press, 1984)

Brooke, Jocelyn, *The Orchid Trilogy* (Harmondsworth: Penguin, 1981)

Brooke, Jocelyn, *Ronald Firbank* (London: Arthur Barker, 1951)

Brooke, Jocelyn (ed.), *The Denton Welch Journals* (London: Hamish Hamilton, 1973)

Brophy, Brigid, *Prancing Novelist: A Defence of Fiction in the Form of a Critical Biography in Praise of Ronald Firbank* (London: Macmillan, 1973)

Brown, Frederick, *An Impersonation of Angels: A Biography of Jean Cocteau* (London: Longmans, 1969)

Bruccoli, Matthew J., *Scott and Ernest: The Authority of Failure and the Authority of Success* (London: Bodley Head, 1978)

Bruccoli, Matthew J., *Some Sort of Epic Grandeur: The Life of F. Scott Fitzgerald* (London: Cardinal, 1991)

Buckle, Richard, *Diaghilev* (London: Hamish Hamilton, 1984)

Buckle, Richard, *Nijinsky* (Harmondsworth: Penguin, 1975)

Buckle, Richard (ed.), *Self Portrait with Friends: The Selected Diaries of Cecil Beaton* (London: Pimlico, 1991)

Burgess, Anthony, *Ernest Hemingway and His World* (London: Thames & Hudson, 1978)

Burgin, Diana Lewis, 'Mother Nature Versus the Amazons: Marina Tsvetaeva and Female Same-Sex Love', *Journal of the History of Sexuality* 6, 1 (1995), pp. 62–88

Burroughs, William S., *The Naked Lunch* (London: Corgi, 1968)

Burton, Humphrey, *Leonard Bernstein* (London: Faber, 1995)

Burton, Peter, *Parallel Lives* (London: GMP, 1985)

Burton, Richard D.E., *Francis Poulenc* (London: Absolute, 2002)

Buruma, Ian, *The Missionary and the Libertine: Love and War in East and West* (London: Faber, 1996)

Butt, Gavin, *Between You and Me: Queer Disclosures in the New York Art World, 1948–1963* (Durham, NC: Duke University Press, 2005)

Byrd, Rudolph P., and Beverly Guy-Sheftall (eds), *Traps: African American Men on Gender and Sexuality* (Bloomington & Indianapolis: Indiana University Press, 2001)

Byron, Robert, *The Road to Oxiana* (London: Picador, 1994)

Cabrera Infante, G., *Mea Cuba* (London: Faber, 1994)

Calder, John, *The Garden of Eros: The Story of the Paris Expatriates and the Post-War Literary Scene* (London: Alma, 2014)

Callow, Simon, *Charles Laughton: A Difficult Actor* (London: Methuen, 1987)

Callow, Simon, *Orson Welles: The Road to Xanadu* (London: Cape, 1995)

Calvet, Louis-Jean, *Roland Barthes: A Biography* (Bloomington & Indianapolis: Indiana University Press, 1995)

Calvino, Italo, *Hermit in Paris: Autobiographical Writings* (London: Penguin, 2003)

Campbell, James, *Talking at the Gates: A Life of James Baldwin* (London: Faber, 1991)

Campbell, Roy, *The Collected Poems of Roy Campbell, Volume One* (London: Bodley Head, 1949)

Campbell, Roy, *The Collected Poems of Roy Campbell, Volume Two* (London: Bodley Head, 1957)

Campbell, Roy, *Lorca: An Appreciation of his Poetry* (Cambridge: Bowes & Bowes, 1952)

Canetti, Elias, *The Torch in My Ear* (London: Granta, 1999)

Capote, Truman, *Answered Prayers* (London: Penguin, 2001)

Carey, John, *The Intellectuals and the Masses: Pride and Prejudice among the Literary Intelligentsia, 1880–1939* (London: Faber, 1992)

Carey, John, *William Golding, the Man Who Wrote* Lord of the Flies: *A Life* (London: Faber, 2009)

Carlston, Erin G., *Double Agents: Espionage, Literature, and Liminal Citizens* (New York: Columbia University Press, 2013)

Carpenter, Edward, *Anthology of Friendship: Ioläus* (London: George Allen & Unwin, 1929)

Carpenter, Edward, *Days with Walt Whitman, with Some Notes on His Life and Work* (London: George Allen, 1906)

Carpenter, Humphrey, *Benjamin Britten: A Biography* (London: Faber, 1992)

Carpenter, Humphrey, *The Brideshead Generation: Evelyn Waugh and His Friends* (London: Faber, 1989)

Carpenter, Humphrey, *W.H. Auden: A Biography* (London: George Allen & Unwin, 1981)

Carter, William C., *Marcel Proust: A Life* (New Haven & London: Yale University Press, 2000)

Cavafy, C.P., *Collected Poems* (New York: Alfred A. Knopf, 2009)

Cerio, Edwin, *The Masque of Capri* (London: Thomas Nelson, 1957)

Cernuda, Luis, *Selected Poems of Luis Cernuda* (Riverdale-on-Hudson, New York: Sheep Meadow Press, 1999)

Cestaro, Gary P., *Queer Italia: Same-Sex Desire in Italian Literature and Film* (New York: Palgrave Macmillan, 2004)

Chandler, Raymond, *Later Novels and Other Writings* (New York: Library of America, 1995)

Chandler, Robert, Boris Dralyuk and Irina Mashinski (eds), *The Penguin Book of Russian Poetry* (London: Penguin, 2015)

Chauncey, George, *Gay New York: Gender, Urban Culture, and the Making of the Gay Male World, 1890–1940* (New York: BasicBooks, 1994)

Cheever, John, *The Journals* (London: Cape, 1991)

Chester, Alfred, *Behold Goliath* (London: Deutsch, 1965)

Chester, Alfred, *The Exquisite Corpse* (London: Sphere, 1971)

Christie, Agatha, *The Mystery of the Blue Train* (London: Harper, 2001)

Chylińska, Teresa, *Szymanowski* (New York: Twayne & The Kościuszko Foundation, 1973)

Claridge, Laura, *Tamara de Lempicka: A Life of Deco and Decadence* (London: Bloomsbury, 2001)

Clark, Adrian, and Jeremy Dronfield, *Queer Saint: The Cultured Life of Peter Watson, Who Shook Twentieth-Century Art and Shocked High Society* (London: John Blake, 2015)

Clark, Kenneth, *Another Part of the Wood: A Self-Portrait* (London: Book Club Associates, 1974)

Clark, Thekla, *Wystan and Chester: A Personal Memoir of W.H. Auden and Chester Kallman* (London: Faber, 1995)

Clarke, Gerald, *Capote: A Biography* (London: Cardinal, 1989)

Cleminson, Richard, and Francisco Vásquez García, *'Los invisibles': A History of Male Homosexuality in Spain, 1850–1940* (Cardiff: University of Wales Press, 2007)

Clifford, Colin, *The Asquiths* (London: John Murray, 2003)

Clughen, Lisa, *'Lorca's Anorexics: Hunger Strike in the Cause of Selfhood', Bulletin of Hispanic Studies* 79, 3 (July 2002), pp. 309–324

Clum, John M., *Acting Gay: Male Homosexuality in Modern Drama* (New York: Columbia University Press, 1994)

Cocteau, Jean, *A Call to Order* (London: Faber & Gwyer, 1926)

Cocteau, Jean, *Les Enfants Terribles* (London: Penguin, 1961)

Cocteau, Jean, *My Contemporaries* (London: Peter Owen, 1967)

Cocteau, Jean, *Opium: The Diary of an Addict* (London: George Allen & Unwin, 1933)

Cocteau, Jean, *Past Tense: Volume II Diaries* (London: Methuen, 1990)

Cocteau, Jean, *Souvenir Portraits: Paris in the Belle Époque* (London: Robson, 1991)

Cocteau, Jean, *The White Paper* (London: Brilliance Books, 1983)

Cohen, Rachel, *A Chance Meeting: Intertwined Lives of American Writers and Artists* (London: Vintage, 2005)

Colette, *Earthly Paradise: An Autobiography Drawn from Her Lifetime Writings by Robert Phelps* (Harmondsworth: Penguin, 1974)

Colette, *The Pure and the Impure* (Harmondsworth: Penguin, 1971)

Collins, Ian, *John Craxton* (Farnham, Surrey: Lund Humphries, 2011)

Collis, Louise, *Impetuous Heart: The Story of Ethel Smyth* (London: William Kimber, 1984)

Collis, Rose, *Portraits to the Wall: Historic Lesbian Lives Unveiled* (London: Cassell, 1994)

Connolly, Cyril, *Enemies of Promise* (Harmondsworth: Penguin, 1961)

Connolly, Cyril, *The Rock Pool* (Oxford: Oxford University Press, 1981)

Connolly, Cyril, 'Where Engels Fears to Tread', in Marie Jacqueline Lancaster (ed.), *Brian Howard: Portrait of a Failure* (London: Blond, 1968), pp.602–613

Connon, Bryan, *Beverley Nichols: A Life* (London: Constable, 1991)

Connon, Bryan, *Somerset Maugham and the Maugham Dynasty* (London: Sinclair-Stevenson, 1997)

Cook, Bruce, *The Beat Generation* (New York: Charles Scribner's Sons, 1971)

Cooper, Wayne F., *Claude McKay: Rebel Sojourner in the Harlem Renaissance, A Biography* (Baton Rouge & London: Louisiana State University Press, 1987)

Cordle, Thomas, *André Gide* (New York: Twayne, 1969)

Core, Philip, *Camp: The Lie That Tells the Truth* (London: Plexus, 1984)

Cornish, Kimberley, *The Jew of Linz: Wittgenstein, Hitler and Their Secret Battle for the Mind* (London: Century, 1998)

Cortázar, Julio, 'To Reach Lezama Lima', in José Lezama Lima, *Selections* (Berkeley, California: University of California Press, 2015)

Corvo, Baron, Frederick Rolfe, *The Venice Letters* (London: Cecil Woolf, 1987)

Cowell, Henry, and Sidney Cowell, *Charles Ives and His Music* (New York: Oxford University Press, 1955)

Cowley, Malcolm, *Exile's Return: A Literary Odyssey of the 1920s* (New York: Penguin, 1994)

Crane, Hart, *The Complete Poems and Selected Letters and Prose of Hart Crane* (London: Oxford University Press, 1972)

Crawford, Robert, *Young Eliot: From St Louis to* The Waste Land (London: Cape, 2015)

Crevel, René, *Babylon* (London: Quartet, 1988)

Crisp, Quentin, *The Naked Civil Servant* (London: Fontana, 1977)

Croall, Jonathan, *John Gielgud: Matinee Idol to Movie Star* (London: Methuen, 2011)

Croft, Andy, *Red Letter Days: British Fiction in the 1930s* (London: Lawrence & Wishart, 1990)

Croft-Cooke, Rupert, *Feasting with Panthers: A New Consideration of Some Late Victorian Writers* (London: W.H. Allen, 1967)

Crosby, Caresse, *The Passionate Years* (London: Alvin Redman, 1955)

Cunningham, Valentine, *British Writers of the Thirties* (Oxford: Oxford University Press, 1988)

Curtin, Kaier, *'We Can Always Call Them Bulgarians': The Emergence of Lesbians and Gay Men on the American Stage* (Boston: Alyson, 1987)

Curtis, James, *James Whale: A New World of Gods and Monsters* (Minneapolis: University of Minnesota Press, 2003)

D'Arch Smith, Timothy, *Love in Earnest: Some Notes on the Lives and Writings of English 'Uranian' Poets from 1889 to 1930* (London: Routledge & Kegan Paul, 1970)

Darlow, Michael, and Gillian Hodson, *Terence Rattigan: The Man and His Work* (London: Quartet, 1979)

Dauster, Frank, *Xavier Villaurrutia* (New York: Twayne, 1971)

Davenport-Hines, Richard, *Auden* (London: Heinemann, 1995)

Davenport-Hines, Richard, *A Night at the Majestic: Proust and the Great Modernist Dinner Party of 1922* (London: Faber, 2006)

David, Hugh, *The Fitzrovians: A Portrait of Bohemian Society, 1900–1955* (London: Michael Joseph, 1988)

David, Hugh, *Stephen Spender: A Portrait with Background* (London: Heinemann, 1992)

Davidson, Michael, *The World, the Flesh and Myself* (London: GMP, 1985)

Davis, Miles, with Quincy Troupe, *Miles: The Autobiography* (London: Macmillan, 1990)

De Becker, Raymond, *The Other Face of Love* (London: Sphere, 1969)

Deford, Frank, *Big Bill Tilden: The Triumphs and the Tragedy* (London: Gollancz, 1977)

De Jongh, Nicholas, *Not in Front of the Audience: Homosexuality on Stage* (London: Routledge, 1992)

De-la-Noy, Michael, *Denton Welch: The Making of a Writer* (Harmondsworth: Viking, 1984)

De-la-Noy, Michael, *Eddy: The Life of Edward Sackville-West* (London: Arcadia, 1999)

Delavenay, Emile, *D.H. Lawrence and Edward Carpenter: A Study in Edwardian Transition* (London: Heinemann, 1971)

D'Emilio, John, and Estelle B. Freedman, *Intimate Matters: A History of Sexuality in America* (New York: Perennial Library, 1988)

Denneny, Michael, Charles Ortleb and Thomas Steele (eds.), *The Christopher Street Reader* (New York: Wideview/Perigee, 1983)

Dhondy, Farrukh, 'Farrukh Dhondy Talks to V.S. Naipaul', *Literary Review* 278 (August 2001), pp. 28–36

Dick, Bernard F., *The Apostate Angel: A Critical Study of Gore Vidal* (New York: Random House, 1974)

Dickinson, G. Lowes, *The Autobiography of G. Lowes Dickinson and Other Unpublished Writings* (London: Duckworth, 1973)

Dickson, Lovat, *Radclyffe Hall at the Well of Loneliness: A Sapphic Chronicle* (London & Toronto: Collins, 1975)

Dillon, Millicent, *You Are Not I: A Portrait of Paul Bowles* (Berkeley & LA: University of California Press, 1998)

Döblin, Alfred, *Berlin Alexanderplatz* (Harmondsworth: Penguin, 1978)

Dolin, Anton, *Last Words: A Final Autobiography* (London: Century, 1985)

Dollimore, Jonathan, *Sexual Dissidence: Augustine to Wilde, Freud to Foucault* (Oxford: Clarendon Press, 1991)

Domville-Fife, Charles W., *This Is Germany* (London: Seeley Service: [1939])

Donaldson, Scott, *By Force of Will: The Life and Art of Ernest Hemingway* (New York: Viking, 1977)

Donoghue, Emma, *We Are Michael Field* (Bath: Absolute Press, 1998)

Dos Passos, John, *Manhattan Transfer* (Harmondsworth: Penguin, 1986)

Douglas, Norman, *Siren Land* (Harmondsworth: Penguin, 1983)

Douglas, Norman, *South Wind* (Harmondsworth: Penguin, 1953)

Dowling, Linda, *Hellenism and Homosexuality in Victorian Oxford* (Ithaca & London: Cornell University Press, 1994)

Doyle, Kegan, 'The Moral of Glenway Wescott: The Closet and the Second Act', *Canadian Review of American Studies* 28, 1 (1998), pp. 43–61

Drabble, Margaret, *Angus Wilson: A Biography* (London: Secker & Warburg, 1995)

Drabble, Margaret, *Arnold Bennett* (London: Weidenfeld & Nicolson, 1974)

Driberg, Tom, *Ruling Passions* (London: Quartet, 1978)

Duberman, Martin Bauml, *About Time: Exploring the Gay Past* (New York: SeaHorse, 1986)

Duberman, Martin Bauml, Martha Vicinus and George Chauncey, Jr (eds), *Hidden from History: Reclaiming the Gay and Lesbian Past* (London & New York: Penguin, 1991)

Duncan, Robert, *The Collected Early Poems and Plays* (Berkeley, CA: University of California Press, 2012)

Duncan, Ronald, *Working with Britten: A Personal Memoir* (Bideford, Devon: The Rebel Press, 1981)

Dunn, Douglas, *Dante's Drum-Kit* (London: Faber, 1993)

Dynes, Wayne R. (ed.), *Encyclopedia of Homosexuality* (Chicago and London: St James Press, 1990)

Edgar, David, 'Stalking Out', *London Review of Books* 28, 14 (20 July 2006), pp.8–10

Edwards, Gwynne, *Lorca: The Theatre Beneath the Sand* (London & Boston: Marion Boyars, 1980)

Ehrenstein, David, *Open Secret: Gay Hollywood, 1928–2000* (New York: Perennial, 2000)

Eksteins, Modris, *Rites of Spring: The Great War and the Birth of the Modern Age* (London: Black Swan, 1990)

Ellison, Ralph, *Invisible Man* (Harmondsworth: Penguin, 1965)

Ellmann, Richard, *Oscar Wilde* (London: Penguin, 1988)

Evangelista, Stefano (ed.), *The Reception of Oscar Wilde in Europe* (London: Continuum, 2010)

Ewen, David, *American Composers: A Biographical Dictionary* (London: Robert Hale, 1983)

Ewen, Frederic, *Bertolt Brecht: His Life, His Art and His Times* (London: Calder & Boyars, 1970)

Faas, Ekbert, *Young Robert Duncan: Portrait of the Poet as Homosexual in Society* (Santa Barbara, California: Black Sparrow, 1983)

Fairbrother, Trevor, *John Singer Sargent: The Sensualist* (New Haven & London: Yale University Press, 2000)

Faludy, György, *My Happy Days in Hell* (London: Penguin, 2010)

Farnan, Dorothy J., *Auden in Love* (London: Faber, 1985)

Farson, Daniel, *The Gilded Gutter Life of Francis Bacon* (London: Vintage, 1994)

Faulks, Sebastian, *The Fatal Englishman: Three Short Lives* (London: Hutchinson, 1996)

Feder, Stuart, *Charles Ives, "My Father's Song": A Psychoanalytic Biography* (New Haven & London: Yale University Press)

Fernandez, Dominique, *A Hidden Love: Art and Homosexuality* (Munich: Prestel, 2002)

Fernandez, Dominique, *Le rapt de Ganymède* (Paris: Bernard Grasset, 1989)

Ferris, Paul, *Dylan Thomas* (London: Hodder & Stoughton, 1977)

Fest, Joachim, *Plotting Hitler's Death: The German Resistance to Hitler, 1933–1945* (London: Phoenix, 1997)

Fichte, Hubert, *The Gay Critic* (Ann Arbor, Michigan: University of Michigan Press, 1996)

Field, Douglas, *All Those Strangers: The Art and Lives of James Baldwin* (Oxford: Oxford University Press, 2015)

Finlayson, Iain, *Tangier: City of the Dream* (London: Flamingo, 1993)

Firbank, Ronald, *The Complete Firbank* (London: Duckworth, 1973)

Fisher, Clive, *This Fabulous Shadow: A Life of Hart Crane* (New Haven & London: Yale University Press, 2002)

Fitch, Noel Riley, *Sylvia Beach and the Lost Generation: A History of Literary Paris in the Twenties and Thirties* (London: Penguin, 1985)

Fondazione Sandro Penna (eds), *Orgoglio e pregiudizio: L'eros lesbico e omosessuale nella letteratura del Novecento* (Torino: Fondazione Sandro Penna, 1983)

Ford, Charles Henri, *Water from a Bucket: A Diary, 1948–1957* (New York: Turtle Point, 2001)

Ford, Charles, and Parker Tyler, *The Young and Evil* (London: GMP, 1988)

Ford, Ford Madox, *Memories and Impressions* (Harmondsworth: Penguin, 1979)

Ford, Mark, *Raymond Roussel and the Republic of Dreams* (London: Faber, 2000)

Forster, E.M., *Maurice* (Harmondsworth: Penguin, 1972)

Forster, E.M., *Two Cheers for Democracy* (Harmondsworth: Penguin, 1965)

Foster, David William, *Gay and Lesbian Themes in Latin American Writing* (Austin, Texas: University of Texas Press, 1991)

Foster, David William (ed.), *Latin American Writers on Gay and Lesbian Themes: A Bio-Critical Sourcebook* (Westport, Connecticut: Greenwood, 1994)

Fountain, Tim, *Quentin Crisp* (London: Absolute Press, 2002)

Fowlie, Wallace, *André Gide: His Life and Art* (New York: Macmillan, 1965)

Franck, Dan, *The Bohemians: The Birth of Modern Art, Paris 1900–1930* (London: Weidenfeld & Nicolson, 2001)

Fry, Michael, *Hitler's Wonderland* (London: John Murray, 1934)

Fryer, Jonathan, *André and Oscar: Gide, Wilde and the Gay Art of Living* (London: Allison & Busby, 1999)

Fryer, Jonathan, *Isherwood* (London: New English Library, 1977)

Furbank, P.N., *E.M. Forster: A Life* (Oxford: Oxford University Press, 1979)

Fussell, Paul, *The Great War and Modern Memory* (London: Oxford University Press, 1975)

Galgoczi, Erzsebet, *Another Love* (San Francisco: Midnight Editions, 2007)

Galgut, Damon, *Arctic Summer* (London: Atlantic, 2014)

Garber, Eric, 'A Spectacle in Color: The Lesbian and Gay Subculture of Jazz Age Harlem', in Martin Bauml Duberman, Martha Vicinus and George Chauncey, Jr (eds), *Hidden from History: Reclaiming the Gay and Lesbian Past* (London & New York: Penguin, 1991), pp. 318–331

Garnett, David (ed.), *Selected Letters of T.E. Lawrence* (London: Reprint Society, 1941)

Garrigues y Díaz-Cañabate, Emilio, 'Al teatro con Federico García Lorca', *Cuadernos hispanamericanos* 340 (1978), pp.99–117

Genet, Jean, *Funeral Rites* (New York: Grove, 1969)

Genet, Jean, *Lettres au petit Franz (1943–1944)* (Paris: Le Promeneur, 2000)

George, Stefan, *Poems* (New York: Schocken Books, 1967)

Gibson, Ian, *Federico García Lorca: A Life* (London: Faber, 1989)

Gibson, Robert, *Roger Martin du Gard* (London: Bowes & Bowes, 1961)

Gibson, Robin, *Glyn Philpot, 1884–1937: Edwardian Aesthete to Thirties Modernist* (London: National Portrait Gallery, 1984)

Gide, André, *Corydon: Four Socratic Dialogues* (New York: Farrar, Straus & Co., 1950)

Gide, André, *If It Die* (Harmondsworth: Penguin, 1977)

Gide, André, *The Immoralist* (Harmondsworth: Penguin, 1960)

Gide, André, *Oscar Wilde* (London: William Kimber, 1951)

Gill, Jonathan, *Harlem: The Four Hundred Year History from Dutch Village to Capital of Black America* (New York: Grove, 2011)

Gilmore, Bob, *Harry Partch: A Biography* (New Haven & London: Yale University Press, 1998)

Ginsberg, Allen, *Collected Poems 1947–1980* (London: Viking, 1985)

Ginsberg, Allen, *Indian Journals, March 1962–May 1963* (San Francisco: City Lights, 1970)

Ginsberg, Allen, *Journals, Early Fifties Early Sixties* (New York: Grove, 1977)

Girard, Xavier, *Mediterranean from Homer to Picasso* (New York: Assouline, 2001)

Glass, Charles, *Americans in Paris: Life and Death Under Nazi Occupation* (NY: Penguin, 2009)

Glassco, John, *Memoirs of Montparnasse* (Toronto & New York: Oxford University Press, 1970)

Glendinning, Victoria, *Vita: The Life of Vita Sackville-West* (Harmondsworth: Penguin, 1984)

Glur, Guido, *Kunstlehre und Kunstanschauung des Georgekreises und die Aesthetik Oscar Wildes*, special issue of *Sprache und Dichtung* (Neue Folge Band 3), 1957

Goering, General Hermann, *Germany Reborn* (London: Elkin Mathews & Marrot, 1934)

Gombrowicz, Witold, *Polish Memories* (New Haven & London: Yale University Press, 2004)

Gooch, Brad, *City Poet: The Life and Times of Frank O'Hara* (New York: Knopf, 1993)

Goytisolo, Juan, *Forbidden Territory and Realms of Strife* (London: Verso, 2003)

Graves, Robert, *Lawrence and the Arabs* (London: Cape, 1934)

Graves, Robert, and Alan Hodge, *The Long Week-End: A Social History of Great Britain, 1918–1939* (Harmondsworth: Penguin, 1971)

Gray, Dominic, *Amaze Me! Paris Between the Wars* (Leeds: Opera North, 2002)

Gray, Simon, *The Smoking Diaries: The Year of the Jouncer* (London: Granta, 2006)

Green, Julian, *Diary 1928–1957* (London: Collins & Harvill, 1964)

Green, Julian, *The Other Sleep* (London: Pushkin, 2001)

Green, Julian, *Paris* (London: Marion Boyars, 1993)

Green, Martin, *Children of the Sun: A Narrative of 'Decadence' in England After 1918* (London: Pimlico, 1992)

Green, Michelle, *The Dream at the End of the World: Paul Bowles and the Literary Renegades in Tangier* (New York: HarperCollins, 1991)

Greer, Germaine, *The Boy* (London: Thames & Hudson, 2003)

Griffin, David [Robin Maugham], *The Wrong People* (New York: Peacock, 1967)

Griffin, Peter, *Less Than a Treason: Hemingway in Paris* (New York & Oxford, Oxford University Press, 1990)

Grigg, M.P., Sir Edward, *Britain Looks at Germany* (London: Nicholson & Watson, 1938)

Grove, Valerie, *A Voyage Round John Mortimer* (London: Penguin, 2008)

Grünzweig, Walter, *Constructing the German Walt Whitman* (Iowa City: University of Iowa Press, 1995)

Guédras, Annie (ed.), *Jean Cocteau: Erotic Drawings* (Köln: Evergreen, 1999)

Gussow, Mel, *Edward Albee: A Singular Journey* (New York & London: Applause, 2001)

Haag, Michael, *Alexandria: City of Memory* (New Haven & London: Yale University Press, 2004)

Haden-Guest, Anthony, *The Last Party: Studio 54, Disco, and the Culture of the Night* (New York: William Morrow, 1997)

Häger, Bengt, *Ballets Suédois* (London: Thames & Hudson, 1990)

Hale, Keith (ed.), *Friends and Apostles: The Correspondence of Rupert Brooke and James Strachey, 1905–1914* (New Haven & London: Yale University Press, 1998)

Hall, Radclyffe, *The Well of Loneliness* (London: Virago, 1982)

Hallam, Paul, *The Book of Sodom* (London: Verso, 1993)

Halperin, David M., *One Hundred Years of Homosexuality, and Other Essays on Greek Love* (New York & London: Routledge, 1990)

Hamecher, Peter, 'Der männliche Eros im Werke Stefan Georges', *Jahrbuch für Sexuelle Zwischenstufen* 14 (1914), pp. 10–23

Hamer, Emily, *Britannia's Glory: A History of Twentieth-Century Lesbians* (London: Cassell, 1996)

Hammelmann, H.A., *Hugo von Hofmannsthal* (London: Bowes & Bowes, 1957)

Hancock, Eleanor, '"Only the Real, the True, the Masculine Held Its Value": Ernst Röhm, Masculinity, and Male Homosexuality', *Journal of the History of Sexuality* 8, 4 (1998), pp. 616–641

Harding, James, *Agate* (London: Methuen, 1986)

Harris, Derek, *Luis Cernuda: A Study of the Poetry* (London: Tamesis Books, 1973)

Hart, Liddell, *T.E. Lawrence: In Arabia and After* (London: Cape, 1935)

Hart-Davis, Rupert, *Hugh Walpole: A Biography* (London: Rupert Hart-Davis, 1952)

Harvey, Ian, *To Fall Like Lucifer* (London: Sidgwick & Jackson, 1971)

Hassall, Christopher, *Rupert Brooke: A Biography* (London: Faber, 1972)

Hawkeswood, William G., *One of the Children: Gay Black Men in Harlem* (Berkeley: University of California Press, 1996)

Hayman, Ronald, *Tennessee Williams: Everyone Else Is an Audience* (New Haven & London: Yale University Press, 1993)

Hayman, Ronald, *Thomas Mann: A Biography* (London: Bloomsbury, 1996)

Hedín, Sven, *Germany and World Peace* (London: Hutchinson, 1937)

Heilbut, Anthony, *Thomas Mann: Eros and Literature* (London: Macmillan, 1996)

Hemingway, Ernest, *A Moveable Feast* (London: Cape, 1964)

Hibberd, Dominic, *Wilfred Owen: A New Biography* (London: Weidenfeld & Nicolson, 2002)

Hicks, Michael, 'The Imprisonment of Henry Cowell', *Journal of the American Musicological Society* 44 (1991), pp. 92–119

Higgins, Patrick, *Heterosexual Dictatorship: Male Homosexuality in Post-War Britain* (London: Fourth Estate, 1996)

Higgins, Patrick (ed.), *A Queer Reader* (London: Fourth Estate, 1993)

Higgs, David (ed.), *Queer Sites: Gay Urban Histories Since 1600* (London & New York: Routledge, 1999)

Hillier, Bevis, *Young Betjeman* (London: John Murray, 2003)

Hitchens, Christopher, *Hitch-22: A Memoir* (London: Atlantic, 2011)

Hitler, Adolf, *Mein Kampf* (London: Hurst & Blackett, 1939)

Hoare, Philip, *Noël Coward: A Biography* (London: Arrow, 1997)

Hoare, Philip, *Serious Pleasures: The Life of Stephen Tennant* (London: Penguin, 1991)

Hoare, Philip, *Wilde's Last Stand: Decadence, Conspiracy and the First World War* (London: Duckworth, 1997)

Hoffman, Nicholas von, *Citizen Cohn: The Scandalous Life and Times of Roy Cohn, Lawyer, Fixer, Destroyer* (London: Abacus, 1989)

Hofmannsthal, Hugo von, 'Preface', in St.-John Perse, *Anabasis* (London: Faber, 1959), pp.84–86

Holroyd, Michael, *Lytton Strachey* (London: Vintage, 1994)

Homans, Jennifer, *Apollo's Angels: A History of Ballet* (London: Granta, 2010)

Honig, Edwin, *García Lorca* (London: Cape, 1968)

Horst, *Portraits: Paris, London, New York* (London: National Portrait Gallery, 2001)

Horton, Philip, *Hart Crane: The Life of an American Poet* (New York: Viking, 1957)

Houlbrook, Matt, *Queer London: Perils and Pleasures in the Sexual Metropolis, 1918–1957* (Chicago & London: University of Chicago Press, 2005)

Howes, Keith, *Outspoken: Keith Howes'* Gay News *Interviews, 1976–83* (London: Cassell, 1995)

Howes, R.W., 'Fernando Pessoa, Poet, Publisher, and Translator', *British Library Journal* 9, 2 (1982), pp. 161–170

Hughes, Langston, *The Big Sea: An Autobiography* (London: Pluto, 1986)

Hughes, Robert, *Goya* (London: Harvill, 2003)

Hughes-Hallett, Lucy, *The Pike: Gabriele D'Annunzio, Poet, Seducer and Preacher of War* (London: Fourth Estate, 2014)

Huxley, Aldous, *Those Barren Leaves* (Harmondsworth: Penguin, 1951)

Hyde, H. Montgomery, *The Other Love: An Historical and Contemporary Survey of Homosexuality in Britain* (London: Mayflower, 1972)

Hyde, H. Montgomery, *Stalin: The History of a Dictator* (London: Rupert Hart-Davis, 1971)

Hyde, H. Montgomery, *The Trials of Oscar Wilde* (London: Hodge, 1948)

Hyde, Mary (ed.), *Bernard Shaw and Alfred Douglas: A Correspondence* (London: John Murray, 1982)

Ireland, G.W., *André Gide: A Study of His Creative Writings* (Oxford: Clarendon Press, 1970)

Ireland, G.W., *Gide* (Edinburgh: Oliver & Boyd, 1963)

Irwin, Robert, *The Arabian Nights: A Companion* (London: Allen Lane, Penguin, 1994)

Isherwood, Christopher, *All the Conspirators* (Harmondsworth: Penguin, 1976)

Isherwood, Christopher, *Christopher and His Kind, 1929–1939* (London: Eyre Methuen, 1977)

Isherwood, Christopher, *Down There on a Visit* (London: Four Square, 191964)

Isherwood, Christopher, *Exhumations: Stories, Articles, Verses* (London: Methuen, 1966)

Isherwood, Christopher, *Goodbye to Berlin* (Harmondsworth: Penguin, 1945)

Isherwood, Christopher, *Liberation: Diaries, Volume Three, 1970–1983* (London: Chatto & Windus, 2012)

Isherwood, Christopher, *Lions and Shadows: An Education in the Twenties* (London: Methuen, 1953)

Isherwood, Christopher, *Lost Years: A Memoir, 1945–1951* (London: Vintage, 2001)

Isherwood, Christopher, *My Guru and His Disciple* (London: Eyre Methuen, 1980)

Isherwood, Christopher, *A Single Man* (Harmondsworth: Penguin, 1969)

Ivry, Benjamin, *Francis Poulenc* (London: Phaidon, 1996)

Jaggi, Maya, 'Voice of the Maghreb', *The Guardian: Review* (May 6, 2006), p. 11

James, Burnett, *Manuel de Falla and the Spanish Musical Renaissance* (London: Gollancz, 1979)

James, Clive, *Unreliable Memoirs* (London: Picador, 1981)

Jarman, Derek, *Smiling in Slow Motion* (London: Vintage, 2001)

Jarroway, David R., *Going the Distance: Dissident Subjectivity in Modernist American Literature* (Baton Rouge: Louisiana State University Press, 2003)

Jarry, Alfred, *The Supermale* (London: Cape, 1968)

Jimenez-Fajardo, Salvador, *Luis Cernuda* (Boston: Twayne, 1978)

Jóhannesson, Guðni Thorlacius, *The History of Iceland* (Santa Barbara, California: Greenwood, 2013)

Johnson, James Weldon, *The Autobiography of an Ex-Colored Man* (New York: Penguin, 1990)

Johnson, Robert B., *Henry de Montherlant* (New York: Twayne, 1968)

Johnston, Jill, *Jasper Johns: Privileged Information* (New York & London: Thames & Hudson, 1996)

Jonas, Ilsedore B., *Thomas Mann and Italy* (University, Alabama: University of Alabama Press, 1979)

Jones, James W., *'We of the Third Sex': Literary Representations of Homosexuality in Wilhelmine Germany* (New York: Peter Lang, 1990)

Jowitt, Deborah, *Jerome Robbins: His Life, His Theater, His Dance* (New York: Simon & Schuster, 2004)

Judt, Tony, *Reappraisals: Reflections on the Forgotten Twentieth Century* (London: Vintage, 2009)

Jullian, Philippe, *D'Annunzio* (London: Pall Mall, 1972)

Kaes, Anton, Martin Jay and Edward Dimendberg (eds), *The Weimar Republic Source Book* (Berkeley: University of California Press, 1994)

Kaiser, Charles, *The Gay Metropolis* (London: Weidenfeld & Nicolson, 1998)

Kaplan, Fred, *Gore Vidal: A Biography* (London: Bloomsbury, 1999)

Kaplan, Fred, *Henry James: The Imagination of Genius* (Baltimore & London: Johns Hopkins University Press, 1999)

Kaplan, Fred (ed.), *Travelling in Italy with Henry James* (London: Hodder & Stoughton, 1994)

Kaplan, Morris B., *Sodom on the Thames: Sex, Love, and Scandal in Wilde Times* (Ithaca, New York: Cornell University Press, 2005)

Karlinsky, Simon, 'Kuzmin, Gumilev and Cvetaeva as Neo-Romantic Playwrights', in Malmstad, John E. (ed.), *Studies in the Life and Works of Mikail Kuzmin*, Wiener Slawistischer Almanach, Sonderband 24 (n.d.), pp. 17–30

Karlinsky, Simon, *Marina Tsvetaeva: The Woman, Her World and Her Poetry* (Cambridge: Cambridge University Press, 1986)

Karlinsky, Simon, 'Russia's Gay Literature and Culture: The Impact of the October Revolution', in Martin Bauml Duberman, Martha Vicinus and George Chauncey, Jr (eds), *Hidden from History: Reclaiming the Gay and Lesbian Past* (London & New York: Penguin, 1991), pp. 347–364

Karpeles, Eric, *Paintings in Proust: A Visual Companion to* In Search of Lost Time (London: Thames & Hudson, 2008)

Kashner, Sam, *When I Was Cool: My Life at the Jack Kerouac School, A Memoir* (London: Century, 2004)

Katz, Jonathan D., *Gay American History: Lesbians and Gay Men in the U.S.A.* (New York: Avon, 1978)

Katz, Jonathan D., and David C. Ward, *Hide/Seek: Difference and Desire in American Portraiture* (Washington, D.C.: Smithsonian Books, 2010)

Kauffmann, Stanley, 'Homosexual Drama and Its Disguises', *New York Times* (23 January 1966), section 2, p.1

Kavanagh, Julie, *Rudolf Nureyev: The Life* (London: Fig Tree, 2007)

Kay, Jackie, *Bessie Smith* (Bath: Absolute Press, 1997)

Kazantzakis, Nikos, *Report to Greco* (London: Faber, 1973)

Keeley, Edmund, *Cavafy's Alexandria: Study of a Myth in Progress* (London: Hogarth, 1977)

Kelley, Kitty, *Nancy Reagan: The Unauthorized Biography* (New York: Bantam, 1992)

Kellner, Bruce, *Carl Van Vechten and the Irreverent Decades* (Norman, Oklahoma: University of Oklahoma Press, 1968)

Kellogg, Stuart (ed.), *Essays on Gay Literature* (New York: Harrington Park Press, 1983)

Kelly, Catriona, and David Shepherd (eds), *Russian Cultural Studies: An Introduction* (Oxford: Oxford University Press, 1998)

Kennedy, Hubert, *Ulrichs: The Life and Works of Karl Heinrich Ulrichs, Pioneer of the Modern Gay Movement* (Boston: Alyson, 1988)

Kenner, Hugh, *The Pound Era* (London: Faber, 1975)

Kerouac, Jack, *Desolation Angels* (London: Flamingo, 2001)

Kessler, Count Harry, *The Diaries of a Cosmopolitan: 1918–1937* (London: Weidenfeld & Nicolson, 1999)

Kiernan, Robert F., *Gore Vidal* (New York: Frederick Ungar, 1982)

King, Francis, 'Broken Butterfly', *Gay Times* 281 (February 2002), p.78

King, Francis, *E.M. Forster and His World* (London: Thames& Hudson, 1978)

King, Francis, *Yesterday Came Suddenly* (London: Constable, 1993)

King, Tom, *David Geffen: A Biography of New Hollywood* (London: Hutchinson, 2000)

Kirkup, James, *A Poet Could Not But Be Gay: Some Legends of My Lost Youth* (London: Peter Owen, 1991)

Kirstein, Lincoln, *Mosaic: Memoirs* (New York: Farrar, Straus & Giroux, 1994)

Kirstein, Lincoln, *Paul Cadmus* (San Francisco: Pomegranate Artbooks, 1992)

Klyuev, Nikolai, *Poems* (Ann Arbor, Michigan: Ardis, 1977)

Knobel, Paul, *An Encyclopedia of Male Homosexual Poetry and its Reception History* (Sydney, New South Wales : Homo Poetry, 2002)

Knox, James, *Robert Byron* (London: John Murray, 2004)

Koestenbaum, Wayne, 'Call It Hollywood', *London Review of Books* 26, 24 (16 December 2004), pp. 31–32

Koestenbaum, Wayne, *Double Talk: The Erotics of Male Literary Collaboration* (New York & London: Routledge, 1989)

Koestler, Arthur, *Arrow in the Blue* (London: Collins, 1952)

Kramer, Jane, *Paterfamilias: Allen Ginsberg in America* (London: Gollancz, 1970)

Kubizek, August, *Young Hitler: The Story of Our Friendship* (London: Allan Wingate, 1954)

Kuzmin, Mikhail, 'Alexandrian Songs' in Richard McKane (ed.), *Ten Russian Poets: Surviving the Twentieth Century* (London: Anvil, 2003), pp. 19–47

Kuzmin, Mikhail, *Wings* (London: Hesperus, 2007)

Kuzmin, Mikhail, *Wings: Prose and Poetry* (Ann Arbor, Michigan: Ardis, 1972)

Lambert, Gavin, *Mainly About Lindsay Anderson* (London: Faber, 2000)

Lamos, Colleen, *Deviant Modernism: Sexual and Textual Errancy in T.S. Eliot, James Joyce, and Marcel Proust* (Cambridge: Cambridge University Press, 1998)

Lane, Christopher, *The Ruling Passion: British Colonial Allegory and the Paradox of Homosexual Desire* (Durham, North Carolina: Duke University Press)

Larivière, Michel, *Homosexuels et bisexuals célèbres: le dictionnaire* (Paris: Delétraz, 1997)

Lasch, Christopher, *The Agony of the American Left* (New York: Vintage, 1969)

Laurents, Arthur, *Original Story By: A Memoir of Broadway and Hollywood* (New York & London: Applause, 2000)

Lawrence, D.H., *Selected Letters* (Harmondsworth: Penguin, 1950)

Lawrence, D.H., *Women in Love* (London: Grafton, 1988)

Lawrence, T.E., *Seven Pillars of Wisdom: A Triumph* (London: The Reprint Society, 1939)

Léautaud, Paul, *Journal of a Man of Letters, 1898–1907* (London: Chatto & Windus, 1960)

Leddick, David, *Intimate Companions: A Triography of George Platt Lynes, Paul Cadmus, Lincoln Kirstein, and Their Circle* (New York: St Martin's Press, 2000)

Lee, Hermione, *Virginia Woolf* (London: Chatto & Windus, 1996)

Lee, Hermione, *Willa Cather: A Life Saved Up* (London: Virago, 1989)

Lees-Milne, James, *Harold Nicolson: A Biography, Vol. 1, 1886–1929* (London: Chatto & Windus, 1980)

Lehmann, John, *Christopher Isherwood: A Personal Memoir* (London: Weidenfeld & Nicolson, 1987)

Lehmann, John, *I Am My Brother: Autobiography II* (London: Longmans, 1960)

Lehmann, John, *In the Purely Pagan Sense* (London: GMP, 1985)

Leiris, Michel, *Manhood* (London: Cape, 1968)

Lesk, Andrew, 'Having a Gay Old Time in Paris: John Glassco's Not-So-Queer Adventures', in Terry Goldie (ed.), *In a Queer Country: Gay and Lesbian Studies in a Canadian Context* (Vancouver: Arsenal Pulp, 2001), pp. 175–187

Leslie, Shane, *Long Shadows* (London: John Murray, 1966)

LeSueur, Joe, *Digressions on Some Poems by Frank O'Hara: A Memoir* (New York: Farrar, Straus & Giroux, 2003)

Levenstein, Harvey, *Seductive Journey: American Tourists in France from Jefferson to the Jazz Age* (Chicago & London: University of Chicago Press, 1998)

Levi, Carlo, *The Watch* (South Royalton, Vermont: Steerforth Italia, 1999)

Levi, Carlo, *Words Are Stones: Impressions of Sicily* (London: Hesperus, 2005)

Levine, Suzanne Jill, *Manuel Puig and the Spider Woman: His Life and Fictions* (London: Faber, 2000)

Lewis, David Levering, *When Harlem Was In Vogue* (New York: Oxford University Press, 1989)

Lewis, Jr, Robert W., *Hemingway on Love* (New York: Haskell, 1973)

Lewis, Roger, *The Real Life of Laurence Olivier* (London: Century, 1996)

Lewis, Wyndham, *The Apes of God* (London: Nash & Grayson, [1930])

Lewis, Wyndham, *The Hitler Cult* (London: Dent, 1939)

Lewis, Wyndham, *The Roaring Queen* (London: Secker & Warburg, 1973)

Leyland, Winston (ed.), *Gay Sunshine Interviews, Volume One* (San Francisco: Gay Sunshine, 1978)

Leyland, Winston (ed.), *Gay Sunshine Interviews, Volume Two* (San Francisco: Gay Sunshine, 1982)

Lezama Lima, José, *Selections* (Berkeley: University of California Press, 2005)

Li, Zhisui, *The Private Life of Chairman Mao: The Memoirs of Mao's Personal Physician* (London: Arrow, 1996)

Liddell, Robert, *Cavafy: A Critical Biography* (London: Duckworth, 1974)

Liddell, Robert, *Unreal City* (London: Peter Owen, 1993)

Lilly, Mark, *Gay Men's Literature in the Twentieth Century* (London: Macmillan, 1993)

Lindqvist, Sven, *Desert Divers* (London: Granta, 2000)

Lisboa, Eugénio, and L.C. Taylor (eds), *Fernando Pessoa: A Centenary Pessoa* (Manchester: Fyfield/Carcanet, 2003)

Littlejohn, David (ed.), *Gide: A Collection of Critical Essays* (Englewood Cliffs, N.J.: Prentice-Hall, 1970)

Logue, Christopher, *Prince Charming: A Memoir* (London: Faber, 1999)

Londré, Felicia Hardison, *Federico García Lorca* (New York: Frederick Ungar, 1984)

Lorca, Federico García, *Poet in New York* (London: Penguin, 1990)

Lorca, Federico García, *The Public and Play without a Title* (New York: New Directions, 1983)

Lorca, Federico García, *A Season in Granada: Uncollected Poems and Prose* (London: Anvil, 1998)

Lorca, Federico García, *Selected Poems* (Newcastle upon Tyne: Bloodaxe, 1992)

Lorde, Audre, *Zami: A New Spelling of My Name* (London: Pandora, 1996)

Lucas, John, *Next Year Will Be Better: A Memoir of England in the 1950s* (Nottingham: Five Leaves, 2010)

Ludington, Townsend, *Marsden Hartley: The Biography of an American Artist* (Boston: Little, Brown, 1992)

Macey, David, *The Lives of Michel Foucault* (London: Vintage, 1994)

Machlin, Mitt, *The Gossip Wars: An Exposé of the Scandal Era* (no place specified: no publisher specified, 1981)

Mackay, John Henry, *The Hustler* (Boston: Alyson, 1985)

Mackenzie, Compton, *Extraordinary Women: Theme and Variations* (London: Icon, 1967)

Mackenzie, Compton, *My Life and Times: Octave Two, 1891–1900* (London: Chatto & Windus, 1963)

Mackenzie, Compton, *Vestal Fire* (London: Cassell, 1927)

Mackridge, Peter, 'The Protean Self of Costas Taktsis', *European Gay Review* 6/7 (n.d.), pp. 172–184

MacNeice, Louis, *The Strings Are False* (London: Faber, 1965)

Mahieux, Viviane, 'The Chronicler as Streetwalker: Salvador Novo and the Performance of Genre', *Hispanic Review* (Spring 2008), pp. 155–177

Malaparte, Curzio, *Kaputt* (New York: Dutton, 1946)

Malaparte, Curzio, *The Skin* (London: Panther, 1964)

Malmstad, John E., *Marina Tsvetaeva: The Woman, Her World and Her Poetry* (Cambridge: Cambridge University Press, 1986)

Malmstad, John E. (ed.), *Out of the Blue: Russia's Hidden Gay Literature, An Anthology* (San Francisco: Gay Sunshine, 1997)

Malmstad, John E., and Nikolay Bogomolov, *Mikhail Kuzmin: A Life in Art* (Cambridge, Massachusetts, & London: Harvard University Press, 1999)

Mann, Golo, *Reminiscences and Reflections: Growing Up in Germany* (London: Faber, 1990)

Mann, Klaus, *André Gide and the Crisis of Modern Thought* (London: Dennis Dobson, 1948)

Mann, Klaus, *Mephisto* (New York: Penguin, 1995)

Mann, Klaus, *The Pious Dance* (London: GMP, 1988)

Mann, Klaus, *The Turning Point: Thirty-five Years in This Century* (London: Gollancz, 1944)

Mann, Thomas, *Death in Venice, Tristan, Tonio Kröger* (Harmondsworth: Penguin, 1955)

Mann, William J., *Behind the Screen: How Gays and Lesbians Shaped Hollywood, 1910–1969* (New York: Penguin, 2002)

Mann, William J., *Wisecracker: The Life and Times of William Haynes, Hollywood's First Openly Gay Star* (New York: Penguin, 1999)

Manrique, Jaime, *Eminent Maricones: Arenas, Lorca, Puig, and Me* (Madison, Wisconsin: University of Wisconsin Press, 1999)

Mansel, Philip, *Levant: Splendour and Catastrophe on the Mediterranean* (London: John Murray, 2010)

March, Harold, *Gide and the Hound of Heaven* (New York: A.S. Barnes, 1961)

Marks, Steven G., *How Russia Shaped the Modern World: From Art to Anti-Semitism, Ballet to Bolshevism* (Princeton, New Jersey: Princeton University Press, 2003)

Marr, David, *Patrick White: A Life* (London: Cape, 1991)

Marr, David, 'A Note on *The Hanging Garden*', in Patrick White, *The Hanging Garden* (London: Vintage, 2013), pp. 217–224

Martel, Frédéric, *The Pink and the Black: Homosexuals in France Since 1968* (Stanford, California: Stanford University Press, 2000)

Martin, Robert K., *The Homosexual Tradition in American Poetry* (Austin, Texas, & London: University of Texas Press, 1979)

Martin, Robert K. (ed.), *The Continuing Presence of Walt Whitman: The Life After the Life* (Iowa City: University of Iowa Press, 1992)

Martin, Robert K., and George Piggford (eds), *Queer Forster* (Chicago & London: University of Chicago Press, 1997)

Martin du Gard, Roger, *Notes sur André Gide, 1913–1951* (Paris: Gallimard, 1951)

Massey, Ian, *Patrick Procktor: Art and Life* (Norwich: Unicorn, 2010)

Massine, Léonide, *My Life in Ballet* (London: Macmillan, 1968)

Masters, Brian, *The Life of E.F. Benson* (London: Pimlico, 1993)

Mathews, Marcia M., 'Richmond Barthé, Sculptor', *South Atlantic Quarterly* 74 (1975), pp.324–339

Maugham, Robin, *Escape from the Shadows* (London: Robin Clark, 1981)

Mauriès, Patrick, *Jean Cocteau* (London: Thames & Hudson, 1998)

Maxwell, William J., *F.B. Eyes: How J. Edgar Hoover's Ghostreaders Framed African American Literature* (Princeton, N.J.: Princeton University Press, 2015)

McAlmon, Robert, and Kay Boyle, *Being Geniuses Together, 1920–1930* (London: Hogarth, 1984)

McBrien, William, *Cole Porter: The Definitive Biography* (London: HarperCollins, 1998)

McCourt, James, *Queer Street: Rise and Fall of an American Culture, 1947–1985* (New York: Norton, 2005)

McDonald, Robert, 'Jumping About Like Quanta', in Earl G. Ingersoll (ed.), *Lawrence Durrell: Conversations* (Cranbury, New Jersey: Associated University Presses, 1998), pp.149–162

McKay, Claude, *A Long Way from Home* (London: Pluto, 1985)

McKinlay, Neil C., *The Poetry of Luis Cernuda: Order in a World of Chaos* (London: Tamesis Books, 1999)

McVay, Gordon, *Esenin: A Life* (London: Hodder & Stoughton, 1976)

Meaker, Marijane, *Highsmith: A Romance of the 1950s* (San Francisco: Cleis Press, 2003)

Medley, Robert, *Drawn from the Life: A Memoir* (London: Faber, 1983)

Meier, Paul L., *The Flames of Rome* (Grand Rapids, Michigan: Kregel, 1981)

Melville, Joy, *Diaghilev and Friends* (London: Haus, 2009)

Mendelsohn, Daniel, 'Introduction', in C.P. Cavafy, *Collected Poems* (New York: Alfred A. Knopf, 2009), pp. xv–lix

Mendelson, Maurice, 'Life and Work of Walt Whitman: A Soviet View', in Gay Wilson Allen and Ed Folsom (eds), *Walt Whitman and the World* (Iowa City: University of Iowa Press, 1995), pp. 336–338.

Merrill, James, *A Different Person: A Memoir* (San Francisco: HarperCollins, 1994)

Metzger, Michael M., and Erika A. Metzger, *Stefan George* (New York: Twayne, 1972)

Meyers, Jeffrey, *The Enemy: A Biography of Wyndham Lewis* (London & Henley: Routledge & Kegan Paul, 1980)

Meyers, Jeffrey, *Hemingway: A Biography* (London: Macmillan, 1985)

Meyers, Jeffrey, *Homosexuality and Literature, 1890–1930* (London: Athlone, 1977)

Mhrabet, Mohammed, *Love with a Few Hairs* (London: Arena/Anchor, 1986)

Middleton Murry, John, *Between Two Worlds: An Autobiography* (London: Cape, 1935)

Miles, Barry, *The Beat Hotel: Ginsberg, Burroughs and Corso in Paris, 1957–1963* (London: Atlantic, 2001)

Miles, Barry, *Ginsberg: A Biography* (New York: Viking, 1990)

Miller, Arthur, *Timebends* (London: Methuen, 1999)

Miller, Carl, *Stages of Desire: Gay Theatre's Hidden History* (London: Cassell, 1996)

Miller, David A., *The Novel and the Police* (Berkeley, California: University of California Press, 1988)

Miller, Henry, *The Colossus of Maroussi* (Harmondsworth: Penguin, 1972)

Miller, Henry, *Letters to Anaïs Nin* (London: Peter Owen, 1965)

Miller, Henry, *Quiet Days in Clichy* (New York: Grove, 1965)

Miller, Henry, *Tropic of Cancer* (London: Harper Perennial, 2005)

Miller, James, *The Passion of Michel Foucault* (Cambridge, Mass.: Harvard University Press, 2000)

Miller, Leta E., and Fredric Lieberman, *Lou Harrison: Composing a World* (New York & Oxford: Oxford University Press, 1998)

Miller, Neil, *Out of the Past: Gay and Lesbian History from 1869 to the Present* (London: Vintage, 1995)

Miłosz, Czesław, *Native Realm: A Search for Self-Definition* (Berkeley & Los Angeles: University of California Press, 1981)

Miłosz, Czesław, *Post-War Polish Poetry* (Harmondsworth: Penguin, 1970)

Miłosz, Czesław, *Proud to Be a Mammal: Essays on War, Faith and Memory* (London: Penguin, 2010)

Miłosz, Czesław, *The Witness of Poetry* (Cambridge, Massachusetts: Harvard University Press, 1983)

Mishima, Yukio, *Confessions of a Mask* (London: Sphere, 1967)

Mishima, Yukio, *Forbidden Colours* (Harmondsworth: Penguin, 1971)

Mitchell, Donald, *Britten and Auden in the Thirties: The Year 1936* (London: Faber, 1981)

Mitchell, Leslie, *Maurice Bowra: A Life* (Oxford: Oxford University Press, 2009)

Mitford, Jessica, *Hons and Rebels* (Harmondsworth: Penguin, 1962)

Mitford, Nancy, *The Pursuit of Love, and Love in a Cold Climate* (Harmondsworth: Penguin, 1980)

Money, James, *Capri: Island of Pleasure* (London: Hamish Hamilton, 1986)

Montagu of Beaulieu, Lord, *Wheels Within Wheels: An Unconventional Life* (London: Weidenfeld & Nicolson, 2000)

Moore, Marianne, *The Selected Letters of Marianne Moore* (London: Faber, 1998)

Morand, Paul, *Venices* (London: Pushkin, 2002)

Morgan, J.H., *Assize of Arms: Being the Story of the Disarmament of Germany and Her Rearmament (1919–1939) in Two Volumes*, Volume One (London: Methuen, 1945)

Morgan, Ted, *Literary Outlaw: The Life and Times of William S. Burroughs* (New York: Avon, 1990)

Morley, Sheridan, *John G: The Authorised Biography of John Gielgud* (London: Hodder & Stoughton, 2001)

Morris, C. Brian, *Son of Andalusia: The Lyrical Landscapes of Federico García Lorca* (Liverpool: Liverpool University Press, 1997)

Morwitz, Ernst, 'Stefan George', in Stefan George, *Poems* (New York: Schocken Books, 1967), pp. 9–36

Mosley, Charlotte (ed.), *The Letters of Nancy Mitford* (London: Sceptre, 1994)

Moss, Kevin (ed.), *Out of the Blue: Russia's Hidden Gay Literature, An Anthology* (San Francisco: Gay Sunshine, 1997)

Mowrer, Edgar Ansel, *Germany Puts the Clock Back* (London: John Lane the Bodley Head, 1933)

Mrabet, Mohammed, *Love with a Few Hairs* (London: Arena, 1986)

Muggeridge, Malcolm, *Chronicles of Wasted Time, I: The Green Stick* (London: Collins, 1972)

Mulvagh, Jane, *Madresfield: One Home, One Family, One Thousand Years* (London: Black Swan, 2009)

Munro, H.H., *The Penguin Complete Saki* (London: Penguin, 1982)

Murray, Douglas, *Bosie: A Biography of Lord Alfred Douglas* (London: Hodder & Stoughton, 2000)

Nabokov, Vladimir, *The Eye* (London: Penguin, 1992)

Nabokov, Vladimir, *Speak, Memory* (Harmondsworth: Penguin, 1969)

Nabokov, Vladimir, *Strong Opinions* (London: Penguin, 2011)

Nadal, Rafael Martínez, *Lorca's* The Public: *A Study of His Unfinished Play (*El Público*) and of Love and Death in the Work of Federico García Lorca* (London: Calder & Boyars, 1974)

Näslund, Erik, 'The Ballet Avant-Garde I: The Ballets Suédois and Its Modernist Concept', in Marion Kant (ed.), *The Cambridge Companion to Ballet* (Cambridge: Cambridge University Press, 2007), pp. 201–211

Näslund, Erik, *Rolf de Maré: Art Collector, Ballet Director, Museum Creator* (Alton, Hampshire: Dance Books, 2009)

Nathan, John, *Mishima: A Biography* (Cambridge, Massachusetts: Da Capo, 2000)

Nelson, Emmanuel S. (ed.), *Contemporary Gay American Novelists: A Bio-Bibiliographical Critical Sourcebook* (Westport, Connecticut: Greenwood Press, 1993)

Nelson, Emmanuel S. (ed.), *Critical Essays: Gay and Lesbian Writers of Color* (New York: Harrington Park Press, 1993)

Neruda, Pablo, *Memoirs* (Harmondsworth: Penguin, 1978)

Nicholls, David (ed.), *The Whole World of Music: A Henry Cowell Symposium* (Amsterdam: Harwood, 1997)

Nichols, Beverley, *All I Could Never Be: Some Reflections* (London: Cape, 1949)

Nichols, Beverley, *Oxford—London—Hollywood: An Omnibus* (London: Cape, 1931)

Nichols, Beverley, *The Sun in My Eyes: Or How Not to Go Round the World* (London: Heinemann, 1969)

Nichols, Beverley, *The Sweet and Twenties* (London: Weidenfeld & Nicolson), 1958

Nichols, Beverley, *The Unforgiving Minute: Some Confessions from Childhood to the Outbreak of the Second World War* (London: W.H. Allen, 1978)

Nicholson, Virginia, *Among the Bohemians: Experiments in Living, 1900–1939* (London: Penguin, 2003)

Nicolson, Harold, *Diaries and Letters, 1945–1962* (London: Collins, 1968)

Nicolson, Nigel, *Long Life* (London: Weidenfeld & Nicolson, 1997)

Nicolson, Nigel, *Portrait of a Marriage* (London: Weidenfeld & Nicolson, 1973)

Niles, Blair, *Strange Brother* (London: T. Werner Laurie, 1931)

Norse, Harold, *Memoirs of a Bastard Angel* (London: Bloomsbury, 1990)

Norton, Robert E., *Secret Germany: Stefan George and His Circle* (Ithaca & London: Cornell University Press, 2002), pp. 98–107

O'Connor, Sean, *Straight Acting: Popular Gay Drama from Wilde to Rattigan* (London: Cassell, 1998)

Orwell, George, *Down and Out in Paris and London* (Harmondsworth: Penguin, 1974)

Orwell, George, *Essays* (London: Everyman, 2002)

Orwell, George, *Keep the Aspidistra Flying* (London: Penguin, 1989)

Orwell, George, *A Life in Letters* (London: Penguin, 2011)

Orwell, George, *The Road to Wigan Pier* (Harmondsworth: Penguin, 1962)

Osborne, Charles, *W.H. Auden: The Life of a Poet* (New York & London: Harcourt Brace Jovanovich, 1979)

Osborne, John, *Almost a Gentleman: An Autobiography, Volume II, 1955–1966* (London: Faber, 1992)

Osborne, John, *A Better Class of Person: An Autobiography, 1929–1956* (Harmondsworth: Penguin, 1982)

Ouditt, Sharon, *Impressions of Southern Italy: British Travel Writing from Henry Swinburne to Norman Douglas* (London: Routledge, 2013)

Owen, Wilfred, *Collected Poems* (London: Chatto & Windus, 1967)

Padilla, Heberto, *Sent Off the Field: A Selection from the Poetry of Heberto Padilla* (London: André Deutsch, 1972)

Page, Norman, *Auden and Isherwood: The Berlin Years* (London: Macmillan, 1998)

Painter, George D., *André Gide: A Critical Biography* (London: Weidenfeld & Nicolson, 1968)

Painter, George D., *Marcel Proust: A Biography, Volume I* (London: Chatto & Windus, 1959)

Painter, George D., *Marcel Proust: A Biography, Volume II* (London: Chatto & Windus, 1965)

Parker, Peter, *Ackerley: A Life of J.R. Ackerley* (London: Cardinal, 1990)

Parker, Peter, *Isherwood: A Life* (London: Picador, 2004)

Pasolini, Pier Paolo, *The Letters of Pier Paolo Pasolini, Volume I: 1940–1954* (London: Quarter, 1992)

Pasolini, Pier Paolo, *The Scent of India* (London: Olive Press, 1984)

Pasternak, Boris, *The Last Summer* (Harmondsworth: Penguin, 1960)

Paterson, Michael, *Winston Churchill: Personal Accounts of the Great Leader at War* (Newton Abbot, Devon: David & Charles, 2005)

Patrick, Robert, 'The Insider-Outsider' in Jackson R. Bryer and Mary C. Hartig (eds), *William Inge: Essays and Reminiscences on the Plays and the Man* ((Jefferson, North Carolina: McFarland, 2014), pp. 25–29

Paz, Octavio, 'Luis Cernuda: The Edifying Word', in Luis Cernuda, *Selected Poems* (Riverdale-on-Hudson, NY: The Sheep Meadow Press, 1999), pp.xiii-xli

Pearsall, Ronald, *The Worm in the Bud: The World of Victorian Sexuality* (Harmondsworth: Penguin, 1971)

Pearson, Hesketh, *The Life of Oscar Wilde* (London: Methuen, 1946)

Pearson, John, *Façades: Edith, Osbert and Sacheverell Sitwell* (London: Fontana, 1980)

Pecora, Elio, *Sandro Penna: una cheta follia* (Milano: Frassinelli, 1984)

Pensa, Mario, *Stefan George: saggio critico* (Bologna: Nicola Zanichelli Editore, 1961)

Perry, Gill, *Women Artists and the Parisian Avant-Garde* (Manchester: Manchester University Press, 1995)

Pessoa, Fernando, *The Book of Disquiet* (London: Serpent's Tail, 1991)

Pessoa, Fernando, *The Collected Poems of Álvaro de Campos, Volume Two: 1928–1935* (Exeter: Shearsman, 2009)

Pessoa, Fernando, *A Little Larger Than the Entire Universe: Selected Poems* (London: Penguin, 2006)

Pessoa, Fernando, *Selected Poems* (Harmondsworth: Penguin, 1974)

Peters, Arthur King, *Jean Cocteau and André Gide: An Abrasive Friendship* (New Brunswick, N.J.: Rutgers University Press, 1973)

Peters, Margot, *May Sarton: A Biography* (New York: Knopf, 1998)

Peyrefitte, Roger, *The Exile of Capri* (London: Panther, 1969)

Phelan, Nancy, *Charles Mackerras: A Musicians' Musician* (London: Gollancz, 1987)

Phillips, Richard, Diane Watt & David Shuttleton (eds.), *De-centring Sexualities: Politics and Representations Beyond the Metropolis* (London & New York: Routledge, 2000)

Philp, Richard, and Mary Whitney, *Danceur: The Male in Ballet* (New York: McGraw-Hill, 1977)

Plant, Richard, *The Pink Triangle: The Nazi War Against Homosexuals* (Edinburgh: Mainstream, 1987)

Plante, David, *Becoming a Londoner: A Diary* (London: Bloomsbury, 2013)

Plomer, William, *At Home* (Harmondsworth: Penguin, 1961)

Plomer, William, *Museum Pieces* (Harmondsworth: Penguin, 1961)

Pollard, Patrick, *André Gide: Homosexual Moralist* (New Haven & London: Yale University Press, 1991)

Polmar, Norman, and Thomas B. Allen, *The Encyclopedia of Espionage* (New York: Gramercy Books, 1998)

Portuges, Catherine, 'Jewish Immigrant Directors and their Impact on Hollywood', in Daniel Bernardi, Murray Pomerance and Hava Tirosh-Samuelson (eds), *Hollywood's Chosen People: The Jewish Experience in American Cinema* (Detroit, Michigan: Wayne State University Press, 2013), pp. 35–52

Poulenc, Francis, *My Friends and Myself* (London: Dennis Dobson, 1978)

Powell, Anthony, *Agents and Patients* (Harmondsworth: Penguin, 1961)

Powell, Anthony, *Under Review: Further Writings on Writers, 1946–1989* (London: Heinemann, 1991)

Praz, Mario, *The Romantic Agony* (London: Oxford University Press, 1970)

Priestley, J.B., 'Thoughts in the Wilderness: Block Thinking', *New Statesman and Nation* 46, 1182 (31 October 1953), pp. 515–516

Pritchett, V.S., *The Tale Bearers: Essays on English, American and Other Writers* (London: Chatto & Windus, 1980)

Proctor, Patrick, *Self-Portrait* (London: Weidenfeld & Nicolson, 1991)

Proust, Marcel, *Cities of the Plain, Part One* (London: Chatto & Windus, 1968)

Proust, Marcel, *Time Regained* (London: Chatto & Windus, 1970)

Proust, Marcel, *Within a Budding Grove, Part Two* (London: Chatto & Windus, 1967)

Pryce-Jones, Alan, *The Bonus of Laughter* (London: Hamish Hamilton, 1987)

Puig, Manuel, *Blood of Requited Love* (London: Faber, 1989)

Puig, Manuel, *The Buenos Aires Affair* (London: Faber, 1989)

Puig, Manuel, *Kiss of the Spider Woman* (London: Arena, 1984)

Purser, Philip, *Where Is He Now? The Extraordinary Worlds of Edward James* (London: Quartet, 1978)

Putnam, George F., 'Vasilii V. Rozanov: Sex, Marriage and Christianity', *Canadian Slavic Studies* 5, 3 (Fall 1971), pp. 301–326

Queneau, Raymond, *Odile* (Normal, Illinois: Dalkey Archive, 1988)

Queneau, Raymond, *Zazie in the Metro* (London: Penguin, 2001)

Quiroga, José, *Tropics of Desire: Interventions from Queer Latino America* (New York: New York University Press, 2000)

Radiguet, Raymond, *Count d'Orgel* (London: Calder & Boyars, 1968)

Raphael, Frederic, *The Glittering Prizes* (Harmondsworth: Penguin, 1976)

Raphael, Frederic, *Somerset Maugham and His World* (London: Book Club Associates, 1978)

Rawsthorn, Alice, *Yves Saint Laurent: A Biography* (London: HarperCollins, 1996)

Re, Lucia, 'Alexandria Revisited: Colonialism and the Egyptian Works of Enrico Pea and Giuseppe Ungaretti', in Patrizia Palumbo (ed.), *A Place in the Sun: Africa in Italian Colonial Culture from Post-Unification to the Present* (Berkeley: University of California Press, 2003), pp.163–196

Read, Piers Paul, *Alec Guinness: The Authorised Biography* (London: Simon & Schuster, 2003)

Reade, Brian (ed.), *Sexual Heretics: Male Homosexuality in English Literature from 1850 to 1900* (London: Routledge & Kegan Paul, 1970)

Reavey, George, 'Russian Poetry: Introduction', in Willis Barnstone et al. (eds), *Modern European Poetry* (Toronto, New York & London: Bantam, 1966)

Rebellato, Dan, *1956 and All That: The Making of Modern British Drama* (London & New York: Routledge, 1999)

Reed, Christopher, *Art and Homosexuality: A History of Ideas* (Oxford: Oxford University Press, 2011)

Reed, Christopher, *Bloomsbury Rooms: Modernism, Subculture, and Domesticity* (New Haven & London: Yale University Press, 2004)

Reich-Ranicki, Marcel, *Thomas Mann and His Family* (London: Collins, 1989)

Renault, Mary, *The Charioteer* (London: Virago, 2013)

Reynolds, Michael, *Hemingway: The American Homecoming* (Oxford: Blackwell, 1992)

Richardson, John, *The Sorcerer's Apprentice: Picasso, Provence and Douglas Cooper* (London: Cape, 1999)

Richelson, Jeffrey T., *A Century of Spies: Intelligence in the Twentieth Century* (New York & Oxford: Oxford University Press, 1995)

Riding, Alan, *And the Show Went On: Cultural Life in Nazi-Occupied Paris* (London: Duckworth Overlook, 2011)

Rifkin, Adrian, *Street Noises: Parisian Pleasure, 1900–1940* (Manchester: Manchester University Press, 1995)

Robb, Graham, *Strangers: Homosexual Love in the Nineteenth Century* (London: Picador, 2003)

Robinson, Christopher, *Scandal in the Ink: Male and Female Homosexuality in Twentieth-Century French Literature* (London: Cassell, 1995)

Rodriguez, Suzanne, *Wild Heart, A Life: Natalie Clifford Barney and the Decadence of Literary Paris* (New York: Ecco, 2003)

Rorem, Ned, *Knowing When to Stop: A Memoir* (New York: Simon & Schuster, 1994)

Rorem, Ned, *A Ned Rorem Reader* (New Haven & London: Yale University Press, 2001)

Rorem, Ned, *The Paris Diary of Ned Rorem* (New York: George Braziller, 1966)

Rosenfeld, Emmy, *L'Italia nella poesia di Stefan George* (Milano: Malfasi Editore, 1948)

Ross, Alex, *The Rest is Noise: Listening to the Twentieth Century* (London: Harper Perennial, 2009)

Rossiter, Frank R., *Charles Ives and His America* (London: Gollancz, 1976)

Rowbotham, Sheila, *Edward Carpenter: A Life of Liberty and Love* (London: Verso, 2008)

Rowse, A.L., *Friends and Contemporaries* (London: Methuen, 1989)

Rowse, A.L., *Homosexuals in History: A Study of Ambivalence in Society, Literature and the Arts* (London: Weidenfeld & Nicolson, 1977)

Rule, Jane, *Lesbian Images* (New York: Pocket Books, 1976)

Russo, Vito, *The Celluloid Closet: Homosexuality in the Movies* (New York: Harper & Row, 1987)

Saba, Umberto, *Ernesto* (Manchester: Carcanet, 1987)

Sackville-West, Vita, *The Edwardians* (London: Virago, 1983)

Said, Edward, *Orientalism* (London: Penguin, 1991)

Saikaku, Ihara, *Comrade Loves of the Samurai* (Rutland, Vermont, & Tokyo: Charles E. Tuttle, 1972)

St.-John Perse (Alexis Leger), trans. T.S. Eliot, *Anabasis* (London, Faber, 1959)

Samson, Jim, *The Music of Szymanowski* (London: Kahn & Averill, 1980)

Sarduy, Severo, *Cobra and Maitreya* (Normal, Illinois: Dalkey Archive, 1995)

Sarton, May, *The Education of Harriet Hatfield* (London: Virago, 1990)

Sarton, May, *Mrs Stevens Hears the Mermaids Singing* (London: Women's Press, 1993)

Savage, Catharine, *Roger Martin du Gard* (New York: Twayne, 1986)

Savigneau, Josyane, *Marguerite Yourcenar: Inventing a Life* (Chicago & London: University of Chicago Press, 1993)

Sawyer, Roger (ed.), *Roger Casement's Diaries: 1910, The Black and the White* (London: Pimlico, 1997)

Schehr, Lawrence R., *Alcibiades at the Door: Gay Discourses in French Literature* (Stanford, California: Stanford University Press, 1995)

Schenkar, Joan, *Truly Wilde: The Unsettling Story of Dolly Wilde, Oscar's Unusual Niece* (London: Virago, 2000)

Schouvaloff, Alexander, *The Art of Ballets Russes* (New Haven & London: Yale University Press, 1997)

Schulze, Franz, *Philip Johnson: Life and Work* (New York: Knopf, 1994)

Schwartz, Barth David, *Pasolini Requiem* (New York: Pantheon, 1992)

Schwarz, A.B. Christa, *Gay Voices of the Harlem Renaissance* (Bloomington & Indianapolis: Indiana University Press, 2003)

Schweitzer, Viktoria, *Tsvetaeva* (London: Harvill, 1992)

Scott, Cyril, *Bone of Contention: Life Story and Confessions* (London: Aquarian Press, 1969)

Scott, Cyril, *My Years of Indiscretion* (London: Mills & Boon, 1924)

Seabrook, Mike, *Max: The Life and Music of Peter Maxwell Davies* (London: Gollancz, 1994)

Sedgwick, Eve Kosofsky, *Epistemology of the Closet* (Hemel Hempstead, Hertfordshire: Harvester Wheatsheaf, 1991)

Seel, Pierre, *I, Pierre Seel, Deported Homosexual: A Memoir of Nazi Terror* (New York: Basic Books, 2011)

Segal, Naomi, *André Gide: Pederasty and Pedagogy* (Oxford: Clarendon Press, 1998)

Sentein, François, *Minutes d'un libertin (1938–1941)* ([Paris]: Le Promeneur, 2000)

Sentein, François, *Nouvelles minutes d'un libertin (1942–1943)* ([Paris]: Le Promeneur, 2000)

Servadio, Gaia, *Luchino Visconti: A Biography* (London: Weidenfeld & Nicolson, 1981)

Seton, Marie, *Sergei M. Eisenstein: A Biography* (London: Bodley Head, 1952)

Seymour, Miranda, *Ottoline Morrell: Life on a Grand Scale* (London: Sceptre, 1998)

Seymour, Miranda, *A Ring of Conspirators: Henry James and His Literary Circle, 1895–1915* (London: Hodder & Stoughton, 1988)

Seymour-Jones, Carole, *Painted Shadow: A Life of Vivienne Eliot* (London: Constable, 2001)

Seymour-Smith, Martin, *Guide to Modern World Literature* (London: Wolfe, 1973)

Seymour-Smith, Martin, *Robert Graves: His Life and Work* (London: Hutchinson, 1982)

Shakespeare, Nicholas, *Bruce Chatwin* (London: Vintage, 2000)

Shattuck, Roger, *The Banquet Years: The Origins of the Avant-Garde in France, 1885 to World War I* (New York: Vintage, rev. edn, 1968)

Shelden, Michael, *Friends of Promise: Cyril Connolly and the World of* Horizon (London: Hamish Hamilton, 1989)

Shelden, Michael, *Orwell: The Authorised Biography* (London: Minerva, 1992)

Shepherd, Simon, 'Gay Sex Spy Orgy: The State's Need for Queers', in Simon Shepherd and Mick Wallis (eds), *Coming On Strong: Gay Politics and Culture* (London: Unwin Hyman, 1989), pp. 213–230

Sheridan, Alan, *André Gide: A Life in the Present* (London: Penguin, 2000)

Sherry, Michael S., *Gay Artists in Modern American Culture: An Imagined Conspiracy* (Chapel Hill, North Carolina: University of North Carolina Press, 2007)

Shukman, Harold, *Rasputin* (Stroud, Gloucestershire: Sutton, 1997)

Siciliano, Enzo, *Pasolini* (London: Bloomsbury, 1987)

Silver, Philip, '*Et In Arcadia Ego': A Study of the Poetry of Luis Cernuda* (London: Tamesis Books, 1965)

Sinfield, Alan, *Cultural Politics—Queer Reading*, 2nd edn (Abingdon, Oxon: Routledge, 2005)

Sinfield, Alan, *Literature, Politics and Culture in Postwar Britain* (Berkeley & Los Angeles: University of California Press, 1989)

Sinfield, Alan, *Out on Stage: Lesbian and Gay Theatre in the Twentieth Century* (New Haven & London: Yale University Press, 1999)

Sinfield, Alan, *The Wilde Century: Effeminacy, Oscar Wilde and the Queer Moment* (London: Cassell, 1994)

Skidelsky, Robert, *John Maynard Keynes, 1883–1946: Economist, Philosopher, Statesman* (London: Pan, 2004)

Smith, Paul Julian, *The Body Hispanic: Gender and Sexuality in Spanish and Spanish American Literature* (Oxford: Clarendon Press, 1989)

Smyth, Ethel, *Impressions That Remained: Memoirs* (London: Longmans, Green & Co., 1923)

Snyder, Timothy, *The Red Prince: The Fall of a Dynasty and the Rise of Modern Europe* (London: Vintage, 2009)

Solway, Diane, *Nureyev: His Life* (London: Weidenfeld & Nicolson, 1998)

Sontag, Susan, 'Notes on "Camp"', *Partisan Review* 31, 4 (Fall, 1964), pp. 515–530

Souhami, Diana, *Gertrude and Alice* (London: Phoenix, 2000)

Souhami, Diana, *Mrs Keppel and Her Daughter* (New York: St Martin's Griffin, 1997)

Souhami, Diana, *The Trials of Radclyffe Hall* (London: Weidenfeld & Nicolson, 1998)

Souhami, Diana, *Wild Girls: Paris, Sappho and Art: The Lives and Loves of Natalie Barney and Romaine Brooks* (London: Weidenfeld & Nicolson, 2004)

Southworth, James G., *Sowing the Spring: Studies in British Poets from Hopkins to MacNeice* (Oxford: Blackwell, 1940)

Spalding, Frances, *Duncan Grant: A Biography* (London: Chatto & Windus, 1997)

Spencer, Colin, *Which of Us Two? The Story of a Love Affair* (London: Penguin, 1991)

Spender, Stephen, *Collected Poems 1928–1953* (London: Faber, 1955)

Spender, Stephen, *Journals 1939–1983* (London: Faber, 1992)

Spender, Stephen, *The Temple* (London: Faber, 1988)

Spender, Stephen, *The Thirties and After: Poetry, Politics, People (1933–75)* (London: Fontana, 1978)

Spender, Stephen,(ed.), *W.H. Auden: A Tribute* (London: Weidenfeld & Nicolson, 1975)

Spender, Stephen, *World Within World* (London: Readers Union, 1953)

Sprigge, Elizabeth, & Jean-Jacques Kihm, *Jean Cocteau: The Man and the Mirror* (London: Gollancz, 1968)

Spring, Justin, *Fairfield Porter: A Life in Art* (New Haven & London: Yale University Press, 2000)

Spurr, Barry, 'Camp Mandarin: The Prose Style of Lytton Strachey', *English Literature in Transition* 33, 1 (1990), pp. 31–45

Stainton, Leslie, *Lorca: A Dream of Life* (New York: Farrar, Straus & Giroux, 1999)

Stambolian, George, and Elaine Marks (eds), *Homosexualities and French Literature: Cultural Contexts/Critical Texts* (Ithaca & London: Cornell University Press, 1979)

Steegmuller, Francis, *Cocteau: A Biography* (London: Constable, 1986)

Steel, Johannes, *Hitler As Frankenstein* ([London]: Wishart & Co., n.d.)

Stein, Gertrude, *The Autobiography of Alice B. Toklas* (Harmondsworth : Penguin, 1966)

Stein, Gertrude, *Paris France* (London: Brilliance, 1983)

Steiner, George, *Lessons of the Masters* (Cambridge, Mass. & London: Harvard University Press, 2003)

Steiner, George, *On Difficulty, and Other Essays* (Oxford: Oxford University Press, 1978)

Stevens, Hugh, and Caroline Howlett (eds), *Modernist Sexualities* (Manchester: Manchester University Press, 2000)

Stevenson, Jane, *Edward Burra: Twentieth-Century Eye* (London: Pimlico, 2008)

Steward, Samuel M., *Chapters from an Autobiography* (San Francisco: Grey Fox, 1981)

still, Judith and Michael Worton (eds), *Textuality and Sexuality: Reading Theories and Practics* (Manchester: Manchester University Press, 1993)

Stokes, John, 'Wilde at Bay: The Diaries of George Ives', *English Literature in Transition* 26 (1983), pp. 175–186

Stoltzfus, Ben, *Gide's Eagles* (Carbondale & Edwardsville: Southern Illinois University Press, 1969)

Stone, Charles, 'What if Hitler Was Gay?', *Gay and Lesbian Review* 9, 3 (May–June, 2002), pp. 29–34

Stoneley, Peter, *A Queer History of the Ballet* (London & New York: Routledge, 2007)

Storrs, Ronald, *Orientations* (London: Ivor Nicholson & Watson, 1937)

Strachey, Lytton, *Eminent Victorians* (London & Glasgow: Collins, 1959)

Strachey, Lytton, *The Letters of Lytton Strachey* (London: Viking, 2005)

Stuart, Otis, *Perpetual Motion: The Public and Private Lives of Rudolf Nureyev* (London: Simon & Schuster, 1995)

Stuhlmann, Gunther (ed.), *Henry Miller: Letters to Anaïs Nin* (London: Peter Owen, 1965)

Stutterheim, Kurt von, *The Two Germanys* (London: Sidgwick & Jackson, 1939)

Summers, Claude J., *Gay Fictions: Wilde to Stonewall, Studies in a Male Homosexual Literary Tradition* (New York: Continuum, 1990)

Summerscale, Kate, *The Queen of Whale Cay* (London: Fourth Estate, 1997)

Sutherland, John, *Offensive Literature: Decensorship in Britain, 1960–1982* (London: Junction Books, 1982)

Sutherland, John, *Stephen Spender: The Authorized Biography* (London: Viking, 2004)

Swafford, Jan, *Charles Ives: A Life with Music* (New York: Norton, 1996)

Swansea, Bruce, and José Ramón Enríquez, 'Homosexuality in the Spanish Generation of 1927: A Conversation with Jaime Gil de Biedma', *Gay Sunshine* 42/43 (Spring 1980), pp. 18–20, 14

Sweetman, David, *Mary Renault: A Biography* (London: Chatto & Windus, 1993)

Sykes, Christopher, *Evelyn Waugh: A Biography* (London: Penguin, 1977)

Sylvester, David, *Interviews with Francis Bacon* (London: Thames & Hudson, 1975)

Symons, Julian, *The Thirties: A Dream Revolved* (London: Faber, 1975)

Szerb, Antal, *Journey by Moonlight* (London: Pushkin, 2007)

Tamagne, Florence, *A History of Homosexuality in Europe: Berlin, London, Paris, 1919–1939* (New York: Algora, 2004)

Taubman, Howard, 'Not What It Seems', *New York Times* (5 November 1961), section 2, p. 1

Taylor Jr, Clark L., 'Mexican Gaylife in Historical Perspective', *Gay Sunshine* 26/27 (Winter 1975–1976), pp.1–3

Tedeschi, Richard (ed.), *Selected Letters of André Gide and Dorothy Bussy* (Oxford: Oxford University Press, 1983)

Thomas, Dylan, *The Collected Letters of Dylan Thomas* (London: Dent, 1985)

Thomas, Lowell, *With Lawrence in Arabia* (London: Hutchinson, n.d.)

Thomsen, Christian Braad, *Fassbinder: The Life and Work of a Provocative Genius* (London: Faber, 1997)

Thomson, Virgil, *Virgil Thomson* (New York: Knopf, 1967)

Thurman, Judith, *Secrets of the Flesh: A Life of Colette* (London: Bloomsbury, 1999)

Thwaite, Ann, *Edmund Gosse: A Literary Landscape* (London: Tempus, 2007)

Tilley, Sue, *Leigh Bowery: The Life and Times of an Icon* (London: Sceptre, 1997)

Timmons, Stuart, *The Trouble with Harry Hay: Founder of the Modern Gay Movement* (Boston: Alyson, 1990)

Tippett, Michael, *Those Twentieth Century Blues: An Autobiography* (London: Pimlico, 1994)

Todd, Pamela, *Bloomsbury at Home* (London: Pavilion, 1999)

Tóibín, Colm, *Love in a Dark Time: Gay Lives from Wilde to Almodóvar* (London: Picador, 2002)

Toklas, Alice B., *The Alice B. Toklas Cookbook* (London: Folio Society, 1993)

Tomkins, Calvin, *Off the Wall: Robert Rauschenberg and the Arts World of Our Times* (New York: Doubleday, 1980)

Tommasini, Anthony, *Virgil Thomson: Composer on the Aisle* (New York & London: Norton, 1997)

Trevor-Roper, Hugh (ed.), *The Goebbels Diaries: The Last Days* (London: Secker & Warburg, 1978)

Trotsky, Leon, *Literature and Revolution* (Ann Arbor: University of Michigan Press, 1960)

Tsvetaeva, Marina, *Bride of Ice: New Selected Poems* (Manchester: Carcanet, 2009)

Tsvetaeva, Marina, *Selected Poems* (Harmondsworth: Penguin, 1974)

Tytell, John, *Naked Angels: The Lives and Literature of the Beat Generation* (New York: McGraw-Hill, 1976)

Unterecker, John, *Voyager: A Life of Hart Crane* (London: Blond, 1970)

Vaill, Amanda, *Everybody Was So Young: Gerald and Sara Murphy, A Lost Generation Love Story* (London: Warner, 1999)

Van Vechten, Carl, *The Blind Bow-Boy* (New York: Knopf, 1925)

Van Vechten, Carl, *Parties: A Novel of Contemporary New York Life* (New York & London: Knopf, 1930)

Viano, Maurizio, *A Certain Reality: Making Use of Pasolini's Film Theory and Practice* (Berkeley & Los Angeles, California: University of California Press, 1993)

Vickers, Hugo, *Cecil Beaton: The Authorized Biography* (London: Weidenfeld & Nicolson, 1985)

Vidal, Gore, *The City and the Pillar* (London: John Lehmann, 1949)

Vidal, Gore, *Palimpsest: A Memoir* (London: Abacus, 1996)

Vidal, Gore, *Point to Point Navigation: A Memoir, 1964 to 2006* (London: Abacus, 2007)

Vidal, Gore, *Sexually Speaking: Collected Sex Writings* (San Francisco: Cleis Press, 1999)

Viénot, Pierre, *Is Germany Finished?* (London: Faber, 1931)

Vincent, John, *Queer Lyrics: Difficulty and Closure in American Poetry* (New York: Palgrave Macmillan, 2002)

Vogel, Bruno, *Alf* (London: GMP, 1992)

Waelti-Walters, Jennifer, *Damned Women: Lesbians in French Novels, 1796–1996* (Montreal & Kingston: McGill-Queen's University Press, 2000)

Waite, Robert G.L., *The Psychopathic God: Adolf Hitler* (New York: Basic Books, 1977)

Walkowitz, Judith R., *Nights Out: Life in Cosmopolitan London* (New Haven & London: Yale University Press, 2012)

Watson, Peter, *The German Genius: Europe's Third Renaissance, the Second Scientific Revolution and the Twentieth Century* (London: Simon & Schuster, 2010)

Watton, Lindsay F., 'Constructs of Sin and Sodom in Russian Modernism, 1906–1909', *Journal of the History of Sexuality* 4, 3 (1994), pp. 369–394

Waugh, Evelyn, *Black Mischief* (London: Penguin, 2000)

Waugh, Evelyn, *Brideshead Revisited: The Sacred and Profane Memories of Captain Charles Ryder* (Harmondsworth: Penguin, 1962)

Waugh, Evelyn, *Decline and Fall* (Harmondsworth: Penguin, 1937)

Waugh, Evelyn, *The Ordeal of Gilbert Pinfold* (London: Penguin, 1998)

Waugh, Evelyn, *Put Out More Flags* (London: Penguin, 1943)

Waugh, Evelyn, *The Sword of Honour Trilogy* (London: Penguin, 1984)

Waugh, Evelyn, *Vile Bodies* (London: Eyre Methuen, 1978)

Weeks, Jeffrey, *Coming Out: Homosexual Politics in Britain, from the Nineteenth Century to the Present* (London: Quartet, 1977)

Weinberg, Jonathan, *Speaking for Vice: Homosexuality in the Art of Charles Demuth, Marsden Hartley, and the First American Avant-Garde* (New Haven & London: Yale University Press, 1993)

Welch, Denton, *Dumb Instrument: Poems and Fragments* (London: Enitharmon, 1976)

Welch, Denton, *Extracts From His Published Works* (London: Chapman & Hall, 1963)

Wescott, Glenway, *The Pilgrim Hawk: A Love Story* (New York: New York Review Books, 2001)

West, Rebecca, *Cousin Rosamund* (London: Virago, 1988)

Wheen, Francis, *Karl Marx* (London: Fourth Estate, 1999)

Wheen, Francis, *The Soul of Indiscretion: Tom Driberg, Poet, Philanderer, Legislator and Outlaw* (London: Fourth Estate, 2001)

White, Chris (ed.), *Nineteenth-Century Writings on Homosexuality: A Sourcebook* (London & New York: Routledge, 1999)

White, Edmund, *The Burning Library: Writings on Art, Politics and Sexuality, 1969–1993* (London: Picador, 1995)

White, Edmund, *City Boy: My Life in New York During the 1960s and 1970s* (London: Bloomsbury, 2009)

White, Edmund, *The Flâneur: A Stroll Through the Paradoxes of Paris* (London: Bloomsbury, 2001)

White, Edmund, *Genet* (London: Chatto & Windus, 1993)

White, Edmund, *My Lives* (London: Bloomsbury, 2005)

White, Patrick, *Flaws in the Glass: A Self-Portrait* (Harmondsworth: Penguin, 1983)

White, Patrick, *The Hanging Garden* (London: Vintage, 2013)

White, T.H., *The Age of Scandal* (London: Folio, 1993)

Wilcox Michael, *Benjamin Britten's Operas* (Bath: Absolute Press, 1997)

Wilde, Oscar, *The Complete Letters of Oscar Wilde* (London: Fourth Estate, 2000)

Wilde, Oscar, *De Profundis, and Other Writings* (Harmondsworth: Penguin, 1973)

Wildeblood, Peter, *Against the Law* (Harmondsworth: Penguin, 1957)

Williams, James S., *Jean Cocteau* (London: Reaktion, 2008)

Wilson, Angus, *Hemlock and After* (London: Granada, 1979)

Wilson, Angus, *No Laughing Matter* (London: Granada, 1979)

Wilson, Angus, *Reflections in a Writer's Eye: Writings on Travel* (London: Secker & Warburg, 1986)

Wineapple, Brenda, *Genêt: A Biography of Janet Flanner* (London: Pandora, 1994)

Winmar, Frances, *Wings of Fire: A Biography of Gabriele d'Annunzio and Eleonora Duse* (London: Alvin Redman, 1957)

Wolfenden, John, *Turning Points: The Memoirs of Lord Wolfenden* (London: Bodley Head, 1976)

Wolff, Charlotte, *Magnus Hirschfeld: A Portrait of a Pioneer in Sexology* (London: Quartet, 1986)

Wolff, Charles, *Journey Into Chaos* (London: Hutchinson, n.d.)

Woods, Gregory, *Articulate Flesh: Male Homo-eroticism and Modern Poetry* (New Haven and London: Yale University Press, 1987)

Woods, Gregory, 'Foreword' to Pierre Seel, *I, Pierre Seel, Deported Homosexual: A Memoir of Nazi Terror* (New York: Basic Books, 2011), pp. xi–xxxi

Woods, Gregory, 'Gay and Lesbian Urbanity', in Kevin R. McNamara (ed.), *The Cambridge Companion to the City in Literature* (New York: Cambridge University Press, 2014), pp. 233–244

Woods, Gregory, 'High Culture and High Camp: The Case of Marcel Proust', in David Bergman (ed.), *Camp Grounds: Style and Homosexuality* (Amherst: University of Massachusetts Press, 1993), pp. 121–133.

Woods, Gregory, *A History of Gay Literature: The Male Tradition* (New Haven and London: Yale University Press, 1998)

Woods, Gregory, 'The Injured Sex: Hemingway's Voice of Masculine Anxiety', in Judith Still and Michael Worton (eds.), *Textuality and Sexuality: Reading Theories and Practices* (Manchester: Manchester University Press, 1993), pp. 160–172

Woods, Gregory, 'Modernism, Homosexuality and Speech', *Meridian: The La Trobe University English Review* 19, 1 (November 2008), pp. 39–56

Woods, Gregory, 'Queer London in Literature', *Changing English* 14, 3 (December 2007), pp. 257–270

Woods, Gregory, *Quidnunc* (Manchester: Carcanet, 2007)

Woods, Gregory, 'Roger Peyrefitte, *The Exile of Capri*', in Tom Cardamone (ed.), *The Lost Library: Gay Fiction Rediscovered* (New York: Haiduk, 2010), pp. 151–158

Woods, Gregory, *This Is No Book: A Gay Reader* (Nottingham: Mushroom, 1994)

Worsley, T.C., *Fellow Travellers* (London: GMP, 1984)

Wright, Adrian, *Foreign Country: The Life of L.P. Hartley* (London: André Deutsch, 1996)

Wright, Adrian, *John Lehmann: A Pagan Adventure* (London: Duckworth, 1998)

Yardley, Michael, *Backing into the Limelight: A Biography of T.E. Lawrence* (London: Harrap, 1985)

Yeats-Brown, F., *European Jungle* (London: Eyre & Spottiswoode, 1939)

Yingling, Thomas, *Hart Crane and the Homosexual Text: New Thresholds, New Anatomies* (Chicago: University of Chicago Press, 1990)

Young, Ian, 'Claus von Stauffenberg and the Stefan George Circle', *Gay Sunshine* 31 (1977), pp. 14–15

Young, Ian (ed.), *The Male Homosexual in Literature: A Bibliography* (Metuchen, N.J.: Scarecrow, 1975)

Zaborowska, Magdalena J., *James Baldwin's Turkish Decade: Erotics of Exile* (Durham, North Carolina: Duke University Press, 2009)

Zeldin, Theodore, *France 1848–1945: Intellect and Pride* (Oxford: Oxford University Press, 1980)

Ziegler, Philip, *Mountbatten: The Official Biography* (London: Guild, 1985)

Ziegler, Philip, *Osbert Sitwell: A Biography* (London: Pimlico, 1999)

Zweig, Stefan, *Confusion: The Private Papers of Privy Councillor R Von D* (London: Pushkin, 2002)

Zweigenhaft, Richard L., and G. William Domhoff, *Diversity in the Power Elite: Have Women and Minorities Reached the Top?* (New Haven & London: Yale University Press, 1998)

# INDEX